HISTORY AND SOURCES OF THE COMMON LAW

TORT AND CONTRACT

D0146871

HISTORY AND SOURCES
OF THE
COMMON LAW

TORT AND CONTRACT

BY

C. H. S. FIFOOT, M.A.

Of the Middle Temple, Barrister-at-Law;
Fellow of Hertford College, Oxford;
All Souls Reader in English Law

GREENWOOD PRESS, PUBLISHERS
NEW YORK

Originally published in 1949
by Stevens & Sons Ltd., London

First Greenwood Reprinting 1970

SBN 8371-2814-5

PRINTED IN UNITED STATES OF AMERICA

CONTENTS

PREFACE

THIS book is an attempt to follow two branches of the common law from their sources. I have not explored the manuscripts, but have confined myself to the printed materials: to the literature of the law from Glanvill to Blackstone and to the reports, with especial emphasis upon the Year Books as they have been published in the Rolls Series, in the volumes of the Selden Society and of the Ames Foundation, and in the black letter editions. In the translation of these last I hope that, amid their ambiguities and corruptions, I have guessed aright. My debt to the acknowledged masters, to Ames and Holmes, to Maitland and Holdsworth, is obvious and inevitable and is none the less real because on occasion, in the light cast by later researchers, I have ventured to differ from their conclusions. To provoke new and alien views is at once the penalty and the reward of genius. It will be equally clear that I am heavily indebted to such contemporary historians as Professors Woodbine and Winfield, Plucknett and Potter.

I had at first intended to leave the evidence, with as little commentary as possible, to speak for itself. But I came to feel that, in a book designed primarily for students, this course was too austere. I have therefore introduced each subject with a narrative, which may serve to provide a context for the sources and which has enabled me to refer to authorities too numerous to cite in full. In these narratives I have been led from time to time into controversy, and I have not scrupled, when I have formed my own conclusion, to declare it. To confirm or to correct, the reader has only to turn to the sources, and perhaps, as I hope, to explore further on his own account.

In all anthologies a major difficulty is that of selection. Where, as in the present context, the history of doctrine is imbedded in the history of process, the difficulty is aggravated. While I have tried to shun the vice of interpreting the past in the light of the present, I have had to remember that the student will chiefly be interested in those phenomena which, if rather by chance than by design, have determined the character of the living law and the history of which is rich enough to justify portrayal. This is why, on the one hand, I have not dealt with Replevin, once of great importance but now almost a closed chapter in the law, and why, on the other hand, I have omitted such torts as Fraud and Conspiracy, where, despite their current importance, historical continuity is lacking.

From many friends I have received help and encouragement Two have laid upon me a special burden of gratitude. Dr. F. H. Lawson, Professor of Comparative Law in the University of Oxford, read the book in manuscript. He not only checked and corrected my translations from Glanvill and Bracton, but, with his imaginative insight and from his great store of learning, suggested analogies which, left to myself, I should have missed. Mr. Eric Ronald Guest, M.A., B.C.L., one of the Magistrates of the Police Courts of the Metropolis, repeating the generous office of friendship he performed when I wrote my first book eighteen years ago, read the proofs. With unerring literary tact he has saved me from many faults of style, and, combining an eager interest in legal and historical scholarship with a long professional experience, he has challenged or approved my interpretation of events.

I have to acknowledge with gratitude the ready courtesy of those who have allowed me to cite the transcriptions to be found among the sources in this book, the provenance of which will be found each in its place: of His Majesty's Stationery Office for the citations from the Rolls Series, of the Secretary of the Selden Society for those from its storehouse of learning, of the Trustees of the Ames Foundation, and of the Delegates of the Clarendon Press for the excerpts from Volume IV of the Oxford Studies in Social and Legal History. Finally, I should indeed be churlish if I were not to thank the publishers and the printers who have met exigent demands with unfailing skill and patience.

C. H. S. FIFOOT.

HERTFORD COLLEGE,
OXFORD.
May, 1949.

TABLE OF CASES

[The cases printed in black type will be found set out in the Sources, and the black-printed numerals indicate the pages at which they may be so found. The letters R.S. indicate the Rolls Series, and the letters S.S. the Selden Society.]

TABLE OF LAWS AND STATUTES

PART ONE

TORT

⚛ *1* ⚛

NUISANCE

THE modern torts, for the most part, are the offspring of that prolific 'action on the case' which began to be developed in the later years of the fourteenth century. Before its emergence, however, the common law had invented and developed several forms of action which, in greater or in less degree, have helped to mould the modern pattern of civil liability. Of these the writs of Nuisance, Detinue and Trespass are of major importance.[1] Before discussing them it is proper to offer a preliminary word at once of warning and of explanation. The temptation to translate the past into the terms of the present is one which every student of history finds as difficult to resist as it is easy to reprove. The student of legal history in particular has to take constant care not to apply to mediæval conditions the current categories of tort, contract and property. In the England of the twelfth and thirteenth centuries the King's officers, after their preliminary duty of keeping the peace, were preoccupied with the task of defining and sanctioning the system of tenure upon which society depended. It is not surprising, therefore, that an exploration of the origins of tort should lead back to the roots of the land law. Nuisance, Detinue and Trespass were all concerned more or less intimately with the incidents of property; and Nuisance, in substance if not in form the earliest of the three, was essentially and indeed exclusively an encroachment upon the rights of the freeholder. The very name—*nocumentum*—suggests the damage which he had suffered by conduct which nevertheless fell short of an actual dispossession. A history of tort must thus be prefaced by a brief excursion into the remedies available to the freeholder for the protection or recovery of his estate.

The first book of the common law—*Tractatus de legibus et consuetudinibus regni Angliæ*—appears to have been completed between 1187 and 1189, and is traditionally ascribed to Ranulf Glanvill, Chief Justiciar to Henry II.[2] The author, as was to be expected, was mainly

---

[1] Of the other early writs, *Deceit* lay only for an abuse of the judicial process and its history has been intermittent and fragmentary. See P. & M. II 534-536; Holdsworth, H.E.L. III. 407-8; Potter, *Historical Introduction to English Law*, 3rd ed., pp. 414-8. *Replevin* was an action of great importance in the middle ages as a means of regulating the process of distress, but to the student it is a closed chapter which it is scarcely necessary to re-open. See Plucknett, *Concise History of the Common Law*, 4th ed., pp. 348-9, and Holdsworth, H.E.L. III. 283-7; and for a rare modern example, with some interesting historical discussion, *Swaffer* v. *Mulcahy* [1934] I K.B. 608.

[2] Glanvill was made Chief Justiciar by Henry II in 1180 and died in 1190. Though the book is generally given his name and it will be convenient to refer to it under

3

concerned with the land law; and of the land law, as viewed by the royal officers, the core was the Writ of Right. This generic writ had two principal species. It issued to a sheriff in the form of a *Præcipe,* instructing him to order a person seised of a freehold estate to restore it to a complainant or show cause before the King's Justices for his failure to do so. It thus served, after a *locus pœnitentiæ,* to originate proceedings in the King's courts. It issued, on the other hand, as a *Breve de recto tenendo,* to a lord in whose jurisdiction the case lay, commanding him to do justice, with the threat that failure would entail removal of the case from his authority.[3] Doctrinaires might insist that a *Præcipe* was appropriate only where the complainant was a tenant-in-chief and where the King, as the arch feudal lord, had undoubted jurisdiction. But Henry II was bold or naughty enough to disregard scruple and, on one pretext or another, to draw most litigation upon freehold estates into his courts.[4] The Writ of Right, moreover, was as protean in scope as in form. It might be used to vindicate not only the freehold itself, but the appurtenances without which the estate would be sterile. Glanvill thus offered a precedent wherein the sheriff is to command the defendant ' that he permit (*quod permittat*) the plaintiff to have his easements in the wood and pasture of such a vill as he ought to have and is wont to have '; and the word ' easements,' while not yet clothed with the precise significance of later days, introduces at least one facet of the modern law of nuisance.[5]

From his discussion of the Writ of Right Glanvill turned to the newly invented Assize of Novel Disseisin.[6] Here again he had a theme which admitted of variation. A freeholder might be disseised, not of the whole estate, but of some useful or vital concomitant. The plaintiff's dykes were alleged to have been destroyed or his water-mill obstructed, or he had been ousted from his common of pasture; and in two at least of these precedents the injury was said to have been done *ad nocumentum liberi tenementi.*

his name, it is universally admitted to be doubtful if he wrote it. Pollock and Maitland suggested that the true author might have been Hubert Walter, who later himself became Chief Justiciar. The suggestion—on less learned lips it might be called a guess—is based on a passage in Bracton, f. 188b. Pollock and Maitland themselves say, ' We should not be surprised if it were the work ' of Hubert Walter; Professor Winfield says it may ' possibly ' be so; Holdsworth in H.E.L. II at p. 189 thought there was ' considerable probability ' in the suggestion, while in his *Sources and Literature of English Law,* at p. 25, this has become ' very probable.' The evidence, however, remains as slender as ever. See, on Glanvill generally, P. & M. I. 162-8; H.E.L. II. 188-192; Winfield, *Chief Sources of English Legal History,* 256-8.

[3] Glanvill, Bk. I, Cap. 5 and 6; Book XII, Cap. 1, 2, 3. *Infra,* pp. 11-12.
[4] Glanvill, Bk. I, Cap. 5, *infra,* p. 11. The feudal lords won a temporary victory by asserting feudal doctrine against the King in *Magna Carta,* c. 34: ' The writ called *Præcipe* shall not for the future be issued to anyone concerning any tenement whereby a free man may lose his court.' But the victory was illusory, and the King's officers evaded the clause, *inter alia,* by developing writs of entry. See McKechnie, *Magna Carta,* pp. 348-355; H.E.L. I. 58-9; P. & M. II. 65. For a different interpretation of the clause, see Hurnard, *Studies in Mediæval History presented to F. M. Powicke* [1948] p. 157.
[5] Glanvill, Bk. XII, cap. 9, 13, 14; *infra,* pp. 12-13.
[6] Glanvill, Bk. XIII, cap. 32-37. *Infra,* pp. 13-15; P. & M. II. 46-56.

In the fifty years after the appearance of Glanvill's book both remedies were freely used. The case of *Wildeker* v. *Ros* in 1232[7] illustrates the value of *Quod Permittat* in protecting the freeholder's rights of timber. It is possible to detect in the pleadings in this case some vacillation from the strict pattern of the Writ of Right. The Writ of Right was proprietary rather than possessory, the Assise possessory rather than proprietary:[8] in the former the demandant[9] asserted that he or his ancestor was seised not only 'as of fee' but also 'as of right' (*ut de feodo et ut de iure*), in the latter he need be seised only 'as of fee.' In *Wildeker* v. *Ros* the demandant, claiming as heir, declared only that his father ' was seised as of fee on the day of his death ' of timber rights pertaining to his freehold. But the tenant denied that the father was ever ' seised of that estover as of fee *and of right,*' and, as issue was joined upon this traverse, propriety perhaps was satisfied. At least the form of the writ given in the earliest extant Register, ascribed by Maitland to the beginning of Henry III's reign, followed Glanvill's model.[10]

It was, however, through the Assise of Novel Disseisin that most experiments were made in the sphere of what is now the law of nuisance.[11] These may conveniently be grouped under four heads. The surviving records exhibit in the first place a pleasing variety of agricultural diversions falling short of total disseisin. The plaintiff complained that the defendant had destroyed his dyke or his hedge *ad nocumentum liberi tenementi;*[12] or that he had been deprived of pasture for his cattle or of pannage for his pigs; or, by a *placitum porcariæ levatæ,* that evil-disposed persons had unjustly and without a judgment overthrown his piggery.[13] In the year 1204 two cases were recorded, one at Worcester and one at Westminster, where interference was alleged with fishing rights. In the case at Worcester ' an assise came to recognize whether Reynold Folet unjustly and without judgment disseised Robert le Bret of his common fishery in Wilderemareis, which belonged to his tenement in Birtsmorton. The jurors said that in truth Robert had a boat which wandered about (*errantem in*) that fishery in Reynold's time and the time of Reynold's

---

[7] B.N.B., Plea 685; *infra*, p. 16.

[8] It would be unhistorical to express the distinction with more precision. See P. & M. II. 74-8.

[9] In a Writ of Right the plaintiff is ' the demandant,' the defendant ' the tenant.'

[10] *Infra*, p. 18. See also *Bishop of Carlisle* v. *Mulcastre* (1310) S.S. Vol. 22, p. 201.

[11] See generally S.S. Vol. 62 (1943). Sir C. T. Flower, Chap. XVIII.

[12] See *Bracton's Note-Book*, Plea 806 (A.D. 1233): Plea 1804 (A.D. 1222): Plea 1953 (A.D. 1221).

[13] S.S. Vol. 62 (1943), pp. 330-1. ' The right of pannage is simply a right granted to an owner of pigs—the grant was usually to an owner of land of some kind who kept pigs—to go into the wood of the grantor of the right and to allow the pigs to eat the acorns or beech-mast which fall upon the ground. . . . The pigs have no right to take a single acorn or any beech-mast off the tree, either by themselves or by the hands of those who drive them. There is not even a right to shake the tree. It is only a right to eat what has fallen to the ground.'—*per* Jessel, M.R. in *Chilton* v. *Corporation of London* [1878] 7 Ch.D. 562 at p. 565.

father; but they knew not whether it was by favour or as of fee, because Robert had no land near that fishery within three bowshots whereby he ought to have common there. Judgment: Robert is to take nothing in the fishery."[14] The second group comprised obstructions to rights of way. These rights usually depended upon express and elaborate grants. Thus in 1203 William de Cirinton warranted his charter, whereby ' for the salvation of his own soul and those of William, son of Helto, his uncle, and of all his ancestors, he gave to the church of Bermondsey the mill of Farningham with all its appurtenances, especially the path leading from his court to the mill through his demesne and the path from the mill in Chimbhams and the path which led to Boxherse so far as his land extended, so that, whenever they wished and ought so to do, men could go to the mill with their grist by the said paths in peace and without hindrance."[15]

In the third group is a large number of cases which attest the importance of the water-mill both as an element of the mediæval economy and as a lucrative feudal monopoly.[16] A record of the reign of King John is typical: ' The Assise comes to recognize if Jordan the Miller unjustly and without a judgment has raised the mill-pool of his mill in Weston to the nuisance of the freehold of Simon of Merston within the time of the assise. The jurors say that he has so raised his pool. Judgment, that the pool be destroyed and that Jordan be in mercy one half-mark. Damages, three shillings."[17] In this case the issue admitted of a simple verdict; but in many instances the finding of the jurors was elaborate in its topographical detail or in the demarcation of rival interests.[18] It is curious, however, that the right of the lord to exact from his tenants exclusive service at his mill was vindicated not by an Assise but by a separate writ of *Secta ad Molendinum.*[19]

[14] S.S. Vol. 62, pp. 24 and 56.
[15] S.S. Vol. 62, pp. 331-2. See the case of the Abbot of Meaux (A.D. 1218), S.S. Vol. 56, Plea 91, *infra,* p. 15, and S.S. Vol. 56 (A.D. 1219), Plea 404. Compare P. & M. II. 145-6.
[16] See Coulton, *The Mediæval Village,* Chap. VI. Norwich Priory had nine mills, which in 1299-1300 made a profit of £21-13-2d. Dr. Coulton cites the Chartulary of Ramsey Abbey: ' All the tenants owe suit to the mill, whereunto they shall send their corn. And if they cannot, on the first day, grind as much wholemeal as may keep their household in bread for that day, the mill must grind it. . . . From August 1 to Michaelmas each man may grind where he will, if he be unable to grind at my lord abbot's mill on the day whereon he has sent the corn. Moreover, if it chance that my lord's mill be broken or his milldam burst, so that the tenant cannot grind there, he may take it elsewhere at his will. If the tenant be convicted of having failed to render suit to my lord's mill, he shall give 6d. before judgment; or, if he has gone to judgment, he shall give 12d.'
[17] S.S. Vol. 62, pp. 159-160. See S.S. Vol. 56, pl. 94, *infra,* p. 16.
[18] e.g., S.S. Vol. 62, pp. 327-8.
[19] *Infra,* p. 18. The reason for the refusal of the Assise is not clear. Prof. Woodbine (*Glanvill,* p. 290) thinks that it is because the ' tenement ' could not be put in view, as required in an Assise, and cites B.N.B. pl. 1979. This case does not seem conclusive, for the plaintiff here did not specify any tenement, so that of necessity view could not be granted. It is true, however, that, at least in the 13th and 14th centuries, view was not granted in a writ of *Secta ad Molendinum* (*Burnhill* v. *Ringtherose* (1310) Y.B. 3 Ed. II., S.S. Vol. 20, p. 201); though Fitzherbert states otherwise in the 16th century (F.N.B. 123).

Finally, the Assise was used to protect the right to hold a fair or market which had been granted to a feudal lord by royal charter and the profits of which were now diminished by the activities of a rival. Such franchise rights were analogous to rights of common and were keenly contested. In the reign of King John, the Abbot of St. Edmunds complained that the Bishop of Ely was holding a market at Lavenham to the injury of his own market at Bury St. Edmund's; and the Count of Aumale challenged the right of the Abbot of Abingdon to hold a fair at Shillingford to the nuisance of his own fair at Wantage. In the early years of Henry III, the Earl of Essex complained that his market at Moreton Hampstead was impoverished by a rival market established by the defendant at Chagford, and the ' free and lawful men of the vicinage' were asked whether or not the latter existed before the creation of the former.[20] A crucial feature of these cases was the question of damages. Assessment was often speculative and difficult; but the plaintiff would fail if no damage was proved.[21]

Already, therefore, in the early years of the thirteenth century cases of nuisance were not uncommon; but there had been no attempt at generalisation. The attempt was made by Bracton, the author of the second great book of the common law.[22] Bracton introduced a

[20] *Infra*, p. 15; and S.S. Vol. 62, pp. 332-4.
[21] *Infra*, p. 15; and B.N.B. Plea 494.
[22] *NOTE ON BRACTON*. (See Maitland, *Bracton's Note-Book*, I. 13-25; P. & M. I. 206-10; H.E.L. II. 232-290; Winfield, *Chief Sources of English Legal History*, 258-262; Kantorowicz, *Bractonian Problems* (1941).) Holdsworth began his biographical account with the words, ' There are no striking facts in the life of Bracton.' Our knowledge of him, at least, is limited. He was born about 1200, became a judge in 1245, and is known to have been alive in 1268. He came from Devonshire and studied law at Exeter (*non Oxon sed Exon*). In the MSS. of his book more than sixty variants of his name appear, but ' Bracton' is hallowed by tradition and vindicated by Kantorowicz. The book itself, though eight times as long as the Institutes, was left unfinished at his death, and its date has been variously estimated. Maitland, Holdsworth and Winfield have ascribed it to the years 1250-1258; but Kantorowicz offered reasons for ante-dating it. 'It can no longer be upheld,' he concluded at p. 36, ' that the Treatise was written in the main between 1250 and 1258 by Bracton the judge of King Henry III. It was written before 1239 by Bracton the clerk of William Raleigh ' (himself a judge in 1229). The difficulty of reaching a conclusion upon dates is shown by the state of the manuscripts, which Kantorowicz thus described. ' The Bracton as handed down to us in the manuscript is . . . a redaction of [Bracton's own work] by [an unknown man, possibly] Bracton's clerk. Bracton's original is probably lost for ever, but from the extant manuscripts we can guess that it must have been in an appalling state of disorder after several years of drafting and about thirty years of adding to it. . . . A great many of the extant manuscripts were copied immediately after his death, whereas there is not one that can be dated or traced to his lifetime.' But ' its success must have been instantaneous. There are still about 30 manuscripts reliably ascribed to the late 13th or early 14th centuries. . . . [We may] estimate the number of all manuscripts perished or extant at about 300.' In these circumstances the task of an editor is formidable, and it has certainly proved discouraging. The first printed edition, by Tottell, was published in 1569, and the second, by Sir Travers Twiss, in 1878-1883. Of the first Selden said, in his *Dissertatio ad Fletam* at p. 464, ' *Menda sunt perplurima eaque crassissima, partim e librariorum inscitia, partim ex operarum incuria.*' Of the second, Vinogradoff, recalling Selden's dual criticism, said, ' Sir Travers Twiss has contrived to add to both classes ' (*Coll. Papers*, I. 79). The third is still in course of production by Professor Woodbine. Four volumes have so far appeared, containing an *apparatus criticus* and a text, and a commentary is promised. Of the first and second volumes Kantorowicz declared (at

long discussion with the resounding words, *Nocumenta infinita sunt*.[23]
He then offered two general propositions: that a nuisance is essentially
an injury to a servitude, and that, to be actionable, it must not only
have caused damage, but must also be of a type selected by the law
for condemnation.[24]   Of these propositions it may be remarked that,
to a modern lawyer, the first is misleading, since Bracton, naturalising
the alien term ' servitude,' applied it to circumstances not envisaged
by Roman jurists, and that, while the burden of the second—the
possibility of *damnum sine injuria*—is sufficiently familiar, it has the
familiarity which breeds incoherence if not contempt.   It may, therefore, be more helpful to state the three types of ' nuisance ' which
Bracton mentioned.   The first was interference with easements and
profits *stricto sensu*—rights of way, of pasture, of drawing water.
The rights might be created by grant or by prescription, and the interference might be total or partial.   The second reflected the competition
between rival markets which has already been noticed.   B. might have
been granted a franchise or liberty to hold a market on the express
condition that it be not ' to the nuisance ' of a similar franchise
previously granted to A.   Such a condition was an invitation to
controversy which contemporary records show was not declined.   It
is the third which betrays the ambiguity of Bracton's ' servitude.'
' If,' he says, ' a servitude is imposed upon a man's land by the law,
though not by the grant of a man, whereby he is forbidden to do on
his own land what may harm his neighbour, as if he should raise the
level of a pond on his own land or make a new one whereby his
neighbour is harmed, as for example if his neighbour's land is thus
flooded, this will be to the injurious nuisance of his neighbour's
freehold unless his neighbour has given him permission to do it.'[25]
Unneighbourly conduct of this kind was not an invasion of a Roman
servitude or of an English incorporeal hereditament, but an attack
upon the ordinary amenities of land-holding, or, in the now established
if optimistic phrase, upon ' natural rights.'   To Bracton, concerned
with procedure rather than analysis, the distinction was not important;
but it induced a confusion not removed until the nineteenth century
and the echoes of which still disturb the modern law.[26]

p. 131): ' The collation of selected passages in the first and a considerable portion
of the work in the second volume look reliable and will probably not have to be
done again.   But, apart from this, the work must unfortunately be started over
again.'   The justice of this severe criticism may, however, be questioned.   See
Schulz, 59 L.Q.R., 172.
       Finally, reference should be made to the collection of some 2,000 cases now
known as *Bracton's Note-Book*, the great majority of which come from the years
1216-1240.   Maitland, acting on Vinogradoff's suggestion, concluded that they were
collected by Bracton to help him in his treatise.   See his Introduction to the Note-
Book, and H.E.L. II. 235.
[23] f. 231b, *infra*, p. 18.
[24] f. 231b, *infra*, p. 18; and see f. 221a.
[25] f. 232, *infra*, p. 19. See also f. 232b, *infra*, p. 19; and compare f. 221a.
[26] H.E.L. III. 153-7; H.E.L. VII. 328-333; and see Winfield, *Text-Book of the Law of
Tort*, 4th ed. pp. 436-7.

Whatever the impropriety of his language, Bracton made it clear that the law of nuisance was an accessory of the land law. No one might complain unless he had an interest in land; and that interest must be one of freehold. 'It is necessary to view the tenement to which the injurious harm has been done, because if the complainant has no tenement which can be harmed, the complaint is not valid; . . . wherefore it is necessary that the complainant should have a free tenement, because no one can acquire a servitude over any estate in land unless he has himself an estate and a freehold estate at that.'[27] The restriction, while it may be associated with Bracton's loose application of 'servitude,' followed almost inevitably from the conception of nuisance as a species of disseisin. No one could be disseised save the freeholder, and the assise was thus denied to one who held only in wardship or for a term of years or who was *in possessione* only in another's name.[28]

If the injury were flagrant the plaintiff might abate the nuisance at once without recourse to law. The period of self-help, as in all cases of disseisin, was limited to four days.[29] If he let this time go by, he must seek a writ from the King, which, in Bracton as in Glanvill, might be either a *Quod Permittat* or an Assise of Novel Disseisin.[30] But Bracton made mention for the first time of a new remedy, the Assise of Nuisance. The choice between the old and the new Assise depended upon the site of the injury. If the wrongful act were done upon the plaintiff's land, Novel Disseisin was appropriate; if upon the defendant's land it was more remote from the conception of disseisin, and the Assise of Nuisance was to be brought. Acts done partly on the one land and partly on the other called strictly for both remedies, but for convenience Bracton allowed the plaintiff to confine himself to the Assise of Nuisance.[31]

After Bracton the same remedies continued to be available, with amendment and extension. A new form of *Quod Permittat* was developed. The Writ of Right, upon which it had originally been based, had for some time been disliked by the King's officers both for technical and for political reasons, and they had devised as an alternative a series of so-called 'Writs of Entry.' These writs, of which there was a rich variety, were all marked by a common feature. Whereas the Writ of Right left at large the whole question of title as between

---

[27] Bracton, f. 234, *infra,* p. 20. In most real actions a 'view' could be demanded by the defendant in order to identify the tenement in question. See Booth, *Real Actions,* pp. 37-42, and *supra,* p. 6, n.

[28] See Bracton, ff. 167b and 168, and the authorities collected in Woodbine's *Glanvill,* at p. 290.

[29] Bracton, f. 231b and f. 233; *infra,* p. 20. 'He may ride one day east, another west, another north, another south, to collect friends and arms, and must perpetrate the re-ejectment on the fifth day at the latest'; P. & M. II. 50, citing Bracton, f. 209b. See also Maitland, *Coll. Papers,* I. 416-7.

[30] ff. 231b, 232, 233b; *infra,* pp. 18-20.

[31] f. 234b; *infra,* p. 21.

the parties, the Writs of Entry confined the issue by alleging a flaw
in the defendant's title beyond which argument was not to range.
The defendant was said to have entered on the estate only through
or after the act of a third party in disseising the plaintiff, or by virtue
of a conveyance made by a person who, while himself lawfully
occupying, had no powers of alienation; and it was upon this particular
defect that the whole question was made to turn.[32] *Quod Permittat*
was therefore re-fashioned upon this new model.[33] In 1258, moreover, both *Quod Permittat* and the Assise received a desirable extension.
Neither was available at common law when, after the cause of action
had arisen, the land involved had been alienated; and to supply this
deficiency the Statute of Westminster II, c. 24, expressly provided
suitable variants.[34]

It was with reluctance, however, that Nuisance was divorced from
the context of Disseisin. At the end of the thirteenth and the beginning of the fourteenth centuries no settled policy prevailed. On
the one hand, lawyers spoke readily enough of ' Writs of Nuisance.'
In an anonymous case of 1293 the plaintiff brought two separate
actions against the defendant, the one on a ' writ of Novel Disseisin '
for digging so deeply on his three acres of land that he lost all profit
from it, and the other on a ' writ of Nuisance ' for ' tortiously con-
structing a pool to the nuisance of his freehold.' The defendant sought
to impale the plaintiff upon a dilemma by asserting that there was
but one estate in question, of which for the purpose of the first action
he must declare himself disseised and for that of the second seised;
but the plaintiff avoided this delicate point by referring to two separate
estates.[35] In 1294, the Prior of Spalding brought a ' writ of Nuisance '
against a defendant because ' he had held a market in the vill of P. to
the nuisance of his own market,' and because the defendant had been
so unprincipled as to invite customers to his market free of toll, ' so
that he has drawn all persons to the vill of P. and they have quitted
the plaintiff's market.'[36] In 1303 the Prior of Holy Trinity, Canterbury, brought a ' writ of Nuisance ' against a defendant for construct-
ing a weir above the Prior's mill, ' whereby the water was retarded

---

[32] On the Writs of Entry and the reasons for their origin, see P. & M. II. 62-74, and
supra, p. 4, n. 4; and for specimens see Maitland, *Forms of Action*, p. 85.
Blackstone (III. 184) absurdly says that they were known to ' our Saxon ancestors '
and were older than Assises. Early specimens were in fact known in the reign of
John, and their development was complete before the death of Henry III.
[33] The following specimen is given by Booth, *Real Actions*, at p. 238:—*Rex vicecomiti
salutem. Præcipe A. quod iuste ct sine dilatione permittat B. habere communiam
pasturam in N. quæ pertinet ad liberum tenementum suum in eadem villa [vel alia]
de qua idem A. [vel W. pater prædicti A. cuius heres ipse est] iniuste disseisivit R.
patrem prædicti B. cujus heres ipse est. . . .* ' This writ,' says Booth, 'is in nature of
a writ of entry sur disseisin done to the ancestor.' The older model of *Quod
Permittat* remained available and was sometimes used. See *Bishop of Carlisle* v.
Mulcastre (1310) S.S. Vol. 22, p. 201.
[34] *Infra*, p. 78.
[35] Y.B. 20 & 21 Ed. I. (R.S. pp. 414-9). *Infra*, p. 21.
[36] Y.B. 21 & 22 Ed. I. (R.S. p. 568).

and did not run so readily as it was wont to do,' and not only did the mill grind less but the surrounding land was flooded.[37] On the other hand, in 1313 a similar interference with a mill was redressed by an Assise of Novel Disseisin, and in 1315 the Assise was again used to vindicate a common of pasture.[38] But by the middle of the fourteenth century it was common practice to speak in terms of nuisance, and attention was focussed on the scope rather than on the form of the action.[39] Finally, in 1359 Bracton's test to determine the boundaries of Nuisance and Novel Disseisin was abandoned. To an assise of Nuisance for the diversion of a watercourse the defendant argued that the acts complained of had been done on the plaintiff's freehold, so that Novel Disseisin and not Nuisance was appropriate. But the argument was rejected; and henceforth it may be said that nuisance, though still exclusively an injury to land, was an individual wrong.[40]

SOURCES

GLANVILL[41]

BOOK I

Cap. 5

When anyone complains to our lord the King or to his Justices as to his fee or freehold, if the complaint is such that it should be brought into the King's court, or our lord the King so wills it, then the complainant shall have the following writ of summons.

Cap. 6

Rex vicecomiti salutem. Præcipe N. quod iuste et sine dilatione reddat R. unam hidam terræ in villa illa unde idem R. queritur quod prædictus N. ei deforciat. Et nisi fecerit, summone eum per bonos summonitores quod sit coram me vel iustitiis meis in crastino post octabas clausi Paschæ apud locum illum ostensurus quare non fecerit. Et habeas ibi summonitores et hoc breve. Teste Ranulpho de Glanvilla apud Clarendunam.

The King to the sheriff greeting. Command N. that justly and without delay he render to R. one hide[42] of land in such a vill whereof the same R. complains that the aforesaid N. deforces him. And unless he will do this, summon him by good summoners that he be

---

[37] Y.B. 30 & 31 Ed. I. (R.S. p. 404).
[38] Y.B. 6 & 7 Ed. II. (S.S. Vol. 36, p. 76); Y.B. 8 Ed. II. (S.S. Vol. 41, p. 1).
[39] *Smeteborn* v. *Holt* (1348) Y.B. Hil. 21 Ed. III, f. 2, pl. 5. *Infra*, p. 22; and see Y.B. 19 Ed. 3 (R.S. p. 340), A.D. 1345, an Assise of Nuisance for a right of way.
[40] Y.B. Lib. Ass. 32 Ed. III. pl. 2. *Infra*, p. 23.
[41] All the passages from Glanvill cited in this book are from the text of Professor Woodbine's edition (1932), but the translation is mine.
[42] For the 'hide,' see Maitland, *Domesday Book and Beyond*, Essay III.

before me or my justices on the morrow after the octave of Easter
at such a place to show why he has not done it. And have there the
summoners and this writ. Witness Ranulph Glanvill at Clarendon.

BOOK XII

Cap. 1

The aforesaid pleas of right[43] come directly and at first instance
into the court of our lord the King and are there discussed and ended.
Again, sometimes certain pleas of right, although they do not come at first
instance into the court of our lord the King, are yet removed thither when
it is proved that the courts of the various lords have failed to do right. For
then, through the medium of the County Court, they may be removed, for
divers reasons stated above, to the chief court of our lord the King.[44]

Cap. 2

When anyone thus claims a free service or a freehold as held
of another by free service, he cannot draw the defendant into litigation without a writ from our lord the King or from his justices. He shall therefore
have a Writ of Right (*breve de recto*) directed to his lord, of whom he claims
to hold. And if the plea concerns land, it will be as follows:—

Cap. 3

Rex comiti W. salutem. Præcipio tibi quod sine dilatione teneas
plenum rectum N. de decem carucatis terræ in Middeltune quas clamat
tenere de te per liberum servitium feodi unius militis pro omni servitio . . .,
quas R. filius W. ei deforciat. Et nisi feceris vicecomes de Notingeham
faciat, ne amplius clamorem inde audiam pro defectu iustitiæ. Teste, etc.

> The King to the Earl of W. greeting. I command you that
> without delay you hold full right to N. of ten carucates of land in
> Middleton which he claims to hold of you by the free service of one
> knight's fee for all services . . . and of which R. the son of W. deforces
> him. And if you do not, let the Sheriff of Nottingham do it, so that
> I hear no more clamour for want of justice. Witness, etc.

But writs of right of this kind are varied in many ways for divers causes,
as will appear from the divers forms of writ set out below. . . .[45]

Cap. 9

Thus to the sheriff belong the aforesaid writs of right where the
courts of lords are proved to have failed to do right. And certain other such
pleas also belong; as where one complains to the court concerning his lord,
that he exacts from him customs and services that are not due or more
service than is due for the freehold which he holds from him . . .; and
generally all things for which the sheriff has the writ of our lord the King
or of his Chief Justice for the purpose of doing justice in any matter. . . .
And some of these things appear from the following writs.

---

[43] i.e. pleas in the nature of *Præcipe*: *supra*, Bk. I, Cap. 6.
[44] Pleas were removed from the lord's court to the county court by writ of *Tolt*, and
from the county court to the King's court by writ of *Pone*. For an account of the
County Court, see P. & M. I. 532-556.
[45] In Cap. 4 and Cap. 5 Glanvill gives examples; e.g. a claim to one hundred shillings
of rent held by free service.

Cap. 13

Rex vicecomiti salutem. Præcipio tibi quod iuste et sine dilatione facias amensurari pasturam de illa villa unde I. quæ fuit uxor P. et R. soror sua queruntur quod S. eas iniuste superonerat. Nec permittas quod præfatus S. in ea pastura plura averia habeat quam habere debeat et quam habere pertinet secundum quantitatem feodi sui quod ipse habet in eadem villa, etc.

The King to the sheriff greeting. I command you that justly and without delay you cause to be assessed the pasture of that vill whereof I., who was the wife of P., and R. her sister complain that S. unjustly overstocks. And that you do not permit the aforesaid S. to have in that pasture more beasts than he ought to have and than pertains to him according to the extent of his fee which he has in the same vill, etc.

Cap. 14

Rex vicecomiti salutem. Præcipio tibi quod sine dilatione præcipias R. quod iuste et sine dilatione permittat habere H. aisiamenta sua in bosco et in pastura de villa illa quæ habere debet ut dicit, sicut ea habere debet et habere solet; et non permittas quod præfatus R. vel alius ei inde molestiam vel iniuriam faciat. Ne amplius, etc.[46] Teste, etc.

The King to the sheriff greeting. I command you that without delay you command R. that justly and without delay he permit H. to have his easements in the wood and pasture of such a vill which he ought to have, as he says, just as he ought to have and is wont to have; and that you do not permit the aforesaid R. or any other to do him in this regard molestation or injury. Lest further, etc. Witness, etc.

Book XIII

Cap. 32

Lastly, it remains to speak of that recognition[47] which is called Novel Disseisin. Thus, when anyone, within the assise of our lord the King, that is, within the time appointed for such purpose by our lord the King with the advice of his lords (which time may be longer or shorter), has disseised another unjustly and without a judgment of his freehold, the disseised person can avail himself of the benefit of this ordinance, and he shall have the following writ.

Cap. 33

Rex vicecomiti salutem. Questus est mihi N. quod R. iniuste et sine iudicio desaisiavit eum de libero tenemento suo in illa villa post ultimam transfretationem meam in Normaniam; et ideo tibi præcipio quod si præfatus N. fecerit te securum de clamore suo prosequendo, tunc facias tenementum illud resaisiari de catallis quæ in ipso capta fuerunt et ipsum tenementum cum catallis esse in pace usque ad clausum Paschæ. Et interim facias duodecim liberos et legales homines de visneto videre terram illam et nomina eorum imbreviari facias. Et summone eos per bonos summonitores quod tunc sint coram me vel iustitiis meis parati inde facere recognitionem. Et

[46] See Glanvill, Book XII, Cap. 3, *supra*, p. 12.
[47] *Recognitio* is at first synonymous with *Jurata*, and then becomes appropriated both to the process with which the jury is concerned and with the verdict given.

pone per vadium et salvos plegios prædictum R., vel baillivum suum si ipse non fuerit inventus, quod tunc sit ibi auditurus illam recognitionem. Et habeas, etc.

> The King to the sheriff greeting. N. has complained to me that R. unjustly and without a judgment has disseised him of his freehold in such a vill since my last crossing into Normandy; and so I command you that, if the aforesaid N. shall give you security for pursuing his claim, you shall then cause that tenement to be reseised of the chattels which were taken on it and the same tenement with the chattels to be in peace until the close of Easter. And meanwhile you shall cause twelve free and lawful men of the neighbourhood to view that land and their names to be put in the writ. And summon them by good summoners to be before me or my justices ready to make recognition thereupon. And put by gage and safe pledges the aforesaid R. or his bailiff, if he himself shall not be found, that he come then and there to hear that recognition. And have, etc.

Cap. 34

The writs of Novel Disseisin are varied in diverse manner according to the diversity of the tenements on which disseisins take place. For if any dyke[48] be set up or thrown down, or if the level of any mill-pond be raised, to the nuisance of the freehold of anyone within the assise of our lord the King, then these writs are varied in the following manner.

Cap. 35

Rex vicecomiti salutem. Questus est mihi N. quod R. iniuste et sine iudicio levavit quoddam fossatum, vel prostravit, in illa villa ad nocumentum liberi tenementi sui in eadem villa post ultimam transfretationem meam in Normaniam. Et ideo præcipio tibi quod si præfatus N. fecerit te securum de clamore suo prosequendo, tunc facias duodecim liberos, etc. videre fossatum illud et tenementum, et nomina eorum imbreviari facias. Et summone per bonos summonitores, etc., ut prius.

> The King to the sheriff greeting. N. has complained to me that R. unjustly and without a judgment has set up, or thrown down, a certain dyke in such a vill to the nuisance of his freehold in the same vill since my last crossing into Normandy. And so I command you that, if the aforesaid N. shall give you security for pursuing his claim, you shall then cause twelve free, etc. to view that dyke and freehold, and shall cause their names to be put in the writ. And summon by good summoners, etc., as above.

Cap. 36

Rex vicecomiti salutem. Questus est mihi N. quod R. iniuste et sine iudicio exaltavit stagnum molendini sui in illa villa ad nocumentum liberi tenementi sui in eadem villa vel in alia villa post ultimam transfretationem meam in Normaniam. Et ideo præcipio tibi quod si præfatus N. fecerit te securum de clamore prosequendo, tunc facias duodecim liberos, etc. videre stagnum illud et tenementum, etc., ut prius.

> The King to the sheriff greeting. N. has complained to me that R. unjustly and without a judgment has raised the level of his mill-

---

[48] *fossatum*: dyke or ditch, often implying the existence of embankments on either side. See S.S. Vol. 40, Intro. p. xxvii.

pond in such a vill to the nuisance of his freehold in the same vill or in another vill since my last crossing into Normandy. And so I command you that, if the aforesaid N shall give you security for pursuing his claim, you shall then cause twelve free, etc. to view that pond and tenement, etc., as above.

Moreover, if a disseisin be done in a common of pasture, then the writ shall be thus : —

Cap. 37

Rex vicecomiti salutem. Questus est mihi N. quod R. iniuste et sine iudicio desaisiavit eum de communi pastura sua in illa villa quæ pertinet ad liberum tenementum suum in eadem villa vel in alia villa post ultimam transfretationem meam in Normaniam. Et ideo tibi præcipio quod si præfatus N. fecerit te securum de clamore suo prosequendo, tunc facias duodecim liberos, etc., videre pasturam illam et tenementum. Et nomina eorum, etc., ut prius.

The King to the sheriff greeting. N. has complained to me that R. unjustly and without a judgment has disseised him of his common of pasture in such a vill which pertains to his freehold in the same vill or in another vill since my last crossing into Normandy. And so I command you that, if the aforesaid N. shall give you security for pursuing his claim, you shall then cause twelve free, etc. to view that pasture and tenement. And their names, etc., as above.

SELECT CIVIL PLEAS—A.D. 1200-1203
S.S. Vol. 3

Plea 136. Suffolk. Michaelmas, 1202

The Jury, by sixteen knights, with the consent and at the wish of the parties, comes to recognize if the market of the Bishop of Ely at Lavenham is so injurious to the market of the Abbot of St. Edmund's at the town of Bury St. Edmund's, that it ought not to be there and cannot by the custom of England. The jurors say that the market of Lavenham is injurious to the market of Bury St. Edmund's, because dead flesh and living and fish and corn and much merchandise which were wont to be carried to Bury St. Edmund's (where the Abbot has the customs) and sold there, are now brought to Lavenham and sold there, so that the Abbot loses the customs. And the knights, being asked what damage the Abbot has sustained by that market, say that they do not know, nor can it be known, nor does any one know save God alone.[49]

ROLLS OF THE JUSTICES IN EYRE FOR YORKSHIRE, A.D. 1218-9
S.S. Vol. 56

Plea 91

The Assise[50] came to recognize whether the abbot of Meaux unjustly and without judgment has obstructed a certain way in Wharram to the nuisance

[49] Cf. *B.N.B.*, plea 494 (A.D. 1231) where the plaintiff, in a similar complaint, failed because he could prove no damage to his market.

[50] Here and in Plea 94, *infra*, the editor, translating, uses the words 'Assise of Nuisance.' The word 'nuisance,' however, does not appear to be used, save in the body of the report. I have made a few other alterations in the translation.

of William of Sankeston's free tenement in the same vill within the assize, etc., by the writ of King John. And the abbot by his attorney has come and has said nothing wherefore the assize should stand over.

The jurors say that the abbot has so obstructed that way as the writ says. And so the abbot is in mercy and William is to have his seisin. Precept to the sheriff. Damages, 6d.

Plea 94

The Assise came to recognize whether Ralph of Ecclesall unjustly and without judgment has raised the level of a certain mill-pool in Dalton to the nuisance of the free tenement of Robert of Wentworth in the same vill within the assise, etc., by the writ of King Henry. And Ralph has come and has said nothing wherefore the assize should stand over.

The jurors say that Ralph has so raised the level of the pool as the writ says, and they say that this Ralph and this Robert share that pool, and they say that Ralph impleaded this Robert in his lord's court touching his whole land, so that the duel was pledged, armed and fought therein, and at length concord was made between them, and Robert acknowledged that the land was the right of Ralph, and for that acknowledgment Ralph granted Robert the half of that land with the half of the aforesaid mill to hold of him, and Robert did homage to him for it. And because the jurors attest that Ralph has raised the level of his part of the pool above Robert's part and to the nuisance of his free tenement, therefore Ralph is to be in mercy. Damages, 12d.[51]

WILDEKER v. ROS

BRACTON'S NOTE BOOK, PLEA 685

A.D. 1232

Walter of Wildeker claims against William of Ros, whom the Prior of Kintham calls to warranty[52] . . . that he permit him to have his reasonable estover in the wood of Husum, and as to which he claims that he permit him to have in that same wood house-bote and hay-bote and plough-bote, for burning and for hedging and for other uses,[53] whereof Hugo his father, whose heir he is, was seised as of fee on the day of his death and which yet pertained to his freehold in Winston in the time of King Richard . . ., and whereof he claims the seisin of his father as being his father's heir; and he says that by reason that he [the defendant] deforces him of that estover he has suffered loss, etc. . . .

[51] For another case of nuisance to a mill, see S.S. Vol. 62, p. 327, where, in 1212, Samson of Molesey was summoned to show why he diverted the water-course of Molesey to the nuisance of the free tenement of the Prior of Merton, removing in the process the Prior's men, his barrows, spades and sieves, to his damage 40/-.

[52] For ' voucher to warranty,' see P. & M. II. 662-3.

[53] ' Common of estovers (from *estoffer,* to furnish) is a liberty of taking necessary wood for the use or furniture of a house or farm from off another's estate. The Saxon word *bote* is of the same signification with the French *estovers;* and therefore house-bote is a sufficient allowance of wood to repair, or to burn in, the house, which latter is sometimes called fire-bote. Plough-bote and cart-bote are wood to be employed in making and repairing all instruments of husbandry, and hay-bote or hedge-bote is wood for repairing of hays, hedges or fences.' Blackstone, II. 35.

And William comes and defends his right and says that the aforesaid Hugo was never seised of that estover as of fee and of right nor as pertaining to his aforesaid tenement of Winston . . .; and that he was not seised of that estover as of his fee nor died thus seised as pertaining to his tenement of Winston, he puts himself upon the country and offers the lord King 40 shillings to have a jury. . . .

And Walter says that his father was so seised and died thus seised . . ., and puts himself on the country.

Wherefore it is commanded to the sheriff that he cause to come (*venire faciat*) before the justices at Westminster 12 knights, etc. to recognize on their oaths whether the aforesaid Hugo died thus seised of the aforesaid estover as appurtenant to his freehold. . . .

AN EARLY THIRTEENTH-CENTURY REGISTER OF WRITS[54]

ELSA DE HAAS

UNIV. OF TORONTO L.J. VOL. 7 (1947) p. 196

De superoneratione pasture[55]

Rex vicecomiti salutem. Questus est nobis A. quod B. iniuste superoneraverit communem pasturam suam in C., ita quod in ea pluria habet animalia et pecora quam habere debet et ad eum pertinet secundum liberum tenementum. Et ideo tibi precipimus quod iuste et sine dilatione amensurari facias pasturam illam. . . .

Of the over-stocking of pasture

The King to the sheriff greeting. A. has complained to us that B. has unjustly over-stocked his common of pasture in C., so that he has therein more beasts and cattle than he ought to have and than pertains to him according to his freehold. And so we command you that justly and without delay you cause that pasture to be assessed. . . .

De domo muro piscaria et huiusmodi loquelis[56]

Vicecomiti salutem. Questus est nobis A. quod B. iniuste et sine iudicio levavit quandam domum murum vel piscinam in tali villa ad nocumentum liberi tenementi sui in eadem villa vel alia post ultimum redditum Domini J. regis patris nostri de Hybernia in Angliam. Et ideo tibi precipimus quod loquelam illam audias et postea ipsum A. inde iuste deduci facias. Ne amplius, etc., pro defectu, etc.

Of house, wall, fishery and similar suits

To the sheriff greeting. A. has complained to us that B. unjustly and without a judgment has made a certain house, wall or fishery in such a vill to the nuisance of his freehold in that same vill or in

---

[54] The learned author here transcribes the items comprising the register referred to by Maitland, *Coll. Papers* II. p. 135, as 'a Cambridge MS., [which] may, I think, be safely ascribed to the early years of Henry III.' The learned author of the article does not offer any more exact date, but describes the register as covering 'fourteen pages at the end of a small quarto, written in Latin on parchment in an even and neat formal hand of the *second* half of the thirteenth century.' I offer my own translation, varying in some slight degree from that of the learned author.

[55] At p. 212. In mediæval Latin, *e* often equals *æ*. Hence, *pasture = pasturæ; precipe = præcipe: terre = terræ,* etc.

[56] At p. 225.

another, since the last return of the lord King John our father from
Ireland into England. And so we command you that you hear that
suit and afterwards give the said A. a just deliverance therefrom.
Lest we hear further complaint for default of justice, etc.

Quod permittat[57]

Vicecomiti salutem. Precipimus tibi quod iusticies A. quod iuste et sine
dilatione permittat B. habere rationabile estoverium suum in bosco vel
turbaria in tali villa quod habere debet et solet, ut dicit, sicut rationabiliter
monstrare poterit quod ei facere debeat. Ne amplius, etc. pro defectu, etc.

To the sheriff greeting. We command you that you constrain A.
that justly and without delay he permit B. to have his reasonable
estover in wood or turbary[58] in such a vill as he ought to have and is
wont to have, as he says, in so far as he can reasonably show that he
ought there to do. Lest we hear further complaint, etc.

Secta ad hundredum vel molendinum[59]

Vicecomiti salutem. Precipimus tibi quod iusticies talem quod iuste et
sine dilatione faciat sectam tali ad hundredum suum vel molendinum suum
de tali villa quam ei facere debet, ut dicit, sicut rationabiliter monstrare
poterit quod ei facere debeat. Ne amplius, etc.

Suit to Hundred Court or Mill

To the sheriff greeting. We command you that you constrain
such an one that justly and without delay he do suit to such an one
at his hundred court or his mill at such a vill, such as he ought to
do, as he says, in so far as he can reasonably show that he ought to do
to him, etc.

BRACTON[60]

f. 231b

. . . Nuisances are infinite, according to what will be said below, and
either they wholly impair servitudes or at least so impede them that they
are less useful. It is to be observed that one nuisance is both injurious and
causes damage, while another causes damage but is not injurious; wherefore, when complaint is made of a nuisance, it must be asked what is the
damage involved and it must be seen whether it is injurious as well as the
cause of damage, and, if so, then it must be abated.[61] But if, though causing
damage, it is not injurious, it must be endured. And this may be seen from
the following case. If a person has a servitude and a right of pasture in
another's land, then he has a free entrance to and exit from the land. But
if the owner of the land does something at the entrance whereby he cannot

---

[57] At p. 226.
[58] For *estover* and *turbary*, see Blackstone, II. 34-5, and *supra*, p. 16, n.
[59] At p. 226.
[60] The citations from Bracton are from the text of Professor Woodbine's edition, but the translation is mine.
[61] ' *Et sciendum quod nocumentorum aliud iniuriosum et damnosum, aliud damnosum et non iniuriosum, unde cum fiat querela de nocumento quæri oportet ad quod damnum aliquod fiat; et videndum utrum sit damnosum et iniuriosum, et tunc tollendum.*'

enter at all or only the less conveniently, as where the owner makes a wall, a ditch or a hedge, he commits an injurious nuisance. And what has thus been done, while the injury is still recent and flagrant, can be removed and destroyed even without a writ; but after a time not without a writ. The same rule applies if anyone is granted a right of way across another's land, and the way is in any wise obstructed or narrowed so that he cannot go at all or only with the less ease. So, too, if a right to draw water is thus granted, and it is diverted to his nuisance in whole or in part. So, too, a person can share a right of common with another and a right to dig, just as he may have a right of pasture. . . . And in all the aforesaid cases and in many others an assise of novel disseisin will lie. . . .

f. 232

. . . Again, if a servitude is imposed upon a man's land by the law, though not, as above, by the grant of a man, whereby he is forbidden to do on his own land what may harm his neighbour, as if he should raise the level of a pond on his own land or make a new pond whereby his neighbour is harmed, as for example if his neighbour's land is thus flooded; this will be to the injurious nuisance of his neighbour's freehold, unless his neighbour has given him permission to do it. And just as one can have a servitude over a neighbour's land by express creation, so also one can have it without express creation by long user with the knowledge and sufferance of the owner, because long sufferance is taken for consent. . . .

All the rights noted above and all servitudes concern the appurtenances of tenements and belong to one tenement over another; and appurtenances of this kind have their own appurtenances, as a right of way and free entrance and exit pertain to a right of pasture and to the actual exercise of it. . . . And just as such rights and servitudes can be taken away by disseisin so that no one may use them, so too can injurious nuisances be done to the appurtenances of appurtenances, whereby a person cannot conveniently enjoy his said servitudes or cannot enjoy them at all; as if one should altogether obstruct a road-way or a drove-way, whereby a man is wont to enter a pasture, by making a ditch or a wall. Such a nuisance does not much differ from a disseisin; and so, since it is unlawful, it should be abated at the cost of the wrongdoer, provided it has been done on the wrongdoer's land. But if it be done on another's land, that other will have an assise of novel disseisin concerning his free tenement, and, in accordance with the rule that the assise of novel disseisin includes the nuisance because every disseisin causes harm, by this means the nuisance can be abated and the damage made good to the complainant, as well that which flows from the disseisin of the freehold as that which flows from the nuisance; which would not be the case if the action were confined to the nuisance. . . .

f. 232b

. . . Again, by the act of the parties (*ex constitutione hominum*[62]) a servitude may be imposed whereby one man has the right of drawing water across another's land. . . . It is also a rule of law (*constitutio iuris*[62]) that no one shall act injuriously on his own land, that is to say, that he shall not make a pond or raise or lower its level so that harm happens to his neighbour, as if by the flowing-back of the water his neighbour's tenement is flooded. . . . And just as one can commit an injurious nuisance by doing an act, so one may do so by not acting, and that on one's own land or on another's: as if a man be bound by grant (*ex constitutione*[62]) to stop and close or to cleanse and repair, and he does not do what he is bound to do. Again, just as one can cause harm by not acting, so one can harm by not permitting an act to be done; as if a man does not permit another to carry out his obligation of stopping and closing or of cleansing and repairing, when he is bound to do so by grant (*ex constitutione*[62]) or by long custom. . . .

f. 233

Those things which have been constructed or thrown down and destroyed to the injurious nuisance of another can, as in the case of other disseisins, by acting at once while the wrongdoing is still flagrant, be demolished or repaired, if the complainant is able to do so. If not, recourse must be had [to the following writ] . . .

[Then Bracton gives specimen writs to bring the complaint within the jurisdiction of the sheriff.]

f. 233b

. . . But, if the King wishes that nuisances of this kind shall be ended by proceedings before any of his justices, then the writ shall be in this form.

Rex vicecomiti salutem. Questus est nobis talis quod talis iniuste, etc., levavit quoddam fossatum . . . in tali villa ad nocumentum liberi tenementi sui in eadem villa vel in alia post ultimum redditum, etc. Et ideo tibi præcipimus quod si idem talis fecerit te securum, etc., tunc facias duodecim liberos et legales homines de visneto illo videre fossatum illud et tenementum illud, et nomina eorum imbreviari. Et summone eosdem per bonos summonitores quod sint coram iustitiariis nostris ad primam assisam, etc., parati inde facere recognitionem. Et pone per vadium et salvos plegios præfatum talem vel ballivum eius, etc. . . .

> The King to the sheriff greeting. Such an one has complained to us that such another unlawfully, etc., has raised a certain dyke . . . in such a vill to the nuisance of his freehold in the same vill or in another vill since our last return, etc. And so we command you that, if the said complainant shall give you security, etc., you shall then cause twelve free and lawful men of that neighbourhood to view that dyke and that freehold, and you shall enter their names on the writ. And summon them by good summoners to be before our justices at the first assise, etc., ready to make recognition. And put by gage and safe pledges the aforesaid party or his bailiff, etc.

f. 234

. . . Again, it is necessary to view the tenement to which the injurious harm has been done, because if the complainant has no tenement which can be harmed the complaint is not valid; . . . wherefore it is necessary that the complainant should have a free tenement, because no one can acquire a servitude over any estate or land unless he himself has an estate, and a freehold estate at that; nor can anyone owe a servitude save he who has an estate, and a freehold estate at that. . . .

---

[62] The word *constitutio* is used ambiguously; sometimes, it would seem, to denote a general rule of law—*constitutio iuris*—sometimes to indicate a private act of the parties—*constitutio bominum*. Cf. the use of the word in Just. Inst. II. 3, 4.

f. 234b

... Again, if the level of a pond or weir be raised or lowered so as to cause an injurious nuisance, it must be seen whether this is done wholly on the tenement of the complainant, as in a case where he has a tenement on both banks of a stream. In this case there will be a disseisin of his freehold rather than an assise of nuisance. But if it be raised or lowered wholly on the defendant's tenement, then there will be an assise of nuisance rather than a disseisin of the freehold, since the act is done wholly on another's land. But if part is on the complainant's land and part on the other's land (as if a line were drawn between them down the middle of the stream), then for that part which is on the complainant's land the assise of novel disseisin of the freehold will apply, and for that part which is on the other's land the assise of nuisance will apply; and so there will be two assises for one act. But since it is burdensome to pursue both, we must see which is the better remedy, so as to cure the whole wrong, lest part be remedied and part be left untouched. If you should wish by the assise of novel disseisin to correct all that has been done affecting your freehold, this is not possible, since that assise does not include an assise of nuisance for what has been done on another's land. It is therefore better to proceed by the assise of nuisance, whereby both wrongs may be amended. ...

f. 235

.... Among other nuisances, the grant of a franchise may result in a nuisance to an earlier franchise; as where a man is granted a franchise to hold a market in a certain place only on condition that it is not to the nuisance of a neighbouring market. ...

STAFFORDSHIRE EYRE
ANON.
Y.B. 20 & 21 Ed. I. (R.S. pp. 414-9)
A.D. 1293

Adam brought a *writ of Novel Disseisin* against B., saying that he had tortiously disseised him of his freehold in N.; and he put in his view three acres of land and two acres of meadow, etc.; and he stated the manner in which he had been disseised, saying that B. had dug so deep in the three acres that he (A.) could have no profit from his land, and that he had carried thence with his cart full six cartloads of earth, and that he (A.) could not come to or till his land or make his profit thereof; ready, etc., by the assise.

And, besides this, he brought a *writ of Nuisance,* and complained that he had tortiously constructed a pool to the nuisance of his freehold in N.; and he put in his view a portion of the meadow.

Lowther: Sir, whereas he complains that we have tortiously disseised him of two acres of meadow and two [*sic*] acres of land in N.; by that writ of Nuisance he supposes that he is seised of the freehold to which the pool is a nuisance; and we tell you, Sir, the same place which he puts in his view in the writ of Novel Disseisin he puts into the view in his other writ of Nuisance; and thus by his writ of Novel Disseisin he supposes that he is out of seisin, and by his writ of Nuisance he supposes that he is in seisin; and consequently one is contrary to the other: judgment of the inconsistency.

Howard said that they were different places and not one place. . . .

[After further argument—e.g., the defendant saying that the pond was of old standing, the plaintiff that it was new—the case went to the Assise.]

The Assise said, as to the *Novel Disseisin,* that Adam was disseised by B. of the three acres of land; for they said that he had dug the earth and carried away full three carts' load of earth to his damage of half a mark: and B. was in mercy. And as to the meadow, they said that Adam was not disseised; and therefore he was in mercy. As to the *Nuisance,* they said that the level of the pool was raised and that it was not newly constructed, inasmuch as there had been a pool there, but that it was totally broken down and destroyed, so that there was only left there a space of the same dimensions, but in the same condition as the land adjoining it, and that he raised its level.

And so the writ was quashed.

SMETEBORN v. HOLT
Y.B. HIL. 21 ED. III. f. 2, pl. 5
A.D. 1348

Johanna Smeteborn brought an Assise of Nuisance against one Robert Holt and Clarissa his wife; and she complained for that, whereas she had a mill in the vill of B. and in the same vill a weir to retain the water, to which weir and mill she ought to have a way over the land of the said Robert and Clarissa to carry her timber and to draw a boat to the aforesaid water full of timber and of all other things needed for the repair of the said mill, the said Robert and Clarissa his wife had built a house across her aforesaid way; whereby she said she could not go to her mill as she was wont to do, but must go two leagues round.

Skipwith: Sir, we say that the land over which she claims the way and the weir and mill to which she claims it were, since the time of memory, in the hand of one William, so that this way cannot be claimed as appendant; wherefore it cannot be that she may maintain the Assise without showing title.

Mowbray: Sir, we say to you that, before the seisin of William of which he speaks, the mill and the weir were in one hand and the land in another hand and always thus continued since the time of memory until the seisin of William. And we say that William had issue two daughters, of whom this Clarissa is the one and Johanna, the now plaintiff, is the other; and that between them partition was made, so that the land was allotted as her share (*a la purparty*)[63] to Clarissa and the mill and the weir were assigned as her share to the other sister. And agreement was made between them that she [Johanna] should have the way over the land of Clarissa, to use as it had been wont to be used as of yore. And this we are ready to aver; and we demand judgment and pray the Assise.

Skipwith: At least they have acknowledged that, when William was seised, it was not appendant, and the partition which they have alleged can found no claim. And inasmuch as they say that agreement was made between the two sisters that [the plaintiff] should have the way, and this lies in specialty, of which they show nothing, we demand judgment whether they should have the Assise.

[63] *Purparty* = *propars,* the share of a co-parcener. See P. & M. II. 306.

Hillary, J.: A thing granted *in purparty* can be good without specialty; for if one coparcener grants a rent-charge to the other because the value of her share is greater than that of the other, I say that the coparcener shall have an action for this rent without specialty.[64] So it is here in this case.

Sharshulle, J.: Even though she might have the way without specialty, this does not prove that she shall have the Assise if she be disturbed in it. For suppose I grant to you a way over my land to such a mill by specialty and at this time you are not seised of the mill, but you purchase the mill afterwards; I say that, though I afterwards disturb you in this way, you can not have the Assise, but you must have recourse to your writ of Covenant. Wherefore in this case also.

Thorpe: In your case there is nothing to wonder at, for he could not have the Assise because, at the time that the way was granted, he had not the freehold to which the way belonged, and the later purchase of the free-hold could not sustain the action. But in the case here we have had the freehold in respect of which we claim the way for as long time as the way itself. And moreover there is no word in our writ which supposes that the way was appendant rather than that it began by grant; for our writ says only *quod obstruxit quandam viam ad nocumentum liberi tenementi sui*, and all this is true that we have shown to you.

And then, after consideration, the Assise was granted.

ANON.

Y.B. Lib. Ass. 32 Ed. III. pl. 2

A.D. 1359

An assise of Nuisance was brought at Salisbury for the diversion of a water-course. And the nuisance assigned was that he had made a trench across a stream called R., whence the plaintiff's mill drew its water, so that the water was diverted, and, as a result, the mill, which used to grind day and night three quarters of each manner of corn, can now grind only one bushel; and also that the said water floods fifteen acres of meadow belonging to the plaintiff and adjacent to the said mill, so that, where he was wont to have therefrom forty cart loads of hay, he can now have only seven, and, where he was wont to have in the same meadow, after the hay was cut and taken away, pasture for forty great beasts, he can now have pasture only for six. . . .

. . . It was found that the place [where the nuisance was done] was the plaintiff's freehold, and that the defendant had made a trench on that soil to his nuisance, as set out above, to the plaintiff's damage two marks.[65].

Persey: By the writ it is alleged that the defendant has diverted the water to the nuisance, etc.; by which writ it must be supposed that the free-hold where the nuisance is levied is in the defendant. But now it is found that the place where the nuisance is done belongs to the plaintiff, for which the proper remedy is by Assise of Novel Disseisin or by Writ of Trespass.

[But the Court gave judgment for the plaintiff, awarding him damages and ordering the nuisance to be abated.]

[64] See Blackstone, Comm. II. 323-4.
[65] A mark is 13s. 4d. In the 12th century money was reckoned both by tale, *ad numerum*, i.e. 12 pennies make a shilling, 20 shillings a pound, and by weight, *ad pensum*, i.e. 20 pennies make one ounce of silver, 8 ounces make a mark, 13s. 4d. See Poole, *The Exchequer in the Twelfth Century*, pp. 82-3.

❧ 2 ❧

DETINUE

A NOTE upon classification may precede the history of Detinue. Ames, in his Lectures on Legal History,[1] confidently urged its contractual character. 'The appeal, trespass and replevin were actions *ex delicto*. Detinue, on the other hand, in its original form was an action *ex contractu* in the same sense that Debt was a contractual action. It was founded on a bailment; that is, upon a delivery of a chattel to be re-delivered.' He proceeded to relate eight phenomena which 'showed' this 'contractual nature.' Thus, 'in the first place, the count must allege a bailment, and a traverse of this allegation was an answer to the action. . . . Fourthly, the gist of the action of detinue was a refusal to deliver up the chattel on the plaintiff's request; that is, a breach of contract. . . . Fifthly, bailees were chargeable in *assumpsit*, after that action had become the common remedy for the breach of parol contracts. . . .'[2] Eighthly, one for whose benefit a bailment was made could have detinue although not owner of the property bailed. Thus, on bailment of a charter by A. to B. to deliver to C., who was not owner of the land, C. recovers by priority[3] of bailment.'

Ames' conclusion, it will be observed, rests upon four assumptions: that Detinue was originally in intimate association with Debt, that Debt was contractual, that the scope of Detinue was co-terminous with that of bailment, and that bailment is, or was, a matter of contract. The first of these assumptions is universally admitted; the second was denied by such authoritative names as Holmes, Pollock and Maitland and Holdsworth. The same jurists allowed the third, though Holdsworth's language reveals some slight uneasiness, and its examination may be postponed to a discussion of the cases upon which its validity must depend.[4] Even if it be just, it will not avail to support Ames' thesis without the aid of the fourth assumption, and this last, it is suggested, is demonstrably false. The very facts offered by Ames in evidence betray the weakness of the argument. He is driven to identify the refusal by a bailee to re-deliver a chattel with the breach of a contract, and to suppose a contractual relationship between the bailee and a third party. Bailment, in truth, is *sui generis*—an elementary and unique transaction, the practical necessity of which is self-evident and

---

[1] Lecture VI, especially pp. 71-3.
[2] A remarkable instance of *ex post facto* historical treatment.
[3] *Sic*: *quare*, is this a misprint for 'privity'?
[4] *Infra*, p. 26. See Holmes, *The Common Law*, Lectures V and VII, esp. at p. 252; P. & M. II. 172-180; H.E.L. II. 366-8 and III. 324-8.

self-explanatory, and if in later years it is most often, though not invariably,[5] associated with a contract, this is not, and never has been, its essential characteristic. It was a familiar fact, as Detinue and Debt were familiar words, before contract was a generic conception.

Detinue, therefore, is not to be affiliated to contract. To-day it is expressed in terms of tort, though not without *malaise* and, in part at least, as the accident of statutory interpretation.[6] As a remedy for the recovery of chattels, moreover, it maintains relations with the Law of Property. The mediæval writ lay across the categories of modern analysis, and to force it into one or other of them is to be guilty of anachronism.

In the beginning Detinue was but part of Debt. Glanvill in his tenth book gave the writ to be used by a person who sued in the King's court for a ' debt which is due to him.'[7] It followed, as precisely as the context would admit, the pattern of the Writ of Right: there was the same direction to render the object of complaint to the plaintiff or show cause for default, and the same allegation that the plaintiff had been ' unjustly deforced.' The difference lay in the subject-matter. In Glanvill's example the claim was not for a hide of land, as in the Writ of Right, but for one hundred marks which the defendant was said to ' owe.' Later in the same book Glanvill explained that the debt might be demanded for several causes, and, among others, *ex causa commodati,* on a gratuitous loan of a chattel to be used and returned. But whether it be a sum of money or a specific chattel which was in question, the plea was still a ' plea of debt ' and the same writ was employed—the composite writ of Debt-Detinue.[8]

Bracton added little to Glanvill's account, but from the few reported cases of the thirteenth century and from the evidence of Registers and Statutes some reconstruction may be attempted. Six early cases between 1200 and 1234 deserve attention. In *Maltravers* v. *Turberville* in 1200, the plaintiff, as heir, claimed three charters which the defendant's wife ' had in her keeping,' and five breastplates which had belonged to his father and which were ' unjustly detained from him.'[9] In 1202, the plaintiff, as the elder brother and represen-

---

[5] See *R.* v. *McDonald* (1885) 15 Q.B.D. 323 and *Meux* v. *G.E. Ry.* [1895] 2 Q.B. 387.
[6] See *Bryant* v. *Herbert* (1878) 3 C.P.D. 389; and Winfield, *Province of the Law of Tort,* Chap. V.
[7] Glanvill, Book X. Cap. 1, 2, 3, 13. *Infra,* p. 233.
[8] When the claim was for a chattel, its value must be stated in the writ. Pollock and Maitland (P. & M. II, 173-7), basing themselves on Bracton, f. 102b, maintained that, as a result, the defendant always enjoyed the option to pay value instead of returning the chattel and that for this reason English law refused a ' real action ' for movables. Bracton does indeed say this and does draw this conclusion. Glanvill, however, is less categorical. By his account the defendant must restore the chattel if it still exists: only if it has meanwhile disappeared is he to pay the value. See also *Wulghes* v. *Pepard, infra,* p. 37, where restitution of a book was awarded by the Court.
[9] S.S. Vol. 3, Plea 8; *infra,* p. 35. ' Charters ' in these cases represent the title-deeds to land.

tative of Ralph St. Germain, claimed from Sarah St. Germain ' two charters of the hereditaments which belonged to Walter St. Germain, their uncle, . . . and which the said Walter delivered to Sarah to keep in this way, that if anything should happen to Walter, Sarah should deliver those charters to Ralph, as Walter's heir."[10]   In 1220 William of Cantelupe claimed from the Prior of Broc certain charters which, he said, belonged to an heir, whose guardian he was.   The Prior admitted that he had received the charters from a third party, John d'Egville, contained in a coffer and sealed with John's seals, and declared himself ready to give them up to William, if only John would consent; but, so far from consenting, John was harassing him with proceedings in the ecclesiastical courts, and he dared not part with them.[11]   In 1222 John Stolke demanded the return of a horse valued at thirty-two shillings, and alleged that the defendant had assaulted the plaintiff's servant while he was riding the horse and hoping to sell it at Stamford Fair, had unseated him and imprisoned him, and had taken and kept the horse; whereby ' *vexatus est et gravatus et deterioratus et dampnum habet ad valenciam centum solidorum.*'[12]   In 1224 the plaintiff claimed five marks and one sword which he alleged to have been formally granted to him in settlement of a previous injury—*pro transgressione.*[13]   In 1234 an heir demanded from the Prior of St. Frideswide's in Oxford fourteen charters which he said that his father, on his departure for the Holy Land, had delivered ' to be safely kept.'[14]

Of these six cases three, indeed, originated in bailment.   The plaintiff, however, sued, not as bailor, but as an heir whose ancestor, or some third party, had deposited title-deeds for safe custody with the defendant, and the action seems to have been brought as an aid to secure the inheritance.   The others were not cases of bailment at all.   The first was, once more, a stage on the perilous road of the mediæval heir, the fourth an anticipation of Trespass,[15] and the fifth the compromise of an action.   The whole seems hardly to justify the intimate or inevitable association of Detinue and Bailment.

The cases are as interesting in form as in substance.   The word ' *deforciat,*' reminiscent of the Writ of Right, is to be found in none, nor does it appear in the specimen writ given in a Register dated 10 November 1227 and intended for Irish litigation.[16]   In other

---

[10] S.S. Vol. 3, Plea 137.
[11] B.N.B. Plea 1366.
[12] B.N.B. Plea 194.
[13] B.N.B. Plea 936. *Transgressio* is clearly used in a non-technical sense.
[14] B.N.B. Plea 832; *infra*, p. 35.
[15] Or possibly recalled the old claim for recovery of *res adiratæ* (*adextratum*—' gone from the hand '). This old remedy, if indeed it existed in any precise form, is too obscure to receive detailed treatment, but is a possible antecedent of Detinue. See P. & M. II. 160-2; H.E.L. III. 320-6; Potter, *Historical Introduction to English Law*, 3rd edn., pp. 386-7.
[16] Maitland, *Collected Papers*, II. 130-4.

respects the method of pleading seems not to have crystallised. In the first, third and sixth cases ' *detinet* ' was used without ' *debet*,' in the fourth the horse was claimed as one ' *quem ei debet et iniuste detinet*,' in the fifth the plaintiff averred a ' *detinet* ' and the defendant denied a ' *debet*.' The fluid language and the tendency to rely on ' *detinet* ' alone suggest that the time was not far distant when the composite writ of Debt-Detinue would be broken. The breach took place about the middle of the century. The Register of 1227 offered still but a single form of writ: in a later collection, judged by Maitland at least to be older than 1259, the parts have separated. The plaintiff claimed ' *xii. marcas quas ei debet et iniuste detinet*,' but ' *catallum ad valenciam x. marcarum quod ei detinet*.'[17] The demarcation was emphasised when the Statute of 1284 prescribed the process for the new courts of conquered Wales and distinguished the formulæ appropriate on the one hand for money and on the other hand for goods.[18]

By the close of the thirteenth century a separate writ of Detinue had thus emerged. But it was one thing to insist on the individuality of Debt and Detinue and another to determine their boundaries. The approach was through the subject-matter, and particularly by distinguishing claims for money or other *res fungibiles* and claims for specific chattels. Thus in 1292 Roger Mortimer brought a ' writ of Detinue of a Charter ' against Dame Maud Mortimer. The defendant admitted the bailment, but said that it had taken place while she was still married, so that she could bind herself no more than if she had received a loan of thirty marks. The plaintiff replied that the gist of his action was not the bailment of the charter during the marriage but its detinue now that she was a widow, and that the hypothetical loan of money offered no analogy. ' The case is not similar; for, whereas in a writ of Debt you would say *debet*, here you would say *quam iniuste detinet*.'[19] The line of demarcation, though indicated, was not·yet firmly drawn. In the following year a plaintiff brought Debt for the price of wheat sold to the defendant and declared that the latter 'tortiously detained' £4, without any allegation of 'debet.'[20] Practice, however, was hardening throughout the reign of Edward II, and the crucial cases were those where money had indeed been delivered to the defendant, but enclosed in a chest or other receptacle so that it should not be used as current coin. In *Luffenham* v. *Abbot of Westminster* in 1313[21] the plaintiff sued in a ' Bref de detenue de chattels ' for a box, containing money, bailed to the defendants.

---

[17] Maitland, *Collected Papers*, II. 141-154, esp. at p. 145.
[18] *Infra*, p. 238. The Statute codified procedure for a new jurisdiction, and may therefore have been more precise than current litigious practice.
[19] *Mortimer* v. *Mortimer*, Y.B. 20 & 21 Ed. I. (R.S.) pp. 189-191.
[20] *Richard* v. *Verdon*, Y.B. 21 & 22 Ed. I. (R.S.) p. 293; *infra*, p. 241. See also the cases cited by Barbour, *History of Contract in Early English Equity*, at pp. 27-8.
[21] Y.B. Hil. 6 Ed. II. (S.S. Vol. 43, p. 65).

> *Scrope* (for the defendants): We ask judgment of the writ, for the writ speaks of chattels only, and he has counted of both chattels and money.

> BEREFORD, C. J.: He is not counting in debt or in covenant, but he says that he bailed into your custody the box under seal. Answer over.

In an anonymous case of 1339 the argument was repeated and received as conclusive.[22] A father had bailed to an Abbot a sealed bag, containing pots, linen and twenty pounds in coin, to be delivered to his daughter when she came of age. The defendant again challenged the form of action on the ground that money was claimed and that such a claim necessitated Debt, but the challenge again failed. It was the bag with all its contents, whatever they might be, which was the object of the bailment, and the transaction was not *mutuum,* but *depositum.* The rule was thus settled that money and other *res fungibiles* were to be claimed by Debt, charters and other specific chattels by Detinue. The distinction was reflected in, though not invariably translated into, the language of the writs. It may not be said that the two words ' *debet* ' and ' *detinet* ' were invariably found in Debt, since the former might be omitted if the action was not between the original parties;[23] but at least it is true that ' *debet* ' was never used in Detinue.

Two points of procedure should be noted. It is a familiar statement that Detinue was subject to Wager of Law and that this defect occasioned the subsequent preference for an action on the Case. Wager of Law, however, was not always allowed. It was certainly refused, in Detinue as in Debt, where the original parties, or one of them, had died; executors and administrators could not wage the law of the deceased.[24] But for a time at least judges inclined to refuse it, even as between the original parties, when the facts appeared so notorious that the testimony of witnesses could be received. In 1306 in *Croke* v. *Ellis,*[25] chattels to the value of £40 were alleged to have been given on the occasion of a marriage which later proved to be a nullity. HENGHAM, C.J., insisted on a jury.

> ' To the law you shall not get, for the contract was not made privily in a chamber between Agnes's father and you; for it may be that the marriage was so made that your friends and her friends saw when you appropriated the chattels and beasts, so that the Court can be certified by the county. . . . And so to the jurors.'

Three years later, in a simple case between bailor and bailee, BEREFORD, C.J., made the same point with characteristic vehemence.

[22] Y.B. 12 & 13 Ed. III (R.S.) p. 245.
[23] *Infra,* p. 217.
[24] Y.B. 2 & 3 Ed. II, A.D. 1309 (S.S. Vol. 19, p. 15).
[25] Y.B. 2 & 3 Ed. II. (S.S. Vol. 19, Appendix I, p. 194).

' God forbid that he should get to his law about a matter of which the county may have knowledge; for then with a dozen or half-a-dozen ruffians he might swear an honest man out of his goods.' [26]

Later in the century the point of notoriety was abandoned. In *Thornhill's Case* in 1344,[27] counsel for the plaintiff contended that the defendant should not be allowed to wage his law ' in respect of a bailment which falls so manifestly within the knowledge of the county.' But the contention was rejected, and the rejection affirmed the following year in *Manston's Case*.[28] Henceforth wager of law was always a potential thorn in the path of the plaintiff.

The second point concerns the question of damages. Professor Woodbine has asserted that, in the time of Glanvill, there was no possibility of recovering damages in a writ of Debt-Detinue. What, then, he asks, ' would the bailor recover where the *res* bailed was a thing which, though of little value in itself, represented great value, as a charter, when the *res* was lost or destroyed? '[29] The assertion, whatever be its validity for the reign of Henry II, does not represent the later law. The reports of the fourteenth century are full of such claims. In 1312 £40, and in 1313 £100, were demanded for the detention of charters[30]; and thirty years later the precise question put by Professor Woodbine was answered. In ' Detinue of a writing ' it was found by the jury that the charter had been burnt by the defendant. Plaintiff's counsel suggested that his client might be prejudiced in defending his title and asked for damages to include such prejudice. The Court allowed the damages, though it assessed them at the somewhat inadequate figure of half a mark, and made a presumably fruitless order for restitution of the deed.[31] A still more significant case occurred in 1346. The defendant was found guilty of the ' detinue of a writing,' and damages were assessed at ten marks ' in case the writing had not been either burnt or eloigned ' and at twenty marks if it had. An optimistic demand was immediately made for the higher sum, but the case was remitted to Nisi Prius to discover the fate of the charter.[32]

The content of the fourteenth-century cases confirms the suspicion that bailment was not the single root of Detinue. There were certainly many instances of simple bailment; of sacks of wool, of boxes or bags,

[26] Y.B. 2 & 3 Ed. II. (S.S. Vol. 19, Appendix I, p. 195). See also *Yelverton* v. *Yelverton* (1311) Y.B. 4 Ed. II. (S.S. Vol. 26, p. 15). Contrast with these cases *Wulghes* v. *Pepard* (1310) Y.B. 4 Ed. II. (S.S. Vol. 26, p. 14), *infra*, p. 37, where the alleged bailment was not a matter of notoriety.
[27] Y.B. 17 & 18 Ed. III. (R.S.) p. 510. *Infra*, p. 41.
[28] Y.B. 19 Ed. III. (R.S.) p. 328.
[29] Glanvill, pp. 257-8, and see 33 Yale L.J. 802-11.
[30] *Lyndesey* v. *Suth*, Y.B. 6 Ed. II. (S.S. Vol. 34, p. 166), and *Anon* v. *Anon* (S.S. Vol. 27, p. 16), *infra*, pp. 37-9. See also *Wulghes* v. *Pepard* (1310) (S.S. Vol. 26, p. 14), *infra*, p. 37.
[31] Y.B. 17 & 18 Ed. III. (R.S.) p. 2.
[32] Y.B. 20 Ed. III. (R.S.) p. 74.

sealed or unsealed and alleged to contain money or jewels, and, on occasion, of valuable books.[33] But the range of Detinue was wide. The plaintiff's claim in *Croke* v. *Ellis,* already noticed for the Court's refusal to award wager of law,[34] was based on what modern lawyers would be tempted to describe as a total failure of consideration. Richard Croke had arranged a marriage between his daughter and the defendant, and, to encourage the bridegroom, gave him £40 worth of goods. The marriage was celebrated, but the defendant was later found to have been already married to a certain Isabel. The plaintiff, now that her marriage was void, sued the bigamist for the goods or their value. In another context a group of cases illuminates the obscure but curious law of 'legitim.' The mediæval power of testamentary disposition, even of movables, was not unfettered. A childless widower might indeed do what he pleased. If, however, he left either widow or child, but not both, he could deal freely only with one half of his chattels, and, if he left both widow and children, they were divided into three parts, the 'wife's part,' the 'bairns' part,' and the 'dead's part,' and the last alone was at his disposal. Such seems to have been the general law of the twelfth and thirteenth centuries, and, though questioned in the fourteenth, it survived to the close of the middle ages.[35] An anonymous case of 1308 is instructive.[36] A son claimed from his father's executors a third part of the chattels as his 'legitim' or legitimate share, and alleged that 'by the usage of the country the third part ought to remain to the dead man and one part to his wife and one part to his unadvanced children.' The arguments suggest the complexity of the action, and in particular the delicate adjustment of civil and ecclesiastical jurisdiction and the mysteries of 'advancement.' A child, blessed by his father's bounty *inter vivos,* could not claim unless he brought this property into 'hotchpot'; and the plaintiff in the present case was driven to argue that the seisin of thirty acres of land was no 'advancement,' but merely 'shoe-money.'[37]

In this, as in the earlier period, the majority of cases concerned the title-deeds of land. In some they had been bailed by the plaintiff to the defendant, in others by a third party to the defendant, and in others again they had, without any bailment, come into the possession of the

[33] *Wulghes* v. *Pepard* (1310), *infra* p. 37; *Anon* Y.B. 2 & 3 Ed. II. (A.D. 1309) (S.S. Vol. 19, p. 15); *Luffenham* v. *Abbot of Westminster,* Y.B. 6 Ed. II (A.D. 1313) (S.S. Vol. 43, p. 65); *Bowden* v. *Pelleter,* Y.B. 8 Ed. II. (A.D. 1315) (S.S. Vol. 41, p. 136).
[34] Y.B. 2 & 3 Ed. II. (A.D. 1306) (S.S. Vol. 19, App. I, p. 194), *supra,* p. 28.
[35] And, in the Province of York, until 1692. See P. & M. II. 348-356; Plucknett, 4th ed., pp. 705-7. In the modern law of Scotland, a widow may still have her 'terce' and a bairn his 'legitim': Gloag and Henderson, *Introduction to the Law of Scotland* (4th ed.) Chap. XL.
[36] Y.B. 1 & 2 Ed. II. (S.S. Vol. 17, p. 39); *infra,* p. 36. See also *Plenty* v. *Gold and Talbot* (1389) Y.B. 12 Rich. II. (Ames Foundation, Vol. VII, Plea 4), and *Ward's Case* (A.D. 1343) Y.B. 17 Ed. III. (R.S. p. 140), a widow's claim.
[37] *Quare,* the masculine of pin-money? Blackstone, II. 190, describes 'hotchpot' as a 'housewifely metaphor' and explains it in Littleton's words (Co. Litt. 164): 'It seemeth that this word is in English a pudding; for in a pudding is not commonly put one thing alone, but one thing with other things together.'

defendant as executor; but in none was the bailment the gist of the action. In the words of counsel in 1311, ' Detinue of charters is much in the nature of disinheritance,'[38] and the argument in court often took the form of an assertion and a denial of title. In a case heard during the Eyre of Kent, 1313-14,[39] the plaintiff claimed, as heiress of her mother, two charters which she said had been in her mother's custody and which were now detained from her by the mother's executor, and the defendant in turn maintained his right to them as the deeds of an estate of which he was seised by a lawful feoffment. In the record of the case, both Count and Plea set out in some detail the respective titles claimed. It would almost seem that ' Detinue of Charters ' was regarded as a distinct writ or, at least, as a highly individualised species of a generic writ, and it is significant that, when the sixteenth-century lawyers collated the mediæval law, they made separate entries for ' Detinue de biens et chattels' and for ' Detinue de scripts et charters.'[40]

The prevalence of claims for title-deeds and of other cases where bailment was not the vital issue raised a question of pleading. Was this to vary according to the presence or absence of a bailment, or was there some formula which might cover the whole sphere of detinue? In the early years of the fourteenth century a phrase emerged which might well be deemed sufficiently comprehensive. In *Lyndesey* v. *Suth*[41] the plaintiff, as heiress to her grandfather, claimed a charter from the defendant, and declared that, after the grandfather's death, it had ' come into the seisin ' (*devenit in seisinam*) of his second wife, by whom it had been delivered to the defendant. The defendant pleaded that she herself had been enfeoffed of the estate in question by the grandfather, who had naturally given her the title-deeds at the same time, and the plaintiff replied by traversing the feoffment and repeating that the charter had come to the hands (*devenit ad manus*) of the second wife. The defendant argued in Court that the plaintiff should have alleged and proved a bailment, but the plaintiff denied the necessity; a taking or a finding by the defendant would equally make her liable to the action. The case was ultimately sent to the jury to decide how the charter came to be possessed by the defendant, but the language of the count was not repudiated.

The phrase *devenit* or *devenerunt ad manus* became, with variants, common form for over a hundred years, and was manifestly convenient when the precise steps whereby the charter or other chattel had reached

[38] *Yelverton* v. *Yelverton,* Y.B. 4 Ed. II. (S.S. Vol. 26, p. 15).
[39] *Anon* v. *Anon,* Eyre of Kent, 6 & 7 Ed. II, A.D. 1313-4 (S.S. Vol. 27, p. 16), *infra,* p. 39; and *Lyndesey* v. *Suth,* Y.B. 6 Ed. II. (S.S. Vol. 34, p. 166), *infra,* p. 37. See also *Anon* (1388), Bellewe, *Detinue de Charters,* p. 134, a claim by a remainder-man against an executor.
[40] See Brooke, *Abridgment* (ed. 1586), and Bellewe, *The Cases of K. Rich. le Second* (1585).
[41] A.D. 1312, Y.B. 6 Ed. II. (S.S. Vol. 34, pp. 166-8), *infra,* p. 37. See also *Anon* v *Anon* (1313-4), *infra,* p. 39.

the defendant were doubtful or disputed. If, however, there had certainly been a bailment, must this fact be specifically pleaded or might it be merged in the more general *devenerunt ad manus*? In 1323 a plaintiff sued in Detinue for a bond which he declared he had bailed for safe custody to X, and which, after X's death, had come into the hands (*devynt en la mayn*) of the defendant. Counsel objected to the form of the declaration. ' Your count is worth nothing, because you commence it by alleging the bailment to a certain person, and then, whereas you should continue to lay your action against us by force of the bailment, you do not pursue the bailment, as by making us privy to the bailee, but treat us as complete strangers.' The plaintiff, he suggested, ' should have counted that we detain the writing tortiously from you, and tortiously in that the writing *devynt en notre mayn*.'[42] In other words, since the plaintiff had begun by alleging a bailment, he must pursue his allegation to its conclusion and could not be allowed to wander off into a general *devenerunt*; but, had he never alleged a bailment, his declaration would have been good. The argument, if logical, was too refined for the coarse realities of litigation, and it was soon abandoned. If the plaintiff chose to rely on a detinue *sur bailment* he must, of course, prove a bailment and that the defendant was privy to it. But if he declared on a *devenerunt ad manus,* the process whereby the chattel reached the defendant, whether by bailment or otherwise, was irrelevant: it was the detention that constituted the tort. ' In whatever way it came into your possession, whether as executors or because you took it out of the possession of some one else or because you found it, if you detain it, I shall have an action; wherefore, inasmuch as you do not answer as to the detinue, which is the principal matter of the action, I ask judgment.'[43]

To declare upon a *devenerunt* thus became the natural recourse of a plaintiff who could say no more than that he had lost goods, he knew not how, and that the defendant had found them. As against a rightful claimant finding was not keeping.[44] Towards the close of the fourteenth century cases occurred in which it was expressly alleged that goods had been lost and found. In 1389, the plaintiff brought detinue against a husband and wife for a box of charters, and he declared ' that the husband and wife found the box (*troverount le boist*) . . . at Queenhithe in London,' that he asked for the box and that the defendants refused to give it up. The action foundered on the technicalities with which the common law surrounded the marital

---

[42] *Anon.* Y.B. 16 Ed. II. (Trin.) f. 490.

[43] *Green, arguendo* in *Thornhill's Case*, A.D. 1344, Y.B. 17 & 18 Ed. III, (R.S.) p. 150, *infra*, p. 42; and see *Wagworth* v. *Holyday*, A.D. 1356, Y.B. 29 Ed. III. Trin. f. 38b.

[44] *Lyndesey* v. *Suth*, *infra*, p. 37, and *Thornhill's Case*, *infra*, p. 41; and *per* SCROPE, J. (*obiter*) in Y.B. 2 Ed. III. Hil. f. 2, pl. 5—a case of Trespass: ' If you had found the charter in the street, I should have my recovery against you by the *Præcipe quod reddat.*'

state, but no objection was made to the form of the declaration.[45] To allege a *trover* when such was indeed the fact called for little comment. But in the middle of the fifteenth century the allegation was introduced, not as the description of a particular incident in the history of a case, but as a substitute for the general declaration on a *devenerunt*. It was in *Malpas' Case* in 1455 that—almost, it would appear, by accident— the step was taken which was to make so lasting an impression upon the law.[46] The plaintiff claimed a sealed box, containing the title-deeds of land, which ' had come into the hands of the defendant by finding ' (*per inventionem*). It was objected that the plaintiff had not recited his title to the land with sufficient particularity to justify his claim to the deeds. Chief Justice Prisot at first inclined to the objection, but, after Littleton had argued on the other side, it was abandoned. The distinction was re-stated between detinue *sur bailment* and detinue on a *devenerunt ad manus*. In the former the relations between the plaintiff and the defendant must be traced, in the latter it sufficed that the defendant had the chattels in his possession and would not restore them. The reporter concluded with words which have since become familiar. ' And then Littleton said privately (*secrettement*) that this declaration *per inventionem* is a new-found Haliday; for the old declaration has always been in such case that the charters *ad manus et possessionem defendentis devenerunt*.'[47]

While it is evident that Littleton's somewhat oracular words were provoked, not by a change in the substantive law, but by an innovation of pleading, the cause of this innovation is by no means clear. The plaintiff who declared on a *devenerunt* committed himself to little, and his counsel could cull from the history of the case such incidents as industry or ingenuity might suggest. To abandon so safe and generous a course for the hazard of a single allegation would seem strangely unwise. No technical explanation is satisfactory, and the reason may perhaps be sought in the political turmoil of the mid-fifteenth century. Public disorder was private opportunity. Philip Malpas himself, the defendant in the ' new-found Haliday ' case, a London merchant and Lancastrian supporter, had his own house plundered in Cade's rebellion of 1450;[48] and contemporary documents reveal the alacrity with which merchants and country gentlemen sought to enrich their estates at the expense of their neighbours. A typical incident was recorded on the Patent Rolls of 1448. Sir Robert Wingfield complained that the Duke of Norfolk, Gilbert Debenham and others, ' bringing by night

---

[45] *Anon* v. *Anon*. Y.B. 13 Rich. II. (Ames Foundation, ed. Plucknett, p. 56).
[46] Y.B. 33 Hen. VI. Trin. f. 26, pl. 12. *Infra*, p. 42.
[47] Littleton did not become a Judge until April 17, 1466, and this report is a tribute to his reputation even at the Bar. See, for his life and works, H.E.L. II. 571-591. ' Haliday ' = ' holiday,' and was used contemporaneously in the sense of a trifling or irrelevant incident—a quirk or conceit.
[48] Kingsford, *Prejudice and Promise in XVth Century England*, p. 50.

carts and wagons with cannons,' came to his house at Letheringham and ' hurled stones thereat, brake his walls, towers and stone chimneys, sawed asunder the posts and beams of divers houses, set coals of fire in the litters of his beds and in his corn,' and carried off many goods and chattels, including ' chests of charters.'[49] It is significant that among the booty were the title-deeds which might later serve to lend to injury the colour of right and that the complainant was himself the object of a similar petition. Spoliation was not only an agreeable but a mutual pastime, and the victim of to-day, who hoped to be the oppressor of to-morrow, would prefer, when he sought the recovery of his deeds, to avoid allegations of violence which might recoil upon his own head. Where judicial ignorance was bliss, it was folly to induce wisdom. The fiction of a *trover* was as effective and much safer than the fact of an assault.

Whatever the reason, and despite the fastidious reluctance of Littleton, the ' new-found Haliday ' was popular and, with occasional reversions to the more general *devenerunt,* quickly became the normal course of pleading. In 1490 Chief Justice Brian offered a litigant the choice of counting ' sur un trover ' or ' sur un bailment ';[50] and in the early years of the sixteenth century the device of the pleader became the language of the substantive law. All cases which did not depend upon a bailment were classified under the head of *trover,* and *detinue sur bailment* and *detinue sur trover* became an inevitable antithesis.[51]

---

[49] Calendar of Patent Rolls, 1446-52, pp. 137, 226, cited by Miss Haward, *Gilbert Debenham, A Mediæval Rascal in Real Life, History,* Vol. 13, p. 300, at p. 303. See Bennett, *The Pastons and Their England,* Chaps. I, XII and XIII: Mr. Justice Paston himself was not above suspicion. See also Kingsford, *Prejudice and Promise in XVth Century England,* cited above, where Lecture III abounds in similar incidents. Thus one Savage petitioned Chancery in 1461 that he had been robbed of all his goods during the French attack on Plymouth save of certain jewels, ' which he packed in two chests and sent by one of his servants to what he deemed would be a safe place. But the servant was met by a follower of Thomas Carew, who took the chests and gave them to his mistress, by whom they were detained ' (pp. 56-7). Particularly affecting is the fate of Peter Marmion, who was seized by a neighbouring squire and tied up with a dog collar until he executed a deed releasing his manor to his assailant (pp. 60-1).

[50] *Anon,* Y.B. Mich. 6 Hen. VII, pl. 4. See Y.B. Mich. 39 Hen. VI, pl. 7; Y.B. Mich. Ed. IV, pl. 2; Y.B. Hil. 21 Ed. IV, pl. 21; Y.B. Mich. 2 Hen. VII, pl. 1. Compare, for reversion to the *devenerunt,* Y.B. 10 Ed. IV, pl. 7 (S.S. Vol. 47, p. 104), and Y.B. Trin. 27 Hen. VIII, pl. 14. See also Coke, C.J. in *Isaack* v. *Clark,* 2 Bulstrode 306, (*infra,* p. 117), at pp. 312-3.

[51] e.g. Y.B. Pasch. 27 Hen. VIII, pl. 35 (A.D. 1536): ' Note, that FITZHERBERT, J. put a diversity, where one comes to the possession of goods by bailment or by trover. For where one comes to the possession by bailment, there he is chargeable by force of the bailment, and if he bails them over or where they are taken out of his possession, still he is chargeable to his bailor by force of the bailment. But it is otherwise where he comes to the possession by trover, for there he is chargeable only by reason of the possession, and if he is out of possession lawfully before the rightful owner has brought his action, he is not chargeable.' Moreover, while trover might be, and usually was, a fiction, the bailment was a fact which the plaintiff must prove; and to traverse it was therefore an issue which, in Fitzherbert's words, must ' go to the lay gents (*les lais gens*).' The use of this pleasing appellation for the Jury is not uncommon in the Year Books. For a specimen of mid-sixteenth century pleading in Detinue sur trover, see *Rastell's Entries* (1566), *infra,* p. 43.

SOURCES

MALTRAVERS v. TURBERVILLE
SELECT CIVIL PLEAS (A.D. 1200-1203): S.S. VOL. 3
A.D. 1200
Plea 8

John Maltravers demands against Walter de Turberville and Alice his wife two charters of King Henry the grandfather and one of our lord King John, and one charter of the Earl of Striguil, which Alice had in her keeping. And Walter de Turberville comes and admits that he had those charters, but he says that they were stolen from him and burnt when his house was burnt, whereof he appealed the burners of his house and whereof the said John was appealed.

And he, John, demands against them [also] five breast-plates which they unjustly detain from him (*quas ipsi iniuste ei detinent*) and which belonged to John his father. And Walter denies that they [he and his wife] ever had those breast-plates,[52] and says that John, the father of the said John, had no breast-plate but one only, which he gave to a certain son of his, together with ten librates of land, in the seventh year before his death. And John comes and says that his father had those five breast-plates in a certain Welsh war and was bound by the tenure of his land to have them; and he produces sufficient suit thereof, to wit, Reginald de Argentine, who saw them. And he craves that it may be allowed in his favour that Walter admits that he had the charters and that they were lost under his charge after he [John] had begun his plea.

It is ordered that Walter shall be here on the morrow of St. Michael to hear judgment touching the breast-plates, and judgment touching the charters at the same time. . . .

[Walter makes default, and judgment is given for John.]

HILARY, A.D. 1234 — OXFORDSHIRE
BRACTON'S NOTE BOOK
Plea 832

Geoffrey the son of John the son of Hugo demands against the Prior of St. Frideswide's 14 charters which he unjustly detains from him, as he says; and [he says] that John the son of Hugo, when he set out for the Holy Land, delivered these charters to be safely kept, and as to this he produces sufficient suit[53]; and [he says] that they were delivered to the predecessor of the Prior that now is, to wit, one Simon the Prior.

---

[52] ' Defendit quod numquam habuerunt loricas illas.' The word ' defendit ' was often used in the sense of ' deny ' or ' refuse,' as was its English counterpart as late as the fifteenth century. See Wyld in *Essays and Studies*. Vol. XXVI (1941), p. 35, citing Henry V's despatch describing his crossing of the Seine in 1418 ' albeit that our enemys with grete power assembled for to have let and defended us the same passage.'

[53] Suit: *Secta*, i.e. the plaintiff's friends, prepared to support his claim. They were not witnesses in the modern sense (cf. Holmes, *The Common Law*, pp. 255-265, who derives them from the Anglo-Saxon transaction witnesses), though they were sometimes examined by the Court. See Bracton's N.B., Case 1693, A.D. 1226, where the plaintiff lost because they told different stories. But in 1343 the Court refused to examine them, and thereafter they were not even produced (Y.B. 17 Ed. III, f. 48, pl. 14). The formula, however—*et inde produxit sectam*—survived as a mere phrase of pleading, until the Common Law Procedure Act, 1852 (15 & 16 Vict. c. 76, s. 55). See Thayer, *A Preliminary Treatise on Evidence*, pp. 10-16.

And the Prior by his attorney comes and denies against him and his suit that any charter was delivered to him, but he does not know in truth if any charter was delivered to his predecessor; and he asks for a day that he may make inquiry; and he has it. . . .

ANON
Y.B. 1 & 2 ED. II. (S.S. VOL. 17, p. 39)
A.D. 1308

This showeth to you that R. and G., executors of the testament of H., wrongfully (*a tort*) do not render to [the plaintiff] chattels to the value of ten marks; and wrongfully for that the said H., his father, whose executors they are, died at a certain place and had chattels to the value of thirty marks, to wit, corn and barley, etc., and by the usage of the country the third part thereof ought to remain to the dead man and one part to his wife and one part to his unadvanced children; wherefore upon his father's death he came to the executors and prayed them that they would deliver to him the third part of the chattels according to the usage, etc.; but they would not and yet will not, etc.

Malberthorpe demanded a hearing of the writ; and it was in common form.

Malberthorpe: You see well how he demands ten marks' worth of chattels and does not affirm by law how the chattels are due to him, for he does not say that he bought them of us, nor that he bailed them to us, and by no contract (*par nulle contracte*) are we obliged to him. We pray judgment whether he should be answered.

Willoughby: We have assigned a cause, namely, that this is according to the usage of the country, and this suffices us.

STANTON, J.: This matter cannot be debated except in Court Christian.

Herle: We did plead there, and they put forward a prohibition and forbade us, and we could not obtain a consultation.[54]

Passeley: The cause of his writ is a detinue, and this accords with the fact and is explained [by the declaration]. Moreover, the Great Charter[55] wills that the dead man's chattels remain to his executors, ' saving to his wife and children their reasonable shares,' and since the Great Charter wills this and the writ that he has purchased accords [with the facts] and there is no other writ, [we pray judgment]. . . .

. . . STANTON, J.: You must answer to the writ. . . .

> [After further argument, issue was joined on the question whether the plaintiff had been ' advanced ' by a lease of thirty acres of land made to him by his father and had thus ceased to be entitled to the third share of his father's chattels.]

. . . *Herle* confessed that [the plaintiff] had land to this extent, but it was worth no more than forty pence a year, and this his father gave him as shoe-money and not as an advancement.

Malberthorpe: If it was not a disadvancement, it was an advancement.

Westcote: And we pray judgment whether he cannot recover, since the land was given him for shoe-money and not by way of advancement.

---

[54] ' A writ of consultation in effect discharges a prohibition and bids the ecclesiastical court proceed.' *Note by Maitland.*
[55] Magna Carta (1297) c. 18.

Malberthorpe: And we pray judgment since you have confessed that you have the land and so are advanced, and since this action is given by the usage [of the country] to those who are unadvanced, etc.

And thus the case stands for judgment.

WULGHES v. PEPARD
Y.B. 4 ED. II. (S.S. VOL. 26, p. 14)
A.D. 1310

Note from the Record

Master John Pepard was summoned to answer Robert of Wulghes, clerk, on a plea that he render to him a certain book of the price of one hundred shillings, which he unlawfully detains from him, etc. And whereupon Robert by Henry of Gurmundele his attorney says that—whereas on [22 July 1305] the Thursday next before the feast of St. James the Apostle 33 Ed. I at Wolfamcote in the county of Warwick he delivered to Master John a certain book of his which is called Saintgrahel of the price of one hundred shillings to guard, and at Robert's will to redeliver to him, etc.— Master John, though he was often asked to deliver that book to him, still detains and has always hitherto refused to deliver it and still refuses. Whereupon he says that he is injured and has damage to the value of ten pounds; and thereof he brings suit, etc.

And Master John by Robert of Lychefeld his attorney comes and denies tort and force when, etc., and well he denies that the book ever came into his custody and that he detains from him the book as Robert asserts; and this he is ready to defend against him and his suit as the court shall award.

Therefore it is awarded that he wage his law thereof to him twelfth handed, etc. And let him come here with his law on the quindene of St. Hilary. Pledges of the law Robert of Lychfeld and Roger of Podymor of the same county. And the attorney of Master John is told that he cause his lord to come here in his own person at the aforesaid term, etc.

Afterwards at that day came Robert by Henry his attorney, and offered himself on the fourth day against Master John on the aforesaid plea, and Master John did not come, and he wagered his law to him thereof, etc., as appears above, etc. Therefore it is awarded that Robert recover against him the aforesaid book of the price aforesaid and his damages against him as undefended, etc.; and that Master John be in mercy, etc.

Damages ten pounds, whereof forty shillings to the clerk.

LYNDESEY v. SUTH
Y.B. 6 ED. II. (S.S. VOL. 34, pp. 166-8)
A.D. 1312

Note from the Record

Agnes, widow of William Suth, was summoned to answer Alice, the daughter of Roger of Lyndesey, in a plea that she render her a certain charter which she unjustly detains from her, etc. And as to this she says that, whereas one Peter Cathale had enfeoffed one Roger of Lyndesey, the grandfather of the said Alice, whose heiress she is, of one messuage and one bovate of land with the appurtenances in Golkesby and Esterby by his charter whereof she now complains, and whereas that charter after the death of the said Roger, the grandfather, etc., together with other deeds which had belonged to the said Roger, had come into the seisin (*devenit in seisinam*) of one Goditha, who had been the wife of the said Roger, the grandfather, etc., and the mother of the said Agnes,[56] and afterwards into the seisin of the said Agnes by the delivery of the said Goditha, the said Alice did repeatedly request the said Agnes to deliver to her the said charter; yet the said Agnes has hitherto unjustly detained from her the said charter and has refused to render it, whereby she says that she has suffered loss and has damage to the value of £20.   And as to this she produces suit, etc.

And Agnes comes by Eudes of Billesby, her attorney, and denies force and wrong, etc. (*defendit vim et iniuriam*).   And she says that the said Alice does unjustly complain; for she says that the said Roger, the grandfather, etc., of his seisin did enfeoff her, the said Agnes, of the said messuage and land, to be held to herself and her heirs, etc.   And she says that the same Roger at the time of the said feoffment delivered to her the said charter. . . . And this she is ready to aver, etc., and she demands judgment.

And Alice says that the said Roger, the grandfather, etc., did never enfeoff the said Agnes of the said tenements, but died seised thereof in his demesne as of fee, so that the said Goditha, mother of the said Agnes, to whose hands the said charter had come as aforesaid (*ad cuius manus predicta carta devenit*) after the death of the said Roger, did deliver to the said Agnes the said charter, etc.   And she prays that this be inquired of by the country.

And Agnes says that she did not have the said charter by the said Goditha, but by the delivery of the said Roger, the grandfather, etc., in the manner aforesaid.   And as to this she puts herself upon the country.

And Alice does likewise.

Therefore the sheriff is commanded that he cause to come here on the quindene of Easter twelve, etc., by whom, etc.

From the Report

Alice of Lyndesey brought her writ of detinue of charters, and counted that, after the death of her ancestor whose heir, etc., one Goditha had seized the charter together with other chattels, and that Goditha had bailed the charter to this Agnes, against whom the writ is brought.

Toudeby: In counting the count you have not shown that you bailed the charter to us or that we received it from the bailee of any of your ancestors. Judgment whether you ought to be received to such a count.

Scrope: If you disseise me and carry off my charters, and I bring my writ and demand these same charters, it is then no answer to my writ to say that I did not bail you any charter.   Likewise if you should find my charters, you would answer for the detinue.   Judgment whether our count, etc.

Toudeby: We tell you that your grandfather enfeoffed us of the same tenements which are comprised in the charter which you demand, and by virtue of that charter there is reserved to us our voucher to warranty.   And a plea is pending here as to the same tenements.[57]   Therefore, if we were to deliver the charter we would lose our voucher.   And this we are ready to

---

[56] 'It seems a reasonable inference that Alice's mother was a daughter of Roger by a first wife, and Agnes a daughter of Goditha, the second wife.'   Note by the Editors, Vinogradoff and Ehrlich.

[57] 'What is probably meant is some other plea in which the same defendant (Agnes) is sued and vouches to warranty.'   Note by the Editors.

aver in whatever way this Court awards. Judgment whether he can have an action against us for that charter.

Scrope: Our grandfather died seised of the same tenements comprised in the charter, and Goditha bailed the same charter to you. Ready, etc.

Issued joined.

ANON

EYRE OF KENT, 6 & 7 ED. II. (S.S. VOL. 27, p. 16)

A.D. 1313-4

A. Year-Book Report

A. brought a writ of detinue of charters against one William and demanded two charters that were in the custody of B., A.'s mother, which William as B.'s executor detained after her death; and in his declaration he set out the contents of these charters.

Cambridge: We ourselves are tenants of the tenements comprised in the charters. Judgment whether you are entitled to recover the charters from us who are tenants of the tenements comprised in the charters.

STANTON, J.: He tells you that the charters were in the seisin of his mother and in her custody, and that you took them, as executor, after his mother's death and wrongfully (*de vostre tort demene*) detain them. Consequently it is no answer to say that you are the tenant of the tenements unless you also justify your tort.

Cambridge: We tell you that we are seised of the tenements, and if we were impleaded we should vouch as feoffor an assignee under one of the charters; and if we cannot do this we shall lose our voucher, for our feoffor has naught to give us to the value.

GOLDINGTON, J.: But just as great hardship would follow if you were to vouch A., for unless he had the charters he could not vouch over, and he would lose his voucher in circumstances where he would be able to vouch if he had the charters.

STANTON, J. (*ad idem*): If the demandant had the charters you would never be able to recover them from him by way of action. No more, then, can you withhold them from him by means of an exception.

SPIGURNEL, J.: If the charters had been delivered to you by your feoffor together with the land, that would be some argument in your favour, but he tells you that after his mother's death you as executor tortiously took them; wherefore, etc.

Cambridge: We tell you that he who now brings this writ enfeoffed us of these tenements, and delivered seisin thereof and these charters to us at the same time. Judgment, etc.

SPIGURNEL, J.: That is a good answer in bar, etc.

Malberthorpe: [Ready to aver] that you took them tortiously as executor, etc.

And thereon the other side joined issue, etc.

B. Note from the Eyre Roll

The plaintiff, according to the Roll, was Isabella, the widow of Baldwin, the goldsmith of Pulham.

The defendant was Simon, the cutler of Canterbury, executor of the will of Margery, *la Cutillere*.

Plaintiff's Count

' Whereas a certain charter, wherein is recited that one William Cokyn enfeoffed one John Carter, the father of the said Isabella, of one messuage with its appurtenances in the district of Canterbury, and also another charter, wherein is recited that the said John enfeoffed the said Isabella of the same messuage, were, while the said Isabella was under age, in the custody of the aforesaid Margery, while she lived, whose executor is the aforesaid Simon, and whereas these said charters, after the death of the said Margery, on the Wednesday after the feast of the translation of the blessed Thomas martyr in the thirty-fifth year of the reign of King Edward the father of the King that now is came into the hands (*devenerunt ad manus*) of the aforesaid Simon as executor; yet, although the said Simon has been many times requested by the said Isabella to deliver to her the aforesaid charters, he has not delivered them and still refuses to deliver them; whence she says that she has suffered loss and has damage to the value of one hundred pounds, and thereof she produces suit, etc.'

Defendant's Plea

' That he ought not to deliver to her the aforesaid charters, because he says that the aforesaid Isabella of her seisin gave the aforesaid messuage contained in the aforesaid charters to one Roger Aunsel and the aforesaid Margery, then the wife of the said Roger, to have and to hold to the said Roger and Margery and their heirs for ever. And he says that the aforesaid Isabella delivered the seisin of the aforesaid messuage together with the charters to the aforesaid Roger and Margery. And he says that the aforesaid Margery survived the said Roger and afterwards of her seisin enfeoffed the said Simon the son of the said Margery of one half of the aforesaid messuage to have and to hold to the said Simon and his heirs for ever. And afterwards in her last will she left to him the rest of the aforesaid messuage and in her lifetime delivered to him the aforesaid charters. And this he is ready to verify by the country, etc.[58]; wherefore he prays judgment

if he should render the aforesaid charters, etc.'

Plaintiff's Replication

' That she never delivered the aforesaid charters together with the seisin of the aforesaid messuage to the aforesaid Roger and Margery. And that the aforesaid charters after the death of the aforesaid Margery, the aunt of the said Isabella, came into the hands (*devenerunt ad manus*) of the aforesaid Simon as executor of the said Margery, in whose custody they had been to the use (*ad opus*) of the said Isabella.'

Issue was joined on this replication.

Verdict of the Jury

' That the aforesaid Isabella had enfeoffed the aforesaid Roger and Margery of the aforesaid messuage and had delivered seisin thereof to them together with the aforesaid charters, just as the aforesaid Simon says.'

Judgment

' That the aforesaid Simon goes thence without a day and that the aforesaid Isabella takes nothing by that verdict, but be in mercy for her false claim.'

[58] *per patriam*—i.e., by a jury.

THORNHILL'S CASE

Y.B. 17 & 18 Ed. III (R.S. p. 510)

A.D. 1344

Detinue was brought by Brian de Thornhill against three executors in respect of a horse of the value of £20. . . .

And afterwards *Thorpe* demanded judgment, inasmuch as this sounds in the nature of debt, whether they ought to be put to answer without specialty.

Green: In this action of Detinue you are put to answer as to your own act, which is the detinue, and not as to your testator's contract; for here you will not have a traverse as to his receipt nor as to the manner how [he received it], but only as to your detinue.

WILLOUGHBY, J.: He is put to answer as to the manner of the receipt and also as to the detinue; wherefore it is sufficient to answer as to one.

SHARDELOWE, J. (*ad idem*): What is the reason that in an action of Debt the executors do not have to answer without a specialty as to a debt due by their testator? It is that their testator could have waged his law, and that answer is denied to them. So in the matter before us.

Gaynesford: The testator would not have his wager of law in respect of a bailment which falls so manifestly within the knowledge of the county (which was denied by the others)[59]; but I say that executors cannot know, when they find (*quant ils trovent*) goods in the possession of their testator, how they came into his possession, whether by purchase, detinue or in any other manner, if no specialty as to the contract be shown. . . .

Mowbray: In case of Debt the executors shall not answer without a specialty, because they shall not answer as to the goods of the deceased nor be charged without a specialty, but in this case they are nct to be charged in respect of the goods of the deceased, but in respect of their own detinue. . . .

R. Thorpe: In case of Debt, when any one counts of a loan without other contract against a person who is party, wager of law lies; but if the plaintiff counts of a sale of goods or on any other certain contract, wager of law does not lie without answering as to the cause. And in such a case, where the testator himself would be put to answer as to the cause, the executors will possibly answer without a specialty; but we are not in this case.

Green: Neither wager of law nor averment would be given for your testator on the manner of the bailment, but he would answer as to the detinue, which is the principal matter of the suit; and so will you do; and even though your testator was never seised and you have come into possession, you will answer as to the detinue; for, in whatsover manner you have come into possession, you shall answer as to the detinue.

SHARSHULLE, J. (*to Thorpe*): . . . We adjudge that you do answer without a specialty. . . .

Thorpe: The reason why we might be put to answer without a specialty would be that the horse came into our keeping (*devynt en nostre garde*) after the death of our testator; and we tell you that after the death of the testator the horse did not come into our keeping; ready, etc.

---

[59] Gaynesford's argument, that in matters of notoriety wager of law is excluded, had previously been accepted by more than one judge: see *supra*, p. 28. But it is now denied; and see also *Manston's Case* (1345), Y.B. (R.S.), 19 Ed. III, p. 328.

Green: In whatever way it came into your possession, whether as executors or because you took it out of the possession of some one else or because you found it, if you detain it, I shall have an action; wherefore, inasmuch as you do not answer as to the detinue, which is the principal matter of the action, I ask judgment.

Thorpe: Then it is the fact that the horse did not come into our keeping, *ut supra.*

Green: In God's name, do you intend that to be your answer?

Then *Thorpe* said: We tell you that the horse did not come into our keeping, nor do we detain any horse, as he counts; ready, etc.

And the other side said the contrary.

MALPAS' CASE
Y.B. 33 HEN. VI. Trin. f. 26, pl. 12
A.D. 1455

Detinue of Charters against Philip Malpas

The plaintiff counted of a sealed box . . . [containing the title-deeds of certain land, whose purport he set out in his count, and which had] come into the hands of the defendant by finding (*devient al. def. per inventionem*). . . . [After other objections to the count, the defendant's counsel took the point that the plaintiff had not sufficiently set out his title to the land, so that he had no interest in the deeds].

Wangford: . . . Sir, I think that if I lose a box with charters, etc., touching land to which I have no title, yet I shall have action of Detinue.

PRISOT, C.J.: I think not. For in your case you should give notice to the finder and request him to re-deliver them to you, and, if he will not, you shall have an action of Trespass against him; for by the finding itself he commits no tort, but the tort begins by the detaining after he has notice. But if A. has the charters of my land of which I am seised and he loses them and B. finds them, I shall have an action of Detinue against him without any notice, because I would have had a cause of action against A., the loser.

Littleton: It seems to me that in the case that *Wangford* puts the loser of the charter shall have an action of Detinue without having any title. Thus if I distrain for rent and afterwards the termor offers me the rent and arrears and I deny him the distress, yet he shall not have an action of Trespass against me, but a writ of Detinue, because I acted lawfully in the beginning when I took the distress; but if I had killed [the beasts distrained] or worked them on my own work, he shall have an action of Trespass.[60] So here, when he found the charters, this was a lawful act, and for his refusal to deliver them on request he shall not have an action of Trespass but an action of Detinue, because no trespass is yet committed; just as, if a man delivers to me goods to keep and to return to him and I detain them, he shall not have a writ of Trespass, but only a writ of Detinue. But peradventure, if they are burnt or the seals are broken or some such act is done, then the action may be maintained. *Ad quod non fuit responsum.* . . .And then *Littleton* said privately that this declaration *per inventionem* is a new found Haliday; for the old declaration has always been in such case that the charters *ad manus et possessionem defendentis devenerunt* generally, without showing

---

[60] i.e., trespass *ab initio*: see *The Six Carpenters Case,* (1610) 8 Coke, 146a.

how; but if it was on a bailment between the plaintiff and the defendant, it would be otherwise.'

R A S T E L L — C O L L E C T I O N   O F   E N T R I E S[61]
Detinue of Charters, f. 204

J. A. was summoned to answer J. N. of a plea that he render to him a certain box, together with charters, writings and other documents contained in the same box, which he unjustly detains from him.

And as to this, the same J. N., by B. his attorney, says that, whereas he was and still is seised of one messuage, etc., in S. as of fee and was possessed of the aforesaid sealed box, together with the charters, writings and other documents contained in the same box, that is to say, one charter whereby W. W. gave and granted the said messuage, etc., to a certain J. C. and his heirs for ever,

And whereas the same J. N. afterwards, at W. in the county of D. on the day and year, etc., casually lost the aforesaid box with the aforesaid charters, as set out above, and the aforesaid J. A. afterwards, on the same day, found the said box with the aforesaid charter set out above and the other charters and documents in the same box contained, and has had it thereafter in his own keeping and still has it, whereby an action has accrued to the same J. N. to demand and have the aforesaid box from the aforesaid J.A.;

Yet the said J. A., though often requested so to do, has not yet delivered the aforesaid box with the aforesaid charter, etc., to the aforesaid J. N., but so to do has hitherto refused and still refuses and unjustly detains it from him, whereby he says that he has suffered loss and has damage to the value of, etc.

[61] For a note on Rastell, see *infra*, p. 90.

❦ 3 ❧

TRESPASS

THE origin of Trespass is to be sought among the dark places of the law, and the search is complicated by the ambiguity of the word. Like ' negligence ' and like ' malice,' it enjoys both a professional and a popular connotation. The Christian repeating the Lord's Prayer and the pleader conning the Register of Writs are not likely to attach the same meaning to the word, and even the legal context varies with its period. According to the theory advanced contemporaneously but independently by Holmes, Ames and Maitland, and accepted by Holdsworth, it derived from the appeal of felony: it was an ' attenuated felony.'[1] Appeals of felony were proceedings whose essence was some grave breach of the King's Peace but which were instituted by individual citizens, and it was the combination, to modern minds peculiar, of public wrong and private process which provoked Maitland, in a calculated solecism, to describe them as ' criminal actions.'[2] They lay for personal injuries, as for homicide, rape, mayhem, wounding and battery, or for injuries to property, as for arson and larceny, or for such a wrong as robbery, which united these characteristics. Mayhem and battery were at first claimed as the ancestors of Trespass, but a later preference has been indicated for robbery, as suggestive both of trespass to the person and of trespass to goods.[3]

If it is unfair to say that this theory has been more often asserted than argued, it is yet true that the evidence marshalled in its support is more slender than its frequent repetition would suggest. Holmes was content to offer it without comment, and even in Maitland's mind it began as a ' plausible opinion ' and only with time hardened into a conviction.[4] It would seem to rest upon three contentions. The first is a linguistic derivation. The language of Trespass is constant and familiar; the defendant is said to have acted *vi et armis et contra*

---

[1] Holmes, *The Common Law* (1881), pp. 3-4, 100-1; Ames, *Lectures on Legal History* (1886-7), pp. 41-60; Maitland, *Register of Writs* (1889), *Coll. Papers* II, pp. 163-5; *Forms of Action*, pp. 48-50; P. & M. II. 522-7; Holdsworth, H.E.L. II. 358-365; III. 316-320.

[2] *Forms of Action*, p. 48. The best modern account of the appeals is to be found in S.S. Vol. 62 (1943) Part II. Chap. XVII, by Sir C. T. Flower. See also specimens of appeals given by Bracton, *infra*, p. 56.

[3] Holmes and Ames cite mayhem and battery. The appeal of robbery was first offered as the progenitor by Bordwell, *Harvard Law Review*, Vol. 29, p. 392, and accepted by Holdsworth in H.E.L. III, p. 320, n. 2.

[4] Compare *Coll. Papers* II. pp. 163-5 with *Forms of Action*, pp. 48-50 and P. & M. II. 522-7, where Maitland offers reasons for his conjecture.

44

pacem regis. The allegations of the appeal, though reinforced by the serious nature of the charges, in Maitland's view were similar: the appellee *fecit hoc nequiter et in felonia, vi et armis et contra pacem Domini Regis.* If the first half of this phrase be abandoned, the line may be drawn from the earlier formula to the later. The second contention is the ' semi-criminal character ' of Trespass. The defendant is not only accused of a breach of the King's Peace, but, if he fails to appear to the writ, he will be outlawed, and, if he is found guilty, he will be punished by fine and imprisonment. The third is the inadequacy of the appeal as a process in any but primitive ages. Apart from the scrupulous nicety of its pleading and the hazardous possibility of trial by battle, it was a broken reed in the hands of a litigant who sought to use it as a means of recovering a stolen chattel. The appellor must make fresh pursuit after the thief from parish to parish by that ' hue and cry ' which retrospectively seems designed to offer the choicest impediments to justice; he must himself, or at least through one of his cohort of pursuers, seize the thief with the chattel in his possession; and he must then secure a conviction on the appeal.[5] If he failed to satisfy all these conditions, though he might be revenged by the punishment of the thief, he would obtain neither restitution nor damages.[6]

The form of the appeal, as given by Maitland, has been challenged by Professor Woodbine. The cardinal words *vi et armis* were found by him twice only in the ' several thousand earliest cases examined.' *Cum vi sua,* on the other hand, occurs with great frequency, but always to indicate the ' invasion of land by an armed force and never the act of an individual by himself.'[7] The phrase was not, as in Trespass, a formula, but the description of a fact. Even if the later allegations were borrowed from the earlier, the loan would not necessarily imply a common origin or a single conception. No legal inference is more dangerous than one based upon linguistic analogy. There was no plethora of words in the middle ages, and the scanty currency was in constant circulation. To derive Trespass from the appeal on the faith of a phrase is as dubious as to invest Debt and Detinue with all the qualities of a Writ of Right for land because they were modelled upon it.

The second argument is open to similar objection. The attributes chosen to invest Trespass with a ' semi-criminal ' character were not absent from other civil actions. The ' breach of the peace '

[5] Ames, *Lectures on Legal History,* pp. 52-3; H.E.L. II, pp. 256-7, 360.
[6] This seems generally admitted. See Woodbine, 33 Yale L.J., pp. 801-2, where he says: ' The reading of several thousand 12th and 13th century cases from 1199 up till the time that the action of trespass became established has failed to reveal a single instance of damages being recovered in an appeal.' He points out that Ames contradicts himself, stating at one point that the appeal was ' purely for vengeance ' and at another that damages might be recovered. See Ames, *Lectures on Legal History,* pp. 41, 48, 56.
[7] 34 Yale L.J., pp. 360-4. See Bracton, ff. 144 and 145b, *infra,* pp. 56-7.

was paralleled by the *deforciat* in the Writ of Right; outlawry was almost an inevitable process in the often arduous task of compelling the appearance of a defendant and remained a feature of civil process until 1852; punishment, in one form or another, followed a false claim or a vain plea throughout the mediæval law. ' Every cause for a civil action is an offence . . . and in the King's Court is an offence against the King punishable by amercement, if not by fine or imprisonment.'[8] It is indeed unprofitable to disentangle the early strands of crime, tort and property. Detinue, Trespass, the Possessory Assises, all show how closely they are interwoven. The Assises, indeed, were typical in their complexity: criminal, in that a guilty defendant might be fined or even imprisoned, tortious, in that the plaintiff soon obtained the right to damages, proprietary, at least so far as to enable the land to be recovered.[9]

If the second argument proves too much, the third proves too little. The inadequacy of the appeal may be confessed, but the conclusion drawn avoided. Because the writ of Trespass, as ultimately evolved, enabled a plaintiff to escape the complexity and to extend the scope of the appeal, it does not follow that the one was derived from the other. *Post hoc,* even in legal history, is not *propter hoc.* The testimony of Bracton, invoked by all parties to the controversy, is interesting. He admits the convenience, if not the necessity, of a civil action to replace the appeal in certain circumstances, but he does not describe that action as Trespass. The word *transgressio* does, indeed, appear in his book. But when used as an antithesis to felony, it is clearly with a popular and not with a technical meaning, and, when it is invested with technical significance, the context is not that of appeal but of disseisin.[10]

Whether a prima facie case has been established for the derivation of Trespass from the appeals may thus be doubted; but, even if this be assumed, its adherents are involved in a series of embarrassments. Damages, it has been seen, were admittedly not awarded on an appeal: they formed the life-blood of the writ of Trespass. So, too, the appeal might be brought, not only against the immediate offender, but against a third party who obtained the stolen goods either by delivery or by himself depriving the offender: the writ of Trespass, from the beginning to the end of its history, would lie only for an act of direct interference with the plaintiff's person or property. The contrast was emphasised at the close of the middle ages. ' If one take my goods

---

[8] P. & M. II. 572; see also H.E.L. II. 365, n. 4. On Outlawry, see H.E.L. III. 604-7 and IX. 254-6, and Common Law Procedure Act, 1852, s. 24.
[9] Plucknett, *Concise History of the Common Law*, 4th ed., p. 339.
[10] Bracton, ff. 119b, 127b, 145b, 146b, 216b. See *infra,* p. 57. *Transgressio* is commonly used in the 12th and 13th centuries in a wider sense than in the modern law. See Glanvill, X. c. 12, *infra,* p. 234; S.S. Vol. 2, p. 6 (four *placita transgressionis,* A.D. 1246), p. 21 (*transgressio cervisiæ*—breach of the assise of ale, A.D. 1249), pp. 95 and 109 (defamation cases of A.D. 1278 and 1288).

and another take the goods from him I shall have appeal against the second felon; but it is otherwise of trespass."[11] If, again, the most plausible assumption be made that the appeal of robbery is the parent stock, this may indeed suggest the derivation of Trespass to the person and of Trespass to goods, but it will scarcely explain Trespass to land. On the one hand, the plaintiffs in the early cases of Trespass almost always complained of an unlawful entry upon land, and the asportation of crops and other chattels and even any personal assault were accessory to the principal cause of action. On the other hand, there was no appeal for such an entry.[12] Both these facts are admitted, and to reconcile them with Maitland's view demands unusual ingenuity.

If this view be rejected, where is the origin of Trespass to be sought? Ames and Maitland, presumably without prejudice to their major premise, suggested that it was well known in the local before it invaded the royal courts.[13] The suggestion has been most fully developed by Professor Plucknett. Two problems have to be solved —the nature of the remedy and the form in which it came to be enshrined. The essence of the first was the award of damages, and these were awarded at an early date in the local courts. The second is but ' part of the larger question of the origin of all the actions which were directed against a defendant who had done damage to a plaintiff. The original writ in all these cases is in the same form *ostensurus quare,* and the origin of that form is the real root of the matter.' In form, as in substance, Professor Plucknett, with diffidence and with regret for the paucity of available material, believes the King's Court to be adopting methods already in use in the local courts.[14]

The evidence offered in support of this suggestion is slight. While Maitland and Professor Plucknett cite no authorities, Ames relies on ' several cases of the reign of Henry I, collected in Bigelow, *Placita Anglo-Normannica.'* The Index to this collection, made in 1879, contains ·twelve references to ' suits in the nature of Trespass.' A glance suffices to dispel the illusion. A typical entry is the suit of the Abbot of Abingdon against the Men of Stanton in 1105 or 1107.

---

[11] Y.B. 4 Hen. VII. f. 5b, cited in *Possession in the Common Law,* p. 156, and see Ames, *Lectures on Legal History,* p. 60, and H.E.L. III, 323-4.

[12] P. & M. II. 166, and Ames, p. 56 n. 2. See a case at the Lincolnshire Eyre in 1202 (S.S. Vol. 1, Plea 35): ' Hugh de Ruperes appeals John of Ashby for that he *in pace Domini Regis et nequiter* came into his meadows and depastured them with his cattle. . . . And whereas it was testified by the sheriff and the coroners that in the first instance Hugh had appealed John of depasturing his meadows and also of beating his men, and he now wishes to pursue his appeal only as regards his meadows, and whereas an appeal for depasturing meadows does not appertain to the crown, it is adjudged that the appeal is null.'

[13] Ames, p. 179, n. 3: 'Trespass in the popular courts of the hundred and county was doubtless of far greater antiquity than the same action in the Curia Regis.'

Maitland, *Coll. Papers,* II. p. 151, n. 1: ' Of course Trespass was well enough known in local courts. "Trespass" and "Debt" were the two great heads of their civil jurisdiction.'

[14] *Concise History of the Common Law,* 4th ed., pp. 349-352. For the form *ostensurus quare,* see *infra,* pp. 53-4.

'Henry, King of England, to Nigel of Oilly and William, Sheriff of Oxford, greeting. I command you that you do full right to the Abbot of Abingdon concerning his sluice which the men of Stanton broke, so that I hear no more complaint thereof for defect of right, and this under penalty of ten pounds. Witness Ralph the Chancellor, at Westminster.'

This document is described by Bigelow as a 'writ of Trespass for breaking a sluice' and is offered as 'the prototype of the writs of Trespass *quare clausum fregit.*' The resemblance could scarcely be fainter.[15] It is true, indeed, that in the middle of the thirteenth century actions with a reasonable likeness to Trespass, and in some of which damages were claimed, were brought in a diversity of local courts. Two examples may be given of pleas in the manorial courts of the Abbey of Bec.[16] The first was heard at Bledlow in Buckinghamshire on the Saturday before Ascension Day in the year 1246.

'John Sperling complains (*queritur*) that Richard of Newmere on the Sunday next before St. Bartholomew's day last past with his cattle, horses and pigs shamefully destroyed (*enormiter destruxit*) the corn on John's land to his damage (*ad dampnum*) of one thrave of wheat and to his dishonour (*ad dedecus*) of two shillings; and of this he produces suit. And Richard comes and defends the whole. Therefore let him go to the law six-handed. His pledges, Simon Combe and Hugh Frith.'[17]

The second was heard at Weedon in Northamptonshire on the day of St. Peter *ad Vincula* (1st August) in the year 1248.

'Hugh of Stanbridge complains of Gilbert, the Vicar's son, and William of Stanbridge that the wife of the said Gilbert, who is of Gilbert's mainpast,[18] and the said William unjustly, etc., beat and shamefully struck him (*iniuste, etc., ipsum verberaverunt et enormiter percusserunt*) and dragged him by his hair out of his own house to his damage forty shillings and to his dishonour twenty shillings; and he produces suit. And Gilbert and William come and defend the whole fully. Therefore let each of them go to his law six-handed.'

Of the pleas recorded in the volume from which these two instances are taken the earliest is of the year 1246 and the latest of 1294, and if they are to be cited as local predecessors of royal Trespass they are unpunctual visitors. The word itself, while sometimes used with a particular significance, more often imports general misconduct. In the Manorial Courts of the Abbot of Ramsey between 1278 and 1294 a number of defendants found guilty of defamation were in mercy *pro transgressione*; and at Bledlow in 1249 one Miller was fined 2d. for a

---

[15] Bigelow, p. 89. See also pp. 98, 127, 285. For the final form of Trespass *quare clausum fregit*, see *infra*, p. 63.
[16] S.S. Vol. 2, ed. Maitland, pp. 7 and 17-18. See also pp. 56 and 64.
[17] 'Thrave' = 'two shocks or stooks of corn, generally containing twelve sheaves each, but varying in different localities,' *O.E.D.* 'Go to the law six-handed' = 'find five compurgators.'
[18] For 'Mainpast,' see P. & M. II. 530-2.

' trespass against the assise of beer.'[19] Even where the context is that of the modern tort and phrases are used which are later to become technical, it is not easy to identify the writ of Trespass in embryo. The entries, it is true, are not innocent of art. In the court of the Abbot of Ramsey held at Broughton in Huntingdon in 1258 a plaintiff complained that the defendant had taken and driven off his oxen, and the defendant successfully pleaded that the declaration was inadequate: it did not state time or place nor the value of the beasts.[20] Such a conclusion, more agreeable to the artist than to the layman, reflects a growing formalism which is more likely to have percolated from the greater to the lesser than to have ascended from the lesser to the greater courts. It is suggestive that anxious if unavailing attempts were made by lords of the manor to exclude professional practitioners,[21] and that the early years of Edward I saw the circulation of manuals for the use of stewards containing both registers of writs and precedents of royal pleading.[22] Upon the whole, and in default of fuller evidence, a verdict of non proven must be returned to the claim of a local origin. The subject-matter of trespass may have been familiar to the local courts; the forms of action were not indigenous to them.

The most recent and the most richly argued theory is appropriately that of Professor Woodbine, the severest critic of the orthodox view.[23] The essential problems are to determine the circumstances in which the King's courts first awarded damages and to discover a common root for all three branches of Trespass—to land, to goods and to the person. Professor Woodbine finds the answer to both in the Assise of Novel Disseisin.

The occasion for the award of damages may be asserted with confidence. In the writ of Novel Disseisin given by Glanvill the sheriff was ordered ' to cause the tenement to be reseised of the chattels which were taken on it, and the same tenement, with the chattels, to be in peace' until the cause could be heard.[24] The order was more easily made than obeyed. The land itself was passive to endure depredation and to await restitution: the chattels were elusive. It was more realistic to award money compensation, and this step was taken as early as 1198.

> ' The assise comes to recognize if G. F. unjustly and without a
> judgment disseised J. M. of his free tenement in M. . . . The jurors

---

[19] S.S. Vol. 2, pp. 21, 95, 109.
[20] S.S. Vol. 2, p. 56.
[21] *Ibid.* pp. 135-6. ' In 1240 the Abbot of Ramsey forbad his tenants at Brancaster on pain of twenty shillings to introduce pleaders into his court to impede or delay his justice.' Compare *ibid.,* p. 160.
[22] *The Court Baron,* S.S. Vol. 4, ed Maitland and Baildon, esp. pp. 1-13.
[23] The epithet ' orthodox ' is not necessarily a term of reproach. Professor Woodbine's arguments are set out at length in 33 Yale L.J. pp. 799-816 and 34 Yale L.J. pp. 343-370.
[24] Glanvill, Book XIII, c. 33, supra, p. 13.

> say that G. F. did so disseise him. Judgment: Let J. M. have his
> seisin and G. F. be in mercy. And the damage is 40/-.'[25]

It became common practice to order the sheriff to assess the
damages and to levy them, when assessed, out of the defendant's
goods, and the practice was allowed by Bracton to have superseded the
older procedure of Glanvill.[26]   In the fifty years between the two
books the idea of damages was thus familiarised.   In Maitland's
words, ' an action for damages was a novelty. We may doubt whether
Glanvill ever presided at the hearing of such an action. . . . It makes
its appearance in an influential quarter, in the popular assise of novel
disseisin. . . . In a few years all had changed.'[27]

The pursuit of the second problem may well seem to lead back
to the same source. The core of early trespass was the injury to land,
of which the other incidents were concomitants, irritating but sub-
sidiary. Such also was the nature of a disseisin. The very word
invokes a scene of violence, where no assault was out of place and
where, as the form of the writ shows, the asportation of chattels was
a likely consequence. But, even where the disseisin was complete, the
assise might not be available. Entry might have been made when
the possession was vacant, when the land was in the hands of a pledgee
or of a guardian, who, though seised of the wardship, was not seised
of the estate. The disseisor might already have left the land and the
only remaining issue be that of compensation for the damage done,
or the disseisee, after bringing a successful assise, might have failed to
obtain either goods or damages.[28] The conduct of the defendant, on
the other hand, while hostile, might fall short of a complete disseisin.
It is in this context that Bracton speaks of trespass. ' Every disseisin,'
he says, ' is a trespass, but not every trespass is a disseisin.' If a person
enters the land of another against that other's will, but ' not to usurp
the freehold or its rights for himself, he commits not a disseisin but
a trespass.'[29]

To see a fault, however, is not to cure it. The invention of a
remedy to meet these defects was a long process of trial and error. Of
the experiments which immediately followed the first award of damages
in 1198 the most illuminating are the proceedings in *Rande* v. *Malfe*
in 1199.[30] The plaintiff complained that the defendant, who was his

[25] 1 Rot. Cur. Reg. 154, cited by Woodbine, 33 Yale L.J., p. 807.
[26] Bracton, f. 186b. See B.N.B. Plea 165 (A.D. 1222). See also Woodbine's notes to
Glanvill, pp. 288-9.
[27] P. & M. II. 522-4. See also S.S. Vol. 62, Part III, Chap. XII—' Damages.' The
idea quickly spread to other royal actions, e.g. Covenant; but, as Sir C. T. Flower
here says, one of the points which differentiated the assises of Novel Disseisin from
other civil actions was ' that they *habitually* involved the assessment of damages.'
He cites many instances in John's reign.
[28] These various contingencies are discussed by Woodbine, 34 Yale L.J., pp. 344-9 and
pp. 356-7.
[29] Bracton, f. 216b, *infra*, p. 57.
[30] 2 Rot. Cur. Reg. 120, cited by Woodbine, 34 Yale L.J., p. 347.

lord, ' *cum vi et armis* had cut down his wood and *cum forcia* had taken his four horse teams, and even now unjustly held and detained one of them, to his damage of twenty marks.' The defendant pleaded that, when his predecessor enfeoffed the plaintiff's ancestor, the wood and timber were reserved from the grant. The plaintiff then ' put himself on the Grand Assise as to whether he had the greater right of holding the wood.' The exigencies which compelled and the ingenuity which devised this action are alike instructive. The plaintiff could not bring a Possessory Assise since there had been no disseisin, nor Replevin since the beasts had not been taken by way of distress, nor Detinue since three of the teams had apparently been restored. He therefore devised a form of complaint which was at least colourful. The first phrase, *cum vi et armis,* though it foreshadowed Trespass, was clearly descriptive, while the second, *cum forcia,* may recall either the Appeal of Felony or the Writ of Right. The suit began with a claim for damages and ended with a submission to the Grand Assise on a question of title.

This interesting hybrid, it is to be observed, was initiated not by a writ but by a less formal complaint of misconduct. Such informal *querelæ* played a large part in the development of the law throughout the thirteenth century and have formed the subject of recent study.[31] Maitland, upon the basis of Bracton's words, ' *Non potest quis sine brevi agere,*' committed himself to the ' very general rule that no action could be begun in the King's courts, and that no action touching freehold could be begun anywhere, without an " original " or (as we might say) " originating " writ, which proceeded from the chancery and served as the justices' warrant for entertaining that action.' As he had simultaneously to explain the acknowledged fact that the age between the accession of Henry II and that of Edward I was one of exceptional fertility, he attributed the irrigation of the soil to a constant trickle of chancery writs. ' The chancery was doling out actions one by one. There is no solemn *Actionem dabo* proclaimed to the world, but it becomes understood that a new writ is to be had or that an old writ, which hitherto might be had as a favour, is now a " writ of course." '[32] Later research has shown that the source of this fruitfulness is not so clear as Maitland believed. Each successive Register

[31] See Bolland, *Eyre of Kent,* Vol. II (S.S. Vol. 27), especially his Introduction, pp. xxi-xxx, and Richardson and Sayles, *Select Cases of Procedure without Writ under Henry III* (S.S. Vol. 60), upon whose full and learned Introduction this present account is largely based.

[32] P. & M. I. 194-6; II. 558-9. Bracton's words are on f. 413b, and are preceded by a classification of writs. ' And there are some writs formed upon determinate cases (*brevia formata super certis casibus*) agreed and approved as of course (*de cursu*) by the common counsel of the realm, which can in no wise be changed without the consent and will of all. . . . But there are other writs called *magistralia* and which may often be varied according to the variety of cases and complaints.' Coke (2nd Inst. f. 407) says that *magistralia* = ' framed *ad hoc* by the masters in the Chancery.' Mr. Landon supports this (52 L.Q.R. p. 74); Professor Plucknett denies it (31 Col. L.R., p. 793).

of Writs is indeed a memorial to the activity of the Chancery; but the words of Bracton, unless set in their proper context, are misleading. As an unqualified assertion, they described accurately, but must be confined to, the course of a real action in the King's courts. Bracton himself indicated a rival approach to justice through a *querela sine brevi,* and at least thirty of the cases in his Note Book were so begun. It was not so easy to obtain a new writ. The clerks of the Chancery, though their puny efforts would doubtless disgrace a modern official, were still civil servants, and speed and flexibility have never been the prime characteristics of a bureaucracy. Minor changes might be made by them without special authority, and major innovations were certainly accomplished from time to time. But these latter, as Bracton declared, were matters of grave import and demanded the approval of the common council of the realm. It was not every wrong which found a remedy, nor every remedy that came by writ.[33]

A happier approach to royal justice was open to the litigant who had neither the time nor the money nor the influence to stir the Chancery to unusual effort. The records of the thirteenth century are full of complaints and petitions, varied in scope and gravity but constant in their informality. They have been traced back to the earliest extant rolls of 1194 and forward to the reign of Edward III. They were presented, at least at first, to the Common Pleas, more often to the King's Bench, and above all to the Justices in Eyre who were most intimately identified with the Royal Prerogative. Their results, even if favourable, were sometimes ephemeral; sometimes the frequent grant of a remedy induced the ultimate creation of a writ in which they were merged or which they survived as venerable if superfluous alternatives.[34] The clerks who kept the Plea Rolls recognised their presence by the word *querela* or the less frequent but more colloquial *billa,* and the story told by them was introduced by the phrase, ' *A.B. queritur de C.D.*' The written complaints themselves have not survived for the years before the accession of Edward I, though their existence is vouched for by abundant entries in the rolls, but thenceforth some hundreds are preserved in the Public Record Office. They are thus described by Bolland:[35]

> ' They are formed of slips of parchment varying in size with what had to be written upon them. Some of them are barely as wide as

[33] See the whole question discussed in the Introduction to S.S. Vol. 60, especially at pp. xiii-xiv, xxiii-xxv and lx-lxii. The references to Bracton are to f. 112, f. 154b, f. 157, ff. 413b-14b, f. 438b, and those to Bracton's Note-Book are given in S.S. Vol. 60, p. xiii, note 3. There has been controversy as to Bracton's use of the word *libellus.* Mr. Richardson and Dr. Sayles understand it as a contrast to, Professors Woodbine and Hollond as synonymous with, *breve.* The former view on the whole seems preferable. Cf. S.S. Vol. 60, pp. lx-lxii, and Hollond in C.L.J. (1944) pp. 256-7.
[34] For illustrations of survival which, while illogical, testified to the force of tradition, see S.S. Vol. 60, pp. cxxxv-cxlvi. A possible analogy is afforded by Gaius, IV. 47.
[35] S.S. Vol. 27, pp. xxii-iii and xxviii. For a specimen, see *infra,* p. 61.

is a man's little finger. They are almost invariably written in Anglo-French. A very few are in Latin. With exceedingly few exceptions they are addressed *A les Justices nostre Seygnur le Roy.* . . . Not a single one of them is addressed to the King nor to his Council nor to the Chancellor. . . . They are largely used by very poor people. No rules as to form affect them, so that, no expert knowledge being necessary, they can be framed and presented by anyone who can write or can get another to write for him. There is no evidence that any fee was payable. . . .'

The range of this poor person's procedure, or lack of procedure, was catholic. Redress was sought for non-payment of debts, for interference with chattels, for breach of covenant, for conspiracy and abuse of legal process, and, most freely and most pertinently, for wrongs in the nature of trespass.[36]

The process was singularly apt for the experiments designed to supply the deficiencies of the established writs. In 1200 and 1201 complaints were made that the petitioner dared not till his land for fear of the defendant, and in the second of these ' boycott ' cases the land itself had already been recovered by the Assise.[37] In 1221 the petitioner succeeded in obtaining seisin where the fact that the land was held in wardship would have been fatal to the Assise, and the offenders were to be in mercy ' *pro transgressione.*'[38] In 1202 an Appeal for ' depasturing meadows ' had been disallowed: in 1230 a *querela* prevailed.[39] Besides these ' *innominate* ' cases, the plea rolls contain a large number which may be described generically as *Quare* actions: the defendants were required to explain *why* they had done the acts alleged against them, and, most frequently in the earlier years of the thirteenth century, *quare intruserunt se in terram.* ' Intrusion ' was here used to include any encroachment upon land less than a disseisin, and around this central feature were grouped a rich variety of aggravating incidents—the destruction of corn, the asportation of chattels, assault upon master or man.[40] Soon after 1230 the word disappeared from the language of the *querelæ,* possibly because it was absorbed into the *writ of entry sur intrusion,*[41] but the *quare* actions

---

[36] S.S. Vol. 27, p. xxiii, and S.S. Vol. 60, pp. lxix-cxxxiv. For trespass in particular, S.S. Vol. 60, pp. cviii-cxxxix. In some instances the petitioner may be a person of importance who presses no claim, but seeks a declaration of his legal position. ' We have an early example of what is essentially a petition of right in the Hilary term of 1231. Richard Siward, who believed he had a good claim to the lordship of the hundred of Bullingdon in Oxfordshire, says expressly that he brings forward no plaint, but he wishes to know to what rights he and his wife (for he claimed through her) are entitled,' p. lxx.

[37] Select Civil Pleas (S.S. Vol. 3) pl. 7, and Woodbine, 34 Yale L.J., pp. 348-9.

[38] B.N.B. Plea 1520, *infra,* p. 58.

[39] B.N.B. Plea 378. Cf. *supra,* p. 47, n.

[40] B.N.B. Pleas 85, 566, 1104, *infra,* pp. 58-9. See Woodbine, 34 Yale L.J., pp. 349-356.

[41] See Bracton ff. 324-5; F.N.B. 203E-204E. In these writs ' intrusion ' is technical: ' the entry of a stranger, after a particular estate of freehold is determined, before him in remainder or reversion ' (Blackstone, III. 169).

themselves became ever more prolific and bore an ever closer resemblance to the ultimate form of Trespass. Phrases were repeated and familiarised: *contra pacem regis, cepit et asportavit, verberaverunt et male tractaverunt,* and, though clearly no mere figure of speech, *vi et armis.* But neither claim nor procedure were yet stereotyped. The case of the Men of Chalgrove in 1237 was a successful attempt to settle a question of common rights, and, as late as 1250, wager of law was awarded on an issue of assault.[42]

The force of precedent, however, was irresistible. Under the pressure of repeated incident phrase hardened into formula and Querela into Writ. In a gradual process precise dates are misleading, but a case of 1253 is significant. Henry Organ complained ' by the King's writ' that four named persons came *vi et armis* upon land of which he was the lessee and assaulted him *contra pacem domini regis.* The defendants objected to the form of action: it was neither an appeal nor a querela, but a writ to which they need not answer. The objection was overruled and the case went to the jury on the facts. In the same year before the same Justices in Eyre a plaintiff again complained ' by the King's writ,' and in this case no objection was taken.[43] For another ten years litigants vacillated between the one form and the other,[44] but by the accession of Edward I the Writ of Trespass was established. A tract of 1267 gave instruction in the manner of its pleading,[45] and the Statute of Westminster II in 1285 cited it as a familiar analogy.[46]

A comment upon Professor Woodbine's theory may now be not impertinent. In the atmosphere which his researches have evoked it is alluring. The origin of damages, the scope of the Assize, the focussing of attention upon the injury to land, all suggest the substitution of ' attenuated disseisin ' for ' attenuated felony.' But temptation must reluctantly be resisted. It is proper to find in the avowed and crippling limitations of Novel Disseisin the occasion for the experiments whose ultimate evolution was the Writ of Trespass. To identify the one as the child of the other is to betray too casual a view of fatherhood. The charge of inconsequence with which Professor Woodbine visited his predecessors might be returned upon his own head. The parents of Trespass were the complainants whose impor-

---

[42] S.S. Vol. 60, Pleas 19 and 57, *infra,* pp. 59-60. Other instances are given in the same volume, e.g. Pleas 1, 37, 39, 40, 54.

[43] Compare S.S. Vol. 60, Plea 59, *infra,* p. 60, and Plea 61: ' Roger of Duston *conqueritur per breve domini regis* of four defendants *quod ei insultum dederunt et ipsum vulneraverunt et maletractaverunt contra pacem domini regis.*

[44] See S.S. Vol. 60, Plea 96 (A.D. 1259) and Pleas 125 and 129 (A.D. 1260-1), which, though they contain the familiar allegations, seem not to be writs.

[45] The tract is entitled *Fet Asaver* and is one of the *Four Thirteenth Century Law Tracts* ed. by Woodbine (1910).

[46] Stat. of West. II. c. 35. See also Woodbine, 34 Yale L.J., p. 358, and the cases there cited. A contributory factor in the formulation of the writ may well have been the turmoil of the Barons' war. See Maitland, *Coll. Papers,* II. 154, and Plucknett, *Concise History,* 4th ed., p. 351.

tunity disturbed royal justice for fifty years: any more remote ancestry is lost in the darkness of unrecorded time.[47]

The new writ was at once popular. The rolls of the Common Pleas for the Easter term, 1271, contain no less than 85 entries of Trespass, those of the King's Bench for Michaelmas, 1273, 181 out of a total of 310 cases, and those of the same court for Trinity, 1307, 827 out of 1,068.[48] The natural result of abundance was differentiation. Trespass to the person and to goods began to separate from the basic stock of Trespass to land. In 1276 Richard Lombe brought a writ of Trespass against five defendants, and alleged that they had assaulted him at the Fair of St. Ives and ' beat and wounded him and slit his left ear and so ill-treated him that his life was despaired of,' to his damage of a hundred pounds and against the peace—

> *quare in ipsum Ricardum Lombe insultum fecerunt et ipsum ver-*
> *beraverunt vulneraverunt et auriculam eius sinistram fiderunt et eum*
> *maletractaverunt ita quod de vita eius desperabatur ad dampnum*
> *ipsius Ricardi centum librarum et contra pacem....*[49]

In 1280 Matilda Lorimer sued Walter Comyn and alleged that he had assaulted her at Salisbury and ' beat, wounded, imprisoned and ill-treated her, and robbed her of her goods and chattels, and other outrages there did to her (*et alia enormia ei intulit*) to her damage of a hundred shillings and against the peace."[50] In neither case was there any suggestion of a trespass to land, nor indeed were the words *vi et armis* included in the writ.[51] But in each there was an assault and battery, described in language already a little worn with use, and in the second an additional allegation of false imprisonment. In a third case in 1292 the plaintiff complained of a trespass to goods committed *vi et armis et contra pacem,* but unconnected with land and not even described as an asportation.[52]

By the close of the thirteenth century the process of differentiation was complete and the adoption of set terms had clipped the exuberance

---

[47] It is proper to say that Professor Woodbine's views have not been accepted by Professor Plucknett (*Concise History*, 4th ed., p. 350), Professor Hollond (C.L.J. (1944) p. 252) or Mr. Richardson and Dr. Sayles (S.S. Vol. 60, pp. cxxviii-cxxxiv).

[48] See P. & M. II. 565-7, and S.S. Vol. 57, pp. cxxi-iii. The writ is not in the earliest Registers of Edward I, but does appear in two of uncertain date in that reign: see Maitland, *Coll. Papers*, pp. 161-5. The omission may suggest that the language of the writ was not yet stereotyped or it may mean no more than clerical inertia.

[49] *Lombe* v. *Clopton* (1276) S.S. Vol. 55, p. 30.

[50] *Lorimer* v. *Comyn* (1280) S.S. Vol. 55, p. 64.

[51] In a case of 1290 both *vi et armis* and *contra pacem regis* occur, but in other respects it is a curiosity rather than a precedent. Trespass was brought by John Waleys, the messenger of the Archbishop of Canterbury, against two defendants. The plaintiff served upon the defendants the Archbishop's letters of citation for ' outrages committed against God and the Church,' but the defendants, it was alleged, had taken ' the aforesaid John le Waleys at London within the precincts of the King's verge during the King's parliament and *vi et armis* did compel him to eat the aforesaid letters, and did beat, wound and ill-treat him, to the manifest contempt of God and Holy Church and also of the King, and to the no slight loss and hurt of the aforesaid John and against the peace': *Waleys' Case* (1290) S.S. Vol. 57, p. 18.

[52] *Toht's Case* (1292) S.S. Vol. 57, p. 113. *Infra*, p. 62.

of earlier litigants or their pleaders. But when phrase becomes formula, fact declines into fiction. No sooner was the language of Trespass fixed than it was divorced from reality. In two cases in 1304 Chief Justice Bereford made the position clear. In the first, the writ ran ' *verberaverunt, vulneraverunt et ipsum ceperunt et imprison-averunt.*' The Jury found that the defendants had indeed taken and imprisoned the plaintiff, but that they had not beaten or wounded him. In the second, the plaintiff alleged that the defendants ' came tor-tiously *vi et armis* and cut and carried away his wood.' The Jury found that they did cut his trees, but not with force and arms. In each case Chief Justice Bereford disregarded the superfluous words as mere formalities and gave judgment for the plaintiff.[53] Three years later the plaintiff's counsel, who in his writ of Trespass had alleged that the defendant had carried off his corn and broken his hedges—*quare clausum fregit*—was allowed to explain away the latter words as inserted only ' to serve our writ.'[54] The accession of Edward I saw the establishment of Trespass as a writ, his death its species distinct and its language set in a mould which was to endure until the holocaust of the nineteenth century.[55]

S O U R C E S

B R A C T O N
APPEALS

f. 144. *Of the peace and of wounds inflicted against the peace*
. . . The appeal is made in these words.

The words of the appeal

A. appeals B. that, whereas he was in the peace of our lord the King on such a day in such a place, or whereas he was going in the peace of our lord the King on the King's highway between such and such a vill on such a day before or after such a feast in such a year and such an hour, the said B. came with his force (*cum vi sua*) and against the peace of our lord the King (*contra pacem domini regis*) feloniously and with a premeditated assault made an onslaught upon him and gave him a certain wound in such a place with such manner of arms, and that he did this wickedly and feloniously he offers to prove against him by his body as the court shall award.

B. comes and denies

And B. comes and denies (*venit et defendit*) the breach of our lord the King's peace and the felony and the wound and whatever is against the

---

[53] Both are anonymous cases and are reported in 32 and 33 Ed. I (R.S.) at pp. 258-9. A later case, where the phrase *vi et armis* was again treated as an empty form, is *Anon.* Y.B. 11 Ed. II (S.S. Vol. 61) p. 290, A.D. 1318.
[54] *Anon.* Y.B. 1 & 2 Ed. II (S.S. Vol. 17) p. 36, A.D. 1307.
[55] See the precedents, *infra*, pp. 63-5.

peace of our lord the King and altogether word by word whatever is imputed to him and in manner as it has been imputed to him, and [this he will defend] by his body according as the court of our lord the King shall award. . . .

f. 145b. . . . The appeal of peace and imprisonment

. . . The words of the appeal

A. appeals B. that, whereas he was in the peace of our lord the King, etc., *ut supra,* the said B. came with his force (*cum vi sua*) against the peace, etc., *ut supra,* and took him to such a court or to such a place and there put him in chains and in irons and in the stocks and there kept him in prison for so long a time and wounded him and maimed him until he was released by the bailiff of our lord the King or until A. gave so much money for his ransom. . . .

B. comes and denies

And B. comes and denies the force and the injury (*venit et defendit vim et iniuriam*) and the breach of our lord the King's peace and the taking and the imprisonment, etc. . . .

But in the appeal of peace and of wounds and imprisonment it is possible to proceed civilly although the act done is criminal. Thus a man may speak as one complaining of a wrong (*de iniuria*), without adding an allegation of felony. . . . And in this case bodily punishment does not follow, but only a money payment by reason of the damage suffered, which is not the case if an allegation of felony is added. . . .

f. 146. . . . Of a criminal action, as of peace and robbery, and of the appeals thereof

. . . The words of the appeal

A. appeals B. that, whereas he was in the peace of our lord the King on such a day in such a place, etc. *ut supra,* the said B. came with his force (*cum vi sua*) and wickedly and feloniously and against the peace of our lord the King (*et nequiter et in felonia et contra pacem domini regis*) by robbery took from him one hundred shillings and three pennies and one horse of such a price and one green robe of such a price. . . .

B. denies

And B. comes and denies the breach of the peace and the felony. . . .

DISSEISIN AND TRESPASS

f. 216b

. . . Sometimes the assise is turned into a jury on account of the trespass; as where a person insists on using another's land against the will of the owner or, against the will of his co-tenant, uses the common land and makes it his own or makes excessive use of it. . . . Every disseisin is a trespass, but not every trespass is a disseisin. Thus, if with the above intent [i.e. to use only] a person enters the land of another, and not to usurp the freehold or its rights for himself, he commits not a disseisin but a trespass. But, when it is uncertain with what intent he acted, the complainant will proceed by the assise. . . . A regular course of conduct changes the trespass into a disseisin, so that, if a person is always trespassing and then answers to the assise that he claims no right in the freehold or no right for himself in the common, and thus thinks to evade the penalty of a disseisin, he will not be heard, but he will undergo the penalty for disseisin and for repeated disseisin.

BRACTON'S NOTEBOOK
DEVONSHIRE. A.D. 1220
PLEA 85

The sheriff was commanded that, if Richard of Baggetor should [give him security for pursuing his claim], he should have before the justices, etc., Matthew Morel, Thomas Ferrars, Robert Grosseteste, Almeric the Reeve, Roger the Reeve, William Bedel and Richard Bedel, to answer to the aforesaid Richard why against the peace of our lord the King they intruded with force and arms (*quare contra pacem domini Regis vi et armis intruserunt se*) into his houses and land of Baggetor and carried away his chattels and ejected him thence and beat down his corn. . . .'

[The sheriff is ordered to inquire the damages involved.]

SUFFOLK. A.D. 1221
PLEA 1520

Agnes of Freston made complaint that William the son of Eutropus and [seven others] with many other armed men came to her house at Freston, which she holds in wardship with her son Philip by gift of the Earl Roger Bigod, and ejected the said Agnes and her son from the aforesaid house and by force and unjustly and against the peace of our lord the King maintained themselves therein, and destroyed the corn and the food and other things belonging to the said Agnes, etc. Wherefore the sheriff was commanded to have before the justices the bodies of all the aforesaid, and of the others who came there in that array (*in forcia*) to answer for the said trespass. . . .

[The defendants denied the breach of peace and pleaded that Agnes' title was defective and that they themselves entered peacefully into their own inheritance.]

It was adjudged that she should have her seisin and her chattels . . . and that they should be in mercy for the trespass.

SUSSEX. A.D. 1225
PLEA 1104

Felicia Harang was attached to answer William of Ouinges why she intruded (*quare ipsa intrusit se*) into one carucate of land with the appurtenances thereof in Bromhurst and by force and arms (*vi et armis*) maintained herself in that same land, whereof John of Ouinges, the father of the aforesaid William, whose heir he is, was seised as of fee on the day of his death; and as to which the said William complains that, whereas he himself, after the death of John his father, was seised of the same land as of his inheritance, the same Felicia with a multitude of armed men in hauberks and breastplates and with iron helmets and with all manner of arms ejected him by force, and wasted and destroyed his chattels found in his house, such as corn, hay, fodder and whatsoever they found there, and laid waste his garden and laid low his houses and did other destruction; whereby he suffered loss and has damage (*per quod deterioratus est et dampnum habet*) to the value of 40 marks; and thereof he produces suit.

And Felicia comes and denies force and injury and intrusion (*venit et defendit vim et iniuriam et intrusionem*), but [says that] in truth she holds that land as her right and her inheritance. And, asked whether John died seised of that land, she says that in truth he did die so seised. And so it is adjudged that William recover his seisin and that Felicia be in mercy.

The sheriff is ordered by the oath of lawful men diligently to inquire what damage the said Felicia did to the said William as touching his houses, gardens, parks and the rest. . . .

OXFORDSHIRE. A.D. 1231

PLEA 566

Hugh Druval and others were attached to answer William Sutton why they intruded into 7 hides of land with the appurtenances in, etc. . . .

. . . [The complainant says that] the aforesaid Hugh and all the others beforenamed came and threw him off the horse on which he was sitting and broke his saddle and beat him and basely and dishonestly treated him (*eum verberaverunt et turpiter et inhoneste eum tractaverunt*), and afterwards entered the houses of the said William and took his palfrey and led it away and took hay and other things which they found there and cut down the trees and took rent from his men, so that he suffered damage. . . .

> [The defendants *veniunt et defendunt vim et injuriam,* and lengthy allegations were made as to the respective rights of the parties to the land.]

. . . It was adjudged that William recover his seisin and that the said Hugh satisfy him as to damages and that all the trespassers be kept in custody.

SELECT CASES OF PROCEDURE WITHOUT WRIT UNDER HENRY III

S.S. VOL. 60

A.D. 1237

PLEA 19, pp. 23-4

The abbot of Abingdon, the abbot of Thame, the master of the Temple at Cowley, the lady of Rofford, Reginald the forester and others complain to the King that in Easter week last the men of Chalgrove came with force and arms and great commotion (*cum vi et armis et magno tumultu*) to their meadows at Lewknor and, setting a watch, they wrongfully depastured them with their own cattle and those of others in breach of the King's peace (*contra pacem domini regis*). Wherefore they say that they have suffered loss to the amount of forty marks (*unde dicunt quod dampnum habent ad valenciam xl. marcarum*).

And the men come and deny the injury (*et homines veniunt et defendunt iniuriam*) and say that they lawfully depastured that meadow-land because they ought at such time of year to have common there with the abbots and the others. . . . And they expressly deny that they were present with arms or in any other way than simply as the shepherds and keepers of the cattle or that any cattle were there save their own. And thereof they put themselves on the country. Therefore let an inquest be made by twelve men who do not belong to the honour of Wallingford, and let them come this next Friday before the King to speak the truth.

Afterwards the parties come to an agreement, and the men of Chalgrove give the King five marks for leave to do so. . . .

[The agreement settles the question of common rights as between the parties.]

A.D. 1250
PLEA 57, pp. 73-4

Simon of Cockfield complains that, whereas he was in the peace of the King and of the justices on Tuesday before St. Simon and St. Jude's day (25 October, 1250) on his estate at Wilby which he holds in wardship because John, son and heir of Robert of Cockfield, is under age and in his wardship, Robert of Holme came with force and arms and a host of armed men (*cum vi et armis et cum multitudine armatorum*) to that estate and beat and maltreated (*verberaverunt et male tractaverunt*) William of Holme, his bailiff of the estate, against the peace of our lord the King and of the justices and within the summons of their eyre. And thereby he says that he has suffered loss and has damage to the value of a hundred shillings (*unde dicit quod deterioratus est et dampnum habet ad valenciam C. solidorum*). And thereof he produces suit, etc.

And Robert comes and denies the force and injury (*defendit vim et iniuriam*). And he expressly denies that he or anyone on his behalf beat or maltreated William, Simon's bailiff. And he offers to defend this statement against him and his suit as the court shall award. And therefore it is awarded that he is to wage his law against him, himself the twelfth hand. And let him come with his compurgators to-morrow. . . .

Afterwards they come to an agreement, and Simon gives half a mark for leave to make a concord. . . .

[The concord includes an admission by Robert of Simon's right to the wardship.]

A.D. 1253
PLEA 59, pp. 75-6

Henry Organ of Guilden Morden complains by the King's writ (*per breve domini regis*) against Robert the parson of Guilden Morden's brother, Robert Russell, Nicholas, son of Beatrice, and Reginald his brother, that Robert and the others came with force and arms to the land of William of Culworth in Weston, which Henry Organ had let to him, and found Henry there and beat, wounded and maltreated him against the peace of our lord the King (*verberaverunt, vulneraverunt et maletractaverunt contra pacem domini regis*). . . .

And Robert and the others come and pray judgment whether they ought to answer, inasmuch as Henry Organ neither by way of appeal nor by way of complaint (*nec per modum appelli nec per modum querimoniæ*) makes any count against them whereby they ought to be put to answer. . . .

Afterwards they come and deny the force and injury, etc. And they expressly deny that they ever came to the aforesaid land or beat, wounded and maltreated Henry against the peace, etc., as the writ has it. And as to this they put themselves on the country. . . .

[The inquest finds against Nicholas and Reginald and for the other defendants.]

And because Nicholas and Reginald are proved to have wounded and beaten Henry in breach of the King's peace, therefore let them be kept in custody. And likewise let Henry be kept in custody for a false plaint against Robert and all the others. . . . And let Robert and all the others be acquitted. . . . Afterwards Nicholas and Reginald came and made fine by half a mark only, because they were poor, on the security of Thomas de Picquigny and Thomas Knight.

BOLLAND

Introduction to S.S. Vol. 27

Specimen Querela or Bill, pp. xxiii-xxiv

A.D. 1292[56]

Fesrekyn's Complaint

Cher sire joe vus cri merci issi cum vus estis mis en lu nostur seinur le Roy pur dreit fere a poveris e a riches. Joe Johan Fesrekyn face pleint a deu e a vus Sire Justice ke Richard le Carpenter Clerk du bayli de Salopesburie ke le vaundist Richard me de teent vi. mars le queuz Joe li bayla par escrit ke il meme Richard moy Johan duce trouer me sustinaunce pur le deners le queus il resu de moy e ne fe mie cum covenaunt fu entre nous mes ausi tot com il avoit le deners il me desoula e me fit sere par le trunc e me dona un leyke de pain ausi com ce fu un povere homme ke demaunds un pain pur deu e me morit pres de feim. E pur ce Cher Sire Joe vus cri merci pur deu ke vus me facers aver me deners avaunt ke vus partus ors de sete vile autrement ne recoverai jammes me deners ke sachers le riche gent tendrunt a semble ke le povere gent naverunt nul dreit en sete vile. Ausi tot moun seynur ki Joe ai me deners Joe me vois en le tere saint e priera pur le Roy de Engleterre e pur vus nomement Sire John de Berrewyke. Ke sachers ki Joe nai dener ne mayl pur pleyter. E pur ce Cher Sire ei merci de mey ki Joe ei me deners.

Dear Sir, of you who are put in the place of our lord the King to do right to poor and to rich, I cry mercy. I, John Fesrekyn, make my complaint to God and to you, Sir Justice, of Richard the carpenter that is clerk of the bailiff of Shrewsbury, that the said Richard detains from me six marks which I paid him upon receiving from him an undertaking in writing by which he bound himself to find me in board and lodging in return for the money he had from me[57]; and he keeps not what was agreed between us, but as soon as he had gotten hold of the money he abandoned me and constrained me by my body[58] and gave me a scrap of bread as though I had been

---

[56] 'The date of this bill is almost certainly 20 Edward I.': Bolland. The learned editor adds that 'the pathos of its illiteracy is untranslatable,' but he fortunately contrives to give a rendering of the 'Anglo-French,' which follows immediately.

[57] This type of private pension was common, if hazardous, in the middle ages. If granted by a religious house, it was called a *corody*. See P. & M. II. 134-5.

[58] 'Probably with a chain round it. The use of *"trunc"* for the living body is uncommon but warrantable': Bolland.

but a pauper begging his bread for God's sake, and through him I all but died for hunger. And for all this I cry you mercy, dear Sir, and pray, for God's sake, that you will see that I get my money back before you leave this town, or else never shall I have it back again, for I tell you that the rich folk all back each other up to keep the poor folk in this town from getting their rights. As soon, my Lord, as I get my money I shall go to the Holy Land, and there I will pray for the King of England and for you by your name, Sir John de Berewick; for I tell you that not a farthing I have to spend on a pleader. And so for this, dear Sir, be gracious to me that I may get me my money back.' [59]

SELECT CASES IN THE COURT OF KING'S BENCH: EDWARD I, Vol. II

S.S. Vol. 57

A.D. 1292

Toht's Case

Plea 44, pp. 113-5

Roger Toht [and eleven other named defendants] were attached to answer Robert, son of Henry, merchant of Northampton, of a plea wherefore, when the said Robert, son of Henry, had caused his cloths and merchandise at Northampton to be tied up and made ready for carrying to Stamford Fair in order there to make his profit therefrom, the aforesaid Roger [and the other defendants] did with force and arms obstruct the aforesaid Robert, son of Henry, when he wanted to carry those cloths and merchandise in his carts, and maliciously did tear them and violently throw them down in filthy places in the main street, whereby a great part of that merchandise perished; and thus the said Robert, son of Henry, was not able to make his profit of the remainder at the aforesaid fair. And other outrages they did to him (*et alia enormia ei intulerunt*), to his, the said Robert, son of Henry's, damage of forty marks, and against the peace, etc.

And thereof he complains that the aforesaid Roger and the others did the aforesaid trespass (*fecerunt predictam transgressionem*) on the Friday before Mid-Lent in the twentieth year of the reign of the King that now is [7 March, 1292], and tore and violently threw down his cloths, to wit, scarlet cloths, striped cloths, blue cloths, burnet cloths, camlot cloths and other cloths, into filthy places, whereby he says that he has suffered loss and has damage to the value of forty marks (*unde dicit quod deterioratus est et dampnum habet ad valenciam quadraginta marcarum*). And thereof he produces suit, etc.

And the aforesaid Roger and the others come and deny the force and injury, etc. . . .

[Nine of the defendants plead not guilty and put themselves on the country.]

And the aforesaid Roger Toht [and two others] say that the aforesaid Robert, son of Henry, was for a long time mayor of the town of

<hr/>

[59] 'This bill bears the endorsement *Cognoscit et concordati sunt per licentiam*, so we may suppose that John recovered at any rate a substantial portion of his "deners" from the bailiff's clerk': Bolland. Sir John de Berewick, though, *semble*, never a Justice of one of the Benches, was a Justice Itinerant from c. 1291-c. 1307.

Northampton so that he received from the community of the town about five hundred marks whereof he refused to render account, although often asked so to do. And they, as mayor and bailiffs of the aforesaid town, . . . attached the said Robert, who was evading the aforesaid account, by some cloths of his, according to the custom of the same town hitherto observed, until he had found them security that he would render his account; and they deny that they tore and violently threw any of the said Robert's cloths into filthy places or did him any other trespass. And as to this they put themselves on the country. . . .

> [After a replication by the plaintiff, the case is sent to an inquest of twenty-four: twelve from Northampton and twelve from the neighbouring districts.]

REGISTRUM BREVIUM[60]

f. 93. Trespass to the Person

Rex vicecomiti Lincolniæ salutem. Si A. fecerit te securum de clamore suo prosequendo, tunc pone per vadium et salvos plegios B. quod sit coram iustitiariis nostris apud Westmonasterium[61] in octavis sancti Michaelis ostensurus quare vi et armis in ipsum A. apud N. insultum fecit et ipsum verberavit vulneravit et maletractavit ita quod de vita eius desperabatur, et alia enormia ei intulit, ad grave damnum ipsius A. et contra pacem nostram. Et habeas ibi nomina plegiorum et hoc breve.

> The King to the sheriff of Lincoln greeting. If A. shall give you security for pursuing his claim, then put by gage and safe pledges B. that he be before our justices at Westminster on the octave of St. Michael to show wherefore with force and arms he made an assault upon the same A. at N. and beat wounded and ill-treated him so that his life was despaired of, and other outrages there did to him, to the grave damage of the same A. and against our peace. And have there the names of the pledges and this writ.

f. 110. Trespass to Land and Goods

Rex vicecomiti Lincolniæ salutem. Si A. fecerit te securum de clamore suo prosequendo, tunc pone per vadium et salvos plegios B. quod sit coram iusticiariis nostris apud Westmonasterium in octavis sancti Michaelis ostensurus quare vi et armis clausum ipsius A. apud T. fregit et arbores suas ibidem nuper crescentes succidit, et in separali piscaria sua ibidem piscatus fuit, et herbam suam ibidem nuper crescentem falcavit, et fænum inde proveniens ac piscem de piscaria prædicta necnon arbores prædictas et alia bona et catalla sua ad valentiam viginti marcarum, ac quadraginta

---

[60] The two following specimens are given by Holdsworth, H.E.L. III. 663. They are taken from the edition of 1687. On the Register generally, see Maitland, *Coll. Papers,* II. 110, and Holdsworth, H.E.L. II. 512-525 and Appendix V. The earliest Register seen by Maitland is dated 10 November, 1227, and it expanded greatly until the close of the reign of Henry VI, after which few additions were made. The earliest copies comprise a dozen pages, the latest seven hundred; and the first printed edition is dated 1531 and concludes—'Thus endyth thys booke called the Register of the wryttes oryggynall and judiciall, pryntyd at London by William Rastell, and finished the xxviii day of September in the yere of our lorde 1531.' The edition of 1687 is said by Maitland to be a reproduction of the volume printed in 1531.

[61] These words occur if the case is to come into the Common Pleas: if into the King's Bench the form would be—*quod sit coram nobis ubicumque tunc fuerimus in Anglia.*

libras de denariis suis in pecunia numerata ibidem inventa cepit et asportavit, et alia enormia ei intulit, ad grave damnum ipsius A. et contra pacem nostram. Et habeas ibi nomina plegiorum et hoc breve.

The King to the sheriff of Lincoln greeting. If A. shall give you security for pursuing his claim, then put by gage and safe pledges B. that he be before our justices at Westminster on the octave of St. Michael to show wherefore with force and arms he broke the close of the same A. at T., and cut down his trees there lately growing and fished there in his several fishery and mowed his grass there lately growing, and took and carried away the hay thus made and the fish from the aforesaid fishery and also the aforesaid trees and other of his goods and chattels to the value of twenty marks and also forty pounds of his money in coined money there found, and other outrages there did to him, to the grave damage of the same A. and against our peace. And have there the names of the pledges and this writ.

JOHN LILLY: A COLLECTION OF MODERN ENTRIES[62]

A. Trespass to the Person

(Assault, Battery and False Imprisonment)

LEE v. SCARMER

A.D. 1694

Northampton, to wit[63]: *William Lee*, gent., complains of *William Scarmer* and *Francis Adams* in the custody of the marshal, etc., for this, that they

[62] Lilly's Entries were first published in 1723. The precedents here cited are from the edition of 1791, at pp. 453 and 431 respectively. It will be observed that they are not original writs. The reason is that, by the end of the 17th century, the original writ, though still in principle the first move in a case, was rarely used in personal actions, as being both technical and expensive. It was usual to begin with a judicial writ of *Capias ad respondendum* which strictly was the process whereby the sheriff was directed to arrest a defendant who would not answer to an original writ, but had become simply a device to start litigation. Thus Blackstone, *Comm.* III. 282: ' it is now usual in practice [in the Common Pleas] to sue out the *capias* in the first instance . . . and afterwards a fictitious original is drawn up, with a proper return thereupon, in order to give the proceedings a colour of regularity'; and III. 285: ' [in the King's Bench] the more usual method of proceeding is without any original, but by a peculiar species of process entitled a *bill of Middlesex*, and therefore so entitled because the court now sits in that county. . . . The bill of Middlesex is a kind of *capias*, directed to the sheriff of that county and commanding him to take the defendant and have him before our lord the king at Westminster on a day prefixed, to answer to the plaintiff of a plea of trespass. . . . When once the defendant is taken into the custody of the marshall, or prison-keeper of this court, for the supposed trespass, he, being then a prisoner of this court, may here be prosecuted for any other species of injury. Yet, in order to found this jurisdiction, it is not necessary that the defendant be actually the marshall's prisoner; for, as soon as he appears, or puts in bail, to the process, he is deemed by so doing to be in such custody of the marshall as will give the court a jurisdiction to proceed.'

The allegation of trespass might thus be a fiction, designed only to introduce the real cause of action. In the three precedents here cited from Lilly, however, the plaintiff is actually suing in trespass.

[63] ' The " to wit " placed after the name of a county at the beginning of a legal record represents a mere flourish ꝝ, dividing the name of the county from the beginning of the story. This was mistaken for a long S, which was supposed to be the abbreviation of *scilicet*,' Maitland, Letter of 14 February, 1904, quoted in *F. W. Maitland*, by H. A. L. Fisher, p. 151.

on the 14th day of March in the fifth year of the reign of the lord and lady William and Mary, now King and Queen of England, etc., with force and arms on him the said *William Lee* at Daventry in the county aforesaid did make an assault, and him the said *William Lee* did then and there beat, wound and abuse, take and imprison, and him in prison there for a long time, to wit, for the space of twenty-four hours from thence next ensuing, without any reasonable and lawful cause and against the law and custom of this kingdom of England and until the said *William Lee* paid to them the said *William Scarmer* and *Francis Adams* a fine of 5s. 6d. to obtain his liberty, did detain, and other outrages on him then and there committed, against the peace of the said lord and lady the now King and Queen and to the damage of the said *William Lee* 40 l. And therefor he produces the suit, etc.

B. TRESPASS QUARE CLAUSUM FREGIT

HIGGINS v. SMITH

A.D. 1692

Warwick, to wit: *John Higgins* complains of *Thomas Smith* the younger, *John Dickins* and *Thomas Wooton* in the custody of the marshal, etc., for this, that they on the 20th day of November in the third year of the reign of the lord and lady William and Mary, now King and Queen of England, etc., with force and arms the close of the said *John,* called *Cliffe Bank* in the parish of *Alveston* in the county aforesaid, broke and entered, and the grass of him the said *John* in the same close then growing to the value of 40s. with their feet by walking trod down and consumed, and other outrages on him then and there committed, against the peace of the said lord and lady the now King and Queen and to the damage of him the said *John,* 40 l. And therefor he produces the suit, etc.[64]

C. TRESPASS QUARE CLAUSUM FREGIT
AND
TRESPASS DE BONIS ASPORTATIS

HENDERSON v. CROSS

A.D. 1696

Middlesex, to wit: *Thomas Henderson* complains of *Robert Cross, John Furbeck* [and others] in the custody of the marshal, etc., for this, that they on the 4th day of October in the sixth year of the reign of the lord and lady William and Mary, now King and Queen of England, etc., with force and arms the house of him the said *Thomas* in the parish of *St. Margaret, Westminster,* in the county of Middlesex, did break and enter, and 20 barrels filled with strong beer to the value of 40 l., and 10 butts filled with strong ale to the value of 50 l., of him the said *Thomas,* in the cellar of the same house of him the said *Thomas* then and there being found, did then and there take and carry away and to their own use did convert and dispose, and other outrages on him the said *Thomas* did then and there commit, against the peace of the said lord and lady the now King and Queen and to the damage, etc.

[64] Many of the cases of *Trespass q. cl. fr.* arise out of a claim of right by the defendant. Thus, in the above case, the defendants pleaded a right of fishery.

⤳ 4 ⤳

THE DEVELOPMENT OF ACTIONS
ON THE CASE

THE writs established at the accession of Edward I offered a respectable measure of redress for injury to property and, less amply, for personal injury. But their limitations were patent. Even Trespass, potentially the most fruitful, would lie only for a direct and unauthorised interference with land, goods or person. A plaintiff could not use it who had voluntarily submitted himself or his property to the defendant's ministrations, as where he complained of the carelessness of a doctor or a farrier or a veterinary surgeon. A bailor could not use it if the bailee damaged or destroyed the goods.[1] It would not avail where the injury was not the direct but the merely consequential result of the defendant's misfeasance. So, if the defendant by operations on his own land succeeded in flooding other land of which the plaintiff was a lessee for years, the latter had no remedy.[2] Finally, the plaintiff could not sue where he was injured not by an act, but by an omission: ' not doing is no trespass.'[3] It is common knowledge that these gaps were in time filled by the development of actions on the case; but the origin of these actions has provoked as pretty a controversy as that of Trespass itself. The modern literature is considerable. Sir William Holdsworth and Mr. Landon stand opposed to Professor Plucknett and Miss Dix, and Professor Potter, in a dispassionate review of the contest, takes refuge in agnosticism.[4]

Mr. Landon has named three schools of thought. The ' modernists,' represented by Ames, Jenks and Mr. Sutton, think ' that the action on the case originated in the Statute of Westminster II and even that it received its name from the word *casu* in the phrase *in consimili casu,*' contained in chapter 24 of that Statute.[5] The ' revolutionary ' school of Professor Plucknett and Miss Dix will have nothing to do with the Statute. The ' traditionalists,' with whom Mr. Landon is ranged, profess a *via media* and contend that the ' action on the case existed

---

[1] See *Anon.* Y.B. Hil. 13 Rich. 2 (Ames Found.) p. 103, A.D. 1390; *infra,* p. 83. If the goods, though damaged, were returned, neither Trespass nor Detinue would lie: *infra,* p. 102.
[2] The Assise of Nuisance lay only for a freeholder: *supra,* p. 9.
[3] So stated *per Curiam* as late as 1610 in the *Six Carpenters' Case,* Co. Rep. 146a. The Assise of Nuisance might lie in certain circumstances: *supra,* p. 19.
[4] See Professor Plucknett, (1931) 31 Columbia L.R., 778, and (1936) 52 L.Q.R. 220; Holdsworth, (1931) 47 L.Q.R. 334; Mr. Landon, (1936) 52 L.Q.R. 68; Miss Dix, (1937) 46 Yale L.J. 1142; Professor Potter, *Hist. Intro. to English Law,* 3rd ed., 292-7.
[5] Ames, *Lectures on Legal History,* p. 442; Jenks, *Hist. of Eng. Law,* p. 137; Sutton, *Personal Actions at Common Law,* pp. 24-6.

before the Statute,' but that ' its development and ultimate transmutation into Trespass on the Case would not have been possible without the powers which Parliament in c. 24 conferred upon the Chancery clerks.'[6]   The core of the problem is thus to be found in this particular chapter of the Statute of Westminster II, 1285.[7]

A word must be said upon the background of the Statute.   If, in England as elsewhere, the first half of the thirteenth century was a period of juristic expansion, the second half was one of contraction. This not unnatural reaction was assisted both by technical and by political forces.   The elaboration of the royal courts tended to the uniformity of thought as of procedure.   The Chancery was becoming ever more ominously a government department, where the quality of imagination seemed incompatible with administrative efficiency.   Such a process as the evolution of the Writ of Trespass out of the Quare actions might itself be represented as the triumph of certainty over elasticity.   English law, in short, was passing through a stage familiar to all students of legal history.   Dr. Schulz has described the phenomena as universal.   ' At Rome, as elsewhere, actional formalism passed through three stages of development.   In the earliest, the jurists regarded the forms as what in fact they were, namely as creations of their own untrammelled cautelary science; at this stage the forms were plastic, adaptable and capable of being added to.   In the second stage the forms became petrified; the jurists felt that they ought not to be further altered, and thus their canon became closed.   In the third stage the forms were either simply disused or observed as an ancestral rigmarole to be gabbled with a smile.'[8]   In law, as in other projections of human intelligence, the creature is ever in wait to devour the creator.

This growing professionalism was accompanied and balanced by the evolution of Parliament.   The word was as yet no term of art,[9] nor must it be invested with the attributes of nineteenth-century sovereignty.   It was still the framework for the operations of the King's Council, still but one of the channels through which the King's grace percolated.   But for a space, under the influence of the astute Chancellor, Robert Burnell,[10] it was an instrument of law-making without

---

[6] Mr. Landon cites, among the ' traditionalists,' Coke (*Litt.* s. 67; 2nd Inst., 407; *Webb's Case,* 8 Co. Rep. at pp. 48-9) and Blackstone, III. 50-1.   Maitland, *Forms of Action,* pp. 51-2, said: ' [The Statute of Westminster II, c. 24] is regarded as the statutory warrant for the variation of the writs of trespass so as to suit special cases.'

[7] For text and translation, see *infra,* pp. 78-9.

[8] Schulz, *Roman Legal Science,* p. 26.

[9] Powicke, *King Henry III and the Lord Edward,* p. 341.

[10] Chancellor, 1274-1292. 'Edward, with this busy, trusty, congenial, immoral man by his side, was more the master of his fate than any king since the Conqueror,' Powicke, *supra,* p. 595.   See Tout, 7 D.N.B. 386-9, and Plucknett, 31 Col. L.R., pp. 791-7, and *Concise Hist. of the Common Law* (4th ed.), p. 658: ' For eighteen years he held the Great Seal, and for eighteen years there flowed the vast stream of reforming legislation which extends from the Statute of Westminster the First to *Quia Emptores.'*

precedent in England and for centuries without successor. If the Justices of the Bench were timid or divided, if the clerks of the Chancery were indolent or hidebound, the King in his Parliament could redress all grievances and end all doubts. Such, at least, was the vision which dazzled contemporary eyes before it faded. ' The King has his court in his council in his parliaments, where, being present the prelates, the earls, the barons, the chief men and other learned men, the doubts which have arisen upon judgments are resolved and for new injuries which have emerged new remedies are devised, and to each is there awarded the justice which he deserves.'[11]

Against this background the rival schools may be assessed. The ' modernist' view that writs on the case originated in the Statute of Westminster and derived their name from its clause *in consimili casu* may be dismissed. Mr. Landon himself has pointed out that such a derivation would suggest as their title not writs *sur le cas* or *super casum*, but *en le cas* or *in casu*. It is clear, on the contrary, that actions on the case were so called because of the loquacity of the writ by which they were begun. In such a writ as Trespass the plaintiff confined himself to conventional words and reserved his substantial allegations for the Declaration. But in actions on the case the naked facts upon which he relied were thrust into the writ itself. Mr. Landon has summoned impressive testimony from the sixteenth to the nineteenth centuries.[12] Rastell, in his law-dictionary, first printed in 1527, defined ' Action sur le case ' as ' a writ brought against a person for some offence without force . . . where the whole case is contained in the Writ.[13] Two and a half centuries later Blackstone repeated the explanation. ' This action of *trespass,* or transgression, *on the case* is . . . so called because the plaintiff's whole case or cause of complaint is set forth at length in the original writ.'[14]

The ' traditionalist' view rests upon two assumptions. The first is that writs on the case were issued by the clerks of the Chancery in the earlier years of the thirteenth century, and were none other than the *brevia magistralia* whose varying content Bracton contrasted with the fixed and determinate *brevia de cursu*.[15] The second is that, after an interval of conservatism which provoked and explained its terms, Chapter 24 of the Statute of Westminster II gave the clerks

---

[11] *Fleta* (c. A.D. 1290), Lib. II. c. 2. For his book, see P. & M. I. 210 and H.E.L. II. 321-2.

[12] 52 L.Q.R. pp. 69-71. Cf. the contrast in the classical Roman law between *actiones in factum* and *in jus*: Gaius IV, 46.

[13] These words are cited by Mr. Landon from the edition of 1567. John Rastell's work, which in fact precedes in date the earliest English general dictionary, passed through twenty-nine editions, the last of which was in 1819, and is usually known as his *Termes de la Ley*. See Cowley's *Bibliography of Abridgments* (S.S. 1932), pp. lxxxi-lxxxiv.

[14] Blackstone, III. 122. See also *Anon* (A.D. 1429), Y.B. 7 Hen. 6, f. 45, and *The Bishop of Salisbury's Case* (A.D. 1459) Y.B. 38 Hen. 6, f. 9, *infra*, pp. 84-6.

[15] *Supra*, p. 51, n.

enlarged powers which, with persistent enthusiasm, they used to invent
the new writs upon which so much of the modern law is based. The
'tradition' is under-written by the august names of Coke and Blackstone; but, despite its prevalence and dignity, it would seem to have
been destroyed by the criticism of Professor Plucknett and Miss Dix.

To describe the first half of the thirteenth century as an age of
expansion is legitimate.[16] To identify the instruments of that expansion with the writs on the case not only requires more evidence than
has been offered,[17] but involves the most tortuous essays in chronology.
The actions which entered the law during the reign of Henry III were
based not upon writs, but upon formless *querelæ,* and were sanctioned
by the authority not of the clerks but of the justices. Whatever the
significance of Bracton's cryptic *brevia magistralia,* the writ of Trespass itself was not established until the accession of Edward I. Until
there was Trespass there could not be Trespass on the case; and the
first of the 'traditional' assumptions requires therefore the reversal
of the normal process of generation and transposes the dates of Case
and Trespass. The strain upon the reader's credulity is not lessened
by the remarkable fact that there is no authenticated instance of an
action *sur le case* before 1367, over eighty years after the passing of
the Statute.[18]

The second assumption, that the writs on the case which appeared
in the fourteenth and fifteenth centuries were invented by the clerks
of the Chancery under the powers given to them by the Statute, is open
to still graver objections. It is necessary to discuss the language of
the Statute and its interpretation by the judges, to contrast the procedure envisaged by the Statute with that actually adopted in the creation
of the writs, and to examine the form of those writs. The general
words always cited to warrant the statutory connexion and which contain the vital phrase *in consimili casu* appear, not at the beginning,
but at the end of chapter 24.[19] They are preceded by an attempt to
cure a particular flaw in the course of justice occasioned by the alienation of an estate or by the death of one of the parties after an injury
done to some species of real property. Three instances are expressed:
where B commits on his land a nuisance to A and then conveys the
land to C, where a parson is disturbed in his common of pasture by
X and one or both of the parties dies, and where a dispute has arisen
upon the status of an estate as frankalmoign or as lay fee and one
church has succeeded to the claim of another. In each of these cases
the common law writ—Assise of Nuisance, Quod Permittat or Assise

---

[16] *Supra,* pp. 51-2.
[17] Mr. Landon contents himself with saying, 'We must admit that the action on the
case existed at common law': 52 L.Q.R., p. 73.
[18] *The Miller's Case, infra,* p. 80.
[19] *Infra,* p. 79. The Statute of Westminster II contains 50 chapters, dealing with a
heterogeneous collection of problems. It is not so much a Statute in the modern
sense, as a series of statutes enacted at one session.

Utrum[20]—failed because of the conveyance or successsion, and in each the Statute declared that an analogous writ was to be framed. ' Henceforth, when a writ is granted in one case, and in like case a corresponding remedy is needed, there shall be a writ.' The general words follow only upon the particular instances, and, without attributing the *ejusdem generis* rule to the fourteenth century, it is not pedantic to require those words to be read in their context.

The interpretation of a thirteenth or fourteenth century statute is not to be approached with the same almost pathological interest which attends the reaction of a modern judge to a modern Act of Parliament. On the one hand, the mediæval statute had not the pre-eminence of its successors, and, as a source of law, was at most but *primus inter pares*. The King might legislate with no less authority by writ or charter, by provision or ordinance. On the other hand, the mediæval judge was a more intimate attendant at its birth. ' Do not gloss the statute,' said Chief Justice Hengham to counsel, ' we understand it better than you, for we made it.'[21] The judicial reaction to chapter 24 is thus of peculiar importance. For twenty-five years after its enactment few cases are recorded in which counsel relied upon the general words of that chapter and in none of them did the appeal succeed.[22] But in 1310 three cases occurred where they were cited and applied by the court. In the first, the King's Bench allowed a writ of ' Ravishment of Ward,' already available to a guardian in knight service, to be used by a guardian in socage.[23] In the second and third the scope of the writ of entry was extended. Before 1278 a writ of entry *ad communem legem* enabled the reversioner to recover if a tenant for life, in dower or by the curtesy, wrongly conveyed the estate to X— but only after the death of such tenant. The Statute of Gloucester, 1278, c. 7, allowed the writ during the lifetime of a tenant in dower but in no other case (*writ of entry in casu proviso*). As a result of the two cases of 1310 a writ of entry *in consimili casu* was allowed during the life of a tenant for life or by the curtesy.[24] Seven years later, a plaintiff brought a writ of Waste under chapter 14 of the Statute of

---

[20] On the Assise Utrum, see P. & M. I. 246-250.

[21] *Aumeye's Case* (1305) Y.B. 33-35 Ed. I (R.S. pp. 78-82). Thus the ' Statute concerning the Sheriff and his Clerks,' designed in 1298 to meet the inconveniences of sheriffs who, ' putting so much faith in the acts of their clerks, affect not themselves in any way to intermeddle in the overlooking or examining of writs directed to them,' is said to be made by the Treasurer, the Chancellor, three Bishops, ' John de Cobham and his Companions, Barons of the Exchequer,' the ' Justices of both Benches and others of the King's Council, being assembled at the Exchequer at Westminster': Statutes of the Realm, I. 213. The classical example of drastic judicial interpretation is that of Bereford, C.J. and the Statute *De Donis*: Plucknett, *Concise History*, 4th ed., pp. 521-3. On the whole question see Plucknett, *Statutes and their Interpretation in the Fourteenth Century*.

[22] The references to a number of unsuccessful attempts in 1304 are given by Plucknett, 31 Col. L. Rev., at p. 783. See also *St. Michael* v. *Beauchamp* (1307) Y.B. 33-35 Ed. I (R.S.), p. 426, *infra*, p. 71.

[23] *Frowyk* v. *Leukenore* (1310) Y.B. 2 & 3 Ed. II. (S.S. Vol. 19, pp. 157-163).

[24] *Devereux* v. *Tuchet* (1310) Y.B. 3 Ed. II (S.S. Vol. 20, pp. 16-19), and *Stirkeland* v. *Brunolfshead* (1310) Y.B. 3 Ed. II. (S.S. Vol. 20, pp. 106-9).

Westminster II, whereby the defendant was required to show why, ' whereas by the Common Council of the King's Realm it is provided that no one may do waste, sale or destruction of lands, houses, woods, gardens or men leased to him for a term of life or of years,' the defendant had ' made waste, sale, destruction *and exile* of the lands, etc.' The writ was challenged because the Statute made no mention of ' exile '; but it was upheld by Chief Justice Bereford on the strength of chapter 24. ' It was good by virtue of the Statute which gives a writ " in like case when like remedy needeth." '[25]

Beyond these instances no other writ is reported as framed upon the general clause. In 1307, indeed, the court had refused a writ of entry to a remainderman, because ' the Statute of Westminster II directs that in a similar case there shall be a similar remedy; but these two things, reversions and remainders, are not similar.'[26] In each of the instances, moreover, the land law was in question. It is natural, as Sir William Holdsworth observed, that the first employment of the clause should be thus confined,[27] but, if its implications were as generous and as evident as the ' traditionalists ' have claimed, it is strange that even this step was not taken for twenty-five years and that no attempt at a writ of Trespass on the Case was recorded for another half-century.

These applications of the general clause are significant not only because they are so few and so belated. The clause itself was precise in the recipe which it prescribed. The initiative lay with the clerks of the Chancery, who were to ' agree in making a writ,' and, if they found any difficulty, they were to refer ' to the next Parliament.' Not a word was said upon the function of the Judges.[28] The statutory

---

[25] *Walkefare* v. *Munpinceon* (1317) Y.B. 11 Ed. II (S.S. Vol. 61, pp. 8-12). The plaintiff in his Declaration alleged, as the incidents of waste, etc., ' digging ditches and making pits in 3 acres of land and selling thereof the marl and clay to the value of 40/-, breaking down a barn of the value of £10, a stable of the value of 10 marks, a mill of the value of 10 marks, cutting down and selling in the wood of the same manor 20 oaks each of the value of 3/-, 80 ash-trees each of the value of 2/-, 40 small ash-trees each of the value of 12 pence, and in the gardens of the same manor 20 apple-trees each of the value of 2/-, 40 pear-trees each of the value of 2/-, and making exile of one Walter Hune, a villein of the aforesaid manor, who held 14 acres of land of the villeinage of the same manor, and of one Gilbert Cloveleke, a villein of the aforesaid manor, who held a messuage and 6 acres of land with the appurtenances of the villeinage of the same manor, by grievous and intolerable distresses.' ' Exile of villeins,' according to Coke, is ' making them poor, where they were rich when the tenant came in, whereby they depart from their tenures ': Co. Litt., 53b.

[26] *St. Michael* v. *Beauchamp* (1307) Y.B. 33-35 Ed. I (R.S.) p. 426. As Miss Dix says (46 Yale L.J. at p. 1154), ' If the likeness had to be more apparent than that between remainders and reversions, what reason is there to think that the similarity between an injury done with force and an injury done without force could have been regarded as sufficiently close?'

[27] 47 L.Q.R. pp. 334-6.

[28] It is true that in 1293, *Howard*, arguing for the plaintiff on an assise of Novel Disseisin and finding it likely that the Court would rule the facts to lie outside the scope of the assise, said: ' If we cannot have a remedy by this writ at common law, give us a remedy.' (*Anon*, Y.B. 20 & 21 Ed. I, R.S., p. 429). This *cri de cœur* fell on deaf ears; but the remarkable fact is not that it should have failed to move the Court, but that it should have been uttered at all—at least, if the Statute of Westminster II was as dominating a feature of Edward I's reign as is traditionally asserted. *Howard* might have been expected to lay his petition at the feet of the Clerks of the Chancery rather than before the judges.

procedure was followed in the three cases of 1310 already described. In the case of ' Ravishment of Ward,' Chief Justice Brabazon said, ' The writ is given by the Statute, which says " let not the complainants leave the Chancery without remedy "; and it has been fashioned by the common counsel of the clerks of the Chancery.'[29] The two cases upon the scope of the writ of entry are peculiarly interesting. In *Devereux* v. *Tuchet* Chief Justice Bereford at first quashed the writ as supported neither at the common law nor by the Statute of Gloucester. The plaintiff then complained to the clerks of the Chancery, from whom, doubtless at a good price, he had bought the writ. The sequel is not without piquancy. The clerks of the Chancery summoned the Chief Justice to attend upon them and explain his conduct, and, after they had delivered a lecture on the Statute, the Chief Justice, usually so masterful, surrendered. ' Blessed be he who made that statute! Make the writ and we will maintain it.'[30] In *Stirkeland* v. *Brunolfshead* Chief Justice Bereford again quashed the writ and was again called before the Clerks; but this time a model writ was settled in conference between them.[31] It is intelligible that the drastic powers given to the clerks should have perturbed the judges and intrigued the reporters; but these vivid incidents are in strange contrast to the absence of excitement attendant upon the writs of Trespass on the Case. If the latter were in truth a species of writ *in consimili casu,* some reference might be expected to their statutory origin. None is recorded throughout their history.[32]

The form of the writ is as instructive as its mechanics. In writs with an undoubted statutory origin one of two features may be noticed. If the parent statute contained not only general directions but an exact precedent, it sufficed to follow the model without citing the statute. If no pattern was prescribed, the subsequent writs rehearsed the statute or at least referred to it. The Year-Books teem with instances. Writs based on the Statutes of Labourers, on the Statute of Marlborough, on the Statutes of Forcible Entry, all rehearse the source of their creation.[33] No specimen form is offered in the general clause of chapter 24; and yet in no reported action on the case is the Statute of Westminster mentioned in the writ or in the declaration,

---

[29] *Frowyk* v. *Leukenore*, Y.B. 2 & 3 Ed. II (S.S. Vol. 19) at p. 161.

[30] *Devereux* v. *Tuchet*, Y.B. 3 Ed. II (S.S. Vol. 20) esp. at p. 19. See also Bolland, *Chief Justice Sir William Bereford* (1924), pp. 13-19.

[31] Y.B. 3 Ed. II (S.S. Vol. 20), esp. at p. 109.

[32] See Plucknett, 52 L.Q.R., at pp. 222-4, citing Holdsworth, 47 L.Q.R. at p. 336, and commenting on Landon, 52 L.Q.R. at pp. 77-8.

[33] For writs based on the Statutes of Labourers, see Y.B. Trin. 18 Hen. 6, f. 13, pl. 2, Y.B. Hil. 19 Hen. 6, f. 53, pl. 15, Y.B. Trin. 22 Hen. 6, f. 58, pl. 8; on the Statute of Marlborough, c. 4, see Y.B. Pasch. 22 Ed. 4, f. 11, pl. 30; on the Statutes of Forcible Entry, many instances throughout the reigns of Hen. 6 and Ed. 4, especially Y.B. 14 Hen. 6, f. 13, pl. 44, Y.B. 35 Hen. 6, f. 6, pl. 8, Y.B. 5 Ed. 4, f. 34. So, too, in 27 Hen. 8 occur a number of actions on the new statute of non-residence—that spiritual persons must reside in their benefices—and in each the writ recites the statute, e.g. 27 Hen. 8, f. 21, pl. 12. See also the instances given in F.N.B. 89O to 90C; and *infra*, the writ *of monstravit de compoto*, p. 268, n.

by counsel or by judge. Sir William Holdsworth apologised for this silence by denying the necessity of speech. 'Writs on the case were not directly given by the Statute: the Statute was addressed to the clerks of the Chancery, and ordered them to make writs in cases similar to those in which a writ was already provided.'[34] Unfortunately in the cases of 1310 and 1317 already cited the statutory reference occurred. In *Devereux* v. *Tuchet* the plaintiff in his writ alleged conduct 'against the form of the statute in this case provided,' and the defendant denied the existence of any such Statute—*non est aliquod statutum in quo huiusmodi breve sit formatum.*[35] In *Stirkeland* v. *Brunolfshead* the form of writ finally settled in conference declared that the land should revert to the plaintiff by the form of the Statute provided in a like case—*per formam statuti in casu consimili provisi.*[36] In *Walkefare* v. *Munpinceon* the writ rehearsed the provision of the Common Council of the King's Realm and declared the waste to be against the form of that provision—*contra formam provisionis predictæ.*[37]

A final comment must be offered upon the 'great names' of the tradition, the men who, in Mr. Landon's words, 'were far better acquainted with their sources than we can ever hope to be.'[38] It is admitted that no lawyer before the seventeenth century observed a connexion between the writs on the case and the Statute of Westminster. Coke appears to have made the suggestion, which was embraced *con amore* by Blackstone and by him transmitted to the Victorian jurists.[39] The latter were moved neither to doubt nor to verify, and neither Coke nor Blackstone was remarkable for historical scholarship. Coke was sceptical or credulous as might serve his turn and did not scruple to tamper with his sources: Blackstone, though with more interest in legal history, was capable of ludicrous errors.[40] Contemporary inquirers, equipped with the tools and chastened by the results of modern research, are more likely to be 'acquainted with the sources' than Stuart or Hanoverian dogmatists. Sir William Holdsworth's last words on the question reveal the insubstantial nature of the tradition. 'The relation of the Statute to writs on the case [is] not unlike the relation of certain clauses of Magna Carta to certain important constitutional doctrines—there is a real historical connexion,

---

[34] 47 L.Q.R. pp. 334-6. Cf. Plucknett in 52 L.Q.R., pp. 222-3.
[35] Y.B. 3 Ed. II (S.S. Vol. 20) at p. 19.
[36] Y.B. 3 Ed. II (S.S. Vol. 20) at p. 109.
[37] Y.B. 11 Ed. II (S.S. Vol. 61) at p. 11.
[38] 52 L.Q.R. at p. 78.
[39] A reference is made by Lambard in his *Archeion*, apparently written in 1591, but not published until 1635: see Plucknett, 31 Col. L. Rev. p. 778. For Coke, see *Second Institute*, 407 and *Webb's Case*, 8 Co. Rep. at pp. 48-9. For Blackstone, see *Comm.* III. 50-1. Ames is didactic: 'They were all the product of a few lines in a statute enacted near the end of the thirteenth century,' *Lectures*, p. 442. He makes no attempt at historical examination.
[40] See, e.g., *supra*, p. 10, n. 32.

though that connexion is not quite so clear or so immediate as our old lawyers supposed."[41] The analogy of Magna Carta is damning. If such is the relation of Case to the Statute of Westminster, it must be diagnosed as a conscious anachronism.[42]

Whatever test be applied, the ' traditionalist ' view seems untenable. The action on the case derived, not from the statutory powers of Chancery clerks, but from the fiat of the judges. In the course of the fourteenth century, indeed, the status of the Chancery clerks declined.[43] At the beginning of the century even the formidable Chief Justice Bereford had been prepared to treat them as his equals and to recognise that the creation of writs *in consimili casu* was essentially their function. But when, in the last third of the century, the actions on the case began to be developed, no more is heard of the clerks and their powers. The new instruments were the product not of bureaucratic but of judicial initiative. It would, therefore, have been improper to refer to the Statute of Westminster, since by that statute no creative powers were given to the judges. Of their inherent and abundant vitality Case was the most striking testimony and the most fruitful result. On the rare occasions when a judge found it necessary to examine the nature of the writ, the answer was given without hesitation and received without challenge. In the words of Hill, J. in 1409, ' the action was taken at common law.'[44] The compilers and commentators of the sixteenth century were equally without doubt. Fitzherbert, in his *New Natura Brevium,* first published in 1534, allocated distinct sections to writs of *Trespass sur le Case* and to writs *in consimili casu*: the latter appear only in two references, and in each instance as incidental to a discussion of the Assise Utrum.[45] Rastell, in his *Collection of Entries,* first published in 1566, offered 54 examples of *Accion sur le Case,* in none of which may any statutory flavour be detected: under the title of *Consimili Casu* is placed a solitary writ of entry drafted *per formam Statuti in consimili casu.*[46]

An attempt may now be made to indicate the course of the remedy evolved by the common lawyers to meet the acknowledged deficiencies of the older writs. The stock selected for grafting was Trespass, and the earliest reported experiment was in 1367.[47] A ' writ of Tres-

[41] 47 L.Q.R. at p. 336.
[42] See, on the curious historical vicissitudes of Magna Carta, Butterfield, *The Englishman and his History* (1944).
[43] See Wilkinson, *The Chancery under Edward III,* pp. 184-8, and Holdsworth, 47 L.Q.R., at p. 336.
[44] *Anon,* Y.B. Mich. 11 Hen. 4, f. 33, pl. 60, *infra,* p. 340. So also in *Anon,* Y.B. 21 Hen. 7, f. 30, pl. 5, counsel for the defendant argued that ' one shall never have an action on the case where he can have *other* action at the common law.'
[45] *F.N.B.* ff. 92E-95D, *infra,* p. 88; and f. 49 D and F.
[46] *Rastell,* ff. 2-13, *infra,* p. 90; and f. 121.
[47] *The Miller's Case,* Y.B. 41 Ed. 3, f. 24, pl. 17, *infra,* p. 80. There has been some diversity of opinion on the chronology of these early instances: see Maitland, *Forms of Action,* p. 66, and Street, *Foundations of Legal Liability,* III, 249. But the discrepancy is not great, and is due largely to the failure of the sixteenth century

pass *sur le case* [48] was brought against a miller who had carried off two bushels of corn which the plaintiff was attempting to grind at the mill. While the ultimate question at issue was the right to take toll, the occasion of the dispute was the asportation of chattels, and it was not surprising that the Court should have dismissed the action on the ground that a ' common writ of Trespass ' was available. Two years later the experiment was repeated, and this time with success. A pilgrim to Canterbury brought a writ of Trespass ' on all the matter according to the case ' against an innkeeper upon a general custom of the realm to keep safely the property of his guests. He alleged that, having taken a room in the inn, he left his chattels there while he went out to do his shopping, and, when he returned, they had been removed ' by evil doers through the default of the innkeeper and his servants.' He won his action. [49] During the next thirty years a number of cases were reported where Trespass *vi et armis* would not have availed because the plaintiff had voluntarily put himself or his goods into the defendant's hands. In *Waldon* v. *Marshall* in 1370 [50] the plaintiff succeeded in an action against a veterinary surgeon who had undertaken to cure his horse but had negligently killed him; in 1373 a writ of Trespass *en son case* was sustained against a farrier for laming a horse; [51] and in 1375 an action of Trespass *sur son case* failed against a surgeon, who had negligently pursued his undertaking to heal the plaintiff's hand, only because the writ did not specify the *locus in quo*. [52]

At the end of the fourteenth century it was possible to contrast the old ' general ' Trespass with the new ' special ' Trespass, framed on the individual facts of each case but designed to assist the plaintiff where there had been no direct and unauthorised interference with his person or property. Thus in *Waldon* v. *Marshall* [53] defendant's counsel objected that the plaintiff ' could have a writ of Trespass, that he killed your horse, *generalement*,' and received the reply that this was impossible, ' because the horse was not killed by force, but died by default of his cure.' In an anonymous case of 1390 the contrast was fatal to a plaintiff who had ignored it. He had brought Trespass *vi et armis* against husband and wife for killing his horse,

compilers to classify with precision the forms of action. Thus Fitzherbert in his *Abridgment* (1565) offers for the 14th century 18 examples of *Accion sur le Case*, but 7 only are properly so called: the others are either Trespass *vi et armis* or rested not on writs but on bills. See also the failure to appreciate the character of the *Humber Ferryman* case, *infra*, p. 330.   On the whole question see Miss Dix, 46 Yale L.J., pp. 1157-1162, to whose account of the action on the case all students of legal history are indebted.

[48] The reporter thus describes the writ, while counsel for the plaintiff speaks of a writ ' taken *sur ma matter*,' i.e. upon the individual circumstances of his case. The phrase is surely remote from any association with the *in consimili casu* clause of the Statute.
[49] *The Innkeeper's Case*, Y.B. 42 Ed. 3, f. 11, pl. 13, *infra*, p. 80.
[50] Y.B. 43 Ed. 3, f. 33, pl. 38, *infra*, p. 81.
[51] *The Farrier's Case*, Y.B. 46 Ed. 3, f. 19, pl. 19, *infra*, p. 81.
[52] *The Surgeon's Case*, Y.B. 48 Ed. 3, f. 6, pl. 11, *infra*, p. 82.
[53] Y.B. 43 Ed. 3, f. 33, pl. 38, *infra*, p. 81.

but was forced to admit in court that the horse had been bailed and that he should have proceeded by a *brief sur son cas*.[54] The distinction was marked in the language of the writs. The words '*vi et armis et contra pacem regis*,' which emphasised the association of 'general' Trespass with immediate misconduct, were inappropriate to 'special' Trespass. The phrase '*vi et armis*,' though it appeared in the initial experiment in 1367, was omitted in 1373,[55] and its presence or absence served as the test of the two writs in the anonymous case of 1390.[56] The phrase '*contra pacem regis*' appeared in the plaintiff's writ in the *Innkeeper's Case* of 1369;[57] but in *Waldon* v. *Marshall* the court expressed their hypothetical disapproval of it,[58] and in an anonymous case of 1372 they quashed the writ because it had been used.[59] In the *Surgeon's Case* in 1375 the defendant offered to wager his law. The plaintiff objected that such a course was not open on a writ of Trespass, whose concomitant was trial by jury; but the court supported the defendant. 'This writ does not suppose "force and arms" nor "against the peace," so that wager of law is to be allowed.'[60] The decision was eccentric and unique, but it serves to mark the essential contrast.

Throughout the fifteenth century these experiments were multiplied and extended. That the parent stock of Trespass was not ignored is shown by a case of 1429, where the plaintiff brought *Trespass sur le cas* for a false imprisonment, apparently because the defendant had not personally imprisoned him, but had indirectly secured his arrest.[61] But its ancestry receded in memory as in time. A number of cases depended, in subject-matter though not in name, upon the analogy of nuisance: litigants sought to avoid the technicalities of the Assise or to transcend its boundaries.[62] A second group would be classified by modern analysis under the rubric of contract rather than of tort. Already in the fourteenth century plaintiffs had alleged conduct in breach of an undertaking; but the undertaking was incidental to the misfeasance upon which the action depended and was in the nature

[54] *Anon*, Y.B. 13 Rich. 2 (Ames Foundation), pp. 103-4, *infra* p. 83.

[55] *The Farrier's Case*, *infra*, p. 81.

[56] *Anon*, *infra*, p. 83.

[57] *Infra*, p. 80.

[58] *Infra*, p. 81.

[59] Y.B. Trin. 45 Ed. 3, f. 17, pl. 6: an early attempt to use '*un briefe de Trespass compernant tiel matter*' on an issue of nuisance.

[60] *Infra*, p. 82. Practice remained uniform in rejecting *vi et armis* in Trespass on the Case, but there was later uncertainty about *contra pacem regis*. The latter phrase occurs in some, but not in all, precedents given by Fitzherbert in his *New Natura Brevium*. Cf. 86 H, 92 E and 94 A. See *infra*, p. 88.

[61] *Anon*, Y.B. 7 Hen. 6, f. 45, pl. 24, *infra*, p. 84.

[62] e.g., *Rickhill* v. *Two Parsons of Bromaye* (1400) Y.B. 2 Hen. 4, f. 11, pl. 48, *infra*, p. 83: *The Prior of Nedeport's Case* (1443) Y.B. Mich. 22 Hen. 6, f. 14, pl. 23, *infra*, p. 96: *Erich's Case* (1455) Y.B. Mich. 34 Hen. 6, f. 4, pl. 11: *The Bishop of Salisbury's Case* (1459) Y.B. 38 Hen. 6, f. 9, pl. 20, *infra*, p. 85: *The Prior of Southwark's Case* (1498) Y.B. 13 Hen. 7, f. 26, pl. 4, *infra*, p. 87.

of a recital rather than an operative part of the writ.[63] In 1400 and again in 1409 a writ ' on the special matter ' was brought where the plaintiff could prove no more than the failure to implement an undertaking. Both actions were lost; and, although in a third case of 1425 the Court was divided, issue was ultimately joined on the question whether in fact the defendant had performed his obligations.[64] That the judges should hesitate to apply to cases of nonfeasance a writ still regarded as related, however distantly, to Trespass is not surprising. But the very fact that the attempt was made shows that the original ties were almost severed.

Ultimate severance is seen retrospectively to have been inevitable. The name of ' Special Trespass ' comforted lawyers with the insinuation that they were participating in a prudent evolutionary process; but the absence of force and of direct interference had always in truth been incompatible with the very nature of Trespass. To abandon a friendly phrase, however, is ungrateful. Fitzherbert in 1534 retained the dichotomy of *Writ of Trespass* and *Writ of Trespass sur le Case,* though the examples collected under the latter heading revealed the archaism.[65] Meanwhile the non-committal ' Action on the Case ' was growing in favour. It was a frequent synonym in the Year-Books of the fifteenth century,[66] and a Statute of 1503, designed to equate the procedure in Case with that of Trespass, used it as a familiar term.

> ' Forasmuch as before this time there hath been great delays in actions of the case, that hath been sued as well before the King in his bench as in his court of his common bench, because of which delays many persons have been put from their remedy . . . it is ordained, enacted and established . . . that like process be had hereafter in accions upon the case, as well sued and hanging as to be sued in any of the said courts, as in actions of trespass or debt.' [67]

Finally, in 1566 Rastell adopted *Accion sur le case* as a suitable title for the fifty-four varieties of precedent which he offered to practitioners.[68]

However described, Case had become by the sixteenth century a distinct and generic form of action. Its one essential feature was that the plaintiff should set out at large in his writ the facts upon which

---

[63] *Supra,* p. 75.
[64] *Watton* v. *Brinth* (1400) Y.B. 2 Hen. 4, f. 3, pl. 9, *infra,* p. 340; *Anon* (1409) Y.B. 11 Hen. 4, f. 33, pl. 60, *infra,* p. 340; *Watkins' Case* (1425) Y.B. 3 Hen. 6, f. 36, pl. 33, *infra,* p. 341. See also *The Shepherd's Case* (1486) Y.B. 2 Hen. 7, f. 11, pl. 9, *infra,* p. 86.
[65] *Infra,* p. 88.
[66] e.g. in *Watkins' Case* (1425), *infra,* p. 341, the phrases ' Writ of Trespass,' ' Writ sur tiel matter,' ' Writ of Trespass sur le matter,' are all used. In the *Bishop of Salisbury's Case* (1459), *infra,* p. 85, ' Trespass sur le cas,' ' Writ sur le cas,' ' Especial briefe sur son cas' are found; and in the *Prior of Southwark's Case* (1498), *infra,* p. 87, ' Writ of Trespass sur le cas,' ' Writ sur le cas,' ' Action sur mon cas.'
[67] Stat. 19 Hen. 7, c. 9. The Statute is headed *De Processibus super accionibus specialibus faciend.'*
[68] *Infra,* p. 90.

he sought redress.[69] This necessity had been emphasised throughout the preceding century. In the False Imprisonment case of 1429, Chief Justice Babington quashed the writ because it did not contain the ' special matter ' required.[70] In the *Bishop of Salisbury's Case* of 1459 the adequacy of the detail was discussed at length and with a diversity of views, but all agreed that the conventional language of *Trespass vi et armis* would not suffice and that a too reticent writ could not be supplemented by a more informative Declaration.[71] Litigants were thus offered a wide choice in the framing of writs to meet the substance of their complaints, and, within the limits of professional decency, judges had equal liberty to accord or to withhold their sanction as expediency or temperament might dictate. The opportunity offered was eagerly grasped. Not only did the judges sustain what, in substance if not in name, were writs of Nuisance on the Case and Detinue on the Case, but they were prepared to envisage actions where no basic analogy existed at all. The way was open for the development of such modern torts as Defamation and Negligence.

SOURCES

STATUTE OF WESTMINSTER II., CAP. XXIV.
13 Ed. I. (A.D. 1285)

In casibus quibus conceditur breve in Cancellaria de facto alicuius, de cetero non recedant querentes a curia Regis sine remedio pro eo quod tenementum transfertur de uno in alium et in registro de Cancellaria non est inventum aliquod breve in illo casu speciale; sicut de domo, muro, mercato, conceditur breve super eum qui levavit, et si transferatur domus, murus, et his consimilia, in aliam personam breve denegatur; sed de cetero cum in uno casu conceditur breve et in consimili casu simili remedio indigente sicut prius fit breve[72]:

> Questus est nobis A. quod B. iniuste, etc. levavit domum, murum, mercatum et alia quæ sunt ad nocumentum:

si huiusmodi levata transferantur in aliam personam de cetero fiat breve sic:

> Questus est nobis A. quod B. et C. levaverunt, etc.

Eodem modo sicut persona alicuius ecclesiæ recuperare potest communiam pasturæ per breve Novæ disseisinæ, eodem modo de cetero recuperet successor super disseisitorem vel eius heredem per breve quod permittat, licet huiusmodi breve prius a Cancellaria non fuit concessum.

---

[69] cf. *supra,* p. 68.
[70] *Anon,* Y.B. 7 Hen. 6, f. 45, p. 24: *infra,* p. 84.
[71] *Infra,* p. 85.
[72] The text here is obscure. I offer below a possible translation.

Eodem modo sicut conceditur breve utrum aliquod tenementum sit libera elomisina alicuius ecclesiæ vel laicum feodum talis, de cetero fiat breve utrum sit libera elemosina talis ecclesiæ, vel alterius ecclesiæ, in casu quo libera elemosina unius ecclesiæ transfertur in possessionem alterius ecclesiæ.

Et quotienscumque de cetero evenerit in Cancellaria quod in uno casu reperitur breve et in consimili casu cadente sub eodem iure et simili indigente remedio non reperitur, concordent clerici de Cancellaria in brevi faciendo vel atterminent querentes in proximo parleamento et scribant casus in quibus concordare non possunt et referant eos ad proximum parleamentum et de consensu iurisperitorum fiat breve; ne contingat de cetero quod curia diu deficiat querentibus in iusticia perquirenda.

> In cases in which a writ is granted in the Chancery concerning an act done by some person, the complainants shall not henceforth depart from the King's Court without remedy by reason of the fact that the tenement has been transferred from one person to another and no writ to meet that special case is to be found in the register of the Chancery. Thus, a writ is granted against him who builds a house or a wall or sets up a market; but if that house or wall or the like is transferred to another person the writ is denied. Henceforth, however, when a writ is granted in one case and in like case a corresponding remedy is needed [there shall be a writ]. Thus there is already this writ:

> A. has complained to us that B. unjustly, etc., built a house or wall or set up a market, etc., to the nuisance, etc.

Now if the things so built or set up shall be transferred to another person, there shall henceforth be this writ:

> A. has complained to us that B. and C. have built, etc.

Likewise, just as the parson of a church can recover his common of pasture by a writ of Novel Disseisin, in the same way from henceforth shall his successor recover against the disseisor or his heir by a writ of Quod Permittat, although such a writ was not heretofore granted by the Chancery. Likewise, just as a writ is granted to try whether a certain tenement is the free alms of a church or the lay fee of some person, so from henceforth there shall be a writ to try whether it is the free alms of this church or of another church, in a case where the free alms of the one church have been transferred into the possession of another church.[73]

And whensoever from henceforth it shall happen in the Chancery that in one case a writ is found and in a similar case falling under the same law and needing a similar remedy there is no writ found, the clerks of the Chancery shall agree in making a writ, or they shall adjourn the complainants to the next Parliament and they shall write down the cases in which they cannot agree and refer them to the next Parliament, and a writ shall be made by the consent of those learned in the law; so that from henceforth it shall not befall that the court shall fail those who seek justice.

[73] For 'free alms' or 'frankalmoign,' see P. & M. I. 240-251.

THE MILLER'S CASE
Y.B. MICH. 41 ED. 3, f. 24, pl. 17
A.D. 1367

A writ of *Trespass sur le case* was brought against a Miller, and the plaintiff counted that, whereas he was wont to grind his corn at the mill of T. for himself and his ancestors for all time without toll and he had brought his corn there to be ground, the defendant came and took two bushels' weight with force and arms, etc. And the writ ran: *Quod cum prædictus Johannes, etc. et antecessores sui a tempore cujus memoria non existit molere debuerunt sine multura, etc., prædictus defendens, etc. prædictum querentem sine multura molere vi et armis impedivit, etc.*

Cavendish: You see well how the writ runs, that he will not suffer him to grind without toll, and he has declared in his count that he took toll; and in this case he should have a general writ (*general briefe*) that he carried off the corn with force and arms, and not this writ: judgment of the writ.

Belknap: The writ is taken *sur ma matter*, and, if he has taken toll where he should not have taken it, I shall have a writ against him.

THORPE, C.J.: You shall have *Quod Permittat*[74] against the tenant of the soil and thus it shall be tried, and not on a writ against the defendant.

Belknap: If a market be set up to the nuisance of my market, I shall have against him such a writ of *Quod Permittat*; but if a stranger disturbs folks (*gents*) so that they cannot come to my market, I shall have against him such a writ as this and shall make mention of the circumstances; and so here I shall have a writ of Trespass against him, because I cannot have *Quod Permittat*.

WICHINGHAM, J.: Suppose he had taken all your corn or the half of it, should you have such a writ as this, because he had taken more than he should take by way of toll? You should not have it, but a common writ of Trespass; and so you shall have here. Wherefore take nothing by your writ.

THE INNKEEPER'S CASE
Y.B. EASTER 42 ED. 3, f. 11, pl. 13
A.D. 1369

Trespass was brought by one W. against one T., an innkeeper, and his servants; and he counted that, whereas throughout the whole kingdom of England it was the custom and use, where a common inn was kept, that the innkeeper and his servants should keep (*garde*) the goods and chattels which their guests had in their rooms within the inn while they were lodged there, the said W. came there on such a day, etc., into the town of Canterbury to the said T. and there lodged with him together with his horse and other goods and chattels, to wit, clothes, etc. and twenty marks of silver in a purse, and he took a room there and put these goods and chattels and the silver in the room, and then went into the town for other things; and while he was in the town, the said goods and chattels and silver were taken out of his room by evil doers through the default of the innkeeper and his servants in keeping them, *per tort et encounter le peace*, to his damage, etc. And he had a writ *sur tout le mattere accorde al cas.*

---

[74] *Supra*, pp. 13 and 18.

And the innkeeper demanded judgment, because he had not alleged in his count, nor in his writ, that he had delivered to him the goods and silver, nor that the goods were taken by them, so that he had supposed no manner of blame in them; and also he had delivered to him a key of his room to keep the goods therein; and he asked judgment if this action lay: and on this matter they demurred.

And it was adjudged by KNIVET, J. that the plaintiff should recover against them. And the court taxed the damages, and he will not get the damages just as he counted them. . . .

WALDON v. MARSHALL
Y.B. MICH. 43 ED. 3, f. 33, pl. 38
A.D. 1370

William Waldon brought a writ against one J. Marshall, and alleged by his writ *quod prædictus Johannes manucepit equum prædicti Willelmi de infirmitate [curare], et postea prædictus Johannes ita negligenter curam suam fecit quod equus suus interiit.*

Kirton: We challenge the writ, because it makes mention of *contra pacem,* and in his count he has counted of his cure *ita negligenter* so that the horse died, so that he should not have said ' against the peace.'

And the Judges were of opinion that the writ was ill framed. And then the writ was read, and he had *not* said *contra pacem* in the writ, and the writ was held to be good.

Kirton: Because he has counted that he had undertaken to cure his horse of his malady, for which he should have had an action of covenant, judgment of the writ.

Belknap: That we cannot have without a Deed; and this action is brought because you did your cure *ita negligenter* that the horse died, wherefore it is right to maintain this special writ according to the case; for we can have no other writ.

Kirton: You could have a writ of Trespass, that he killed your horse, *generalment.*

Belknap: A general writ we could not have had, because the horse was not killed by force, but died by default of his cure. . . .

And then the writ was adjudged good. . . .

THE FARRIER'S CASE
Y.B. TRIN. 46 ED. 3, f. 19, pl. 19
A.D. 1373

Trespass was brought against a farrier for that he had lamed his horse, and the writ contained the words *quare clavem fixit in pede equi sui in certo loco per quod proficium*[75] *equi sui per longum tempus amisit,* etc.

Persay: He has brought a writ of trespass against us and it does not contain the words *vi et armis*: judgment of the writ.

FINCHEDON, C.J.: He has brought his writ *en son case,* so his writ is good.

[75] i.e. profits.

Persay: The writ should say *vi et armis* or *maliciose fixit*, and it has neither the one nor the other: judgment. Also he has not supposed in his count that he bailed us the horse to shoe, so otherwise it should be understood that if any trespass was done, it should be against the peace; wherefore judgment.

And then the writ was adjudged good, and issue was joined that he shod the horse, without this,[76] that he lamed it, etc.

THE SURGEON'S CASE
Y.B. HIL. 48 ED. 3., f. 6, pl. 11
A.D. 1375

A man brought a writ of *Trespass sur son case* against one J. M., surgeon, and the writ ran thus, that, whereas the plaintiff's right hand was wounded by one T. B., the defendant undertook (*emprist*)[77] to cure him of his malady in his hand, but that by the negligence of the said J. and his cure, the hand was so injured that he was maimed *a tort et a ses damages*. And note that in this writ there was no mention in what place he undertook, etc., but in his count he declared that he undertook in London in Tower Street in the parish of B. And the writ was not *vi et armis* nor *contra pacem*, etc.

Gascoigne: He did not undertake to cure him of the malady, as he has alleged: ready to wage our law.

Honnington: This is an action of Trespass and of a matter which lies within the cognisance of the country, in which case wager of law is not to be granted: wherefore, for default of answer, we demand judgment and pray our damages.

CAVENDISH, C.J.: This writ does not allege 'force and arms' nor 'against the peace,' so that wager of law is to be allowed. . . . And this is the opinion of the whole court. . . .

[The case was then adjourned.]

Afterwards he waived the tender of law and said that he did not undertake to cure his hand: ready, etc.

Issue was joined on this.

Gascoigne: Now, Sir, you see well that the writ does not mention in what place he undertook to cure him, so that the writ is defective in this matter, for the court cannot know from what neighbourhood the jury shall come.

Persay: He has not defined the place in his writ; wherefore we demand judgment of the writ.

Honnington: Because we have assigned in our count the place where he undertook our cure, therefore, though it is not mentioned in the writ, it is yet sufficient to bring together the jury from the place where we have affirmed the undertaking to have been made. Wherefore judgment if our writ be not good.

CAVENDISH, C.J.: At this stage it is seasonable to challenge the writ for that he has not assigned the place of the undertaking, because it is necessary to summon the jury from that place; but if he had waged his law according to our first issue, then it would not have been necessary to have assigned

---

[76] *absque hoc*: On this form of pleading, see *infra*, p. 143, n.

[77] *Emprist* is the reporter's translation from the Latin of the writ. The writ is not given, so that the original word may possibly have been *assumpsit*, though more probably *manucepit*, as in *Waldon* v. *Marshall*, *supra*, p. 81.

a place in the writ. Moreover, this action of covenant of necessity is maintained without specialty, since for every little thing a man cannot always have a Clerk to make a specialty for him. . . .

. . . And then, because the place was not named in the writ where the cure was said to have been undertaken, the action abated. And the plaintiff was in mercy.

ANON
Y.B. HIL. 13 RICH. 2. (AMES FOUNDATION, ED. PLUCKNETT), pp. 103-4
A.D. 1390

In trespass brought against a man and wife, *Woodrow* counted of a horse killed at a certain place with force and arms.

Gascoigne: We protest that we do not admit coming with force and arms, for we say that the wife had the horse as a loan from the plaintiff to ride to a certain place, and we ask judgment whether he can maintain this action against us.

And this was held a good plea.

Woodrow, for the plaintiff: The truth of the matter is that the wife had the horse as a loan to ride to a certain town; and we say that she rode to another town, whereby the horse was enfeebled to the point of death; then she brought him back to the place named, and there the husband and wife killed him; and we demand judgment.

Gascoigne: And now we demand judgment of his writ, which says ' with force and arms,' for upon his own showing he ought to have had *brief sur son cas.* (*Quod nota.*)

So *Woodrow* said, we wish to imparl.[78]

RICKHILL v. TWO PARSONS OF BROMAYE
Y.B. MICH. 2 HEN. 4, f. 11, pl. 48
A.D. 1400

Sir William Rickhill Justice, William Brinchley,[79] and William Makene, together with others, sued a writ of Trespass against two Parsons of Bromaye.

And their writ comprised the following matter (*comprent tiel matter*), that, whereas the said plaintiffs were seised of 14 acres of land in the manor of Bromaye and of certain meadows in the same vill, from which land the plaintiffs and all who held the same estate from time whereof the memory runneth not to the contrary had the use of a way over three acres of land of the said defendants as far as to their said meadows, the said defendants of malice had disturbed them in their way to their damage of 40/-.

And they joined issue, as it appeared, last term on [the title of the plaintiffs]. And this term the inquest came to the bar, and they found for the plaintiffs to their damage of half a mark. And on another day,

THIRNING, C.J. said to *Tirwit,* who was for the defendants, Have you aught to say why the plaintiffs should not have their judgment? . . .

---

[78] Imparlance or *licentia loquendi*: leave to ' end the matter amicably without farther suit, by talking with ' the other party. See Bl. Comm. III, 298.

[79] *Rickhill* and *Brinchley* were both judges of the Common Pleas, in which this action was brought. Perhaps they were seised as feoffees to uses, for which purpose distinguished lawyers, not excluding judges, were much in demand: see Fortescue, *De Laudibus Legum Angliæ,* Intro. by Chrimes, p. lxxi.

[*Tirwit* first took a point as to the several ownership of the two defendants, so that they should not have been joined in the writ.]

... THIRNING, C.J.: This matter is not greatly to the purpose. But let us see whether this action is maintainable or not, and in particular whether this matter which is done by the defendants in their freehold, that is to say, on their own soil, can be said to be an impediment to or disturbance of the plaintiffs' way, and whether it can be redressed or amended by this action—this will be good matter to speak of.

MARKHAM, J.: If a man makes a dyke or hedge across my road, I shall have an Assize of Nuisance for this, and not such a writ as this.

Skrene: This writ is not *contra pacem,* but it is a writ *sur nostre case;* and if they had disturbed me with swords or staves or other weapons, I should have made a good declaration against them *contra pacem.* But here I should well maintain this action *sur ma matter*.

THIRNING, C.J.: That may well be in the case you put, for the trespass you suppose is not a thing incident or pertaining to the freehold. But see now if this matter pertains to his freehold, which the law gives him as in his own proper soil, so that it cannot be said to be such a disturbance to you that you should maintain such an action as this.

MARKHAM, J.: If you should have common of pasture in my land and I plough up all my land so that your beasts cannot have pasture, shall you have a writ of *trespass sur votre mattere* for this? I think not. But I know well that you shall have a good assize. . . . So it seems to me that this action of yours is not maintainable for this thing.

Read: If a water-course runs to your mill and I make part of this water to take another course in my own soil, so that your mill which used to grind ten quarters a day now grinds only one quarter a day, you shall have such a writ as this.

MARKHAM, J.: You shall not have it, but an assize; so, if you have reasonable estovers in my wood and I cut all the wood so that you cannot have them, you shall have the assize and no other remedy. . . .

[Similar arguments follow, including a suggestion by *Rickhill* himself.]

... Afterwards, by the assent of all the Judges except the plaintiff, that is to say, Rickhill, the writ was abated. *Quod nota.*

ANON
Y.B. TRIN. 7 HEN. 6, f. 45, pl. 24
A.D 1429
Trespass sur le cas

The plaintiff alleged that, when he was coming to answer to a writ which R. had pending against him in the Common Pleas, the defendant had caused him to be arrested in London tortiously and against the privilege of the King's Court and to the contempt of the King, and he prayed his damages, etc. And he counted that he came to answer to a writ pending against him and that the defendant caused him to be arrested, and he sued out a *Corpus cum causa,*[80] by force of which he was remitted and

[80] A species of *Habeas Corpus*: see Bl. Comm. III, 130.

discharged; and then on the next day he returned to London for his proofs, and the defendant, knowing that the writ was pending against him, had him arrested afresh, *a tort,* etc.

Fulthorpe: The writ is *general* and the count is *especial sur le cas,* in which case the writ too should be special, *comprendant le substance del matter.* Wherefore judgment of the count as not warranted by the writ.

Cottesmore: In every writ of Trespass one shows more in the count than in the writ: wherefore, etc.

BABINGTON, C.J.: The writ is *fonde sur le cas*; in which case it should have contained special matter, and that it has not done. Wherefore take nothing by your writ, but be in mercy.

THE BISHOP OF SALISBURY'S CASE
Y.B. MICH. 38 HEN. 6, f. 9, pl. 20
A.D. 1459

Trespass sur le cas by the Bishop of Salisbury. And he counted that King Richard II by Letters Patent had granted to John, then Bishop of Salisbury, predecessor of the said Bishop, Assise and Assay of Bread and Ale, fines and amercements and other points of the View of Frankpledge in all the lands and fees, etc., and that the said John, then Bishop, was seised of the vill of Salisbury[81] in his demesne as of fee and in right of his aforesaid Church, and that the plaintiff was seised of the said vill in right of his Church, and that, on such a day and year, the plaintiff, thus seised of the said vill, distrained for his amercements by such an one, his Bailiff, and that the defendants obstructed him tortiously and to his damage. And the writ was *sur le cas* and rehearsed [the title, as above].

. . . . And the defendant demanded judgment of the writ, because it is a writ *sur son cas,* in which *tout sa matter* should be expressed, or otherwise the writ is worthless. And he has alleged in his writ that the now Bishop is seised in his lands and fees of New Salisbury, but he has not alleged that the said John, Bishop of Salisbury, his predecessor, to whom the grant was made, was seised at the time of the grant of the vill of New Salisbury where he has alleged the trespass to be done; and if the predecessor was not seised of the said vill at the time of the grant, but the plaintiff has come to this vill by purchase or descent or in some other manner, the Letters Patent do not extend to this, but only to the lands and fees of which the predecessor was seised at the time of the said grant. Wherefore he demanded judgment of the writ.

Choke: It seems to me that the writ is good enough. For the writ is that King Richard granted to John, then Bishop of Salisbury, and to his successors, that they should have the Assise, etc., in all lands and fees; which grant enures to his successors as well as to himself and to those lands which come afterwards as well as to those of which the said John was seised at the time of the grant. And seeing that we have counted in our count that

---

[81] 'Counties are divided into hundreds . . . and hundreds again into vills, under which name boroughs and cities are included.' Fortescue, *De Laudibus Legum Angliæ,* Cap. XXIV. The defendant's argument, it will be seen, is that, while the *Declaration* recited the predecessor's seisin of the vill of New Salisbury, the *Writ* did not; and that in a writ *sur son cas* this omission of a relevant fact was fatal.

the said John at the time of the grant was seised of the said vill, this suffices; for everything cannot be expressed in the writ, and it will suffice to make the matter more certain in the declaration.

Billing: . . . As to the point that the count will make the writ good . . . this is not so; for a writ *sur son cas* must contain in itself all the material facts and show on what question issue may be taken. . . .

DANVERS, J.: The writ seems good enough . . . in so much as the writ cannot comprise all the matter, and what is lacking in his writ will be declared by his count.

PRISOT, C.J.: I think the writ is bad; for the King's grant is not to be understood save as to the lands which his predecessor had at the time of the grant and to no others save those expressed in the grant, as *Billing* has said. . . . And as to the point that the matter in the count will make the writ good, that is not so; for it is one of the most particular points in the writ which ought to be observed, and especially when it is an *especial brief sur son cas,* that it must comprise all material facts as clearly as the count. . . .

DANBY, J.: I think the writ is good. . . . [He then argued that it contained enough matter for the necessary inferences to be drawn: *quod* DANVERS *concessit*].

But at last the opinion of the Court was that the writ ought to show that Salisbury was parcel of the lands and fees which belonged to the predecessor at the time of the grant, and that the grant would not have effect save as to such lands and fees.

[The case was adjourned; and the reporter adds, *Quære forma brevis.*]

THE SHEPHERD'S CASE

Y.B. 2 HEN. 7, HIL. f. 11, pl. 9

A.D. 1486

The case was this. A person had 100 sheep to keep, and *negligenter* by his default he suffered them to be drowned.

Rede: It seems to me that the action does not lie; because for a nonfeasance *Action sur le cas* does not lie; but on this the party shall have a writ of Covenant. For if a person has clothes to keep, and they are wasted by moths or spoilt, no *action sur le cas* lies, but an action of Detinue.

Wood: I think the action lies well. For suppose that a person undertakes to carry glasses or pots, and he breaks them by negligence, I shall have an *Action sur mon cas*.

Keble said that nonfeasance does not support *Action sur le cas*. For, before the Statute of Labourers, if a servant was retained and he was unwilling to do service for his master, for his nonfeasance no action lay. But it is admitted that, if any act were done by the party, then the action would lie well enough; as if I bail a chest with obligations and he breaks it open, or if I bail a horse to ride 10 leagues and he rides it 20 leagues, *Action sur le cas* lies. Wherefore in this case, if the party had driven the sheep into the water, for this an *Action sur le cas* lies.

TOWNSHEND, J.: Since the party had taken on himself (*assumpsit super se*) to take charge of the sheep, and afterwards suffered them to perish by his default, in as much as he had entered on and executed his bargain and had them in his custody, and afterwards did not watch over them, the Action lies; for here his act, that is to say, his agreement and *assumpsit* and afterwards the breach on his part together form the cause of the action. Suppose a horse to be bailed to a man to keep, and afterwards he gives him no food and he dies, an *Action sur le cas* lies. Again, if a carrier takes my goods to carry them and afterwards he loses or breaks them, an action lies well for their return because he has not executed his bargain and has taken upon himself to do this thing. But if a covenant is made with me to keep my horse or to carry my goods and nothing more done, then the action of Covenant lies and no other action; for in these cases he only fails to execute his promise.

THE PRIOR OF SOUTHWARK'S CASE

Y.B. TRIN. 13 HEN. 7, f. 26, pl. 4

A.D. 1498

A Prior brought a writ of *Trespass sur le cas,* and he alleged that he himself and all his predecessors had been seised of certain houses and of certain gardens in Southwark in right of their houses from time whereof the memory does not run, and that they, through their tenants of the same houses, for the same time have had a water-course or stream running into a ditch of the river Thames near to the said houses and gardens and running between all the said houses and gardens, to dye their clothes, to water their beasts, to bake and to brew, and for other easements; and that the defendant had made a lime-pit for calf-skins and sheep-skins so close to the stream that the corruption of the said lime-pit had corrupted the said stream, wherefore the tenants had left the said houses.

Keble came and challenged the writ because he had alleged that the defendant had made the lime-pit *ibidem,* which must be taken to be in the plaintiff's soil; in which case he ought to have had a general writ of *Trespass quare vi et armis* and not a writ *sur le cas.* And the opinion of the Court was that the challenge was good and that the writ should be abated.

Wherefore the plaintiff, with the defendant's assent, amended the writ and alleged that the pit was made in the defendant's soil.

Keble then said that the plaintiff had no rights in the water save in common with a stranger unnamed: judgment of the writ. And the opinion was that the plea was not good.

Then he said that the plaintiff had no rights in the land covered by the water otherwise than in common: judgment of the writ.

BRIAN, C.J.: I put the case that I and a stranger are tenants in common of a stream, and I have houses adjoining for which I have an easement of such water, as in the case here, and my companion commits such a nuisance as this and corrupts the water; shall I not have an *action sur mon cas* against him? I think so: for this nuisance is done to my soil, since he has no rights in the houses to which the nuisance is done.

Keble: Sir, his complaint is as to what is done to the water, and to this I have made answer: wherefore the writ should abate.

BRIAN was of the contrary opinion, as above.

And the case was adjourned.

FITZHERBERT : NEW NATURA BREVIUM[82]
Writ de Trespass sur le Case
92 E.

There is another form of writ of trespass upon the case, which is to be sued in the common pleas or king's bench; and in that writ he shall not say *vi et armis,* etc., but in the end of the writ he shall say *contra pacem;* and the form is as follows:

> The king to the sheriff, etc. If Maud of D. etc., then put J., etc., that he be, etc., to answer as well us as Maud wherefore, seeing that the same Maud lately in our court obtained our certain writ of prohibition against the aforesaid J. that he should not prosecute any plea in the court christian touching chattels and debts which do not concern testament or matrimony, and the same Maud delivered our said writ to the aforesaid J. at C., he the said J., having received our said writ there, cast it into the dirt and trod it under his feet, and also hath prosecuted the plea aforesaid in the same court christian, in contempt of us and to the great damage of the said Maud, and against our peace, etc.

Another writ;

92 F.

> Wherefore he fixed piles across the water of Plim, along which, between Humber and Gaunt, there is a common passage for ships and boats, whereby a certain ship, with thirty quarters of malt of him the said W., was sunk under water, and twenty quarters of the malt of the price of one hundred shillings perished; and other wrongs, etc.

93 G.

And a man shall have an action of trespass upon the case against his neighbour who hath lands betwixt him and the sea and ought to make banks and mound certain ditches and sewers betwixt him and the sea, and he doth not cleanse them as he ought to do, by reason whereof his land is surrounded, etc.; he shall have his action upon the case against him for this nonfeasance.

94 A.

And if a man promise and take upon him to make for another man certain carts for carriages, or other thing, and take money beforehand to do the same, and afterwards he do not make them according to his promise and undertaking; the other may have an action upon the case against him, and the writ shall be such:

> If W., etc., then put J., etc., to show wherefore, whereas he the said J. undertook to make and build three carriages for conveying victuals and tackle of him the said W. to parts beyond sea for a certain sum of money, one part whereof he beforehand received, within a certain term between them agreed; he, the same J., did not take care to make and build the carriages aforesaid within the term aforesaid, by which he the said W. hath wholly lost divers his goods and chattels, to the value of one hundred marks, which ought to have been conveyed in the carriages aforesaid, for want thereof to the great damage of him the said W., as it is said, etc.

[82] See Winfield, *Chief Sources of English Legal History,* pp. 302-3. The first edition was published in 1534 and the last in 1794.

94 *B*.

And if a man be lodged in any inn, and any of his goods be taken from thence by a stranger, he shall have an action upon the case against the innkeeper, and the writ shall be such:

> The king to the sheriff, etc. If A. shall make you secure, etc., then put, etc., B. that he be, etc. to show, etc. wherefore, whereas according to the law and custom of our realm of England innkeepers, who keep common inns to entertain persons passing by the places where such inns are and lodging in the same, are bound to keep the goods of such persons deposited therein without subtraction night and day, so that by the default of them the innkeepers or their servants no damage may come in any manner to the guests: certain malefactors took and led away a certain horse of the price of forty shillings of him the said A. entertained within the said inn of the aforesaid B. at S., by the neglect of him the said B., and other wrongs, etc., to the great damage, etc.

94 *C*.

If a man sell unto another man a horse, and warrant him to be sound and good, etc., if the horse be lame or diseased, that he cannot work, he shall have an action upon the case against him.

And so if a man bargain and sell unto another certain pipes of wine and warrant them to be good, etc., and they are corrupted, he shall have action upon the case against him.

But note: it behoveth that he warrant it to be good, and the horse to be sound, otherwise the action will not lie. For if he sell the wine or horse without such warranty, it is at the other's peril, and his eyes and his taste ought to be his judges in that case.

94 *D*.

But if a smith prick my horse with a nail, etc., I shall have my action upon the case against him without any warranty by the smith to do it well; and the writ shall be,

> Wherefore he fixed a certain nail in one foot of a certain horse of J. at N. by which it became putrid, so that the same horse for a long time could not work, and he the said J. during that time lost the benefit of his horse aforesaid, to the damage, etc.

For it is the duty of every artificer to exercise his art rightly and truly as he ought.

95 *D*.

And if a man play with another at dice, and he have false dice with which he playeth and get the other's money with these false dice, he who loseth his money may have his action upon the case for this deceit, and the form of the writ is such:

> The king to the sheriff, etc. If A. shall make you secure, then put, etc. T. of D., etc., that he be, etc., to show wherefore, whereas the aforesaid T. of D., contriving deceitfully to defraud him the said A. and to extort divers sums of money from the same A., excited and procured the said A. to play at dice with him the said T. at a certain game called 'the dozen' for divers sums of money at Burton upon Trent, and the said A. there played with him at dice at the game

aforesaid, the aforesaid T. certain dice truly titled delivered to him the said A. to throw, and when the said dice happened to come to the hands of him the said T., he the same T. falsely and fraudulently threw certain other false dice and deceitfully titled, which he knew would turn up number twelve and no other number at every throw, by which he the said A. lost great sums of money to him the said T. at that game, and the said T. falsely and deceitfully took and carried away those sums under colour of gain, to the damage of him the said A. of five pounds, as it is said: and have you there the names of the pledges and this writ. Witness, etc.

RASTELL : COLLECTION OF ENTRIES[83]

Accion sur le Case

Under this general heading Rastell gives 54 sub-headings, which are set out below with comments by the present writer.

1. *sur Assumption.* This sub-heading contains many cross-references to other sub-headings, e.g. Carrier, Disceit, Nonfeasans, Promise, etc.

2. *vers Attorney ou Counseller.* Allegations that the defendant *falso et fraudulenter decepit ad damnum, etc.,* with significant and pleasing details, e.g. that the defendant was 'ambidexter.'[84]

3. *pour seignior de Auncien Demesne*[85] *sur recovery al common ley.* The precedent given seems to be based on the analogy of a Writ of Entry.

4. *vers Baily.* See 48, *infra.*

5. *sur Bailment.*

6. *vers Barber pur raser la barbe inartificialiter.* R. S. nuper de N. barber attach. fuit ad respondendum H. B. de placito quum idem R. ad barbam ipsius H. bene et artificialiter cum novacula munda et salubri[86] radere apud N. assumpsisset, præpdictus R. barbam ipsius H. cum quadam novacula immunda et insalubri tam negligenter et inartificialiter radit ut facies ipsius H. morbola et scabiola devenit ad damnum. . . .

7. *vers cestui qui promise a Carier et ne fait.* This is an assumpsit: the defendant is not described as a common carrier.

8. *pur nyent trover Chaplen que ad este use per prescription,* i.e. failure to fulfil a prescriptive duty to find a chaplain.

9. *concernant Charters. vide* Detinue, fol. 204.

10 *pur misfeasans de Chien.* There is a cross-reference to Trespass for damage thus done by a dog, fol. 558, in scattering 220 sheep.

11. *concernant Chimin.* i.e. case for nuisance.

12. *pur misuser le Chivall.* An *assumpsit* for negligent custody of a horse.

---

[83] The first edition is dated 1566: the precedents here cited are from the edition of 1574. Rastell was the nephew of Sir Thomas More and the grandson of More, J., some of whose precedents Rastell used in his own Collection. See Chambers, *Sir Thomas More,* p. 54.

[84] i.e. a solicitor who, retained by one party to litigation, abandons him for his adversary. See *Annison v. Blofield* (1671) Rolle, Abr. 55, Carter, 214.

[85] See Holdsworth, H.E.L. III, 263-9.

[86] 'with a clean and wholesome razor.'

13. *concernant Comen.* i.e. ' Action on the case against one who makes trenches across a road, whereby the plaintiff cannot get to his common.'

14. *sur Conspiracy.* i.e. conspiring to indict for felony.

15. *vers Counsellor. vide* Attorney, *supra.*

16. *pur misuser de Cranage.* i.e. a customary due for loading or discharging goods on or from a ship. The declaration alleges the work to be done *tam imprudenter et negligenter.*

17. *vers cestuy que ad chose Deliver a luy par le plaintiff.* An *assumpsit* to re-deliver to the plaintiff for payment.

18. *in lieu de action de Dett.* There are three examples given of Case instead of Debt, based on *assumpsit.*

19. *in lieu de action de Detinewe.* (a) vers cestuy que trove biens et eux vend. (b) pur charters et escripts nient deliver a cestuy que purchase le terre. The facts supposed in the Declaration in (b) are that R. W. owned freehold estates, that he deposited the title-deeds with R. R. for safe custody, that he sold the estates to T. F., that T. F. demanded the title-deeds from R. R. and that R. R. refused to deliver them to T. F.

20. *concernant Disceit.* Vide *Assumption.*

21. *a Discharger et saver harmless.* See 49 *infra.*

22. *concernant Distress.* This refers to a claim to hold a court leet.

23. *sur Disturbance de exerciser de office.* The form given complains of a disturbance to the plaintiff in his office of Steward of courts, with a consequent loss of profits.

24. *pur nient faire Estate.* i.e. failure to implement the sale of an estate.

25. *concernant Estray.*[87]

26. *vers Executour ou Administer.*

27. *pur misuser de Fait.* i.e. for defacing and injuring a *scriptum obligatorium*[88] delivered to the defendant for safe custody.

28. *pur negligent garder son Few.* This precedent for damage done by the defendant's fire refers to the custom of the realm for safe keeping of fire and alleges that the defendant kept his fire *tam negligenter et improvide* to the damage of the plaintiff and against the custom.

29. *pur Forger des Faits.*

30. *concernant Franchis et Liberties. vide supra* 22 and 23.

31. *vers cestuy que prise chose en Gage.* i.e. against a lender who takes a pledge and will not re-deliver it when repaid. The precedent supposes an *assumpsit.*

32. *vers Gaylor que lessa prisoner escape.* The gaoler, in this precedent, ' machinans subtiliter ad defraudandum [the plaintiff] ad suum proprium largum ire permisit.' There is a cross-reference to Debt.[89]

33. *concernant Garde.*[90]

34. *vers cestuy que assume a Garder chose a luy baile.* The declaration alleges (a) a bailment of a chest with money for safe custody, (b) an *assumpsit* to keep safely, (c) that the defendant ' tam negligenter custodivit.'

[87] See Blackstone, Comm. I, 297.
[88] See *infra,* p. 220.
[89] *Infra,* p. 168.
[90] for Ravishment of Ward, see Blackstone, Comm. III, 141.

35. *vers cestuy que vend chose et Garrant ceo d'estre bon.* Two precedents for warranty of quality on a bargain and sale of goods.

36. *vers Hosteler.* Declaration against a 'common innkeeper' on the custom of the realm for the safe keeping of goods, and that *pro defectu* the innkeeper or his servants the goods were removed by third parties to the damage of the plaintiff and against the custom. There is no allegation of negligence.[91]

37. *pur false Imprisonment.*

38. *pur Misfeasans.* An *omnium gatherum* with cross-references to 6, 11, 12, 16, etc.

39. *pur nusans a Molyn.* Three precedents are here given for nuisance to the plaintiff's mill. Of these, two are in fact Trespass *vi et armis,* with short and uninformative counts, and the third is Case, with a declaration setting out in detail the plaintiff's title to the mill.

40. *pur Nonfesans.* 'Vide in Assumption totum.' . . .

41. *pur Nusans.*

42. *pur Occider* de beastes.

43. *sur assumption de Paier money.* A normal *assumpsit.*

44. *versus Physition ou Surgeon.* . . . ' quare cum idem A. ad sinistram tibiam ipsius C. casualiter læsam bene et competenter curandam apud G. pro quadam pecuniæ summa eidem A. pro manibus soluta assumpsisset, idem A. curam suam circa eam tibiam prædictam curandam tam negligenter et improvide apposuit et nervos et venas eiusdem tam inartificialiter scidit quod tibia prædicta claudica devenit ad dampnum, etc.'

45. *concernant Pledge.* See 31, *supra.*

46. *sur le Promise.* 'Vide in Assumption totum.'

47. *pur nient faire Reparations per quel le meson del plaintiff est destroy.* An action on the case for nuisance, based upon a prescriptive duty to repair. No negligence is alleged.

48. *vers Vicecomes ou Baily per false Retourn.*[92]

49. *vers cestuy que promise a saver harmless le plaintiff que fuit oblige pour le defendant.* Another *assumpsit.*

50. *pur Slaunder.* Four precedents are given, including the original Writ (a rare occurrence in Rastell).[93]

51. *pur planter de Spines*[94] *negligenter.* Another *assumpsit.*

52. *concernant Tolls.* Nuisance, based on a prescriptive duty.

53. *pur mitter cattes in son Warren.* This seems in fact to be Trespass *vi et armis,* whereby the plaintiff complains that the defendant has put cats —*quosdam catos*—into his warren, which have destroyed 2,000 conies.

54. *pur claymer le plaintiff Villeine.*[95].

---

[91] Compare Fitzherbert, 94B, *supra,* p. 89.
[92] See Blackstone, Comm. III, 163: 'if the sheriff wilfully makes a false return [to a writ] . . ., the party aggrieved shall have an action on the case.'
[93] *Infra,* p. 141.
[94] i.e., *thorns.*
[95] See Holdsworth, *H.E.L.* III, 500-510.

☙ 5 ❧

ACTION ON THE CASE FOR
NUISANCE

THE value of the Assise of Nuisance was diminished by its derivation from Novel Disseisin. It could not be used save by a
plaintiff who was seised of a freehold estate. Around this limitation
the arguments revolved in *Smeteborn* v. *Holt* in 1348, where Sharshulle, J. declared that, if a right of way were granted by deed to a
grantee who at the time had no estate, a subsequent purchase would
not cure the flaw and the only possible remedy was by writ of
Covenant.[1] Practitioners had not yet imagined an action on the case;
but the subsequent innovation was soon exploited in the field of
nuisance. In 1372 a Prior brought *un briefe de Trespass compernant
tiel matter* against a defendant whose failure to repair the banks of
a stream had flooded his land, and, though the writ was quashed
because it contained the words ' *contra pacem regis,*' its propriety
in such a context was not challenged.[2] In 1400 in *Rickhill* v. *Two
Parsons of Bromaye*[3] a similar writ was brought for the obstruction
of a right of way, but was disallowed on the express ground that, as
the parties on each side were freeholders, the Assise was exclusively
appropriate. The denial of concurrent remedies on a single cause of
action harmonised with mediæval sentiment, and it is not clear why
the plaintiffs in this case, among whose number were two judges, chose
to affront it. But to the use of the new writ where the Assise was
defective no such objection could be taken. In *Chedder* v. *Dyer* in
1410 the reporter drew attention to the *obiter dictum* of Chief Justice Hankford that ' of a way in gross a man shall not have Assise
of Nuisance, but *le breve sur son cas,*' to which the other judges
agreed.[4] In the *Prior of St. Nedeport's Case* in 1443,[5] the scope of
the two writs was eagerly discussed. The Prior brought a writ of
Trespass on the Case to establish the right of suit to his mill and,
despite some support from Paston, J., was forced once more to admit
the superior claims of the Assise. But in the course of the argument
two contingencies were suggested in which the writ would be
sustained. If, it was said, the defendant's conduct ' impaired the

[1] Y.B. 21 Ed. 3, f. 2, pl. 5: *supra*, p. 22.
[2] *Anon* (1372) Y.B. Trin. 45 Ed. 3, f. 17, pl. 6. See *supra*, p. 76.
[3] Y.B. 2 Hen. 4, f. 11, pl. 48: *supra*, p. 83.
[4] (1410) Y.B. Mich. 11 Hen. 4, f. 25, pl. 48, at f. 26.
[5] Y.B. 22 Hen. 6, f. 14, pl. 23: *infra*, p. 96.

plaintiff's freehold,' the Assise alone lay; but if the freehold was not impaired, the plaintiff would be ' put to an *accion sur son cas.*' So, too, if a right of way were obstructed by the owner of the servient tenement, the Assise must be brought; but if the obstruction were the work of a stranger, he must be sued in Case.

During the second half of the fifteenth century similar cases were reported from time to time, and there are indications of a growing judicial sympathy.   In 1455 the familiar objection that Assise was available was not upheld by the Court, and in 1498 Chief Justice Brian proclaimed his adherence to the new action.[6]   But in each instance the issue was taken on another point, and it was not until 1523 that the inevitable, if belated, step was taken.   In an anonymous case of that year the Court was unanimous that for a total obstruction of a right of way the Assise lay and for a partial obstruction Case; and Brooke, J. added that ' *accion sur le cas* lies where there is no other action provided for a wrong.'[7]   The two remedies were to be complementary.   If the plaintiff were seised when the nuisance was committed, and if he complained of a total obstruction by another free-holder, he must bring the Assise.   If he had no freehold at the crucial time,[8] or the obstruction were only partial or by a stranger, he must bring Case.   The new writ had come, not to destroy, but to fulfil the old.

The exercise of a nice discrimination would thus keep the Register tidy; but litigants might be forgiven if they felt the purchase of an archaic writ too heavy a price to pay for the preservation of juristic elegance.   In 1560 a tenant for life crossed the frontiers of the two actions and brought Case where the Assise was clearly available.[9] The invasion was repelled, but it was only premature.   In the last decade of the sixteenth century the diversity of opinion was reflected in a number of actions, of which two in the year 1596 are typical. In *Beswick* v. *Cunden*[10] a freeholder complained in Case that the defendant had flooded his land, and the Court held that he should have brought an Assise or a Quod Permittat.   ' A man shall never have an action on the case, where he may have any other remedy by any writ found in the register; for this is only given where there wants such a remedy.'   In *Alston* v. *Pamphyn*,[11] on the other hand,

[6] *Erich's Case* (1455) Y.B. Mich. 34 Hen. 6, f. 4, pl. 11; *The Prior of Southwark's Case* (1498) Y.B. 13 Hen. 7, f. 26, pl. 4, *supra*, p. 87.   See also the *Bishop of Salisbury's Case* (1459) Y.B. 38 Hen. 6, f. 9, pl. 20, where *Trespass sur le cas* was brought to vindicate a franchise, and objection was taken, not to the propriety of the writ in the context, but to the inadequacy of its detail.   *Supra*, p. 85.

[7] *Anon* (1523) Y.B. 14 Hen. 8, f. 31, pl. 8, *infra*, p. 97.   The actual decision is some-what curious, inasmuch as Bracton had expressly declared the Assise to be avail-able as well for a partial as for a total obstruction: *supra*, p. 19.

[8] See *Westbourne* v. *Mordaunt* (1591) Cro. Eliz. 191, where Gawdy, J. allowed Case to a plaintiff who became seised only after the nuisance had been committed.

[9] *Yevance* v. *Holcomb* (1560) 2 Dyer, 250b.

[10] (1596) Cro. Eliz. 520.

[11] (1596) Cro. Eliz. 466.   See also *Leverett* v. *Townsend* (1591) Cro. Eliz. 198.

the plaintiff was offered Case or the Assise at his election, and Chief Justice Popham said that 'he had seen it so in experience divers times.' The pressure of convenience was, in truth, too great to be long withstood. In *Cantrel* v. *Church* in 1601 the Court of Exchequer Chamber confirmed the right of election between the two writs and abandoned the distinction previously taken between the total and the partial obstruction of a right of way.[12] Henceforth the older precedents were no more than memories. 'The plaintiff,' said Chief Justice Rolle in 1649, 'may have an assise or an action upon the case at his election, although there be a disturbance of his freehold and although the antient books say the contrary."[13]

The inheritance to which Case succeeded, though enlarged in scope, retained its original character. The plaintiff, if he need no longer be a freeholder, must still complain of an injury to land or its appurtenances. The interests affected could still be sub-divided into 'servitudes'[14] and 'natural rights,' and each class still awaited definition. Coke in his commentary on Littleton was able to discuss with some particularity the Common of Pasture and to say something of other profits.[15] Rights of way and similar easements were the recurrent object of contemporary litigation. But it was not until the nineteenth century that the English law of 'servitudes' obtained coherence.[16] The elucidation of 'natural rights' would seem an even sterner task. Who is to prescribe the amenities of life? The judges were faced with the problem in *Aldred's Case* in 1611,[17] and gave an answer which, stripped of the pedantry dear to Coke's generation, has survived three centuries as a not unreasonable compromise. A householder may obtain redress for an obstruction of light or a pollution of air which sensibly affects habitation, but he cannot complain if his outlook is spoilt. The law of nuisance, in the last resort, is the observance of neighbourly conduct, and to the seventeenth, as to the twentieth-century Englishman, comfort and not æsthetics offered the criterion.

By the time of Coke nuisance could thus be defined as a tort to land redressed by an action on the case. But the name might be found in another context. If a person were guilty of acts offensive or injurious to the community as a whole, he could be punished in the local courts. But was this 'common' or 'public' nuisance a tort as well as a crime so as to enable a private citizen to obtain redress? The question was put and answered as early as 1535. An action on the

---

[12] (1601) Cro. Eliz. 845, *infra*, p. 98. See also *Pollard* v. *Casy* (1611) 1 Bulst. 47.
[13] *Ayre* v. *Pyncomb* (1649) Style, 164.
[14] And such analogous rights as franchises: *supra*, pp. 7-8.
[15] Co. Litt. 122a.
[16] Mainly under the influence of Gale, whose book on Easements was first published in 1839 and who borrowed extensively from Roman Law. On the whole development of Incorporeal Hereditaments, see H.E.L. VII. 312-342.
[17] 9 Coke Rep. 57b, *infra*, p. 99.

case would lie if, but only if, the defendant's conduct had inflicted upon the plaintiff peculiar damage or an inconvenience other than that endured by the public at large.[18] The position was summarised by Coke and by him transmitted to future generations. If a highway be obstructed by digging a ditch across it, ' the law for this common nuisance hath provided an apt remedy, and that is by preferment in the leete or in the torne, unlesse any man hath a particular damage; as if he and his horse fall into the ditch, whereby he receive hurt or losse, there for this special damage, which is not common to others, he shall have an action upon his case.'[19]

SOURCES

THE PRIOR OF ST. NEDEPORT'S CASE
Y.B. Mich. 22 Hen. 6, f. 14, pl. 23
A.D. 1443

The Prior of St. Nedeport[20] brought a writ of *Trespass sur son cas* against John Weston, and counted by *Bingham* that he was lord of St. Nede and that he and all his predecessors, lords of the same vill, had had within the same vill three free mills from time whereof, etc., and that no one had within the same vill any mill save the Prior and his predecessors from time whereof, etc.; and that all the tenants of the said Prior within the same vill and all others residing therein ought from time whereof, etc., to have their corn ground at the said mill and pay toll for the grinding; and that the said defendant, one of the tenants of the said Prior, had set up within the said vill a mill at which those residing in the said vill ground their corn, tortiously and to the damage of the plaintiff. . . .

[After argument on the question of prescription]: —

Bingham: I think that we should have this action or else we are without remedy. For against those who grind at this new mill and who of right should grind at our mill we cannot have other action, since a writ of *Secta facta ad molendinum*[21] does not lie save where a man holds by fealty and by suit to the mill, and here the suit is by reason of residence and not by reason of tenure.

NEWTON, C.J.: In this very case *Secta ad molendinum* lies the more properly. For where one holds by fealty and suit to his mill, there, if he will not do his suit, he can distrain him; but he cannot do so in this case. And if all the tenants of Dale ought to grind at my mill, and that by prescription, why shall I not have *Secta ad molendinum* against them?

PASTON, J.: . . . Suppose I have a market or a fair on Saturdays and another sets up a market or a fair on the same day in a town adjoining my market so that my market or fair is impaired, I shall have against him *Assise*

---

[18] *Anon* (1535) Y.B. 27 Hen. 8, f. 27, pl. 10, *infra*, p. 98. See also *Anon* (1584) Moore, 180, and *Williams's Case* (1592) 5 Coke Rep. 72b, in each of which the plaintiff failed as he could not prove special damage.

[19] Co. Litt. 56A: see also Coke, Fourth Inst., Chap. LIII and LIV. For the Sheriff's Tourn, see H.E.L. I. 76-82, and for the Court Leet, H.E.L. I. 134-7.

[20] *Quaere*, St. Neots?

[21] For this writ, see Y.B. 12 & 13 Ed. III (R.S.), p. 122, and *supra*, p. 18.

of *Nuisance* or *Action sur mon cas.* And the law is the same if I have from ancient time a ferry in a vill and another starts another ferry on the same bank near my ferry so that the profits of my ferry are impaired; I shall have against him an *Action sur mon cas.* So here.

NEWTON, C.J.: Your case of the ferry differs from the case at bar. For in your case you are bound to maintain the ferry and keep it in repair for the ease of people in general, and for this you are answerable to the Sheriff in his tourn and also before the Justices in Eyre. But in this case at bar, if the lord of the mills should suffer them to go to ruin or even destroy them, he cannot be punished. And as for your case of the market or fair, this is not in point; for in the King's grant [of the market or fair] is this clause—' provided always that it be not to the nuisance of any other market or fair '; so that the very creating of it is a nuisance. . . .

PASTON, J.: Suppose the King grants me a market without such a provision; then, if one afterwards sets up another market which is a nuisance to my market, I shall have *Assise of Nuisance* against him.

FULTHORPE, J.: It seems to me that in the case at bar he should have an *Assise of Nuisance* and not this action.

Markham: No, Sir. But if a man builds a house which stops the light of my house or which causes the rain to run down and on to my house, or if he does anything which impairs my freehold, there I shall have the *Assise* against him. But in this case, and in the case put of the ferry, my freehold is not impaired, and for this reason I am put to an *Accion sur mon cas.*

Moyle: If I have a way appendant to my land over your land and you make a hedge on the land so that I am stopped of my way, I shall have an *Assise of Nuisance* against you; but if a stranger without your assent makes such a hedge on your land, I shall not have the *Assise,* but an *Accion sur mon cas.*

And then at the end of the Term the defendant traversed the point of the writ; and they joined issue. And then because of the above matters, and also for other matters, he abandoned this writ. . . .

ANON

Y.B. EASTER, 14 HEN. 8, f. 31, pl. 8

A.D. 1523

One John brought an *Accion sur le cas* against S., for that, whereas the stream of S. ran by such a Vill, he had built a mill so that the stream no longer ran as it used to do; and he showed that the defendant had made flood-gates so that the stream ran on to the fields and flooded the land.

Rowe: It seems that here he should have an *Assise of Nuisance* and not an *Accion sur le cas*; just as I should have *Assise of Nuisance* if you were to stop a conduit.

POLLARD, J.: There is a difference where he stops all your way so that you cannot pass, for there you shall have an *Assise of Nuisance,* and where he stops part only so that you can pass but narrowly, for there you shall have an *Accion sur votre cas*; and so there is a difference where he withholds part [of the stream water] and where he withholds all.

Quod omnes Justiciarii concesserunt.

BROOKE, J.: *Accion sur le cas* lies where there is no other action provided for a wrong.

ANON

Y.B. Mich. 27 Hen. 8, f. 27, pl. 10

A.D. 1535

One brought a *Writ sur son cas* against another. He alleged that, whereas the plaintiff had used to have a way from his house to a close over the King's highway for carriage and re-carriage, etc., the defendant had stopped the King's highway, so that the plaintiff could not go to his aforesaid close, to his tort and damage.

BALDWIN, C.J.: It seems to me that this action does not lie to the plaintiff for the stopping of the highway; for the King has the punishment of that, and he has his plaint in the Leet and there he has his redress, because it is a common nuisance to all the King's lieges, and so there is no reason for a private particular person to have an *accion sur son cas*; for if one person shall have an action for this, by the same reason every person shall have an action, and so he will be punished a hundred times on the same case.

FITZHERBERT, J. to the contrary: I agree well that each nuisance done in the King's highway is punishable in the Leet and not by an action, unless it be where one man has suffered greater hurt or inconvenience than the generality have; but he who has suffered such greater displeasure or hurt can have an action to recover the damage which he has by reason of this special hurt. So if one makes a ditch across the highway, and I come riding along the way in the night and I and my horse are thrown into the ditch so that I have great damage and displeasure thereby, I shall have an action here against him who made this ditch across the highway, because I have suffered more damage than any other person. So here the plaintiff had more convenience by this highway than any other person had, and so when he is stopped he suffers more damage because he has no way to go to his close. Wherefore it seems to me that he shall have this action *pour ce special matiere*; but if he had not suffered greater damage than all others suffered, then he would not have the action. *Quod Nota.*

CANTREL v. CHURCH

(1601) CROKE, ELIZ. 845

Error,[22] for that in action upon the case the plaintiff declares that he was seised in fee of a house and land in D. whereto he had common appurtenant in such a place; and that he, and all those whose, etc., had had a way from the said place wherein, etc., and that the defendant *totaliter* hath stopped up his way, whereby he could not come to his common, but had altogether lost the use thereof, etc.

The defendant pleaded not guilty; and it was found against him and judgment given for the plaintiff; and error assigned because he ought not to have had an action upon the case, but an assise of nuisance, in regard that the inheritance is in question.

And so upon the first motion held divers of the justices and Barons; but after divers motions and considerations had of the books of 8 *Eliz. Dyer,*

---

[22] i.e. the decision of a lower court has here been brought, on a Writ of Error, to the Exchequer Chamber: see Bl. Comm. III. 405-11.

250, *b.*, 11 *Hen.* 4,[23] 2 *Hen.* 4[24] and others, they resolved that the action was well brought, for he hath election to bring either the one or the other. For, although there had a difference been taken, where the way is so stopped up that he loseth the use thereof altogether and thereby his common, there an assise shall lie, but where it is estopped but in part and not totally, that there an action upon the case lies and not an assise, they conceived it not to be any difference, for he hath election to have either the one or the other action; especially as this case is, where it appears not that the stopping was made by him who is the tenant of the freehold, but it might be done by a stranger who hath nothing to do with the land, or by one who hath but a term therein.

Wherefore they all resolved that the action was well brought; and thereupon the judgment was affirmed.

ALDRED'S CASE
(1611) 9 COKE REP. f. 57b

William Aldred brought an action on the case against Thomas Benton . . . that whereas the plaintiff, 29 *Septemb' anno* 6 *Jac.*, was seised of a house and a parcel of land in length 31 feet and in breadth 2 feet and a half next to the hall and parlour of the plaintiff of his house aforesaid in Harleston in the county of Norfolk in fee; and whereas the defendant was possessed of a small orchard on the east part of the said parcel of land. *prædictus Thomas, malitiose machinans et intendens ipsum Willielmum de easiamento et proficuo* (profit) *messuagii et parcell' terræ suorum prædictorum impedire et deprivare,* the said 29th day of September *anno* 6 *Jacobi quoddam magnum lignile* (wooden shed) *in dicto horto* (orchard) *ipsius Thomæ construxit et erexit ac illud adeo exaltavit, etc., quod per lignile illud, etc., tam omnia fenestra et luminaria ipsius Willielmi aulæ et camerarum suarum quam ostium* (entrance) *ipsius Willielmi aulæ prædictæ penitus obstupata fuerunt* (were obstructed), *etc.; et prædictus Thomas ulterius, machinans et malitiose intendens ipsum Willielmum multipliciter prægravare* (oppress) *et ipsum de toto commodo, easiamento et proficuo totius messuagii sui prædicti penitus deprivare, prædicto 29 die Sept' an' 6 supradicto quoddam ædificium pro suibus* (sows) *et porcis suis in horto suo prædicto tam prope aulam* (hall) *et conclave* (chamber) *ipsius Willielmi prædicti erexit, ac sues et porcos suos in ædificio in horto illo pascuit* (fed) *et illos ibidem per magnum tempus custodivit, ita quod, per fœtidos et insalubres ordores sordidorum prædictorum suum et porcorum prædicti Thomæ in aula et conclave prædictis ac alias partes prædicti messuagii ipsius Willielmi penetrantes et influentes, idem Willielmus et famuli sui ac aliæ personæ in messuagio suo prædicto conversantes existentes* (then dwelling) *absque periculo infectionis in aula et conclave prædictis ac aliis locis messuagii prædicti continuare seu remanere non potuerunt: prætextu cujus* (by reason of which) *idem Willielmus totum commodum, usum, easiamentum et proficuum maximæ partis messuagii sui prædicti per totum tempus prædictum totaliter perdidit et amisit ad damnum ipsius Willielmi* 40 *l., etc.*

And the defendant pleaded not guilty, and at the assises in Norfolk he was found guilty of both the said nuisances, and damages assessed.

---

[23] Y.B. Mich. II, Hen. 4, f. 25, pl. 48. In this case, *Chedder* v. *Dyer,* where an Assise of Nuisance was brought for obstructing a right of way, Hankford, J. said *obiter,* ' For a way in gross a man shall not have an assise of nuisance, but a writ *sur son cas*'—*Quod alii Justiciarii concesserunt.*

[24] *Supra,* p. 83.

And now it was moved in arrest of judgment, that the building of the house for hogs was necessary for the sustenance of man, and one ought not to have so delicate a nose that he cannot bear the smell of hogs; for *lex non favet delicatorum votis.*

But it was resolved that the action for it is (as this case is) well maintainable. For in a house four things are desired, *habitatio hominis, delectatio inhabitantis, necessitas luminis et salubritas æris;* and for nuisance done to three of them an action lies, *sc.* (1) To the habitation of a man, for that is the principal end of a house. (2) For hindrance of the light, for the ancient form of an action on the case was significant, *sc. quod messuagium horrida tenebritate obscuratum fuit*[25]; . . .

And as to this there was a case adjudged in the King's Bench, Trin. 29 Eliz.—Thomas Bland brought an action on the case against Thomas Moseley and declared how that James Bland was seised in fee of an ancient house in Netherousegate in the parish of St. Michael in the county of the City of York, and that the said James, and all those whose estate he had in the said house, from time whereof, etc., have had and have used to have for them and their tenants for life, years and at will, in the west side of the said house seven windows or lights against a piece of land containing half a rood in the parish aforesaid adjoining to the said house, which piece of land from time whereof, etc., was without any building until the 28th day of September *anno* 28 Eliz., and shewed the length and breadth of the said windows for all the time aforesaid, by force of which windows the said James and all those whose estate he had in the said house from time whereof, etc., have used to have for them and their tenants aforesaid divers wholesome and necessary easements and commodities by reason of the open air and light, etc. And that the said James the 20 September *anno* 28 Eliz. demised to the plaintiff the said house for 3 years; and that the defendant, maliciously intending to deprive him of the said easements *et obscurare messuagium prædictum horrida tenebritate,* etc. 20 *Nov. anno* 29 *Eliz.* had erected a new building on the said piece of land, so near etc., that the said seven windows were stopped; whereby the plaintiff lost the said easements, etc., *et maxima pars messuagii prædicti horrida tenebritate obscurata fuit,* etc. . . .

[The defendant here pleaded in bar a custom of York entitling him so to build.]

. . . It was adjudged by Sir Christopher Wray, Chief Justice, and the whole Court of King's Bench that the bar was insufficient in law to bar the plaintiff of his actions, for two reasons:

1. When a man has a lawful easement or profit by prescription from time whereof, etc., another custom, which is also from time whereof, etc., cannot take it away, for the one custom is as ancient as the other: as if one has a way over the land of A. to his freehold by prescription from time whereof, etc., A. cannot allege a prescription or custom to stop the said way.

2. It may be that before time of memory the owner of the said piece of land has granted to the owner of the said house to have the said windows without any stopping of them, and so the prescription may have a lawful beginning.

[25] Reference is here made to 7 Ed. 3, 50b: 11 Hen. 4, 47: 22 Hen. 6, 14.

And Wray, C.J. then said[26] that for stopping as well of the wholesome air as of light an action lies, and damages shall be recovered for them, for both are necessary; for it is said *et vescitur aura ætherea;* and the said words *horrida tenebritate,* etc. are significant and imply the benefit of the light. But he said that for prospect, which is a matter only of delight and not of necessity, no action lies for stopping thereof, and yet it is a great commendation of a house if it has a long and large prospect, *unde dicitur, laudaturque domus longos qui prospicit agros.* But the law does not give an action for such things of delight. And Solomon says, Ecclesiast. 11. 7, *Dulce lumen est et delectabile oculis videre solem . . .*; and if the stopping of the wholesome air, etc. gives cause of action, *a fortiori* an action lies in the case at Bar[27] for infecting and corrupting the air. And the building of a lime-kiln is good and profitable; but if it be built so near a house that when it burns the smoke thereof enters into the house so that none can dwell there, an action lies for it. So if a man has a watercourse running in a ditch from the river to his house for his necessary use, and if a glover sets up a lime-pit for calve-skins and sheep-skins so near the said watercourse that the corruption of the lime-pit has corrupted it, for which cause his tenants leave the said house, an action on the case lies for it, as it is adjudged in 13 Hen. 7, 26,b.,[28] and this stands with the rule of law and reason, *sc. Prohibetur ne quis faciat in suo quod nocere possit alieno, et sic utere tuo ut alienum non lædas. . . .* So in the case at Bar, forasmuch as the declaration is that the defendant, maliciously intending to deprive the plaintiff of the use and profit of his house, erected a swine stye. . . . To which declaration the defendant pleaded not guilty and was found guilty of the matter in the declaration.

It was adjudged that the plaintiff should recover.

[26] i.e. in the case of *Bland* v. *Moseley.*
[27] i.e. *Aldred's Case.*
[28] *Supra,* p. 87

∾ 6 ∾

TROVER AND CONVERSION

HISTORIANS have compiled a dismal catalogue of defects to which Detinue was subject and which invited the use of Case. A plaintiff, at least where the action was between the original parties and not their representatives, might be debarred from fighting on the facts by the defendant's insistence upon wager of law.[1] The possibility was itself a severe deterrent. But the writ offered substantial as well as procedural disadvantages. If a bailee damaged the goods or charters bailed to him and then returned them, there was no detention and the bailor could not sue.[2] If he damaged them, but continued to hold them, Detinue would indeed lie but offered the bailor barren satisfaction. Damages were awarded only in lieu of restitution: the Court in such a case would order the bailee to restore the goods, and, if he complied, their condition was immaterial.[3] It has also been suggested that a stranger to the bailment was not liable in Detinue if by his misconduct he had made delivery impossible. Sir William Holdsworth was positive upon the point, though Professor Potter, like Ames, is content to doubt.[4] The authority cited is a case of 1472, where A. bailed goods for safe custody to B., who bailed them over to C. C. so used them as to destroy their value. In an action *sur le case*, Chief Justice Brian gave judgment for the defendant, C., since he was 'a stranger to the first bailee,' but the other Judges found for the plaintiff.[5] The case justifies the suggestion only by the inference that the plaintiff was driven to Case because he could not sue in Detinue, and, even if this inference be just, its rationale is not evident. A bailee guilty of similar misconduct would clearly be liable,[6] and, while a plaintiff who sued in Detinue *sur bailment* might find difficulty in establishing relations between himself and a stranger, no such objection could be taken to Detinue *sur trover*. The defects of Detinue may thus have been

---

[1] *Supra*, p. 28.

[2] See Y.B.B. 39 Hen. 6, f. 44, pl. 7 (wrongly cited by Ames, *Lectures*, p. 83, as 33 Hen. 6); 18 Ed. 4, f. 23, pl. 5, *infra*, p. 113; and 2 Hen. 7, f. 11, pl. 9, *supra*, p. 86.

[3] Y.B. 18 Ed. 4, f. 23, pl. 5 (A.D. 1479), *infra*, p. 113; and *Anon* (1510) Keilway, 160, *infra*, p. 114.

[4] See H.E.L. III, 350; Ames, *Lectures*, p. 84; Potter, *Hist. Intro. to Eng. Law*, 3rd edn., p. 396.

[5] Y.B. Mich. 12 Ed. 4, f. 13, pl. 9 (A.D 1472).

[6] See Y.B. 20 Hen. 6, f. 16, pl. 2 (A.D. 1442). *Brown* (arguendo): 'If you bail to me a thing which is wastable, as a tun of wine, and peradventure I drink it up with other *bons compagnons* without payment, you cannot have Detinue for this, because it is not *in rerum natura*, but by Account before auditors its value will be found.' NEWTON, C.J.: 'If one bails such a thing to me to bail over to another, which peradventure I have wasted while it is in my hands, shall he have Account against me? Why no, but a writ of Detinue.'

102

exaggerated. But they were irksome enough for litigants to cast eager eyes upon the more fashionable action on the case.

The case of 1472 showed that the new action was already available. But there were earlier precedents. In 1461 a bailor brought *Trespass sur son cas* against a bailee who had ' defaced ' a deed committed to his charge; and in the following year Littleton, as counsel, sought to illustrate the difference between Trespass and Case by saying that if ' I bail my cloak to you and you burn it, I will have an action of *Trespass sur le case* against you.'[7] In the contemporary law of Nuisance, Case had similarly been used to supplement the Assise, but it was long before it was allowed to supplant it.[8] Propriety might seem to demand the same jealous differentiation in Detinue; but if scruples were felt, they were faint and quickly overborne. In 1505 a buyer brought an *action sur son cas* against a seller for non-delivery, and the relation of the new writ to its predecessors was discussed at length.[9] Chief Justice Frowicke admitted that Case and the Assise were incompatible, but only because they came of different stock. Case was a personal and the Assise a real action, and the two could not meet. But no such impediment barred the union of Case and Detinue.

> ' If I bail my goods to a man for safe keeping and he take the custody upon himself, and my goods are lost for default of good custody, I shall have action of Detinue or action on my case at my pleasure. . . . And if I sue my action of Detinue and he wages his law, I shall be barred in my action on my case because I had my choice and chose Detinue, and this was at my peril, and I have lost the advantage of the action on my case.' [10]

Five years later counsel sought to impose a limit upon the plaintiff's freedom of choice, but the Court reiterated the right of election.[11]

The precedents so far considered were but so many examples of Case as a generic writ. The index of the Common Law knew as yet no such title as Trover and Conversion, though it is significant that in 1479 a bailor complained that a bailee had broken open certain hampers of silver and ' converted them to his use.'[12] Mere damage by a bailee, indeed, never became conversion and was remediable only by an ' innominate ' action.[13] But in the second half of the sixteenth century Trover emerged as a distinct species of Case. The process may be traced through the pleadings. In 1554 in *Lord Mounteagle* v. *Countess of Worcester*[14] the plaintiff counted that,

[7] Y.B. 39 Hen. 6, f. 44, pl. 6; and Y.B. 2 Ed. 4, Pasch. pl. 9.
[8] *Supra*, p. 94.
[9] *Anon* (1505) Y.B. 20 Hen. 7, Mich. f. 8, pl. 18, *infra*, p. 351.
[10] See the report of the same case in Keilway, at pp. 77-8: *infra*, p. 353.
[11] *Anon* (1510) Keilway, p. 160: *infra*, p. 114.
[12] *Anon*, Y.B. 18 Ed. 4, f. 23, pl. 5: *infra*, p. 114. See also *The Carrier's Case* (1473), S.S. Vol. 64, p. 30, *infra*, p. 300.
[13] See *Symons* v. *Darknoll* (1628) Palmer, 523.
[14] 2 Dyer, 121a.

'Whereas he was possessed of a chain of gold of the price of one hundred marks as of his proper chattels, and, being so possessed thereof, at London in the parish, etc., casually lost the said chain, which afterwards came to the hands and possession of the said Countess at London in the parish and ward aforesaid by finding;

Yet the said defendant, knowing that the said chain was the chattel of the said plaintiff, but contriving subtilly to defraud and deceive the said plaintiff of the same, there sold the said chain to divers persons unknown to the said plaintiff for divers sums of money and received the money for the same and converted it to her own use.'

It is instructive to compare these four allegations with their predecessors in Detinue sur Trover.[15] The first three—the possession, the loss and the finding—were with slight variation common to both: the fourth was an innovation. The defendant was charged in the old action with a refusal to deliver on request and a consequent detention of the goods, and in the new action with their conversion to his own use. The formula, however, was still experimental. Rastell, in the specimen offered in his Collection of Entries in 1566, borrowed more largely from the language of Detinue. The plaintiff alleged (1) that he was possessed of specified goods of a certain value ' as of his own proper goods,' (2) that, being so possessed, he ' casually lost them out of his possession,' (3) that they afterwards ' came into the hands and possession of the defendant by finding,' (4) that the defendant, though often requested so to do, had failed to deliver them to the plaintiff, and (5) that he had converted them to his own use.[16] For the next fifty years practitioners extemporised happily upon their theme. As late as 1614 the plaintiff in the leading case of *Isaack* v. *Clark* not only omitted from his declaration the ' refusal to deliver on request,' but substituted for the ' trover ' the more primitive *devenerunt ad manus.*[17] But Rastell's five allegations ultimately became common form and were adopted by Coke as a precedent in his own Book of Entries.[18]

Of these allegations the ' losing ' was almost at once treated as fictitious. In *Gumbleton* v. *Grafton* in 1600[19] the plaintiff in his declaration alleged that he had delivered to the defendant ' certain wools to keep and that the defendant had converted them to his own use.' The defendant objected that, as the plaintiff had not lost the wools, Detinue alone would lie; but the objection failed. In 1626 the Court of Exchequer Chamber expressly stated that ' the losing is but a surmise and not material, for the defendant may take it in the pres-

---

[15] Cf. Rastell, *Collection of Entries. Detinue of Charters*, f. 204; *supra*, p. 43.

[16] *Ibid*, f. 4: ' Action sur le case in lieu de action de Detinue vers cestuy que trove biens et eux vend.'

[17] (1614) 2 Bulstrode, 306, *infra*, p. 117.

[18] *Infra*, p. 116.

[19] Croke, Eliz. 781.

ence of the plaintiff or any other who may give sufficient evidence.'[20] The ' finding ' was equally insubstantial. In *Ratcliff* v. *Davies* it was held that ' a Trover and Conversion well lies, although [the defendant] came unto them by a lawful delivery and not by trover ';[21] and in *Isaack* v. *Clark* the Court disregarded as irrelevant the jury's verdict that the defendant was ' not guilty *de inventione*.'[22] The Judges, indeed, had to reduce both charges to fictions if they were to allow the action on the case as a substitute for Detinue sur Bailment as well as Detinue sur Trover. The first allegation with its confusion of ' possession ' and ' property ' contained the germs of lively controversy; but it remained to a future generation of lawyers to realise and to exploit the rich and subtle implications.[23] It will be convenient, therefore, to concentrate for the moment upon the last two allegations and to attempt, through their medium, to define the act of conversion.

That such an act was of the essence of the plaintiff's case was repeatedly asserted in the closing years of the sixteenth century. ' The action is *sur le conversion* ': ' the conversion is the substance of the action ': ' the conversion is the special cause of this action.'[24] Upon this assumption three problems fell to be examined. In the first place, was conversion to be defined so as to be satisfied merely by the proof of negligence? The question was put to the Court in 1590 in *Walgrave* v. *Ogden*.[25] The plaintiff sued for the ' trover and conversion of twenty barrels of butter and declared that by negligent keeping of them they were become of little value.' The defendant demurred, and his demurrer was upheld. ' If a man finds my garments,' said Walmsley, J., ' and suffereth them to be eaten with moths by the negligent keeping of them, no action lieth; but if he weareth my garments it is otherwise, for the wearing is a conversion.' The distinction here drawn was adopted in *Isaack* v. *Clark,* where it was said that no action of conversion would lie for the ' ill and negligent keeping ' of goods by a finder, ' because this is but a non feasans.'[26] A conversion, therefore, must comprise some act of positive misconduct.

The judges had, in the second place, to consider the effect of a refusal to deliver the goods on request. The allegation was a vital element in Detinue, whether *sur trover* or *sur bailment,* and had found its way into the accepted formula of the action on the case for Trover. Was such a refusal to be deemed an irrebuttable presumption of

[20] *Kinaston* v. *Moore* (1626) Croke, Car. 89.
[21] (1611) Croke, Jac. 244, *infra*, p. 115.
[22] *Infra*, p. 117.
[23] *Infra*, pp. 110-3.
[24] *The Countess of Rutland's Case* (1588) Moore, p. 266; *Stransham's Case* (1588) Croke, Eliz. 97, per Coke, *arguendo*: *Vandrink* v. *Archer* (1590) 1 Leonard, 221.
[25] 1 Leonard, 224.
[26] *Infra*, p. 118. Cf. Trevor, C.J., in *Anon* (1705) 2 Salk. 655: ' Trover lies not against a carrier for negligence, as for losing a box; but it does for an actual wrong, as if he break it to take out goods, or sell it.'

conversion or might the defendant offer some ground of justification? There was a period of judicial hesitation. In an anonymous case of 1591 the plaintiff alleged the conversion of a bag of money, and the defendant was allowed to justify his non-delivery by pleading that it had been put into his hands as stakeholder to await a decision which had not yet been given.[27] In *Easton* v. *Newman*,[28] on the other hand, the Jury found specially that the defendant had refused to restore the goods and ' prayed the discretion of the Court if this were a conversion.' It was considered to be such by three judges to one, but the case was adjourned and no final decision is recorded. This diversity of opinion lent peculiar emphasis to the judgment in *Isaack* v. *Clark*.[29]

> A. had obtained judgment against B. for £40. B. did not pay and disappeared. Execution was then ordered upon the goods of C., who was one of B.'s pledges. and D., a court official, accordingly seized three butts of wine. E., a friend of C., sought to stop the sale of the wine and proposed to ask A. to abandon the execution against C. It was therefore arranged that D. should temporarily return the wine to C., and, as security for its re-delivery to D. if A. continued to insist on the execution, E. deposited with D. a purse containing £22. E. now sued D. for the conversion of the purse and money.

The Jury returned a special verdict (1) that A. had not been induced to stay the execution, (2) that E. had asked D. to return the purse and money and that D. had refused, and left it to the King's Bench to rule whether upon these facts the defendant was guilty of a conversion. The Court unanimously gave judgment for the defendant, and Chief Justice Coke examined the whole nature of the action. Upon the precise point at issue he was clear. A refusal to deliver was but a fact to be considered in relation to its context. If it were unqualified and unreasonable, it might indeed amount to a conversion; but if the defendant could satisfy the Court that there were adequate grounds for his refusal, the presumption which it had raised against him was rebutted. Such grounds were amply present in the instant case, where the purse and money were being held to await a condition not yet satisfied.[30]

The solution here offered was generally adopted. Thus, in *Robinson* v. *Walter*[31] a stranger had lodged in the defendant's inn and had left a horse behind him as security for the payment of a bill. The plaintiff discovered the horse to be his, demanded it from the

---

[27] *Anon* (1591) 1 Leonard, 247.
[28] (1596) Moore, 460: Croke, Eliz. 495.
[29] (1614) 2 Bulstrode, 306, *infra*, p. 117.
[30] See also *The Case of the Chancellor of the University of Oxford* (1614) 10 Coke Rep. 53b: ' It is good evidence *prima facie* to prove a conversion, that the plaintiff requested the defendant to deliver and he refused . . .; but yet it is but evidence.'
[31] (1616) 3 Bulstrode, 269. See also *Hartfort* v. *Jones* (1698) 1 Ld. Raym. 393, where goods were allowed to be detained until payment of salvage.

innkeeper, and, on the latter's refusal, sued him in conversion. Judgment was given for the defendant by Chief Justice Montague. 'Here in this case the innkeeper said to the plaintiff, Prove the horse to be yours, pay for his meat, and you shall have him. This is no denial nor yet any conversion. He claims no property at all; he only detains the horse till he is satisfied for his meat, and so he may well do by the law.' The distinction between an absolute and a conditional refusal, upon which the solution rested, might seem at first sight to have been obscured by the judgment in the later case of *Baldwin* v. *Cole*.[32] A carpenter had been temporarily employed in the ' Queen's Yard,' and, when he sought to leave, the royal surveyor refused to let him take his tools, ' pretending an usage to detain tools to enforce workmen to continue until the Queen's work was done.' Chief Justice Holt declared that ' the very denial of goods to him that has a right to demand them is an actual conversion and not only evidence of it, as has been holden.' But the facts of the case and the succeeding words of the judgment reveal the assertion as no more than the characteristically vigorous indulgence of a generous mind; and, if it was imprudent, the subsequent definition made ample atonement. ' What is a conversion, but an assuming upon one's self the property and right of disposing of another's goods; and he that takes upon himself to detain another man's goods from him without cause takes upon himself the right of disposing of them.'

The third problem was to determine the principle of liability upon which the tort was based. Must the plaintiff prove fault in the defendant, or, to transpose the question, was innocence a defence? As early as 1590 the Court was confronted with a situation that in the modern law has become painfully familiar. The owner of goods sued a bona fide purchaser for value into whose hands they had come. Judgment was given upon a flaw in the manner of pleading, and on the point of substance the Court was divided.[33] For another hundred years the cases were few and equivocal and were not made more helpful by an occasional inability to distinguish Trover and Trespass; but, so far as a judicial opinion emerged, it inclined to regard innocence as a defence.[34] It was not until the eighteenth century that the ground was cleared and the doubt resolved. In *Hartop* v. *Hoare* in 1743 the jury found a special verdict that the plaintiff, as the owner of certain jewels, had bailed them to X. and that X. had improperly pawned them

[32] (1705) 6 Mod. 212.
[33] *Vandrink* v. *Archer* (1590) 1 Leonard, 221. Cf. WINDHAM, J.: ' The plaintiff declares of a conversion of his own goods and the defendant justifies because the property of the goods was in a stranger who sold them to him, which cannot be any good title for him without a traverse, unless he had showed that he bought them in an open market,' and PERIAM, J., ' Where a man buys goods of one who comes to them by trover, he may sell them and shall not be answerable for them.'
[34] e.g. *Bayley* v. *Bunning* (1665) 1 Siderfin, 272: *Lechmere* v. *Thorowgood* (1690) Comberbatch, 123: *Cole* v. *Davies* (1700) 1 Ld. Raym., 724. See also *Mires* v. *Solebay* (1678) 2 Mod. 242.

to the defendants. The plaintiff obtained judgment. ' As to the defendants, though they came honestly by them, yet they are within the general rule of *caveat emptor* unless something appears particularly to exempt them.'[35] Thirteen years later Lord Mansfield affirmed the conclusion that innocence was no defence and disposed of the more embarassing of the seventeenth-century cases by the convenient device of denouncing the integrity of the reporters. Of three cases cited against him by counsel, the first appeared in Siderfin, who ' did not seem to know what the court was going upon,' the second in Comberbatch, who did not understand the argument and whose account of the judgment ' was the only sensible part of the whole report,' and the third in some ' notes of Lord Raymond, taken as short hints for his own use and too inaccurate to be relied on as authorities.'[36]

The issue had been complicated and the conclusion delayed by a number of cases where the defendant was a servant acting on the behalf and with the authority of his master. It was at first thought that public policy required him to be excused, at least if he committed no palpable offence. ' The action,' said Scroggs, J., in 1678,[37] ' will not lie against the servant; for it being in obedience to his master's command, though he had no title, yet he shall be excused. And this rule would extend to all cases where the master's command was not to do an apparent wrong. . . . For otherwise it would be a mischievous thing if the servant upon all occasions must be satisfied with his master's title and right before he obey his commands.' But here as elsewhere the clear intelligence of the eighteenth century exposed the fallacy. The question was not what the defendant was or what he had thought, but what he had done. If his acts fell within the range of conduct stigmatised as conversion, if, in Holt's words, he had ' assumed upon himself the property and right of disposing of another's goods,' he was liable whether he were a servant or a master, honest or dishonest. He had committed a tort and must pay for it.[38]

The judges, in their efforts to define the meaning of conversion, had repeatedly to review the relation of Trover to the older writs. The fact that it was available in certain circumstances as a substitute for Detinue, whether *sur Trover* or *sur Bailment,* has already been noticed and was indeed essential to its development. But the two forms of action, though they might overlap, were not coincident. It was the anxiety to distinguish them which led Coke to assert in *Isaack v. Clark* that a refusal to deliver, if it was to be a conversion, must be absolute. ' If a denyer only shall make a conversion, by this you will confound all form; for then, this way, every action of detinue shall be an action

---

[35] 2 Strange, 1187: 1 Wilson, 8.
[36] *Cooper* v. *Chitty* (1756) 1 Burrow, 20. For the cases chastised by Lord Mansfield, see *supra*, p. 107, n. 34.
[37] *Mires* v. *Solebay*, 2 Mod. 242.
[38] *Perkins* v. *Smith* (1752) 1 Wilson, 328, *infra*, p. 122.

upon the case upon a trover, because there is a denyer.'[39]   The distinction may be traced both in the character of the acts done and in the nature of the remedy offered.   Any act or omission which made it impossible for the defendant to deliver the goods to the plaintiff sufficed for Detinue.   For conversion there must be some conduct, however innocent in its intent, which amounted in effect to a denial of the plaintiff's rights in the goods.   So Chief Justice Hale ruled in 1673 that ' if a carrier loseth goods committed to him, a general action of trover doth not lie against him,'[40] and Lord Mansfield a hundred years later was equally emphatic.   A refusal to deliver might or might not be a conversion: a mere failure could never be.[41]   The nature of the redress sought likewise differed, although the difference tended to be lost in the single-hearted devotion of the Common Law to the award of damages.   In principle at least, a plaintiff in Detinue looked to the return of his goods, even if in practice he must be content with their value: in Trover the claim was for damages only.   The cases of *Kettle* v. *Bromsall*[42] and *Olivant* v. *Berino*[43] offer an interesting contrast.   In the former the plaintiff claimed in Detinue ' a handle of a knife with an old English inscription purporting it to be a deed of gift to the monastery of St. Alban's ' and ' a ring with an antique stone with one of the Cæsars' heads upon it.'   Chief Justice Willes not only insisted upon the peculiar relevance of Detinue in dealing with objects of *vertu,* but went so far as to contemplate an order of specific restitution.   ' In trover only damages can be recovered; but the things lost may be of that sort, as medals, pictures or other pieces of antiquity, that no damages can be an adequate satisfaction, but the party may desire to recover the things themselves, which can only be done in detinue.'[44]   In the latter, a defendant, sued in Trover for the value of certain pictures, sought to be quit of his liability by returning them to the plaintiff.   But the Court refused the option.   ' This action is for damages, and you cannot oblige the plaintiff to accept the thing itself.'   The difference was, perhaps, academic rather than practical, but it reflected a wider, if vaguer, doctrine as to the transfer of property.   It was said by Chief Justice Anderson in *Bishop* v. *Viscountess Montague*[45] that the action of Detinue ' affirmed the property ' in the

---

[39] *Infra*, p. 118.   See also *per Curiam* in *The Countess of Rutland's Case* (1588) Moore, p. 266: in Trover ' le accion est sur le conversion,' but in Detinue ' le point del accion est le non redelivery.'

[40] *Owen* v. *Lewyn* (1673) 1 Ventris, 223.

[41] *Ross* v. *Johnson* (1772) 5 Burrow, 2825, *infra*, p. 123.

[42] (1738) Willes, 118.

[43] (1743) 1 Wilson, 23.

[44] The general opinion is certainly that, before the Common Law Procedure Act, 1854, s. 78, the defendant in Detinue had always the option of keeping the goods and paying their value.   But there are indications, apart from the remarks in *Kettle* v. *Bromsall,* that the principle was not universal.   See Blackstone III. 151-2; *Wulghes* v. *Pepard, supra*, p. 37, and *Anon* (1479), *infra*, p. 113.

[45] (1601) Croke, Eliz. 824, *infra*, p. 114.

plaintiff, and by Chief Justice Coke in *Isaack* v. *Clark* that the judgment in Trover 'changed the property' from the plaintiff to the defendant.[46] It was a natural inference that the plaintiff should assert in Detinue his desire for his own goods and must in Trover transfer his interest to their value.

Trover might be preferred, not only to Detinue, but to Trespass. The advantage of this particular preference was not obvious since Trespass was never subject to wager of law, and litigants may merely have been in pursuit of a fashionable remedy. Whatever the reason, the propriety of such an alternative was much canvassed in *Bishop* v. *Viscountess Montague* and, after judicial vacillation, was admitted.[47] But, as with Trover and Detinue, so with Trover and Trespass, it was not in every case that the plaintiff might elect between them. It is, indeed, possible to find in the reports loose talk, repeated sometimes by those who should have known better, that 'whenever Trespass for taking goods will lie, that is, when they are taken wrongfully, Trover will also lie.'[48] But the judges sought to correct these wide statements and to delimit the boundaries of the two actions. On the one hand, there might be an act of conversion without any direct interference with the plaintiff's possession, as where an innocent purchaser from a thief refused to deliver the goods to the true owner. Here Trover lay, but not Trespass. 'You say that trespass will lie wherever trover will. It is a manifest mistake; for trespass lies not on a bare denial, as trover will on a demand and denial.'[49] Conversely, there might be a Trespass, but no Trover. The slightest interference with the plaintiff's goods, if unauthorised, was a trespass, and no challenge to his rights need be shown; in conversion such a challenge was the essence of the tort. So in *Bushell* v. *Miller* the defendant, by shifting a parcel a yard from its site to suit his own convenience, was guilty of a trespass but not of a conversion, and the subsequent loss of the parcel was an unfortunate incident which could not alter the character of the tort.[50]

It is now time to return to the first allegation in the plaintiff's declaration in Trover, that he was 'possessed of the goods as of his

---

[46] *Infra*, p. 118. In the modern law of Conversion it is not the judgment itself, but the satisfaction of the judgment, which operates to transfer the property. But this seems a nineteenth-century innovation: see per Willes, J. in *Brinsmead* v. *Harrison* (1871), L.R., 6 C.P. 584.

[47] (1601) Croke, Eliz. 824, *infra*, p. 114. The possibility of Trover as alternative to Trespass was affirmed in *Kinaston* v. *Moore* (1626) Croke, Car. 89.

[48] So Serjt. Williams in a note to his edition of Saunders' Reports, on the case of *Wilbraham* v. *Snow* (1670) 2 Saunders, 47. For the case itself, see *infra*, p. 119.

[49] Pemberton, C.J., in *Putt* v. *Royston* (1683) 2 Shower 211, *infra*, p. 120. The denial, as seen above, must be unqualified. Cf. *Bishop* v. *Viscountess Montague*, *infra*, p. 114, where there was a tortious taking.

[50] (1731) 1 Strange, 128, *infra*, p. 121. A further distinction between Trespass and Trover, dependent on the plaintiff's relation to the goods, will be considered later. See *infra*, p. 112.

own property ' or ' as of his proper goods.' The phrase would seem to contain a patent ambiguity. Was the plaintiff's case to depend upon possession or upon ownership? The development of pleading, however, was not an analytical but a historical process, and its language was not to be subjected to the prim scrutiny of the jurist. Definition even to-day is perilous, and well into the nineteenth century ' property ' might imply at discretion any one of the three conceptions of ownership, right to possess or possession. A languid effort at discrimination may be observed in the antithesis of the ' general ' or ' absolute ' property of the owner and the ' special ' property of the bailee or other person with only a limited interest.[51] But such epithets do not err upon the side of precision, and it is not surprising that the task of determining the particular relationship between the plaintiff and the goods which would suffice for Trover was arduous and protracted.

The first attempt was made in 1611 in *Ratcliffe* v. *Davies.*[52] The plaintiff pawned a chattel to John Whitlock who delivered it to the defendant and died. The plaintiff then tendered the sum due on the pledge to Whitlock's executrix and demanded the chattel from the defendant. The executrix refused to receive the money and the defendant refused to return the chattel. It was held that the plaintiff, though he was out of possession at the moment of conversion, could maintain Trover because the 'special property' re-vested in him by the tender. In other words, ' possession,' as used in the first allegation, must be taken to include ' right to possess.' In the second half of the seventeenth century two cases raised the question whether possession, without more, would suffice for Trover. In each of them it was argued for the defendant that, while such a relationship was the essence of Trespass, Trover rested upon the idea of ' property,' but in each the argument was repelled. A bailee or a sheriff executing a writ could sue a third party for the conversion of the goods entrusted to him.[53] The principle was extended in the familiar case of *Armory* v. *Delamirie*[54] so as to place the action at the disposal of a plaintiff into whose hands the goods had come without any prior authority. As against a wrongdoer possession alone sufficed in Trover as in

[51] e.g. *Ratcliff* v. *Davies* ('special' property of a bailee), *infra*, p. 115; *Wilbraham* v. *Snow* (of a sheriff), *infra*, p. 119. See also *Arnold* v. *Jefferson* (1697) 1 Ld. Raym. 275, and *Bushell* v. *Miller*, *infra*, p. 121. In *Webb* v. *Fox* (1797) 7 T.R. 391, LAWRENCE, J., said: 'Absolute property is where one, having the possession of chattels, has also the exclusive right to enjoy them and which can only be defeated by some act of his own. Special property is where he who has the possession holds them subject to the claims of other persons.'

[52] Croke, Jac. 244: *infra*, p. 119.

[53] *Wilbraham* v. *Snow* (1670), *infra*, p. 119; and *Arnold* v. *Jefferson* (1697), 1 Ld. Raym. 275.

[54] (1722) 1 Strange, 505. It was ruled by Pratt, C.J. at Nisi Prius that ' the finder of a jewel, though he does not by such finding acquire an absolute property or ownership, yet he has such a property as will enable him to keep it against all but the rightful owner, and consequently may maintain trover.'

Trespass, and the second half of the phrase ' possessed as of his own property ' was to be interpreted no more literally than the first.

At the end of the eighteenth century the judges were confronted with the further question whether a plaintiff could maintain Trover who, while the undoubted owner of the goods, had, at the crucial time, neither possession nor yet the right to possess. In *Ward* v. *Macauley*[55] Lord Kenyon, taken at a disadvantage, was incautious. The plaintiff owned a house which he let furnished to X. The defendants levied execution upon X. and seized the furniture, and the plaintiff sued them in Trespass. Lord Kenyon was clear that Trespass would not lie where there was no direct interference with the possession, but he hazarded the suggestion that the plaintiff should have brought Trover. ' The distinction between the actions of trespass and trover is well settled: the former is founded on possession, the latter on property. Here the plaintiff had no possession; his remedy was by an action of trover founded on his property in the goods taken.' Five years later in *Gordon* v. *Harper*[56] a plaintiff took Lord Kenyon at his word, and on similar facts sued in Trover. His Lordship was forced to recant, and paid vicariously the price of imprudence. Trover was a more ample remedy than Trespass in that it embraced the right to possess without the possession itself, but, despite the brave words of property in the writ, it did not avail to vindicate a bare right of ownership.[57]

A corollary of the distinction between Trespass and Trover may finally be noted. A defendant may wish to plead that the title to the goods, though not in himself, is not in the plaintiff either but in a third party. Logic would seem to require this defence of Jus Tertii to be allowed or refused according as title is or is not in issue. English law has perhaps been fortunate in that the judges have sometimes shrunk from the consequences of their own arguments, but here at least they have manfully drawn their conclusions. In Trespass, where possession alone is relevant, the Jus Tertii may not be pleaded.[58] In Trover a distinction is taken. If the plaintiff can rely on his possession, he is as secure as in Trespass;[59] but if he is not in possession he puts in issue his right to possess, and the defendant may take up the challenge. In *Leake* v. *Loveday*[60] the plaintiff was the holder of a bill of sale upon the furniture of a Mr. Cox of Oxford. The effect of the bill was to leave the possession of the goods in Cox, but to transfer to the plaintiff the ownership and, on Cox's failure to pay the money

[55] (1791) 4 T.R. 489.
[56] (1796) 7 T.R. 9: *infra*, p. 124.
[57] In certain circumstances an ' innominate' action on the case may be available to protect such a bare right, but the judges have not developed the idea. See *Mears* v. *L. & S.W. Ry.* (1862), 11 C.B.N.S. 850, and *Halliday* v. *Holgate* (1868), L.R. 3 Ex. 299.
[58] For the somewhat confused position in the peculiar species of Trespass known as Ejectment, see Winfield, *Textbook on the Law of Tort*, 4th ed., pp. 334-8.
[59] *Webb* v. *Fox* (1797) 7 T.R. 391.
[60] (1842) 4 M. & G. 972.

due under the bill, the immediate right to possess. Cox then became a bankrupt, and the title to the furniture, as it was in his ' order and disposition,' passed to his assignees in bankruptcy. But, before they could realise their assets, the furniture was seized by the defendant, the sheriff of the County of Oxford, in execution of a debt owed to yet other creditors. The plaintiff sued the defendant in Trover and the latter pleaded the Jus Tertii. The defence succeeded. As the plaintiff was not in possession, he had to prove his right to possess, and the sheriff could therefore assert the superior title of the assignees in bankruptcy although he himself did not act under their authority and had no common cause with them.

S O U R C E S

ANON
Y.B. HIL. 18 ED. 4, f. 23, pl. 5
A.D. 1479

In an *action sur le cas* the plaintiff declared that he bailed certain hanapers of silver to the defendant for safe keeping and that the defendant broke them open and converted them to his use (*convert a son œps*), etc.

Tremayle: It seems that the action does not lie, for it would appear that he can have a writ of Detinue; for the property is not altered and, although he can recover the thing itself,[61] yet he can also recover damages.

CHOKE, J.: The contrary seems to be true; and it will be against reason to force him to sue in an action of Detinue, for when he has sued, he will not have the results of his suit, since it will be vain. For the nature of an action of Detinue is to recover the thing itself, or its value in damages if it cannot be found; and here it is apparent that it is too late and he cannot recover the thing itself.[61] So lately there was an action sued here, and the plaintiff counted that he bailed to the defendant certain cloth of gold and that he [the defendant] had made clothes of it, and, because it appeared to the Court that he could not recover the thing itself, the action was upheld, etc.

Catesby: It seems that he could have had the one action or the other; as if I deliver £20 to *Catesby* to deliver to *Pigot,* he can have either a writ of Account against *Catesby* or a writ of Debt. And so, if you borrow from me my horse to ride to York and you ride on to Carlisle, I shall have a writ of Detinue and recover the horse, and afterwards I shall have an *accion sur mon cas* and recover damages for the labour of my horse outside the covenant; and in the same way, if I bail to you my robes to keep and you wear them so that they are spoilt, I shall have an action of Detinue, for in all these cases the property is not altered; and afterwards I shall have an *accion sur le cas* and recover damages for the loss sustained by the use of the robes. So here he can have the one or the other.

BRIAN, C.J.: It seems to me that he shall have an action of Detinue in this case and no other action; and as to what has been said that he shall

---

[61] In these two passages, and later in the remarks of Brian, C.J., there seems some confusion between the hanaper (i.e. basket, hamper) which was in fact recoverable and the silver, its contents, which were not.

have an action of Debt or of Account, I say that he shall have an action of Account and not of Debt. For on what matter shall his action of Debt be founded? He cannot declare on a contract, as on a sale or on a loan, and so such an action must fail. And I put this question to you: if I bail to you my hanaper to keep and you break it into four parts and you keep these in your chest, is the property changed or not? I think not; so it is clear that he shall have an action of Detinue, where the property is in him, so that he can recover the thing itself. And I take it for clear law that he shall not have any *accion sur le cas* if he can recover the thing itself. And, again, the defendant in an action of Detinue can wage his law, but by the action of the plaintiff in this case he will be ousted from it.' [62]

ANON
MICH. 2 HEN. 8, KEILWAY, 160, pl. 2
A.D. 1510

In the Common Pleas *Moore, Sjt.* showed a diversity where a man shall have an *action sur le case* and where an action of Detinue. For if I bail goods to a man to keep safely and he undertakes to do this, either for or without reward, and by his default the goods spoil, I shall have in this case an *action sur mon case*; for if I bring an action of Detinue, as I can if I wish, then I shall recover the thing as it is, and it is my folly to bring such an action when I can have a better. But if the case is that he sells the goods to another, I shall have against my bailee an action of Detinue and not *sur mon case*.

And several of the Judges said that the party shall in the last case put have an *action sur le case* against his bailee, for he has misdemeaned himself in that he has sold my goods to another, on which misdemeanour by the bailee the *action sur le case* is always founded, notwithstanding that the party can have an action of Detinue if he wishes.

And FAIRFAX, J. said that, if I bail a chest to one and the bailee breaks open the chest, I shall have against him a general action of Trespass; which was not denied. [63]

And REDE, C.J. said that, if one robs me of my goods and another robs him of the said goods, I shall have against the first robber an appeal of robbery and against the second also, because the property of the goods remains always in me. . . . [64]

BISHOP v. VISCOUNTESS MONTAGUE
(1601) CROKE, ELIZ. 824: CROKE, JAC. 50
CROKE, ELIZ. 824

Action sur trover and conversion of five oxen. The defendant pleaded not guilty. By special verdict it was found that one J. S. as bailiff to the defendant took those beasts as for heriots due to the defendant, where there were not any due, and without any command from the said *Viscountess*

---

[62] Holdsworth, H.E.L. III. 350, n. 6, speaks of Brian, C.J. as 'dissenting'; but the report offers only the two conflicting opinions, that of Choke, J. and that of Brian, C.J.

[63] See *The Carrier's Case* (1473) S.S. Vol. 64, p. 30, *infra*, pp. 300-1.

[64] On the scope of the appeal, see *supra*, p. 46.

Montague; but that afterwards she agreed thereto, and converted them; and after that the bailiff died; and whether this action lies, or that he should have brought a general action of Trespass, was the question.

WALMESLEY and KINGSMILL, J.J. held that this action lies not. For when the bailiff took them tortiously, the property and the possession is divested out of the plaintiff, so that he cannot suppose that he was possessed of them until he lost them and until they came to the defendant's hands; and the defendant, by assenting to the taking, is a trespasser *ab initio*. . . . Wherefore, where he might have had a general writ of Trespass, he cannot have any other manner of action; especially not this action, which differs from it in nature and quality.

ANDERSON, C.J. and WARBERTON, J.: *e contra*. They agreed that an assent before or after the taking of the goods made her a trespasser *ab initio* and to be punished as a trespasser. . . . But, although Trespass lies, yet he may have this action if he will, for he hath his election to bring either. And as he may have Detinue or Replevin for goods taken by a trespass, which affirms always property in him at his election, so he may have this action; for one may qualify a tort, but not increase a tort. So he hath election to make it a tortious prisal or not. . . . Wherefore here he might maintain the one writ or the other at his election.

CROKE, JAC. 50[65]

. . . WARBERTON, J.: . . . Trespass and Trover are contrary actions; for it cannot be that he should have property and no property at one and the same time. And there is not here any word of the writ true, for he hath not any property at the time of the conversion. . . .

But ANDERSON, C.J., WALMESLEY, J. and KINGSMILL, J.: *e contra;* and that he had election to bring either of the actions at his pleasure.

Wherefore it was adjudged for the plaintiff.

RATCLIFF v. DAVIES
(1611) CROKE, JAC. 244

Action sur trover and conversion of an hatband set with pearls and diamonds. Upon not guilty pleaded, a special verdict was found: that the plaintiff was possessed thereof and pawned it to *John Whitlock* for £25, but no certain time appointed for the redemption thereof; that, *Whitlock* being sick, his wife, in his presence and with his assent, delivered it to the defendant; and afterwards he made his said wife his executrix and died, who proved the will; that the plaintiff tendered to the said executrix the said £25, who refused it, and afterwards demanded the hatband of the defendant, who refused to deliver it, but converted it to his own use; whereupon, etc.

And in this case three points were moved: First, there being no time appointed for the redemption, whether it may be made after the death of him to whom it was pawned or ought to be in the lives of both parties. And all the Justices resolved, It may be well made after the death of him to whom it was pledged, but not after the death of him who pledged it.

[65] If this is another report of the same hearing, it varies in important circumstances; e.g. the first report shows an equal division of judicial opinion, the second a majority for the plaintiff. It may, however, represent a second argument, with a change of judicial opinion. Thus Walmesley and Kingsmill, J.J. now agree with Anderson, C.J. to give judgment for the plaintiff, while Warberton, J. transfers his allegiance to the defendant.

YELVERTON[66] and CROKE[66] doubted, and held that it could not; for he at his peril ought to redeem it in his time, as it is upon a mortgage. But FLEMING[66] and the others against it; for pledging doth not make an absolute property, but it is a delivery only until he pays, etc. So it is a debt unto the one and a retainer of the thing unto the other, for which there may be a re-demand at any time upon the payment of the money. For the pledge delivered is but as security for his money lent, so that he who borrows the money is to have again his pledge when he repays it, and his tender gives him interest therein. And there is a difference between mortgage of land and pledging of goods; for the mortgagee hath an absolute interest in the land, but the other hath but a special property in the goods, to detain them for his security. . . .

Secondly, it was resolved that, by this delivery of the said goods by the *feme*, with the assent of the *baron*, to the defendant, there passed no interest in them to the defendant, but (as it were) a custody only; and therefore the tender of the redemption ought to be made to the executrix and not to the defendant.

Thirdly, that when he tendered the money to the executrix, and she refused, it was as good as payment, and the special property of the goods is revested in the plaintiff. Then, when he demanded them of the defendant, and he refused to deliver them, but converted them to his own use, a *Trover and Conversion* well lies, although he came unto them by a lawful delivery and not by trover.

Wherefore it was adjudged for the plaintiff.

COKE : A BOOK OF ENTRIES[67]

f. 38d—THE DECLARATION IN FERRER'S CASE, 6 COKE. REP. f. 7a

Action sur le Case

Pur Trover

Warwickshire, s.s.—Robertus Arden alias Ardern nuper de Parkhall in comitatu predicto, armiger, attachiatus fuit ad respondendum Humfrido Ferrers, militi, Willielmo Colmer, generoso, et Willielmo Holt, generoso, de placito,

Quare, cum iidem Humfridus, Willielmus et Willielmus decimo die Junii anno regni dominæ Reginæ nunc tricesimo octavo apud Aston iuxta Birmingham in comitatu predicto possessionati fuissent de quodam bove coloris nigri pretii sex librarum ut de bove ipsorum Humfridi, Willielmi et Willielmi proprio,

et, sic inde possessionati existentes, iidem Humfridus, Willielmus et Willielmus bovem illum postea, scilicet quarto decimo die Octobris anno regni dictæ dominæ Reginæ nunc tricesimo octavo supradicto, apud Aston iuxta Birmingham predictam extra manus et possessionem suas casualiter amiserunt,

qui quidem bos postea, scilicet nono die Novembris anno supradicto apud Aston iuxta Birmingham predictam ad manus et possessionem predicti Roberti per inventionem devenit,

[66] Fleming was Chief Justice, and Yelverton and Croke Justices of the King's Bench. The other Justices were Fenner and Williams.
[67] 1st edition in 1614.

predictus tamen Robertus, sciens bovem illum fore bovem ipsorum Humfridi, Willielmi et Willielmi predictorum et ad ipsos Humfridum, Willielmum et Willielmum de iure spectare et pertinere, machinansque ipsos Humfridum, Willielmum et Willielmum de bove illo callide decipere et defraudare, bovem illum eisdem Humfrido, Willielmo et Willielmo, licet postea, scilicet vicesimo tertio die Novembris anno regni dictæ dominæ Reginæ nunc tricesimo nono, apud Aston iuxta Birmingham predictam requisitus fuit, hucusque non deliberavit,

sed bovem illum postea, scilicet tertio decimo die Decembris anno tricesimo nono supradicto, apud Aston iuxta Birmingham predictam ad usum suum proprium convertit et disposuit, ad damnum ipsorum Humfridi, Willielmi et Willielmi quadraginta librarum.

ISAACK v. CLARK

(1614) 2 BULSTRODE, 306

In an action upon the case for a trover and conversion, the plaintiff counts that 9 *Februarii, 6 Jac.,* he was possessed of a bag of money, and that 12 *Februarii,* in the same year, he lost the same; that the last day of the same February this came to the hands of the defendant; and that he, the same last day of February, did convert this to his own use: for which conversion the action was brought.

Upon *non culp.* pleaded, the jury found a special verdict. They find that one Rich. Adams did recover against one Lewis in the County Court £40. 13s. 4d. for damages; upon this a *capias ad satisfaciendum*[68] issued out against Lewis, and a return of *non est inventus*[68] by Clark the defendant, serjeant of the mace; upon which a writ of *fieri facias*[68] issued out against Watkins, one of his pledges, to be executed upon his goods, and upon this three buts of sack taken in execution. Isaack, the plaintiff, being there present, and to stay the sale of these three buts of sack so taken by virtue of this writ, the said purse and £22 in it then and there did pawn and leave *in deposito* in the hands of Clark, to the intent and purpose that he should keep the same *usque* 13 *Martii* next ensuing, being the Court-day; and this only as a pledge for the re-delivery of the said three buts of sack unto Clark upon his request, if Watkins in the interim did not obtain from Adams to·spare the levying of this execution. The jury find no request made nor that Watkins had procured the sparing of the execution; but they find the request made by the plaintiff of the defendant, to deliver the purse with the money in it, and his refusal so to do; and so do conclude that, if upon the whole matter the Court shall judge this to be a conversion, then they do find the defendant *culp.,* but if they shall adjudge this to be no conversion, then they find the defendant *non culp.*

[Judgment was given for the defendant by all the judges of the King's Bench: COKE, C.J., HAUGHTON, DODDERIDGE and CROKE, J.J.]

COKE, C.J.: [He first posed five questions[69]:

---

[68] cf. Blackstone III. 414-7. A writ of *capias ad satisfaciendum* is a species of execution against the person, whereby the debtor is to be imprisoned 'till satisfaction be made for the debt, costs and damages. . . . If a *non est inventus* is returned thereon, the plaintiff may sue out a process against the bail, if any were given. . . . The next species of execution is against the goods and chattels of the defendant, and is called a writ of *fieri facias* from the words in it where the sheriff is commanded *quod fieri faciat de bonis,* that he cause to be made of the goods and chattels of the defendant the sum or debt recovered.'

[69] At p. 311.

1. May Case on a Trover and Conversion be brought on a Bailment?
    Yes : ' the judge is not to look unto the bailment, if you can lay and well prove a conversion, which is the chief point of the action.'

2. What is recoverable in an action on the Case, the whole value of the thing, or damages for the detaining?
    ' The value of the thing, but not damages for the detaining.'

3. ' Whether the property be changed by the judgment and execution? '
    ' The property is changed.'

4. In what circumstances may a finder be guilty of a conversion?

5. ' Whether here be any conversion in this case or not? '

The judgment is concerned mainly with the last two questions.]

[70]. . . He which finds goods is bound to answer for them to him who hath the property; and if he deliver them over to any one unless it be unto the right owner, he shall be charged for them; for at the first it is in his election whether he will take them or not into his custody, but, when he hath them, one only hath then right unto them, and therefore he ought to keep them safely. If a man therefore finds goods, if he be wise, he will then search out the right owner of them and so deliver them unto him. If the owner comes unto him and demands them and he answers him that it is not known unto him whether he be the true owner of the goods or not, and for this cause he refuseth to deliver them, this refusal is no conversion, if he do keep them for him. . . . If a man finds goods, an action upon the case lieth for his ill and negligent keeping of them, but no trover and conversion, because this is but a non feasans. . . .[71] The next matter considerable is the conversion, and what shall make a conversion. As to this, there ought to be an act done to convert one thing to another, and whether a denyer only shall make a conversion, by this you will confound all form; for then, this way, every action of detinue shall be an action upon the case upon a trover, because there is a denyer. . . . If one do find goods [and] the owner demands them [and] he refuseth to deliver them, an action of detinue lieth and not an action upon the case. *In usum suum proprium convertit et disponit,* these are the words that make a conversion; and therefore it shall be very absurd if every denyer should be said to be a conversion. The party makes a request to have his goods, the other does not deliver them; it should be a hard case to make him by this to be a trespasser and subject unto an action upon the case for a trover and conversion only by his denyer to deliver them, being demanded. But there ought to be some other act done by him to make him thereby to be such a trespasser, as that *in usum suum proprium convertit et disponit.* But upon a bare refusal to deliver the goods, being demanded, no action upon the case *sur trover and conversion* lyeth for this . . . I agree that in some cases a denyer to deliver the same shall make a conversion, as if it be of money, which cannot be known from other money (as if it be out of a bag), thereupon his refusal to deliver the same, being demanded, for this an action upon the case *sur trover* lieth; but if it be for money in a bag, there, upon his denyer, no trover lyeth, but an action of detinue.[72] . . .

[70] At p. 312.
[71] At p. 313.
[72] See *Core's Case* (1537) Dyer, 20a, *infra,* p. 287.

. . . [In the case at bar the defendant] did not know whether the condition was performed or not, so this refusal is good evidence to a jury, but no good conversion in point of law. As to the verdict and the exceptions to it, which have been well and truly taken (*de inventione et conversione*), they find the defendant guilty, [but] upon the whole matter he is not guilty *de inventione*, for they do find *quod pigneravit.* Herein I agree in opinion that this finding of theirs is not material. *Ad quæstionem facti* the Judges are not to answer, *ad quæstionem iuris non iuratores*: juries are to meddle with matters of fact, but not with the matter here of a conversion; being matter in law, this is only to be determined by the Judges. I agree also in this, that, until the three buts of sack are delivered to him, the plaintiff is not to have his money . . ., and therefore he is to keep and detain the money for his satisfaction and therewith to satisfie the execution. So that in this case we do all of us agree in this, that prima facie a denyer upon a demand is a good evidence to a jury of a conversion; but if the contrary be shewed, then the same is no conversion.

And so the Judges all agreed in this case, upon the whole matter to them appearing, for the defendant and against the plaintiff, that he had no just cause of action; and according to this the judgment of the Court was pronounced and so entered, *quod quærens nil capiat per billam.*

WILBRAHAM v. SNOW

(1670), 1 Modern Reports, 30[73]

Trover and conversion—Upon issue *not guilty,* the jury find a special verdict, viz., that one Talbot recovered in an action of debt against one Wimb, and had a *fieri facias* directed to the Sheriff of Chester, whereupon the sheriff took the goods into his possession; and that, being in his possession, the defendant took them away and converted them, etc.

The sole point was whether the possession which the sheriff has of goods by him levied upon an execution is sufficient to enable him to bring an action of trover.

Winnington: I conceive the action does not lie. An action of trover and conversion is an action in the right, and two things are to be proved in it, viz., a property in the plaintiff and a conversion in the defendant. I confess that in some cases, though the plaintiff have not the absolute property of the goods, yet as to the defendant's being a wrong-doer, he may have a sufficient property to maintain the action against him. But I hold that in this case the property is not at all altered by the seizure of the goods upon a *fieri facias* (for which he cited Dyer, 98, 99,[74] and *Ayre* v. *Aden,* Yelverton, 44). This case is somewhat like that of commissioners of bankrupts. They have power to sell and grant and assign; but they cannot bring an action: their assignees must bring all actions. It is true, a sheriff in this case may bring an action of trespass, because he has possession. But trover is grounded upon the right, and there must be a property in the plaintiff to support that; whereas the sheriff takes the goods by virtue of a naked authority: as when a man deviseth that his executors shall sell his land, they have but a naked authority.

[73] The case is reported in a number of different reports—e.g. 2 Saunders, 47; 1 Levinz, 282; 1 Ventris, 52—but always inadequately. The above is the best of a poor choice.
[74] *Milton* v. *Eldrington* (1553) 1 Dyer, 98b.

PER CURIAM: The sheriff may well have an action of trover in this case. As for the case in Yelverton, 44, there the sheriff seized upon a *fieri facias;* then his office determined; then he sold the goods, and the defendant[75] brought trover. And it was holden that the property was in the defendant by reason of the determining of the sheriff's office, and because a new *fieri facias* must be taken out; for that a *venditioni exponas*[76] cannot issue to the new sheriff. They compared this case to that of a carrier, who is accountable for the goods that he receives, and may have trover or trespass at his election.

TWISDEN, J. said: The commissioners of bankrupts might have an action of trover if they did actually seize any goods of the bankrupts, as they might by law.

RAINSFORD, J. said: Let[77] the property after the seizure of goods upon an execution remain in the defendant or be transferred to the plaintiff, since the sheriff is answerable for them and comes to the possession of them by law, it is reasonable that he should have as ample remedy to recover damages for the taking of them from him, as a carrier has that comes to the possession of goods by the delivery of the party. . . .

TWISDEN, J.: I know it hath been urged several times at the assizes that a sheriff ought to have trespass and not trover; and counsel have pressed hard for a special verdict.[78]

MORETON, J.: My Lord Chief Justice Bramston said, he would never deny a special verdict while he lived, if counsel did desire it.

Judgment was given for the Plaintiff.[79]

PUTT v. ROYSTON
(1683), 2 SHOWER, 211

Trover and conversion for goods. The defendant pleads in bar *trespass* brought for the same goods, and that, upon *not guilty* pleaded, there was a verdict for the defendant. The plaintiff demurs.

There was urged *Coke's Entries, f.* 38,[80] and *Ferrer's Case,* 6 Co. 7, that, if the plea be to the action, and he be barred by judgment upon demurrer, confession or verdict in a personal action, it is a bar for ever. . . .

The case was twice argued. On the second argument: —

Saunders, for the plaintiff: A *recovery* in trespass is a bar in detinue or trover for the same thing; and the reason is because, by the damages given, the property of the goods is altered and out of the plaintiff; the recompense being given to him for them in damages. But otherwise where a man mistakes his action. . . .

Pollexfen, for the defendant: If another action of trespass had been brought, and the former trespass pleaded in bar, that would be agreed a

---

[75] i.e. the defendant in the action of debt as a result of which the goods had been seized.
[76] A writ authorizing the sale of the goods.
[77] i.e. 'whether.'
[78] i.e. in order to test the law upon the point.
[79] See the report in 1 Levinz, 282: 'It was argued . . . that the sheriff might have trespass, but not this action. But the whole Court to the contrary: the sheriff has a special property to maintain this action.'
[80] *Supra,* p. 116.

good plea. Then, supposing it so, the question is, if it be a good bar in trover? When one is bound by judgment, confession or verdict, he is bound not only in that action, but in every action of that nature. . . . Now these actions are of the same nature, and the variance is only nominal, and the coming of the goods to the defendant's hands is the main matter in both, for damages are to be recovered in both: they are more of the same nature than any two actions in the world. . . .

L.C.J. [PEMBERTON]: I take *Ferrer's Case* to be good law and not at all to be shaken; and I reckon the difference and reason to be this. Where the same evidence will maintain one or the other, there without question a bar in the one will be so in the other, as in *Ferrer's Case*; but where the evidence will not, it is otherwise. You say that trespass will lie wherever trover will. It is a manifest mistake; for trespass lies not on a bare denial, as trover will on a demand and denial. . . .

See another report, *sub. nom. Put and Hardy* v. *Rawsterne*, Sir T. Raymond, 472: —

Trover of divers goods. The defendants plead an action of Trespass *vi et armis* brought against them formerly for taking and disposing of the same goods; and upon Not Guilty pleaded, a verdict for the defendants: judgment *si actio*.

The plaintiff demurs; and adjudged for the plaintiff in this action of trover, because trover and trespass are actions sometimes of a different nature. For trover will sometimes lie where trespass *vi et armis* will not lie; as if a man hath my goods by my delivery to keep for me and I afterwards demand them and he refuses to deliver them, I may have an action of trover but not trespass *vi et armis*, because here was no tortious taking. And sometimes the case may be such that either the one or the other will lie; as where there is a tortious taking away of goods and detaining them, the party may have either trover or trespass, and in such case judgment in one action is a bar to the other. And the rule for this purpose is that, wheresoever the same evidence will maintain both the actions, there the recovery or judgment in one may be pleaded in bar of the other; but otherwise not. And so this judgment will not clash with *Ferrer's Case*, 6 Co., which is good in law; for here it is to be presumed that the plaintiffs in the first action had mistaken their action, for that they had brought a trespass *vi et armis* whereas they had no evidence to prove a wrongful taking, but only a demand and denial, and therefore the verdict passed against them in that action, and so were forced to begin in this new action of trover.

This judgment was given positively by Pemberton, Jones and myself, Dolben *hæsitante*.[81]

BUSHELL v. MILLER
(1731), 1 STRANGE, 128
At Nisi Prius

Upon the Custom-House quay there is a hut, where particular porters put in small parcels of goods if the ship is not ready to receive them when they are brought upon the quay. The porters who have a right in this hut have each particular boxes or cupboards, and as such the defendant had one.

---

[81] The Court of King's Bench consisted of Pemberton, C.J., and Jones, Raymond and Dolben, J.J.

The plaintiff, being one of the porters, puts in goods belonging to A., and lays them so that the defendant could not get to his chest without removing them. He accordingly does remove them about a yard from the place where they lay towards the door, and without returning them into their place, goes away, and the goods are lost. The plaintiff satisfies A. of the value of the goods, and brings trover against the defendant.

And upon the trial two points were ruled by the Chief Justice [PRATT].

1. That the plaintiff, having made a satisfaction to A. for the goods, had thereby acquired a sufficient property in them to maintain trover.

2. That there was no conversion in the defendant. The plaintiff, by laying his goods where they obstructed the defendant from going to his chest, was in that respect a wrong-doer. The defendant had a right to remove the goods, so that thus far he was in no fault. Then, as to the not returning the goods to the place where he found them, if this were an action of trespass perhaps it might be a doubt; but he was clear it could not amount to a conversion.

PERKINS v. SMITH

(1752), 1 WILSON, 328

In trover the jury find a special verdict, which in substance is shortly this: that upon 22 September, 1749, Hughes was possessed of the goods in the declaration as his own property and became a bankrupt that day; that the plaintiff is assignee under the commission; that upon 23 September, 1749, the defendant Smith, who is servant and riding clerk to Mr. Garroway, to whom the bankrupt was considerably indebted, went to the bankrupt's shop to try to get his master's money and found it shut up; and that the bankrupt delivered to Smith the goods in the declaration, who gave a receipt for the same in the name of his master and sold the same for his master's use.

It was objected that the action was improperly brought against the servant Smith, who acted wholly in this matter for his master; and that the conversion is found to be to the use of his master, which is the gist of an action of trover. After two arguments at the Bar, the Court gave judgment for the plaintiff.

LEE, C.J.: The point is whether the defendant is not a tort-feasor; for, if he is so, no authority that he can derive from his master can excuse him in this action.

Hughes, the bankrupt, had no right to deliver these goods to Smith. The gist of trover is the detainer or disposal of goods (which are the property of another) wrongfully; and it is found that the defendant himself disposed of them to his master's use, which his master could give him no authority to do; and this is a conversion in Smith, this disposal being his own tortious act. The act of selling the goods is the conversion, and, whether to the use of himself or another, it makes no difference. I am very well satisfied that this servant has done wrong and that no authority that could be derived from his master before or after the fact can excuse him.

The finding that the defendant disposed of the goods for his master's use is only the conclusion of the jury and does not bind the Court. The taking upon him to dispose of another's property is the tortious act and the gist of this action. Judgment for the plaintiff, *per totam curiam*.

ROSS v. JOHNSON

(1772), 5 BURROW, 2825

An action of trover was brought by Hugh Ross, Esq. against John Johnson and William Dowson for certain goods mentioned in the declaration. *Not guilty* was pleaded, and issue joined. The cause came on to be tried at Guildhall before Lord Mansfield at the sittings after Michaelmas term, 1771; when the plaintiff was nonsuited, subject to the opinion of the Court on the following case.

The goods in question, being the property of the plaintiff, were delivered by the captain of a vessel to the defendants as wharfingers, for the use and upon the account of the plaintiff, to whom they were directed; but were stolen or lost out of their possession; and afterwards, before the commencement of this action, were demanded by the plaintiff of the defendants, to whom he tendered the wharfage for the same; but the goods were not delivered to him.

The question for the opinion of the Court was, "whether this action will lie." If the Court shall be of the opinion " that this action will lie," then the nonsuit to be set aside, and a verdict entered for the plaintiff for £92 damages and 40s. costs.

Mr. Mansfield, for the plaintiff, argued that trover would lie. In trover, nothing more is necessary to be proved than the property being in the plaintiff, and that the defendant has converted them. It is not necessary to prove actual conversion. A demand and non-delivery are evidence of a conversion, and are sufficient unless the defendant can give some legal excuse for the non-delivery. The goods being stolen or lost is no excuse to a wharfinger, who takes them for hire: *Isaack v. Clark.*[52] A pawnee is bound to deliver the goods pawned.

Mr. Walker, contra, for the defendants, argued that this action of trover could not be maintained. Trover can't be maintained unless the defendant uses the plaintiff's goods as his own. Goods may be withholden by a person who has a lien upon them; and he instanced in pawns, distresses, and carriers detaining till paid for the carriage. Bare withholding is not making use of them as his own; and, without that, trover will not lie. He was not obliged, he said, to maintain " that no other action would lie ": it was enough for his purpose " that the present action will not lie." A demand and refusal is only evidence of a conversion. And trover will not lie for mere negligence, for losing the goods, without any actual wrong.

Mr. Mansfield agreed that, where a lawful reason is shown for not delivering the goods, the defendant is not to be considered as guilty of a conversion. But here is no lawful reason shown why they are not delivered; and therefore the mere non-delivery does amount to a conversion. If they are in fact lost or stolen, what is that to the owner? It does not alter the obligation which the defendants are under to deliver them to the owner; nor can the owner know what is become of them.

LORD MANSFIELD declared his disapprobation of nonsuits, founded upon objections which had no relation to the merits of a cause. But he looked upon it as established upon principles and authorities, that trover would not lie in the present case; but that it must be an action upon the case. It is impossible, he said, to make a distinction between a wharfinger and a common carrier. They both receive the goods upon a contract. Every case

[52] *Supra,* p. 117.

against a carrier is like the same case against a wharfinger; but, in order to maintain trover, there must be an injurious conversion. This is not to be esteemed a refusal to deliver the goods. They can't deliver them: it is not in their power to do it. It is a bare omission.

ASTON, WILLES and ASHURST, J.J. concurred. . . . The Court ordered that the nonsuit should stand.

GORDON v. HARPER
(1796), 7 T.R. 9

In trover for certain goods, being household furniture, a verdict was found for the plaintiff, subject to the opinion of this Court on the following case. On October 1, 1795, and from thence until the seizing of the goods by the defendant, as after mentioned, Mr. Biscoe was in possession of a mansion-house at Shoreham and of the goods in question, being the furniture of the said house, as tenant of the house and furniture to the plaintiff, under an agreement made between the plaintiff and Mr. Biscoe, for a term which at the trial of this action was not expired. The goods in question were on October 24 taken in execution by the defendant, then sheriff of the county of Kent, by virtue of a writ of *testatum fieri facias* issued on a judgment at the suit of J. Broomhead and others, executors of J. Broomhead deceased, against one Borret, to whom the goods in question had belonged, but which goods, previous to the agreement between the plaintiff and Mr. Biscoe, had been sold by Borret to the plaintiff. The defendant after the seizure sold the goods. The question is, whether the plaintiff is entitled to recover in an action of *trover*. . . .

[Counsel for the plaintiff cited *Ward* v. *Macauley* (1791), 4 T.R. 489.[83]]

LORD KENYON, C.J.: The only point for the consideration of the Court in the case of *Ward* v. *Macauley* was, whether in a case like the present the landlord could maintain an action of *trespass* against the sheriff for seizing goods, let with a house, under an execution against the tenant; and it was properly decided that no such action could be maintained. What was said further by me in that case, that trover was the proper remedy, was an extra-judicial opinion, to which upon further consideration I cannot subscribe. The true question is whether, when a person has leased goods in a house to another for a certain time, whereby he parts with the right of possession during the term to the tenant and has only a reversionary interest, he can notwithstanding recover the value of the whole property pending the existence of the term in an action of trover. The very statement of the proposition affords an answer to it. If, instead of household goods, the goods here taken had been machines used in manufacture which had been leased to a tenant, no doubt could have been made but that the sheriff might have seized them under an execution against the tenant, and the creditor would have been entitled to the beneficial use of the property during the term: the difference of the goods then cannot vary the law. . . . I forbear to deliver any opinion as to what remedy the landlord has in this case, not being at present called upon so to do: but it is clear that he cannot maintain trover.

ASHHURST, J.: I have always understood the rule of law to be that, in order to maintain trover, the plaintiff must have a right of property in

[83] See *supra*, p. 112.

the thing and a right of possession, and that unless both these rights concur the action will not lie. Now here it is admitted that the tenant had the right of possession during the continuance of his term, and consequently one of the requisites is wanting to the landlord's right of action. It is true that in the present case it is not very probable that the furniture can be of any use to any other than the actual tenant of the premises; but supposing the things leased had been manufacturing engines, there is no reason why a creditor seizing them under an execution should not avail himself of the beneficial use of them during the term.

GROSE, J.: The only question is whether trover will lie where the plaintiff had neither the actual possession of the goods taken at the time, nor the right of possession. The common form of pleading in such an action is decisive against him; for he declares that, being possessed, etc., he lost the goods; he is therefore bound to show either an actual or virtual possession. If he had a right to the possession, it is implied by law.

LAWRENCE, J.: to the same effect.

Judgment for the defendant.

ॐ 7 ॐ

DEFAMATION

BEFORE the sixteenth century the common law took little direct interest in defamation. It was not that mediæval men and women indulged the impulse to evil-speaking and uncharitableness less frequently or with more discretion than their descendants, but that their words echoed in homelier tribunals. The surviving records of the thirteenth century show the local courts hard at work to secure redress for verbal and sometimes for written licence.[1] In many instances they were concerned primarily to keep the peace against vulgar abuse or the parochial activities of the common scold;[2] but in others a plaintiff complained of injured reputation in circumstances more nearly akin to a modern action of slander or libel. Such cases were sufficiently frequent in the later years of the century to warrant, or at least to invite, the introduction of technical pleading,[3] and several claims were made for 'special damage.' Thus one plaintiff complained that the defendant, by defaming him in words to one person and by letter to another, had prevented him from renewing a lease, a second alleged the loss of a profitable bargain and a third the failure to secure a loan.[4]

The rivals of the local courts were the Courts Christian. Their jurisdiction over defamation was acknowledged in 1285 by the document called *Circumspecte Agatis,* which, though it has found a place among the Statutes of the Realm, was issued in the form of instructions to the Judges.[5]

> 'The King to the Judges, greeting. Use yourselves circumspectly in all matters concerning the Bishop of Norwich and his clergy, not punishing them if they hold pleas in Courts Christian concerning things as be meer spiritual.'

The ground upon which the judges were to walk delicately included

[1] See the Index to S.S. Vol. 2 (Select Pleas in Manorial Courts), to S.S. Vol. 18 (Borough Customs, Vol. I), to S.S. Vol. 21 (Borough Customs, Vol. II), and to S.S. Vol. 23 (Select Cases covering the Law Merchant).

[2] See the later Hereford Custumal of 1486: 'It was decided as concerning female scolds that much mischief arose in the city through such persons, to wit, quarrelling, blows, defamation, disturbance of night's rest, and strife between neighbours often thence arising. . . . Wherefore, whenever scolds shall be taken and convicted, they shall have the judgment of the cucking-stool without making any ransom. And there they shall stand with bare feet and their hair down, during such time as they may be seen by all passers-by upon the road.' (S.S. Vol. 18, pp. 79-80.) The cucking-stool was 'an instrument of punishment formerly in use for scolds, disorderly women, fraudulent tradespeople, etc., consisting of a chair (sometimes in the form of a close-stool), in which the offender was fastened and exposed to the jeers of the bystanders, or conveyed to a pond or river and ducked': *O.E.D.*

[3] e.g. *Grayling* v. *Dike* (1288) *infra*, p. 137; *Swindon* v. *Stalker* (1294), *infra*, p. 138; *Woodfool* v. *Pors*, (1295), *infra*, p. 138.

[4] *Swindon* v. *Stalker* (1294) *infra*, p. 138; *Woodfool* v. *Pors* (1295) *infra*, p. 138; and *Mor's Case* (1333), *infra*, p. 139.

[5] 13 Ed. I. See Graves, 43 *Eng. Hist. Rev.*, p. 1.

the field of defamation, as to which 'it hath been granted elsewhere that it should be tried in Court Christian, provided that money be not demanded, but the suit is prosecuted for punishment of sin.' The language of this document betrayed the uneasy relations between the ecclesiastical and the common lawyers. Each served a jealous God, whose attributes it was hard for finite intelligence to comprehend and harder to define. The sanctions available to the Courts Christian and the limits of their jurisdiction were alike uncertain. If defamation were a sin, the sinner must do penance, but the victim could not be allowed to make a profit; and the common lawyers were ready with their writs of Prohibition to prevent any attempt to award damages. The capacity of the Courts Christian to fine was more doubtful. Why should not the penance take the form of alms and oblations? A Statute of 1315 ordained that 'in Defamation the Prelates shall correct in manner abovesaid [by penance], the King's Prohibition notwithstanding; first injoyning a Penance Corporal, which, if the offender will redeem, the Prelate may freely receive the money, though the King's Prohibition be shewed.'[6] The scope of the ecclesiastical jurisdiction remained in dispute throughout the middle ages. The common lawyers might not understand the meaning of sin, but they did know a crime when they saw it; and they insisted at least upon the negative rule that the Courts Christian should not meddle with any matter for which the common law provided a remedy. Thus, in the early years of the fourteenth century, defendants who had been acquitted on indictment were tempted to cite before the Courts Christian the grand jurors who had presented them. This attempt, under the name of defamation, to ignore the writ of Conspiracy and to anticipate the tort of malicious prosecution was too palpable an encroachment upon the common law and was restrained by a Statute of 1327.[7] But it was rare for the issue to be so clearly presented. The hapless litigant had more often to run the gauntlet of the rival weapons of Prohibition, of Excommunication and of Contempt before he could learn to which, if either, of the courts he should have applied.[8] The Judges did little more than indicate the extent of the ecclesiastical powers by determining the limits of their own. The jurisdictions were mutually exclusive, and 'things spiritual' could be defined only as the antithesis of 'things temporal.' In 1497 the King's Bench discussed at length the propriety of Prohibition where a woman had been cited before a Church Court for slander. Chief Justice Fineux gave a number of instances in which the writ would lie, 'but here in the case at bar,' he said, 'it is quite otherwise; for the case of defama-

---

[6] *Articuli Cleri*, 9 Ed. II, Stat. 1, c. 4.
[7] 1 Ed. III, Stat. 2, c. 11.
[8] See the *Case of the Abbot of St. Alban's* (1482) Y.B. 22 Ed. 4, f. 20, pl. 47, and f. 29, pl. 9: Holdsworth, H.E.L. III, 410-1, and Plucknett, *Concise History* (4th ed.), p. 462.

tion is wholly a spiritual offence . . . and not determinable at the common law.'[9]

A single species of defamation was made criminal by Parliament. It was provided by chapter 34 of the Statute of Westminster the First[10] that,

> 'Forasmuch as there have been oftentimes found in the country devisers of tales whereby discord or occasion of discord has many times arisen between the king and his people or great men of this realm, for the damage that hath and may therefor ensue it is commanded that from henceforth none be so hardy to cite or publish any false news or tales whereby discord or occasion of discord or slander may grow between the king and his people or the great men of the realm; and he that doth so shall be taken and kept in prison until he hath brought him into the court which was the first author of the tale.'

The statute was re-enacted in 1378, when the 'great men' or 'magnates' were defined, and again in 1388 when the punishment of offenders was entrusted to the Council.[11] The offence of *Scandalum Magnatum*, thus created, is little more than a historical curiosity. It was imagined as a political weapon, it was put into the hands of the Council rather than of the common lawyers, and it was seldom used. Coke recalled 'two notable records' which may be relevant: the case of Adam de Ravensworth who was convicted in 1337 of calling Richard of Snowshall 'Roy de Raveners,' and that of John of Northampton who complained in 1345 of the indolence of His Majesty's judges.[12] A third may be cited from the Rolls of Parliament for 1384, when John Cavendish, a London fishmonger, was convicted of falsely accusing the Chancellor, Michael de la Pole, of taking a bribe of £40, three yards of scarlet cloth and a load of herring, sturgeon and other fish, delivered free at his house.[13] With these exceptions the Statutes, at least until the troubles of the Tudor succession, remained an empty threat.[14]

The position at the beginning of the sixteenth century thus left much to be desired. The local courts, once so lively an arena, were in decay. The Courts Christian, though their powers were still unimpaired, could act only within ill-defined but comparatively narrow limits and could not award damages. The common law, quick to resent encroachment, offered no positive remedy. Attempts had, indeed, been made in the reign of Edward IV to use Trespass *sur le*

[9] *Anon*, Y.B. 12 Hen. 7, f. 22, pl. 2.
[10] 3 Ed. I (A.D. 1275).
[11] 2 Rich. II, Stat. 1, c. 3, and 12 Rich. II, c. 11.
[12] Coke, *Third Institute*, 174. It is possible, indeed, that the second of these cases is not a case of *Scandalum Magnatum* at all: see H.E.L. III, pp. 392 and 409.
[13] 3 Rot. Par. 168-170.
[14] They were re-enacted in 1554 and in 1559, and a few cases were decided upon them: but the Star Chamber, when it developed a crime of libel, struck out a new line for itself. *Infra*, p. 131: and see Plucknett, *Concise History* (4th ed.), pp. 456-458, and Holdsworth, H.E.L. III, p. 409, n. 8.

cas where a defendant had attacked the plaintiff's status as a freeholder and claimed him as his villein.   But even where the slander thus closely affected the rights of property, it was admitted to be without redress unless accompanied by assault or, at the very least, by the threat of assault.   ' There are divers cases in our law where a man has *dampnum absque injuria,*' said the Court in 1478, and defamation, of whatever nature, was among them.[15]

A new and material age was not likely to be content with empty maxims, and the evolution of Case as a generic form of action offered the opportunity of experiment even where no basic analogy existed. It was not unnatural that the first actions on the case should concern those accusations of crime which the common law had banned from the Courts Christian without admitting them to its own.   In 1535 and in 1536 two successful actions were brought for accusing the plaintiff of theft,[16] and, in the latter year, a reporter judged it profitable to offer, as a novelty, an elaborate specimen of a writ in which £100 damages were claimed for proclaiming the plaintiff ' thief and larcener.'[17]   Once admitted, actions on the case for words multiplied apace.   It was not so much, as Chief Justice Wray lamented, that ' the intemperance and malice of men had increased,'[18] as that thin skins and offended susceptibilities might now be capitalised.   These new developments required the common lawyers to re-state their relations with the Courts Christian and to offer some deterrent to predatory litigation, and the dual task demanded a nice and not uncongenial discrimination.   To call a man ' heretic ' or ' adulterer ' was ' merely spiritual '; to call him ' thief ' or ' murderer ' or ' traitor ' supported an action on the case; to call him ' knave ' or ' villain ' was to indulge idle words without peril in this world or the next.[19]   By 1585 the

[15] *Browne* v. *Hawkins* (1478) Y.B. 17 Ed. 4, f. 3, pl. 2, *infra*, p. 139; and see Y.B. Pasch. 2 Ed. 4, f. 5, pl. 10 (1462).

[16] Y.B. 26 Hen. 8, Hil. f. 9, pl. 1, and Y.B. 27 Hen. 8, Trin. f. 22, pl. 17.   In the latter case the defendant argued unsuccessfully that as the sheep, which it was alleged the plaintiff had stolen, were not declared to be worth one shilling, this was but petty larceny, and, if a felony, not such as involved loss of life, and therefore that no action lay for so miserable an accusation.

[17] Y.B. 27 Hen. 8, f. 11, pl. 27: *infra*, p. 141.

[18] *Stanhope* v. *Blyth* (1585) 4 Coke Rep. 15a, *infra*, p. 142.

[19] Cf. *Anon* (1536) 27 Hen. 8, f. 14, pl. 4 and *Anon* (1561) Moore, Case 92, p. 29, *infra*, p. 142.   The jurisdiction of the ecclesiastical courts was invoked well into the eighteenth century; see a case in the Archdeacon's Court of Exeter as late as 1788— *Carslake* v. *Mapledoram*, 2 T.R. 473.   The distinctions drawn were sometimes ludicrous.   Thus in *Achery* v. *Barton* (1705) 2 Salkeld, 693, it was resolved, after long argument, that to say of a woman that she was a ' brandy-nosed whore ' charged incontinence rather than intemperance and was therefore a fit subject for spiritual redress.   Henry Consett, in his book on ' The Practice of the Spiritual or Ecclesiastical Courts,' published in 1685, explained how the Penance, enjoined by the ecclesiastical court for the defamation, was to be done (at pp. 343-4).   'If the defamatory words were uttered in a publick place, then the Penance is to be done publickly; though it is wont to be done in the Parish Church of the party defamed in time of Divine Service in presence of the party. . . .   But if these defamatory words are uttered in a private place, then the Penance is to be done in the house of the party defamed or in the house of some honest neighbour, and the said Penance is wont to be enjoined on this manner: the party defaming must say

judges realised that, if they were not to be overwhelmed by trumpery actions, they must adopt a deliberate policy of repression, and in *Stanhope* v. *Blyth* they declared that they would allow no redress for mere abuse and that, if the words complained of were ambiguous, they would give the defendant the benefit of the doubt. ' Actions for scandals should not be maintained by any strained construction or argument, nor any favour given to support them.'[20]

The words sufficient to maintain an action were grouped into three classes.[21] The first, as chronology demanded, concerned criminal charges. The plaintiff must prove the express allegation of a specific offence, and the defendant was allowed every technical advantage. It was not actionable to say of a plaintiff that he had ' stolen half an acre of corn,' since it was not alleged that the corn had already been cut and there could be no larceny of standing crops; nor that he had ' burnt the defendant's barn,' unless it could be shown that the barn was parcel of a dwelling-house.[22] Perhaps the most pleasing example of judicial indulgence is afforded by the case of *Holt* v. *Astgrigg*.[23] An action was brought for the words, ' Sir Thomas Holt struck his cook on the head with a cleaver and cleaved his head; the one part lay on the one shoulder and another part on the other.' The defendant argued that, as it was not expressly averred that the cook was dead, no precise offence had been charged, and the Court accepted the argument. ' Slander ought to be direct, against which there may not be any intendment. But here, notwithstanding such wounding, the party may yet be living, and it is then but trespass.' The second class comprised imputations of unfitness for some particular trade, profession or office. An attorney thus succeeded in 1585 on an allegation of corrupt practice. ' The said words,' it was declared, ' scandalise him in the duty of his profession, by which he gets his living.'[24] While the legal profession might expect protection, a word so comprehensive as ' office ' required interpretation, and it is not surprising that an unpaid justice of the peace should at one time be brought within

---

publickly, that, in saying such and such words, he hath defamed the plaintiff, and therefore he must first beg pardon of the Almighty and then of the party defamed for uttering these words.' If the defendant should refuse to do Penance, he must be excommunicated.

[20] *Stanhope* v. *Blyth* (1585) 4 Coke Rep. 15a, *infra*, p. 142. See also Coke, C.J. in *Crofts* v. *Brown* (1609) 3 Bulstrode, 167: ' We will not give more favour unto actions upon the case for words than of necessity we ought to do, where the words are not apparently scandalous, these actions being now too frequent.' The repeated judicial denunciations suggest that the methods of repression were not wholly effective.

[21] There were one or two isolated additions; e.g. imputations of disease calculated to cause the plaintiff's society to be shunned. See *James* v. *Rutledge* (1599), Moore, 573; 4 Coke Rep. 17a.

[22] *Castleman* v. *Hobbs* (1595) Moore, 396, and *Barham* v. *Nethersole* (1602) 4 Coke Rep. 20a.

[23] (1607) Croke, Jac. 184.

[24] *Birchley's Case* (1585) 4 Coke Rep. 16a. The barrister did not obtain similar redress until 1611: *Bestney* v. *Dyson*, 13 Coke Rep. 71.

its scope and at a later date excluded.[25] But at least the generalisation had been framed and admitted by 1602.[26] If a case did not fall within these two classes, a plaintiff had yet a third chance of success. He was allowed to prove that the defendant's words, otherwise irreproachable, had caused him material loss. If by the accusation of incontinency a woman had missed a good marriage or forfeited a lease, or if the charge of heresy had cost a parson his preferment, this 'special damage' deserved a temporal remedy and enabled the common law to rescue lucrative causes from the cold comfort of the spiritual courts.[27]

By the death of Elizabeth the judges had recognized and gone far to define the civil action of defamation. Reasons of state induced a parallel process in the criminal law. The Star Chamber, partly upon the venerable, if vague, pattern of *Scandalum Magnatum,* but chiefly by its own intrinsic authority, was evolving the offence of libel. Recurrent political crises, aggravated by the new powers of the press, stimulated a precocious activity, particularly at the close of the reign. Hudson, in his book on the Star Chamber, observed with pious exaggeration that 'in all ages libels have been severely punished in this court, but most especially they began to be frequent about 42 and 43 Elizabeth, when Sir Edward Coke was her attorney-general.'[28] Coke was never remiss to discharge the task of prosecution, and in 1606 his report of the case *De Libellis Famosis* summarised the aims and powers of the Court.[29] The defendant was accused of 'composing and publishing an infamous libel in verse, by which John, Archbishop of Canterbury (a prelate of singular piety, gravity and learning) now dead, . . . and Richard, Archbishop of Canterbury, who now is, were traduced and scandalized.' It was resolved that the law of God, revealed in the Old Testament, no less than the law of man, required the punishment of libels, whether upon the quick or the dead and whether upon public or private persons. Attacks upon the former scandalized the Government in Church or State, and upon the latter

---

[25] In *Stuckley* v. *Bulhead* (1602) 4 Coke Rep. 16a, a justice of the peace was allowed to sue on the ground that improper conduct might 'put him out of the commission'; but in *Bill* v. *Neal* (1663) 1 Levinz, 52, it was ruled that no action lay against a defendant, who said of a magistrate that he was 'a fool and an ass and a beetle-headed justice,' because 'words which sound in disability only are not actionable except they are spoken of one who gains his living by that thing wherein the words do disable him.' But it was agreed 'that the defendant deserved to be bound to his good behaviour for his sauciness to a magistrate.'

[26] *Brittridge's Case* (1602) 4 Coke Rep. 18b, *infra,* p. 145.

[27] *Davis* v. *Gardiner* (1593) 4 Coke Rep. 16b, *infra,* p. 144. See, for the eighteenth century law, Blackstone, III, 124: 'With regard to words that do not thus apparently and upon the face of them import such defamation as will of course be injurious, it is necessary that the plaintiff should aver some particular damage to have happened; which is called laying his action with a *per quod.*'

[28] *Hudson on the Star Chamber,* p. 100. On his life and treatise, see H.E.L. V. 164-6. He was called to the Bar in 1605, practised chiefly in the Star Chamber and died in 1635.

[29] 5 Coke Rep. 125a. For a general account of the Star Chamber's jurisdiction in Libel, see Holdsworth, H.E.L. V. 205-212, and Plucknett, *Concise History* (4th ed.), pp. 458-461.

less directly, but none the less gravely, threatened the general peace by provoking the victims to take the law into their own hands. ' Even Job, that mirror of patience, became *quodammodo* impatient when libels were made of him.' Proceedings might be taken, it was added, either in the Star Chamber or by indictment at the common law. In a review of these contemporary developments it is tempting to speak of a crime of libel and a tort of slander, and such terms reflect not unfairly the bias of each jurisdiction. But there were cases in which the Star Chamber punished words and the Common Law gave compensation for writing, and Libel and Slander must not yet be accepted as terms of art.[30]

On the abolition of the Star Chamber the common lawyers, as its residuary legatees, re-examined the relations between the crime and the tort of defamation. On the one hand, they refused to allow a prosecution for speech as opposed to writing: 'to encourage indictments for words would make them as uncertain as actions for words are.'[31] On the other hand they distinguished two branches of their tort, to which the names Libel and Slander became technically appropriate. It was ruled by Sir Matthew Hale in 1668 that a plaintiff might sue for written words which, if spoken, would not be actionable without proof of special damage,[32] and the ruling, after argument by eminent counsel, was repeated in 1684.[33] For the next hundred years the law remained in a curious state of suspended animation. No case was reported where the distinction was denied,[34] but on the few occasions when it was brought to their notice, the judges received it with reluctance and found evident difficulty in explaining it. Sir Matthew Hale saw more malice in the written than in the spoken word;[35] Mr. Justice Gould felt it hard to deny an action for conduct admitted to be criminal;[36] while in *Harman* v. *Delany*[37] the court stressed the ' diffusive effect of a libel in a publick newspaper.' Academic jurists of the eighteenth century treated the distinction with indifference. Wood, in the ninth edition of his Institutes, condescended to notice it,[38] but Blackstone ignored it. ' What was said with regard to words spoken will also hold in every particular with regard to libels by printing or writing and

---

[30] In *Broughton's Case* (1583) Moore, 141, the King's Bench upheld a verdict of £300 damages for a letter written by the Bishop of Coventry, and in *Dalton* v. *Heydon* (1632) Cases in the Star Chamber, 71, the Court declared that ' a libel may be by word as well as in writing.'

[31] Per Holt, C.J. in *Reg.* v. *Langley* (1704) 6 Mod. 125.

[32] *King* v. *Lake,* Hardres, 470.

[33] *Austin* v. *Culpepper* (1684) 2 Shower, 313: *infra,* p. 146.

[34] In *Bell* v. *Stone* (1798) 1 B. & P. 331, Macdonald, C.B. ruled against it, but, on further argument, the Court ' expressed themselves clearly that any words, written and published, throwing contumely on the party, were actionable.'

[35] *King* v. *Lake* (1668) Hardres, 470.

[36] *Villers* v. *Monsley* (1769) 2 Wilson, 403.

[37] (1731) 2 Strange, 898: Fitzgibbon, 122, 253.

[38] *Institutes,* 9th ed., Book IV. Chap. IV., at p. 554. This edition was published in 1763.

the civil actions consequent thereon."[39]   It was not until the case of
Thorley v. *Lord Kerry* in 1812 that it was finally confirmed by Sir
James Mansfield, C.J., as a canon of the common law.[40]   No judge
could have reached a conclusion with less enthusiasm. He exposed the
sophistries by which it had been excused and discovered no alternative
basis of support, but he had to allow that the chain of authority, however slender, was too long to be broken. Its original reception and
the subsequent fitful attempts at rationalisation present as a whole a
phenomenon by no means without interest. It is difficult in retrospect to deny the influence of the criminal law, but it was an influence
felt rather than understood and rather endured than exploited. The
first decisions were taken almost without premeditation and certainly
without foresight, and they survived because criticism was mobilised
only when it was too late. The phenomenon is not unique in legal
history, and the results have rarely been happy.

The means available to rebut a prima facie case of defamation
were not elaborated until late in the history of the common law. The
idea of justification, indeed, was inherent in the nature of the action.
The plaintiff sued for injury to his good name, and he must fail if it
could be shown that he did not deserve it. The point was taken in
the earliest cases and was a contributory factor in the persistent efforts
of the judges to distinguish temporal and spiritual offences: they could
appreciate the truth in the one case but not in the other.[41]   It was
also inevitable that the question should be raised of repetition as
opposed to origination of a slander.   In 1535 the defendant had
accused the plaintiff of stealing sheep, and the court rejected his plea
that such was ' the common voice and fame of the countryside.'[42]
While a defendant was not to escape under cover of common gossip,
his position might be happier if he not only claimed to be repeating
with accuracy the statement of another but identified his informant.
This additional fact was pleaded before the Star Chamber in 1613,
and the Court was of opinion that, while it was no defence to a
charge of *Scandalum Magnatum,* it might afford matter of justification
in an action on the case, since the victim would then have his remedy
against the originator.[43]   The opinion was sustained so late as 1796
and was not finally repudiated until 1829.[44]   But although, or perhaps
because, the judges were thus forced to discuss the truth of the allega-

---

[39] Commentaries, III. 126. But see Comyns, Digest, *tit. Libel.*
[40] 4 Taunton, 355; *infra*, p. 149.
[41] *Anon* (1535) Y.B. 26 Hen. 8, Hil. f. 9, and *Anon* (1536) 27 Hen. 8, f. 14, pl. 4, *infra,*
p. 141. See also *Lucas* v. *Cotton* (1566) Moore, p. 79, where the defendant stated
facts to support his words that ' George Lucas is a false knave and worthy to stand
upon the pillory,' and the Court held that there was ' bon justification.'
[42] *Anon* (1535) Y.B. 26 Hen. 8, Hil. f. 9.
[43] *Earl of Northampton's Case* (1613) 12 Coke Rep. 132. The offence of Scandalum
Magnatum was originally directed against repetition: *supra*, p. 128.
[44] Cf. *Davis* v. *Lewis* (1796) 7 T.R. 171, and *McPherson* v. *Daniels* (1829) 10 B. & C.
269.

tions in their endeavour to define the tort itself, it was not until the eighteenth century that justification was separated from the initial case made by the plaintiff and particularised as an individual defence. In 1743 a full meeting of the judges was called to consider an earlier ruling of Chief Justice Holt that the truth might be offered without notice in mitigation of damages, and it was resolved that henceforth matter of justification must be specially pleaded.[45] So in *J'anson* v. *Stuart* the plaintiffs sued for a libel in the Morning Post alleging them to be swindlers, and the defendant simply pleaded that in truth they were. The plaintiffs demurred that the plea was too general and the demurrer was upheld. A defendant, if he sought to justify, ' must be prepared with the facts which constitute the charge in order to maintain the plea, and he ought to state those facts specifically, to give the plaintiff an opportunity of denying them; for the plaintiff cannot come to the trial prepared to justify his whole life.'[46]

The history of Privilege, if still more belated, was akin to that of Justification. It was ruled in 1585 and again in 1591 that no action would lie for a statement made, by whatever person and with whatever motive, in the course of legal proceedings. But the immunity was conceived, not as the special defence of an individual in peculiar circumstances, but as an obvious and necessary incident in the administration of justice. ' If actions should be permitted in such cases, those who had just cause for complaint would not dare to complain for fear of infinite vexation,' and therefore, if occurring in ' the course of justice, no action lies although the matter is merely false.'[47] The business of Parliament might seem to warrant, only less urgently, a similar indulgence; but the bitterness of politics combined with professional jealousy to postpone the acceptance of the analogy. It was not until after the Restoration that the judges admitted that papers printed for a Committee of Parliament were beyond the scope of their scrutiny.[48] Between such cases of absolute, and those comprised within the modern designation of qualified, privilege, there is little in common but their name, and the gulf fixed in time is as wide. Lord Mansfield was the first to suggest that a defendant might deserve a special, if conditional, protection in the conduct of private life. A master, he said, was not liable ' for giving the true character ' of his former servant, ' unless there should be extraordinary circumstances

---

[45] *Underwood* v. *Parks* (1743) 2 Strange, 1200, reversing the ruling of Holt, C.J. at *nisi prius* in *Smithies* v. *Harrison* (1701) 1 Ld. Raym. 727. See also *Smith* v. *Richardson* (1737) Willes, 24.

[46] (1787) 1 T.R. 748. But, while justification thus became a special plea, its *raison d'être* remained unaltered. So Blackstone, III. 125: ' If I can prove the tradesman a bankrupt, the physician a quack, the lawyer a knave, and the divine a heretic, this will destroy their respective actions; for, though there may be damage sufficient accruing from it, yet, if the fact be true, it is *damnum absque injuria.*'

[47] *Cutler* v. *Dixon* (1585) 4 Coke Rep. 14b, and *Buckley* v. *Wood* (1591) 4 Coke Rep. 14b: *infra*, p. 143.

[48] *Lake* v. *King* (1669), 1 Levinz, 240: 1 Wms. Saunders, 120, 131.

of express malice.' The suggestion, first made obiter in 1769, was adopted as the *ratio decidendi* of *Weatherston* v. *Hawkins* in 1786, but the language of the judgments was far from happy.[49] In his earlier impromptu Lord Mansfield failed to distinguish Justification, where the defendant maintains that his words are true, and Privilege, where he admits them to be false, and, although counsel in the later case emphasised the distinction, it was not clearly proclaimed by the court.

The development of the defence, thus clumsily introduced, was hindered by a second cause of confusion. Lord Mansfield had spoken of ' extraordinary circumstances of express malice ' and Mr. Justice Buller of the plaintiff's need to prove the words ' malicious as well as false.'[50] The lawyer has often been tempted to think that, if he could withdraw his language, if not his doctrine, from popular contamination, he might yet become a scientist. It is at least certain that few words have proved a more potent source of confusion than that of ' malice.' It was a familiar term of opprobrium in most actions on the case and notably in defamation, and familiarity bred an early contempt. In *Mercer* v. *Sparks* in 1586 the defendant objected to its omission from the plaintiff's declaration, but the court thought it sufficed that the ' words themselves were malicious and slanderous.'[51] The word, as used by the plaintiff, was no more than an impolite fiction and need not be proved. But its implications were not so easily exorcised. The indolence or timidity of pleaders retained it in their vocabulary, and, when in the eighteenth century it became identified in vulgar speech with malevolence, the authority of *Mercer* v. *Sparks* was temporarily impaired. It was said in the Exchequer Chamber in 1737 that malice was the gist of the action and that evidence was admissible to ' prove the manner and occasion of speaking the words ' so as to shew that they were spoken without it.[52] The statement was made *obiter* and was not developed in later cases; but that the term was used loosely and without reflection appears from Blackstone's Commentaries. After discussing the scope of slander he adds, ' Words of heat and passion, as to call a man rogue and rascal, if productive of no ill consequence and not of any of the dangerous species before-mentioned, are not actionable; neither are words spoken in a friendly manner, as by way of advice, admonition or concern, without any tincture or circum-

---

[49] *Hargrave* v. *Le Breton* (1769) 4 Burr. 2422, at p. 2425, and *Weatherston* v. *Hawkins* (1786) 1 T.R. 110: *infra*, p. 147.

[50] *Ibid.*

[51] Owen, 51.

[52] *Smith* v. *Richardson*, Willes, 24. The plaintiff had been ' beer butler of the College of Christ Church in Oxford,' but had been dismissed because the defendant had accused him of stealing his beer. The trial judge refused to allow evidence of the truth of the allegation to be given on the general issue, but reserved the point for the consideration of all the judges. His refusal was upheld by eight judges to four. The scope and meaning of 'malice' was thus not the *ratio decidendi* of the case; and the words cited above are contained in the reasons for their view of the principal matter given by the four judges in the minority.

stance of ill will: for, in both these cases, they are not *maliciously* spoken, which is part of the definition of slander.'[53]   In the first of these instances the word is only a compendium to indicate the technical limits of the action, in the second it is given its popular connotation; and Blackstone himself seems unaware of the transference of his thought.

It is not surprising, therefore, that in the new context of Qualified Privilege the ambiguity, hitherto latent and comparatively innocuous, should have become virulent.   Judicial definition, however, requires the previous accumulation of adequate material.   It was not until 1825 that Mr. Justice Bayley clarified the law by recognizing 'two descriptions of malice,' to which, perhaps unfortunately, he attached the two titles 'malice in law' and 'malice in fact.'   The first was technically a part of the plaintiff's case, but was meaningless.   The second imposed a real burden upon him where he sought to overcome an otherwise staunch defence of Qualified Privilege, and it could be discharged by showing that the defendant was actuated by some motive other than the discharge of the duty or the protection of the interest for which alone the privilege was accorded.[54]

The latest of the defences to emerge from the struggles of litigants to avoid the consequence of their words was that of Fair Comment. It appeared at the close of the eighteenth and the beginning of the nineteenth centuries as an attempt to discipline literary and dramatic criticism.   Three *nisi prius* cases are of especial interest.   In the first, the defendant in his newspaper had attacked the conduct of the plaintiff's music-hall.[55]   Lord Kenyon admitted as his premise the liberty of the press, but qualified the admission by a familiar if unfortunate phrase.   The liberty must be used 'fairly and without malice': if the comment were 'malevolent or exceeding the bounds of fair opinion,' it would be actionable.   To say that the criticism must not 'exceed the bounds of fair opinion' was merely to re-state the question: to say that it must not be 'malevolent' was to assume the identity of 'malice' and 'ill-will.'   The other two cases were tried by Lord Ellenborough in 1808.   In *Tabart* v. *Tipper*[56] the plaintiff was a publisher of children's books, and the defendant in a review had

---

[53] Commentaries, III. 125.
[54] *Bromage* v. *Prosser* (1825) 4 B. & C. 247, *infra*, p. 151. See also *Hooper* v. *Truscott* (1836) 3 Bing. N.C. 457, where the defendant, suspecting that the plaintiff had stolen goods from him, accused him to his relations. The plaintiff sued him in defamation and the defendant pleaded privilege.   The jury was satisfied that the defendant's object was not to promote a proper inquiry but to induce the relatives to purchase his silence.   It was held that the absence of personal spite did not preclude a finding of malice.
[55] *Dibdin* v. *Swan* (1793) 1 Espinasse, 28.   Charles Dibdin, the plaintiff, was a most prolific author and composer, and, besides many plays and operas, wrote over 900 songs, of which the most celebrated is *Tom Bowling*. Espinasse, the reporter, did not enjoy a high reputation.   Chief Baron Pollock, when counsel cited him, is said to have answered, 'Espinasse! Oh, yes, he was that deaf old reporter who heard one half of a case and reported the other half.'
[56] 1 Campbell, 347.

detected immoral tendencies. Lord Ellenborough proclaimed free criticism as the foundation alike of ' purity of taste and morals, the truth of history and the advancement of science,' and directed the attention of the jury to the presence or absence of malice. ' The main question here is *quo animo* the defendant printed the article—whether he meant to put down a nuisance to public morals or to prejudice the plaintiff.' In *Carr* v. *Hood*[57] he took advantage of a preliminary argument with counsel to enlarge his views. Towards the definition of malice, indeed, he did no more than demand express proof of its existence and refuse to infer it merely from the severity of the criticism. But he drew two lines beyond which the defendant was not to pass. First, if he made assertions, they must be fact and not fiction: a comment based upon a lie could not be fair. Secondly, he must confine his remarks to the matter of public interest which alone should properly have excited them, and he must not attack private life under the cover of literary criticism.

These three cases raised, perhaps, as many questions as they answered. The meaning of ' malice ' still awaited Mr. Justice Bayley's clarification, and it remained to the Victorian judges to examine, if not to elucidate, the relation of Fair Comment to Privilege.[58] But it is at least fair to say that the potentialities of the defence were no sooner realised than exploited, and that it is upon the principles indicated by Lord Ellenborough that the modern law has developed.

S O U R C E S

GRAYLING v. DIKE

S.S. Vol. 2, p. 109

A.D. 1288

Manor Court of King's Ripton[59]

Hugh Grayling complains of John Dike for that the said John defamed him by calling him thief and accused him of other enormities (*defamavit ipsum vocando furem et alia enormia ei intulit*) on the Friday next after the feast of St. Scholastica last past against the peace and to the damage of the said Hugh one half-mark.

And John comes and denies, etc., and says that he did not defame him nor did he accuse him of other enormities to his damage, etc. (*et Johannes venit et defendit, etc. et dicit quod ipsum non defamavit nec alia enormia ei intulit ad dampnum, etc.*); and he desires that this may be inquired of according to the custom of the manor. And Hugh does the like.

---

[57] 1 Campbell, 355, note: *infra*, p. 148.
[58] Cf. *Campbell* v. *Spottiswoode* (1863) 3 B. & S. 769 and *Henwood* v. *Harrison* (1872) L.R. 7 C.P. 606. The relations of the two defences can hardly yet be said to be finally settled: see Salmond on Torts, 10th ed., pp. 419-421, and Winfield on Torts, 4th ed., pp. 281-2.
[59] A manor of the Abbot of Ramsey.

The jurors say that John defamed the said Hugh in such wise as Hugh alleges against him to his damage, etc. Therefore it is considered that the said John be in mercy for his trespass (*pro transgressione in misericordia*) and that the said Hugh do recover his damages, etc. The damages are remitted except 6d., for which Nicholas Newman and Ivo Walter's son are pledges.

SWINDON v. STALKER
S.S. VOL. 2, p. 116
A.D. 1294
MANOR COURT OF KING'S RIPTON

Henry of Swindon complains of John Stalker for that he on the Saturday next before the . . . of St. Mary last past came to Margery wife of Nicholas Hall and there defamed the said Henry by saying that he was a thief, a seducer and a manslayer and other grievous things, and said that he, Henry, slew his son Nicholas, who really is still living; and, not content with this, on the Sunday following sent a letter to Sir Roger of Ashridge, clerk of our lord the king and rector of the church of King's Ripton, in which he violently defamed him by the said words and other enormities written in the said letter (*violenter defamavit per verba predicta et alia enormia in predicta littera scripta*), adding that he was not fit to dwell in the vill of King's Ripton nor in any other vill because he is a manslayer and slew his son Nicholas, who in fact is alive; for which cause the said Sir Roger cut off three years from the term which he [Henry] has in the church of King's Ripton by lease from the said Roger,[60] to his detriment 30s. and to his grave damage 20s. (*ad detrimentum suum triginta solidorum et ad grave damnum viginti solidorum*), and that this is true he produces suit. . . .'

WOODFOOL v. PORS
S.S. VOL. 23, p. 71
A.D. 1295
FAIR COURT OF ST. IVES

Robert Woodfool complains of Robert Pors, for that, whereas on Monday last he [Woodfool] was in the vill of St. Ives in front of the house of John Poke, the said Robert Pors came there and insulted him with vile words (*insultavit ipsum turpibus verbis*), calling him thief and faithless merchant, by which defamation he lost credit until the following Michaelmas for three quarters of wheat, which a certain Simon Ginnel was to have delivered to the said Robert Woodfool, to his great damage a half-mark.

The said Robert Pors is present and denies all word for word and wages his law (*defendit totum de verbo ad verbum et est ad legem*); pledges of his law, Henry Lewine and Hugh King. And Robert Woodfool puts in his place William of Fulletby.

Afterwards the said Robert Pors came and failed in his law, for that he came three-handed when he ought to have come six-handed.

[60] Maitland, as editor, notes: 'perhaps Henry was a vicar to whom the church was leased. It will be noticed that his plea with its allegation of special damage raises a question much debated in these later days; see *Vicars* v. *Wilcox* in Smith's Leading Cases [1803, 8 East, 1].'

Therefore he is in mercy 6d., and the damages are taxed at 12d., of which half is given to the clerk of the court. Pledges of both, Henry Lewine and Hugh King.

MOR'S CASE
A.D. 1333[61]
COUNTY COURT OF BEDFORD

John, son of Robert atte Mor of Ampthill, senior, complains of John, son of Ralph atte Mor of Ampthill, by a plea of trespass. William le Taillour and John, son of Robert atte Mor, junior, are pledges for prosecuting.[62]

And the aforesaid John, son of Ralph, is attached to answer by John Herm and Maur de Ronhale. And thereupon the aforesaid John, son of Robert, complains that the aforesaid John, son of Ralph, on [February 5, 1332] Wednesday next after the feast of the Purification of the Blessed Mary in the sixth year of the present King Edward at Ampthill called this same John son of Robert a false and faithless fellow; whereby the same John son of Robert lost credit with John de Morteyn concerning forty shillings which he would have borrowed of him, from the said Wednesday until [March 26, 1332] Thursday after the feast of the Annunciation of the Blessed Mary next following, whereby he says that he has suffered loss to the damage of twenty shillings and more, and thereof he brings his suit.

And the aforesaid John, son of Ralph, comes and denies all tort and force and whatever, etc., and denies that he is in anywise guilty thereof. And of this he is ready to make his law. And he is at his law. Pledges for his law: Richard Tyvill and William Archier.

BROWNE v. HAWKINS
Y.B. 17 ED. 4, TRIN. f. 3, pl. 2
A.D. 1478

Thomas Browne brought an action *sur son cas* against one Hawkins for that, whereas the said Thomas Browne was of good fame and condition, the said Hawkins had on such a day and in such a place claimed him as his villein, and with force and arms (*vi et armis*) lay in the way to take and imprison him and to treat him as his villein, whereby he knew not how to go about his business. And he had judgment to recover damages because he was free and of free estate. And now the said Hawkins sued a writ of Error in the King's Bench.

Wood: It seems to me that the judgment should be reversed, for the matter is not sufficient in itself to maintain the action. For I take for one argument that a man shall not have an action for a thing which depends solely on the intent of another person, for this cannot properly be tried; as if I should say that I would break down your house, and then I come near to your house but do nothing, you will not have an action, and yet perchance my intent was to do as I said before. *E fortiori* in the case at bar,

---

[61] Text and translation by Professor Plucknett in *The County Court*, 42 H.L.R. 639, at pp. 668-9.
[62] Professor Plucknett notes that ' Robert atte Mor has two sons, both named John,' and refers to Bolland, S.S. 6 Ed. 2 (1313) Vol. 2, at p. xxiii.

for it is lawful for me to claim one as a villein, when I believe him to be so. So, if I claim to take one as a ward or servant, without any act done I will not be punished. So, too, as it seems to me, the lying-in-wait will not be actionable for the same cause, if he has not proved the act done which he has alleged. . . .

Townsend: The form of the action here is inconsistent. For if I take my horse to a farrier to be shod and by his negligence he kills him, and I bring an action *sur mon cas,* reciting the special matter and concluding *vi et armis equum suum interfecit,* I take nothing by my writ. For I have put matters for two actions in the writ, viz., the one for action on the case and the other for a general writ of Trespass. So here in this action on the case he has these words in his writ, *vi et armis, etc.,* which, with the matter preceding, comprises two actions of divers natures. Wherefore, etc. Also, the substance of the action is not good. For none of the matters disclosed suffices for an action, neither the claim nor the lying-in-wait, and when they are put together, still they do not any the more give an action. For, as to the first, viz., the claim, this is but an " infamy," as if a man call me thief, which gives no action in our law. And, as to the second, here is no tort, for without an act done a mere intent will not suffice. . . .

Genney, to the contrary: Even if it be assumed that he cannot have an action for the claim, yet as he laid in wait in pursuance of his claim, by reason whereof he dared not go about his business, this gives him a cause of action. So if one lies in wait in the High Street and says that he will beat me if I come to Westminster Hall, and a friend of mine tells me this so that I dare not come to plead, shall I not have an action? Why, yes; and yet he did not speak any words to me. And it is a common thing to indict a man for lying in wait in the highway, and it is contained in the commission of Justices of the Peace.

THE COURT: By our souls, if such an indictment comes before us, the defendant will be discharged.

Genney: As to the statement that for a claim a man shall have no action, that is not so; and especially for such a matter as will cause a man and all his blood to be corrupt. . . .

FAIRFAX, J.: I agree that the claim and the lying-in-wait alone give no cause of action. But in so far as he says in addition *per quod circa negotia sua palam intendere non audebat,* all this together is good matter for an action. And I agree that the words are not material, for a man shall have an action *sur son cas* where no word is spoken; as if I write on a scroll that I will beat J.S. if he comes out of his house and then throw this scroll into the house of J.S., whereby he dare not come out on his business, in this case he shall have an action *sur son cas.* And yet no word is spoken.

NEEDHAM, J. and BILLING, C.J. to the contrary: As it is agreed that neither the claim nor the menaces give any cause of action, which are antecedent, how can the consequences give an action? They cannot do so; wherefore it will be the folly of the plaintiff that he does not go out on his business. And there are divers cases in our law where a man has *dampnum absque injuria,* such as defamation in calling a man thief or traitor: this is damage, but no tort in our law. And if two conspire to indict a man, he shall have no remedy unless he be indicted in fact and also be acquitted of the charge; and so in our case. But because this is the first time that this matter has been argued, we would consider of it.

ANON

Y.B. Easter, 27 Hen. 8, f. 11, pl. 27

A.D. 1536

One brought a Writ *sur son cas,* and the writ was thus.

If R.C. of A. [shall give you security, etc.], then put [by gage and safe pledges] J.B., late of W. in the county, etc. [that he be before our justices, etc.] to show wherefore, whereas the said R. is a true liege of our lord the King that now is and has borne and held himself as a true liege of his progenitors, lately Kings of England, from the time of his birth until this present time, and has been of good name, fame and condition and has always hitherto been declared and reported of good conversation and repute among very many of the lieges of our lord the King; yet the aforesaid J., contriving unjustly to prejudice the aforesaid R. and to deprive him of the good name and fame which he has hitherto borne from the day of his birth and to harm, detract from and corrupt the fame and report of his said good name and also to draw the said R. into perturbation and infamy, at B. in the aforesaid county did falsely and maliciously impute to the said R. the crime of Theft and Larceny and publicly and there and then expressly said, asserted and proclaimed him to be Thief and Larcener, by the recital of these very words, or by other words tending to the same office or meaning, in the presence and hearing of very many of the lieges of our said lord the King, and there did oftentimes repeat these words; and afterwards the said J., at the Sessions held at J. in the county aforesaid on the Monday next after the Feast, etc., did cause to be written a certain Bill of Indictment of and concerning the said R. and the same Bill to be presented before the faithful and beloved Justices of our Lord the King at the Assizes then held in the aforesaid County, and also did cause the said R. to be kept in the Gaol of our lord the King at B. among the prisoners there lying, by reason whereof the said R. was then and there examined of the Felony aforesaid by the Justices aforesaid and was then and there declared not guilty of such Felony in the presence of the said Justices and by the testimony of many faithful and creditable lieges; and by reason of the said words thus proclaimed and published the said R. has not only been harmed and prejudiced and has suffered despite in his good name, fame and condition, but also, by reason of such aforesaid false imputation of crime, has been greatly injured and damnified by much labour and expense; to the grave damage of the said R. one hundred pounds, etc.[63]

ANON

Y.B. Trin. 27 Hen. 8, f. 14, pl. 4

A.D. 1536

Action sur le cas was brought for that the defendant had called the plaintiff ' Heretic and a man of the new learning.'

Willoughby questioned if this action lay here, for it was a spiritual matter.

[63] The above is a free rendering of the abbreviated Latin in the Blackletter edition. Compare Rastell, *Entries, Action sur le Cas pur Slaunder* (1566), where, contrary to Rastell's usual practice, a specimen writ is given, and Coke, *Entries, Action sur le Cas pur Slaunder del Person* (1614), where seven precedents of Declarations are offered, exhibiting a generous choice of abusive epithets.

FITZHERBERT and SHELLEY, J.J.: It is clear that this action does not lie here; for it is merely spiritual. And if the defendant would justify that the plaintiff was a heretic and would show in what point, we could not judge whether it was heresy or not. But if it were a matter where we could decide the principal point, as 'Thief' or 'Traitor' or such, for these words an action lies here, for we have cognisance of what matter is Treason or Felony. But if he had called him an adulterer, or as the case is here, no action lies for the reason aforesaid. . . .[64]

STANHOPE v. BLYTH

(1585), 4 COKE REP. 15a

The plaintiff recited in his declaration that, whereas he was a justice of peace, surveyor of the Duchy of Lancaster and had divers other offices, the defendant said of him, ' M. Stanhope hath but one manor, and that he hath gotten by swearing and forswearing ' ; and it was adjudged that the said words were not actionable.

1. Because they were too general; and words which shall charge any one with an action in which damages shall be recovered ought to have convenient certainty.

2. The defendant doth not charge the plaintiff with swearing or forswearing, for he may recover or get a manor by swearing or forswearing and yet he was not procuring or assenting to it; and words which maintain an action ought to be directly applied to the plaintiff, and not by collection or inference; for the damages ought to be given to the plaintiff in regard to the damage which he has by the scandal.

3. If one charges another that he has forsworn himself, it is not actionable for two reasons: 1. Because he may be forsworn in common conversation, *quia benignior sententia in verbis generalibus seu dubiis est præferenda.* 2. It is an usual word of passion and anger for one to say, that another has forsworn himself; as if one says of another, that he is a villain or a rogue or a varlet *vel similia,* these or such like will not maintain an action, for *boni Judicis est lites dirimere.* But if one says of another, that he is perjured or that he has forsworn himself in such a Court, for such words an action shall be maintained; for by these words it appears that he has forsworn himself in a judicial proceeding: *sed hæc ita in promptu sunt ut res probatione non egeant.* For all these cases have been often adjudged.

And WRAY, Chief Justice, said that, although slanders and false imputations are to be suppressed, because many times *a verbis ad verbera perventum est,* yet he said that the Judges had resolved that actions for scandals should not be maintained by any strained construction or argument nor any favour given to support them; forasmuch as in these days they more abound than in times past and the intemperance and malice of men increase, *et malitiis hominum est obviandum;* and in our books *actiones pro scandalis*

---

[64] Cf. *Anon* (1561) Moore, Case 92, p. 29: 'Action on the case was brought for that the defendant called the plaintiff adulterer, and was not maintainable, in that there is no punishment for this at common law, but by the spiritual law. But if he had called him murderer, it would be otherwise. And if a man calls him a knave or a villain, action on the case lies not.'

sunt rarissimæ, and such which are brought are for words of eminent slanders and of great import.[65]

BUCKLEY v. WOOD

(1591), 4 COKE REP., 14b

The case was that Owen Wood exhibited a bill in the Star Chamber against Sir R. Buckley, and charged him with divers matters examinable in the same Court; and further, that he was a maintainer of pirates and murderers and a procurer of murders and piracies, which offences were not determinable in the Star Chamber. Sir R. Buckley brought an action on the case against Owen Wood, and declared that the said Owen had exhibited the said bill, containing (*inter alia*) that the said Richard was a maintainer of pirates and murderers and a procurer of murders and piracies, and that the said Owen at B. in the county of Salop, speaking of the matters contained in the said bill, said *in auditu quamplurimorum* that the said bill and matters contained therein were true. The defendant confessed the exhibiting of the bill in the Star-Chamber and that he in the said Court of Westminster said the said words, *absque hoc*[66] that he spoke the words in the county of Salop before or after the day mentioned in the declaration; by which he excluded the day itself and answered not to it, for which cause the bar was held insufficient *per totam Curiam*.

And it was resolved *per totam Curiam* that for any matter contained in the bill that was examinable in the said Court no action lies, although the matter is merely false, because it was in course of justice; and this agrees with the opinion in 11 Eliz. Dyer 285, and with the judgment in *Cutler and Dixon's Case* before.[67]

It was resolved and adjudged that for the said words *not* examinable in the said Court an action on the case lies, for that cannot be in a course of justice; for the Court has no power or jurisdiction to do that which appertains to justice nor to punish the said offences; and if such matters may be inserted in bills exhibited in so high and honourable a Court in great slander of the parties, and they cannot answer it to clear themselves, nor

---

[65] Cf. Coke, closing his collection of 'actions for slander,' 4 Co. Rep. 12b-20b, at p. 20b: 'These resolutions concerning scandals (which I amongst many others for my private instruction have observed) at the importunate request and desire of my good friends, some in the realm of Ireland and others dwelling in the remote parts of England out of the meridian of Westminster, I have reported, but in a summary. and succinct manner, as you see, omitting many others which I do not think necessary to be published, my opinion always being *quod multo utilius est pauca idonea effundere, quam multis inutilibus homines gravari.* And nevertheless these brief resolutions and the reason of them, being well understood and observed, will peradventure give great direction and instruction *pro multis aliis,* and will deter men, for words which are but wind, from subjecting themselves to actions in which damages and costs are to be recovered, which sometimes trench to the great hindrance and impoverishment of the speakers.

[66] These words indicate that the defendant's plea is not a *general traverse,* i.e. a direct and general denial, but a *special traverse,* where he first makes a positive statement and then adds a particular denial. 'The affirmative part of the special traverse is called its *inducement;* the negative part is called the *absque hoc*—those being the Latin words formerly used and from which the modern expression, *without this,* is translated.' Stephen on Pleading, 2nd ed. (1827), pp. 205-9.

[67] *Cutler* v. *Dixon* (1585) 4 Coke Rep. 14b: 'It was adjudged that if one exhibits articles to justices of peace against a certain person, containing divers great abuses and misdemeanors, not only concerning the petitioners themselves but many others, and all this to the intent that he should be bound to his good behaviour; in this case the party accused shall not have for any matter contained in such articles any action upon the case, for they have pursued the ordinary course of justice in such case; and if actions should be permitted in such cases, those who have just cause for complaint would not dare to complain for fear of infinite vexation.'

have their actions as well to clear themselves of the crimes as to recover damages for the great injury and wrong done them, great inconvenience will ensue; but the said libel, without any remedy given the party, will remain always on record to his shame and infamy, which will be full of great inconvenience. . . .

Judgment for the plaintiff.

DAVIS v. GARDINER
(1593), 4 COKE REP. 16b

The plaintiff declared that she was a virgin of good fame, etc., and free from all suspicion of incontinency, etc. And whereas Anthony Elcock, citizen and mercer of London of the substance and value of three thousand pounds, desired her for his wife and had thereupon conferred with John Davis her father and was ready to conclude it, the defendant (*præmissorum non ignarus*), to defame the said Anne and to obstruct the said Anthony's proceeding, uttered and published of the said Anne these words: ' I know Davis's daughter well (*innuendo prædictam Annam*), she dwelt in Cheapside and there was a grocer that did get her with child ' ; and the defendant being there and then admonished that he should be advised *quid dixerat de præfata Anna, ulterius de eadem dixit*: ' I know very well what I say, I know her father and mother and sister, and she is the youngest sister and had the child by the grocer ' ; by reason of which words the plaintiff was greatly defamed, *et ratione inde dictus Anthonius ipsam Annam in uxorem ducere penitus recusabat*. And the defendant pleaded not guilty, and at Nisi Prius in the County of Bucks the jurors found for the plaintiff and assessed damages to two hundred marks.

And it was now moved in arrest of judgment by the defendant's counsel, that the said defamation of incontinency concerned the spiritual and not the temporal jurisdiction; and therefore, as the offence should be punished in the Spiritual Court, so her remedy for such defamation should be there also. So if a man is called bastard or heretic or miscreant or adulterer, (forasmuch as these belong to the ecclesiastical jurisdiction) no action lies at the common law; and in proof thereof 12 Hen. 7. 22, and 27 Hen. 8, 14,[68] were cited.

But it was answered by the plaintiff's counsel and resolved *per totam Curiam* that the action was maintainable for two reasons.

1. Because, if the woman had a bastard, she was punishable by the statute of 18 Eliz. cap. 3. . . .

2. It was resolved, if the defendant had charged the plaintiff with bare incontinency, yet the action should be maintainable: for in this case the ground of the action is temporal, *sc.* that she was to be advanced in marriage and that she was defeated of it, and the means by which she was defeated was the same slander, which means tending to such end shall be tried by the common law. So if a divine is to be presented to a benefice, and one, to defeat him of it, says to the patron, ' that he is an heretic or a bastard or that he is excommunicated,' by which the patron refuses to present him (as he well might if the imputations were true), and he loses his preferment, he shall have his action on the case for these slanders tending to such end. And if a woman is bound that she shall live continent and chaste, or if a lease is made to her *quamdiu casta vixerit*, in these cases incontinency shall be tried by the common law. . . .

[68] *Supra*, p. 141.

BRITTRIDGE'S CASE

(1602), 4 COKE REP. 18b

Brittridge brought an action upon the case for these words, ' Mr. Brittridge is a perjured old knave, and that is to be proved by a stake parting the land of H. Martin and Mr. Wright.'

The defendant pleaded not guilty, and was found guilty; and now in arrest of judgment it was moved that these words are not actionable.

1. Because [in] this word, ' a perjured old knave,' the noun is ' knave,' and ' perjured ' is spoke adjectively; as if a man says, one is a seditious or thievish knave, these words are not actionable, because the words do not import that he hath made sedition or felony, but are adjective, which imply an inclination to it.

2. That the Court ought to judge upon all the words together and collect the defendant's intention upon all his words, and not to take his words by parcels. And it was said that the last words extenuate the genuine and proper sense of the first words, for perjury shall be intended in some Court upon judicial proceeding; but when he adds, ' and that is to be proved by a stake parting, etc.,' that explains, for any thing that appears to the Court, that this perjury was not in any Court, but an unadvised oath extrajudicial about the placing of a stake for a partition.

As to the first, it was resolved by POPHAM, Chief Justice, GAWDY, FENNER and YELVERTON, Justices, that . . . sometimes adjective words will maintain an action and sometimes not. They are actionable, (1) when the adjective presumes an act committed, (2) when they scandalise one in his office or function or trade, by which he gets his living; so if a man says that one is ' a perjured knave,' there must be an act done or otherwise he cannot be perjured, as was resolved before. So if one says of an officer or a Judge that he is a corrupt officer or judge,[69] an action lies for both causes: 1. Because it implies an act done : 2. It is slanderous to him in respect of his office. . . . So if one says of a merchant that he is a ' bankruptly knave, or bankrupt knave,' although there bankrupt be spoken adjectively, yet an action lies, as it was adjudged in *Mitton's Case* in C.B. Mich. 43 & 44 Eliz. Or if one says of a merchant ' that he will be bankrupt in two days,' which implies but inclination, yet an action lies, 6 Ed. 6, Dyer, 72,[70] for that defames him in his trade by which he gets his living. But when the words do not imply an act done, but an inclination to an act which doth not scandalize the party in the duty of any office or function nor in his trade of living, there an action upon the case doth not lie; as to say that he is a ' seditious or thievish knave,' these do not import any act to be done, but an intent or inclination to it, which is not punishable by the common law.

As to the second, it was resolved in the case of *Brittridge*, that upon all the words taken together no action lay; for the latter words extenuate the first and explain his intent, that he did not intend any judicial perjury. Also it is impossible that a stake can prove him perjured, and therefore upon consideration of all the words, for the impossibility and insensibility of them, they are not actionable; as it has been adjudged that, where one says to another ' thou art a thief, for thou hast stolen my apples out of my orchard,' or ' for thou hast robbed my hop ground,' [these] latter words

---

[69] ' Skinner, a merchant of London, said of Manwood, Chief Baron, that he was a corrupt Judge; and it was adjudged that the words are actionable ': *Birchley's Case* (1585), 4 Coke Rep. 16a.
[70] *Kemp's Case* (1553), 1 Dyer, 72.

prove it no felony, and so qualify the proper sense of this word thief, which of itself, although it is generally spoken, will bear an action. And so it was adjudged *inter Dobbins and Franklin,* Mich. 43 & 44 Eliz., in C.B. . . . So in the case at Bar, ' thou art a perjured old knave, and that will be proved by a stake parting, etc.' For the office of Judges is upon consideration of all the words to collect the true scope and intention of him who speaks them. . . .

Judgment for the Defendant.

AUSTIN v. CULPEPPER
(1684), 2 SHOWER, 313

Case, wherein the plaintiff declares that, whereas there was a cause depending in the Court of Chancery between the said parties and witnesses sworn and examined on the behalf of the plaintiff, the defendant, to scandalise the plaintiff, did forge and counterfeit an order of the said Court of Chancery, that Sir John Austin should stand committed, unless cause, etc., and this did cause to be written and published as an Order of the said Court; and afterwards, (viz.) the same day, did make the picture and representation of a pillory and under the same did write these words, ' For Sir John Austin and his suborned, forsworn witnesses.'

Mr. Pollexfen moves in arrest of judgment. This Declaration consists of two parts, (viz.) the forgery of the Order and the Figure with the words underwritten, and the damages are entire. Now if either of them be not actionable the plaintiff ought not to have judgment; as suppose a man should bring an action for malicious prosecution of a crime and for words imputing the said crime, and damages given entirely; if the words happen not to be actionable, 'twill be naught. Then for the words themselves, if they had been spoken, they had not been actionable; for to call a man *forsworn* is not actionable, unless it do appear that 'twas in a Court of Justice. Now the forgery itself is not actionable, for he lays no damage or trouble accrued to him thereby.

Mr. Holt, e contra: 'Tis all but one complicated act, and the action is for libelling him in that manner. Now, supposing the words themselves were not actionable, yet, being published by way of libel, they are so. There was the case of *Colonel King* v. *Lake* before my Lord Hale, where the action was for printing a petition, which he delivered to several members of the House of Commons (having a complaint there against him), containing scandalous matter concerning him, as that he was dishonest and unjust and had abused him; and yet none of these words printed would have born an action if spoken; yet the action was held to lie, and judgment affirmed upon a Writ of Error.[71] And an action lies for a libel as well as an indictment, and a libel may be either *per scripta* or *per signa.* . . .

PER CURIAM: It is but one complicated act, and an action lies for scandalising a man by writing those words, which will not, being spoken, bear an action. . . .

Judgment for the Plaintiff.

---

[71] *King* v. *Lake* (1668), Hardres, 470. Hale, C.B.: ' Although such general words spoken once, without writing or publishing them, would not be actionable; yet here, they being writ and published, which contains more malice than if they had been but once spoken, they are actionable.'

WEATHERSTON v. HAWKINS

(1786), 1 T.R. 110

This was an action on the case by a servant against the defendant, who was his former master, for words, and also for falsely and maliciously writing and publishing the following letter (stated in the declaration) to one Collier, respecting the plaintiff's character as a servant: . . . [The letter contained allegations of dishonesty against the servant in the discharge of the master's business]. . . . This was tried at the sittings at Guildhall after last Michaelmas term before Lord Mansfield, when a verdict was found for the plaintiff on the last count, containing the letter (the words not being proved), subject to the opinion of the Court on the following case.

'The plaintiff was brother-in-law to Mr. Collier. He was in the service of the defendant and was by him turned away. Rogers, to whom the plaintiff was recommended to be taken as a servant, applied to the defendant for a character, which, not being advantageous, but to the effect stated in the Declaration, he (Rogers) did not take him. Collier upon this repeatedly called on the defendant; upon which the letter stated in the Declaration was written with an intent to prevent an action by the plaintiff for the words spoken by the defendant to Rogers. The writ was sued out on the same day the letter was written.

The question for the opinion of the Court is whether this action lies.'

Wood, for the plaintiff: This action is maintainable on the letter, which is a false and malicious libel. This does not differ from the case of common libels; for it has the two essential parts which constitute a libel, namely, slander and falsehood. That it is slanderous is extremely clear, for it charges the plaintiff with specific acts of fraud, almost amounting to felony. It is likewise false; for had it been true, the defendant might have justified. And though in his letter he said 'he could prove it,' yet, as he did not at the trial, the Court must now take it for granted that it is false. It is not necessary in an action for a libel to prove express malice: if it be slanderous, malice is implied. And on trials for libels it is sufficient to prove publication; the motives of the party publishing are never gone into. The same doctrine holds in an action for words, where, though the declaration allege them to be spoken 'falsely and maliciously,' no express malice need be proved. . . . If it be contended that the master of a servant is exempted from the general rule on account of his relative situation, such a principle is not warranted by any determination in the books. And this is very different from the case of a master giving a general bad character of a servant; for here the defendant has made specific charges of fraud. . . .

LORD MANSFIELD: I have held more than once that an action will not lie by a servant against his former master for words spoken by him in giving a character of the servant.[72] The general rules are laid down as Mr. Wood has stated; but to every libel there may be a necessary and implied justification from the occasion. So that what, taken abstractedly, would be a publication, may from the occasion prove to be none; as if it were read in a judicial proceeding. Words may also be justified on account of the subject-matter or other circumstances. In this case, instead of the plaintiff's shewing

[72] e.g. *Hargrave* v. *Le Breton* (1769), 4 Burr. 2422—a case of Slander of Title—where Lord Mansfield said, at p. 2425: 'No action lies for giving the true character of a servant, upon application made to his former master to inquire into his character with a view of hiring him; unless there should be extraordinary circumstances of express malice.'

it to be false and malicious, it appears to be incident to the application by Rogers to the master of the servant. And the letter was written to the brother-in-law of the plaintiff for the express purpose of preventing an action being brought.

BULLER, J.: This is an exception to the general rule on account of the occasion of writing the letter. Then it is incumbent on the plaintiff to prove the falsehood of it. And in actions of this kind, unless he can prove the words to be malicious as well as false, they are not actionable. On this case it evidently appears that the defendant has been entrapped, because the letter was written on the application of the plaintiff's brother-in-law. And, besides, it is stated that the writ was sued out on the same day the letter was written.

Judgment for the Defendant.

CARR v. HOOD
(1808), 1 CAMP., 355, note

[The plaintiff was the author of certain books, such as 'The Stranger in France,' 'A Northern Summer,' 'The Stranger in Ireland,' etc. The defendants published a brochure entitled ' My Pocket Book, or Hints for a Righte Merrie and Conceited Tour,' ridiculing the plaintiff's books and containing a caricature of the plaintiff.]

. . . LORD ELLENBOROUGH, as the trial was proceeding, intimated an opinion that, if the book published by the defendants only ridiculed the plaintiff as an author, the action could not be maintained.

Garrow, for the plaintiff, allowed that, when his client came forward as an author, he subjected himself to the criticism of all who might be disposed to discuss the merits of his works. But that criticism must be fair and liberal; its object ought to be to enlighten the public and to guard them against the supposed bad tendency of a particular publication presented to them, not to wound the feelings and to ruin the prospects of an individual. If ridicule was employed, it should have some bounds. . . . The object of the book published by the defendants clearly was, by means of immoderate ridicule, to prevent the sale of the plaintiff's works and entirely to destroy him as an author. In the late case of *Tabart* v. *Tipper* (1 Camp., 350) his Lordship had held that a publication by no means so offensive or prejudicial to the object of it, was libellous and actionable.

LORD ELLENBOROUGH: In that case the defendant had falsely accused the plaintiff of publishing what he had never published. Here the supposed libel has only attacked the works of which Sir John Carr was the avowed author; and one writer, in exposing the follies and errors of another, may make use of ridicule, however poignant. Ridicule is often the fittest weapon that can be employed for such a purpose. If the reputation or pecuniary interests of the person ridiculed suffer, it is *damnum absque injuria.* Where is the liberty of the press, if an action can be maintained on such principles? Perhaps the plaintiff's *Tour through Scotland* is now unsaleable[73]; but is he to be indemnified by receiving a compensation in damages from the person who may have opened the eyes of the public to the bad taste and inanity of his compositions? . . . Reflection on personal character is another thing. Shew me an attack on the moral character of this plaintiff, or any attack

---

[73] It had at least inspired a spirited review by Sir Walter Scott in the first number of the *Quarterly Review*: Lockhart, *Life of Scott*, Chap. XIX.

upon his character unconnected with his authorship, and I shall be as ready as any Judge who ever sate here to protect him; but I cannot hear of malice on account of turning his works into ridicule.

The counsel for the plaintiff still complaining of the unfairness of this publication and particularly of the print affixed to it, the trial proceeded. . . .

LORD ELLENBOROUGH [directed the Jury]: Every man who publishes a book commits himself to the judgment of the public and anyone may comment on his performance. If the commentator does not step aside from the work or invent fiction for the purpose of condemnation, he exercises a fair and legitimate right. In the present case, had the party writing the criticism followed the plaintiff into domestic life for the purpose of slander, that would have been libellous; but no passage of this sort has been produced; and even the caricature does not affect the plaintiff except as the author of the book which is ridiculed. The works of this gentleman may be, for aught I know, very valuable; but, whatever their merits, others have a right to pass their judgment upon them—to censure them if they be censurable, and to turn them into ridicule if they be ridiculous. The critic does a great service to the public, who writes down any vapid or useless publication, such as ought never to have appeared. He checks the dissemination of bad taste and prevents people from wasting both their time and money upon trash. I speak of fair and candid criticism; and this everyone has a right to publish, although the author may suffer a loss from it. . . .

The Chief Justice concluded by directing the jury that, if the writer of the publication complained of had not travelled out of the work he criticised for the purpose of slander, the action would not lie; but if they could discover in it anything personally slanderous against the plaintiff, unconnected with the works he had given to the public, in that case he had a good cause of action, and they would award him damages accordingly.

Verdict for the Defendants.

THORLEY v. LORD KERRY
(1812), 4 TAUNTON, 355

[The original plaintiff, Lord Kerry, brought an action of defamation against the original defendant, Thorley, for a letter addressed by the defendant to the plaintiff and delivered unsealed to a servant to carry to the plaintiff. The servant opened and read it. The jury found for the plaintiff with £20 damages, and judgment was given for the plaintiff in the King's Bench. The defendant went to the Exchequer Chamber on a writ of error. The opinion of the court of Exchequer Chamber was delivered by Sir James Mansfield.[74]]

SIR JAMES MANSFIELD: This is a writ of error brought to reverse a judgment of the Court of King's Bench, in which there was no argument. It was an action on a libel published in a letter, which the bearer of the letter happened to open. The declaration has certainly some very curious recitals. It recites that the Plaintiff[75] was tenant to Archibald, Lord Douglas, of a messuage in Petersham; that, being desirous to become a parishioner and to attend the vestry, he agreed to pay the taxes of the said house; that the Plaintiff in error[76] was churchwarden; that the Defendant in error gave him

---

[74] Chief Justice of the Common Pleas, 1804-1814: see *infra*, p. 438.
[75] i.e. the original plaintiff, now the defendant in error.
[76] i.e. the original defendant.

notice of his agreement with Lord Douglas; and that the Plaintiff in error, intending to have it believed that the said earl was guilty of the offences and misconducts thereinafter mentioned (offences there are none, misconducts there may be), wrote the letter to the said earl which is set forth in the pleadings.

There is no doubt that this was a libel, for which the Plaintiff in error might have been indicted and punished; because, though the words impute no punishable crimes, they contain that sort of imputation which is calculated to vilify a man and bring him, as the books say, into hatred, contempt and ridicule. For all words of that description an indictment lies; and I should have thought that the peace and good name of individuals was sufficiently guarded by the terror of this criminal proceeding in such cases.

The words, if merely spoken, would not be of themselves sufficient to support an action. But the question now is whether an action will lie for these words so written, notwithstanding that such an action would not lie for them if spoken; and I am very sorry it was not discussed in the Court of King's Bench, that we might have had the opinion of all the twelve judges on the point, whether there be any distinction as to the right of action between written and parol scandal. For myself, after having heard it extremely well argued, and especially in this case by Mr. Barnewall, I cannot, upon principle, make any difference between words written and words spoken as to the right which arises on them of bringing an action. For the Plaintiff in error it has been truly urged that in the old books and abridgments no distinction is taken between words written and spoken. But the distinction has been made between written and spoken slander as far back as Charles the Second's time,[77] and the difference has been recognized by the Courts for at least a century back. It does not appear to me that the rights of parties to a good character are insufficiently defended by the criminal remedies which the law gives, and the law gives a very ample field for retribution by action for words spoken in the cases of special damage, of words spoken of a man in his trade or profession, of a man in office, of a magistrate or officer; for all these an action lies. But for more general abuse spoken, no action lies.

In the arguments both of the judges and counsel in almost all the cases in which the question has been, whether what is contained in a writing is the subject of an action or not, it has been considered whether the words, if spoken, would maintain an action. It is curious that they have also adverted to the question whether it tends to produce a breach of the peace; but that is wholly irrelevant and is no ground for recovering damages. So it has been argued that writing shows more deliberate malignity; but the same answer suffices, that the action is not maintainable upon the ground of the malignity, but for the damage sustained. So it is argued that written scandal is more generally diffused than words spoken, and it is therefore actionable; but an assertion made in a public place, as upon the Royal Exchange, concerning a merchant in London, may be much more extensively diffused than a few printed papers or a private letter. It is true that a newspaper may be very generally read, but that is all casual.

These are the arguments which prevail on my mind to repudiate the distinction between written and spoken scandal; but that distinction has been established by some of the greatest names known to the law, Lord

[77] See *supra*, p. 132.

Hardwicke, Hale, I believe Holt, C.J., and others. Lord Hardwicke, C.J., especially has laid it down that an action for a libel may be brought on words written, when the words, if spoken, would not sustain it. *Co. Dig. tit. Libel,* referring to the case in *Fitzg.* 122, 253,[78] says there is a distinction between written and spoken scandal, and by his putting it down there, as he does, as being the law, without making any query or doubt upon it, we are led to suppose that he was of the same opinion.[79] I do not now recapitulate the cases[80]; but we cannot, in opposition to them, venture to lay down at this day that no action can be maintained for any words written, for which an action could not be maintained if they were spoken. Upon these grounds we think the judgment of the Court of King's Bench must be affirmed. The purpose of this action is to recover a compensation for some damage supposed to be sustained by the Plaintiff by reason of the libel. The tendency of the libel to provoke a breach of the peace, or the degree of malignity which actuates the writer, has nothing to do with the question. If the matter were for the first time to be decided at this day, I should have no hesitation in saying that no action could be maintained for written scandal, which could not be maintained for the words if they had been spoken.

Judgment affirmed.

BROMAGE v. PROSSER

(1825), 4 BARNEWALL AND CRESSWELL, 247

BAYLEY, J.[81]: This was an action for slander. The plaintiffs were bankers at Monmouth, and the charge was that, in answer to a question from one Lewis Watkins whether he, the defendant, had said that the plaintiffs' bank had stopped, the defendant's answer was, ' it was true, he had been told so.' The evidence was that Watkins met defendant and said, ' I hear that you say the bank of Bromage and Snead at Monmouth has stopped. Is it true?' Defendant said, ' Yes it is: I was told so.' He added, ' It was so reported at Crickhowell and nobody would take their bills, and that he had come to town in consequence of it himself.' Watkins said, ' You had better take care what you say: you first brought the news to town and told Mr. John Thomas of it.' Defendant repeated, ' I was told so.' Defendant had been told at Crickhowell that there was a run upon plaintiffs' bank, but not that it had stopped or that nobody would take their bills, and what he said went greatly beyond what he had heard.

The learned Judge considered the words as proved, and he does not appear to have treated it as a case of privileged communication; but as the defendant did not appear to be actuated by any ill-will against the plaintiffs, he told the jury that if they thought the words were not spoken maliciously, though they might unfortunately have produced injury to the plaintiffs, the defendant ought to have their verdict; but if they thought them spoken maliciously, they should find for the plaintiffs. And the jury having found for the defendant, the question upon a motion for a new trial was upon the propriety of this direction.

[78] *Harman* v. *Delany* (1731), Fitzgibbon, 122, 253: *per Curiam* at p. 254, ' words published in writing will be actionable, tho' not so when barely spoken.'
[79] 'He' is Comyns, L.C.B. (1738-40), whose Digest was published between 1762 and 1767.
[80] See *Villers* v. *Monsley* (1769), 2 Wilson, 403.
[81] Delivering the judgment of the King's Bench on a motion for a new trial.

If in an ordinary case of slander (not a case of privileged communication) want of malice is a question of fact for the consideration of a jury, the direction was right; but if in such a case the law implies such malice as is necessary to maintain the action, it is the duty of the judge to withdraw the question of malice from the consideration of the jury; and it appears to us that the direction in this case was wrong. That malice, in some sense, is the gist of the action, and that therefore the manner and occasion of speaking the words is admissible in evidence to shew they were not spoken with malice, is said to have been agreed (either by all the judges or at least by the four who thought the truth might be given in evidence on the general issue) in *Smith* v. *Richardson*[82]; and it is laid down in 1 Com. Dig. *Action upon the case for defamation G* 5 that the declaration must shew a malicious intent in the defendant, and there are some other very useful elementary books in which it is said that malice is the gist of the action. But in what sense the words ' malice ' or ' malicious intent ' are here to be understood, whether in the popular sense or in the sense the law puts upon those expressions, none of these authorities state.

Malice in common acceptation means ill-will against a person, but in its legal sense it means a wrongful act done intentionally without just cause or excuse. If I give a perfect stranger a blow likely to produce death, I do it ' of malice,' because I do it intentionally and without just cause or excuse. If I maim cattle without knowing whose they are, if I poison a fishery without knowing the owner, I do it ' of malice,' because it is a wrongful act and done intentionally. If I am arraigned of felony and wilfully stand mute, I am said to do it ' of malice,' because it is intentional and without just cause or excuse. And if I traduce a man, whether I know him or not and whether I intend to do him an injury or not, I apprehend the law considers it as done of malice, because it is wrongful and intentional. It equally works an injury whether I meant to produce an injury or not, and, if I had no legal excuse for the slander, why is he not to have a remedy against me for the injury it produces? And I apprehend the law recognises the distinction between these two descriptions of malice, malice in fact and malice in law, in actions of slander.

In an ordinary action for words it is sufficient to charge that the defendant spoke them falsely, it is not necessary to state that they were spoken maliciously. This is so laid down in Styles, 392, and was adjudged upon error in *Mercer* v. *Sparks*.[83] The objection there was that the words were not charged to have been spoken maliciously, but the Court answered that the words were themselves malicious and slanderous, and therefore the judgment was affirmed. But in actions for such slander as is prima facie excusable on account of the cause of speaking or writing it, as in the case of servants' characters, confidential advice, or communications to persons who ask it or have a right to expect it, malice in fact must be proved by the plaintiff. . . . So in *Hargrave* v. *Breton*[84] Lord Mansfield states that no action can be maintained against a master for the character he gives a servant unless there are extraordinary circumstances of express malice. But in an ordinary action for a libel or for words, though evidence of malice may be given to increase the damages, it never is considered as essential nor is there any instance of a verdict for a defendant on the ground of want

[82] (1737) Willes, 24. *Supra,* p. 135.
[83] (1586) Owen, 51.
[84] (1769) 4 Burrow, 2422, at p. 2425.

of malice. Numberless occasions must have occurred (particularly in cases where a defendant only repeated what he had heard before, but without naming the author), upon which, if that were a tenable ground, verdicts would have been sought for and obtained, and the absence of any such instance is a proof of what has been the general and universal opinion upon the point.

Had it been noticed to the jury how the defendant came to speak the words, and had it been left to them as a previous question whether the defendant understood Watkins as asking for information for his own guidance and that the defendant spoke what he did to Watkins merely by way of honest advice to regulate his conduct, the question of malice in fact would have been proper as a second question to the jury, if their minds were in favour of the defendant upon the first. But as the previous question I have mentioned was never put to the jury, but this was treated as an ordinary case of slander, we are of opinion that the question of malice ought not to have been left to the jury. . . .

The rule was made absolute for a new trial.

ᗏ 8 ᕑ

NEGLIGENCE

I T is generally agreed that little or nothing akin to the modern idea of negligence is to be found in the common law before the evolution of Case. The royal courts in the age of Bracton did not discuss it, and, despite a few despondent suggestions, there is no real evidence that it interested the local courts.[1] But the same unanimity does not attend the efforts to disentangle among the ramifications of Case the threads which at last, after many vicissitudes, were woven into a general tort of negligence. Professor Winfield in his explorations has detected a number of diverse influences which may here be examined under four heads: the liability in certain cases of nuisance and for the breach of prescriptive duties analogous to nuisance, liability based on the control of dangerous things, the duty voluntarily accepted in assumpsit, and the duty cast upon bailees and upon persons pursuing a ' public ' or ' common ' calling.[2]

It is true that Bracton mentions a type of nuisance dependent upon the failure to repair or to maintain,[3] and that it was sanctioned at a later date by an action on the case. Thus in 1372 a Prior brought Trespass on the Case against a defendant,

> ' for that, whereas he [the defendant] held a house and four acres of land in the vill, whereby he ought to keep in repair certain ditches and banks, etc., and whereas the tenants of these tenements for all time have been wont to keep the said ditches and banks in repair, the said [defendant] had not repaired the said ditches, so that 40 acres of land of the said Prior were flooded and he lost the profits of the land for five years to his damage 30 pounds ' [4]

Instances may also be found of analogous duties similarly enforced, as of the Hundred which would not give its bailiff his immemorial ration of beer or of the Abbot who denied more spiritual refreshment by failing to appoint a chaplain.[5] But the mere recital of such facts emphasises their remoteness from the tort of negligence. The defendant is sued, not because he has been careless, but because, where he should have done something, he has done nothing.

---

[1] See P. & M. II, 527-8, and Winfield, 42 L.Q.R., pp. 184-5.
[2] Winfield, 42 L.Q.R., 37-51 and 184-201: (1931) C.L.J., pp. 203-5: 34 Columbia L.R., pp. 44-58.
[3] Bracton, f. 232b, *supra*, p. 19.
[4] *Anon* (1372) Y.B. Trin. 45 Ed. 3, f. 17, pl. 6. The writ was quashed because it contained the words *contra pacem*: see *supra*, p. 76.
[5] The Beadle's case appears in Rolle, *Abridgment, Action sur case, N* (1), under the bare citation 19 Rich. II: the Abbot's case is Y.B. Hil. 22 Hen. 6, f. 46. See Winfield, 42 L.Q.R., p. 191.

In the class of dangerous things for whose escape a man may be liable Professor Winfield includes unruly animals and fire. The first of these categories offers little help. An action on the case for damage done by animals was known as early as 1387; but the writ, though it imputed to the defendant knowledge of a dangerous propensity, made no mention of negligence. The plaintiff complained ' *quare quendam canem ad mordendos oves consuetum scienter retinuit.*'[6] Throughout the mediæval law the language of the writ remained constant, and it was endorsed as late as 1661.[7] In 1700 a plaintiff attempted a variant by omitting the *scienter* and substituting a complaint that he had been bitten in the calf through the defendant's lack of control over a savage mongrel mastiff—*pro defectu debitæ curæ et custodiæ canis molossi valde ferocis.* Chief Justice Holt repudiated the innovation. ' For anything that appears to the contrary, the owner might not have had this dog but one day or two before and did not know of his fierce nature. . . . Otherwise if the defendant had known before . . ., for then he ought to have kept him in at his peril.'[8] Despite the severity of these last words, the allegation of *scienter* would seem designed to impute some degree of fault in the defendant; but throughout the history of this branch of Case the word ' negligence ' is never used.

The second category of dangerous things is more fruitful. The peril of fire, perennial though it was in the conditions of mediæval town life, provoked little legal discussion before the advent of Case.[9] The *locus classicus* is the report of *Beaulieu* v. *Finglam* in 1401.[10] The plaintiff complained that the defendant kept his fire *tam negligenter* that for lack of due keeping the plaintiff's house and furniture were burnt. The defendant, after objecting that the fire could not be called his since no man could have property in the elements, argued strenuously that he was not to be held liable without fault. The Court overcame the argument by the counter-doctrine of vicarious liability; but the report does not suggest that their view would have been the same had no member of the defendant's household been to blame. Three hundred years later the language of pleading remained unaltered. In 1693 Dorothea Panton complained of Sir Justinian Isham that in the parish of St. Martin in the Fields he had kept his fire ' in so negligent and careless a manner that, for default of due care, her houses had

---

[6] Glanville Williams, *Liability for Animals,* pp. 278-284. See especially the reference given at p. 278, note 2.
[7] Aston, *A Book of Entries* (1661), *Counts per Tort, Pur un chien ad mordend' oves consuet.*
[8] *Mason* v. *Keeling* (1700) 1 Ld. Raym. 606, 12 Mod. 332. The old form is resumed by Lilly in his *Collection of Modern Entries* (1723) in his precedent, *sub. nom. King* v. *Peach*—' Case for keeping a dog accustomed to bite sheep.'
[9] Professor Winfield refers in his *Law of Torts,* 4th ed., p. 495, to the possibility of suing by a Writ of Trespass *vi et armis* and cites 42 Lib. Ass. pl. 9. The action here, which in fact failed, was significantly brought in 1369, before Case was really established, and seems to be unique.
[10] Y.B. 2 Hen. 4, f. 18, pl. 6: *infra,* p. 166. See also Y.B. Pasch. 28 Hen. 6, f. 7 (A.D. 1450).

been destroyed."[11]   In 1697 in *Turberville* v. *Stamp*,[12] the defendant
'so negligently and improvidently kept his fire' in a certain 'close
of heath' that, 'for want of due keeping,' a neighbouring close was
burnt.   The defendant not unreasonably sought to distinguish domestic
and other fires, but a majority of the Court, including Chief Justice
Holt, refused the distinction.   Once 'it is found to have been by his
negligence, it is the same as if it had been in his house.'   That the
allegation of negligence was no mere forensic flourish appears from
an examination of Rastell's Entries in 1566.   In his 'accion sur le
case pur negligent garder son few (fire),' he insists on the adverbs
'negligenter et improvide,' whereas in his specimen writ and declaration for failure to discharge a prescriptive duty, no hint of negligence
is to be found.[13]

The rich promise of Assumpsit was in vivid contrast to these scattered and uncertain precedents.   From the moment when the judges
first entertained an action on the case for the breach of a voluntary
undertaking, they opened their ears and so their minds to the language
of negligence.   In 1370 a plaintiff complained that the defendant, after
accepting the cure of his horse, had done his work so carelessly—*ita
negligenter curam suam fecit*—that the horse had died.   The allegation
was regarded as of the essence of his action, and it was repeated five
years later against a surgeon.[14]   In the course of the fifteenth century
recurrent attempts were made to enlarge the scope of this species of
Case, but after much hesitation the judges came to insist on the combination of two factors: proof of an assumpsit and proof of positive
misconduct.   Unless there were a prior undertaking no amount of
negligence would make a defendant liable, and, even where that
undertaking existed, the negligence charged must be something more
than the mere failure to implement it.[15]   In the early years of the
sixteenth century the action was allowed for nonfeasance no less than
for misfeasance, and a general remedy for the breach of a promise
was created.   But the association of assumpsit with contract, though
now predominant, was not exclusive.   It continued to be alleged on
occasion, not for contractual purposes, but to support an action for
negligent conduct, imagined as an independent wrong.   Thus in *Coggs*
v. *Bernard* in 1703[16] it was used to explain the circumstances in which
the defendant came into control of the plaintiff's goods and to justify

---

[11] *Panton* v. *Isham* (1693) 3 Levinz, 356.
[12] 3 Ld. Raym. 375: 12 Mod. 152, *infra*, p. 167.
[13] Rastell, *Collection of Entries, Accion sur le case, pur negligent garder son few*, and
pur nient faire Reparations: supra, p. 90.
[14] *Waldon* v. *Marshall*, Y.B. 43 Ed. 3, f. 33, pl. 38, *supra*, p. 81; and *The Surgeon's
Case*, Y.B. 48 Ed. 3, f. 6, pl. 11, *supra*, p. 82.
[15] See *Watton* v. *Brinth* (1400) Y.B. 2 Hen. 4, f. 3, pl. 9, *infra*, p. 340: *Anon* (1409)
Y.B. 11 Hen. 4, f. 33, pl. 60, *infra*, p. 340: *Marshal's Case* (1441) Y.B. 19 Hen. 6. f.
49, pl. 5, *infra*, p. 345: *The Shepherd's Case* (1486) Y.B. 2 Hen. 7, f. 11, pl. 9, *supra*,
p. 86.   For the general evolution of Assumpsit, see *infra*, pp. 330-40.
[16] 2 Ld. Raym. 909, *infra*, p. 173.

a consequent obligation to be careful. So, too, negligence in the discharge of a professional duty, as it was recognised before, so it survived on its own credentials after, the evolution of contract. In *Russell* v. *Palmer* the plaintiff alleged that the defendant, ' being retained or employed as the plaintiff's attorney or agent,' and ' undertaking and faithfully promising ' to execute his duty with discretion, ' so negligently and inadvertently conducted and behaved himself in his said employment that by reason of his said negligence and omission ' the plaintiff was damaged. The language was contractual, but the duty was tortious. ' We are all of opinion,' said the Court, ' that this action is well conceived and lies against Mr. Palmer for negligence.'[17]

The search for principle in the law of bailment has provoked a variety of supplementary questions and a corresponding diversity of answers. It has raised in particular the problem of the ' public ' or ' common ' calling. What mediæval trades were comprised within this term, what liability was thereby involved and what were its relations to bailment in general? Professor Winfield[18] favours a miscellaneous catalogue, which would include the carrier and the innkeeper, the surgeon and the marshal or veterinary surgeon, the smith or farrier and, in a descending scale of probability, the ferryman, the carpenter, the shepherd and the barber. He lays special stress upon the familiar remark of Fitzherbert in 1534 that ' it is the duty of every artificer to exercise his art rightly and truly as he ought.'[19] But its significance in this context is not obvious. It occurs only as a pendant to a specimen writ against a smith which makes no reference to a ' common calling,' and it is paralleled by two precedents given by Rastell against a barber and a surgeon with similar omissions.[20] Holmes, in his Common Law, was content with the innkeeper, the carrier and the smith. Pollock denied the title of the smith, and Professor Plucknett has doubted even the carrier.[21] The latter's position is interesting. On the one hand, no reference to his legal condition can be traced before 1523.[22] On the other hand, contemporary evidence amply attests his rôle in the social and economic life of the fifteenth century. The Paston letters refer constantly to the Norwich carrier;[23] a witness in the Star Chamber in 1484 deposed that ' he was used to carry Linen cloth and other merchandises from Exeter to

---

[17] *Russell* v. *Palmer* (1767) 2 Wilson, 325; and see *Slater* v. *Baker* (1767) 2 Wilson, 359—an action against a surgeon. For the legacy of confusion left by the supposed necessity of associating assumpsit irrevocably with contract, see Cheshire and Fifoot, *The Law of Contract*, 2nd ed., pp. 60-3.

[18] 42 L.Q.R., pp. 185-190.

[19] F.N.B. 94d, *supra*, p. 89.

[20] *Collection of Entries, Accion sur le case* 6 and 44, *supra*, p. 90.

[21] Holmes, *The Common Law*, pp. 183-198; Pollock on Torts, 14th ed. at p. 429; Plucknett, *Concise History*, 4th ed., pp. 451-3.

[22] Doctor and Student, c. 38. Cf. *infra*, p. 160.

[23] See Bennett, *The Pastons and their England*, pp. 159-164.

London by the space of thirty-five years last past ';[24] and the University carrier was favoured as a nurse for undergraduates too tender to travel alone.[25]   It would seem on the whole that, at least by the sixteenth century, he was admitted to share with the innkeeper the responsibilities of the ' common calling,' but that no other tradesman may safely be included in the description.   The absence, moreover, of any examination of these responsibilities before the development of Case[26] suggests that neither the innkeeper nor the carrier is to be regarded as a genuine antique and that each may, without impropriety, be discussed with bailees in general.

Upon the major question issue has been joined between Holmes, supported by Sir William Holdsworth, on the one side and Professor Plucknett and Dr. Fletcher on the other.[27]   According to Holmes, the law of bailment, as befitted a stock of ' pure German descent,'[28] was based upon a principle of strict liability and retained its canon uncorrupted not only throughout the middle ages but as late as the dawn of the eighteenth century.   It was only in the degenerate days of Holt that its primitive simplicity was marred by the strain of negligence and that the ' common callings ' were left as survivors of a stronger age.[29]   Professor Plucknett and Dr. Fletcher are unable to draw so uncompromising a conclusion from the mediæval records.   So far as these may be interpreted, they tend to rebut rather than to support the theory of strict liability.   Such a theory, according to this view, was an innovation in the time and under the influence of Coke, and Holt's judgment in *Coggs* v. *Bernard* was a necessary attempt to reconcile the new precedents and the old.

The evidence, marshalled by Dr. Fletcher, merits attention both for its intrinsic importance and for the light shed upon the place of negligence in the law.   Of the text-books, Glanvill undoubtedly required the *commodatarius* to pay the value of a chattel lost, for whatever cause, while in his custody; but he confined his attention

[24] S.S. Vol. 16, p. 84.

[25] A deed of 1459, designed to settle the respective jurisdictions of the Chancellor of the University and of the Mayor of the City of Oxford, accorded the privileges of the University to ' alle common caryers, bryngers of Scolers to the Universite, or their money, letters, or any especiall message to eny Scoler or clerk or fetcher of any Scoler or clerk fro the Universite for the tyme of fetchyng or bryngyng or abydyng in the Universite for that entent.' The deed is given in *Munimenta Academica*, ed. Anstey (1868) I, pp. 346-7, and is cited by Bennett, *The Pastons and their England*, p. 163, and by Mallet, *History of the Univ. of Oxford*, I, pp. 332-3.

[26] The first reference to the Innkeeper is in 1369: *supra*, p. 80.

[27] Holmes, *The Common Law*, Lecture V, and Holdsworth, H.E.L. III, 336-350 and VII, 450-5; Plucknett, *Concise History*, 4th ed., pp. 447-453; and Fletcher, *The Carrier's Liability* (1932), a most valuable monograph.   Professor Beale, *Essays in Anglo-American Legal History*, III, 148, has also criticised Holmes, while P. & M. II, 170, are noncommittal.

[28] *The Common Law*, p. 175.   The hypothesis of an original reservoir of Teutonic law, presumably of exceptional purity, intrigued the nineteenth-century jurists, but seems to be wholly romantic.

[29] *Coggs* v. *Bernard* (1703) 2 Ld. Raym. 909: *infra*, p. 173.

to the single case of the gratuitous borrower.[30] Bracton distinguished between one bailee and another: he affirmed the strict duty of the borrower, but held the hirer and the pledgee liable only for *culpa* and the depositary only for *dolus*.[31] His account may be received, according to taste or prejudice, as an empty Romanesque flourish or as an intelligent, if over-refined, deduction from the contemporary law. From the mediæval cases Holmes, in support of his thesis, had selected two as especially significant. In *Bowdon* v. *Pelleter* in 1315 the plaintiff sued the defendant in Detinue, and alleged that he had bailed to her a variety of chattels ranging from a bed to a purse and that she had refused to re-deliver them. The defendant offered a double plea: that the chattels had been bailed to her locked in a chest and that the chest was stolen from her together with other goods of her own.[32] Holmes assumed that the first of these pleas was alone relevant, since, if the plaintiff had delivered a locked chest, there was no bailment of the chattels as such. But it is clear from the record that issue was taken upon both pleas and that proof of the theft would have excused the defendant. The suggestion that the defendant's own goods had been simultaneously stolen was presumably made to justify the inference that she had taken as much care of the bailor's property as of her own.

In the *Case of the Marshalsea* in 1455 the plaintiff sued the Keeper of the King's Bench prison for the escape of a debtor committed to his charge.[33] The defendant pleaded that the prison had been broken open and the prisoners released by ' a great multitude of the King's enemies ' and that such an act afforded him as ample a defence as would the Act of God. Holmes supposed the Court to have distinguished an entry by alien and by domestic enemies. The former was a valid defence, but the latter was not, since the defendant would have his action against the third parties and so would be liable to his bailor.[34] Such an interpretation, and certainly the larger inference thereby implied, are not warranted by the report of the case. The form of action was not Detinue, but Debt; the defendant was not the bailee of a chattel; the analogy on which he relied was the law, not of bailment, but of waste; and no decision was recorded. Of the two judges whose remarks survive, Danby, J., did indeed rest liability on the possibility of a remedy over against a third party, but Prisot, C.J., spoke in terms of negligence. The case is therefore inconclusive.

---

[30] Glanvill, Book X, Chap. 13: *infra,* p. 234.
[31] Bracton, Book III, f. 99a, b.
[32] Y.B. 8 Ed. II (S.S.) Vol. 41, pp. 136-7.
[33] Y.B. 33 Hen. 6, f. 1, pl. 3, *infra,* p. 168.
[34] The general argument is obscured by the question, repeatedly posed by Holmes, whether the bailee was answerable to the bailor because he could sue a third party or whether he could sue the third party because he was answerable to the bailor. The answer may well have had practical consequences, but historically the question resembles too nearly the riddle of the chicken and the egg.

Elsewhere, however, the judges admitted limitations upon the liability of a bailee. In 1355 it was said that ' if one bails me goods to keep and I put them with mine and they are stolen, I will not be charged ';[35] and in 1431 that, ' if I give goods to a man to keep to my use and by his misguard they are stolen, he shall be charged, but if he be robbed of them he is excusable.'[36] The suggestion of carelessness, though faint, is perceptible, and it grows stronger in the early years of the sixteenth century. Chief Justice Frowicke in 1505 emphasised the necessity of ' good custody,'[37] and in the passage in *Doctor and Student*, where reference is first made to the ' common carrier,' he is to be liable ' if he go by the way that be dangerous for robbers or drive by night or in other inconvenient time, and be robbed, or if he overcharge a horse whereby he falls into the water or otherwise so that the stuff is hurt or impaired.'[38]

The mediæval evidence, while it allows no positive deduction, can hardly be said to reveal a relentless insistence upon strict liability. The picture may be enlarged or relieved by a glance at the cognate subject of carriage by sea.[39] This was governed not by the common but by the civil law, administered in the Court of Admiralty. No files were kept by the Court before 1524 and no reports published until 1764; but it is clear from the records of the reign of Elizabeth that the ultimate criterion was fault. The shipmaster was liable to the cargo owner, not for simple failure to deliver, but for *dolus* or *culpa,* and the atmosphere of negligence was pervasive. Two qualifications must be made. The parties could vary the incidence of risk by suitable provisions in the bills of lading,[40] and the onus of proof, in contrast to the common law procedure, was cast upon the defendant. It was for him to prove diligence and not for the plaintiff to prove fault. Thus in *Proctor* v. *Downes*[41] the plaintiff alleged that the defendant had received on board his ship, the ' Christopher ' of Ipswich, eight casks of wine for carriage from Bordeaux to London and that they had been damaged in transit. The defendants pleaded that the ship had met heavy storms in the Bay of Biscay and that the damage, if any, was

[35] *Per* Thorpe, B. in *Anon,* 29 Lib. Ass. f. 163, pl. 28. The bailee in this case was a pledgee.
[36] *Per* Cottesmore, J. in *Anon,* Y.B. 10 Hen. 6, f. 21, pl. 69.
[37] *Anon,* Keilway, at p. 78: *infra,* p. 353.
[38] c. 38, *supra,* p. 157. Dr. Fletcher, at p. 26, depreciates the weight of this passage on the ground that ' its author, St. Germain, was primarily a student of the canon law and interested in the development of equity, and still more so in theology.' His work, therefore, can hardly be regarded ' as an authoritative exposition of the contemporary common law.' St. Germain, however, was a successful practitioner, and his book would seem, on the whole, to be intended as a defence of the common law, of whose doctrines it is a sound exposition.
[39] See Fletcher, *The Carrier's Liability,* pp. 51-101.
[40] The earliest known English bill of lading is dated 1538. See Fletcher, p. 85, and *Select Pleas of the Admiralty* (S.S. Vol. 6) Vol. I, p. 61. In 1545 a bill of lading is recorded with a clause expressly exempting the master from all liability, while in a bill of 1602, on the other hand, the cargo owner found it desirable expressly to impose all risks upon him: Fletcher, pp. 86 and 90.
[41] (1580) Fletcher, p. 70.

caused ' by the said sea and tempest and without fault or negligence on the part of the master or mariners.' In *Guallerottie* v. *Utwicke*[42] the plaintiff at Hamburg loaded on the defendant's ship ' Sampson ' a bale of silk for carriage to London, and alleged non-delivery. According to the defendant, the ship had been boarded off Emden by ' Teuton pirates ' who had overpowered the crew and seized the silk. The ship had been fully manned (with four men), and it was customary, in time of peace, to sail from Hamburg to London without escort. The defendant therefore urged, and the Court held, that the cargo had been lost *sine dolo aut culpa* and that he was not liable.

The seventeenth century opened with the important case of *Southcote* v. *Bennet*.[43] The plaintiff declared that he had delivered goods to the defendant for safe custody and that they had not been returned. The defendant pleaded that he had been robbed of them by a third party. The plaintiff replied that the third party was in truth the defendant's servant. The Court, dismissing the reply as irrelevant and glossing the case of the Marshalsea to serve as their authority, gave judgment for the plaintiff. The simple delivery of goods charged the defendant ' to keep them at his peril.' The case, whether it be acclaimed as the triumph of historical continuity or reproved as an innovation, clearly sought to base the law of bailment upon the ground of strict liability. But it contained two features which forbid too rash a generalisation. On the one hand, the success of Assumpsit had popularised the advantages of contract, and the Court tempered the severity of their doctrine, at least to future litigants, by reminding the defendant that he had only himself to blame for not having secured the protection of a special agreement. This course, indeed, was recommended to bailees by Coke in a note to his report. On the other hand, the form of action was in Detinue, and it is by no means sure that the result would have been the same had the plaintiff sued in an action on the case. The position was tested within the next thirty years, and three possibilities emerged. If the defendant were sued in assumpsit, he was liable according to the precise tenor of his undertaking.[44] If he were sued as a common carrier, he was strictly liable, according to ' the custom of the realm,' for failure to deliver the goods at the proper place and in good condition.[45] If the plaintiff, while suing in case, relied neither on an assumpsit nor on a common calling, he would succeed only by proving negligent misconduct.[46]

[42] (1571) Fletcher, p. 72.
[43] (1601) Croke, Eliz. 815; 4 Coke Rep. 83b: *infra*, p. 169.
[44] *Rogers* v. *Head* (1610) Croke, Jac. 262. Compare the words of the Court in the familiar case of *Paradine* v. *Jane* (1647), Aleyn, 26: ' When the party by his own contract creates a duty or charge upon himself, he is bound to make it good, if he may, notwithstanding any accident by inevitable necessity, because he might have provided against it by his contract.'
[45] *Rich* v. *Kneeland* (1613) Hobart, 17.
[46] *Symons* v. *Darknoll* (1628) Palmer, 523.

A further complication followed the waning fortunes of the Admiralty. Under the influence of Coke, jealous to preserve and to enhance the powers of the Common Law, a fiction had been devised to bring within the jurisdiction of the latter cases which might more properly have fallen within the province of the Law Merchant.[47] The nature and effect of this fiction may be judged from the counter-attack made upon the Common Law by Prynne in his *Animadversions on the Fourth Part of Coke's Institutes.*[48] He resented the ' new strange poetical fiction,' whereby contracts made in foreign parts were alleged to be made

> ' in the Parish of Bow in Cheapside within the City of London or in the Parish of Hackney, Stepney or Islington within the County of Middlesex . . .; and so, by this new-coyned, untraversable fiction, which must be admitted for truth, though never so false and impossible, transporting whole Kingdoms, Countries, Cities, Rivers, Ports, Creeks, Shores in foreign parts, into Cheapside in London or Islington in Middlesex (which no Miracle or Omnipotency itself can do, because a direct contradiction repugnant to nature, experience, scripture and God's own constitution, who hath inviolably and immutably severed them by distinct bounds and large distances from each other), they pretend and resolve that the contract, bargain or thing done beyond the Sea is now become triable only at the Common Law, and not in the Admiralty by the Law of Merchants, Oleron or the Civil Law; and restrain the plaintiffs and the Admiralty by Prohibitions to proceed any further in them.'

But the protest, though spirited, was belated, and after the Restoration the Common Law encroached ever more nearly upon the province of its rival. At first, indeed, it had been content to take the profits of the litigation without its principles, and negligence, as in the Maritime Law of the previous century, remained the criterion of liability.[49] But it was impossible, within the same jurisdiction, long to segregate as distinct species the sea and the land carrier, and any process of assimilation was bound to be at the expense of the former.

This medley of common and civil law, of tort and contract, of strict liability and negligence, had somehow to be reconciled. The

---

[47] *Dowdale's Case* (1606) 6 Coke Rep. 46b.

[48] Published in 1669. Coke's Fourth Institute concerned the jurisdiction of Courts. Prynne's defence of the Admiralty is at pp. 75-133 of his work. He did not condemn fictions as such, but their improper use where, as here, the Admiralty offered an adequate remedy. So the Common Law fictions of *venue* ' are against the end, use and nature of all legal fictions, which are to do right and justice to persons injured in an extraordinary way and manner, when they cannot do it by ordinary means and methods; else no fiction is to be afforded.' Prynne himself suffered many and strange vicissitudes. He lost his ears in the Star Chamber for a gross attack upon Queen Henrietta Maria, he was a leading member of the Long Parliament, he attacked the rule of the army after the death of Charles I and was imprisoned by Cromwell for three years without trial, and he ended his career as Keeper of the Tower Records under Charles II.

[49] Thus in *Pickering* v. *Barkley* (1648) Styles, 132, an action of covenant for breach of a charter-party was decided by the Common Bench upon the evidence of mercantile custom.

first attempt was made by Sir Matthew Hale in *Morse* v. *Slue*.[50] In an action on the case the plaintiff declared against the defendant on two counts: as a common carrier by custom of the realm and in negligence as a bailee for reward. The second count, though it involved a heavier burden of proof, would be needed if he failed to associate a shipmaster with the ' public callings ' of the common law. After two arguments Sir Matthew Hale gave judgment for the plaintiff. As the ship was in the Port of London the Admiralty jurisdiction was excluded and her master was in the same position as a carrier by land. In default of any special agreement to the contrary, he was held strictly responsible for the safety of the goods. The decision would thus appear to have been taken upon the first count and to have established at least the liability of such persons as could be said to follow a ' public ' or ' common calling.'

It still remained to determine whether the decision in *Southcote* v. *Bennet,* imposing a strict liability upon the bailee in general as opposed to the particular calling of the common carrier and of the innkeeper, applied in Case as in Detinue. The problem was faced by Chief Justice Holt in *Coggs* v. *Bernard*.[51] The plaintiff declared in an action on the case that the defendant had undertaken (*assumpsisset*) to move for him several hogsheads of brandy and that he had done the work so carelessly (*tam negligenter et improvide*) that much of the brandy was spilt. The defendant objected that the declaration neither described him as a common carrier nor alleged that he was a bailee for reward. Judgment was unanimously given for the plaintiff. Holt sought to rationalise the law by classifying bailments according to the recipe of Justinian as adapted for English minds by Bracton —' an old author,' he admitted, but one whose doctrine was ' agreeable to reason and to what the law is in other countries.' He was able to enumerate six classes. The depositary, acting solely for the bailor's benefit, was answerable only for ' gross neglect.' The gratuitous borrower and the bailee to whom goods were hired were each liable for the ' least neglect.' The pledgee owed no more than ' ordinary care.' Carriers and other bailees trusted with the management of goods must be sub-divided: if they exercised a ' common calling ' they were under a strict liability, but if, without such status, they practised for reward, they must show ' reasonable care.' Finally, the *mandatarius,* or manager without reward, while under no obligation to keep his promise to act, was yet liable if he entered upon his task and injured the bailor's goods by a ' neglect in his management.' Holt thus accepted, while limiting, the authority of *Morse* v. *Slue,* but exposed the pretensions of the Court in *Southcote* v. *Bennet* to masquerade as the guardians of ancient tradition and to prescribe a single

[50] (1671) 1 Ventris, 190, 238: *infra,* p. 171.
[51] (1703) 3 Ld. Raym. 909: *infra,* p. 173.

doctrine of strict liability which should extend from Detinue to Case. The attempt to mark the degrees of carelessness was neither happy nor successful, but the judgment as a whole settled the law of bailment upon the basis of negligence and isolated the common carrier and innkeeper as persons who exercised special trades and owed special duties.

By the beginning of the eighteenth century the judges were familiar with the name and idea of negligence. While it flowed strongly through the channels of assumpsit and bailment, its influence was diffused over most of the branches of Case.[52]   It was, however, too early to speak boldly of an action of negligence.   The books of the period, if unduly conservative, showed how much must be done before such a generalisation could be attempted.   Comyns in his Digest offered, as examples of the ' Action on the Case for Negligence,' such indiscriminate items as Assumpsit, Bailment and Fire, where the word was appropriate, Prescriptive Duties, where it had always been irrelevant, and Common Callings, where it had been decisively repudiated.[53] Blackstone's treatment was still more curious.[54]. He included liability for negligence in his discussion of ' Contracts implied by reason and construction of law,' which ' arise upon the supposition that every one who undertakes any office, employment, trust or duty, contracts with those who employ or entrust him to perform it with integrity, diligence and skill.   And, if by his want of either of those qualities any injury accrues to individuals, they have therefore their remedy in damages by a special action on the case.' Here, it might be thought, was at least a comprehensive formula, however strangely constructed; but the ' few instances ' which he deemed sufficient to ' illustrate this matter ' were no more than the stale miscellanea which contented Comyns.

The prime factor in the ultimate transformation of negligence from a principle of liability in Case to an independent tort was the luxuriant crop of ' running-down' actions reaped from the commercial prosperity of the late eighteenth and early nineteenth centuries. Their significance lay rather in their number than in their nature. So long as they could be indulged as the occasional accidents of litigation, they called for no special attention; but when they became a daily occurrence, the judges were forced to recognize a formidable phenomenon which could not be confined, without too gross an artificiality, within the conventional categories. The pressure was felt by sea as well as land. Between 1790 and 1800 many actions were brought against

---

[52] e.g. the precedent offered by Lilly in his *Collection of Modern Entries* from the case of *Browne* v. *Davis* (1706): *infra*, p. 180.
[53] Sir John Comyns was Chief Baron of the Exchequer from 1738 to his death in 1740. His *Digest of the Laws of England* was published posthumously between 1762 and 1767.
[54] *Commentaries*, III, pp. 163-5.

defendants for ' negligently, carelessly and unskilfully navigating ' their ships or for ' so incautiously, carelessly, negligently and inexpertly managing, steering and directing ' them, that the plaintiff's vessel was struck and injured.[55] But it was the drastic improvement in the condition of the roads together with a wider distribution of material comforts which filled so happily the judges' lists and turned their minds from the old setting of negligence to the new.[56] It was no longer, as in assumpsit and bailment, one only of several elements all of which the plaintiff must prove to succeed, but the central feature around which his declaration was framed. The ' action on the case for negligence,' which in Comyns' Digest was an empty title, had become a reality. Nor could this orientation of thought, once effected, be restricted to a single, if prolific, class of action. It must slowly but inexorably permeate every type of careless damage.

The new judicial outlook was revealed, none the less vividly because its facts were the merest commonplace of the law, by the case of *Govett* v. *Radnidge* in 1802.[57] The plaintiff declared against three defendants that, for a certain reward, they had undertaken to load a hogshead of treacle and had done their work ' so carelessly, negligently and unskilfully ' that it had been staved and the treacle lost. At the trial the jury had found against one defendant but in favour of the others, and it was argued that the claim was essentially contractual and that, as the transaction was joint, the acquittal of one or more of the contractors involved the acquittal of all. Lord Ellenborough, however, held that the plaintiff might declare at his option in contract or in tort and that the count on which the verdict was taken might be construed as the latter so as to warrant recovery against a single defendant. The ' employment for hire ' could be set aside as incidental and the ' tortious negligence ' interpreted as the breach of an autonomous 'duty.' The judgment, consciously or unconsciously, foreshadowed the development of a century. Lord Ellenborough strove, in the first place, to free the idea of negligence from the influence of contract to which it had been subjected by its long association with assumpsit. That the attempt was perhaps premature and certainly indecisive was shown by the preoccupation with ' privity ' which embarrassed his successors, but its partial success need not detract

---

[55] e.g. *Drewry* v. *Twiss* (1792) 4 T.R. 558: *Sedgworth* v. *Overend* (1797) 7 T.R. 279: *Ogle* v. *Barnes* (1799) 8 T.R. 188: *Williams* v. *Holland* (1833) 10 Bing. 112, *infra*, p. 209.

[56] For a single example of innumerable declarations, see *Morley* v. *Gaisford* (1795) 2 H. Bl. 442, *infra*, p. 180. The rich variety of conveyance encouraged by the new roads may be judged by the slightly later evidence of a Turnpike Act of 1833 which imposed a toll of 6d. for every ' coach, sociable, chariot, berlin, landau, vis-a-vis, barouche, phaeton, curricle, calash, chaise, chair, gig, whiskey, caravan, hearse and litter.' When a whiskey met a vis-a-vis, almost anything might be expected.

[57] 3 East, 62, *infra*, p. 181. Cf. Tindal, C.J. in *Williams* v. *Holland* (1833) 10 Bing. 112, *infra*, p. 209: ' carelessness and negligence is, strictly and properly in itself, the subject of an action on the case.'

from its audacity. He seemed, in the second place and even more boldly, to reach beyond the limits of Case and to anticipate the independent and vigorous tort which was revealed by the procedural reforms of the Victorian Age and which has since come to dominate the whole law of civil liability. Finally, he introduced the concept of duty which is still admitted to be the necessary correlative of negligence. The invention was not altogether happy, but it may well have seemed inevitable to judges who sought a substitute for that almost automatic limit upon the legal consequences of carelessness which the forms of action had provided.

S O U R C E S

BEAULIEU v. FINGLAM
Y.B. 2 HEN. 4, f. 18, pl. 6
A.D. 1401

One brought this writ. *Si Willielmus Beaulieu [fecerit te securum de clamore suo prosequendo tunc] pone Rogerum Finglam [quod sit coram justiciariis nostris ostensurus] quare, cum secundum legem et consuetudinem regni nostri Angliæ hactenus obtentas quod quilibet de eodem regno ignem suum salvo et secure custodiat et custodire teneatur ne per ignem suum dampnum aliquod vicinis suis ullo modo eveniat, prædictus Rogerus ignem suum apud Carlion tam negligenter custodivit, quod pro defectu debitæ custodiæ ignis prædicti bona et catalla ipsius Willielmi ad valentiam quadraginta librarum in domibus ibidem existentia ac domus prædicta adtunc et ibidem per ignem illum combusta extiterunt, ad dampnum ipsius Willielmi, etc.* And he counted accordingly.

Hornby: Judgment of the count; for he has counted upon a common custom of the realm, and he has not said that this custom has been used [from time whereof, etc.].

To which TOTA CURIA said: Answer over; for the common custom of the realm is the common law of the realm.

THIRNING, C.J. said that a man shall answer for his fire, which by misfortune burns another's goods.

And some were of the opinion that the fire could not be said to be his fire, because a man cannot have any property in fire; but that opinion was not upheld.

MARKHAM, J.: A man is held to answer for the act of his servant or of his guest in such a case; for if my servant or my guest puts a candle by a wall and the candle falls into the straw and burns all my house and the house of my neighbour also, in this case I shall answer to my neighbour for his damage; *quod concedebatur per Curiam.*

Hornby: Then he ought to have sued out a writ, *quare domum suam ardebat vel exarsit.*

Hull: This will be against all reason, to put blame or default in a man, where he has none in law; for the negligence of his servants cannot be termed his feasance.

THIRNING, C.J.: If a man kills or slays a man by misfortune, he shall forfeit his goods, and he must obtain his charter of pardon as an act of grace. *Ad quod Curia concordat.*

MARKHAM, J.: I shall answer to my neighbour for each person who enters my house by my leave or my knowledge, or is my guest through me or through my servant, if he does any act, as with a candle or aught else, whereby my neighbour's house is burnt. But if a man from outside my house and against my will starts a fire in the thatch of my house or elsewhere, whereby my house is burned and my neighbours' houses are burned as well, for this I shall not be held bound to them; for this cannot be said to be done by wrong on my part, but is against my will.

Hornby: This defendant will be undone and impoverished all his days if this action is to be maintained against him; for then twenty other such suits will be brought against him for the same matter.

THIRNING, C.J.: What is that to us? It is better that he should be utterly undone than that the law be changed for him.

And then they joined issue that the plaintiff's house was not burned by the fire of the defendant.

TURBERVILLE v. STAMP

PLEADINGS: 3 LD. RAYMOND, 375

A.D. 1697

Dorsetshire, (to wit).—Be it remembered that heretofore, to wit, in the term of Easter last past before our lord the King at Westminster came Thomas Turberville the younger, Esq., by Edward Lawrence his attorney, and brought into the Court of our said lord the King then and there his certain bill against John Stamp, gent., in the custody of the marshal, etc. of a plea of trespass upon the case; and there are pledges of prosecuting, to wit, John Doe and Richard Roe; which said bill followeth in these words, to wit,

Dorsetshire, to wit: Thomas Turberville the younger, Esq., complains of John Stamp, gent., being in the custody of the marshal of the Marshalsea of the lord the King before the King himself, for that, to wit, that, whereas according to the law and custom of this realm of England hitherto used and approved every man of the same realm is bound to keep his fire safely and securely by day and by night, lest for want of the due keeping of such fire any damage in any manner happen to any person of the same realm; and whereas the said Thomas on the 6th day of April in the 9th year of the reign of our Lord William the Third now King of England, etc., was possessed of a certain close of heath lying and being in the parish of Stoke in the county aforesaid; and also whereas the said John the same day and year above said was likewise possessed of a certain other close of heath next adjoining to the aforesaid close of him the said Thomas in the parish and county aforesaid; the said John on the day and year and at the place aforesaid so negligently and improvidently kept his fire in the said close of heath of him the said John, that for want of the due keeping of the said fire the heath and furzes of him the said Thomas to the value of forty pounds in the said close of heath of him the said Thomas then growing and being were burnt, to the great damage of him the said Thomas and contrary to the custom aforesaid; whereupon he saith that he is injured and hath sustained damage to the value of £40, and thereupon he brings suit, etc.

And now here at this day, to wit, Friday next after the morrow of the Holy Trinity in this same term, until which day the said John had leave to imparl to the said bill and then to answer, etc. before the lord the King at Westminster, comes as well the said Thomas by his attorney aforesaid as the said John by Samuel Brewster his attorney; and the said John defends the force and injury when, etc., and saith that he is not guilty thereof; and of this he puts himself upon the country, and the aforesaid Thomas likewise, etc. . . .

PROCEEDINGS IN THE KING'S BENCH: 12 MOD. 152

Action upon the case on the custom of the realm for negligently keeping of his fire; declaring that the plaintiff was possessed of a close of heath, that the defendant was possessed of another close next adjoining, and that the defendant *tam improvide custodivit ignem suum* in his field that it burnt the plaintiff's heath in his field.

After verdict for the plaintiff, it was moved in arrest of judgment that such an action on the case lies only for a negligent keeping of his fire in his house; and that in this case he should have his action specially if he be damaged, and not count on the general custom for negligence.

TURTON, J.: There is difference between fire in a man's house and in the fields. In some countries it is a necessary part of husbandry to make fire on the ground, and some unavoidable accident may carry it into a neighbour's ground and do injury there; and this fire, not being so properly in his custody as the fire in his house, I think is not actionable, as it is laid.

But by HOLT, C.J., ROKEBY and EYRE, J.J.: Every man must so use his own as not to injure another. The law is general. The fire which a man makes in the fields is as much his fire as his fire in his house; it is made on his ground with his materials and by his order, and he must at his peril take care that it does not, through his neglect, injure his neighbour. If he kindle it at a proper time and place, and the violence of the wind carry it into his neighbour's ground and prejudice him, this is fit to be given in evidence. But now here it is found to have been by his negligence; and it is the same as if it had been in his house.

Judgment was given for the Plaintiff.

THE CASE OF THE MARSHALSEA

Y.B. HIL. 33 HEN. 6, f. 1, pl. 3

A.D. 1455

Debt was sued against the Marshal of the King's Bench. And he counted on the Statute,[58] and that one T., who was condemned to the plaintiff in a certain sum in an Assise of Novel Disseisin, sued a writ of Error before the King and then the judgment was affirmed, and the said T. was committed

---

[58] *Quare*, what Statute? Statutory provision was made for Debt to lie against a Gaoler for the escape of a prisoner in special cases—e.g. Statute of Merchants (1285), *infra*, p. 239, Statute of Westminster II (as to accountants), *infra*, p. 278, and 1 Rich. II c. 12 (against the Warden of the Fleet). But no Statute seems to prescribe Debt against the Marshal of the Marshalsea. Perhaps the Blackletter text is here, as in too many instances, corrupt. It is significant that neither Fitzherbert (Abr. Barre, 57) nor Brooke (Abr. Dette, 22), in their notes of the case, refer to any Statute; nor does any such reference appear in the precedents in Rastell, Entries, f. 167b *et seq.*

into the keeping of the Marshal for the sum; and that he let him go at large, *a tort et a ses damages.*[59]

Choke: No action lies: for he says that a great multitude of the King's enemies on such a day and year came to Southwark, and there they broke into the prison of our lord the King and took the prisoners there found out of the said prison, and among them the said T., and took them against the will of the said Marshal; *without this,* that he let him go at large or in any other manner as alleged. If enemies from France or other enemies of the King had been here, the Marshal would be discharged; just as, if they had burned the house of a tenant for life, or if his house were burned through a sudden tempest, he would be discharged from liability for Waste. So here.

DANBY, J.: In your case of the King's enemies or of the sudden tempest, that is reasonable, for there he has no remedy over against anyone; but it is otherwise where the King's lieges thus act, for then you may have action against them.

Choke: Sir, the captain is dead, and all the others are unknown.

PRISOT, C.J.: If they were the King's lieges, they would not be called the King's enemies, but traitors, for enemies are those who are outside the allegiance; though, if they were alien enemies, this would be a good plea without any doubt. But if there were 12 or 20 persons, lieges of the King and unknown, and one night they broke into the prison and there took [the prisoners] outside, etc.; in this case the Marshal would be charged for his negligent keeping. So here. But if it were by sudden adventure of fire and the prison were burned and they escaped, peradventure it would be otherwise.

Choke: If a stranger comes to my house, and by his folly it is burned, and the house of my neighbour is also burned, I shall not be charged with setting fire to my neighbour's house. And, Sir, if the King's liege joins himself with the King's enemies and takes equal part with them, and afterwards he comes and does this thing, he will be taken to have done it as himself an enemy of the King.

PRISOT, C.J.: In your case he would not be deemed to be a prisoner, to make his ransom as an enemy would; but he will be taken as a traitor to the King.

Choke: Then we say that there were four Scotsmen here and others of the King's enemies, together with other traitors.

DANBY, J.: Then you must show the matter with more particularity (*plus specialment*), and give their names.

Et adjornatur.

SOUTHCOTE v. BENNET
A.D. 1601
A. REPORT IN CROKE, ELIZ. 815

Detinue of goods; and counts that he delivered them to the defendant to keep safely, etc. The defendant confesseth the delivery, and that afterwards

---

[59] Supplementary information from the Plea Rolls is given by Dr. Fletcher in his *Carrier's Liability* (1932) App. IV. The plaintiff was John Combe and the defendant John Gargrave. The escape was alleged as on 12 August, 1450, and by 1455, when the action was brought, Gargrave had ceased to be Marshal. The case was adjourned seven times from Hilary, 1455, to Michaelmas, 1456, and no final entry appears to have been made on the roll.

J. S. feloniously robbed him of them. Wherefore, etc. The plaintiff replies, *protestando* that J. S. did not rob him,[60] for plea saith that the said J. S. was servant to the defendant. And it was thereupon demurred.

And after argument at the Bar, GAWDY and CLENCH [J.J.], *ceteris absentibus,* held that the plaintiff ought to recover, because it was not a special bailment—that the defendant accepted to keep them as his proper goods, and not otherwise—but it is a delivery, which chargeth him to keep them at his peril. And it is not any plea in a *detinue* to say that he was robbed by one such; for he hath his remedy over by trespass or appeal, to have them again. And that is the reason of 33 Hen. 6, pl. 1,[61] that, if a gaol be broke open by thieves and the prisoners let at large, yet the gaoler is chargeable, because he hath his remedy over; but if it be broken by the Queen's enemies, it is otherwise.

And although it was moved that the replication was vicious, for that the protestation is repugnant to the matter confessed, and then, the replication being ill, although the bar be vicious, the plaintiff cannot have judgment, as 2 Eliz. *Dautrie's Case* is; yet it was held to be but a default of form and not of substance; and, the demurrer being general, no advantage can be taken thereof.

Wherefore it was adjudged for the plaintiff.

B. REPORT IN 4 COKE REP. 83b

Southcote brought *detinue* against Bennet for certain goods, and declared that he delivered them to the defendant to keep safe: the defendant confessed the delivery, and pleaded in bar that after the delivery one J. S. stole them feloniously out of his possession: the plaintiff replied that the said J. S. was the defendant's servant retained in his service, and demanded judgment, etc. And thereupon the defendant demurred in law, and judgment was given for the plaintiff.

And the reason and cause of their judgment was, because the plaintiff delivered the goods to be safe kept, and the defendant had took it upon him by the acceptance upon such delivery, and therefore he ought to keep them at his peril, although in such case he should have nothing for his safe keeping. So if A. delivers goods to B. *generally* to be kept by him, and B. accepts them without having anything for it, if the goods are stole from him, yet he shall be charged in *detinue;* for to be kept, and to be kept safe, is all one. But if A. accepts goods of B. to keep them as he would keep his own proper goods, there, if the goods are stolen, he shall not answer for them; or, if goods are pawned or pledged to him for money and the goods are stolen, he shall not answer for them, for there he doth not undertake to keep them but as he keeps his own; for he has a property in them and not a custody only, and therefore he shall not be charged, as it is adjudged in 29 *Ass.* 28. But if, before the stealing, he who pawned them tendered the money and the other refused, then there is fault in him; and then the stealing after such tender, as it is there held, shall not discharge him. So if A. delivers to B. a chest locked to keep and he himself carries away the key, in that case if the goods are stolen B. shall not be charged, for A. did not trust B. with them nor did B. undertake to keep them, as it is adjudged in 8 *E.* 2. So the doubts which were conceived upon sundry differ-

[60] i.e., 'while not admitting that J. S. robbed him.'
[61] *Supra,* p. 168.

ing opinions in our books, in 29 *Ass.* 28: 3 *H.*7.4: 6 *H.*7.12: 10 *H.*7.26, of Keble and Fineux, are well reconciled; *vide* Bract. lib. 2, fol. 62b. But in *accompt* it is a good plea before the auditors for the factor that he was robbed, as appears by the books in 12 *E.*3; *Accompt*, 111: 41 *E.*3.3 and 9 *E.*4.40. For if a factor (although he has wages and salary) does all that which he by his industry can do, he shall be discharged; and he takes nothing upon him, but his duty is as a servant to merchandise the best that he can, and a servant is bound to perform the command of his master. But a ferryman, common innkeeper or carrier, who takes hire, ought to keep the goods in their custody safely, and shall not be discharged if they are stolen by thieves: *vide* 22 *Ass.* 41: *Br. Action sur le Case*, 78.

And the Court held the replication idle and vain, for *non refert* by whom the defendant was robbed: *vide* 33 *H.* 6. 31*a. b.*[62] If traitors break a prison, it shall not discharge the gaoler: otherwise, of the King's enemies of another kingdom; for in the one case he may have his remedy and recompense, and in the other not.

Nota, reader: it is good policy for him who takes any goods to keep, to take them in special manner, *scil.* to keep them as he keeps his own goods, or to keep them the best he can at the peril of the party, or, if they happen to be stolen or purloined, that he shall not answer for them; for he who accepteth them ought to take them in such or the like manner, or otherwise he may be charged by his general acceptance. So if goods are delivered to one to be delivered over, it is good policy to provide for himself in such special manner, for doubt of being charged by his general acceptance, which implies that he takes upon him to do it.

M O R S E v. S L U E

(1671), 1 VENTRIS, 190, 238

An action upon the case was brought by the plaintiff against the defendant; and he declared that, whereas according to the law and custom of England masters and governors of ships which go from London beyond sea and take upon them to carry goods beyond sea are bound to keep safely day and night the same goods without loss or subtraction, *ita quod pro defectu* of them they may not come to any damage; and whereas the 15th of May last the defendant was master of a certain ship called 'The William and John,' then riding at the port of London, and the plaintiff had caused to be laden on board her three trunks, and therein 400 pair of silk stockings and 174 pounds of silk, by him to be transported for a reasonable reward of freight to be paid, and he then and there did receive them and ought to have transported them etc.; but he did so negligently keep them that, in default of sufficient care and custody of him and his servants, 17 May, the same were totally lost out of the said ship.

Upon not guilty pleaded, a special verdict was found, *viz*:

That the ship lay in the river of Thames in the port of London in the parish of Stepney in the county of Middlesex, etc.

That the goods were delivered by the plaintiff on board the ship, etc., to be transported to Cadiz in Spain.

[62] The reference is 33 H.6.1., pl. 3: *supra*, p. 168.

That the goods being on board, there were a sufficient number of men for to look after and attend her left in her.[63]

That in the night came eleven persons on pretence of pressing of seamen for the King's service, and by force seized on these men (which were four or five, found to be sufficient, as before), and took the goods.

That the master was to have wages from the owners, and the mariners from the master.

That she was of the burthen of 150 ton, etc.

So the question was, upon a trial at Bar, whether the master was chargeable upon this matter.

It was insisted on for the plaintiff that he who took goods to carry them for profit ought to keep them at his peril.

To which it was answered, that there was no negligence appeared in the master. By the civil law, if goods were taken by pirates, the master shall not answer for them; and this is not the case of a carrier, for tho' here the goods are received on land, yet they are to be transported, and, being one entire contract, they shall not be under one law in the port and another at sea. The master is not liable in case of fire or sinking the ship; everyone knows the ship is liable to inevitable accidents, and there is no case of this nature in experience. And *Serjeant Maynard* added that this differed from the case of a carrier, for that he is paid by the owner of the goods; but here the master is servant to the owner of the ship, and he pays him, and not the merchant.

The Court inclined strongly for the defendant, there being not the least negligence in him; but it was appointed to be argued. . . . It was agreed on all hands that the master should have answered in case there had been any default in him or his mariners.

Report continued, 1 VENTRIS, 238

The case was argued two several terms at the Bar, by Mr. Holt for the plaintiff and Sir Francis Winnington for the defendant; and Mr. Molloy for the plaintiff and Mr. Wallop for the defendant; and by the judgment of the whole Court judgment was given this term for the plaintiff.

HALE, C.J. delivered the reasons as followeth: First, by the admiral civil law[64] the master is not chargeable *pro damno fatali,* as in case of pirates, storm, etc.; but where there is any negligence in him, he is. Secondly,this case is not to be measured by the rules of the admiral law, because the ship was *infra corpus comitatus.*

Then the first reason wherefore the master is liable is because he takes a reward; and the usage is that half wages is paid him before he goes out of the country.

Secondly, if the master would, he might have made a caution for himself, which he omitting and taking in the goods generally, he shall answer for what happens. There was a case (not long since) when one brought a box to a carrier, in which there was a great sum of money, and the carrier demanded of the owner what was in it. He answered that it was filled with silks and such like goods of mean value, upon which the carrier took it and was robbed; and resolved that he was liable. But if the carrier had told the owner that it was a dangerous time and, if there were money in it, he durst not take

---

[63] According to the report in 2 Keble, 866, there were four men: the gunner, two cooks and a cooper.

[64] i.e. the civil law as administered in the Court of the Admiral.

charge of it, and the owner had answered as before, this matter would have excused the carrier.

Thirdly, he that would take off the master in this case from the action must assign a difference between it and the case of a hoyman, common carrier or innholder.

'Tis objected, that the master is but a servant to the owners.

Answer: The law takes notice of him as more than a servant. 'Tis known that he may impawn the ship if occasion be, and sell *bona peritura*: he is rather an officer than a servant. In an escape the gaoler may be charged, tho' the sheriff is also liable; for *respondeat superior;* but the turnkey cannot be sued, for he is but a mere servant. By the civil law the master or owner is chargeable at the election of the merchant.

'Tis further objected, that he receives wages from the owners.

Answer: In effect the merchant pays him, for he pays the owners' freight, so that 'tis but handed over by them to the master. If the freight be lost, the wages are lost too; for the rule is, freight is the mother of wages. Therefore, tho' the declaration is that the master received wages of the merchant, and the verdict is that the owners pay it, 'tis no material variance.

Objection: 'Tis found that there were the usual number of men to guard the ship.

Answer: True, for the ship; but not with reference to the goods; for the number ought to be more or less as the port is dangerous and the goods of value. 33 *H*.6.1.[65]: if rebels break a gaol so that the prisoners escape, the gaoler is liable; but it is otherwise of enemies. So the master is not chargeable, where the ship is spoiled by pirates. And if a carrier be robbed by an hundred men, he is never the more excused.

COGGS v. BERNARD
(1703), 2 Ld. Raymond, 909

In an action upon the case the plaintiff declared *quod cum Bernard,* the defendant, the 10th of November, 13 Will. 3, at etc., *assumpsisset salvo et secure elevare* (*anglice,* to take up) several hogsheads of brandy then in a certain cellar of D., *et salvo et secure deponere* (*anglice,* to lay them down again) in a certain other cellar in Water Lane; the said defendant and his servants and agents *tam negligenter et improvide* put them down again into the said other cellar, *quod per defectum curæ ipsius* the defendant, his servants and agents, one of the casks was staved and a great quantity of brandy, *viz.,* so many gallons of brandy, was spilt. After not guilty pleaded, and a verdict for the plaintiff, there was a motion in arrest of judgment, for that it was not alleged in the declaration that the defendant was a common porter, nor averred that he had anything for his pains. And the case being thought to be a case of great consequence, it was this day argued *seriatim* by the whole court. . . .

[The whole court, Holt, C.J., Gould, Powys and Powell, J.J. delivered judgments in favour of the plaintiff.]

Holt, C.J.: The case is shortly this. This defendant undertakes to remove goods from one cellar to another, and there to lay them down safely; and he managed them so negligently that for want of care in him some of the goods were spoiled. Upon not guilty pleaded, there has been a verdict for the plaintiff, and that upon full evidence, the cause being tried before

---

[65] *Supra*, p. 168.

me at Guildhall. There has been a motion in arrest of judgment, that the declaration is insufficient because the defendant is neither laid to be a common porter nor that he is to have any reward for his labour, so that the defendant is not chargeable by his trade; and a private person cannot be charged in an action without a reward.

I have had a great consideration of this case; and because some of the books make the action lie upon the reward, and some upon the promise, at first I made a great question whether this declaration was good. But upon consideration, as this declaration is, I think the action will well lie. In order to show the grounds upon which a man shall be charged with goods put into his custody, I must show the several sorts of bailments. And there are six sorts of bailments. The first sort of bailment is a bare naked bailment of goods, delivered by one man to another to keep for the use of the bailor; and this I call a *depositum*, and it is that sort of bailment which is mentioned in *Southcote's Case*.[66] The second sort is, when goods or chattels that are useful are lent to a friend *gratis*, to be used by him; and this is called *commodatum*, because the thing is to be restored in *specie*. The third sort is when goods are left with the bailee to be used by him for hire; this is called *locatio et conductio*, and the lender is called *locator*, and the borrower *conductor*. The fourth sort is, when goods or chattels are delivered to another as a pawn, to be a security to him for money borrowed of him by the bailor; and this is called in Latin, *vadium*, and in English, a pawn or a pledge. The fifth sort is, when goods or chattels are delivered to be carried, or something is to be done about them, for a reward to be paid by the person who delivers them to the bailee, who is to do the thing about them. The sixth sort is, when there is a delivery of goods or chattels to somebody who is to carry them, or do something about them, *gratis*, without any reward for such his work or carriage, which is this present case. I mention these things, not so much that they are all of them so necessary in order to maintain the proposition which is to be proved, as to clear the reason of the obligation which is upon persons in cases of trust.

1. *Depositum.*—As to the first sort, where a man takes goods in his custody to keep for the use of the bailor, I shall consider for what things such a bailee is answerable. He is not answerable if they are stole without any fault in him, neither will a common neglect make him chargeable, but he must be guilty of some gross neglect. There is, I confess, a great authority against me; where it is held that a general delivery will charge the bailee to answer for the goods if they are stolen, unless the goods are specially accepted to keep them only as you will keep your own. But my Lord Coke has improved the case in his report of it[67]; for he will have it, that there is no difference between a special acceptance to keep safely, and an acceptance generally to keep. But there is no reason or justice, in such a case of a general bailment, and where the bailee is not to have any reward but keeps the goods merely for the use of the bailor, to charge him without some default in him. For if he keeps the goods in such a case with an ordinary care, he has performed the trust reposed in him. But according to this doctrine the bailee must answer for the wrongs of other people, which he is not, nor cannot be, sufficiently armed against. If the law be so, there must be some just and honest reason for it, or else some universal settled rule of law upon which it is grounded; and therefore it is incumbent

---

[66] *Supra*, p. 169.
[67] *Southcote* v. *Bennet, supra*, p. 169.

upon them that advance this doctrine to show an undisturbed rule and practice of the law according to this position. But to show that the tenor of the law was always otherwise, I shall give a history of the authorities in the books in this matter; and by them show, that there never was any such resolution given before *Southcote's Case*. The 29 Ass. 28 is the first case in the books upon that learning; and there the opinion is, that the bailee is not chargeable, if the goods are stole. As for 8 Edw. 2, Fitzh. Detinue 59: where goods are locked in a chest, and left with the bailee, and the owner took away the key, and the goods were stolen, it was held that the bailee should not answer for the goods: that case they say differs, because the bailor did not trust the bailee with them. But I cannot see the reason of that difference, nor why the bailee should not be charged with goods in a chest, as well as with goods out of a chest: for the bailee has as little power over them when they are out of a chest, as to any benefit he might have by them, as when they are in a chest; and he has as great power to defend them in one case as in the other. The case of 9 Edw. 4, 40 b, was but a debate at bar; for Danby was but a counsel then. Though he had been Chief Justice in the beginning of Edw. 4, yet he was removed, and restored again upon the restitution of Hen. 6, as appears by Dugdale's *Chronica Series*. So that what he said cannot be taken to be any authority, for he spoke only for his client; and Genny, for his client, said the contrary. The case in 3 Hen. 7, 4, is but a sudden opinion; and that by half the court; and yet, that is the only ground for this opinion of my Lord Coke, which besides he has improved. But the practice has been always at Guildhall, to disallow that to be a sufficient evidence to charge the bailee. And it was practised so before my time, all Chief Justice Pemberton's time, and ever since, against the opinion of that case. When I read *Southcote's Case* heretofore, I was not so discerning as my brother Powys tells us he was, to disallow that case at first; and came not to be of this opinion till I had well considered and digested that matter. Though I must confess, reason is strong against the case, to charge a man for doing such a friendly act for his friend; but so far is the law from being so unreasonable, that such a bailee is the least chargeable for neglect of any. For if he keeps the goods bailed to him but as he keeps his own, though he keeps his own but negligently, yet he is not chargeable for them; for the keeping them as he keeps his own is an argument of his honesty. *A fortiori*, he shall not be charged where they are stolen without any neglect in him. Agreeable to this is Bracton, lib. 3, c. 2, 99 b: ' *Is apud quem res deponitur, re obligatur, et de eâ re, quam accepit, restituendâ tenetur, et etiam ad id, si quid in re depositâ dolo commiserit; culpæ autem nomine non tenetur, scilicet desidiæ vel negligentiæ, quia qui negligenti amico rem custodiendam tradit, sibi ipsi et propriæ fatuitati hoc debet imputare.*' [68] As suppose the bailee is an idle, careless, drunken fellow, and comes home drunk, and leaves all his doors open, and by reason thereof the goods happen to be stolen and his own; yet he shall not be charged, because it is the bailor's own folly to trust such an idle fellow. So that this sort of bailee is the least responsible for neglects, and under the least obligation of any one, being bound to no other care of the bailed goods than he takes of his own. This Bracton I have cited is, I confess, an old author; but in this his doctrine is agreeable to reason, and to what the law is in other countries. The civil law is so, as you have it in Justinian's Inst. lib. 3, tit. 14. There the law goes further;

[68] See *Bracton and Azo* (S.S. Vol. 8) ed. Maitland, pp. 144-7.

for there it is said: '*Ex eo solo tenetur, si quid dolo commiserit : culpæ autem nomine, id est, desidiæ ac negligentiæ, non tenetur. Itaque securus est qui parum diligenter custoditam rem furto amiserit, quia qui negligenti amico rem custodiendam tradit, non ei, sed suæ facilitati, id imputare debet.*' So that such a bailee is not chargeable without an apparent gross neglect. And if there is such a *gross neglect*, it is looked upon as an *evidence of fraud*. Nay, suppose the bailee undertakes safely and securely to keep the goods, in express words; yet even that would not charge him with all sorts of neglects; for if such a promise were put into writing, it would not charge so far, even then.   Hob. 34, a covenant, that the covenantee shall have, occupy, and enjoy certain lands, does not bind against the acts of wrong-doers. 3 Cro. 214, acc., 2 Cro. 425, acc., upon a promise for quiet enjoyment.   And if a promise will not charge a man against wrong-doers, when put in writing, it is hard it should do it more so, when spoken.   Doct. and Stud. 130 is in point, that though a bailee do promise to re-deliver goods safely, yet if he have nothing for the keeping of them, he will not be answerable for the acts of a wrong-doer.   So that there is neither sufficient reason nor authority to support the opinion in *Southcote's Case.*   If the bailee be guilty of gross negligence, he will be chargeable, but not for any ordinary neglect.

2.   *Commodatum.*—As to the second sort of bailment, *viz.*, commodatum, or lending *gratis*, the borrower is bound to the strictest care and diligence to keep the goods, so as to restore them back again to the lender, because the bailee has a benefit by the use of them; so as if the bailee be guilty of the least neglect he will be answerable; as if a man should lend another a horse to go westward, or for a month, if the bailee go northward, or keep the horse above a month, if any accident happen to the horse in the northern journey, or after the expiration of the month, the bailee will be chargeable; because he has made use of the horse contrary to the trust he was lent to him under, and it may be, if the horse had been used no otherwise than he was lent, that accident would not have befallen him.   This is mentioned in Bracton *ubi supra*: his words are: '*Is autem cui res aliqua utenda datur, re obligatur, quæ commodata est, sed magna differentia est inter mutuum et commodatum; quia is qui rem mutuam accepit, ad ipsam restituendam tenetur, vel ejus pretium, si forte incendio, ruinâ, naufragio, aut latronum vel hostium incursu, consumpta fuerit, vel deperdita, subtracta vel ablata. Et qui rem utendam accepit, non sufficit ad rei custodiam, quod talem diligentiam adhibeat, qualem suis rebus propriis adhibere solet, si alius eam diligentius potuit custodire; ad vim autem majorem, vel casus fortuitos non tenetur quis, nisi culpa sua intervenerit. Ut si rem sibi commodatam domi, secum detulerit cum peregre profectus fuerit, et illam, incursu hostium vel prædonum, vel naufragio, amiserit, non est dubium quin ad rei restitutionem teneatur.*'   I cite this author, though I confess he is an old one, because his opinion is reasonable, and very much to my present purpose, and there is no authority in the law to the contrary.   But if the bailee put this horse in his stable, and he were stolen from thence, the bailee shall not be answerable for him.   But if he or his servant leave the house or stable doors open, and the thieves take the opportunity of that, and steal the horse, he will be chargeable; because the neglect gave the thieves occasion to steal the horse.   Bracton says, the bailee must use the utmost care; but yet he shall not be chargeable, where there is such a force as he cannot resist.

3.   *Locatio rei.*—As to the third sort of bailment, *scilicet locatio*, or lending for hire, in this case the bailee is also bound to take the utmost

care, and to return the goods when the time of the hiring is expired. And here again I must recur to my old author, fol. 62 b: '*Qui pro usu vestimentorum, auri vel argenti, vel alterius ornamenti, vel jumenti, mercedem dederit vel promiserit, talis ab eo desideratur custodia, qualem diligentissimus paterfamilias suis rebus adhibet, quam si præstiterit, et rem aliquo casu amiserit, ad rem restituendam non tenebitur. Nec sufficit aliquem talem diligentiam adhibere, qualem suis rebus propriis adhiberit, nisi talem adhibuerit, de quâ superius dictum est.*' From whence it appears that, if goods are let out for a reward, the hirer is bound to the utmost diligence, such as the most diligent father of a family uses; and if he uses that, he shall be discharged. But every man, how diligent soever he be, being liable to the accident of robbers, though a diligent man is not so liable as a careless man, the bailee shall not be answerable in this case, if the goods are stolen.

4. *Vadium.*—As to the fourth sort of bailment, *viz. vadium,* or a pawn, in this I shall consider two things; first, what property the pawnee has in the pawn or pledge; and secondly, for what neglects he shall make satisfaction. As to the first, he has a special property, for the pawn is a securing to the pawnee, that he shall be repaid his debt, and to compel the pawnor to pay him. But if the pawn be such as it will be the worse for using, the pawnee cannot use it, as clothes, &c.; but if it be such as will be never the worse, as if jewels for the purpose were pawned to a lady, she might use them. But then she must do it at her peril; for whereas, if she keeps them locked up in her cabinet, if her cabinet should be broke open and the jewels taken from thence, she would be excused; if she wears them abroad, and is there robbed of them, she will be answerable. And the reason is, because the pawn is in the nature of a deposit, and, as such, is not liable to be used. And to this effect is Ow. 123. But if the pawn be of such a nature, as the pawnee is at any charge about the thing pawned, to maintain it, as a horse, cow, &c., then the pawnee may use the horse in a reasonable manner, or milk the cow, &c., in recompence for the meat. As to the second point, Bracton, 99 b, gives you the answer: '*Creditor, qui pignus accepit, re obligatur, et ad illam restituendam tenetur; et cum hujusmodi res in pignus data sit utriusque gratiâ, scilicet debitoris, quo magis ei pecunia crederetur, et creditoris, quo magis ei in tuto sit creditum, sufficit ad ejus rei custodiam diligentiam exactam adhibere, quam si præstiterit, et rem casu amiserit, securus esse possit, nec impedietur creditum petere.*' In effect, if a creditor takes a pawn, he is bound to restore it upon the payment of the debt; but yet it is sufficient if the pawnee use true diligence, and he will be indemnified in so doing, and, notwithstanding the loss, yet he shall resort to the pawnor for his debt. Agreeable to this is 29 Ass. 28, and *Southcote's Case* is. But, indeed, the reason given in *Southcote's Case* is, because the pawnee has a special property in the pawn. But that is not the reason of the case; and there is another reason given for it in the book of Assize, which is indeed the true reason of all these cases, that the law requires nothing extraordinary of the pawnee, but only that he shall use an ordinary care for restoring the goods. But, indeed, if the money for which the goods were pawned be tendered to the pawnee before they are lost, then the pawnee shall be answerable for them; because the pawnee, by detaining them after the tender of the money, is a wrong-doer, and it is a wrongful detainer of the goods, and the special property of the pawnee is determined. And a man that keeps goods by wrong must be answerable for them at all events; for the detaining of them by him is the reason of the loss. Upon the same difference

as the law is in relation to pawns, it will be found to stand in relation to goods found.

5. *Locatio operis faciendi.*—As to the fifth sort of bailment, *viz.* a delivery to carry or otherwise manage, for a reward to be paid to the bailee, those cases are of two sorts; either a delivery to *one that exercises a public employment,* or a delivery to *a private person.* First, if it be to a person of the first sort, and he is to have a reward, he is bound to answer for the goods at all events. And this is the case of the common carrier, common hoyman, master of a ship, &c.: which case of a master of a ship was first adjudged, 26 Car. 2, in the case of *Mors* v. *Slue,* Sir T. Raym. 220, 1 Vent. 190, 238.[69] The law charges this person, thus entrusted, to carry goods against all events, but acts of God and of the enemies of the king. For though the force be never so great, as if an irresistible multitude of people should rob him, nevertheless he is chargeable. And this is a politic establishment, contrived by the policy of the law, for the safety of all persons, the necessity of whose affairs oblige them to trust these sorts of persons, that they may be safe in their ways of dealing; for else these carriers might have an opportunity of undoing all persons that had any dealings with them, by combining with thieves, &c., and yet doing it in such a clandestine manner as would not be possible to be discovered. And this is the reason the law is founded upon in that point. The second sort are bailees, factors, and such like. And though a bailee is to have a reward for his management, yet he is only to do the best he can. And if he be robbed, &c., it is a good account. And the reason of his being a servant is not the thing; for he is at a distance from his master, and acts at discretion, receiving rents and selling corn, &c. And yet if he receives his master's money, and keeps it locked up with reasonable care, he shall not be answerable for it, though it be stolen. But yet this servant is not a domestic servant, nor under his master's immediate care. But the true reason of the case is, it would be unreasonable to charge him with a trust, further than the nature of the thing puts it in his power to perform it. But it is allowed in the other cases, by reason of the necessity of the thing. The same law of a factor.

6. *Mandatum.*—As to the sixth sort of bailment, it is to be taken, that the bailee is to have no reward for his pains, but yet that by his ill management the goods are spoiled. Secondly, it is to be understood, that there was a neglect in the management. But thirdly, if it had appeared that the mischief happened by any person that met the cart in the way, the bailee had not been chargeable. As if a drunken man had come by in the streets, and had pierced the cask of brandy; in this case the defendant had not been answerable for it, because he was to have nothing for his pains. Then the bailee having undertaken to manage the goods, and having managed them ill, and so by his neglect a damage has happened to the bailor, which is the case in question, what will you call this? In Bracton, lib. 3. 100, it is called *mandatum.* It is an obligation which arises *ex mandato.* It is what we call in English an acting by commission. And if a man acts by commission for another *gratis,* and in the executing his commission behaves himself negligently, he is answerable. Vinnius, in his commentaries upon Justinian, lib. 3. tit. 27. 684,[70] defines *mandatum* to be *contractus quo aliquid gratuito gerendum committitur et accipitur.* This undertaking obliges the

[69] *Supra,* p. 171.
[70] In modern editions of the Institutes, this is Bk. 3, tit. 26.

undertaker to a diligent management. Bracton, *ubi supra,* says, ' *Contrahitur etiam obligatio, non solum scripto et verbis, sed et consensu, sicut in contractibus bonæ fidei, ut in emptionibus, venditionibus, locationibus, conductionibus, societatibus et mandatis.*' I do not find this word in any other author of our law, besides in this place in Bracton, which is a full authority, if it be not thought too old. But it is supported by good reason and authority.

The reasons are, first, because in such a case a neglect is a deceit to the bailor. For when he entrusts the bailee upon his undertaking to be careful, he has put a fraud upon the plaintiff by being negligent, his pretence of care being the persuasion that induced the plaintiff to trust him. And a breach of a trust undertaken voluntarily will be a good ground for an action; 1 Roll. Abr. 10; 2 Hen. 7, 11; a strong case to this matter. There the case was an action against a man who had undertaken to keep an hundred sheep, for letting them be drowned by his default. And the reason of the judgment is given, because ' when the party has taken upon him to keep the sheep, and after suffers them to perish in his default, inasmuch as he has taken and executed his bargain, and has them in his custody, and, after, he does not look to them, an action lies; for here is his own act, *viz.* his agreement and promise, and that after broke on his side, that shall give a sufficient cause of action.' [71]

But, secondly, it is objected, that there is no consideration to ground this promise upon, and therefore the undertaking is but *nudum pactum.* But to this I answer, that the owner's trusting him with the goods is a sufficient consideration to oblige him to a careful management. Indeed, if the agreement had been executory, to carry these brandies from the one place to the other such a day, the defendant had not been bound to carry them. But this is a different case, for *assumpsit* does not only signify a future agreement, but, in such a case as this, it signifies an actual entry upon the thing, and taking the trust upon himself. And if a man will do that, and miscarries in the performance of his trust, an action will lie against him for that, though nobody could have compelled him to do the thing. The 19 Hen. 6, 49, and the other cases cited by my brothers, show that this is the difference. But in the 11 Hen. 4, 33,[72] this difference is clearly put, and that is the only case concerning this matter which has not been cited by my brothers. There the action was brought against a carpenter, for that he had undertaken to build the plaintiff a house within such a time, and had not done it, and it was adjudged the action would not lie. But there the question was put to the court—what if he had built the house unskilfully? —and it is agreed in that case an action would have lain. There has been a question made. If I deliver goods to A., and in consideration thereof he promise to re-deliver them, if an action will lie for not re-delivering them; and, in Yelv. 4, judgment was given that the action would lie. But that judgment was afterwards reversed; and, according to that reversal, there was judgment afterwards entered for the defendant in the like case; Yelv. 128. But those cases were grumbled at; and the reversal of that judgment in Yelv. 4 was said by the judges to be a bad resolution, and the contrary to that reversal was afterwards most solemnly adjudged, in 2 Cro. 667, Tr. 21 Jac. 1,[73] in the King's Bench, and that judgment affirmed upon a writ of

[71] *Supra,* p. 86.
[72] *Infra,* p. 340.
[73] *Wheatley* v. *Low,* Cro. Jac. 668.

error. And yet there is no benefit to the defendant, nor no consideration in that case, but the having the money in his possession and being trusted with it, and yet that was held to be a good consideration. And so a bare being trusted with another man's goods must be taken to be a sufficient consideration, if the bailee once enter upon a trust and take the goods into his possession. The declaration in the case of *Mors* v. *Slue*,[74] was drawn by the greatest drawer in England in that time; and in that declaration, as it was always in all such cases, it was thought most prudent to put in, that a reward was to be paid for the carriage. And so it has been usual to put it in the writ, where the suit is by original. I have said thus much in this case, because it is of great consequence that the law should be settled in this point; but I do not know whether I may have settled it, or may not rather have unsettled it. But however that happen, I have stirred these points, which wiser heads in time may settle.

And judgment was given for the plaintiff.

JOHN LILLY : A COLLECTION OF MODERN ENTRIES

BROWNE v. DAVIS (1706)[75]

(Case against the master of a hoy for falling foul of and sinking the plaintiff's dung-boat)

Middlesex, to wit. William Browne complains of John Davis in the custody of the marshal, etc. for this, to wit, that, whereas the said William on the 6th day of March in the 4th year of the reign of the lady Anne now Queen of England, etc., at the parish of Chelsea in the county aforesaid was lawfully possessed of a certain flat-bottomed boat, then loaded with dung and riding at anchor in the river Thames within the parish aforesaid, as of his own proper boat; and the said John Davis then and there was master and pilot of a certain barge then sailing in the river Thames aforesaid within the parish aforesaid towards the city of London; that the said John Davis then and there his said barge so negligently, carelessly and unskilfully managed and steered, that the said barge, for want of good and sufficient care and management thereof, in and upon the said boat of him the said William, so as aforesaid loaded, then and there fell foul, and the said boat broke and sank; and the said William by reason thereof not only his dung aforesaid in the said boat loaded totally lost, but likewise lost the whole use, profit and benefit of his said boat for the space of six days then next following, and also expended and laid out great sums of money in and about the raising and repairing of his said boat; whereby the said William says that he is prejudiced, and hath damage to the value of £30. And therefor he produces suit, etc.

MORLEY v. GAISFORD

(1795), 2 H. BL. 442

This was an action on the case, and the declaration, which consisted of only one count, stated that the Plaintiff on etc. at etc., was lawfully possessed of

[74] *Supra,* p. 171.
[75] at p. 38.

a certain carriage called a chaise and of a certain horse then and there drawing the same; and the Defendant was then and there also possessed of a certain cart and a certain horse, then and there drawing the said cart, and then and there, by a certain then servant of him the said Defendant, had the care, conduct and management of the said horse and cart of the said Defendant and of the driving thereof, to wit, at etc.; yet the said Defendant by his said servant then and there so negligently and unskilfully managed and behaved himself in the premises, and so badly, ignorantly and negligently drove, managed, guided and governed the said cart and horse of the said Defendant, that the said cart for want of good and sufficient care and management thereof and of the said horse so then and there drawing the same as aforesaid then and there struck and ran to and against the said chaise of the said Plaintiff with great force and violence, and then and there pulled, forced and dragged the same to a great distance, and then and there broke to pieces, destroyed and damaged the said chaise and one of the wheels of the said chaise and the shaft thereof, to wit, at etc.; whereby the said chaise of the said Plaintiff then and there became and was crushed, broken, damaged and injured, and he the said Plaintiff was forced and obliged to lay out and expend, and did lay out and expend a large sum of money, to wit, the sum of £30, in and about the repairs and amendment thereof, to wit, at etc., to the damage, etc.

A verdict having been found for the Plaintiff, *Cockell,* Serjt. now moved in arrest of judgment on the ground that the action ought to have been trespass and not case, as the injury was direct and not consequential.[76] It was not necessary, he said, that the act done should be unlawful, to make it a ground of trespass; as if a man lift up a stick to defend himself and by accident strike another, there, though the act was lawful, yet trespass lies. *A fortiori,* therefore, where the act is unlawful, as in the present instance, trespass is the proper remedy. And he cited *Day* v. *Edwards,* 5 T.R. 648, and *Savignac* v. *Roome,* 6 T.R. 125,[77] where the ground of the decision was, not that the act was wilful, as the counsel contended, but that there was a direct and not a consequential injury.

The Court[78] seemed at first inclined to refuse the rule, saying that it was difficult to put a case where the master could be considered as a trespasser for an act of his servant which was not done at his command; but they said that respect for the decisions of the Court of King's Bench would induce them to give the point further consideration; and accordingly a rule to shew cause was granted. But a few days afterwards *Cockell* acknowledged that the rule could not be supported; in which the Court concurred, being clearly of opinion that case, and not trespass, was the proper form of action. Rule discharged.

GOVETT v. RADNIDGE

(1802), 3 EAST, 62

. . . LORD ELLENBOROUGH, C.J. . . . delivered the opinion of the Court.

This was an action brought by E. Govett against W. Pulman, M. Gimble and J. Radnidge, in which he declared in the first count, upon which alone he obtained a verdict, that the defendants had the loading of a certain hogs-

[76] On Trespass and Case, see *infra,* pp. 184-7.
[77] See *infra,* pp. 185-6.
[78] of Common Pleas.

head of treacle upon a certain cart for a reasonable reward, to be therefore
paid by the plaintiff to the two first defendants, and a certain other reasonable reward to the last named defendant. And that the three defendants so
carelessly, negligently and unskilfully behaved and conducted themselves in
the loading such hogshead of treacle, that by reason thereof the hogshead
was staved and the treacle lost. To this declaration the defendants pleaded
not guilty, and a verdict was found for the two first named defendants, and
against the last defendant.

A motion in arrest of judgment has been made upon this ground; that
the cause of action stated in the first count, and upon which the question
arises, is founded in contract, or at least quasi ex contractu, as it is said;
and that being so, the finding of not guilty as to two of the defendants
negatives the existence of such a joint contract by all the three defendants
as must be proved if the declaration be founded on contract; and therefore
that the plaintiff is not entitled to have any judgment given for him upon
this record.

That this is to be considered as an action founded on contract has been
mainly contended, on the part of the defendant, on the authority of the case
of *Boson* v. *Sandford*; which is reported in 1 & 2 Shower; Levinz; 3 Mod.;
Salk. 440, and in other places.[79] That was the case of certain shipowners
who were charged by the declaration to have received certain goods on
board their ship to be 'safely transported for the plaintiff from London
to Topsham, for reasonable freight and salary by the plaintiff to the defendants for such carriage thereof to be paid' ; and who had undertaken (for so
it is expressly laid) to transport and carry them accordingly . . .; and against
whom it was charged that they, disregarding their duty and fraudulently
intending to injure the plaintiff, so negligently placed, carried and kept the
goods in the ship, that the goods were damnified by sea water. Upon not
guilty pleaded, one question was whether the action was maintainable
against these defendants alone, certain other part owners of the ship not
having been joined as defendants. Another question was whether, if the
action ought to have been brought against all, this matter ought not to have
been pleaded in abatement, and not given in evidence (as it had been) on
the general issue. . . .

> [Lord Ellenborough then considered the *ratio decidendi* of
> *Boson* v. *Sandford* and, observing that it turned upon a point of
> pleading which had since been determined otherwise, concluded that]

this case may therefore be laid out of the question as an authority for
some of the propositions therein determined.

And as to the necessity of considering a count against carriers for hire,
framed as this is upon alleged neglect of duty and not upon the breach
of any undertaking, as a count in assumpsit and as distinguished from tort,
with all its consequences (which consequences are these, viz., of letting in a
plea in abatement for want of joining all the parties; of entitling the defendant
to a general verdict if the cause of action should not be proved as against all;
and of excluding the right to join therewith a count in trover); the case of
Dickon v. *Clifton,* 2 Wilson, 319, . . . is a case in point. There L.C.J.
Wilmot considered a count, in terms the same as the present, as a count laid
ex delicto of the defendant, and that a count in trover might therefore be
joined therewith. He says, ' I own that in many books it is reported that
trover and a count against a common carrier cannot be joined, but common

[79] (1689) 1 Shower, 101; 2 Shower, 478; 3 Levinz, 258; 3 Mod. 321.

experience and practice is now to the contrary.' And, to be sure, if the count against the common carrier is laid as this is, not in terms of contract but upon the breach of duty, it is now the daily, and I think the convenient and well warranted, practice to join them.

What inconvenience is there in suffering the party to allege his gravamen, if he please, as consisting in a breach of duty arising out of an employment for hire and to consider that breach of duty as tortious negligence, instead of considering the same circumstances as forming a breach of promise implied from the same consideration of hire? By allowing it to be considered in either way, according as the neglect of duty or the breach of promise is relied upon as the injury, a multiplicity of actions is avoided; and the plaintiff, according as the convenience of his case requires, frames his principal count in such a manner as either to join a count in trover therewith, if he have another cause of action for the consideration of the Court other than the action of assumpsit, or to join with the assumpsit the common counts[80]: if he have another cause of action to which they are applicable. . . . We are of opinion that the acquittal of one defendant in an action founded, as this is, on neglect of duty and not upon breach of promise, does not affect the right of the plaintiff to have his judgment as against the defendant against whom the verdict has been obtained; and that the rule for arresting the judgment ought to be discharged.

[80] *Infra*, pp. 369 and 393.

9

TRESPASS AND CASE

WHEN it was clear that Trespass and Case were to divide between them the incidents of civil liability, it became a matter òf importance to determine their respective limits. In the early years of the eighteenth century the task of definition was accepted with that cheerful confidence which attends failure to perceive the inward nature of a problem. It was all to be a question of comparative proximity. Trespass was appropriate where the plaintiff complained of an immediate attack upon his person or property, Case where the injury was merely consequential upon some otherwise neutral act of the defendant. In 1709 two actions on the case were brought upon facts which lay across the modern frontiers of false imprisonment and malicious prosecution. The plaintiff alleged in the first that the defendant had ' caused him to be arrested and carried to prison without cause,' and in the second that he had ' caused her to be arrested and had falsely and maliciously charged her with a felony before a Justice.' In each case the defendant argued that the action should have been in Trespass, and in each the plaintiff replied by insisting on the distinction between an immediate and a consequential injury.[1]

The distinction was easier to assert than to define, and easier to define than to apply. In *Reynolds* v. *Clarke*[2] in 1726, Fortescue, J. was content with the test of proximity and offered an illustration which was to do duty for many years to come. ' If,' he said, ' a man throws a log into the highway and in that act it hits me, I may maintain trespass because it is an immediate wrong; but if, as it lies there, I tumble over it and receive an injury, I must bring an action upon the case because it is only prejudicial in consequence.' Lord Raymond, in the same case, professed himself equally anxious to distinguish Trespass and Case: ' we must keep up the boundaries of actions, otherwise we shall introduce the utmost confusion.'[3] But he then proceeded to offer a new method of discrimination which served only to cloud the issue. In his opinion, the plaintiff must bring Case if the act of the defendant were *prima facie* lawful, Trespass if it were unlawful *ab initio*. It is not difficult to trace the sequence of thought underlying the first half

---

[1] *Bourden* v. *Alloway,* 11 Mod. 180, and *Slater's Case,* Holt, 22. See also *Kent's Case* (1705) 6 Mod. 138, *Keble* v. *Hickeringill* (1707) 11 Mod. 130, *per* Holt, C.J. at p. 131, and *Leveridge* v. *Hoskins* (1709) 11 Mod. 257.
[2] 1 Strange, 634: *infra,* p. 201.
[3] *Ibid.,* at p. 635.

of this proposition: if a man committed himself or his goods into the hands of another, he could never complain of an act done *vi et armis*. It was by no means so evident that if the interference were illegal from the beginning he should be confined to Trespass. To throw the log into the highway was in any event an unlawful act, and the choice of remedies depended not upon its inherent quality but on its sequel. These diverse views were discussed by the Court of Common Pleas in *Scott* v. *Shepherd*,[4] where all four judges admitted that the plaintiff had just cause of complaint if only their wit could find the right action to allow it to be heard. While Nares and Gould, J.J. adopted Lord Raymond's variant, Chief Justice De Grey and Mr. Justice Blackstone detected and exposed the fallacy and returned to the primitive simplicity of earlier years. But even they, while agreed upon the test, differed in their attempts to apply it to the facts. When did an injury cease to be immediate and become consequential?

Whatever the difficulties of application, the test itself was accepted by their successors and reiterated both by Lord Kenyon and by Lord Ellenborough. The former was rash enough to describe the distinction as ' perfectly clear.' ' If the injury be committed by the immediate act complained of, the action must be trespass; if the injury be merely consequential upon that act, an action upon the case is the proper remedy.'[5] New complexities, however, attended the ' running-down actions ' which filled the courts at the turn of the eighteenth and nineteenth centuries. Attention was focussed not only upon the dominant allegation of negligence, but also, through the repeated attempts to make an employer liable for the conduct of his coachman and a shipmaster for that of his crew, upon the related problem of vicarious liability. In *Savignac* v. *Roome*[6] the plaintiff's counsel, by declaring in Case that ' the defendant, by his servant, wilfully drove ' a coach and horses against the plaintiff's chaise, exposed himself to a dilemma. If the collision were indeed deliberately engineered by the master, the form of action should have been Trespass and not Case; but if, as the evidence suggested, it was the result of the servant's negligence, while the form of action was right, the declaration was wrong. Some at least of these tangled threads were straightened by Lord Kenyon in *McManus* v. *Crickett*.[7] The master could be sued in Trespass only if the act complained of had been done by his express command or was the inevitable consequence of such a command. For the negligence of a servant in the course of his employment the proper remedy

---

[4] (1773) 2 W. Bl. 892: *infra*, p. 202.

[5] *Day* v. *Edwards* (1794) 5 T.R. 648. For similar statements by Lord Kenyon, see *Savignac* v. *Roome* (1794) 6 T.R. 125, and *Ogle* v. *Barnes* (1799) 8 T.R. 188; and by Lord Ellenborough, see *Leame* v. *Bray* (1803) 3 East, 593, *infra*, p. 205, *Covell* v. *Laming* (1808) 1 Camp. 497, and *Lotan* v. *Cross* (1810) 2 Camp. 464.

[6] (1794) 6 T.R. 125.

[7] (1800) 1 East, 106.

was Case, and, where the servant embarked wilfully upon a ' frolic of his own,' the master was not liable at all.[8]

The antithesis implied by the words ' wilful ' and ' negligent ' was unhappily allowed to escape from the environment of vicarious liability and to obscure the distinction between Trespass and Case in much the same way as it had been confused by the excursions of Lord Raymond in a previous generation. In *Ogle* v. *Barnes,* while Lord Ellenborough repeated the test of ' immediate ' and ' consequential ' injuries, Lawrence, J. indulged the new vagary. ' Such an injury as the present,' he said, ' may be occasioned either by the wilful act or by the negligence of the defendants: it is a question of evidence. If the former, trespass is the proper action; if the latter, an action on the case.'[9] It is true that in *Leame* v. *Bray*[10] he recanted, or at least ' explained ' his judgment in the ingenious or disingenuous terms adopted by judges who seek to preserve a reputation for consistency. It is also true that Lord Ellenborough, despite many temptations, remained staunch in the profession of the orthodox creed.[11] But the disturbing spirit was not exorcised. It appeared, moreover, that the boundaries of Trespass and Case were not so inviolable as the brave words of lawyers might suggest. It had been pointed out by Blackstone, J. in *Scott* v. *Shepherd*[12] that a plaintiff in Trespass, though his main complaint was of an act done *vi et armis,* could add a claim for consequential damage and to this extent encroach upon the field of Case. Lawrence, J. recommended such a course to avoid or diminish the perennial risk that the evidence might not support the declaration. If the plaintiff brought Trespass, he would recover whether the evidence showed the defendant's conduct to be wilful or not; but if wilfulness were proved and he had brought Case, he would be nonsuited.[13] Case, on the other hand, had its own peculiar advantages. If in an action of Trespass the plaintiff recovered less than forty shillings, he was entitled to no more costs than damages; but in Case costs followed the event even if the verdict were only for nominal damages.[14]

These discordant elements were resolved into a semblance of harmony by Chief Justice Tindal in *Williams* v. *Holland* and Baron Parke in *Sharrod* v. *L. & N.W.Rly.*[15] The distinction between the immediate

---

[8] The case of *McManus* v. *Crickett* was anticipated by *Morley* v. *Gaisford* (1795) 2 H. Bl. 442, *supra,* p. 180, and followed in *Huggett* v. *Montgomery* (1807) 2 B. & P.N.R. 446 and *Sharrod* v. *L. & N.W. Ry.* (1849) 4 Ex. 580, *infra,* p. 212.

[9] (1799) 8 T.R. 188. Lawrence, J. was supported by Grose, J.

[10] (1803) 3 East, 593; *infra,* p. 205.

[11] See *Covell* v. *Laming* (1808) 1 Camp. 497 and *Lotan* v. *Cross* (1810) 2 Camp. 464, and cf. *Rogers* v. *Imbleton* (1806) 2 B. & P. N.R. 117.

[12] *Infra,* p. 204.

[13] *Leame* v. *Bray* (1803) 3 East, 593; *infra,* p. 208.

[14] *Savignac* v. *Roome* (1794) 6 T.R. 125. Professors Winfield and Goodhart think the balance of advantages to be more decidedly with Case: 49 L.Q.R., 359.

[15] *Williams* v. *Holland* (1833) 10 Bingham, 112, *infra,* p. 209; *Sharrod* v. *L. & N.W. Ry.* (1849) 4 Ex. 580, *infra,* p. 212. Both cases are interesting examples of judicial *finesse.* In the former, Chief Justice Tindal showed what could be done by a judge

act and its consequences was retained as a principle, but refined. Immediate acts were further classified as wilful or negligent. If wilful, the plaintiff must sue in Trespass: if negligent, he might choose between Trespass and Case. But Case was the only remedy both where the injury was merely consequential and when a master was sued for the negligence of his servant. Such was the solution adopted by or forced upon the courts on the eve of the Common Law Procedure Act of 1852 which, by ensuring the destruction of the forms of action, concentrated attention upon the substantive law which they enshrined.

A classification, based in part upon ethical standards, could not but react upon the search for principles of liability. On this question much has been written, and sometimes by writers more eager to mould the cases to their own pattern than to mirror what, to ardent minds, must seem a dim and disappointing reflection. Academic conflict has most frequently raged around the suggestion that English law began with a doctrine, or, if the word be too strong, with a sentiment of strict or even absolute liability, which gradually, as if in obedience to some occult influence, mellowed into the correspondence of fault and compensation agreeable to nineteenth-century liberalism.[16] Holmes, indeed, thought the story too simple to be true. He doubted whether the Common Law ever had a rule of absolute responsibility, ' unless in that period of dry precedent so often to be found midway between a creative epoch and a period of solvent philosophical reaction.'[17] By 1926 scepticism had gone so far as to enable Professor Winfield to entitle an essay, ' The Myth of Absolute Liability,' without incurring the charge of iconoclasm.[18] The literature on the subject offers as a whole a striking and not unentertaining warning against the temptation of historians to assume the presence of some recurrent theme—of evolution or of progress or of action and reaction—and to ' find the facts ' necessary to disclose or to support it. To adventure far into this fascinating realm of wish-fulfilment would be irrelevant to the purpose of the present book. But, since the principles of liability, if any such existed, must be sought historically among the intricacies of Trespass and Case, some slight reference to the question is not impertinent.[19]

---

in relating old precedents to new needs by a drastic process of rationalisation and in breaking through technical difficulties to reach the merits of a case. In the latter, Baron Parke met the new situation produced by the advent of the railway by applying, as an apt and sufficient analogy, the earlier highway law.

[16] See Wigmore, *Responsibility for Tortious Acts*, A.A.L.H. III. 474, and Ames, *Law and Morals, Lectures on Legal History*, pp. 435-452.

[17] *The Common Law*, p. 89.

[18] 42 L.Q.R. 37.

[19] Holmes thought that to seek for great principles by observing the relations of Trespass and Case was unworthy. ' It can hardly be supposed that a man's responsibility for the consequences of his acts varies as the remedy happens to fall on one side or the other of the penumbra which separates trespass from the action on the case.': *The Common Law*, p. 80. But he spoke here as the rationalist, not as the historian.

It may be worth while to observe, through the medium of two modern and familiar cases, the attitude of the judges as they looked back, not without regret, upon the forms of action which had so long sheltered them from the rude elements of responsibility. In *Holmes* v. *Mather*[20] the defendant's horses, driven by his groom in his presence, ran away and knocked down the plaintiff. The jury found, and Bramwell, B. agreed, that neither master nor man were in any way to blame. The Declaration contained two counts: (1) ' that the defendant so negligently drove a carriage and horses in the highway that they ran against the plaintiff and threw her down,' and (2) ' that the defendant drove a carriage with great force and violence against the plaintiff and wounded her.' In the sad days of technical pleading from which practitioners had now been released the first count would have been in Case and the second in Trespass. It was argued for the defendant that, as there was fault in nobody, the action could not be maintained ' in any form,' and, for the plaintiff, that Trespass would lie even where the injury was a pure accident, provided only that it were immediate. Bramwell, B. gave judgment for the defendant.

> ' As to the cases cited, most of them are really decisions on the form of action, whether case or trespass. The result of them is this, and it is intelligible enough. If the act that does an injury is an act of direct force *vi et armis,* trespass is the proper remedy (if there is any remedy) where the act is wrongful, either as being wilful or as being the result of negligence. Where the act is not wrongful for either of these reasons, no action is maintainable, though trespass would be the proper form of action if it were wrongful.'

In *Stanley* v. *Powell*[21] the plaintiff was a beater at a shooting party, who lost an eye through a pellet of shot fired from the defendant's gun. He alleged in his Statement of Claim that the defendant had acted ' negligently and wrongfully and unskilfully,' but the allegation was negatived by the jury. It was nevertheless contended that, upon these facts, ' an action of Trespass would have lain before the Judicature Acts '; but Denman, J., after examining the authorities at some length, found the contention unsupported save by dicta divorced from their context, and dismissed it.

> ' I am of opinion that, if the case is regarded as an action on the case for an injury by negligence, the plaintiff has failed to establish that which is the very gist of such an action; if, on the other hand, it is turned into an action for trespass, and the defendant is (as he must be) supposed to have pleaded a plea denying negligence and establishing that the injury was accidental . . ., the verdict of the jury is equally fatal to the action.'

The conclusion here reached, that a defendant was liable neither in Trespass nor in Case unless he had been in some degree at fault, has

[20] (1875) L.R. 10 Ex. 261.
[21] [1891] 1 Q.B. 86, especially at p. 94.

been variously received. Sir William Holdsworth and Professor Winfield agree that the evidence is to be sought rather in dicta than in decisions and that it is negative rather than positive; but while the former detected, the latter denies, a mediæval tendency to strict liability.[22] Dr. Stallybrass accepted *Stanley* v. *Powell* as good modern authority, but thought it represented 'a departure from the earlier precedents.'[23] Pollock, in the eleventh edition of his *Law of Torts,* opposed a number of conflicting dicta, but, after inclining against the view of strict liability, declared that 'the decisive change of opinion took place within our own time.' Mr. Landon, in the fourteenth edition, denounces both *Holmes* v. *Mather* and *Stanley* v. *Powell* as wrong in law, in morals and in history.[24]

To ransack the Year Books for large statements of doctrine made in irrelevant circumstances by judges barely conscious of their significance is neither a pleasing nor a profitable task. Its perils have been noticed in the pursuit of negligence and may again be illustrated from two leading mediæval cases. The *Thorns' Case* of 1466 was an action of trespass to land.[25] The defendant confessed the trespass, but pleaded, by way of justification, that he had been cutting a thorn hedge on his own land, that the thorns had fallen on to the plaintiff's land and that he had simply entered to remove them. His counsel argued that a man was not to be punished merely because a lawful act had untoward consequences. Plaintiff's counsel seized upon the word ' punishment ' to distinguish criminal and civil responsibility: an unintended act, though it would not warrant a prosecution for felony, might well involve an obligation to pay compensation for the resultant damage. Brian, on the same side, put the point with characteristic confidence. ' When any man does an act, he is bound to do it in such manner that by his act no prejudice or damage is done to others.' Though no judgment is recorded, the opinion of the Court was with the plaintiff. The judges, however, approached the question from different angles. Littleton, J. adopted Brian's proposition. ' If a man suffers damage, it is right that he be recompensed.' Chief Justice Choke was less severe. ' As to what has been said that they fell *ipso invito,* this is not a good plea; but he should have said that he could not do it in any other manner or that he did all that was in his power to keep them out.'

The *Tithe Case* of 1506 was an action of trespass to goods.[26] Wheat had been severed from the main crop as tithe due to a parson. It had been removed by the defendant, without authority but with the object of securing it against theft, to the parson's barn, whence it would seem

---

[22] Cf. H.E.L. VIII 453-8 and Winfield, *Text-Book of the Law of Tort,* 4th ed., pp. 42-5.
[23] *Salmond on Torts,* 10th ed., p. 339.
[24] Cf. Pollock, *The Law of Torts,* 11th ed., pp. 136-148, and 14th ed., Excursus B.
[25] Y.B. 6 Ed. 4, f. 7, pl. 18, *infra,* p. 195.
[26] Y.B. 21 Hen. 7, f. 27, pl. 5, *infra,* p. 197.

to have been stolen by third parties. The Court refused to recognize this act of officious kindness as a justification of the trespass, partly because the sequel had shown it to have promoted rather than prevented the loss, and partly on the more academic ground that the parson would in any event have had his action over against the thieves. Chief Justice Rede repeated the distinction between civil and criminal liability and said that in trespass 'the intent is not to be construed, though in felony it shall be.' From each of these cases isolated passages may be and have been taken to support opposing theories, but neither is decisive. In both the trespass itself was designed and admitted, and the Court had only to assess the adequacy of the justification. Nor was clarity of thought assisted by lucidity of language. Chief Justice Rede used the word 'intent' indifferently to indicate a deliberate as against an accidental act and in the sense of motive: the defendant, though it might not excuse him, had 'done a good deed.'

The seventeenth-century cases are equally susceptible of partisan treatment. On the one hand, two cases of 1682 may be cited to support the theory of strict liability. In *Dickenson* v. *Watson*[27] a tax-collector, armed with pistols 'for the better discharge of his office,' shot the plaintiff and pleaded accident. He was held liable, 'for in trespass the defendant shall not be excused without unavoidable necessity, which is not shown here.' In *Bessey* v. *Olliot*,[28] Sir Thomas Raymond declared that 'in all civil acts the law doth not so much regard the intent of the actor as the loss and damage of the party suffering'; but the strength of the dictum is impaired by its appearance in a dissenting judgment. On the other hand, in *Millen* v. *Fandrye*[29] Chief Justice Crew based his decision on the more lenient interpretation of the *Thorns Case* and found for the defendant on the ground that he had 'done his best endeavour' to avoid harm. So, too, in *Gibbons* v. *Pepper*,[30] the defendant, whose horse had run away and injured the plaintiff, lost only through a technical flaw. Had he pleaded the general issue he would have been found not guilty, 'for, if the horse ran away against his will, it cannot be said with any colour of reason to be a battery in the rider.' Most typical, however, in its confusion of language is the case of *Weaver* v. *Ward*.[31] The Court, after stating that 'no man shall be excused of a trespass, except it may be judged utterly without his fault,' proceeded,

> 'As if a man by force take my hand and strike you, or if here
> the defendant had said that the plaintiff ran against his piece when
> it was discharging, or had set forth the case with the circumstances

[27] (1682) Sir T. Jones, 205, *infra*, p. 200.
[28] (1682) Sir T. Raym., 421, 467.
[29] (1626) Popham, 161, *infra*, p. 199.
[30] (1695) 1 Ld. Raym., 38, *infra*, p. 200. On the General Issue, see *infra*, p. 193.
[31] (1616) Hobart, 134, *infra*, p. 198.

so as it had appeared to the Court that it had been inevitable and that the defendant had committed no negligence to give occasion to the hurt.'

'Fault,' 'inevitable accident,' 'negligence,' are words used indiscriminately without reflection and almost without meaning.

Such authority as this scarcely warrants the assumption of a doctrine of strict liability imbedded in the common law. The judges did not, in truth, approach their problems with any *a priori* conception of responsibility. Where, as in the instances discussed, the plaintiff sued in trespass, the defendant might escape if he could prove that he was the sport of the elements or the victim of a third party. His immunity, however, was not based upon ethical grounds, but followed the failure of the plaintiff to prove him guilty of any act committed *vi et armis*. If his tree had fallen on the plaintiff's land or another had taken his hand and struck the plaintiff, he could not be said to have acted at all.[32] It was also necessary to distinguish trespass and felony and, for this purpose, to examine the question of intention. But the only contrast drawn was between intent and accident. Negligence was a *tertium quid,* which, while it might be inferred from the facts, was rarely present to the minds of the judges and which entered the law not through trespass but through case. Until it had become a familiar phenomenon to be set against intention on the one side and accident on the other, no serious examination of the principles of liability was possible. Act and no-act, intent and no-intent, were the only judicial antitheses.

Such an examination might have been expected to follow the acceptance in the eighteenth century of an 'action on the case for negligence.'[33] But this new title in the books was still too incoherent to sustain, or at least to require, analysis, and nothing can be found save a few disconnected and ill-considered dicta. The case of *Underwood* v. *Hewson* in 1724[34] has been cited by modern scholars on the strength of a side-note that 'Trespass lies for an accidental hurt.' The whole report, however, consists of a single sentence, which, meagre as it is, does not distinguish between accident and negligence.

> 'The defendant was uncocking a gun, and, the plaintiff standing to see it, it went off and wounded him; and at the trial it was held that the plaintiff might maintain trespass.'

In *Beckwith* v. *Shordike*[35] the plaintiff sued the defendant in trespass for entering his close with guns and dogs and killing his deer. Both the entry and the killing appeared clearly in evidence, and a verdict

[32] See *The Thorns Case, infra,* at p. 197, and *Weaver* v. *Ward, supra,* p. 190, and *infra,* p. 199.
[33] See *supra,* p. 164.
[34] 1 Strange, 596. See Holmes, *The Common Law,* p. 87.
[35] (1767) 4 Burrow, 2092. Compare Sir William Holdsworth's treatment of the case in H.E.L. VIII, pp. 456 and 466.

for the plaintiff was almost automatic.   In the circumstances Mr. Justice
Aston's attempt to distinguish *Millen* v. *Fandrye* on the ground that
there the trespass was against the defendant's will, while 'the present
case can't be considered as an accidental involuntary trespass,' must
be regarded as an adventure into the obvious rather than a statement
designed for general consumption.[36]   The same fugitive, almost for-
tuitous, interest attaches to Lord Mansfield's declaration that 'in
trespass innocence of intention is no excuse, in case the whole turns
upon it; malice, or the *quo animo*, is the very gist of the action.'[37]   Such
language, at once vigorous and vague, shows it to be unnecessary to
the decision of the case and unrelated to any framework of principle.

The emphasis lent to negligence by the 'running-down actions'
thrust the idea of fault into the foreground.   The nineteenth century
opened with a passage subsequently chosen as their *cheval de bataille*
by the protagonists of strict liability.   In *Leame* v. *Bray* the Court of
King's Bench, concerned to differentiate the forms of action, found
it necessary to deny that wilfulness was essential to Trespass.   Grose,
J. went so far as to assert as a principle that 'if the injury be done
by the act of the party himself at the time or he be the immediate
cause of it, though it happen accidentally or by misfortune, yet he is
answerable in trespass.'[38]   The *non sequitur* is evident: because a
plaintiff need not prove the act to be wilful, it does not follow that
inevitable accident is no defence.   The learned judge was repeating
the old antithesis of intent and no-intent without regard to the intervention of negligence.   The omission was the more curious in that
the defendant had not only admitted carelessness but had used it for
his contention that the plaintiff should have sued in Case.   The dictum
was nevertheless endorsed by such eminent judges as Chief Justice
Tindal and Baron Parke.[39]   But, despite the prominence thus unhappily
accorded to it, it was never the basis of any actual decision and was
balanced by a number of opposing dicta sanctioned by respectable
names and open to less criticism.   In *Wakeman* v. *Robinson*[40] the
plaintiff brought Trespass 'for driving against his horse and injuring
him with the shaft of a gig.'   The evidence showed that the collision
was caused by the defendant's carelessness.   The trial judge directed
the jury that, 'this being an action of trespass, if the injury was occasioned by an immediate act of the defendant, it was immaterial whether
the act was wilful or accidental.'   He did not direct them upon negligence.   The jury found for the plaintiff, and the defendant moved

---

[36] For *Millen* v. *Fandrye*, see *supra*, p. 190; and *infra*, p. 199.

[37] *Tarleton* v. *Fisher* (1781), 2 Douglas, 646, at p. 649.

[38] *Leame* v. *Bray* (1803) 3 East, 593, *infra*, p. 208.   On the influence of Grose, J.'s
dictum, see Wigmore, A.A.L.H. III, pp. 504-8.

[39] See *McLaughlin* v. *Pryor* (1842) 4 Man. & G. 48, and *Sharrod* v. *L. & N.W. Ry.*
(1849) 4 Ex. 580, *infra*, p. 212.

[40] (1823) 1 Bing. 213.

for a new trial on the ground of misdirection. Chief Justice Dallas dismissed the motion, not because he approved the direction, but because the evidence was so clearly against the defendant that substantial justice had been done.

> 'If the accident happened entirely without default on the part of the defendant or blame imputable to him, the action does not lie; but, under all the circumstances that belong to it, I regret that this case comes before the Court. It has been contended, indeed, that the defendant would not have been liable under any form of action; but upon the facts of the case, if I had presided at the trial, I should have directed the jury that the plaintiff was entitled to the verdict, because the accident was clearly occasioned by the default of the defendant. The weight of evidence was all that way.'

In *Goodman* v. *Taylor*[41] the plaintiff brought Trespass for an injury to his horse sustained in a collision with the defendant's pony and chaise. The defendant's witnesses said that his wife 'stood by the head of the pony, holding it by the reins, when a Punch and Judy show coming by frightened the pony and it ran away.' Lord Denman told the jury that, 'If the facts are true as suggested, I very much think you would be disposed to consider this as an inevitable accident, one which the defendant could not prevent.' The jury's verdict for the plaintiff must be taken to reflect rather upon their discretion than upon the propriety of the direction.

The problem of fault was none the less present to the minds of the nineteenth-century judges because it was overlaid by their preoccupation with procedure. The first half of the century was the golden age of the pleaders.[42] A nice discrimination in the use of weapons was the hall-mark of a lawyer, and few questions were more eagerly canvassed than the respective merits of the General Issue and of Special Pleading. A defendant who pleaded the General Issue traversed the plaintiff's Declaration in a set and simple phrase, such as *Not Guilty* to an action of Trespass or Case. If, on the other hand, he employed a special pleader, he staked his fortunes upon a single issue selected with what subtlety he could command. Each course had its merits. The General Issue avoided undue technicality, but, by leaving everything to the Jury, allowed the result to turn upon the hazards of the trial. A Special Plea, while it avoided confusion, was apt to avoid the merits as well.[43] A number of cases between 1800 and 1850 show

---

[41] (1832) 5 C. & P. 410.

[42] The *locus classicus* is Serjeant Stephen's *Treatise on Pleading*, first published in 1824. See also Chitty, *Reports on Practice and Pleading, decided in the King's Bench in 1819*. This volume contained 758 pages of cases, and the learned author was able, in his Preface, to recommend it by saying, 'A very large portion of the time of the Courts is occupied in discussing points of this nature, and the success of a suit depends greatly upon the regularity and accuracy of the proceedings; and when the delay, the expense, and even the failure of justice, which frequently take place from inattention to these particulars, are considered, a favourable reception of this work is anticipated.'

[43] The use of the General Issue was recommended by Blackstone (Comm. III. 305-6), who thus explains it: 'The general issue, or general plea, is what traverses, thwarts

the language of fault struggling for expression through the forms of pleading. In *Knapp* v. *Salisbury*[44] the plaintiff sued in trespass for damage caused to his pony and chaise, and the defendant wished to show that the collision was due to the plaintiff's own carelessness, or at least ' to mere accident without default on his part.' But the fact that he had pleaded the general issue precluded any such inquiry. In the words of Lord Ellenborough,

> ' These facts ought to have been pleaded specially. The only thing to be tried under the plea of Not Guilty is whether the defendant's cart struck the plaintiff's chaise and killed his horse. That it did is now admitted, and the intention of the defendant is immaterial. This is an action of Trespass. If what happened arose from inevitable accident or from the negligence of the plaintiff, to be sure the defendant is not liable; but as he in fact did run down the chaise and kill the horse, he committed the acts stated in the Declaration, and he ought to have put upon the record any justification he may have had for doing so.'

In *Hall* v. *Fearnley*,[45] in an action of Trespass to which the defendant had pleaded the General Issue, Wightman, J. told the jury that they must decide ' whether the injury was occasioned by unavoidable accident or by the defendant's default,' and that, if they found the former, the plaintiff must lose. They returned a verdict for the defendant, but, on a motion for a new trial, the learned judge admitted his error. He did not doubt his law, but remembered, if too late, that the question of fault must be specially pleaded. So, too, in *Cotterill* v. *Starkey*,[46] Patteson, J. directed the jury that, in an action of Trespass, ' if a defendant means to say that the matter did not arise from his fault, that must be stated in a special plea '; and, if so stated, the inquiry must be confined to the precise issue raised.

It is not unfair to conclude that the evidence, fragmentary as it is, confirms Holmes in denying any initial premise of strict liability, and perhaps suggests a doubt as to his ' period of dry precedent ' between more enlightened eras.[47]   The prevailing tenor of judicial opinion in the first half of the nineteenth century, as far as so impalpable a phenomenon may be analysed, would seem to favour rather than to reject the presence of fault as a necessary element of liability both in Trespass and in Case. The judges who decided *Holmes* v. *Mather* and *Stanley* v. *Powell* were more dogmatic than their predecessors,

---

and denies at once the whole declaration, without offering any special matter whereby to evade it. As in trespass either *vi et armis* or on the case, *non culpabilis,* not guilty; in debt upon contract, *nil debet,* he owes nothing; in debt on bond, *non est factum,* it is not his deed; on an assumpsit, *non assumpsit,* he made no such promise.' It was reproved and restricted, on the other hand, by the new rules of procedure adopted in the Hilary Term, 1834: see Stat. 3 & 4 Will. 4, c. 42, s. 1, and the Appendix to 5 B. & Ad. See Fifoot, *Lord Mansfield,* pp. 232-241.

[44] (1810) 2 Campbell, 500.
[45] (1842) 3 Q.B. 919.
[46] (1839) 8 C. & P. 691, *infra,* p. 211.
[47] *Supra,* p. 187.

but it is at least possible that they did no more than express what was already latent and that their decisions need not be condemned as a revolutionary breach with the past.

S O U R C E S

THE THORNS CASE
Y.B. MICH. 6 ED. 4, f. 7, pl. 18
A.D. 1466

A man brought a writ of Trespass *quare vi et armis clausum fregit, etc. et herbam suam pedibus conculcando consumpsit,* and alleged the trespass in 5 acres; and the defendant said, as to the coming, etc. and as to the trespass in the 5 acres, not guilty; and, as to the trespass in the 5 acres, that the plaintiff ought not to have an action; for he says that he [the defendant] has an acre of land on which a thorn hedge grows, adjoining the said 5 acres, and that he [the defendant], at the time of the supposed trespass, came and cut the thorns, and that they, against his will, fell on the said acres of the plaintiff, and that he [the defendant] came freshly on to the said acres and took them, which is the same trespass for which he has conceived this action. And on this they demurred; and it was well argued, and was adjourned.

And now *Catesby* says: Sir, it has been said that, if a man does some act, even if it be lawful, and by this act tort and damage are done to another against his will, yet, if he could by any means have eschewed the damage, he shall be punished for this act. Sir, it seems to me that the contrary is true, and, as I understand, if a man does a lawful act and thereby damage comes to another against his will, he shall not be punished. Thus, I put the case that I drive my cattle along the highway, and you have an acre of land lying next the highway, and my beasts enter your land and eat your grass, and I come freshly and chase them out of your land; now here, because the chasing out was lawful and the entry on the land was against my will, you shall not have an action against me. No more shall you have an action here, for the cutting was lawful and the falling on your land was against my will, and so the re-taking was good and lawful. And, Sir, I put the case that I cut my trees and the boughs fall on a man and kill him; in this case I shall not be attainted as of felony, for my cutting was lawful and the falling on the man was against my will. No more here, therefore, etc.

Fairfax: It seems to me that the contrary is true; and I say that there is a difference where a man does a thing from which felony ensues and one from which trespass ensues; for in the case which *Catesby* puts there was no felony, since felony is of *malice prepense* and, as the act was against his will, it was not *animo felonico*. But if one cuts his trees and the boughs fall on a man and hurt him, in this case he shall have an action of Trespass. So, too, Sir, if a man shoots at the butts and his bow trembles in his hands and he kills a man *ipso invito,* this is no felony, as has been said. But if he wounds a man by his shooting, he shall have a good action of Trespass against him, and yet the shooting was lawful and the tort that the other had was against his will. And so here.

Pigot: To the same intent. I put the case that I have a mill and the water which comes to my mill runs past your land, and you have willows growing by the water, and you cut your willows and against your will they fall in the water and stop the water so that I have not sufficient water for my mill, in this case I shall have an action of Trespass, and yet the cutting was lawful and the falling was against my will. And so if a man has a fish-pond in his manor and he empties the water out of the pond to take the fishes and the water floods my land, I shall have a good action, and yet the act was lawful.

Yonge: The contrary seems to me to be true; and in such a case, where a man has *dampñum absque injuria,* he shall have no action, for if he has no tort he has no reason to recover damages. So in this case, when he came on to his close to take the thorns which had fallen on to it, this entry was not tortious, for when he cut them and they fell on his close *ipso invito,* the property in them was in him and thus it was lawful for him to take them out of his close; wherefore, notwithstanding that he has done damage, he has done no tort.

Brian: I think the contrary. To my intent, when any man does an act, he is bound to do it in such manner that by his act no prejudice or damage is done to others. Thus, in a case where I am building a house and, while the timber is being put up, a piece of it falls on my neighbour's house and damages it, he shall have a good action, and yet the building of the house was lawful and the timber fell *me invito*. So, too, if a man makes an assault upon me and I cannot avoid him, and in my own defence I raise my stick to strike him, and a man is behind me and in raising my stick I wound him, in this case he shall have an action against me, and yet the raising of my stick to defend myself was lawful and I wounded him *me invito*. So in this case.

LITTLETON, J.: To the same intent. If a man suffers damage, it is right that he be recompensed; and to my intent the case which *Catesby* has put is not law; for if your cattle come on to my land and eat my grass, notwithstanding you come freshly and drive them out, it is proper for you to make amends for what your cattle have done, be it more or less. But if cattle stray on to a man's land, the lord cannot distrain them for his rent, because, when a lord distrains for his rent, he must hold the distress until the rent is paid to him, and this he cannot do in the case aforesaid, since, if I will offer him sufficient amends, I shall recover my beasts; and in a writ of *Rescous* of cattle taken *damage feasant,* it is a good plea for the defendant to say that he tendered to the plaintiff sufficient amends. And, Sir, if it were law that he could enter and take the thorns, by the same reasoning, if he cut a great tree, he could come with his carts and horses to carry off the tree, which is not reason, for peradventure he has corn or other crops growing, etc. No more here may he do it, for the law is all one in great things and in small; and so, according to the amount of the trespass, it is proper that he should make amends.

CHOKE, C.J.: I think the same; for when the principal thing is not lawful, then the thing which depends upon it is not lawful. For when he cut the thorns and they fell on to my land, this falling was not lawful, and then his coming to take them away was not lawful. As to what has been said that they fell *ipso invito,* this is not a good plea; but he should have said that he could not do it in any other manner or that he did all that was in his power to keep them out; otherwise he shall pay damages. And, Sir, if the thorns or a great tree had fallen on his land by the blowing of the wind, in this case he might have come on to the land to take them, since the falling had then been not his act, but that of the wind.

THE TITHE CASE
Y.B. TRIN. 21 HEN. 7, f. 27, pl. 5
A.D. 1506

Trespass; where the defendant justified on the ground that the corn, for which the action was brought, had been severed from the rest of the crop as tithe and was in danger of being lost through beasts straying in the fields, and so the defendant took and carried it away and brought it to the barn belonging to the plaintiff, the Parson of the vill, and there put it inside the barn. To this plea the plaintiff Parson demurred.

Brudenell: The plea is not good; for since the corn had been severed as tithe and left there where it had been growing, it was in a place apart and convenient for keeping it safe, and so it was not lawful for anyone to take it away. Thus, if one takes my horse for fear that it will stray, this is not justifiable; and even if it be straying by the highway so that it knows not where it is, yet a man may not take it to his house; unless indeed it be in danger of perishing in the night or of drowning in water. So here, although the corn was in the middle of the field, yet it was in a place set apart and convenient for keeping it, and, if a man takes it, my action lies full well against him. And so the plea is not good.

Palmes: We have alleged that the crops were in danger of being lost, and, if we had not taken them, they would certainly have been lost; which is a sufficient and reasonable cause for us to justify the taking. So, if I see my neighbour's chimney on fire, I may justify an entry into his house to save the things inside and to take them out for their better safety. And here, since it was surmised that the goods were in danger of being lost and we took them to keep them safely to the plaintiff's use, it is good reason to excuse us, and the plea is good.

KINGSMILL, J.: Where the goods of another are taken against his will, it must be justified either as a thing necessary for the Commonwealth or through a condition recognized by the law. First, as a thing concerning the Commonwealth, one may justify for goods taken out of a house when it is purely to safeguard the goods, or for breaking down a house to safeguard others; and so in time of war one may justify the entry into another's land to make a bulwark in defence of King and Country; and these things are justifiable and lawful for the maintenance of the Commonwealth. The other cause of justification is where one distrains my horse for his rent, and that is justifiable because the land was bound by such a condition of distress; and so in the case of other such conditions. Thus for these two reasons one may justify the taking of a thing against the will of its owner. But in this case here we are outside these reasons, for we are not within the cases of the Commonwealth nor in those of a condition; and, although it is pleaded that this corn was in danger of being lost, yet it was not in such danger but that the party could have had his remedy. Thus, if I have beasts *damage feasant*, I shall not justify my entry to chase them out unless I first tender all amends. So here, when the defendant took the plaintiff's corn that it might not be destroyed, yet this is not justifiable. For if it had been destroyed, the plaintiff would have his remedy against those who destroyed it. And as for his having put it into the plaintiff's barn, yet he must keep it safe against any other mischance; and so no advantage thereby comes to the plaintiff. So this plea is not good.

REDE, C.J.: Although the defendant's intent here was good, yet the intent is not to be construed, though in felony it shall be; as where one shoots at the butts and kills a man, this is not felony, since he had no intent to kill him; and so of a tiler on a house where against his knowledge a stone kills a man, it is not felony. But where one shoots at the butts and wounds a man, although it be against his will, yet he shall be called a trespasser against his will. Where executors take the goods of another together with those of the testator, they may excuse the taking in Trespass; and the law is the same where my sheep are mingled with other sheep, and I may justify the driving of the others away with mine, if I drive them into a fold so that I may separate them. And in these cases there is good reason; for in the first case they could not know *prima facie* which goods were the testator's and which the stranger's, and in the second case they could not separate them until they were driven into the fold. Where one justifies the arrest of a man on suspicion of felony, there must be good grounds for suspicion, as where there is a *hue and cry,* or it will not be justifiable; and if the cry be for nothing, then he that raised it shall be punished. So it is necessary always to have a good case to justify; as in Trespass, a license is good justification. . . . But, to return to the case here, when he took the corn, although this was a good deed as regards the damage which cattle or a stranger might do to it, yet this is not a good deed and no manner of justification as regards the owner of the corn; for the latter would have his remedy by action against him who destroyed the corn, if it had been destroyed. Thus, if my beasts are *damage feasant* in another's land, I cannot enter to chase them out; and yet it would be a good deed to chase them out, to save them doing more damage. But it is otherwise where a stranger drives my horses into another's land, where they do damage; for here I may justify my entry to drive them out, since this tort has its beginning in the tort of another. But here, because the plaintiff could have his remedy if the corn had been destroyed, it was not lawful to take them; and it is not like the cases where things are in jeopardy of loss through water or fire and the like, for there the plaintiff has no remedy for the destruction against anyone. So the plea is not good.

FISHER, J. was of the same opinion. *Quod nota.*

WEAVER v. WARD
(1616), HOBART, 134

Weaver brought an action of Trespass of Assault and Battery against *Ward*. The defendant pleaded that he was amongst others, by the commandment of the Lords of the Council, a trained soldier in London of the Band of one *Andrews,* Captain, and so was the plaintiff; and that they were skirmishing with their muskets charged with powder for their exercise *in re militari* against another Captain and his Band; and, as they were so skirmishing, the defendant *casualiter et per infortuniam et contra voluntatem suam,* in discharging of his piece, did hurt and wound the plaintiff; which is the same, etc., *absque hoc* that he was guilty *aliter sive alio modo.*

And upon Demurrer by the plaintiff, judgment was given for him. For though it were agreed that if men tilt or tourney in the presence of the King, or if two Masters of Defence playing their prizes kill one another, that this shall be no felony, or if a Lunatique kill a man, or the like, because felony must be done *animo felonico;* yet in Trespass, which tends only to give damages according to hurt or loss, it is not so. And therefore if a Lunatique hurt a man, he shall be answerable in Trespass; and no man shall be excused of a Trespass (for this is the nature of an excuse, and not of a justification, *prout ei bene licuit*), except it may be judged utterly without his fault. As if a man by force take my hand and strike you, or if here the defendant had said that the plaintiff ran against his piece when it was discharging, or had set forth the case with the circumstances so as it had appeared to the Court that it had been inevitable, and that the defendant had committed no negligence to give occasion to the hurt.

MILLEN v. FANDRYE
(1626), POPHAM, 161

An action of trespass was brought for chasing of sheep. The defendant pleaded that they were trespassing upon certain land, and he with a little dog chased them out, and as soon as the sheep were out of the land he called in his dog; and upon this the plaintiff demurred. The point singly was but this: I chase the sheep of another out of my ground and the dog pursues them into another man's land next adjoining and I chide my dog, and the owner of the sheep brings trespass for chasing of them.

And it was argued by *Whistler* of *Grays Inne,* that the justification was not good. And he cited *Co. lib.* 4. 38 *b,*[48] that a man may hunt cattell out of his ground with a dog but cannot exceed his authority, and an authority in Law which is abused is void in all, and to hunt them into the next ground is not justifiable. The Books differ, if cattell stray out of the highway involuntarily, whether trespass lies, 7 *H.* 7. 2 and *H.* 7. 20, but all agree that they ought to be chased out as hastily as may be.

Littleton argued for the defendant that cattell may be chased out into another man's ground, and he said that a man cannot have such a power upon his dog as to recall him when he pleaseth, and a dog is ignorant of the bounds of land. And he resembled this to other cases of the Law. First, to 21 *E.* 4. 64: in trespass of cattell taken in A. in D. the defendant saith that he was seised of four acres called C. in D., and found the cattell there *damage feasant* and chased them towards the Pound and they escaped from him and went into A., and he presently retook them, which is the same trespass, and admitted for a good plea. And 22 *Ed.* 4. 8: in trespass the defendant justifies by reason of a custom that they which plow may turn their plow upon the land of another, and that for necessity, and it was allowed for a good justification. And he hath more government of his oxen than in our case he can have of his dog. If a man be making of a lawful chase and cannot do it without damage to another, this is *Damnum sine Injuria,* 21 *H.* 7. 27.[49] And he cited a case which was in Mich. 18 Jac. between *Jenning* and *Maystore,* where a man of necessity chased sheep for taking one of his own, in trespass he may justifie it. And also if a dog goes into the land of another (as in this case), trespass does not lye; but otherwise it is of cattell.

CREW, C.J.: It seems to me that he might drive the sheep out with the dog, and he could not withdraw his dog when he would in an instant; and

[48] *Semble, Tyrringham's Case* (1584) 4 Co. Rep. 36b.
[49] *Supra,* p. 197.

therefore it is not like to the case of 38 *E.* 3, where trespass was brought for entering into a warren, and there it was pleaded that there was a pheasant in his land and his hawk flew and followed it into the plaintiff's ground, and there it seems that it is not a good justification, for he may pursue the hawk but cannot take the pheasant. 6 *Ed.* 4[50]: a man cuts thorns and they fall into another man's land, and in trespass he justified for it, and the opinion was that, notwithstanding this justification, trespass lies, because he did not plead that he did his best endeavour to hinder their falling there; yet this was a hard case. But this case is not like to these cases, for here it was lawful to chase them out of his own land, and he did his best endeavour to recall the dog, and therefore trespass does not lye.

[DODDERIDGE and JONES, J.J. gave judgment to the same effect.]

. . . And the same day Judgment was given for the defendant, *Quod quærens nil capiat per billam.*[51]

DICKENSON v. WATSON
(1682), SIR T. JONES, 205

The plaintiff[52] brought Error on a Judgment in the Court of the Sheriff of the City of York, in Trespass for an assault, battery and wounding of the plaintiff's eye, by discharging of a gun charged with powder and hail-shot, by which he lost the sight of his eye.

The defendant pleaded *actio non,* because he is, and at the time of the trespass was, an officer appointed for collecting the duty of hearth-money, and for the better discharge of his office and more sure custody and keeping of the money by him collected and to be collected, he provided himself with fire-arms, and, having one of his pistols in his hands and intending to discharge it *ne aliquod damnum eveniret,* he discharged it (*nemine in opposito visu existente*), and, while he discharged it, the plaintiff *casualiter viam illam præterivit et si aliquod malum ei inde accideret hoc fuit contra voluntatem* of the defendant. *Quæ est eadem transgressio.*

Upon this the plaintiff demurred, and Judgment was given for him; whereupon Error was brought and Judgment was affirmed, nothing being urged besides the sufficiency of the Plea. But the Court held it to be insufficient; for in trespass the defendant shall not be excused without unavoidable Necessity, which is not shewn here. . . .'

GIBBONS v. PEPPER
(1695), 1 LD. RAYMOND, 38

Trespass, assault and battery. The defendant pleads that he rode upon a horse in the King's highway and that his horse being affrighted ran away with him so that he could not stop the horse; that there were several persons standing in the way, among whom the plaintiff stood, and that he called to them to take care, but that, notwithstanding, the plaintiff did not go out of the way but continued there; so that the defendant's horse ran over the

---

[50] *Supra,* p. 195.
[51] In the report of the same case in Latch, 119, it is said that judgment was given for the plaintiff. But this is an evident error: see the further report in 1 Jones, 131—'Resolved by the whole Court, i.e., the four Justices, that the action lay not.'
[52] i.e. the plaintiff in error—the original defendant.

plaintiff against the will of the defendant; *quæ est eadem transgressio*, etc. The plaintiff demurred.

And *Serjt. Darnall* for the defendant argued that if the defendant in his justification shews that the accident was inevitable and that the negligence of the defendant did not cause it, judgment shall be given for him. . . .[53]'

Northey for the plaintiff said that in all these cases the defendant confessed a battery, which he afterwards justified; but in this case he justified a battery, which is no battery.

Of which opinion was the whole court.[54] For if I ride upon a horse, and J. S. whips the horse so that he runs away with me and runs over any other person, he who whipped the horse is guilty of the battery, and not me. But if I by spurring was the cause of such accident, then I am guilty. In the same manner, if A. takes the hand of B. and with it strikes C., A. is the trespasser and not B. And, *per Curiam*, the defendant might have given this justification in evidence upon the general issue pleaded. And therefore judgment was given for the plaintiff.'[55]

REYNOLDS v. CLARKE
(1726), 1 STRANGE, 634[56]

Trespass for entering the plaintiff's yard and fixing a spout there, *per quod* the water came into the yard and rotted the walls of the plaintiff's house. The defendant justifies, that, before the trespass, *John Fountain* was seised in fee of the plaintiff's house and yard and two other houses adjoining, and demised the plaintiff's house and yard to one *Tyler*, except the free use of the yard and privy for the tenants of the other two houses jointly with the tenant of the plaintiff's house. . Then he shews how the house of the defendant, which was one of the two houses, came to him, and that he entered the yard and fixed the spout for his necessary use to carry off the rain, *prout ei bene licuit*. The plaintiff demurs, and

Reeve, pro defendente, insisted that this exception amounted to a license of the party, and that a distinction has always been taken between a license in law, as to go into a tavern, and the license of the party, and that this being of the latter sort, an action of trespass will not lie; but if the spout be a prejudice, the plaintiff must right himself by an action upon the case. 11 *Coke. The Six Carpenters' Case*.[57] This is an action of trespass brought for a nuisance upon our own possession.

Et per Chief Justice [RAYMOND]: Though he had a right to enter into the yard, yet it is considerable whether, if he abuses that right to the detriment of another, he is not in the same case with any other trespasser.

Et per FORTESCUE, J.: Trespass is a possessory action, and how does this invade the plaintiff's possession? The difference between trespass and

---

[53] He cited, *inter alia, Weaver* v. *Ward, supra*, p. 198.

[54] of King's Bench.

[55] Cf. the report in 2 Salkeld, at p. 638: 'not but if the defendant had pleaded Not Guilty, this matter might have acquitted him upon evidence; but the reason of their judgment was because the defendant justified a trespass and does not confess it.'
So the report in 4 Mod. 405: 'he should have pleaded the *general issue*, for if the horse ran away against his will, he would have been found not guilty, because in such case it cannot be said with any colour of reason to be a battery in the rider.' On the General Issue, see *supra*, p. 193.

[56] For a fuller report of the Pleadings and of the arguments of counsel, see 2 Ld. Raymond, 1399.

[57] The reference should be 8 Coke Rep., 146A.

case is that in trespass the plaintiff complains of an immediate wrong, and in case of a wrong that is the consequence of another act.

Et per RAYMOND, C.J.: That distinction is perfectly right. I remember a case in B.R. *Courtney* v. *Collett*,[58] which was for the defendant's diverting his own water-course in his own land, *per quod* the plaintiff's land was overflowed; after a verdict *pro querente,* it was often debated whether this was an action of trespass or upon the case, and at last judgment was for the plaintiff, who had brought trespass only.

The Court said it was a nice case, and therefore they gave not their opinion, but ordered an *ulterius concilium.*

After a second argument to the effect of the former, the Court delivered their opinions this term.

CHIEF JUSTICE: We must keep up the boundaries of actions, otherwise we shall introduce the utmost confusion. If the act in the first instance be unlawful, trespass will lie; but if the act is *prima facie* lawful (as it was in this case), and the prejudice to another is not immediate but consequential, it must be an action upon the case; and this is the distinction. The case I mentioned the last time of *Courtney* v. *Collett* was a plain trespass, and the account I then gave of it from my memory was mistaken. It was Hil. 9 W.3 in B.R., trespass for taking fishes, *necnon pro eo quod* he broke down the bank of the river, *per quod* the water issued and other fishes went away: after verdict for the plaintiff it was moved in arrest of judgment that the latter part was case and not joinable with trespass. But the court held that it was a trespass, and what came under the *per quod* was only matter of aggravation. There was another case in B.R. Hil. 8 Anne, *Leveridge* v. *Hoskins*.[59] That was case for digging trenches, whereby the water was drawn away from the plaintiff's river. It was moved in arrest of judgment that this was trespass; but the court said that, it not being laid to be a digging upon the plaintiff's ground, the action upon the case was most proper. And I take that and this to be the same case; the defendant having a right to enter the yard and do the first act which is here complained of, I think this should have been an action upon the case and that trespass will not lie.

POWYS, J. *accord.*

Et per FORTESCUE, J.: Trespass will not lie for procuring another to beat me. If a man throws a log into the highway and in that act it hits me, I may maintain trespass, because it is an immediate wrong; but if, as it lies there, I tumble over it and receive an injury, I must bring an action upon the case; because it is only prejudicial *in consequence,* for which originally I could have no action at all.

Et per REYNOLDS, J.: The distinction is certainly right. This is only injurious in its consequence, for it is not pretended that the bare fixing of a spout was a cause of action without the falling of any water. The right of action did not accrue till the water actually descended, and therefore this should have been an action upon the case.

Per Curiam. Judgment for the Defendant.

SCOTT v. SHEPHERD
(1773), 2 W. BLACKSTONE, 892

Trespass and assault for throwing, casting and tossing a lighted squib at and against the plaintiff and striking him therewith on the face and so

[58] 1 Ld. Raym., 272.
[59] (1709) 11 Mod. 257.

burning one of his eyes that he lost the sight of it, whereby, etc. On not guilty pleaded, the cause came on to be tried before Nares, J., last Summer Assizes at Bridgwater, when the jury found a verdict for the plaintiff with £100 damages, subject to the opinion of the Court on this case: —

On the evening of the fair-day at Milborne Port, October 28, 1770, the defendant threw a lighted squib, made of gunpowder, etc., from the street into the market-house, which is a covered building supported by arches and enclosed at one end, but open at the other and both the sides, where a large concourse of people were assembled; which lighted squib, so thrown by the defendant, fell upon the standing of one Yates, who sold gingerbread, etc. That one Willis instantly, and to prevent injury to himself and the said wares of the said Yates, took up the said lighted squib from off the said standing and then threw it across the said market-house, when it fell upon another standing there of one Ryal, who sold the same sort of wares, who instantly, and to save his own goods from being injured, took up the said lighted squib from off the said standing, and then threw it to another part of the said market-house, and in so throwing it struck the plaintiff, then in the said market-house, in the face therewith, and, the combustible matter then bursting, put out one of the plaintiff's eyes. *Qu.* If this action be maintainable?

This case was argued last term by *Glyn,* for the plaintiff, and *Burland,* for the defendant: and this term, the Court, being divided in their judgment, delivered their opinions *seriatim.* . . .

BLACKSTONE, J., was of opinion that an action of *trespass* did not lie for *Scott* against *Shepherd* upon this case. He took the settled distinction to be that, where the injury is *immediate,* an action of *trespass* will lie; where it is only *consequential,* it must be an action on the *case: Reynolds* v. *Clarke*[60]; *Haward* v. *Bankes*[61]; *Harker* v. *Birkbeck.*[62] The *lawfulness* or *unlawfulness* of the original act is not the criterion; though something of that sort is put into Lord Raymond's mouth in Strange, 635, where it can only mean that if the act then in question, of erecting a spout, had been in itself unlawful, trespass might have lain; but as it was a lawful act (upon the defendant's own ground), and the injury to the plaintiff only consequential, it must be an action on the case. But this cannot be the general rule; for it is held by the Court in the same case, that if I throw a log of timber into the highway (which is an unlawful act), and another man tumbles over and is hurt, an action on the case only lies, it being a *consequential* damage; but if in throwing it I hit another man, he may bring trespass, because it is an *immediate* wrong. Trespass may sometimes lie for the consequences of a lawful act. If in lopping my own trees a bough accidentally falls on my neighbour's ground, and I go thereon to fetch it, trespass lies. This is the case cited from 6 Edw. IV, 7.[63] But then the entry is of itself an immediate wrong. And case will sometimes lie for the consequence of an unlawful act. If by false imprisonment I have a special damage, as if I forfeit my recognizance thereby, I shall have an action on the case; per Powel, J., 11 Mod. 180. Yet here the original act was unlawful and in the nature of trespass. So that *lawful* or *unlawful* is quite out of the case; the solid distinction is between *direct* or *immediate* injuries on the one hand, and *mediate* or *consequential* on the other. And trespass never lay for the

[60] *Supra,* p. 201.
[61] (1760) 2 Burr., 1113.
[62] (1761) 2 Burr., 1159.
[63] *Supra,* p. 195.

latter. If this be so, the only question will be whether the injury which the plaintiff suffered was *immediate* or *consequential* only; and I hold it to be the latter.

The original act was as against *Yates* a trespass; not as against *Ryal* or *Scott*. The tortious act was complete when the squib lay at rest upon *Yates's* stall. He, or any bystander, had, I allow, a right to protect themselves by removing the squib, but should have taken care to do it in such a manner as not to endamage others. But *Shepherd*, I think, is not answerable in an action of trespass and assault for the mischief done by the squib in the new motion impressed upon it and the new direction given it by either *Willis* or *Ryal*, who both were free agents and acted upon their own judgment. This differs it from the cases put of turning loose a wild beast or a madman. They are only instruments in the hand of the first agent. Nor is it like diverting the course of an enraged ox, or of a stone thrown, or an arrow glancing against a tree; because there the original motion, the *vis impressa*, is continued tho' diverted. Here the instrument of mischief was at rest till a new impetus and a new direction were given it, not once only, but by two successive rational agents. . . .

. . . But it is said, if *Scott* has no action against *Shepherd*, against whom must he seek his remedy? I give no opinion whether Case would lie against *Shepherd* for the consequential damage, though, as at present advised, I think upon the circumstances it would. But I think, in strictness of law, Trespass would lie against *Ryal*, the immediate actor in this unhappy business. Both he and *Willis* have exceeded the bounds of self-defence and not used sufficient circumspection in removing the danger from themselves. The throwing it *across* the market-house, instead of brushing it down or throwing it out of the open sides into the street (if it was not meant to continue the sport as 'tis called), was at least an unnecessary and incautious act. . . .

. . . The same evidence that will maintain *Trespass* may also frequently maintain *Case*, but not *e converso*. Every action of Trespass with a *per quod* includes an Action on the Case. I may bring Trespass for the immediate injury and subjoin a *per quod* for the consequential damages; or may bring Case for the consequential damages and pass over the immediate injury, as in the case from 11 *Mod.* 180 before cited.[64] But if I bring Trespass for an immediate injury and prove at most only a consequential damage, judgment must be given for the Defendant. *Gates* v. *Bailey*, Tr. 6 Geo. 3, 2 Wilson, 313.

It is said by Lord Raymond, and very justly, in *Reynolds* v. *Clarke*,[65] ' We must keep up the boundaries of actions, otherwise we shall introduce the utmost confusion.' As I therefore think no immediate injury passed from the Defendant to the Plaintiff, and without such immediate injury no action of Trespass can be maintained, I am of opinion that in this action Judgment ought to be for the Defendant. . . .

[NARES and GOULD, J.J. and DE GREY, C.J. gave judgment for the Plaintiff.]

DE GREY, C.J.: This case is one of those wherein the line drawn by the law between actions on the case and actions of trespass is very nice and delicate. Trespass is an injury accompanied with force, for which an action of trespass *vi et armis* lies against the person from whom it is received. The

[64] *Bourden* v. *Alloway*, (1709).
[65] *Supra*, p. 202.

question here is whether the injury received by the plaintiff arises from the force of the original act of the defendant or from a new force by a third person. I agree with my Brother Blackstone as to the principles he has laid down, but not in his application of those principles to the present case. The real question certainly does not turn upon the lawfulness or unlawfulness of the original act; for actions of trespass will lie for legal acts when they become trespasses by accident; as in the cases cited of cutting thorns, lopping of a tree, shooting at a mark, defending oneself by a stick which strikes another behind, etc. They may also not lie for the consequences even of illegal acts, as that of casting a log in the highway, etc. But the true question is whether the injury is the direct and immediate act of the defendant: and I am of opinion that in this case it is.

The throwing the squib was an act unlawful and tending to affright the bystander. So far mischief was originally intended; not any particular mischief, but mischief indiscriminate and wanton. Whatever mischief therefore follows, he is the author of it:—*Egreditur personam,* as the phrase is in criminal cases. And though criminal cases are no rule for civil ones, yet in trespass I think there is an analogy. Every one who does an unlawful act is considered as the doer of all that follows. If done with a deliberate intent, the consequence may amount to murder; if incautiously, to manslaughter: Fost. 261. So too, in 1 Ventr. 295, a person breaking a horse in Lincoln's Inn Fields hurt a man; held, that trespass lay: and 2 Lev. 172, that it need not be laid *scienter*.[66] I look upon all that was done subsequent to the original throwing as a continuation of the first force and first act, which will continue till the squib was spent by bursting. And I think that any innocent person removing the danger from himself to another is justifiable; the blame lights upon the first thrower. The new direction and new force flow out of the first force, and are not a new trespass. The writ in the Register, 95a,[67] for trespass in maliciously cutting down a head of water, which thereupon flowed down to and overwhelmed another's pond, shows that the immediate act need not be instantaneous, but that a chain of effects connected together will be sufficient. It has been urged that the intervention of a free agent will make a difference: but I do not consider *Willis* and *Ryal* as free agents in the present case, but acting under a compulsive necessity for their own safety and self-preservation. On these reasons I concur with my Brothers Gould and Nares that the present action is maintainable.

Postea to the plaintiff.[68]

LEAME v. BRAY

(1803), 3 EAST, 593

This was an action of trespass, in which the plaintiff declared that the defendant with force and arms drove and struck a single-horse chaise which the defendant was then driving along the King's highway with such great

---

[66] *Mitchill* v. *Alestree* (1677) 1 Ventris, 295; 2 Levinz, 172. Unfortunately for the Chief Justice's argument, the plaintiff sued in Case.

[67] F.N.B. 95A. As in *Mitchill* v. *Alestree,* so here the precedent given by Fitzherbert is in Case, not Trespass.

[68] 'The verdict, when given, is afterwards drawn up in form and entered on the back of the record of nisi prius. This is done, upon trials in King's Bench in London and Middlesex, by the attorney for the successful party; in other cases, by an officer of the court. Such entry is called the *postea,* from the word with which, at a former period (when the proceedings were in Latin), it commenced': Stephen on Pleading, at p. 119.

force and violence upon and against the plaintiff's curricle drawn by two horses, and upon and against the said horses so drawing, etc., and in which said curricle the plaintiff was then and there riding with his servant, which servant was then driving the said curricle and horses along the King's highway aforesaid, that by means thereof the plaintiff's servant was thrown out of the curricle upon the ground and the horses ran away with the curricle, and, while the horses were so running away with the curricle, the plaintiff, for the preservation of his life, jumped and fell from the curricle upon the ground and fractured his collar bone, etc. Plea: not guilty.

It appeared in evidence at the trial before Lord ELLENBOROUGH, C.J., at the last sittings at Westminster, that the accident described in the declaration happened in a dark night owing to the defendant driving his carriage on the wrong side of the road and the parties not being able to see each other, and that if the defendant had kept his right side there was ample room for the carriages to have passed without injury. But it did not appear that blame was imputable to the defendant in any other respect as to the manner of his driving. It was therefore objected for the defendant that, the injury having happened from negligence and not wilfully, the proper remedy was by an action on the case and not of trespass *vi et armis;* and the plaintiff was thereupon nonsuited.

Gibbs and *Park* now showed cause against a rule for setting aside the nonsuit, and admitted that there were many precedents of trespass *vi et armis* for an injury immediately proceeding from the party although his will did not go along with his act. But here they contended that the injury was consequential and not immediately flowing from the forcible act of the defendant, and in such a case trespass will not lie unless such act be done wilfully; and they compared it to the case of one ship running down another, in all which cases the form of the action has been case and not trespass. . . .

Lord ELLENBOROUGH: I do not find that distinction laid down in any of the cases, that in order to maintain trespass the act must be wilful. In *Scott* v. *Shepherd*[69] Lord C.J. de Grey said that trespass *vi et armis* lay against the person from whom an injury was received by force; and he afterwards adverted to acts that might become trespasses by accident or inadvertency. . . .

LAWRENCE, J.: There certainly are cases in the books where, the injury being direct and immediate, trespass has been holden to lie, though the injury were not intentional: as in *Weaver* v. *Ward*,[70] where the defendant exercising in the trained bands and firing his musket accidentally hurt the plaintiff, and in *Underwood* v. *Hewson*,[71] where one uncocking a gun, it went off and accidentally wounded a bystander. . . .

Gibbs and *Park, arguendo*: Perhaps a defendant might be liable in trespass for that which is the immediate consequence of a forcible act done by himself; but for that which is not the immediate consequence of his own act, but is the consequence of some other act which he negligently, improvidently or unskilfully did, he is only liable in case. . . .

Erskine and *Hovell* in support of the rule: The distinction which was taken in *Reynolds* v. *Clarke*[72] has been adopted in all the subsequent cases, that, where the immediate act itself occasions a prejudice or is an injury to

[69] (1773) 2 W. Bl. 892: *supra*, p. 202.
[70] (1616) Hobart, 134: *supra*, p. 198.
[71] (1724) 1 Strange, 596: *supra*, p. 191.
[72] (1726) 1 Strange, 634: *supra*, p. 201.

the plaintiff's person, etc., there trespass *vi et armis* will lie; but where the act itself is not an injury, but a consequence from that act is prejudicial to the plaintiff's person, etc., there trespass *vi et armis* will not lie, but the proper remedy is by an action on the case. So in *Day* v. *Edwards*,[73] Lord Kenyon said, ' If the injury be committed by the immediate act complained of, the action must be trespass : if the injury be merely consequential upon that act, an action upon the case is the proper remedy.' . . . The declaration there charged that the defendant ' so furiously, negligently and improperly ' drove his cart against the plaintiff's carriage that it overturned and damaged it, but *non constat* that it was done wilfully, however furiously; and, on the contrary, the allegation of its being done negligently as well as furiously rebutted the idea of wilfulness. Yet the Court held that, the injury ensuing upon the immediate act of the defendant, the action ought to have been trespass and not case, as it was laid to be. In *Ogle* v. *Barnes*[74] the Court could not say that the act done was by the immediate agency of the defendants. It was charged to be done by their negligence, carelessness, ignorance and unskilfulness : *non constat* but that the act which produced the mischief was done the day before; they might not have been in the ship when it happened. In none of the cases is it laid down as a branch of the distinction that the act done must be either wilful or illegal or violent in order to maintain trespass : the only question is whether the injury from it be immediate.

Lord ELLENBOROUGH, C.J. : The true criterion seems to be, according to what Lord C.J. de Grey says in *Scott* v. *Shepherd*,[75] whether the plaintiff received an injury by force from the defendant. If the injurious act be the immediate result of the force originally applied by the defendant and the plaintiff be injured by it, it is the subject of an action of trespass *vi et armis* by all the cases both ancient and modern. It is immaterial whether the injury be wilful or not. As in the case alluded to by my brother *Grose,* where one shooting at butts for a trial of skill with the bow and arrow, the weapon then in use, in itself a lawful act and no unlawful purpose in view; yet, having accidentally wounded a man, it was holden to be a trespass, being an immediate injury from an act of force by another.[76] Such also was the case of *Weaver* v. *Ward*,[77] where a like unfortunate accident happened whilst persons were lawfully exercising themselves in arms. So in none of the cases mentioned in *Scott* v. *Shepherd* did wilfulness make any difference. If the injury were received from the personal act of another, it was deemed sufficient to make it trespass. In the case of *Day* v. *Edwards*,[78] the allegation of the act being done furiously was understood to imply an act of force immediately proceeding from the defendant. As to the case of *Ogle* v. *Barnes*,[79] I incline to think it was rightly decided, and yet there are words there which imply force by the act of another. But, as was observed,

---

[73] (1794) 5 T.R. 648.

[74] (1799) 8 T.R. 188. In an action upon the case, the plaintiffs' ship, the ' Anne,' was injured in a collision alleged in the Declaration to be caused by the fact that the defendants ' so incautiously, carelessly, negligently and inexpertly managed, steered and directed ' their ship, the ' Actæon.' The defendants contended that the plaintiffs should have sued not in Case but in Trespass, as ' the injury done was occasioned by the immediate act of the defendants '; but judgment was given for the plaintiffs.

[75] *Supra*, p. 202.

[76] See *The Tithe Case* (1506), Y.B. 21 Hen. 7, f. 27, pl. 5, *supra*, p. 198.

[77] (1616) Hobart, 134, *supra*, p. 198.

[78] (1794) 5 T.R. 648.

[79] (1799) 8 T.R. 188.

it does not appear that it must have been the personal act of the defendants: it is not even alleged that they were on board the ship at the time. It is said indeed that they had the care, direction and management of it, but that might be through the medium of other persons in their employ on board. That therefore might be sustained as an action on the case, because there were no words in the declaration which necessarily implied that the damage happened from an act of force done by the defendants themselves. I am not aware of any case of that sort where, the party himself sued having been on board, this question has been raised. But here the defendant himself was present and used the ordinary means of impelling the horse forward, and from that the injury happened. And therefore, there being an immediate injury from an immediate act of force by the defendant, the proper remedy is trespass; and wilfulness is not necessary to constitute trespass.

GROSE, J.: I am of the same opinion. Looking into all the cases from the Year Book in the 21 H. 7[80] down to the latest decision on the subject, I find the principle to be that, if the injury be done by the act of the party himself at the time or he be the immediate cause of it, though it happen accidentally or by misfortune, yet he is answerable in trespass. The case mentioned from Strange,[81] that in Hobart, and those in the Term Reports, all agree in the principle.

LAWRENCE, J.: I am of the same opinion. It is more convenient that the action should be trespass than case; because if it be laid in trespass, no nice points can arise upon the evidence by which the plaintiff may be turned round upon the form of the action, as there may in many instances if case be brought; for there, if any of the witnesses should say that in his belief the defendant did the injury wilfully, the plaintiff will run the risk of being nonsuited. But in actions of trespass the distinction has not turned either on the lawfulness of the act from whence the injury happened or the design of the party doing it to commit the injury: but, as mentioned by Mr. Justice Blackstone in the case of *Scott* v. *Shepherd,* on the difference between injuries direct and immediate or mediate and consequential; in the one instance the remedy is by trespass, in the other by case. The same principle is laid down in *Reynolds* v. *Clarke.* As to *Ogle* v. *Barnes,*[82] I certainly did not mean to say that the distinction turned on the wilfulness of the act. I only made use of the word 'wilful' to distinguish that from other cases which had been mentioned, where the injurious acts were averred to be wilfully done and where, as the acts complained of were charged as intentional and the injuries done immediately referred to them, trespass was determined to be the proper remedy. And so I understand what was there said by my brother Grose. What I principally relied on there was that it did not appear that the mischief happened from the personal acts of the defendants. It might have happened from the operation of the wind and tide counteracting their personal efforts at the time; or indeed they might not even have been on board. . . .

[LE BLANC, J. delivered judgment to the same effect, and the rule for setting aside the nonsuit was made absolute.]

[80] *The Tithe Case, supra,* p. 197.
[81] *Semble, Underwood* v. *Hewson* (1724), 1 Strange, 596.
[82] (1799) 8 T.R. 188. The actual words of Lawrence, J.'s judgment in that case are thus reported (at pp. 191-2): 'Such an injury as the present may be occasioned either by the wilful act or by the negligence of the defendants; it is a question of evidence. If the former, trespass is the proper action; if the latter, an action on the case.'

WILLIAMS v. HOLLAND

(1833), 10 BINGHAM, 112

The declaration stated that the Plaintiff on, etc., at, etc., was lawfully possessed of a certain cart and of a certain horse drawing the same; in which said cart certain persons, to wit, John Williams, being the son and servant, and Mary Ann Williams, being the infant daughter of the Plaintiff, were then riding in and along a certain public and common highway; and the Defendant was then and there possessed of a certain gig and of a certain other horse drawing the same, which said gig and horse were then and there under the care, government and direction of the Defendant in and along the said highway, to wit, at, etc. Nevertheless the Defendant so carelessly, unskilfully and improperly drove, governed and directed his said gig and horse, that by and through the carelessness, negligence, unskilfulness and improper conduct of the Defendant, the said gig and horse of the defendant then and there ran and struck with great violence upon and against the cart and horse of the Plaintiff, and thereby then and there crushed, broke to pieces and damaged the same; and the said cart of the Plaintiff thereby then and there became and was rendered of little or no value to the Plaintiff; and thereby the said John Williams and Mary Ann Williams were then and there cast and thrown with great force and violence from and out of the said cart to and upon the ground there, and by means of the several premises aforesaid the Plaintiff was deprived of the service of his son and put to expense for doctor's bills, etc. Plea, not guilty.

At the trial before TINDAL, C.J., it appeared that the Plaintiff's cart was standing at the side of a road twenty-four feet wide, with the near wheel on the footway, when the Plaintiff in a gig, and in the act of racing with another gig, drove against the cart, upset and broke it to pieces and severely injured the Plaintiff's children.

The defence was that the Defendant's horse had run away with him. And the Chief Justice left it to the jury to say whether the collision was the result of accident or of negligence and carelessness in the Defendant. The jury found the latter and gave a verdict with damages for the Plaintiff. It was also contended, on the part of the Defendant, that the action was misconceived and ought to have been trespass instead of case. The Chief Justice having reserved that point for the consideration of the Court, *Bompas,* Serjt., obtained thereupon a rule nisi to set aside the verdict and enter a nonsuit.

Jones, Serjt., who shewed cause, contended that the result of all the cases on this subject was that, where the act complained of is immediate and wilful, the remedy is only by action of trespass; where the act is immediate but occasioned by negligence or carelessness, the remedy is either by trespass or case; where the act is unimmediate, the remedy is by case only. . . .

Bompas, in support of his rule, insisted that the effect of all the authorities is that, when the act complained of is immediate, whether it be wilful or the result of negligence, the remedy is by trespass only.

TINDAL, C.J.: . . . The declaration in this case states the ground of action to be an injury occasioned by the carelessness and negligence of the Defendant in driving his own gig; and that such carelessness and negligence is, strictly and properly in itself, the subject of an action on the case would appear, if any authority were wanting, from *Com. Dig. tit. Action upon the Case for Negligence*; and the jury have found, in the very terms of the declaration, that the injury was so occasioned. Under such a form of action, therefore, and with such a finding by the jury, the present objection ought not to prevail unless some positive and inflexible rule of law, or some authority too strong to be overcome, is brought forward in its support. If such are to be found, they must undoubtedly be adhered to; for settled forms of action, adapted to different grievances, contribute much to the certain administration of justice.

But, upon examining the cases cited in argument, both in support of and in answer to the objection, we cannot find one in which it is distinctly held that the present form of action is not maintainable under the circumstances of this case.

For, as to *Leame* v. *Bray*,[83] on which the principal reliance is placed by the Defendant, in which the form of action was trespass and the circumstances very nearly the same as those in the case now under consideration, the only rule established is that an action of trespass might be maintained, not that an action on the case could not. The case of *Savignac* v. *Roome*,[84] in which the Court held that case would not lie where the defendant's servant wilfully drove against the plaintiff's carriage, was founded on the principle that no action would lie against the master for the wilful act of his servant. And in that of *Day* v. *Edwards*,[85] in which it was ruled that trespass was the proper remedy and not case, it should be observed that the question arose upon a special demurrer to the declaration; . . . and, the question, therefore, arising upon a special demurrer, where the Court could look to nothing but the legal construction of the declaration, is very differently circumstanced from this, where the jury have found that negligence was the ground of the injury. On the other hand, the cases of *Rogers* v. *Imbleton*[86] and *Ogle* v. *Barnes*[87] are simply in favour of the proposition that the present form of action is, under the circumstances, maintainable.

We hold it, however, to be unnecessary to examine very minutely the grounds of the various decisions. For the late case of *Moreton* v. *Hardern*[88] appears to us to go the full length of deciding that, where the injury is occasioned by the carelessness and negligence of the Defendant, although it be occasioned by his immediate act, the Plaintiff may, if he thinks proper, make the negligence of the Defendant the ground of his action and declare in case. It has been urged, indeed, in answer to that case, that it was decided on the ground that the action was brought against one of the proprietors who was driving and against his co-proprietors who were absent, but whose servant was on the box at the time; and that as trespass would not have been maintainable against the co-proprietors who were absent, so case was held maintainable in order that all the proprietors might be included. But it is manifest that the Court did not rest their opinion upon so narrow a ground; nor indeed would it have been a solid foundation for the judgment that the master, who was present, should be made liable to a different form of action than he otherwise would have been if the servant of the other proprietors had not been there.

[83] (1803) 3 East, 593, *supra*, p. 205.
[84] (1794) 6 T.R. 125.
[85] (1794) 5 T.R. 648.
[86] (1806) 2 B. & P. (N.R.) 117.
[87] (1799) 8 T.R. 188.
[88] (1825) 4 B. & C. 223.

We think the case last above referred to has laid down a plain and intelligible rule that, where the injury is occasioned by the carelessness and negligence of the Defendant, the Plaintiff is at liberty to bring an action on the case notwithstanding the act is immediate, so long as it is not a wilful act; and, upon the authority of that case, we think the present form of action maintainable to recover damages for the injury.

Rule discharged.

COTTERILL v. STARKEY

(1839), 8 CARRINGTON AND PAYNE, 691

Trespass.—The declaration stated that on the 18th of August, 1838, the defendant drove a cart and horse, which he was then driving along the Queen's highway, against the plaintiff Sarah and threw her on the ground and with the feet of the horse and the wheels of the cart trampled on and ran over her, whereby she was greatly hurt, etc. Pleas, 1st, not guilty; and 2nd, a plea which stated in substance that the accident arose by and through the mere negligent, careless and improper conduct of the plaintiff Sarah.[89]

Replication to the second plea *de injuria*.[90]

It appeared from the evidence for the plaintiff that at about eleven o'clock on the morning of the 18th of August, 1838, the plaintiff and his wife were crossing the Holloway Road and that the defendant, who was driving a light spring cart, turned from the Islington Road into the Holloway Road, and, being on his wrong side of the road, drove against the female plaintiff, who was thrown down and run over and seriously injured. . . .

Evidence was given for the defendant with a view of shewing that Mrs. Cotterill was standing in the road and that the defendant was on the proper side of it and that he pulled up as soon as he possibly could and so suddenly that part of his harness broke.

PATTESON, J., in summing up: This is not an action for negligent driving. If it had been so, the defendant, on a plea of not guilty, would have been

[89] The reporters add the form of the plea, ' as it may be useful in practice.' ' 2nd Plea.—That he, the defendant, just before and at the said time, was driving the said cart and horse, in the said declaration mentioned, in and along the middle of the highway, in the said declaration also mentioned, in a careful, moderate and proper manner; and that whilst he, the defendant, was so driving the same, the said Sarah negligently, carelessly and improperly ran along and across the middle of the said highway near to and against the said cart and horse of the said defendant, and was thereby then cast and thrown to and upon the ground and kicked, trampled upon, and run over and crushed, as in the said declaration mentioned, without any default on the part of the defendant. And so the defendant in fact saith that the said hurt and damage, in the said declaration mentioned, were occasioned and happened to the said Sarah by and through the mere negligent, careless and improper conduct of her, the said Sarah, and not by and through the default or the improper conduct of the defendant; and that, if the said Sarah had exercised ordinary care in that behalf, the same would not have happened, which are the same supposed trespasses in the declaration mentioned and whereof the plaintiffs have above thereof complained against him; and this the defendant is ready to verify.'

[90] The replication *de injuria* was a species of traverse appropriate to a plaintiff in Trespass or Case, when the defendant's plea consisted ' merely of matter of excuse ': *per* Stephen on Pleading, pp. 203-4. Stephen gives an example: ' And as to the said plea by the said defendant last above pleaded, . . . the said A. B. says that, by reason of anything therein alleged, he ought not to be barred from having and maintaining his aforesaid action against the said C. D., because he says that the said C. D. at the said time when, etc., of his own wrong (*de injuria sua propria*) and without the cause in his said last-mentioned plea alleged, committed the said several trespasses. . . .' For an amusing *jeu d'esprit* upon the technicalities involved in the replication, see Hayes, *Crogate's Case: a dialogue in ye shades;* set out in H.E.L. IX. 417-431.

entitled to have shewn that he was not negligent. This is an action of trespass, and if in trespass a defendant means to say that the matter did not arise from his fault, that must be stated in a special plea. That has been done here, and the defendant says that the matter arose from the negligent, careless and improper conduct of Mrs. Cotterill, which is denied by the plaintiff. It is not asserted here, by way of defence, that neither party was in fault and that the matter arose from inevitable accident. You must say whether it arose from the plaintiff's fault or not; but if you should think there was no fault at all anywhere, that will not be a defence here, as there is no plea to that effect, and, before you find for the defendant on the present state of the pleadings, you must be satisfied that the matter arose from the negligent, careless and improper conduct of Mrs. Cotterill. A foot passenger has a right to cross a highway, and I believe that it was held in one case[91] that a foot passenger has a right to walk along the carriage way; but, without going that length, it is quite clear that a foot passenger has a right to cross and that persons driving carriages along the road are liable if they do not take care so as to avoid driving against the foot passengers who are crossing the road; and if a person driving along the road cannot pull up because his reins break, that will be no ground of defence, as he is bound to have proper tackle. . . .

[The jury found that the plaintiff was not at fault and that the defendant was; and judgment was entered for the plaintiff with £15 damages.]

S H A R R O D v. L. & N.W. R y. C o.
(1849), 4 Ex. 580

Trespass for driving a railway engine with great force and violence against and over the plaintiff's sheep, by means whereof they were killed. Plea: not guilty.

At the trial before ROLFE, B. at the Stafford Summer Assizes, 1848, it appeared that the sheep in question had got upon the defendants' line of railway in consequence of the defect of fences and were run over by an express train drawn by a locomotive engine driven by a servant of the Company who had directions to drive at a certain rate per hour; and it was suggested that, while going at that rate in the dusk of the evening, when the accident happened, the driver could not have seen the sheep in sufficient time to avoid the collision. On this state of the facts it was objected on the part of the defendants that the proper form of action was case, not trespass, and a verdict was entered by consent for the plaintiff, leave being reserved to the defendants to move to enter a nonsuit. . . .

PARKE, B.: We are of opinion in this case that an action of trespass will not lie against the Company, the defendants.

The immediate act which caused the damage to the plaintiff's cattle was the impact of a machine which was under the control of a rational agent, the servant of the defendants; not so much so indeed as a horse or a carriage drawn by horses or propelled by mechanical power along an ordinary highway would be, in which cases both the direction and the speed of the machine are under government, but still in such a degree as to make the cases similar for the purpose of deciding the present question. We may treat the case, then, as if the damage had been done by an ordinary carriage

---

[91] See *Boss* v. *Linton* (1832) 5 C. & P. 407.

drawn by horses; and, it being now settled that an action of trespass will lie against a corporation,[92] we may consider, for the present purpose, the defendants as one natural person and the carriage under the care of his servants.

Now the law is well established, on the one hand, that, whenever the injury done to the plaintiff results from the immediate force of the defendant himself, whether intentionally or not, the plaintiff may bring an action of trespass; on the other, that if the act be that of the servant and be negligent, not wilful, case is the only remedy against the master. The maxim *Qui facit per alium facit per se* renders the master liable for all the negligent acts of the servant in the course of his employment; but that liability does not make the direct act of the servant the direct act of the master. Trespass will not lie against him: case will, in effect for employing a careless servant, but not trespass, unless, as was said by the Court in *Morley* v. *Gaisford*,[93] the act was done ' by his command ' ; that is, unless either the particular act which constitutes the trespass is ordered to be done by the principal, or some act which comprises it, or some act which leads by a physical necessity to the act complained of. The former is the case when one, as servant, is ordered to enter a close to try a right or otherwise; the latter, when such a case occurs as *Gregory* v. *Piper*,[94] where the rubbish, ordered to be removed, from a natural necessity fell on the plaintiff's soil. But when the act is that of the servant in performing his duty to his master, the rule of law we consider to be that case is the only remedy against the master, and then only is maintainable when that act is negligent or improper; and this rule applies to all cases where the carriage or cattle of a master is placed in the care and under the management of a servant, a rational agent. The agent's direct act or trespass is not the direct act of the master. Each blow of the whip, whether skilful and careful or not, is not the blow of the master; it is the voluntary act of the servant. Nor can it, we think, be reasonably said that all the acts done in the skilful and careful conduct of the carriage are those of the master, for which he is responsible in an action of trespass, to the same extent as if he had done them himself, because he has impliedly ordered them. But those that were careless and unskilful were not, for he has given no order except to use skill and care.

Our opinion is that, in all cases where a master gives the direction and control over a carriage or animal or chattel to another rational agent, the master is only responsible in an action on the case for want of skill or care of the agent—no more. Consequently, this action cannot be supported. . . .

[92] See *Maund* v. *Monmouthshire Canal Co.* (1842) 4 M. & G. 452.
[93] (1795) 2 H. Bl. 442, *supra*, p. 180.
[94] (1829) 9 B. & C. 591.

PART TWO

CONTRACT

∾ *10* ∾

DEBT

IT has already been observed that the writs of Debt and Detinue emerged from an earlier composite form in the course of the thirteenth century and that the line of demarcation was clearly drawn in the reign of Edward III.[1] If the plaintiff's claim was for a specific chattel or its value, he sued in Detinue: if for money or other *res fungibiles,* he sued in Debt. In the former case he alleged only that the defendant detained his goods, and declared in the *detinet.* In the latter case he alleged, as a general rule, that the defendant both owed and detained—*debet et detinet.* The distinction was sometimes explained by saying that, to justify Detinue, he must already enjoy a ' property ' in the goods claimed—a rationalisation of some importance in the history of Sale.[2] The language of the writ, however, might be misleading. Even where the subject-matter was appropriate to Debt, the word *debet* would be omitted if the action was brought by or against personal representatives. In such a case the duty was not owed to or by the litigants themselves, but to or by the estate of the deceased. A further refinement followed as a logical consequence. If the plaintiff claimed, not as the original creditor nor yet as executor, but as heir, he made the demand *in propria persona* and therefore alleged that the debtor both owed and detained.[3] But while the word *debet* was not an invariable concomitant of the writ of Debt, it never appeared outside it.

While Debt was yet but a component part of Debt-Detinue, Glanvill made some attempt to explain its scope.[4] For this purpose he borrowed the terminology of the Roman, or rather of the Canon, lawyers. A debt must rest upon one of a number of ' causes ':

> ex causa mutui aut ex causa venditionis aut ex commodato aut ex locato aut ex deposito aut ex alia justa debendi causa.

It is difficult to believe that such language aptly expressed the embryonic common law of Henry II; and suspicion deepens when

---

[1] *Supra,* pp. 25-8. See The Statute of Wales, *infra,* p. 238.

[2] Counsel, *arguendo* in Y.B. 50 Ed. III. Trin. f. 16, pl. 8 (A.D. 1377): ' A writ of Detinue can I not have in this case, because I have no property in these same goods beforehand.' The case itself concerned, not the sale of goods, but rent due on a lease; but the argument made its way into Sale. See *infra,* pp. 228-9.

[3] See Y.B. 21 & 22 Ed. I. p. 615 (R.S.), A.D. 1294 (action against a representative): Y.B. 30 & 31 Ed. I., p. 391 (R.S.), A.D. 1303 (action by a representative): *Clare's Case,* Y.B. 12 & 13 Ed. III., p. 168 (R.S.), A.D. 1339 (action between heirs).

[4] *Infra,* pp. 233-6. See Holdsworth, H.E.L. II. pp 191, 204: Plucknett, *Concise History,* 4th ed., pp. 281-2, and 3 Univ. of Toronto Law Journal, at p. 33.

Glanvill must apologise for his scant treatment of contract by the remark that ' private agreements are not usually protected in the court of our lord the king.'[5] The passages which ring most true are those upon *commodatum, emptio venditio* and *mutuum,* and here, while the words are the words of Rome, the law is the law of England. Of these transactions *commodatum* has been discussed under Detinue,[6] *emptio venditio* will take its place in the history of Sale,[7] and *mutuum* alone merits present consideration. Glanvill was interested not so much in the loan itself as in the means whereby the lender strove to anticipate the only too probable contingency of a default. The borrower might be required to offer sureties or to execute a deed, to pledge his faith or, more substantially, his land or his goods, and such expedients served the double purpose of proving the loan and of providing security for its repayment. For a breach of faith the lender must visit the Church Courts to receive spiritual satisfaction: in the pledge of corporeal interests the King's judges were interested, but only if the *res* had actually been deposited with the lender or if an agreement to this end had been enrolled upon their records. By reiterating the royal indifference to ' private agreements,' Glanvill again emphasized the gulf between his words and his law.[8]

Bracton added little to Glanvill's account of Debt, but followed *con amore* the example of his predecessor in using Roman or Romanesque language to adorn or supplement the meagre substance of the English law. He found his material partly at first hand in the Institutes, but mainly in the works of Azo of Bologna, a distinguished civilian of the late twelfth and early thirteenth centuries.[9] Both the extent of his borrowing and the skill with which he exploited it have been variously estimated. Maine was contemptuous:

> ' That an English writer of the time of Henry 3 should have been able to put off on his countrymen as a compendium of pure English law a treatise of which the entire form and a third of the contents were directly borrowed from the Corpus Juris, and that he should have ventured on this experiment in a country where the systematic study of the Roman law was formally proscribed, will always be among the most hopeless enigmas in the history of jurisprudence.[10]

According to Maitland, on the other hand, few passages have contained so many errors in so short a compass. Bracton did not borrow ' a thirtieth part of his book ' from the Corpus Juris, the Roman law

---

[5] Book X, Cap. 18, *infra,* p. 236.
[6] *Supra,* p. 25.
[7] *Infra,* pp. 226-9.
[8] Book X, Cap. 3, 8, 12, *infra,* pp. 234-6. See Professor Woodbine's notes to his edition of Glanvill, pp. 252-4.
[9] Maitland (*Bracton and Azo,* S.S. v. 8, Intro. xviii-xx) thought that, in contract at least, Bracton went straight to the Institutes. Vinogradoff, *Coll. Papers* I, p. 238, maintained that he had recourse throughout to Azo. Kantorowicz, *Bractonian Problems,* pp. 58-9, supported Maitland's view.
[10] *Ancient Law,* Chap. IV, p. 87 (Pollock's ed.).

was not proscribed, formally or informally, in contemporary England, and there was no ' putting off,' if this phrase was designed to suggest the 'passing off' of another's work as his own.[11] But, while he chastised Maine, he was unable to offer a favourable report on Bracton's scholarship. The difference between Bracton and Azo, he said, was ' between a low third class and a high first.'[12] Modern opinion has vindicated Bracton. Vinogradoff and Kantorowicz, Holdsworth, Woodbine and Plucknett, all agree that Bracton understood very well the difference between the Civil and the Common Law and that when he tampered with the former it was to adapt it to the exigencies of the latter. If he drew the outline of English law after a Roman pattern, it was because none other was available, and, if his attempt failed, the fault was not in himself but in his time.[13]

His discussion of contract revolved round the fanciful conception of *causa* with which Glanvill had experimented. A bare agreement was in itself of no interest to the common law. To be actionable it must be clothed with one of the six *causæ* with which the professional wardrobe was so happily supplied.

> Re, verbis, scripto, consensu, traditione,
> Iunctura, vestes sumere pacta solent.[14]

The first four of these *causæ* were the orthodox categories of Roman contract.[15] The foreign models were fitted with varying degrees of elegance to the native anatomy. Three examples will suffice to illustrate the process. In his obligation *per scripturam* Bracton followed the text of Justinian's title *De Litterarum Obligatione,* but abandoned the pretence that the effect of writing was merely evidentiary. A written acknowledgment of a debt was binding by its own intrinsic force. It has been suggested that he had here in mind the almost mystical properties of the English seal; but he made no mention of it, and its peculiar efficacy was not finally accepted until the following century.[16] The language of his ' Verbal Obligations,' with its distinction between judicial and conventional stipulations and its curious or careless reference to the Prætor, would merit the reproach of

---

[11] *Bracton and Azo* (S.S. v. 8), pp. xiv and xxvi. See also Pollock's ed. of Maine's *Ancient Law,* Note G.

[12] *Bracton and Azo,* pp. xviii-xx. So, also, Goudy, *Essays in Legal History,* 1913, p. 223.

[13] See Vinogradoff, *The Roman Elements in Bracton's Treatise,* Coll. Papers I, 237: Kantorowicz, *Bractonian Problems* (1941), pp. 58-79: Holdsworth, H.E.L. II, 267-286: Woodbine, *The Roman Element in Bracton's De Adquirendo Rerum Dominio,* 31 Yale L.J., 827: Plucknett, *The Relations between Roman Law and English Common Law,* 3 Univ. of Toronto L.J., pp. 38-40.

[14] These verses appear in Bracton, f. 16b, but not in Azo. See Maitland, *Bracton and Azo,* pp. 143-4. Bracton's general account of contract is in ff. 99-100b, *infra,* pp. 236-7.

[15] The last two *causæ* were in the nature of addenda. *Traditio* involved a cross-reference to the title *De Donationibus,* where Bracton discusses feoffments and livery of seisin. *Iunctura* recalls the Roman *pacta adjecta*: accessory stipulations which may be added to a principal stipulation, provided that this were done at the time of the original transaction.

[16] Cf. *Bracton and Azo,* pp. 155-6 with P. & M. II. 220, and see *infra,* pp. 257-8.

archaism if it were not redeemed by its content. The ' judicial '
stipulation may be identified with the recognizance, already a prominent feature of court practice.[17] The ' conventional ' stipulations,
though their potentialities were recognized, were dismissed as beyond
or beneath the normal interest of the royal judges. To Bracton, as to
Glanvill, private agreements were scarcely consonant with the dignity
of the common law. But it was, perhaps, his treatment of the ' Consensual Obligations ' which showed most clearly how ill-prepared was
the soil for intensive doctrinal cultivation. He could do little more
than rehearse the Roman names. *Societas* and *Mandatum* were mentioned only to be forgotten. Sale, indeed, received the extended
treatment which its practical importance required; but it was significantly approached, not as a typical contract, but as a means of
acquiring ownership.[18]

Bracton's ambitious and scholarly design was a digression from
the course of contemporary law. Before a conception may be analysed,
it must be perceived to exist. An examination of the scope of Debt,
after its admission as a separate writ, while it reveals a variety of
transactions associated to-day with contract, shows no less clearly the
difficulty of expressing them through a common consensual denomina-
tor. Of the many claims in Debt scattered over the reports of Edward
I, Edward II and Edward III, more than half depended upon the
production of a sealed instrument. They were often for considerable
sums of money,[19] and they served a variety of purposes: to compromise
a suit[20] or to secure the performance of some other and primary undertaking which it might otherwise have been difficult to clothe in
actionable form. Thus in 1309 the plaintiff demanded a hundred
marks ' in which the defendant had bound himself in case he should
not deliver a certain writing on a certain day.' The defendant pleaded
that, at the time specified, he was himself ' in the East,' but that he
' had left the writing at home with our wife for delivery to you.'[21] The
most interesting of such claims were upon the so-called *Scripta
Obligatoria*.[22] Mediæval, like modern, merchants wished to transfer
the right to receive money. As early as the eighth century the Lombards had used documents whereby a debtor undertook to pay either
the creditor or his nominee, and these had certainly spread to England

---

[17] *Bracton and Azo*, p. 152. *Infra*, p. 221.
[18] Bracton, f. 61b-62, *infra*, p. 237.
[19] e.g. £1,000 in *St. Andrew* v. *Stretle* (1310) Y.B. 3 & 4 Ed. II (S.S. Vol. 22), 137.
To estimate the contemporary value of money is speculative and controversial.
Prof. Coulton in *The Mediæval Village*, p. 309, multiplies the figures of Edward I's
reign by twenty to reach the values of 1925. The multiplier required to-day must
be left to taste.
[20] e.g. *Fisher* v. *Newgate* (1309) Y.B. 1 & 2 Ed. II (S.S. Vol. 17), 155.
[21] *Umfraville* v. *Lonstede* (1309) Y.B. 2 & 3 Ed. II (S.S. Vol. 19), 58.
[22] See Postan, *Private Financial Instruments*, 23 Vierteljahrschrift für Sozial-und Wirt-
schaftsgeschichte, 26: Holdsworth, H.E.L. VIII, pp. 115-126: Bailey, *Assignment
of Debts in England*, 48 L.Q.R., pp. 264-271.

by the thirteenth century. Bracton may have had them in mind when
he spoke of *missibilia* or *missilia* as methods of transferring ownership ' *in incertam personam.*'[23] B. acknowledged under seal a debt
due to A. and expressed himself ready to pay A. or his attorney on
production of the writing. By the reign of Edward I actions of Debt
were being brought in the King's Courts on these *scripta obligatoria,*
and they continued to be a feature of the Year Books until the middle
of the fifteenth century.[24] At first the third party had to produce a
formal letter of attorney from the principal creditor, but in later years
the mere production of the *scriptum obligatorium* would suffice. He
sued normally in the name of the original creditor, but occasionally
in his own name. The instruments, it must be observed, were not
negotiable: they did not confer upon the holder a better title than
that of his transferor. They were rather assignments of choses in
action. In the second half of the fifteenth century they were in danger
of falling under the ban of maintenance as an officious intervention
in the suit of a stranger,[25] though as late as 1470 sixty-five actions were
entered upon the rolls of the Common Bench for the Easter Term.[26]
The merchants, however, took alarm and began to experiment with
informal ' bills,' to enforce which they had to go outside the common
law.

Loans of money naturally provoked many actions for Debt.
Lenders, in their insatiable pursuit of security, succeeded in obtaining
two forms of preferential treatment. The first was through the
Recognizance. The debtor acknowledged (*recognoscit*) his debt in
court and conceded that, should he make default, the sheriff might
levy execution. The acknowledgment was entered upon the court rolls
and became known to later lawyers as a ' contract of record.' An
early example appears among the pleas heard before the Justices of
the Bench in the Michaelmas Term, 1201.

> Hugh de Elham, against whom Emma de Luddesdown demands
> ten marks of silver, comes and concedes (*concessit*) that he will give
> the said Emma the ten marks within eight years, to wit, this year
> three marks, and one mark each year following. He concedes also
> that the sheriff may distrain him by his chattels, in the first year at

[23] Bracton, f. 41b.
[24] e.g. *Anon,* Y.B. 20 & 21 Ed. I (R.S.) p. 66 (A.D. 1292), and *Beneyt* v. *Lodewyk*
(1310) Y.B. 3 Ed. II (S.S. Vol. 20) p. 46, *infra,* p. 243. They were the frequent subject
of litigation in the local courts. See *infra,* pp. 296 and 312, where a specimen is
given.
[25] e.g. Y.B. 37 Hen. 6, Hil. f. 13, pl. 3.
[26] The cases entered in the Court rolls for this single term reached the astounding total
of 3,800. Of these, some 2,700 cases were cases of Debt, though many were probably
no more than debt-collecting. See Introduction to S.S. Vol. 47, pp. xvi-xx. The
learned editor observes with justice that ' the Year-Book reports hardly touch the
surface of the great mine of material contained in the Plea Rolls.' The discrepancy
between the selective methods of the mediæval reporters and the rank luxuriance
of the actual litigation adds to the difficulty of presenting any coherent history
of the common law, though it is not unfair to suggest that the Year Books contain
at least those cases of greatest contemporary interest.

Easter to the amount of twenty shillings and at Michaelmas twenty shillings, and in each year following at Michaelmas half a mark and at Easter half a mark.[27]

The device was so gratifying to a lender that he may well have insisted on the enrolment of the Recognizance before he ventured to advance the money.[28] The second method of security was accorded to merchants, and especially foreign merchants, as a matter of state policy. By two complementary Statutes of 1283 and 1285 a merchant might bring his debtor before the Mayor of a town or the Chief Officer of a Fair and require him to acknowledge the debt. The Clerk then drafted a *lettre de obligacion* to which were attached the seals both of the debtor and the King, and, if the debtor made default, he was arrested and, if necessary, his goods and his land were sold.[29]

After the loan, the most frequent occasion for the use of the writ was the demand for money due as the price of goods sold or as rent reserved on a lease.[30] But it was restricted to no particular transaction provided that the plaintiff could claim a precise sum as his debt. The Year Books of Edward III offer a number of instances where reliance was placed upon services rendered to the defendant at his request. In 1343,

> John de H. brought his writ of Debt against one Roger, and demanded 5 marks, which Roger owed him by reason of a contract which was made between them at Arundel to the effect that the said John should be his parker at H. and should take 2 marks and three shillings a year for hunting. And he counted that he had been Roger's bailiff for so long a time that 5 marks of his wages were in arrear.[31]

A few cases may also be found which would now be placed under the heading of Quasi-Contract. In 1294 Chief Justice Metingham said that, if a seller failed to convey land according to his covenant, the buyer might choose whether to ' demand the money by writ of Debt or to demand by writ of Covenant that he perform his covenant.'[32] The offer of such an alternative, though not unique, was rare and does not appear to have survived the thirteenth century.[33] But the following century saw a number of claims for what, to anticipate a later formula,

---

[27] Select Civil Pleas, Vol. I., pl. 102 (S.S. Vol. 3, p. 42).

[28] See P. & M. II, pp. 203-4.

[29] Statute of Merchants, or of Acton Burnell, 1283, and Statute of Merchants, 1285: *infra*, pp. 239-41. See also Y.B. 21 & 22 Ed. I (R.S.) p. 75 (A.D. 1293); Y.B. 12 & 13 Ed. III (R.S.), p. 130 (A.D. 1338); and *Lacy's Case*, Y.B. 16 Ed. III (R.S.), p. 146 (A.D. 1342).

[30] For goods sold, see *infra*, p. 224. For an example of rent reserved on a lease, see *The Prior of Bradstock's Case* (1371) Y.B. 44 Ed. III, f. 42, pl. 46, *infra*, p. 247.

[31] Y.B. 17 & 18 Ed. III. (R.S.), p. 623. See also *Anon* (1338) Y.B. 11 & 12 Ed. III. (R.S.), p. 587, *infra*, p. 247.

[32] Y.B. 21 & 22 Ed. I. (R.S.), p. 598.

[33] Dr. Jackson suggests that such cases ' may be regarded as examples of the "equity" jurisdiction which the common law ceased exercising in the earlier part of the fourteenth century ': *History of Quasi-Contract*, p. 20.

may be termed ' money had and received to the plaintiff's use.'   If A.
gave money to B. to give to C., and B. failed to do so, A. might sue
B. in debt.[34]

The most comprehensive attempt to classify this miscellany was
made in 1410.   It was said that ' each *writ* of Debt is general and in
one form, but the *count* is special and makes mention of the contract,
the obligation or the record, as the case requires.'[35]   Such a classification, by segregating the so-called ' contract of record,' serves at least
to emphasise the extent to which the scope of Debt transcended the
modern notion of agreement.   The recognisance or other acknowledgment entered upon the rolls of the court, while it originated in private
initiative, rested upon judicial sanction; and the writ was equally
available where the liability proceeded *ab initio* from the act not of
the parties but of the law.   Thus it lay to enforce penalties imposed
by statute, bye-law or custom,[36] and to collect judgment debts due
upon proceedings both in the superior and in the inferior courts.   In
a case of 1388, the incumbent of a church at Downham had ' stopped
a road to the nuisance of the country ' and had been fined at a Court
Leet within the jurisdiction of the Earl of Kent.   He did not pay the
fine, and the Earl was allowed to bring a writ of Debt in the Common
Pleas.[37]

Mediæval lawyers, however, were more often content with a dual
classification.   Debt lay either upon an Obligation or upon a Contract.   To appreciate the dichotomy it is necessary to recall the importance of the seal in an illiterate age.   It has already been observed
that in more than half of the cases of Debt reported in the reigns of
the first three Edwards the plaintiff relied upon a sealed instrument.
He might produce either a writing or a tally.   The tally, used as a
receipt for money or chattels, was a narrow wooden stick with notches
of varying dimensions to represent the amount received.   After the
notches had been cut, the stick was split lengthwise into two unequal
pieces.   The longer, which contained a stump or handle and was
called the ' stock,' was given to the person making the payment, and
the shorter, a flat strip called the ' foil,' to the other party.   If the sum
involved was disputed, the two pieces could be fitted one to the other
to see if they would ' tally.'[38]

[34] See *Anon* (1368), Y.B. 41 Ed. III, f. 10, pl. 5, *infra*, p. 285.   C. was not allowed
to use Debt, since, it was said, there was ' no privity.'
[35] *Anon*, Y.B. 11 Hen. 4, f. 73, pl. 11.
[36] See P. & M. II. 209.
[37] *The Earl of Kent's Case*, Y.B. 12 Rich. 2 (Ames Foundation), p. 180.
[38] See Poole, *The Exchequer in the Twelfth Century*, pp. 86-93.   ' A thousand pounds
was marked by cutting out the thickness of the palm of the hand, a hundred by
the breadth of the thumb, a score by the breadth of the little finger, one pound
by that of a swelling barley-corn,' etc.   Dr. Poole added, ' The terminology has
left a permanent imprint on our language.   If you lent money to the Bank of
England, tallies were cut for the amount: the Bank kept the foil and you received
the stock; you thus held " Bank Stock " of the amount recorded upon it.   When
the form of cheque was adopted, it was not indeed called a foil, but the part

Such instruments, whether writings or tallies, and with the necessary seals attached, could be used for one of two purposes. On the one hand, they might support a claim which rested in essence upon some recognized *causa debendi*. Evidence might thus be offered of the buyer's duty to pay the price of goods sold and delivered to him. In 1302, ' Adam Scarlet brought his writ of Debt against the Prior of Bodenne² for ten marks, the price of cloth sold to him, ' and he put forward an obligation under seal ';[39] and in 1304 the plaintiff, claiming £39 on a similar sale of cloth, found himself in difficulty because he produced a deed for only £30[40] The tally was used most often in loans of money; but it gave obvious opportunities of fraud to unscrupulous litigants, and judges were not always prepared to receive it without question. Its uncertain qualities were reflected in two judgments of Chief Justice Bereford. In the first, he rejected with indignation the defendant's offer to wage his law against tallies sealed with his own seal: in the second, he allowed it. ' The tally,' he said ' is a dumb thing and cannot speak. . . . These notches, too; we cannot tell whether they refer to bullocks or to cows or to what else.'[41] Neither writing nor tally, moreover, was essential where the sale or the loan could be proved by other means. In 1292 the plaintiff recovered £20 as money lent to the defendant without the one or the other,[42] and in 1294 Chief Justice Metingham went out of his way to assist a merchant whose tally was inadequate. ' He who demands this debt is a merchant, and therefore if he can give slight proof to support his tally, we will incline to that side. . . . Every merchant cannot always have a clerk with him.'[43] On the other hand, the sealed instrument might be accepted, not as mere evidence of a debt due from some extrinsic cause, but as generating liability by its own inherent validity. A recognizance was naturally so regarded. Counsel argued in 1293 that ' an acknowledgment of Debt or other contract made in court has so great force in itself that he who makes the acknowledgment cannot go against it, but it shall stand good.'[44] The same virtue was accorded early in the fourteenth century to private deeds.

> ' If a man by a writing confesses himself indebted to us, and the writing goes on to say, " and for further security I procure such an one who binds himself," and this latter puts his seal to the writing,

retained by the payer is still the counterfoil; and the word " cheque " itself goes back ultimately to the same root as " exchequer." ' Dr. Poole spoke of the Exchequer tallies, which were used until 1826, and an accumulation of which was responsible for the fire of 1834 which destroyed the old Houses of Parliament. Private tallies naturally varied in detail, but were similar in principle: over two hundred of them are to be found in the Public Records as vouchers to accounts.

[39] Y.B. 30 & 31 Ed. I (R.S.), p. 234.
[40] *Northat* v. *Basset*, Y.B. 32 & 33 Ed. I (R.S. App.), p. 507, *infra*, p. 242.
[41] Cf. *Beneyt* v. *Lodewyk* (1310) Y.B. 3 Ed. II (S.S. Vol. 20), p. 46, *infra*, p. 243, and *Marston* v. *Dalby* (1315) Y.B. 8 Ed. II (S.S. Vol. 41), p. 179, *infra*, p. 246.
[42] Y.B. 20 & 21 Ed. I (R.S.), p. 222.
[43] Y.B. 21 & 22 Ed. I (R.S.), p. 457.
[44] Y.B. 21 & 22 Ed. I (R.S.) 146.

how can you argue that he does not say the same thing as the other says? He affirms it by the fact of putting his seal to it.'[45]

It was only where a plaintiff relied on a deed or tally as possessed of this superior and intrinsic authority that the debt ' lay on an obligation.' In all other cases, whether he offered the instrument in support of some separate *causa debendi,* such as a sale or a loan, or whether he produced none at all, the debt was said to ' lie on a contract,' and its common and essential feature was the receipt by the defendant of a material benefit. If this fact could be proved, the absence of formality was irrelevant.[46] The distinction between the two main classes of Debt was sustained throughout the fourteenth and fifteenth centuries. To a claim for rent in 1371 the defendant objected that the names of the parties, as set out in the writ, varied from those contained in the Deed of Lease which the plaintiff had put in evidence. The objection, which, had the plaintiff sued on the obligation, would have been fatal, was refused. The basis of the claim was the enjoyment of the lease, and ' he could have counted of a contract without having put forward a deed.'[47] In 1385 it was said that ' in Debt on a contract the plaintiff shows in his count for what cause the defendant has become his debtor: otherwise in Debt on an obligation, for the obligation is a contract in itself.'[48] In 1422 the effect was discussed of the merger of a ' simple contract ' in an obligation.

> BABINGTON, J.: If I am your debtor for twenty pounds by a simple contract and I make an obligation to you for the same twenty pounds on the same contract and I am discharged of the contract by obligation; if you bring a writ of debt against me for the contract, I shall plead well that for the same contract and for the same moneys you have an obligation.
>
> *Rolfe*: In the case of the obligation that you have put, I well admit, for the reason that the contract and the obligation are two different contracts, and I am discharged from the lesser by the greater.[49]

The title ' Debt on a Contract ' must not be taken to imply that contemporary lawyers spoke or thought in terms of promise. The defendant was liable, not because he had promised, but because he had received a benefit, which in turn cast upon him a duty to pay.[50] There was here, no doubt, an element of reciprocity which may be allowed to justify the word ' contract '; but the gulf between mediæval and modern thought is shown by the inadequacy of mutual promises

---

[45] *Per* Spigurnel, J. in *Buckland* v. *Leukenore* (1313) Y.B. 6 & 7 Ed. II (S.S. Vol. 27), p. 9, *infra,* p. 266.
[46] See *Richard* v. *Verdon* (1293) Y.B. 21 & 22 Ed. I (R.S.), p. 293, *infra,* p. 241: *Anon* (1338) Y.B. 11 & 12 Ed. III (R.S.), p. 587, *infra,* p. 247.
[47] *The Prior of Bradstock's Case* (1371) Y.B. 44 Ed. III. f. 42, pl. 46, *infra,* p. 247. See also *Warreyn's Case* (1343) Y.B. 17 & 18 Ed. III (R.S.), p. 72.
[48] *Anon,* 8 Rich. II, Bellewe, p. 111.
[49] *Salman* v. *Barkyng,* Y.B. 1 Hen. VI. (S.S. Vol. 50), p. 114, at p. 115.
[50] ' The ground of the action is a duty': Y.B. 7 Hen. 6, f. 5, pl. 9 (A.D. 1428).

to sustain an action unless the plaintiff had performed his part of the bargain. There was no general conception of 'executory parol contracts.' In 1338 the phrase *Quid pro Quo* was used to indicate the necessary correspondence between benefit and duty,[51] and what was at first little more than a casual expression became in the following century a term of art. An anonymous case of 1458 is significant both for the attempt made by the judges to determine its scope and meaning and for the ambiguity of language by which they were embarrassed.[52] The facts of the case were simple. The plaintiff and the defendant had made an informal agreement whereby the plaintiff was to marry the defendant's daughter and the defendant was to pay the plaintiff a hundred marks. The marriage was celebrated, but the money was not paid, and the question was whether, upon these facts, an action of Debt could be sustained. The discussion was confused by the failure to give precise meaning to the words 'contract,' 'accord' and 'covenant.' The Court, however, was agreed that the plaintiff, unless he sued on an obligation, must prove a *Quid pro Quo* and that he could discharge this burden only by showing the receipt of a material benefit. The majority found no difficulty in so describing matrimony. But did it suffice to confer the benefit on a third party at the defendant's request, or must it be conferred directly upon the defendant himself? Upon this issue no conclusion is recorded. Danvers and Moyle, J.J., favoured the plaintiff, Danby J. the defendant, and Chief Justice Prisot vacillated.[53]

The report is of further interest in its revelation of a single but substantial exception to the doctrine of *Quid pro Quo*, which is to be understood only through the history of Sale. Glanvill included Sale in his *causæ debendi*. Seller and buyer were imagined as linked by reciprocal duties. 'The price is owed to the seller and the thing bought to the buyer.' The transaction was binding, not by force of the agreement, but only by the delivery of the thing or by payment of the price in whole or in part; unless one or other of these conditions was satisfied, there was a *locus pœnitentiæ*, subject only to the forfeiture of any earnest which may have been given. The risk was 'generally with him who holds the thing'—a conclusion which would seem to have been reached, not as an inference from any doctrine of ownership or of possession, but as a practical consequence of the situation in which the parties found themselves.[54]

[51] *Anon* (1338) Y.B. 11 & 12 Ed. III (R.S.), p. 587, *infra*, p. 247.
[52] *Anon* (1458) Y.B. 37 Hen. VI, Mich. f. 8, pl. 18, *infra*, p. 249.
[53] See also *Jordan's Case* (1528), *infra*, pp. 339 and 353.
[54] Glanvill, X. 14, *infra*, p. 234. Pollock and Maitland, II. 207-8, observed that 'in substance the conditions mentioned by Glanvill are the very conditions which in the seventeenth century our Statute of Frauds will allow as alternatives in a case of sale to a note or memorandum in writing'—Statute of Frauds, s. 17, and now Sale of Goods Act, 1893, s. 4. But the modern statutory rules are conditions precedent to an action at law and are procedural. Glanvill's conditions are precedent to the validity of the contract. As has been said, 'how was it possible

Bracton, while, with some refinements, he adopted Glanvill's account, distinguished more sharply the formation of the contract, the transfer of the property and the passing of the risk. The transaction was, as in the earlier law, binding only on delivery or, at least, on part payment. The contract, in other words, was real and not—as Bracton's pursuit of his Roman original required him to pretend— consensual. But he marked the difference between a contract and a conveyance. A buyer, even when he had paid the price and could thus sue the seller for the thing or its value, did not become owner until delivery had been made. The risk was still ' with him who holds the thing,' but a rule, which had been no more than the precept of common sense, was now associated with the question of *dominium*. The seller, so long as he kept the thing, undertook the risk because he retained the ownership.[55]

The first stage in the transition from the ' real ' to the ' consensual ' character of Sale may be observed in a remark of counsel in a case of 1348.[56] John Groome of Leicester had covenanted to take one Robert as his apprentice in the ' mystery of saddlery ' for a period of three years and at a fee of eight marks. Robert had enfeoffed John of a freehold estate as security for this fee, but died three weeks later without having paid any part of the money. The defendant, as Robert's heir, ejected John, who brought an assise of novel disseisin. Counsel for the defendant argued that the feoffment was merely security for the payment, that Robert's death prevented the fulfilment of the bargain, that the money ceased to be due and that the estate must be restored. Thorpe, for the plaintiff, denied that there could be any automatic reversion of the right to the estate and offered an analogy from the sale of goods.

> ' I put the case that I make you an obligation for £40 for merchandise bought of you, and you will not deliver the merchandise. I cannot justify the detention of the money; but you can have a writ of Debt against me for the money, and I will be put to my action against you for the thing bought by a writ of Detinue of chattels.'

Belknap, for the defendant, pointed out that Thorpe's case was not an analogy, since, in the case at bar, performance had become impossible; but the Court allowed the assise on the ground that the defendant had taken the law into his own hands instead of suing in Covenant. Thorpe's statement was irrelevant to the issue; but its accuracy was not questioned, and it may be inferred that, by the middle of the fourteenth century, actions could be brought on a sale of goods, even

that legal conditions in 1189 and 1677 should be identical? '—Rabel, 63 L.Q.R., at p. 178. The rôle of earnest, both in Glanvill's and in Bracton's scheme, is distinct from that of delivery or of part payment, and is a matter of evidence rather than of substantive law. It was through the Law Merchant that it altered its character and became comparable to the other conditions. See P. & M. II, pp. 208-9.
[55] *Bracton,* ff. 61b-62, *infra,* p. 237.
[56] *Groome's Case* (1348) Y.B. 21 Ed. III. f. 11, pl. 2.

without delivery or part payment, provided that the buyer had granted the price by deed. The innovation seems to have been a by-product of the special properties ascribed by this date to all documents under seal, and it is not necessary to suppose any profound ratiocination upon the incidents of Sale. The deed bound the buyer to pay in any event, and he could not refuse because the seller failed or refused to deliver. But, as a necessary act of reciprocity, he was allowed a writ of Detinue for the goods.

The transition, thus envisaged, was completed in the course of the fifteenth century. A number of dicta suggest that, by the middle of the century, the common lawyers had accepted the view that the seller could sue in Debt for the price and the buyer in Detinue for the goods[57] as on an executory agreement, and that they explained this result on the ground that the property might pass without delivery. In *Doige's Case* in 1442[58] the plaintiff sued in Deceit on the Case and declared that he had bargained with the defendant for the sale of land and that he had paid the price, but that the defendant had enfeoffed a third party. In the course of a long argument, Chief Justice Fortescue distinguished the sale of land from the sale of goods. In the former the property could be transferred only by livery of seisin, in the latter it might pass by virtue of the agreement. ' If I buy a horse from you, now the property in the horse is in me, and for this you shall have a writ of Debt for the money and I shall have Detinue for the horse on this bargain.' In *Tailbois* v. *Sherman*,[59] where a buyer brought Trespass on the Case against a seller for the non-delivery of two pipes of wine, the mere fact of the bargain was said to have vested the property in the plaintiff; and, in the anonymous case of 1458 already discussed, Chief Justice Prisot assumed the sale of a specific chattel to constitute an exception to the requirement of *Quid pro Quo*.[60]

In the second half of the century, the judges drew the outlines of the modern law. In *Veer* v. *York*,[61] a priest had been retained to chant for the souls of the departed for one year for ten marks. After six months he sickened of his task, and now claimed half the fee. He lost his action, since he had undertaken a single, entire duty, and he must earn all or get nothing. Choke, J. contrasted the case with that of the sale of a horse, where, without anything done to implement the bargain, the property passed to the buyer; although, under the prompting of counsel, he admitted that, while the property might thus be transferred, the possession could not be demanded unless the price had been paid or credit granted. In 1478 an action of trespass was brought for the asportation of corn, and the defendant pleaded that

[57] At least if they were specific.
[58] Y.B. 20 Hen. VI. f. 34, pl. 4, *infra*, p. 347.
[59] (1443) Y.B. 21 Hen. VI, f. 55, pl. 12.
[60] Y.B. 37 Hen. VI, f. 8, pl. 18, *supra*, p. 226 and *infra*, p. 249.
[61] (1470) 49 Hen. VI. (S.S. Vol. 47), p. 163, *infra*, p. 251.

the corn had been sold to him by the plaintiff.[62]   Plaintiff's counsel
argued that, as the defendant had not paid the price, he could not lawfully take the corn, to which it was replied that the sale was on credit.
The Court was of opinion that the sale was for ready money and that
there was thus no right of possession before payment.   Choke, J.,
indeed, forgetful of his own remarks in *Veer* v. *York,* confused the
three questions of contractual liability, transfer of property and right
to possession; but Chief Justice Brian restored the case to its proper
perspective.   On the sale of a specific chattel, the bargain itself vested
the property in the buyer.   But, unless the sale were on credit, he
must pay the price before he could insist on possession.   In the words
of Lord Blackburn, ' his judgment might have been delivered yesterday,
as it is precisely what the law is understood to be after the lapse of
three centuries and a half.'[63]

The tolerance of this ' consensual ' contract in isolated contrast
to the ' real ' character of *Quid pro Quo* was not to be explained as
the outcome of any conscious logical process.   Nor was the accom-
panying rule, that the property in a specific chattel might pass by
simple virtue of the bargain, the conclusion of some grand initial
premise of Sale.   It was, indeed, a denial of that distinction between
contract and conveyance which the more scholarly Bracton had proclaimed.   The judges were only reacting, within the limits of the
mediæval writs, to mercantile pressure.   Once they had allowed a
seller to sue without proving delivery, merely because the buyer had
granted payment under seal, they could never recover their primitive
simplicity.   Continued insistence on the production of a deed in so
essentially commercial a transaction was futile pedantry.   The seller's
writ of Debt must be balanced by the buyer's writ of Detinue, and the
proprietary flavour of the latter was strong enough to suggest the
necessity, or at least the desirability, of attributing ownership to the
party who sought to use it.   A breach of principle, orginating as a
matter of convenience, was thus covered with a veneer of rationalisation.

With this single but important exception, Debt lay only where the
plaintiff could depend upon a formality or could prove a substantial
benefit conferred normally upon the defendant himself, but possibly on
a third party at the defendant's request.   Its scope or value was further
restricted by technical rules.   In the first place, as the duty upon which
it rested must not be indeterminate, it could not be used save to recover
a fixed and certain sum.   The mediæval law knew no *quantum meruit*

[62] *Anon,* Y.B. 17 Ed. IV, f. 1, pl. 2, *infra,* p. 252.   It is to be observed that the corn
was treated throughout as a chattel, though admittedly growing at the time of the
bargain.
[63] Blackburn, *Contract of Sale* (1845), p. 196.   He cites and discusses the case at
pp. 189-197.   For the current law, cf. ss. 18, Rule 1, and 28 of the Sale of Goods
Act, 1893.

count. Thus, in 1426, a plaintiff claimed from executors arrears of salary alleged to be due to him for his service with a deceased 'limner of books.' He failed because, among other reasons, he could not prove that his salary had been ascertained in advance.[64] Fifty years later, Chief Justice Brian reasserted the rule.

> 'If I bring cloth to a tailor to have a cloak made, if the price be not determined beforehand that I shall pay for the making, he shall not have an action of Debt against me.'[65]

It was a corollary of this rule that the plaintiff must recover the precise sum claimed or fail *in toto*. A verdict for less or for more availed him nothing: whether he had been too grasping or too modest, a fatal variation would have been disclosed between the contract or obligation upon which he declared and the facts as they had been found to exist. In 1424, Martin, J. said:

> 'If I demand only £20, and the Inquest says that the defendant owes me £40, the Justices cannot give judgment here. They cannot give me judgment for the £40, because I did not demand £40 . . .; and for the £20 they cannot give me judgment, because they cannot sever the judgment from the verdict, which does not speak only of the £20, but of £40 . . .; nor can they portion it out from the verdict.'[66]

So, too, a special note to a report of 1482 recorded that

> 'the opinion of all the Justices in the Common Bench was that, if a man sold two horses for 40 shillings, and, as plaintiff in an action of Debt, he counts that he has sold one horse for 40 shillings, the defendant can say that he owes him nothing *modo et forma*.[67] And the jury must so find under pain of attaint . . ., because this is not the same contract as was made between them. And the law is the same where one horse is sold for 40 shillings and he counts that he sold two horses for 40 shillings, or if he sold a bullock and he counts of a horse; and so in every case where he varies from the contract.'[68]

In the second place, unless the plaintiff produced a sealed document or other formality either in evidence of a contract or as the obligation upon which he sued, he might expect to be met by wager of law.[69] The defendant, indeed, might prefer a jury, and there are

---

[64] *Timburhill's Case,* Y.B. Pasch. 4 Hen. 6, f. 19, pl. 5.
[65] *Anon* (1473) Y.B. 12 Ed. IV, Pasch. f. 9, pl. 22. But, provided that the claim was for a fixed sum, the plaintiff might be awarded damages for the breach of duty. See *Wyclewode* v. *Waunforde* (1308) Y.B. 1 & 2 Ed. II (S.S. Vol. 17), p. 91, and *Lacy's Case* (1342) Y.B. 16 Ed. III (R.S.), p. 146.
[66] *Anon* (1424) Y.B. Mich. 3 Hen. VI. f. 4, pl. 4.
[67] To deny the allegation *modo et forma*—in the manner and form in which it had been made—remained the proper language of a traverse in the nineteenth century. See *Stephen on Pleading*, pp. 231-2.
[68] *Anon,* Y.B. Pasch. 21 Ed. IV, f 22, pl. 2. The rule and its reason were repeated by Blackstone, Comm. III. 154.
[69] See *Anon* (1338) Y.B. 11 & 12 Ed. III (R.S.), p. 587, *infra,* p. 247, and *The Prior of Bradstock's Case* (1371) Y.B. 44 Ed. III, f. 42, pl. 46, *infra,* p. 247. See also *Ormesby* v. *Loveday* (1311) 4 Ed. II. (S.S. Vol. 26), p. 11, and *Anon* (1311) 4 Ed. II (S.S. Vol. 26), p. 13, where the method of waging law by husband and wife is discussed.

many cases in which he accordingly 'put himself on the country.'[70] On occasion, moreover, a judge would refuse the tender of law. In 1310 a plaintiff brought Debt for £14, due to him as the agreed compensation for being ousted from his church. The defendant denied the ouster and prepared to wage his law.

> *Willoughby* (for the plaintiff): To that you cannot get, for this lies in the knowledge of the country.
>
> BEREFORD, C.J., to *Denom* (counsel for the defendant): Will you have the country?
>
> *Denom*: If you award it.
>
> BEREFORD, C.J.: We will never award the law in this case.[71]

But the reporter added that 'this seemed strange to many people, and in the normal, if not in the invariable course, wager of law remained at the defendant's option. It was ruled as a corollary, in the reign of Edward III, that, wherever a living debtor could have waged his law, no action would lie against his representatives, since they could scarcely be received to wage it for him.[72]

In the third place, if the plaintiff relied on a sealed document, the action was *stricti juris*. The defendant was bound by the deed, the whole deed and nothing but the deed. Once again, the reports of the late thirteenth and early fourteenth centuries offer a few cases where the severity of the doctrine was relaxed. In 1292 a defendant was allowed to plead that a deed of grant, absolute in terms, was in fact conditional upon a marriage which had not been celebrated;[73] and the masterful Chief Justice Bereford allowed himself, and the litigants before him, a latitude from which his more scrupulous or more timid colleagues shrank. He took special notice of soldiers caught in the meshes of the law. In 1311 Edward Burnel was sued for forty pounds due on a deed drafted in complicated and formidable terms. Counsel sought to vindicate the honour of his profession by urging that 'it was no lawyer who drew up such an agreement, but a man-at-arms.' The Chief Justice replied that 'men-at-arms are clever hands at botching work of this sort,' and quashed the writ on a technicality.[74] But these were aberrations from the strict course of

---

[70] See, e.g., *Northat* v. *Basset* (1304) Y.B. 32 & 33 Ed. I (R.S. App.), p. 507, *infra*, p. 242, and *Beneyt* v. *Lodewyk* (1310) Y.B. 3 Ed. II. (S.S. Vol. 20), p. 46, *infra*, p. 243

[71] *Hotot* v. *Richmond* (1310) Y.B. 3 & 4 Ed. II (S.S. Vol. 22), pp. 199-200. Familiar phrases appear in an unfamiliar context in a note to the report. 'Note that the law will suffer a man of his own folly to bind himself to pay on a certain day if he do not make the Tower of London come to Westminster. Whereof said Bereford, C.J., "*Volenti non fit injuria*, although the written law says *Nemo obligatur ad impossibile.*"'

[72] *Anon* (1345) Y.B. 17 & 18 Ed. III (R.S.) 512: cf. *Core's Case*, Dyer, 20a, *infra*, p. 285.

[73] *Anon*, Y.B. 20 & 21 Ed. I (R.S.), p. 366.

[74] *Ford* v. *Burnel* (1311) Y.B. 5 Ed. II (S.S. Vol. 31), p. 140; and see *Anon* (1308) Y.B. 1 & 2 Ed. II (S.S. Vol. 17), p. 160.

orthodoxy which, for the most part, was pursued relentlessly. In *Esthalle* v. *Esthalle*[75] the defendant had executed an absolute deed of grant of one hundred pounds to the two plaintiffs, but, by a second and contemporaneous deed, had made the grant conditional on the failure to levy a fine. Both deeds were deposited for safe custody with one Geoffrey Astwick. The fine was levied, but the deeds remained with Geoffrey and, after his death, came into the hands of his executors, one of whom was a creditor in the first and absolute deed. The latter now sued for the hundred pounds. Spigurnel, J. asked what had become of the second deed, and was told that it was still with the executors, against whom an action was pending for its production. In its absence, the Court could do no more than reprove the defendant for his folly in parting with it and give judgment against him. Even if the money due on a deed had been paid or the debt otherwise discharged, this was no answer to an action, unless the deed had been cancelled and returned to the debtor. In 1343 a defendant, sued for twenty pounds on an obligation, pleaded that the plaintiff had already brought an action for the same debt before the Mayor and Bailiffs of Newcastle-on-Tyne, had recovered judgment and had levied execution.

> SHARDELOWE, J.: He charges you by an obligation; why was it not then cancelled? And you do not produce any acquittance of the debt.
>
> *Mowbray* (for the defendant): That is no default of mine; but since satisfaction has been made to him by execution, and not through any folly of mine, it may be accounted that the deed was cancelled or that I had an acquittance. I pray judgment. ·
>
> SHARDELOWE, J.: The Court adjudges that he do recover his debt and damages assessed by the Court. And see now that the deed be cancelled.[76]

A hundred and fifty years later the doctrine was still pronounced. ' In no case can a man avoid an obligation without a specialty of as high a nature as the original deed.'[77]

The one plea which a defendant might oppose with efficacy to the production of a deed was to deny that it was his—*non est factum*. He did not seek thereby to demean its ' high nature ' or to contradict its terms by extrinsic evidence. He took the simpler and bolder course of undermining the foundations of the plaintiff's case. The plea was recognized in the early years of the fourteenth century, and the issue of fact thus produced was normally submitted to the verdict of a jury.[78]

---

[75] (1313) Y.B. 6 & 7 Ed. II, Eyre of Kent (S.S. Vol. 27), p. 21, *infra*, p. 244. See also Fitzherbert, *Abridgment, Debt*, 169. For the meaning and importance of the ' fine,' mentioned in the case of *Esthalle* v. *Esthalle*, see *infra*, p. 256.
[76] *Denom* v. *Scot* (1343) Y.B. 17 Ed. III. (R.S.), p. 298; and see *Wolfe* v. *Martone* (1310) Y.B. 3 & 4 Ed. II. (S.S. Vol. 22), p. 145.
[77] *Anon* (1485) Y.B. 1 Hen. VII, f. 14, pl. 2.
[78] *Northat* v. *Basset* (1304) Y.B. 32 & 33 Ed. I (R.S. App.), p. 507, *infra*, p. 242. See also the remarks of Inge, J. in *Anon* (1313) Y.B. 7 Ed. II (S.S. Vol. 39), p. 31.

In the course of the fifteenth century the plea was extended so as to enable a defendant who could not read to deny, not the presence of his seal, but the correspondence of the deed with its tenor as rehearsed to him by the draftsman.[79] Such an extension might seem an affront to the sanctity of the instrument, calculated to raise illiteracy from a misfortune to a privilege; but it was a sufficient excuse that not otherwise could an unlearned age be protected. As late as 1582 it was said to be ' the usual form of pleading ' that the defendant was a layman and without learning and that he had been deceived by a distorted recital of the contents.[80] With this exception, any action of Debt, where the plaintiff relied upon a deed, remained *stricti juris*,[81] and a *fait accompli* of two centuries was represented, with the grandiloquence of the sixteenth century, as the fruit of state policy.

> ' Although the truth be that the plaintiff is paid his money, still it is better to suffer a mischief to one man than an inconvenience to many, which would subvert a law; for if matter in writing may be so easily defeated and avoided by such surmise and naked breath, a matter in writing would be of no greater authority than a matter of fact.' [82]

Rhetoric is unpalatable enough to the litigant who has to suffer for his own imprudence, but it becomes odious when invoked to cover official neglect. In 1545 a plaintiff brought Debt on a bond which, in the course of the proceedings, had been placed in the custody of a clerk to the court. Before the day of the trial it had been so eaten by mice that both its terms and the seals attached to it were ' insufficient.' The sole question put to the jury was whether it had been the defendant's deed at the time when the first plea had been pleaded, and, on an affirmative verdict, the plaintiff obtained judgment.[83]

SOURCES

GLANVILL

Book X

Cap. 1

A plea concerning the debts of the laity belongs to the crown and dignity of our lord the King. And so when anyone complains to the court of a

[79] *The Prior of Dunstable* v. *Smyth* (1422) Y.B. 1 Hen. VI (S.S. Vol. 50), p. 23, *infra*, p. 248.
[80] *Thoroughgood's Case* (1582) 2 Co. Rep. 9a. The defence has been grotesquely distorted in the modern law. See Cheshire and Fifoot, *The Law of Contract*, 2nd ed. pp. 180-6.
[81] A note in Keilway, 70b, pl. 6, attributes to Frowyk, C.J. and Kingsmill, J. in 1506 the statement that the plea of *non est factum* might be available on the ground of fraud even to a literate defendant, but there seems no other contemporary evidence to this effect.
[82] *Waberley* v. *Cockerel* (1542) 1 Dyer, 51a.
[83] *Nichols* v. *Haywood* (1545) 1 Dyer, 59a.

debt which is due to him, if he can bring that plea to the court of our lord the King, he shall have the following writ for the first summons.

Cap. 2

Rex vicecomiti salutem. Præcipe N. quod iuste et sine dilatione reddat R. centum marcas quas ei debet ut dicit, et unde queritur quod ipse iniuste ei deforciat. Et nisi fecerit, summone eum per bonos summonitores quod sit coram me vel justitiis meis apud Westmonasterium a clauso Paschæ in quindecim dies ostensurus, etc.

> The King to the sheriff greeting. Command N. that justly and without delay he render to R. one hundred marks which he owes, as he says, and whereof he complains that he unjustly deforces him. And unless he will do this, summon him by good summoners that he be before me or my justices at Westminster within fifteen days of the close of Easter to show [why he hath not done it].

Cap. 3

... The demandant can demand the debt for several causes. For something may be owed *ex causa mutui aut ex causa venditionis aut ex commodato aut ex locato aut ex deposito aut ex alia justa debendi causa. Ex causa mutui* something is owed when one lends to another such things as are counted, weighed or measured. ... When a thing is lent to anyone, the loan is generally accompanied by the giving of sureties, and sometimes by the deposit of a pledge, sometimes by the pledging of faith, sometimes by a deed, and sometimes by the concurrence of several of these modes of security. ...

Cap. 12

When the debtor appears in court on the appointed day, if the creditor has no pledge nor sureties nor any evidence save pledge of faith alone, this is no proof in the court of our lord the King. But for breach of faith or trespass (*de fidei læsione vel transgressione*) action can be brought in a Court Christian. But the ecclesiastical judge, though he may have cognisance of such an offence and may enjoin penitence or satisfaction upon the convicted party, yet, by an assise of the kingdom, he may not in a Court Christian deal with or decide pleas of lay debts or pleas concerning freeholds on the ground that there has been a pledge of faith. Wherefore, if the debtor denies the debt, the creditor must use other modes of proof ...; as by a sufficient witness or by the duel or by deed. ...

Cap. 13

There are also occasions on which something may be owed *ex causa commodati*; as where I lend my chattel to you gratuitously to be taken and used in your service. When the term of service is completed, you are bound to return my chattel to me without deterioration, provided that it still exists. But if the chattel itself has perished or has been lost, in whatever way, while in your custody, you are bound absolutely to render me a reasonable price for it. ...

Cap. 14

Ex causa emptionis et venditionis also something may be owed when one sells his own thing to another. For the price is owed to the seller and the thing bought to the buyer. But the purchase and sale is concluded with effect (*perficitur cum effectu*)[84] from the time when the parties agree upon the price, provided, however, that it is followed by delivery of the thing bought and sold or that the price is paid in whole or in part or at least that something is given and received by way of earnest. But in the first two of these cases neither of the contracting parties can in any way withdraw of his own will from the contract, save for some lawful and reasonable cause; and so, if it is agreed between them that either may withdraw with impunity within a certain time, then either can thus withdraw within that time according to the agreement; for it is usually true that agreement overrides the general law (*quod conventio legem vincit*). Again, if the seller sells his thing to the buyer as being sound and without blemish, and if afterwards the buyer can show by reasonable proof that, at the time of the contract, it was not sound and without blemish, then the seller will be bound to take back his thing. But it is enough that the thing was in good condition at the time of the contract, whatever may afterwards happen to it. I am, however, doubtful within what time such proof or complaint may be made, especially where no pact supervenes. When only earnest has been given, then, if the buyer wishes to withdraw from the contract, he may do so with the loss of his earnest. If in such a case it is the seller who wishes to withdraw, I question if he may do so without penalty. I should think not, for then the seller would be in a better position than the buyer. But if he cannot do so with impunity, what shall be the amount of the penalty? But the risk of the thing bought and sold is generally with him who holds it, unless otherwise agreed.

Cap. 15

The seller and his heirs are bound to warrant the thing sold to the buyer and his heirs, provided it is an immovable. . . . In the case of a movable, if a third party claims it from the buyer on the ground that it had previously been sold or given to him or had been acquired by some other lawful cause, then, provided there is no additional suggestion that he has lost it by felony, the law is the same as in the case of an immovable. But if the thing is claimed from the buyer as having been stolen, then the buyer is required to defend himself precisely from any charge of theft made against him or to vouch [the seller] to warranty. . . .

Cap. 17

. . . The thing owed by sale or by loan should be proved by the general method of proof used in court, that is to say, by writing or by the duel.

Cap. 18

Ex locato et ex conducto a thing may sometimes be owed, as when one lets his thing to another for a certain term, provided that a rent is fixed. Here the letter is bound to give to the hirer the use of the thing lent, and the hirer to pay the rent. It is to be observed that, on the expiration of the term, the letter can lawfully reinstate himself in the thing lent on his own authority. But what if the hirer does not pay the rent at the stated time? In this case also may the letter expel him on his own authority?

[84] Cf. Just. Inst. III. 23. pr.

The above-mentioned contracts, made by the agreement of private persons, we pass over briefly, because, as said above,[85] private agreements are not usually protected in the court of our lord the King, and, as to those contracts which are analogous to private agreements (*quasi quædam privatæ conventiones*), the court of our lord the King does not concern itself.

BRACTON

ff. 99-100b

Unde actio oriatur

We must now see how an action arises. It must be known that it springs from a preceding obligation as a daughter from her mother. And the obligation, which is the mother of the action, itself has its origin and beginning in some preceding cause (*ex aliqua causa præcedente*), whether from contract or quasi-contract, wrong-doing or quasi-wrong-doing. From contract it can arise in many ways, as by agreement (*ex conventione*), by questions and answers, by a form of words which draws into a single consent the wills of the two parties; and such are *pacta conventa*, which are sometimes naked and sometimes clothed. If they are naked, no action follows from them, since from a naked pact no action is born (*ex nudo pacto non nascitur actio*). A pact must therefore have clothes, of which we must speak later. . . .

Quid sit obligatio et qualiter contrahatur

. . . A contract is made *re, verbis, scripto, consensu, traditione, iunctura*, which are all said to be the clothes of pacts.[86] An obligation is contracted *re*, as by way of *mutuum*, which comprises things which may be weighed, counted or measured. . . . For *mutuum* is the name given to that which, instead of being mine, become yours[87]; and sometimes not the very things themselves but others of the same nature are returned to the creditor. But he to whom something is given for his use is bound by a real obligation called *commodatum*. But there is a wide difference between *mutuum* and *commodatum*; for one who has received a thing by way of *mutuum*[88] is bound to return either the same thing or its equivalent, if by fire, the fall of a building, shipwreck or the attack of robbers or enemies it should have been consumed or lost, stolen or carried away. But one who has received a thing for his use must, in guarding it, not be content to take only the

---

[85] See *Cap.* 8, '. . . Sometimes, creditor and debtor agree that a thing is to be pledged by way of security; then, if, after the receipt of the loan by the debtor, the pledge is not in fact delivered, what advice is to be given to the creditor, especially since the same thing may be pledged to other creditors before or afterwards? As to this, it must be noted that the court of our lord the King is not wont to protect or warrant private agreements of this kind for the delivery and receipt of things by way of pledge or of any other kind, if they are made outside the court or even in other courts than that of our lord the King; and so, if these agreements are not kept, the court of our lord the King does not concern itself with them, and thus it will not discuss the rights of the various creditors, prior or subsequent. . . .'

[86] Cf. Bracton, f. 16b:

Re, verbis, scripto, consensu, traditione,
Junctura, vestes sumere pacta solent.

[87] See Just. Inst. III. 14. pr.

[88] I follow here the emendation suggested by Kantorowicz, *Bractonian Problems* (1941), pp. 95-7. See also Holt, C.J. in *Coggs v. Bernard, supra,* p. 173.

same care as he is accustomed to take of his own things, if another person could guard it more carefully; although for *vis major* or mere accident he is not liable, unless his own fault has contributed to the loss, as for instance if he takes with him on a journey a thing lent to be used at home and loses it by the attack of enemies or robbers or by shipwreck; for then there is no doubt that he is bound to make restitution. . . . He with whom a thing is deposited is bound *re,* and he is bound to restore the very thing that he has received. And he is also liable to the extent to which he has committed *dolus* with regard to the thing deposited. But for *culpa,* that is, for sloth or negligence, he is not liable, because he who delivers a thing for custody to a careless friend has only himself and his casual ways to blame for the result. A creditor who receives a pledge (*pignus*) is bound *re,* and is liable to restore it; and, since this sort of thing given by way of pledge is for the benefit of both parties—of the debtor, that the money may be the more readily lent to him, and of the creditor, that his loan may be the better secured—it suffices that *exacta diligentia* be shown in its custody. And if the creditor displays this care and yet loses the thing by chance, he is free from liability and is not prevented from suing on the loan.

An obligation is contracted *verbis* by stipulation. A stipulation is a set form of words, consisting in question and answer, as thus—*Promittis? Promitto. Dabis? Dabo. Facies? Facio. Fideiubes? Fideiubeo.* . . . And a stipulation can be judicial or conventional. It is judicial if made by order of the judge or of the prætor. It is conventional if made by the agreement of both parties and not by order of the judge or of the prætor, and there are almost as many varieties of it as there are objects of contract. But with all these the King's court does not concern itself, save sometimes as a matter of grace. . . .

A person may be bound *per scripturam.* For, if he writes that he owes money, he is bound by the writing whether the money has been advanced or not, and he will not be allowed the defence that the money has not been advanced in contradiction of his writing, because he has written that he owes it. . . .

Again, an obligation is contracted not only by writing and words but also *consensu,* as in *bonæ fidei* contracts such as purchase and sale, letting and hiring, partnership and mandate. And this kind of obligation is said to be contracted *ex consensu* because neither writing nor, in all cases, even the presence of the parties is necessary. . . .

An obligation arises *de traditione* as we have already described in the title *de donationibus.*[89] *Junctura* is where several agreements (*pacta*) about the same thing are included in one stipulation. For several agreements may thus be included in a stipulation, just as several things may be, and, provided they are added to the principal stipulation at the time of the contract, they become part of the contract and add special terms to it; but, if added after an interval of time, it is otherwise. . . .

ff. 61b-62

De adquirendo rerum dominio ex causa emptionis[90]

There is also a certain *causa* of acquiring the ownership of things, which is called *causa emptionis et venditionis.* When a man sells his thing to

---

[89]Cf. Bracton, f. 11 *et seq.* Under this title Bracton treats of feoffments.
[90] Bracton's remarks on Sale and Hire occur, not in his treatment of consensual contracts, but in this title—*De adquirendo rerum dominio.*

another, be it movable or immovable, the buyer is bound to the seller for the price and the seller conversely to the buyer for the delivery of the thing, according to what has been observed above in the case of gifts, for without delivery the ownership of things is not transferred. . . . But the contract of purchase and sale is made when the price is agreed between the contracting parties, so long, at least, as something is received by the seller by way of earnest; since the receipt of earnest is evidence that the contract of purchase and sale has been made. And, if writing is to intervene, the purchase and sale will not be concluded (*perfecta*) until [the writing] is delivered and executed by the parties. And unless and until earnest is given or the writing executed or the thing delivered, there is a *locus pœnitentiæ* and the parties may withdraw from their contract with impunity. But if the price is paid or part of it, and [or][91] delivery is made, the purchase and sale is *perfecta,* and neither of the parties may afterwards withdraw from the contract on the pretext that the price has not been paid in part [or in whole].[91] But the seller may sue to obtain the balance of the price by the appropriate action, though not to recover the thing. . . . Again, when something is paid before delivery by way of earnest, if the buyer repents his purchase and wishes to withdraw from the contract, he loses what he has thus paid. If it is the seller who repents, he must restore to the buyer double the amount of the earnest.

When a seller sells a thing as sound and without blemish, and afterwards it is found to be with blemish or unsound, and it can be proved by the buyer to have been in this state at the time of the contract, the seller will be bound to take it back. . . .

When the contract of purchase and sale has been made as aforesaid, both before and after delivery the risk of the thing bought and sold is generally with him who holds it, unless otherwise agreed at the outset, because in truth a seller who has not yet delivered the thing to the buyer is still the owner of it, since it is by delivery and usucapion, etc., as can be seen above in the case of gifts.[92] . . . But the seller and his heirs are bound to warrant the thing bought to the buyer and his heirs, whether it be movable or immovable; provided that, if it be immovable, the law is as will be stated below about warranties, and, if movable, as we shall state hereafter about theft.[93]

THE STATUTE OF WALES

12 Ed. I. a.d. 1284

The Forms of the King's Original Writs to be pleaded in Wales

. . . The Writ of Debt

Rex Vicecomiti salutem. Precipe A. quod iuste et sine dilatione reddat B. centum solidos quos ei debet et iniuste detinet, ut dicit. Et nisi fecerit et predictus B. fecerit te securum de clamore suo prosequendo, tunc sum-

---

[91] The manuscripts are not clear. It would seem that, if there is either part payment or delivery, the contract is binding, and, in the case of part payment, the seller must deliver and sue for the balance.

[92] *Supra,* p. 237; and cf. the familiar Roman text, *traditionibus et usucapionibus dominia rerum non nudis pactis transferuntur,* Cod. 2. 3. 20.

[93] Bracton has a detailed title *De Warantia* in ff. 380-399b, and deals specifically with warranty in connection with theft in ff. 151-151b.

moneas per bonos summonitores predictum A. quod sit coram Justiciario
nostro ostensurus quare non fecerit. Et habeas ibi summonitores et hoc
breve. . . .[94]

And if chattels, such as sacks of wool, be demanded, the writ shall be as
follows:

Rex Vicecomiti salutem. Precipe A. quod iuste et sine dilatione reddat
B. unum saccum lanæ precii decem marcarum quem ei iniuste detinet, ut
dicit [vel catalla ad valenciam decem marcarum quæ ei iniuste detinet,
ut dicit]. Et nisi fecerit, etc.

And formulæ shall be drafted in similar writs according to the allegation
of the plaintiff and the diversity of the cases. . . .

THE STATUTE OF MERCHANTS[95]
11 Ed. I. a.d. 1283

Forasmuch as Merchants, which heretofore have lent their goods to divers
persons, be greatly impoverished because there is no speedy law provided
for them to have recovery of their debts at the day of payment assigned;
and by reason hereof many merchants do refrain to come into this realm
with their merchandises to the damage as well of the merchants as of the
whole realm:

The King by himself and by his Council hath ordained and established,

That the merchant which will be sure of his debt shall cause his debtor
to come before the Mayor of London or of York or of Bristol and before
the Mayor and a Clerk, which the King shall appoint for the same, for to
acknowledge the debt and the day of payment; and the Recognizance shall
be entered into a Roll with the hand of the said Clerk, which shall be known.
Moreover, the said Clerk shall make with his own hand a Bill Obligatory
(*escrit de obligacion*) whereunto the seal of the debtor shall be put, with the
King's seal that shall be provided for the same purpose, the which seal
shall remain in the keeping of the Mayor and Clerk aforesaid: And if the
debtor doth not pay at the day to him limited, the creditor may come before
the said Mayor and Clerk with his Bill Obligatory (*sa lettre de obligacion*);
and if it be found by the Roll and by the Bill that the debt was acknowledged
and that the day of payment is expired, the Mayor shall incontinent cause
the movables of the debtor to be sold, so far as the debt doth amount,
by the appraising of honest men . . .; and the money without delay shall be
paid to the creditor. . . .

. . . And if the debtor have no movables whereupon the debt may be
levied, then shall his body be taken where it may be found and kept in
prison until that he have made agreement or his friends for him. . . .

THE STATUTE OF MERCHANTS
13 Ed. I. a.d. 1285

Forasmuch as Merchants, which heretofore have lent their goods to divers
persons, be fallen in poverty because there is no speedy remedy provided
whereby they may shortly recover their debt at the day of payment, and

[94] This form corresponds in substance with the specimen cited from the Register in
H.E.L. III. 662.
[95] Otherwise known as the Statute of Acton Burnell.

for this cause many merchants do refrain to come into the realm with their merchandise to the damage of such merchants and of all the realm;

The King by himself and his Council at his Parliament holden at Acton Burnell after the Feast of St. Michael, the eleventh year of his reign, did make and ordain an establishment thereupon for the remedy of such merchants; which ordinance and establishment the King did command to be firmly kept and observed throughout this realm, whereby Merchants have had remedy and less loss and trouble to recover their debts than they have had heretofore. But forasmuch as Merchants after complained unto the King that Sheriffs misinterpreted his Statute and sometimes by malice and false interpretation delayed the execution of the Statute to the great damage of Merchants; the King at his Parliament holden at Westminster after Easter, the thirteenth year of his reign, caused the said Statute made at Acton Burnell to be rehearsed; and for the declaration of certain articles in the statute aforesaid hath ordained and established :

That a Merchant who will be sure of his debt shall cause his debtor to come before the Mayor of London or before some chief Warden of a city or of another good town, where the King shall appoint . . . and he shall acknowledge the debt and the day of payment; and the Recognizance shall be inrolled by one of the Clerks . . ., and the Roll shall be double, whereof one part shall remain with the Mayor or chief Warden and the other with the Clerk that thereto shall be first named; and, further, one of the said Clerks with his own hand shall write an Obligation, to which writing the seal of the debtor shall be put together with the King's seal provided for the same intent. . . .

. . . And if the debtor do not pay at the day limited unto him, then shall the Merchant come to the Mayor and Clerk with his Letter of Obligation; and if it be found by the Roll and by the Letter that the debt was acknowledged and the day of payment expired, the Mayor or chief Warden shall cause the body of the debtor to be taken, if he be Lay, whensoever he happeneth to come in their power, and shall commit him to the prison of the town, if there be any, and he shall remain there at his own costs, until he hath agreed for the debt. And it is commanded that the keeper of the town prison shall retain him upon the delivery of the Mayor or Warden; and if the Keeper of the prison will not receive him, he shall be answerable for the debt, if he have whereof; and if he hath not whereof, he that committed the prison to his keeping shall answer. And if the debtor cannot be found in the power of the Mayor or chief Warden, then shall the Mayor or chief Warden send into the Chancery, under the King's seal, the Recognizance of the debt; and the Chancellor shall direct a Writ unto the Sheriff in whose Shire the debtor shall be found for to take his body, if he be Lay, and safely to keep him in prison until he hath agreed for the debt. And within a quarter of a year after that he is taken, his chattels and lands shall be delivered him, so that by his own he may levy and pay his debt; . . . and if he do not agree within the quarter, then, after the quarter be expired, all the lands and goods of the debtor shall be delivered unto the Merchant by a reasonable extent, to hold them until such time as the debt is wholly levied; and nevertheless the debtor shall remain in prison as before is said, and the Merchant shall find him bread and water; and the Merchant shall have seisin in the lands and tenements delivered unto him or his assignee so that he may maintain a Writ of Novel Disseisin . . . as of freehold, to hold to him and his assigns until the debt be paid; and as soon as the debt is levied and paid, the body of the debtor shall be delivered with his lands. . . . And if the Sheriff return that the debtor cannot be found or that he is a Clerk, the Merchant shall have Writs to all the Sheriffs where he shall have land, that they shall deliver unto him all the goods and lands of the debtor by a reasonable extent, to hold unto him and his assigns in the form aforesaid; and nevertheless he shall have a Writ to what Sheriff he will to take his body, if he be Lay, and to retain it in manner aforesaid. And let the Keeper of the Prison take heed that he must answer for the body or for the debt. . . .

. . . And a Seal shall be provided that shall serve for Fairs, and the same shall be sent unto every Fair under the King's seal by a Clerk sworn, and by the Keeper of the Fair and the Commonalty of Merchants two lawful Merchants of the City of London shall be chosen, who shall take the oath, and the Seal shall be opened before them; and the one piece shall be delivered unto the foresaid Merchants and the other shall remain with the Clerk; and before them, or one of the Merchants if both cannot attend, the Recognizances shall be taken as before is said. And before that any Recognizance be inrolled, the pain of the Statute shall be openly read before the Debtor, so that after he cannot say that any did put another penalty than that whereto he bound himself. . . .

. . . This Ordinance and Act the King willeth to be observed from henceforth throughout his Realm of England and Ireland between any that will of their own accord make such Recognizances, except Jews to whom this Ordinance shall not extend. And by this Statute a Writ of Debt shall not be abated; and the Chancellor, Justices of the one Bench and the other, the Barons of the Exchequer and Justices Errant shall not be estopped to take Recognizances of debts from any who will make such before them. But the execution of Recognizances made before them shall not be done in the form aforesaid, but by the law, usage and manner otherwise provided in other Statutes.

RICHARD v. VERDON

Y.B. 21 & 22 Ed. I. (R.S. p. 293)

A.D. 1293

One Richard brought a writ of Debt against Thomas de Verdon, and said that he tortiously detained from and did not pay to him £4; and tortiously for this, that, whereas the said Richard delivered certain chattels, namely, wheat, etc., to the value of, etc., on such a day in such a year in such a town at such a place, on the terms that he should be paid for them at the feast of St. Michael then next in the same year, Richard often came to the said Thomas and prayed him that he would pay the said £4, but he would not pay them; to his damage, etc.

Thomas denied, etc., and fully acknowledged that Richard delivered to him the chattels to the use of the Bishop of Bath, but not on the terms that he (Thomas) should pay him £4 at the said feast of St. Michael; and he said that he had rendered an account of the chattels to the executors of the Bishop, and so Richard had his action against the said executors. And, said he, Judgment if we ought to answer for these monies, inasmuch as we received the chattels to the use of another person.

Richard: And we pray judgment on your admission that you received the chattels from us, and you cannot deny that the contract for the same chattels was between you and me; and we tell you that it is more natural for your recovery than for ours to lie against the Bishop's executors, since the Bishop received the chattels from your hands.

METINGHAM, J.: For that Thomas has admitted that he received the chattels from Richard, and he cannot deny the contract between himself and Richard, we adjudge that Richard do recover the £4 against Thomas.

NORTHAT v. BASSET

Y.B. 32 & 33 ED. I. (R.S. App., p. 507)

A.D. 1304

Radulfus Basset de Sapecote summonitus fuit ad respondendum Johanni de Northat de placito quod reddat ei XXXIX. libras quas ei debet et injuste detinet.

And as to this, the said John by his attorney says that, whereas one Simon Basset, father of the aforesaid Ralph, whose heir he is, on the Sunday next before the feast of St. Michael in the ninth year of our lord the King that now is at Warwick obliged himself and his heirs to be bound (*obligasset se et hæredes suos teneri*) to the aforesaid John in thirty-nine pounds for cloth bought and received from the said John, to be paid thus: as to fifteen pounds at the feast of the Purification of the Blessed Mary next following, and as to fifteen pounds at the feast of the Ascension of Our Lord next following: the aforesaid Simon, in his life, did not pay the debt, and the aforesaid Ralph, son and heir of the aforesaid Simon, though often thereto requested, has not cared to render the aforesaid debt, but refuses to render it (*prædictum debitum reddere non curavit, sed reddere contradicit*); wherefore he says that he has suffered loss, and has damage to the value of twenty pounds; and as to this he produces his suit (*et inde ducit sectam*). And he puts forward a certain writing under the name of the aforesaid Simon, the father, etc., which witnesses that the same Simon, the father, etc., on the aforesaid day and year obliged himself and his heirs to be bound to the aforesaid John in thirty pounds to be paid as aforesaid.

And the aforesaid Ralph asks if the aforesaid John has aught to show in like manner of the rest of the aforesaid debt. He says that he has naught save his suit.

And Ralph by his attorney comes and denies force and wrong (*defendit vim et injuriam*), etc., and says that by force of the aforesaid writing the aforesaid John cannot demand any part of the aforesaid debt, because he says that the aforesaid writing is not the deed (*non est factum*) of the aforesaid Simon, his father; and thereof he puts himself on the country (*et de hoc ponit se super patriam*). And John does likewise. Wherefore it is commanded to the Sheriff of Warwick that he cause to come hither (*venire faciat*) on the octave of Trinity twelve lawful men, etc.

And as to the rest of the aforesaid debt which is not contained in the aforesaid writing, that is to say, nine pounds, he asks judgment if the aforesaid John can demand the aforesaid debt from the said Ralph as heir, etc., without a specialty (*sine facto speciali*). And because the aforesaid

John shows nothing for the aforesaid balance save that he produces suit, it is adjudged that the aforesaid Ralph as to this goes without a day, and that the aforesaid John take nothing by his writ, but be in mercy for a false claim.

BENEYT v. LODEWYK

Y.B. 3 ED. II. (S.S. VOL. 20, pp. 46-8)

A.D. 1310

Note from the Record

John de Lodewyk, parson of the church of Westowe, was summoned to answer Andrew Beneyt de Wrydewell of a plea that he render to him sixty-three shillings which he owes and unjustly detains, and fifteen quarters of barley and fifteen quarters of rye, price eight pounds and five shillings, which he unjustly detains.

Andrew, by Henry of Lyvemere, his attorney, says that, whereas John on the Sunday next before the feast of St. George the Martyr in 1 Ed. II. [21 April, 1308] at Westowe granted himself to be bound to Andrew in fifty shillings to be paid to Andrew at the feast of the Nativity of the Blessed Mary next following [8 September], and on Sunday the feast of Pentecost in the same year [2 June] at the said vill of Westowe granted himself to be bound in thirteen shillings to be paid to Andrew at the feast of the Exaltation of the Holy Cross next following [14 September], and also on Saturday in the week of Pentecost in the same year [8 June] by his writing obligatory obliged himself to be bound to Andrew in the said corn, to be paid to Andrew at the feast of the Exaltation of the Holy Cross next following; Andrew often required John to render to him the said debt, and John has not rendered it and still refuses to render it to him: damages, ten pounds. And he proffers two sealed tallies, which witness the debt of sixty-three shillings, and a writing obligatory made under John's name, which witnesses the debt of the said corn in form aforesaid.

John, by Ranulph de Trowis, his attorney, denies tort and force. And as to the debt of sixty-three shillings, he denies that he is bound to Andrew in the said monies or in any penny as Andrew surmises against him; and of this he puts himself upon the country. And as to the writing touching the corn, he says that it ought not to hurt him, for he says that the writing is not his deed; and of this he puts himself upon the country.

Issue is joined, and a *venire facias* is awarded for the morrow of St. John Baptist.[96] And be it known that the writing remains in the custody of J. Bacun, the King's clerk.

Afterwards, in the quindene of St. Hilary in A.R.4 [4 Ed. II], in the presence of the parties, the writing was delivered to HERVEY DE STANTON, Justice, to take [a jury] upon it in the country. . . .

Report (p. 47)

A writ of Debt. A writing was produced in respect of part of the debt, and sealed tallies for the residue. The writing was denied [by the defendant], and as to the tallies he tendered his law.

[96] For *venire facias*, see *Northat v. Basset, supra,* p. 242.

Miggeley: To that you cannot get; for we have produced tallies sealed with your seal, and we do not believe that you ought to be admitted to your law against your own deed sealed with your seal.

Passeley: Sir, we saw a case before Sir John of Metingham, etc., where a tally was produced and it was sealed; and it was denied, and found to be [the denier's] deed; and yet he had no punishment as for a deed denied. Wherefore it seems that we are not put to confess or deny [this tally].

BEREFORD, C.J.: Are not the tallies sealed with your own seal? About what would you tender to make law? For shame!

Claver: As to the forty shillings [*sic*] for which the tallies are produced, we owe him no penny. Ready, etc.

Miggeley: We have nothing to do with an averment. Is this your deed or no?

Claver: We have no need to answer that, for we will aver that we owe no penny.

BEREFORD, C.J.: Will you take the averment?

Miggeley: Yes, Sir, if that be your award.

BEREFORD, C.J.: We award it.

Averment received.[97]

ESTHALLE v. ESTHALLE

Y.B. 6 & 7 ED. II. EYRE OF KENT. VOL. II. (S.S. VOL. 27, p. 21).

A.D. 1313

John of Esthalle and Reynard of Herleson made plaint by bill that Richard of Esthalle wrongfully detained from them one hundred pounds which he owed to them.[98]

Cambridge: What proof have you of the debt?

Passeley produced the deed of Richard which testified that he was unconditionally bound to pay to John and Reynard the sum of one hundred pounds upon a certain day.

Malberthorpe claimed inspection of the deed. He imparled[99] upon it; and, when he returned, said that at a certain time negotiations were entered into by the aforesaid John and Reynard and Richard, in the course of which it was agreed that Richard should levy a fine upon a certain day before the Justices of the Bench upon the aforesaid Reynard and John touching certain lands; and the aforesaid Richard bound himself in writing to the aforesaid Reynard and John that he would pay the sum of one hundred pounds to

---

[97] i.e., that nothing was owed.

[98] The plaintiffs declared:—*quod cum predictus Ricardus . . . per scriptum suum obligasset se teneri eisdem Johanni et Reginaldo in predictis centum libris solvendis ipsis Johanni et Reginaldo ad festum Paschæ proximum sequens. Idem Ricardus licet sæpius requisitus fuisset quod predictum debitum eis redderet debitum illud eis semper hucusque reddere contra'ixit et adhuc contradicit. Unde dicunt quod deteriorati sunt et dampnum habent ad valentiam viginti librorum. Et inde producunt sectam et proferunt predictum scriptum quod hoc testatur.* (S.S. Vol. 27, p. 20.)

[99] Cf. Blackstone, III. 298. '[The defendant] is intitled to demand one *imparlance*, or *licentia loquendi*, and may have more granted by consent of the plaintiff; to see if he can end the matter amicably without farther suit, by talking with the plaintiff: a practice which is supposed to have arisen from a principle of religion, in obedience to that precept of the gospel, "agree with thine adversary quickly whilst thou art in the way with him." And it may be observed that this gospel precept has a plain reference to the Roman law of the twelve tables, which expressly directed the plaintiff and defendant to make up the matter while they were *in the way*, or going to the prætor.'

the said Reynard and John upon a certain subsequent day if by the time agreed upon he had not appeared in court to levy the aforesaid fine; and this writing was, by the assent of the parties, deposited in the custody of a neutral party, to wit, in the custody of Geoffrey Astwick, to be delivered to the aforesaid [Richard] if the fine were levied, and to the aforesaid John and Reynard if Richard neglected to levy it; and this was set out in a penalty bond made between the parties, which was indented; and Richard gave his part thereof to this same Geoffrey. And this same Richard came upon the determined day and levied this fine, etc. And we ask judgment whether they can bring an action upon a conditioned bond, when we have performed the condition therein made and are ready to aver performance of it.

Passeley: We have put in evidence your deed which acknowledges this debt, and you have been out to imparl upon it; and yet you make no answer in regard to it, neither admitting it nor denying it. And so we ask for judgment.

And they were driven by the Court to admit the deed or to deny it.

Malberthorpe: We cannot deny the deed. But the deed was conditioned as aforesaid, and it was deposited with Geoffrey after the fashion aforesaid; and we tell you that Richard has fulfilled the condition and consequently he has become entitled to claim the return of the deed from Geoffrey. This same Geoffrey is now dead. He appointed as executors Reynard, the present plaintiff, and others; and Reynard has appropriated the deed binding Richard. We ask judgment whether, seeing that the deed contained such a condition and that we are prepared to aver that we have completely fulfilled that condition, you can derive any right of action from the deed, which you have not received by process of law.

Passeley: And we ask for judgment whether, this deed by which you are bound being unconditional, you can be entitled to aver a condition, of which you bring forward no proof, against your own deed.

Friskeney: We ask for judgment whether, seeing that the deed was delivered to Geoffrey with the assent of the parties until a certain condition was performed, which condition we have now performed, and that we have a right to bring an action against Geoffrey's executors for the return of this deed, the possession of this deed gives you any right of action against us. And you cannot, as executors, retain the deed as against us by your exception.

Cambridge, ad idem: If Reynard, into whose possession, as Geoffrey's executor, this deed has come, were no party to the deed, and John, who is now co-plaintiff with Reynard, were to sue him for the delivery of it to himself, I think that it would be delivered to us and not to John, if we succeed in averring the condition which we are now ready to aver. And we ask judgment whether upon that deed they can have any action, seeing that we have a bill against this same Reynard and Geoffrey's executors pending in this court.

SPIGURNEL, J.: What has become of the deed which testifies to this condition?

Malberthorpe: It was in the custody of Geoffrey; and we have a bill pending against the executors, this Reynard and others, touching this deed and other ones.

SPIGURNEL, J.: It was foolish to let your staff slip from between your fingers.

Malberthorpe: Notwithstanding that, the law can help us by allowing us to make the averment which we are ready to make; and as to that we abide your judgment, seeing that we have a bill demanding this deed pending in this court.

SPIGURNEL, J., with the assent of STANTON, J. and ORMESBY, J.: Since you admit that you were a party to a bond whereby you bound yourself unconditionally, etc., and now seek to upset that bond by alleging a condition of which you offer no proof, the judgment of the Court is that John and Reynard recover their demand of one hundred pounds; and there will be an enquiry as to damages.

Stonore: It seems to us that there is no need for any enquiry as to damages, for you have the deed in court and they have admitted it; and that deed gives the date when the penalty became payable. The assessment of damages is a matter for the Court's discretion.

The Justices agreed to this; and thereupon SPIGURNEL, J. awarded that the plaintiffs should recover damages to the amount of a hundred shillings.

MARSTON v. DALBY

Y.B. 8 ED. II. (S.S. VOL. 41, p. 179)

A.D. 1315

John of Marston brought a writ of debt against Richard Dalby and claimed twenty-five marks, which etc.[1]; and he tendered a sealed tally which had sixteen notches and a writing stating that money was owed.

Toudeby denied the allegations and said that the defendant was willing to make his law that he owed nothing.

Hartlepool: You will not be allowed to do that, for we have tendered a tally sealed with your own seal, which is a proof in the nature of a specialty, and you cannot make your law contrary to a specialty, and therefore you cannot make it here.

Toudeby: The cases are not alike, for a writing proves a grant or an obligation, which this tally does not; and if a man tendered a writing which said merely that he had borrowed money, it would not bind him.

Scrope: There are sixteen notches, and no one can tell whether they mean sixteen shillings or sixteen marks or sixteen pounds, for the inscription speaks only of money, etc.; and, besides, there is nothing to prevent you making as many notches as you like. . . .

. . . *Herle*: There is a writing on the tally, with the seal appendant, which acknowledges that we lent him money on a certain day in a certain year. Judgment.

BEREFORD, C.J.: The tally is a dumb thing and cannot speak, and there is nothing to prevent you taking off this writing and substituting another against his will. These notches, too: we cannot tell whether they refer to bullocks or to cows or to what else, and you may score as many notches as you like; and so we hold this to be no deed which a man must answer, and therefore it is right that he have his law.

[1] 'Idem Ricardus summonitus fuit ad respondendum Johanni de Mershtone de placito quod reddat ei viginti et quinque marcas quas ei debet et injuste detinet . . .' (From the Record, cited at p. 181.) I have, in the above report, collated the two reports given in S.S. Vol. 41, pp. 179-182.

Herle: If you rule that he shall have his law against the tally, we will willingly accept it.

INGE, J.: You may keep your bailiff's account by a tally, and he will not be allowed his law against it; but in the case of this debt we grant the defendant his law notwithstanding the tally.

And *Herle* accepted the law, and the defendant found pledges that he would make it.[2]

A N O N

Y.B. 11 & 12 ED. III. (R.S. p. 587)

A.D. 1338

A writ of Debt was brought against one; and he counted that the plaintiff, by covenant between him and the defendant, had been made his attorney for ten years, taking twenty shillings for every year, which were in arrear.

Pole: This count begins with a covenant and ends with a duty; we ask judgment of such a count as not warranted.

From this objection he was ousted.

Pole: He has nothing showing the covenant.

SHARSHULLE, J.: If one were to count simply of a grant of a debt, he would not be received without a specialty; but here you have his service for his allowance, of which knowledge may be had, and you have *quid pro quo*.

Wherefore *Pole* waged his law that he owed him nothing; and the other counter-pleaded it.

The COURT to *Gayneford*: Will you receive the law at your peril?

Wherefore he received the law.

THE PRIOR OF BRADSTOCK'S CASE

Y.B. 44 ED. III. MICH. f. 42, pl. 46

A.D. 1371

The Prior of Bradstock brought a writ of Debt against John de Knoll, and demanded from him £17; and he said that his predecessor had leased to one W. de C., by a deed which he put before the Court, certain land for the term of three years, rendering to him and to his successors one rose a year, and, after the term, the said tenements were remaindered to the defendant for two years, rendering therefor £8 per annum; and he said that the term was passed, wherefore he brought action.

Cavendish, for John, said that this action was taken on a Deed of Lease, and the deed ran 'John Keynel, clerk,' and the writ ran 'Kenton'; and so there is a variance. Judgment of the writ.

FINCHDON, C.J.: This deed is not like an obligation, where the action is taken on the deed; but the deed is put forward as matter of proof and in maintenance of his action, as in a *Formedon en remainder*[3]; and in all such

---

[2] It appears from the Record that the plaintiff subsequently made default.
[3] See Maitland, *Collected Papers*, II. 174-181, and Humphreys, *Formedon en Remainder at Common Law*, 7 C.L.J. (1941) 238.

cases, when the deed is put forward to support the action, there is no need that the writ accord with the deed, for the action can be maintained without a deed. So if I take a lease of land for the term of my life without a deed, rendering therefor a certain rent, and I die, my executors will answer without a deed.

Belknap: But I say no. If the lease be for the term of the lessee's life, rendering certain rent, and he dies, his executors shall not answer without specialty.

FINCHDON, C.J. denied this; and the other Serjeants said that they understood the law to be otherwise.

Cavendish: In an action of Covenant, if the writ does not accord with the specialty, it is abated.

FINCHDON, C.J.: There, the action is taken on the deed, and without a deed it cannot be maintained. But it is not so here, and the writ must be adjudged good, so far as concerns this challenge.

Thorpe: He could have counted of a contract without having put forward a deed; and then afterwards he can put it in evidence.

Cavendish: So he could. But now in this case I will have recourse to my law, that nothing is owed to him. . . .

THE PRIOR OF DUNSTABLE v. SMYTH

Y.B. 1 HEN. VI. (S.S. VOL. 50, p. 23)

A.D. 1422

From the Record

John Smyth of Battlesdon in the aforesaid county [Bedford], husbandman, was summoned to answer John, prior of Dunstable, on a plea that he should render to him four marks which he owes to him and wrongfully detains, etc. (*quas ei debet et iniuste detinet, etc.*). And whereof the same prior, by John Loughton, his attorney, says that, whereas the aforesaid John Smyth, on the twenty-third day of September in the seventh year of the reign of the lord Henry, late king of England, father of the present lord king, had granted by a certain writing obligatory (*per quoddam scriptum suum obligatorium*) that he was bound and firmly obliged to the aforesaid prior in the aforesaid four marks to pay to the same prior or to his successors on the feast of All Saints then next ensuing, nevertheless the aforesaid John Smyth, although often requested, has not yet rendered the aforesaid four marks to the aforesaid prior, but up to now has refused, and still refuses, to render them to him; whereupon he says that he is injured and has damage to the value of one hundred shillings; and thereof he brings suit, etc. And he proffers here in Court the aforesaid writing, which witnesses the debt aforesaid in the form aforesaid and which is dated on the aforesaid day and year. And in addition he says that the writing aforesaid was made at Dunstable in the same county, etc.

And the aforesaid John Smyth comes by Thomas atte Welle, his attorney. And he denies tort and force when, etc. And he says that he ought not to be burdened with the aforesaid debt by virtue of the writing aforesaid, because he says that, before the time of the drawing up of the aforesaid writing, there was a certain strife and debate between the same John Smyth and the aforesaid prior about and upon the claim and title of a certain annual rent of twelve shillings, which rent the same prior was exacting from the same John Smyth as issuing from a certain messuage belonging to the same John in Battlesdon; so that, to have and re-establish peace between them thereof, the same John Smyth, through the mediation of friends who came between them, conceded to the aforesaid prior to make the aforesaid writing for him under such a condition that, if the same John Smyth would come to some place before the aforesaid prior before the feast of All Saints next ensuing after the date of the aforesaid writing together with his proofs touching the messuage aforesaid, and would show these proofs to the aforesaid prior in order to exclude him from all claim and title of right to the aforesaid rent, then the writing aforesaid should be held for naught; but that otherwise it should remain in its force and strength. And he says that he is himself a layman and illiterate and that the writing aforesaid was read to him together with the aforesaid condition. And the same John Smyth, intending that condition to be specified in the aforesaid writing, made and sealed that writing for the aforesaid prior. And thus he says that the simple and unconditional writing aforesaid now brought against him here in court is not his deed (*non est factum suum*). And of this he puts himself upon the country.

And the aforesaid prior likewise.

Therefore the sheriff is ordered to cause to come in the octave of Hilary twelve, etc. . . . to make recognition, etc. . . . And it should be known that the aforesaid writing remains in the meantime in the keeping of Thomas Belwood, chief clerk of the lord king, for safe and secure keeping, etc.

ANON

Y.B. 37 HEN. VI. MICH. f. 8, pl. 18

A.D. 1458

In a writ of Debt the plaintiff counted that on such a day in such a year at such a place an accord was made between the plaintiff and the defendant that the plaintiff should marry one Alice, daughter to the defendant, for which marriage the defendant should give to the plaintiff one hundred marks; and then he showed that he took the said Alice to be his wife and that the espousals were solemnised between them according to the rites of Holy Church, and he showed when and where they were celebrated; and then the plaintiff came to the defendant and demanded of him the hundred marks, and he would not pay them and has not yet paid them; and so the action accrued to the plaintiff.

PRISOT, C.J.: It seems to me that this writ and count do not suffice to maintain this action. For the action is not founded on such a covenant as a sale, where, if a man buys a cow or a horse from me for twenty shillings, I shall have a good action of Debt against him because of the sale; and yet it may be that the buyer receives no *Quid pro Quo,* for it may be that I have no horse; and yet I shall have a good action of Debt. For it is not a good plea for him to say that I had no horse at the time of the sale, for *caveat emptor.* . . . As if I sell the manor of D., of which I am seised, to a man for a hundred pounds; now I shall have a good action of Debt against him on this contract, and yet by the contract the property of the manor is not in him nor can he enter into the manor by force of the contract without livery of seisin. And so, too, I shall have an action of Debt even if I have no manor; but this is because of the contract.[4] And so a contract is a sufficient matter to maintain an action. So, too, one can have an action of Debt on retaining a man to be one's counsellor at forty shillings per annum, and I shall have a good action on such a contract; but in this case I must declare in my count that I am acting for him or otherwise would have been willing to counsel him, if he should demand counsel from me. So, too, if a servant be retained by me, after he has done his service he shall have a good action of Debt against me; but he must declare that he did his service during this time and show that this was a perfect contract,[5] that there was a retainer and also that there is *quid pro quo*; and he shall have no action unless he has done his service. But in the case at bar he has not declared on a perfect contract, but only that an accord was made, on which it seems to me that this action is not maintainable.

DANVERS, J.: It seems to me that this action is good and maintainable on the matter shown. For, as to the point that it is not a perfect contract, yet it is so in effect; for the accord was that he should take his daughter to wife, whereby the defendant has *Quid pro Quo*. For the plaintiff was charged with the marriage of the daughter and by her espousal he is discharged, and so he has done the thing for which the sum is payable.[6] As if I say to a man that if he will carry twenty quarters of corn from Master Prisot to G. he shall have forty shillings, now because he has carried the twenty quarters he shall have a good action of Debt against me for the forty shillings; and yet the thing is not done to me, but by my commandment. So here, he has shown that he has solemnised the marriage, and so a good action accrues to him. But if he had not solemnised the marriage, then otherwise.

[ASHTON, J. was of opinion that the case, as being one of matrimony, was within the exclusive jurisdiction of the Courts Christian.]

DANBY, J.: It seems to me that he cannot have an action, for it is neither contract nor accord, it is merely covenant, on which there is no action without specialty. For the writ runs *Concordatum est*, and this is neither contract nor accord, but merely covenant. . . . Suppose that this matter had been written in an indenture thus: *Haec indentura, etc. quod concordatum est, quod prædictus J. accipiet in uxore A. filiam prædicti S. et prædictus S. debet ei C. marcarum*: now would he have an action of Debt on this deed? Why, no; because there are no words of grant. But if he had said, *pro qua materia concessit se dare C. marcarum*, peradventure he would have an action of Debt for this word *concessit*. But here there are no words to give an action of Debt, and so, even had it been written down, there would still be no action of Debt: *a fortiori* if not written. So it seems to me that the action is not maintainable.

---

[4] This view of Prisot, C.J. as to the sale of land is heterodox: see Ames, *Lectures on Legal History*, p. 140, n.3.

[5] The text is difficult and perhaps corrupt at this point. The phrase used is 'un mere contract.' The word 'mere' seems to bear, not its modern significance of 'bare' or 'only,' but the contemporary meaning of 'sheer,' 'perfect,' 'absolute.' Thus a 'mere contract' is such a transaction as would justify *Debt on a Contract*, i.e., where the plaintiff proves, not only an agreement, but also that he has conferred the benefit as required by the defendant.

[6] On the use of the word 'charge' in this context, see *infra*, p. 401, n.

MOYLE, J.: I think the contrary. As to what has been said that it sounds in covenant, this is not to the purpose, since the thing has been done. Suppose I retain a carpenter to make me a house and he is to have forty shillings from me for the making. Now if the carpenter makes the aforesaid house, he shall have a good action of Debt against me; and yet this sounds in covenant, and if he will not make the house, I shall [not] have an action against him without specialty, because it sounds in covenant. But when he has made the thing, then the action accrues to him to demand the sum due. If I say to a surgeon that if he will go to one J. who is ill and give him medicine and make him safe and sound he shall have a hundred shillings; now, if the said surgeon gives the said J. medicine and makes him safe and sound, he shall have a good action of Debt against me for the hundred shillings; and yet the thing is done to another and not to the defendant himself. And so, though he has not got *Quid pro Quo,* he has the same in effect. So here, when he promised one hundred marks to take his daughter to wife, which he has done, it seems that the action is maintainable.

PRISOT, C.J.: This is a good case to prove the case at bar, and so is the case put by DANVERS of the carriage of the corn. But now we must see if there is any diversity between the two.

Et adjournatur.

VEER v. YORK

Y.B. 49 HEN. VI. (S.S. VOL. 47, p. 163)

A.D. 1470

In *debt* brought by a priest on the ground that he was retained by the defendant to chant for the soul of one C. for a year for ten marks, the defendant says that within the year the same plaintiff departed out of his service: judgment. And it was discussed whether it was necessary to show at what time he departed, and to pay him for the time he was in service, etc.; as if he had served for half a year, he would have five marks.

Fairfax: This priest cannot be compelled to serve, that is to say, to chant for the soul, etc.; and hence he is not like a common labourer or a priest who is retained to be parish priest.

CHOKE, J.: This duty is entire, and he must serve for a year or otherwise he will have no salary, and he cannot demand his salary until he has served his term; and it is not the same where I buy a horse from a man for twenty shillings, for there the twenty shillings are due to the seller immediately, because by the purchase the property in the horse has passed to me, and I can have possession.

Catesby: If I buy a horse of you for twenty shillings, you can keep the horse until I pay you.

CHOKE, J.: I did not speak to that intent; but I say that the property is vested in me by the purchase, so that if a stranger take him I will have an action of trespass.

Brian, to *Catesby*: Sir, in your case, if you give him a day of payment,[7] you cannot keep the horse. . . .

[7] i.e., credit.

ANON

Y.B. 17 Ed. IV. Pasch. f. 1, pl. 2

A.D. 1478

Trespass for a close broken, and corn, barley and grass taken and carried away.

Catesby. Actio non: For long before the supposed trespass the plaintiff and the defendant bargained in such a ward in London that the defendant should go to the place where, etc., and there view the said corn, barley, etc., as aforesaid, and if they pleased him when he saw them, then he should take the said corn, barley and grass, paying to the said plaintiff 3s. 4d. for each acre, one with the other. And we say that we went there and we viewed them as aforesaid and we were content with the bargain, wherefore we took them, which is the said trespass. Judgment, etc.

Pigot: This is no plea for divers reasons. One is that he has said that the place, etc. is ten acres of corn, etc., whereas he should have said ten acres of land sown with corn, etc. Moreover, he has acknowledged the taking, and has not shown that he has paid us the money according to the bargain; for I believe that it is not lawful for him to take them before he has paid, for it would be most mischievous law that he should have them and not pay. Moreover, when he had viewed the corn, etc., he should have made known to us whether he was content with it or no, so that we should know whether he had taken them for that reason; for it cannot be a perfect bargain if each party be not agreed.

Catesby: The plea is good enough for anything that he has shown. As to the first conceit, that we have called them acres of corn, etc., and not of land, it is so called *vulgariter*. As to the other conceit, that we have not alleged the payment of the money, I believe that most bargains in the kingdom would be void if this were to be law. But I submit that it is lawful for him to take the things on such a bargain as this before any payment; for there is no mischief, because he can have an action of Debt for the money, when we have received the thing; and, to my mind, in every such bargain the law assumes that, as the one puts his trust in the other to have the thing for which they have bargained, so ought the other *e contra*. As for the suggestion that we should certify him of our agreement, it would be very hard that, when we were well content with the view of the thing (which is perchance in another county at a great distance from London), we must return thence to tell this to him. Moreover, the bargain proves that there is no need of this, because he has put his will into our will; that is to say, that, if they pleased us on our view of them, then we should have them. How then could he be better certified than by our taking them?

LITTLETON, J.: As to the payment, it seems to me that it should be alleged, or else it is no plea. As if I come to a draper and ask him how much I shall pay him for such a piece of cloth, and he says so much, and I say that I will have it, but I do not pay him any ready money and yet take the cloth; here he shall have a good action of Trespass against me, and it will be no plea for me to say that I have bought it from him, unless I show that I have paid him. So here.

CHOKE, J.: To the same effect. For a contract cannot be perfect without the agreement of each party. For if you ask me in Smithfield how much you will give me for my horse and I say so much, and you say that you will have him and do not pay the money, do you believe that, for all this, it is my will that you should have him without paying the money? I say no; but I may at once sell him to another and you shall have no remedy against me. For otherwise I shall be compelled to keep my horse for ever against my will, if the property is in you, and you would be able to take him when you pleased, which would be against reason. So here.[8]

BRIAN, C.J.: To the same intent. It seems to me, for any words which have been alleged in this bargain, that it was not lawful for him to enter and take the grain, for it cannot be understood that he intended the defendant to have the grain save on the payment of the money. But if he had said to him, Take them and pay when you please, or if he had given him some day for payment, then I conceive well that he could take them, and that would be a good bar if so pleaded. Further, I say that the property is in the defendant by the bargain in the case at bar, and in your cases of the horse and of the cloth; and yet it is not lawful for him who hath the property to take them without the other's leave. And he[9] shall have a writ of Detinue, but the defendant will be excused by saying that he was ready to render them if the buyer had paid; and if he brings an action of Debt, he shall have the same plea. The case is much the same as where the property remains all the time in me, and yet for a certain time I cannot take it; as where I bail certain sheep to a man to manure his fields for a certain time, here the property is in me, and yet during this time I cannot take them back. As for the other conceit, it seems to me that the plea is not good without showing that he has certified the other of his pleasure; for it is common learning that the intent of a man cannot be tried, for the Devil himself knows not the intent of a man. But had you agreed that, if the bargain pleased you, you should certify this to such a man, then I grant that you need do no more, for this is a matter of fact. Suppose that I am obliged to you in £10 payable two or three days afterwards on condition that, if you please to take a certain horse of mine for some trespass that I have done to you, then [the bond is to be discharged], and you view the horse and do not say whether it pleases you or not, and so I do not pay you the £10, shall the obligation be forfeited? Why, no. Wherefore, etc.

Catesby: Sir, if he does not take the horse and by this act prove his intent, then you forfeit your obligation. And as to what has been said, that there is no need to deliver the thing sold before he pays, in the same way the other need not pay before he has the thing which has been sold. But, as I said before, in law and in reason each shall put trust in the other; and if the payment were material, I think we should have seen issues taken on this fact in our books; but I have never seen them. Suppose you bring a writ of Trespass against me for taking your horse, and I plead that I bought him on a certain day in London in market overt and then committed him to one B. for safe keeping, who gave him to you, and I took him from you, could you say in that case that I had not paid for the horse?

CHOKE, J.: No, for that is not material to the plea.

Pigot: If I am obliged to you in £20 to enfeoff you in such an acre of land on such a day if you are pleased to accept the feoffment, shall you not be bound to show me your pleasure? Yes, verily, as I think.

LITTLETON, J.: I cannot agree that the property is in him who buys by such words without payment; for it is not a clear bargain, but is subject

---

[8] Choke, J. is here confusing the three separate questions of contractual rights, the passing of the property and the right to possession.
[9] i.e. the buyer.

to a condition in law, that is to say, if he pays me it shall be good, and if not it shall be void. Suppose I enfeoff Pigot to enfeoff Catesby: if he will not enfeoff him, my entry is implied by law. So the performance of the condition causes the property to be in him.

Catesby: As to the certifying of the agreement, suppose that he should be stricken dumb after the bargain by act of God and does not know how to write, but he is of sound mind, and it seems to him that the bargain is to his profit, what must he do? Will not his taking be sufficient to prove his will? So here. Wherefore, etc.

ᐯ *11* ᐯ

COVENANT

T HE earliest case of covenant to survive in the records of the law
is from the year 1201.

> Robert of Anmer offered himself on the fourth day against
> William of Anmer of a plea of covenant (*de placito convencionis*)
> made between him and the said William about one hundred and
> seventy-eight acres of land with their appurtenances in Anmer.[1]

It was a common cause of litigation in the reign of Henry III. Sixteen
cases were included in the collection known as Bracton's Note-Book,
and Bracton himself referred, if with a studied lack of precision, to
an *actio de conventione*.[2] It was among the fifty-six *brevia de cursu*
appointed in 1227 to domesticate Irish justice, and a specimen was
given in the contemporary English register cited by Maitland from a
Cambridge manuscript and transcribed in 1947 by Miss de Haas.[3]

> Vicecomiti salutem. Præcipimus tibi quod iusticies A. quod
> iuste et sine dilatione teneat B. conventionem inter eos factam de X.
> acris terræ cum pertinenciis in tali villa, ut dicit, sicut rationabiliter
> monstrare poterit quod ei tenere debeat.

It has been commonly asserted that the writ of covenant, at least
in its early years, was almost exclusively used to protect interests in
land and especially that of the lessee for years.[4] It is true that each
of the precedents in the early Registers and all the sixteen cases in
Bracton's Note-Book derived from the land law. But of these sixteen
cases only four concerned leases,[5] and the rest display a variety of
subject-matter. Plaintiffs claimed on a warranty of title to freehold
estates or asserted the right to feed their pigs without toll in the defen-

---

[1] Select Civil Pleas (Vol. I), S.S. Vol. 3, Plea 89.

[2] Bracton, f. 34.

[3] Maitland, *Coll. Papers*, II., pp. 130-141, and Elsa de Haas, Univ. of Toronto L.J.
Vol. 7, p. 196 at p. 217: see *supra*, p. 17. The form given above is that of a
Justicies, which committed the case to the sheriff, as against a *Præcipe*, which brought
it to the King's court.

[4] Speaking of the two Registers referred to above, Maitland said, 'We may doubt
whether there is as yet any writ as of course which will enforce a covenant not
touching land.' *Coll. Papers*, II. 141. So, too: 'The *placitum conventionis* is
almost always what we should call an action on a lease,' *P. & M*. II. 217. So, too,
'Covenant first manifests itself in connexion with agreements relating to land. . . .
The need for protection of leases brought the writ into existence,' Barbour, *Oxford
Studies in Social and Legal History*, IV., pp. 17-18; 'In the King's Court it is
always a covenant concerning land, apparently,' Plucknett, *Concise History*, 4th
ed., p. 346; 'The remedy was . . . introduced . . . primarily for the protection
of termors,' Potter, *Historical Introduction to English Law*, 3rd ed., p. 445.

[5] See B.N.B. Plea 1739, *Forest* v. *Villy*, *infra*, p. 260.

255

dant's woods:[6] unsavoury disputes arose upon a question of guardianship and upon a conveyance made by a too indulgent father to his
son.[7]   Sir C. T. Flower, moreover, in his *Introduction to the Curia
Regis Rolls,* 1199-1230, *A.D.,* cites a number of cases wholly unconnected with land.   In 1214 a buyer sued a seller on a covenant providing for the delivery of corn at a fixed time and place; and there
were arrangements for the payment of debts by instalments and for
the settlement of disputes.   In one instance, an appeal of murder
was compromised on the terms that the appellee should ' go to Jerusalem and stay there in the service of God for the soul of the dead
man for seven years ' and that a third party, on his behalf, should
solace the kinsman of the deceased with spiritual preferment.[8]

A peculiar and persistent use of the writ was in levying a fine.
A fine—*finalis concordia*—was the compromise of a suit, settled upon
terms approved by the court.   The dispute, while it might be a reality,
was more often fictitious, and was chiefly used as a means of conveying
land.   The procedure was known to and described by Glanvill.[9]

> It often happens that suits originated in the court of our lord the
> king are put an end to by a friendly agreement and final concord,
> provided the consent and license of our lord the king or his justices
> are obtained, whatever be the subject-matter of the suit, whether
> land or anything else.   A final concord of this nature is generally
> reduced to a common writing and takes effect by their common
> consent; and the writing is read before the justices of our lord the
> king and is delivered in their presence to both justices, one part
> being an exact copy of the other. . . .[10]   And note that this is called
> a final concord because it puts an end to the business, so that neither
> of the litigants can thenceforth recede from it.   For if either of them
> does not keep the agreement or will not do what it requires and the
> other complains thereof, the sheriff will be commanded to put the
> recalcitrant party under safe pledges to appear before the justices
> of our lord the king to answer why he has not kept the agreement.

Soon after his book was written, an innovation was made in the procedure which endured until 1833.   The terms of the compromise,
agreed by the parties and approved by the judges, were entered upon
a threefold indenture, one of the parts being given to each of the
litigants and the third—the ' foot ' or bottom of the document—being
kept among the records of the court.   The parties thus obtained
incontestable evidence and abundant security, and either could sue the
other if the agreement were not implemented.   The writ of covenant
was usually chosen to open this pantomime, not through any intrinsic

---

[6] See B.N.B., Pleas 581 and 804, and Plea 1129, *De la Dun* v. *Basset, infra,* p. 261.
[7] B.N.B., Plea 1702, and Plea 36, *Godwin's Case, infra,* p. 260.
[8] S.S. Vol. 62 (1943), pp. 284-8.
[9] Book VIII, Cap. 1-3.   On Fines in general, see P. & M. II. 94-105, Holdsworth,
    H.E.L. III, 236-246, Winfield, *Chief Sources of English Legal History,* 140-4.
[10] Here follows, in Book VIII, Cap 2, the form of the Fine.

propriety, but simply as offering a cheaper and quicker process than the real actions strictly assigned to claims of freehold.[11]

The records of Edward I and Edward II tell the same tale. The draftsman of the Statute of Wales, while he illustrated the use of Covenant from the land law, declared it available for movables as for immovables, and declined a more extended treatment on the ground that, as its variations were infinite, it would be vain to particularise.[12] Of the forty-five cases transcribed for the two reigns in the volumes of the Rolls Series and of the Selden Society thirty-one concerned land, and of those thirty-one sixteen dealt with leases.[13] The others comprised such a diversity of traffic as the loan of a horse for a tournament and the provision of divine service in a private chapel, the guarantee of an apprentice's behaviour and the search for a suitable match for an heiress, the building of mills and the maintenance of sea-walls.[14] It is fair to conclude that Covenant, though its roots were in the land, was a catholic writ.

It might well have seemed, indeed, that Covenant was destined to fulfil the promise of its name and to provide a general contractual remedy. That this expectation was disappointed was due to the introduction of the technical rule that the writ would lie only upon a writing under seal. The cause and date of this rule are alike obscure. Ames declared, with categorical inaccuracy, that ' a seal was always essential.'[15] Pollock and Maitland, Holdsworth and Barbour were content to ascribe it to ' the reign of Edward I.'[16] The evidence is unconvincing. Two cases may be mentioned. *Corbet's Case* in 1292 was cited by Salmond as decisive and by Holdsworth as an action where the absence of a writing was pleaded with ' apparent ' success: Barbour and Pollock and Maitland retorted, and, as the report indicates, with justice, that no conclusion was reached.[17] Barbour, in turn, relied upon an anonymous case of 1304, and Holdsworth thought the rule there to have been ' assumed ' to exist: Pollock and Maitland pointed out that, though counsel argued that 'a covenant is a thing requiring a specialty,' the argument was not accepted by the court.[18] As late as 1311 the

---

[11] The first example of the tripartite indenture is dated 15 July, 1195: P. & M. II. 97. For the procedure in the eighteenth century, see Blackstone, Comm. II. 348-357 and App. IV. The writ used to *enforce* the compromise thus recorded was not Covenant, but, normally at least, *Scire Facias*.

[12] Statute of Wales (1284), 12 Ed. I., Cap. 6 and 10, *infra*, p. 261.

[13] e.g., *Anon* (1311), S.S. Vol. 42, p. 171, *infra*, p. 263.

[14] *Corbet's Case* (1292), *infra*, p. 262: *Anon* (1293) Y.B. 21 & 22 Ed. I. (R.S.) 183: *Wroteham* v. *Canewold* (1311) Y.B. 4 Ed. II (S.S. Vol. 26) 147: *Brandeston* v. *Burgh* (1312), *infra*, p. 264: *Buckland* v. *Leukenore* (1313-4), *infra*, p. 266: *Pessindenne* v. *Potter* (1313-4) Eyre of Kent (S.S. Vol. 27) 12.

[15] *Lectures on Legal History*, p. 98.

[16] P. & M. II. 219-220: Holdsworth, *H.E.L.* III. 417: Barbour, *Oxford Studies*, Vol. IV., 18. See especially the cases cited in P. & M. II. 220, note 1, and in *H.E.L.* III. 417, note 2.

[17] *Corbet's Case, infra*, p. 262: Salmond, *Essays in Jurisprudence and Legal History*, 184; and references as in note (16), *supra*.

[18] See Y.B. 32 & 33 Ed. I. (R.S.) 199, and references as in note (16), *supra*.

issue was doubtful. A case of that year offers so typical an example of forensic technique in the early fourteenth century as to merit examination.[19] A. held nine acres of woodland from B. and leased them to C. C. wrongfully felled the timber. B. sued A. on a writ of Waste and recovered damages. A. now sought to recoup herself by suing C. in covenant. Defendant's counsel at first argued that, as the essence of the complaint lay in the act of destruction, a writ of Waste and not of Covenant was the appropriate remedy; but Chief Justice Bereford rejected the argument as a denial of justice, since no one could bring Waste unless he could complain of an injury to the inheritance and the plaintiff had only an estate for life. Counsel then took the point, made by his predecessor in 1304, that covenant required a specialty and that none had been put in evidence, but again without success. Chief Justice Bereford found no difficulty in the possibility of an unsealed lease and declared that, if either party must produce a deed, it should rather be he who claimed a license to commit waste.

The reign of Edward III, however, found the rule established, for whatever reason, beyond the scope of further argument. In 1346 the judgment of a lower court was reversed on a writ of Error by the King's Bench,

> because the plaintiff counted of a covenant and did not produce any specialty, and exception was taken because the court had ruled that the plaintiff should be answered without producing any specialty, whereas covenant properly falls under the head of specialty.[20]

So, too, in the *Prior of Bradstock's Case* in 1371, the Court distinguished the effect of a deed in an action of Debt upon a lease and in an action of Covenant. In the former it was no more than evidence: in the latter it was all-important. ' The action is taken on the deed, and without a deed it cannot be maintained.'[21] This insistence upon formality stopped the growth of Covenant; but it is interesting to reflect that, had the decision been otherwise, the common law would have enjoyed, at the beginning of the fourteenth century, a general remedy for breach of contract based, not, as ultimately evolved, upon a bilateral bargain, but upon a unilateral promise.

The scope of the writ, thus gravely circumscribed, was further restricted by the rule that, where Debt was a possible, it was the exclusive remedy; and, as Debt was available where a defendant had granted a fixed sum of money by deed, Covenant could be used only upon obligations of a more general character. The rule is said to

---

[19] *Anon* (1311) Y.B. 4 Ed. II. (S.S. Vol. 42) 171, *infra,* p. 263.

[20] *Anon* (1346) Y.B. 20 Ed. III, Vol. II (R.S.) 148.

[21] Y.B. 44 Ed. III. Mich. f. 42, pl. 46, *supra,* p. 247. Once it was established that a deed was essential to Covenant, it followed that the action became *stricti juris* in the same way as Debt *sur* obligation: *supra,* p. 231.

have been established by the close of Edward I's reign, and, though the evidence is negative rather than positive, it is at least clear that such a claim as for rent upon a lease was always made through the medium, not of Covenant, but of Debt. As late as 1613 it was said in the Common Pleas that, ' if a man covenant to pay £10 at a day certain, an action of Debt lieth for the money, and not an action of Covenant.'[22]

A further technical characteristic, if less engrossing, should be noticed. A generation, still suffering from the divorce of common law and equity, may observe, with mingled envy and surprise, the equanimity with which the courts of the thirteenth and fourteenth centuries entertained claims in Covenant for specific relief. Such relief, indeed, was implicit in the language of the writ, which called upon the defendant to keep the agreement which he had made. In *Godwin's Case* in 1219 third parties, to whom the defendant had alienated lands in breach of his covenant, were summoned to explain their conduct, and in *Forest* v. *Villy* in 1226 a lease was to be executed in the plaintiff's favour.[23] In the Statute of Wales the recovery of a tenement was assumed to be a familiar feature of the proceedings in Covenant, although the plaintiff's rights might now be subject to the intervening claims of third parties.[24] The remedy was, in any event, discretionary. In 1305 a plaintiff, who had ' thought to have recovered his term,' had to be content with damages.[25] The disappearance of this power has never been fully explained. It has been argued that a judge, whose only pressure upon a recalcitrant defendant was by distraint, could not compete with a Chancellor who met obstinacy with imprisonment. It has also been suggested that, as the process of the common law courts became ever more technical and the courts themselves ever more autonomous, they ceased to tap the springs of extraordinary justice in the Royal Prerogative. Perhaps, too, the award of damages, originally a poor substitute for specific relief,[26] became ironically such an obsession with the judges as to monopolise their attention. All that can be said with confidence is that a power, still exercised in the fourteenth, had become obsolete in the fifteenth century.[27]

---

[22] *Chawner* v. *Bowes*, Godbolt, 217. The Queen's Bench, however, had in 1585 allowed a plaintiff to elect between Debt and Covenant (*Anon*, 3 Leonard, 119). The rigid demarcation between writs was, at this time, being obscured. See Ames, *Lectures on Legal History*, pp. 152-3. For an example of Debt on a lease, see *The Prior of Bradstock's Case, supra*, p. 247.

[23] *Infra*, p. 260. See also Bracton, f. 220: ' *solent aliquando tales cum eiecti essent infra terminum suum perquirere sibi per breve de conventione.*'

[24] *Infra*, p. 262.

[25] *Anon* (1305) Y.B. 32 & 33 Ed. I (R.S.) 475.

[26] See *supra*, p. 49.

[27] On the whole question, see Hazeltine, *Early History of English Equity* (in *Essays in Legal History*, ed. Vinogradoff) 261: Holdsworth, *H.E.L.* II., pp. 246-8, 344-7: Plucknett, *Concise History*, 4th ed., pp. 639-41.

SOURCES

GODWIN'S CASE
BRACTON'S NOTE-BOOK, PLEA 36
A.D. 1219

Richard, son of Godwin, demands of Godwin, his father, that he keep to him the covenant made between them (*quod teneat ei convencionem factam inter eos*) as to forty acres of land and seven acres of meadow with their appurtenances in Corteseye and as to forty-four acres of land with their appurtenances in Ewesham; as to which the said Richard produces a charter of the said Godwin which testifies that he conveyed to Richard his son and heir in full all his land with its appurtenances, so nevertheless that he should keep two parts of the said land in his own hands all the days of his life to provide for himself and so that he would not grant or sell or pledge or in any way alienate that land or any part thereof to the prejudice of the aforesaid Richard and his heirs after the death of the said Godwin. And now the said Richard complains that, against that charter and covenant, the said Godwin has sold to John Parmer one messuage and seven acres of land in Corteseye and to Warin of Chelsea eight acres of land and one acre of meadow and to Peter of Poddehale one messuage and three acres of land and one acre of meadow and to Ralph Stonor three acres of meadow and to William the priest one acre of land, and has pledged to Ralph the clerk three acres of land for a term of ten years; and as to this he produces his suit.

Godwin comes and acknowledges the charter and covenant and that he has sold and pledged those lands; but he says that he has done this because of his poverty and because he thought that he could well do so.

It was adjudged that the above-mentioned persons be summoned within fifteen days of Michaelmas to show how they came to enter on the aforesaid lands against the covenant made between the said Godwin and Richard by the charter of the said Godwin.

FOREST v. VILLY
BRACTON'S NOTE-BOOK, PLEA 1739
A.D. 1226

Ralph Villy was summoned to answer Hugh Forest as to why he did not keep towards him a covenant made between them as to fifty acres of land in Cunytorpe; as to which the said Hugh said that he [the said Ralph] demised to him the said lands for a term of ten years, whereof nine years were yet to come; and he demanded his term.

And Ralph came and defended the said covenant, but said[28] that he made it in time of war and under duress from the said Hugh; and as to this he put himself on witnesses and on the jury. And Hugh did likewise.

And the sheriff was commanded to hold the inquest thereon; and he commanded the inquest for a certain day. And the verdict was that the said Ralph freely and of his own will and without coercion demised the

---

[28] 'defendit convencionem illam sed dixit.' The word 'defendit' was usually used in the sense of 'deny': see *supra*, p. 35, n. But in the present context the defendant is rather offering a plea of confession and avoidance.

said land to the said Hugh for a term of ten years and that he made the charters which the said Hugh has.

And Ralph did not come; and he had a day *in banco*. Wherefore it was adjudged that the covenant be kept and that Hugh should have his seisin for the term of ten years, counting the year for which the said Hugh had held, etc.; and that Ralph be in mercy, etc.

DE LA DUN v. BASSET
BRACTON'S NOTE-BOOK, PLEA 1129
A.D. 1234

Gregory de la Dun complains of Gilbert Basset that, whereas by a covenant made between Alan Basset, father of the said Gilbert whose heir he is, and William de la Dun, father of the said Gregory whose heir he is, he ought to have in Brocwde which was in the demesne of the lord King Richard the uncle of the lord the King that now is [feeding for] one hundred pigs free of pannage[29] . . ., the said Gilbert does not permit the said Gregory to have his pigs in the said wood as the aforesaid William his father had and as he himself has been wont to have according to the aforesaid covenant; but that he has taken the said pigs and kept them detained against gage and pledge . . .; and of this he puts himself upon the country. . . .

And Gilbert comes and denies the force and the injury (*et defendit vim et injuriam*), and asks judgment if he ought to answer, inasmuch as he [Gregory] produces no suit save his own voice, neither does he show any writing to support the covenant said to be made between their fathers, nor does he offer any certificate of the damages which he claims. . . .

And because the aforesaid Gregory produces no suit save his own single voice nor shows a charter or other evidence of any covenant . . ., it is adjudged that Gilbert go in peace upon this writ, and that Gregory be in mercy.

THE STATUTE OF WALES
12 ED. I. A.D. 1284
Cap. 6.   Breve de Conventione

Rex vicecomiti salutem. Præcipe A. quod iuste et sine dilatione teneat B. conventionem inter eos factam de uno mesuagio et decem acris terræ et quinque acris bosci cum pertinentiis in N. Et nisi fecerit, etc., tunc summoneas prædictum A. quod sit, etc. ostensurus, etc.[30]

. . . And let there be writs of Covenant according to the complaints of the contracting parties and the diversity of the cases. . . .

Cap. 10

Concerning the Third Article in which there is provided the Writ of Covenant, whereby sometimes movables are demanded and sometimes im-

[29] *Pannage* was either the right to turn out swine to feed for a certain period on the beech mast and acorns in another's wood, or, as in the above case, the payment due to the owner of the wood for the exercise of this right. Cf. *supra*, p. 5.

[30] Cf. the specimen cited from the Register of Writs by Holdsworth, H.E.L. III. App., p. 663.

movables by force of a covenant entered into between the parties which may derogate from the law . . ., the proceeding upon the writ is thus. . . .[31]

The plaintiff's complaint being heard and his Declaration, the defendant shall make answer; and upon the affirmation of the one party and the denial of the other they shall proceed to the Inquest, and the business shall be determined by the Inquest of the country. And it is to be known that sometimes a freehold is demanded by the writ of Covenant; as where any man letteth land to another to farm, rendering therefor a certain rent, under a condition added thereto in the writing of the Covenant that, if he be not satisfied for the rent, it shall be lawful for him to enter into the land that he hath demised and hold the same. If he to whom the land hath been demised do not pay the rent and he who demised it hath not the means of entering into the land demised according to the tenor of his writing, by reason of the power of his adversary, in this case he ought to recover the tenement by the writ of Covenant together with damages.

Where sometimes a covenant is made between parties that the one shall enfeoff the other of a certain tenement and shall deliver seisin unto him at a certain day, if afterwards he shall transfer that tenement by feoffment to a third person, since he cannot annul that feoffment by virtue of the prior contract that was not carried into effect, in that case the injured party cannot have other redress by writ of Covenant save satisfaction in money for his damages. And thus in one case there lieth an action to demand a tenement by writ of Covenant, and in another case money as damages or the tenement.

And because contracts in covenants are infinite, it would be difficult to make mention of each in particular. But, according to the nature of each covenant, by the affirmation of the one party and the denial of the other it will either come to be tried by the Inquest upon the facts or it will come to an acknowledgment of the writings brought into judgment and judgment will be awarded according to that acknowledgment; or the writings will be denied and then it will come to an inquiry into the making of the writings by the witnesses named in the writings, if there be such, together with the jury (*cum patria*); and if there should be no witnesses named or they should be dead, then by the jury only.

CORBET'S CASE

Y.B. 20 & 21 Ed. I. (R.S. p. 222)

A.D. 1292

One Thomas Corbet brought a Bill of Covenant[32] against B., saying that, whereas it was agreed (*covynt*) between them on the occasion of a Jousting held in the suburb of Salop that Thomas should lend (*bayla*) his horse worth £20 to the aforesaid B. on condition that, if the horse were maimed or killed in the field so that he could not restore the horse in as good a condition as when he received it, B. should pay to him £20 at the Christmas next ensuing, Thomas delivered the horse to him and the horse was maimed, in consequence whereof it died while in his [B.'s] custody; and that Thomas

---

[31] Here follows an account of the steps to be taken if the defendant makes default.
[32] See a second version of the case given in Appendix II. of the same volume, where it is argued that the plaintiff should have proceeded by writ and not by bill.

came at Christmas and demanded the £20 pursuant to the aforesaid covenant, but that nothing [had been paid] tortiously [*a tort*], etc.

Lowther: What have you to prove the covenant?

Spigurnel: Good suit.

Lowther: Have you anything else?

Spigurnel said not.

Lowther: We ask judgment if we should answer to his suit without a writing.

ANON[33]
Y.B. 4 ED. II. (S.S. VOL. 42, p. 171)
A.D. 1311

One Alice brought her writ of covenant against John de la Rokele of nine acres of wood which this same John held of the lease of this same Alice,[34] who held these same tenements in dower of the inheritance of one Elaine:— Whereas this same John has wrongfully (*a tort*) gone against the covenant and has made waste and sale of the wood aforesaid, that is to say, of one thousand oaks appraised at, etc.[35]; whereupon Elaine, of whose inheritance Alice held this same wood, on a certain day and in a certain year brought a writ of waste before Sir Ralph of Hengham[36] and his fellows, and the waste was found and the damages were taxed at eighteen pounds; whereupon Elaine recovered her damages against this same Alice, so that John has wrongfully, etc., to her damage, etc.

Esthalle: Sir, we do not think that she ought to be answered on such a count and such a writ, for she has laid her action on an act of waste which she assigns; but he who wishes to recover in such a case must recover two things, to wit, the principal and the accessories; therefore, inasmuch as by the law of the land she cannot recover the principal, which would be the soil, without a writ of waste, which is provided as a remedy in such a case, we ask judgment whether she ought to be answered on this writ or this count, for they imply only the recovery of damages.

BEREFORD, C.J.: If she were not answered on this writ, she would be without a recovery, for according to your statement you would drive her to a writ of waste which she could not use, for she could not say that ' he has made waste to her disinheritance, etc.'[37] Therefore answer further.

Esthalle: What have they of the covenant?

Toudeby: We wish to aver that the lease was made to you, as above.

Scotre: And we ask judgment, seeing that they have counted by a covenant, in that they say that 'wrongfully and against covenant, etc.,' which is in its nature a matter of specialty; and she shows no specialty, but offers an averment which ought not to be received in lieu of specialty.

[38]*Toudeby*: It would not be lawful for him to make waste of the tenements leased to him in this fashion if there were no specialty which witnessed

---

[33] Two reports of this case are given in this volume. The present transcription is from the second report, save for interpolations noted as from the first.

[34] According to the first report, the lease was for the life of the lessor without waste.

[35] According to the first report, the oak trees were appraised at half a mark each. Complaint was also made of the felling of a hundred apple trees.

[36] The immediate predecessor as Chief Justice of the Common Pleas of Sir William de Bereford. Hengham died in March, 1309.

[37] On the law of waste, see Holdsworth, H.E.L. III. 121-3.

[38] From the first report.

the covenant. Therefore it seems that we ought to be answered without specialty.

Malberthorpe (on the same side): There would be greater need for you to have specialty to excuse your tort, that is to say, specialty showing that he gave you power to make waste in the wood aforesaid, than for him to have specialty in witness of the covenant. Therefore, etc.

BEREFORD, C.J.: If a man lease tenements to another for a term of years without specialty, do you think that he can make waste? (*quasi diceret, Non*). And as she offers to aver the lease, which you do not deny, it seems that this averment is sufficient. Besides, waste is a thing which implies something against the law. Therefore it lies with you to show a specialty to cover your wrong; for, naturally, a specialty ought, if any there be, always to remain with him to whom the lease is made.

[The parties then went to the country on a traverse of the fact of waste.]

BRANDESTON v. BURGH
Y.B. 5 ED. II. (S.S. VOL. 31, p. 216)
A.D. 1312

NOTE FROM THE RECORD

William of Burgh, Archdeacon of Berkshire, is in mercy for several defaults.

The same Archdeacon was summoned to answer Joan daughter of Margaret that was wife of Hugh of Brandeston of a plea that he execute the agreement made between them (*summonitus fuit ad respondendum . . . de placito quod teneat ei convencionem inter eos factam*) to procure a fit and suitable marriage for the same Joan, such as her estate and the condition of her parentage call for and require, and for the provision of the same Joan in all her necessaries at the charges of the said William until that through him she shall have been so married.

And touching this the same Joan doth say by her attorney that, whereas it was agreed between them on the Wednesday in Easter week in the thirtieth year of the reign of King Edward, father of the lord King that now is, at New Sarum, to wit, that the aforesaid William should procure a fit and suitable marriage for the said Joan such as the estate and condition of her parentage require, etc., and also that he should maintain the said Joan in all her necessaries until that she was married as aforesaid through him, the aforesaid William hath not yet procured a marriage for the aforesaid Joan nor hath he provided her with any of her necessaries in accordance with the tenor of the aforesaid covenant; and although the said William hath been often required to perform the aforesaid covenant he hath hitherto refused to perform it and still doth refuse, whereby she saith that she hath suffered loss and hath damage to the amount of a thousand pounds (*unde dicit quod deteriorata est et dampnum habet ad valenciam mille librarum*). And thereof she doth produce suit, etc. And she makes *profert* of a certain writing in the name of the aforesaid William which doth witness the aforesaid covenant in the form aforesaid, etc. (*et profert quoddam scriptum sub nomine predicti Willelmi quod predictam convencionem testatur in forma predicta*).

And William doth come by his attorney and he doth deny force and injury when, etc. (*et defendit vim et iniuriam quando, etc.*), and he saith that he ought not to answer her to this writ, etc.; for he saith that, while it is contained in the aforesaid writing that the same William is bound to maintain the aforesaid Joan in accordance with the aforesaid covenant until that she be married through the same William as is aforesaid, the same Joan by her count (*per narracionem suam*) is attempting to recover her damages against him on the ground that she is not yet married and also for his failure to maintain her, etc., though he is not bound by his writing to procure a marriage for her within any certain time but only to provide for the same Joan the aforesaid maintenance until that marriage, etc. Wherefore, no breach can be imputed to him by reason of the fact that she is not yet married, etc. And thereof he asks judgment, etc.

A day is given them to hear their judgment here in the quindenes of the Holy Trinity (*a die Sanctæ Trinitatis in XV dies*).

Upon which day came the aforesaid Joan, as well as the aforesaid William by the attorney of the aforesaid William, etc.

And he freely admits the aforesaid writing. But he says that the aforesaid Joan complains unjustly, etc. For he says that he himself, on the Monday next after the close of Easter in the third year of the reign of the lord the King that now is, at New Sarum in the presence of John Poverel, John Chynnot, John Claymund, William Everard, Walter of Sihalcoombe and Henry Baudry, did offer to the same Joan a fit and suitable marriage, to wit with a certain Piers, son and heir of Robert de la Mare, of marriageable age, whose inheritance is worth a hundred pounds a year, the which marriage the same Joan did refuse. And this he is ready to aver (*et hoc paratus est verificare*). And as to the provision of the aforesaid maintenance, etc., he says that at the time of the making of the aforesaid writing the said Joan was dwelling at Yattendon in the county of Berkshire and at Sarum in the county of Wiltshire at the charges of this same William, the which William did provide for the same Joan a fitting maintenance in all things necessary to her in accordance with the tenor of the aforesaid covenant until the aforesaid Monday on which he did offer her the aforesaid marriage, etc. And thereof he asks judgment, etc.

And Joan says that at the time of the making of the aforesaid writing she was dwelling at Lapworth in the county of Warwick, and that she was maintained at the aforesaid vill of Yattendon at the charges of the aforesaid Margaret, her mother, and that the aforesaid William made no provision for her maintenance in accordance with the tenor of the aforesaid covenant, as the same William asserts. And she asks that this be inquired of by the country, etc. And touching that which the aforesaid William says, that she did refuse the aforesaid marriage by him offered to her as aforesaid, the same Joan denies that she ever on the aforesaid day and year did refuse a fitting marriage as the same William charges against her. And this she is prepared to maintain against him and his suit in such manner as the Court shall determine.

A day is given to the aforesaid parties here in the octave of St. John the Baptist, etc.

Afterwards upon that day came both the aforesaid Joan and the aforesaid William in their own persons. And the aforesaid Joan did withdraw herself from her aforesaid writ, etc. So the aforesaid William is to go hence without a day, and the aforesaid Joan and her pledges for prosecution are in mercy.

BUCKLAND v. LEUKENORE

EYRE OF KENT, 6 & 7 ED. II. (S.S. VOL. 27, p. 9)

A.D. 1313-4

Command Roger Leukenore that justly and without delay he perform the covenant entered into between him and John Buckland for the construction of two mills at Maidstone for the use of the said John by and at the cost of the said Roger from new building material and timber. And unless, etc. (*Precipe Rogere Leukenore quod iuste et sine dilacione teneat convencionem Johanni de Bokelonde inter eos factam de duobus molendinis ad opus ipsius Johannis apud Madenstan sumptibus ipsius Rogeri in mæremio et carpentaria de novo construendo. Et nisi, etc.*).

This same John brought similar writs against three others, against each one of them severally; and he counted after the manner following, that they wrongfully (*a tort*) had not kept the covenant made between them as set out in the writ. And wrongfully because, whereas in a certain place, day and year it was agreed (*covynt*) between one Peter the Mason and the said John Buckland that the aforesaid Peter the Mason should build two mills as above at his own cost and by a certain time, and whereas for greater security the aforesaid Roger Leukenore and three others, to wit A., B. and C., had bound themselves together with the aforesaid Peter the Mason to carry out the said works and to perform fully the aforesaid covenant, that is to say each had made himself severally responsible for its full performance; yet nevertheless the said Roger Leukenore has not done according to the aforesaid covenants. And so he has gone against his covenant *a tort*, etc.

Cambridge: Judgment of this count. For at the beginning of the count he counted against us as against a principal party to this covenant: then he said in his declaration that a covenant had been made between this John and one Peter the Mason, etc., and that Roger Leukenore had bound himself for greater security; and so he admits that we are merely a pledge.

SPIGURNEL, J.: No, no; he does not say that you are a pledge. He says that Roger and the others fully bound themselves severally as principals to perform this covenant. So answer over.

Cambridge: Let us have the written covenant read.

The writing recited that the covenant was made between John of B. and Peter the Mason only. Then it went on to say that for greater security Roger Leukenore and A., B. and C. are added, each of whom binds himself severally for the whole performance, etc.

Cambridge: Now we demand judgment, since you have counted that Roger and the others bound themselves, and this is not testified by your writing; for the writing says only that ' for greater security I add such and such,' etc. And so it is Peter alone who is speaking, and not Roger. So we demand judgment.

SPIGURNEL, J.: If a man by a writing confesses himself indebted to us, and the writing goes on to say, ' and for further security I procure such an one who binds himself,' and this latter puts his seal to the writing, how can you argue that he does not say the same thing as the other says? He affirms it by the fact of putting his seal to it. So answer to the deed.

Cambridge: Sir, we fully admit the deed. But we say that Peter the Mason sufficiently completed all he was bound to do about the building of the mills, that is, the provision of the timber and the carpentry; but that this John de B., who should have provided whatever iron was needed, refused to do so, so that the work could not be finished through the fault of that same John. Ready, etc.

And so issue was joined.

And the jury found that the aforesaid Peter had completed all the carpenter's work for the mills, but had not put the timber into position, and that it was still lying in a shed in Maidstone. And they said that the aforesaid John of B. should have provided the iron. But because Peter had not carted the timber on to the site of the mills nor put the carpentered beams into position, they could not blame John de B. for not providing the nails and other iron necessaries before the timber was on the ground and the work begun.

And so it was adjudged that the aforesaid John should recover against Roger the twenty marks which he had paid in advance, etc., and that Roger be in mercy. No regard was to be had to the carpentering or to the work done in the streams where the mills were to have been built, a good hundred trunks of timber having been used that were now perished and rotten, for that was all his fault; and the said John was to pay no compensation for it; and his damages, etc.[39]

---

[39] According to the Eyre Roll, the judgment was:—*quod predictus Johannes de Boklonde recuperet dampna sua quæ taxantur per eosdem Justiciarios ad triginta marcas sex solidos et octo denarios.*

⌘ 12 ⌘

ACCOUNT

IN the year 1200 the bailiff to the Archbishop of Canterbury was brought into the Curia Regis to explain why he had failed to render an account of chattels committed to his charge. Six years later the questions on a ' plea of account ' were submitted to four arbitrators, chosen by the parties, and an independent umpire.[1] By 1232 the pleadings in such actions seem to have crystallised,[2] although no writ of account appeared upon the Register until the middle of the century. When it did so appear, it proved to be but another variant of the writ of right: the defendant was ordered *quod reddat rationabilem compotum suum de tempore quo fuit ballivus suus.*[3] The form was adopted, not because contemporary lawyers detected any proprietary flavour in the proceedings, but simply as a convenient and familiar precedent.

Already the bailiffs administering manorial land formed a professional class, and one of them had even compiled a handy manual for ' cooking accounts.'[4] Where such lucrative temptations were offered to so many men, the meshes of the law might be expected to have been drawn tight around them. They were, in fact, singularly loose. The writ of account depended at common law on process against the land of a bailiff, and, if he had none, it was without effect. It is not surprising, therefore, that the lords of manors should have sought superior aid. The Statute of Marlborough of 1267 provided that defaulting bailiffs, who had no land, should be arrested on a peculiar and stringent writ known as a *Monstravit de Compoto,* and both the scope and the severity of the remedy were extended in 1285 by the Statute of Westminster II.[5] It was to apply not only to bailiffs as such but to ' all manner of receivers,' and their employers were empowered themselves

---

[1] See *Introduction to the Curia Regis Rolls,* 1199-1230, *A.D.* (S.S. Vol. 62), p. 292.
[2] *Hautun* v. *Preston,* B.N.B. Plea 859, *infra,* p. 276.
[3] The first register in which the writ appeared was that described by Maitland as ' older than 1259 ': *Coll. Papers* II. 142, 146.
[4] For a portrait of a professional bailiff of the mid-thirteenth century and his treatise, see *Robert Carpenter and the Provisions of Westminster* in *Collected Papers on Mediæval Subjects,* by N. Denholm-Young, p. 94, esp. at p. 100.
[5] *Infra,* pp. 277-8. The form of the *monstravit de compoto* is thus given in F.N.B. 117H. ' The King to the sheriff, etc. The prior of N. hath shewed unto us that, whereas A. was his bailiff in K., having the care and administration of all his affairs and goods, the same A., his account not being paid, seeking subterfuges, lies hid in your bailiwick, nor can he be found and distrained to render to the said prior his account aforesaid; and because by the common council of our realm it is provided that, if bailiffs who are bound to render account to their lords do withdraw themselves and have not lands or tenements whereby they may be distrained, they shall be attached by their bodies, so that the sheriff in whose bailiwick they be found shall cause them to come to render their account, we command you that, if the aforesaid prior shall make you secure of prosecuting

268

to appoint auditors and, subject to a possible appeal to the Barons of the Exchequer, to secure their imprisonment. Nor did the story end there. The officials responsible for keeping the prisons were enjoined not to release their charges without the consent of the creditors, and they were made liable in Debt for any damages caused by neglect of this injunction. So in 1318 the Sheriffs of the City of London were sued for allowing the plaintiff's debtor to leave Newgate.[6] A nice point of interpretation arose upon these statutes. Could their machinery be used where the person summoned to account indeed possessed land, but where its value was inadequate to satisfy the arrears? Such a case was within the spirit, but against the letter, of the statutes. The letter prevailed, and any interest in land, however slight, sufficed to remit a plaintiff to the barren process of the common law.[7]

Account was of great importance throughout the middle ages, and actions were numerous. Thus, on the plea rolls of the Common Bench for the three terms, Trinity and Michaelmas, 16 Edward III, and Hilary, 17 Edward III, there are no less than 159 entries of Account as against 46 of Debt and 31 of Covenant.[8] The defendant might be sued in one of three capacities: as guardian in socage, as bailiff or as receiver. The liability of the guardian in socage derived expressly from the Statute of Marlborough, and its extent was eagerly canvassed. Thus in 1293 the court discussed the power of a ward to bring the action before he had reached his majority. It was objected that, since no infant could be bound by a release, the guardian might find himself subjected to a second suit after the infant had come of age; but it was generally agreed that the action would lie, provided that the ward acknowledged any final settlement in fact reached by a document recorded upon the rolls of the court.[9] The conduct of the bailiff or estate agent, who, it has been seen, was the earliest type of accountant, was a constant source of litigation, and the sums at stake were sometimes considerable. The bailiff of two manors in Lincolnshire was summoned to give an account of his stewardship for the first eight years of the reign of Edward III, and the damages were laid at £10,000.[10]

his claim, then attach the aforesaid A., so that you may have him before our justices, etc. on such a day, to render to the aforesaid prior his account aforesaid, as he shall reasonably show that he ought to render to him, etc.'
[6] *Thorpe's Case*, 11 Ed. II (S.S. Vol. 61), p. 265.
[7] *Box v. Palmer* (1310) Y.B. 3 Ed. II. (S.S. Vol. 20, p. 91) *infra*, p. 278. So in *Anon* (1313) Y.B. 7 Ed. II. (S.S. Vol. 39, p. 9), counsel said, 'I am entitled to an account for £1,000, and the other party hath naught but a single acre of land,' but he was not allowed to use the machinery of the statutes. On the whole question, see Plucknett, *Statutes and their Interpretation in the Fourteenth Century*, pp. 84-5.
[8] See the statistics offered by Pike, Introduction to Y.B. 20 Ed. III., Vol 2 (R.S.), at p. xxxix. For a survey of Account in general, see pp. xxvii-xxxvii. The learned editor remarks, with justice, that Maitland seriously under-estimated the importance of the writ, when he said (Forms of Action, p. 64), 'that the common law action of Account remains at a low level of development.'
[9] *Nota*, Y.B. 20 & 21 Ed. I (R.S.), p. 318, and see *Anon*, Y.B. 1 & 2 Ed. II (S.S. Vol. 17), p. 107.
[10] Intro. to Y.B. 20 Ed. III, Vol. 2 (R.S.), p. xxxvi.

To sue a defendant as 'receiver' was the most popular as it was the most general of the counts. The Year Books and Plea Rolls testify to the eager commercial life of the fourteenth and fifteenth centuries, and reveal the limits within which the common law was prepared to lend its sanction. In 1305 a plaintiff, expressly declaring on the Law Merchant, described the defendant as 'receiver of his monies in London, Dublin and Cork,' and sought, though without success, to meet the objection that the Irish transactions were beyond the jurisdiction of the English courts by citing a custom of the company of Lombards that 'where the contract is made, there shall the contractor be attached.'[11] In 1312 a defendant was sued for £135, alleged to have been received at Norwich for 'spices and divers merchandises' sold on the plaintiff's account, and the case was remitted to the franchise court of that city.[12] The count was of especial interest as a remedy in partnership, a legal conception which was a complex and ubiquitous feature of mediæval England and the ramifications of which were endless. Archbishop and deacon, widow and taverner, city merchant and London lawyer, hustled each other in the market for wool and silk, for wine and sugar and spice, for precious relics—the bones and blood and even the tears of the saints—for anything and everything, in short, which might seem to offer rich or quick returns.[13] The declaration in such cases soon came to be common form. The defendant was to 'render his reasonable account of the time during which he was the receiver of the monies of the plaintiff, accruing by any cause or from any contract whatsoever to the common profit' of the parties.[14] Foreign as well as native interests were involved. In the year 1343 the great house of the Peruzzi of Florence, with large English connections, went bankrupt, and the legal calendar was filled with actions of account brought by speculators who had invested their capital in the company and who now sought to save what they could from the wreck. Thomas Corpe, merchant, alleged a receipt by the company's agents of £160, entrusted to them at two several times in Sloper's Lane, St. Pancras; Serjeant Pulteney, a familiar figure in the Year Books, sued similarly for £200; a plaintiff, romantically described as John Coupegorge, clerk, claimed no less than £3,000; and the same sum was alleged by William de la Mare and other executors of the

---

[11] *Anon*, Y.B. 32 & 33 Ed. I. (R.S.) 377. See also *Box* v. *Palmer* (1310), *infra*, p. 278.
[12] *Scottow* v. *Birkeleghe* (1312) Y.B. 5 Ed. II (S.S. Vol. 33) 205. For another case remitted to the same court, see *Repps* v. *Repps*, *infra*, p. 282.
[13] Maitland's view, that partnership played little part in the law or economy of mediæval England (*Forms of Action*, 64), cannot be supported. See Plucknett, Y.B. 13 Rich. II (Ames Foundation) xlviii and 153: *Anon* (1306), Y.B. 33 and 35 Ed. I (R.S.) 295: *Anon* (1337), Y.B. 11 & 12 Ed. III (R.S.) 315: *Anon* (1341), Y.B. 15 Ed. III (R.S.) 261: *Salman* v. *Barkyng* (1422), Y.B. 1 Hen. VI (S.S. Vol. 50) 114, where the defendant's ship was chased by Breton pirates on to the Norman coast and there pilfered by wreckers, with the loss, *inter alia*, of loaf sugar, currants and cinnamon belonging to the Bishop of London; and the numerous cases cited in Introduction to Y.B. 20 Ed. III, Vol. 2 (R.S.) xxx-xxxvi.
[14] See *Babbe* v. *Inge* (1315), *infra*, p. 281.

Archbishop of York to have been received by the company ' wherewith to traffic for the Archbishop's profit and whereof they had refused to render an account.'[15]

A plaintiff was often in doubt whether to describe the defendant as a bailiff or as a receiver. The distinction was thus drawn. A bailiff was a man who, as befitted his primary character of estate agent, dealt with farm stock and produce and must answer for the proceeds of their sale. A receiver was one to whom other goods or money had been entrusted by way of trade. Thus in 1309 a *monstravit de compoto* was brought against a defendant as ' *receptor denariorum suorum.*' The plaintiff alleged that he had consigned cloth and wool to the defendant for sale and that no account had been rendered of the result. The writ was challenged on the ground that the defendant should have been sued as ' bailiff,' but was upheld.[16] In *Pirton* v. *Tumby* the plaintiff described the defendant as ' his bailiff of a certain messuage for linens and cloths,' and Chief Justice Bereford declared the writ to be wrongly framed. The defendant might have been bailiff of the messuage, but he could only be receiver of the linen and cloth.[17] In *Repps* v. *Repps* the same learned judge was for once without an answer. The plaintiff had sued the defendant as receiver of money for cattle and corn sold at Norwich by the plaintiff herself. The Chief Justice objected that, as farm produce was in issue, the defendant was a bailiff, not a receiver; but counsel pointed out that the defendant was required to account, not for the sale, which in fact had been conducted by his employer, but for the money thereby realised which had been committed to his charge.[18]

These three categories of accountants, though the appropriate choice might be a matter of nice discrimination, were still only pleading formulæ. A plaintiff was allowed, within limits, to include within one or other of them persons who, in an exact sense, were outside their connotation. The law, in other words, recognised ' constructive ' guardians, bailiffs and receivers. In 1308 an interesting argument took place upon the possibility of using the action given by the Statute of Marlborough in the case of the guardian in socage against a third person to whom the lawful guardian had leased the wardship. The argument was inconclusive, but it was generally agreed that the action would lie at least against a total stranger who, without any colour of right, had usurped the wardship. In the words of counsel, ' we pray

---

[15] See the cases cited and references given in Introduction to Y.B. 20 Ed. III, Vol 2 (R.S.) xxx-xxxv. For an account of the Florentine house of the Peruzzi, see Renouard, *Les Relations des Papes d'Avignon et des Compagnies Commerciales et Bancaires de 1316 á 1378* (pub. Paris, 1941), especially, Part I, Chap. II. They were prepared to receive investments from anyone and put them to any speculation which promised profit. In M. Renouard's words, ' leur but est de gagner de l'argent, et elles ne négligent absolument aucun moyen d'y parvenir ' (p. 64).
[16] *Anon,* Y.B. 2 & 3 Ed. II (S.S. Vol. 19) 34.
[17] (1315) Y.B. 8 Ed. II (S.S. Vol. 41) 59, *infra*, p. 280.
[18] (1315) Y.B. 9 Ed. II (S.S. Vol. 45) 71, *infra*, p. 282.

judgment whether we ought not to have an account, since he who had the profit of the land ought by law to be charged with the account.'[19] So, too, it was accepted that a man who acted as bailiff of an estate, though without prior engagement, was accountable for the results. Chief Justice Brian declared in 1489 that, ' if I have lands and a man receives my rents without my assent, the fact of the receipt will render him liable.'[20] Even the province of the receiver, rich as it was, was extended by a similar process of construction. It was ruled in 1368 that a man might use Account or Debt at his option to recover money which, to borrow the language of a later generation, had been paid on a consideration which had wholly failed, or, in a still more comprehensive phrase, as money received to the plaintiff's use; and in the same case the writ was envisaged as the remedy of the beneficiary upon a trust of money.[21] If A. delivered money to B. to the use of C., and B. failed to pay it to C., A. might sue B. in Debt, but C.'s only remedy was in Account.[22] The position was summarised by Fitzherbert in the early sixteenth century. ' A man shall have a writ of account against one as bailiff or receiver where he was not his bailiff or receiver; for, if a man receive money for my use, I shall have an account against him as receiver, or, if a man deliver money unto another to deliver over unto me, I shall have an account against him as my receiver.'[23] At the end of the century the writ was used, by a further extension, to recover money paid by mistake. In *Framson* v. *Delamere*,[24] the defendant had sued a third party in another action and the plaintiff had acted as the latter's bail. The defendant had won and the plaintiff had paid. It then appeared that, as the third party's name had been mis-spelt in the judgment, the payment was unnecessary, and the plaintiff was allowed to recover the sum in an action of account. In *Hewer* v. *Bartholomew*[25] the plaintiff had paid £100 to the defendant, thinking it to be due under a mortgage which had in fact been discharged. 'Although,' said the Court, ' the plaintiff delivered the £100 to the defendant as his own, not knowing the law therein, supposing it to be due; yet, in regard he did not give it otherwise nor upon other consideration, the defendant received it as the plaintiff's money and is accountable for it.'

---

[19] *Anon*, Y.B. 1 & 2 Ed. II (S.S. Vol. 17) 107.

[20] *The Case of the Dean of St. Paul's*, Y.B. 4 Hen. 7, Pasch. f. 6, pl. 2.

[21] *Anon*, Y.B. Pasch. 41 Ed. III, f. 10, pl. 5, *infra*, p. 285, and see *supra*, p. 223. See also *Core's Case* (1537) Dyer, 20a, *infra*, p. 285. If the subject-matter of the ' use ' were chattels and not money, the appropriate remedy was Detinue: see *Anon* (1339) Y.B. 12 & 13 Ed. III. (R.S.) 245.

[22] It was not until the seventeenth century that Debt was allowed as alternative to Account: *Harris* v. *de Bervoir* (1625) Croke Jac. 687.

[23] F.N.B. 116 Q. On the whole question of ' constructive ' account, see Ames, *Lectures on Legal History*, 117-121, and Jackson, *History of Quasi-Contract*, 10-17 and 30-1.

[24] (1595) Croke Eliz. 458.

[25] (1598) Croke Eliz. 614. See Jackson, *History of Quasi-Contract*, 6-7.

Such divagations from the idea of agreement suggest that the writ, wide as was its scope, was yet remote from the principle of contract. The relations between the plaintiff and the defendant may or may not have derived from a prior arrangement, but the liability to account was in either event imposed *ab extra*. A defendant who, in conventional phrase, pleaded that ' he was never the plaintiff's receiver to render account,' denied not his consent but his status; nor could he voluntarily assume liability unless he chanced to fall within the accepted categories of the law. The affinity of the action was to quasi-contract rather than to contract.[26]

However it was to be rationalised, the writ was clearly a valuable weapon for the protection of agricultural and commercial interests. It would have been still more valuable but for serious flaws in its procedure. In the first place, like Debt and Detinue, it was subject, in theory at least, to wager of law. In the reign of Edward III, indeed, a fiction was adopted to avoid this method of defence. It was ruled in 1340 that a defendant might wage his law where the plaintiff alleged a receipt from his own hands, but that, if the receipt were through a third party, the case must go to a jury.[27] Practitioners seized upon this nice distinction to avoid a process already felt to be archaic, and within two years counsel described a ' custom to count in general terms that the defendant was the plaintiff's receiver, without saying by whose hands; and afterwards, to oust the defendant from his wager of law, the mode was invented of a receipt by the hands of other persons.'[28] But, while wager of law itself might thus be defeated, the complementary rule remained that, wherever in principle this mode of trial was available, no action would lie against personal representatives; and their immunity was sustained until removed by statute in 1706.[29] There is also authority for the further proposition that the writ could not be used by an heir against the original receiver, even if the latter had expressly bound himself to render an account both to the original creditor and to his heirs.[30]

In the second place, the proceedings on the writ involved at least two and possibly three separate stages. When the action first came before the court, the sole question for the judges was whether or not the defendant was liable to account: all details were reserved for examination by the auditors.

> ' Note, that in Account the plea was *Never his Receiver*, and the inquest was taken by SHARDELOWE, J. and SHARSHULLE, J. at Nisi Prius; and the jury found that the defendant was receiver, but of

[26] See Jackson, pp. 15 and 32, and Plucknett, *Concise History*, 4th ed., p. 599.
[27] *Anon*, Y.B. 14 Ed. III (R.S.) 172. The distinction may have turned upon the fact that the third party, unlike the original parties, was allowed to offer his own evidence to the jury.
[28] *Anon*, Y.B. 16 Ed. III (R.S. Vol. II) 24, per *Thorpe, arguendo*, at p. 26.
[29] See *Core's Case* (1537), *infra*, p. 285, and 4 & 5 Anne, cap. 16, s. 27.
[30] *Anon*, Y.B. 18 & 19 Ed. III (R.S.) 406.

much less than the sum of which the plaintiff had counted. And they would not charge the quantity, of how much he was receiver, for that will have to be tried before auditors.'[31]

If the defendant were found liable to account, the case was then sent to auditors, appointed by the court *ad hoc* with some regard to their individual qualifications. Thus in 1329 'two clerks of the Bench' were appointed together with 'one merchant of the city of York who was knowledgeable in merchandise.'[32] The examination before the auditors might be both complicated and protracted. Not only could each item be disputed, but incidental issues of fact might be raised which must themselves be settled either by the production of a sealed document, by wager of law or by the verdict of a jury. In 1346 a defendant offered to the auditors

> 'certain acquittances and also tallies showing payment which were sealed with the plaintiff's seal. As to the acquittances, the plaintiff denied them, and on that matter they joined issue to a jury; and as to the tallies, the plaintiff offered to verify by his law that they were not his tallies.'[33]

When at length the auditors found a precise sum due, the plaintiff, if it were not paid, must bring Debt for its recovery, and the defendant might then challenge afresh the individual items allowed in the examination.

That the division of labour between judge and auditors, while clear in principle, was not without delicacy in practice, appears from the case of the *Bishop of Chichester* in 1338.[34] The Bishop sued the defendant both as bailiff and as receiver, but it was upon the latter claim that the substantial difficulty arose. The defendant admitted the receipt of several sums of money, but said that he had paid over to third parties by the Bishop's orders all of them save one and that this one he had received from the Bishop as a gift. There was no doubt that his admission required him to account in all the cases save in that of the alleged gift, and the assertion that he had disposed of the monies in accordance with his instructions was a point to be made, not to the judges whose function was to determine the duty to account, but to the auditors who would analyse the items actually due to the plaintiff. But what was the appropriate process in the case of the alleged gift? Did this affect the scope of the duty to account or did it lie within the detailed calculations which would ensue only when the limits of that duty had been settled? It was resolved after discussion that the primary liability of the defendant was in question and that a finding by the jury on the allegation of the gift must precede the inquiry by the auditors.

[31] *Anon* (1340), Y.B. 13 & 14 Ed. III (R.S.) 300.
[32] *Anon*, Y.B. 3 Ed. III, f. 10, pl. 30.
[33] *Anon*, Y.B. 20 Ed. III. (R.S. Vol. II) 470.
[34] *The Bishop of Chichester's Case* (1338) Y.B. 11 & 12 Ed. III (R.S.) 489, *infra*, p. 283.

The time and expense involved in these several stages and in the apportionment of the appropriate issues were sufficiently embarrassing to suggest the expediency of an alternative remedy. To sue in Debt would eliminate the proceedings before the auditors, and there were instances in which the plaintiff was allowed to use it at his option.[35] But its efficacy as a substitute was severely limited by the rule that it lay only for a precise sum, and the whole purpose of Account in the majority of cases was to reduce to such a sum an initial indeterminate liability. The solution was found not through the Common Law but in Equity. Dr. Jackson, indeed, has doubted whether the intervention of the Chancellor offered any real prospect of quicker relief.[36] While it is true that expedition is not the most conspicuous feature in the history of English Equity, there is no reason to suppose that his predecessors anticipated either the learning or the prolixity of Lord Eldon's doubts, and earlier litigants may well have been tempted to try their fortunes before a tribunal not yet wholly encumbered with technicality. But Dr. Jackson is surely right in finding the main attraction of Equity in its superior machinery. The rudimentary rules of evidence at the Common Law forbade both the examination of the parties and the discovery of documents, and it was in Account, of all actions, that the plaintiff felt the urge to scrape the conscience of the defendant as closely and as painfully as the law would permit.[37]

An early appeal was made to the Chancellor in 1385, and similar suits in the fifteenth century were not uncommon.[38] But it was not until the latter half of the seventeenth century that cases appeared with any prominence in the reports. During the reign of Charles II the East India Company sought more than once to call its factors to account, and many suits were entertained by and against the representatives of deceased partners.[39] The Chancellor was wedded to no single method of procedure. On one occasion he remitted the case to a committee of merchants with instructions for their guidance, while on another Lord Jeffreys expressed himself in ominous terms upon the methods and capacity of City aldermen.[40] Nor did he claim an exclusive jurisdiction. He recognized the common law powers and intervened at his discretion. Thus in 1688 he allowed the Countess of Plymouth to file a bill against her steward although she had previously attempted an action at law, while in 1692 he dismissed

---

[35] *Supra*, p. 272.
[36] Jackson, *History of Quasi-Contract*, p. 36.
[37] See Blackstone, *Comm.* III. Ch. 9, *infra*, p. 392.
[38] Barbour, *History of Contract in Early English Equity* (Oxford Studies in Social and Legal History, Vol. IV), p. 16.
[39] See *East India Co.* v. *Blake* (1673) Cases in Chancery, *temp.* Finch, 117, and *East India Co.* v. *Mainston* (1677) Cases in Chancery, Part II, 218: *Heyne* v. *Middlemore* (1666) Reports in Chancery, f. 410, and *Fashon* v. *Atwood* (1680) Cases in Chancery, Part II, 6.
[40] See *Holstcom* v. *Rivers* (1670) Cases in Chancery, Part I, 127, and *Newdigate* v. *Johnson* (1685) Cases in Chancery, Part II, 170.

the bill of a widow who had neglected to promote it until long after the dissolution of her husband's partnership.[41]   The common law action itself was made more palatable by the Statute of 1706 which not only allowed representatives to be sued, but also empowered auditors to examine the parties on oath.   But, despite this belated encouragement, it could not compete with equity, and it was said in 1763 that ' actions of Account are almost laid aside.'[42]

A final attempt to revive the common law action was made in 1770 in the case of *Godfrey* v. *Saunders*.[43]   The plaintiff, a London merchant, had shipped a cargo of coral beads to India to be traded with by the defendant and one Solomon Solomons.   The latter had since died, and the plaintiff sued the defendant in account in the Common Pleas.   The pleadings comprised a declaration, three pleas, a replication, a rejoinder and a sur-rejoinder.   The plaintiff obtained a verdict at Nisi Prius in June 1768 and a judgment that the defendant should account in the following Michaelmas.   Three auditors were appointed in the Hilary term, 1769; in Trinity the defendant pleaded before them and the plaintiff demurred to this plea.   The demurrer was twice argued before the full Court and judgment was ultimately given for the plaintiff in Trinity term, 1770.   But Chief Justice Wilmot confessed his inability to determine either the proper form of the judgment or the quantum of damages, and concluded:[44]

> ' It seems to us that judgment should be for the value laid in the declaration; but you will consider of this, because the plaintiff is very old, and, if he dies, it is said in some of the books that the whole is at an end and you must begin again.   Whether this is so, we do not determine, but it is proper to be expeditious; for this cause has been depending fourteen years (though there has been no delay in this court) and it is high time it should be ended.'

' I am glad,' his lordship added, ' to see this action of account revived in this court.'   Litigants might be forgiven if they did not carry a similar sense of gratification so far as to risk a further experiment.

SOURCES

HAUTUN v. PRESTON
BRACTON'S NOTE-BOOK, PLEA 859
A.D. 1232

Theobald Hautun claims against John Preston that he render to him a reasonable account for the time during which he was his bailiff of his

[41] Cf. *Countess of Plymouth* v. *Bladon* (1688) 2 Vernon, 32 and *Sherman* v. *Sherman* (1692) 2 Vernon, 276.
[42] *Wood's Institutes*, 9th ed., Book IV., Chap. IV, p. 553.   See also *Equity Cases Abridged*, 4th ed. (1756), p. 5.
[43] 3 Wilson, 73.
[44] 3 Wilson, at p. 117.

manor of Mereflet (*quod reddat ei compotum racionabilem de tempore quo fuit ballivus suus de manerio suo*), and whereof he says that he is in arrears for three years and that he has suffered loss to the value of two hundred marks.

And John comes and says that he was never bailiff nor did he ever have that manor in his keeping from the said Theobald, but rather from a certain Adam of Mereflet, and that he has rendered his account to the said Adam and has received quittance; and that the said Adam was the bailiff of the said Theobald and was put in that position by Theobald, as the said John says; and of this he calls the said Adam to warranty.

STATUTE OF MARLBOROUGH
(1267) 52 Hen. III
C. 17

It is provided that if land holden in socage be in the custody of the kinsfolk of the heir because the heir is within age, the Guardians shall make no waste nor sale nor any destruction of the same inheritance; but safely shall keep it to the use of the said heir, so that when he cometh to his lawful age they shall answer to him for the issues of the said inheritance by a lawful account (*per legitimam computacionem*), saving to the same Guardians their reasonable costs.

C. 23

It is provided also that if Bailiffs, which ought to make account to their lords (*qui dominis suis compotum reddere tenentur*) do withdraw themselves, and have no lands or tenements whereby they may be distrained; then shall they be attached by their bodies, so that the Sheriff in whose bailiwick they may be found shall cause them to come to make their account (*ad compotum suum reddendum*).

STATUTE OF WESTMINSTER II
(1285) 13 Ed. I
C. 11

Concerning Servants, Bailiffs, Chamberlains and all manner of Receivers, which are bound to yield account (*et quibuscumque receptoribus qui ad compotum reddendum tenentur*), it is agreed and ordained;

That when the Masters of such Servants do assign Auditors to take their account and they be found in arrearages upon the account (all things allowed which ought to be allowed), their bodies shall be arrested and by the testimony of the Auditors of the same account shall be sent or delivered unto the next gaol of the King's in those parts; and shall be received of the Sheriff or Gaoler and imprisoned in iron under safe custody, and shall remain in the same prison at their own cost until they have satisfied their master fully of the arrearages.

Nevertheless, if any person, being so committed to prison, do complain that the Auditors of his account have grieved him unjustly, charging him with receipts that he hath not received or not allowing him expenses or reasonable disbursements, and can find friends that will undertake to bring him before the Barons of the Exchequer, he shall be delivered unto them; and the Sheriff in whose prison he is kept shall give knowledge (*scire faciat*) unto his Master that he appear before the Barons of the Exchequer at a certain day with the rolls and tallies by which he made his account; and in the presence of the Barons or of the Auditors that they shall assign him the account shall be rehearsed and justice shall be done to the parties, so that if he be found in arrearages he shall be committed to the Fleet, as above is said. And if he flee and will not give account willingly, as is contained elsewhere in other statutes,[45] he shall be distrained to come before the Justices to make his account, if he have whereof to be distrained;

And when he cometh to the Court, Auditors shall be assigned to take his account, before whom if he be found in arrearages and cannot pay the arrearages forthwith, he shall be committed to the gaol to be kept in manner aforesaid;

And if he flee, and it be returned by the Sheriff that he cannot be found, Exigents[46] shall go against him from county to county until he be outlawed, and such prisoner shall not be replevisable.[47] And let the Sheriff or keeper of such gaol take heed, if it be within a Franchise or without, that he do not suffer him to go out of prison by the common writ called Replegiare[47] or by other means, without assent of his Master; and if he do and thereof be convict, he shall be answerable to his Master for the damages done to him by such his servant according as it may be found by the country, and the Master shall have his recovery by Writ of Debt. And if the keeper of the gaol have not wherewith he.may be justiced or wherewithall to pay, his superior, that committed the custody of the gaol unto him, shall be answerable by the same writ.

BOX v. PALMER
Y.B. 3 ED. II. (S.S. VOL. 20, p. 91)
A.D. 1310

Note from the Record

Henry Palmer was attached by his body to answer John Box of a plea that he render to him a reasonable account of the time for which he was the receiver of John's money.

The plaintiff, by his attorney, says that, whereas the defendant was the receiver of his money at Kingston on Hull from the Sunday before Christmas in 35 Ed. I. to the Conversion of St. Paul in 3 Ed. II. and received by parcels a hundred and ten pounds to trade with (*ad mercandisandum*), he refused and still refuses to render an account: damages, a hundred pounds.

---

[45] Statute of Marlborough, c. 23. *Supra*, p. 277.

[46] See Blackstone, Comm. III. 283: 'Where a defendant absconds and the plaintiff would proceed to an outlawry against him . . . a *capias* [must be sued out]. And if the sheriff cannot find the defendant upon the first writ of *capias* and returns a *non est inventus*, there issues out an *alias* writ, and after that a *pluries*. . . . And, if a *non est inventus* is returned upon all of them, then a writ of *exigent*, or *exigi facias* may be sued out, which requires the sheriff to cause the defendant to be proclaimed, required or exacted, in five county courts successively, to render himself; and, if he does, to take him, as in a *capias;* but if he does not appear and is returned *quinto exactus*, he shall then be outlawed.'

[47] For the writ *de homine replegiando*, see F.N.B. 66E—68C.

The defendant comes . . . and says that he ought not to answer him to this writ; for he says that this writ of *monstravit*[48] aids those who exact an account in cases where such receivers or bailiffs have no lands or tenements whereby they may be distrained to render such account, and he says that he has lands and tenements in the vill of Pontefract and elsewhere in the said county by which he may be distrained to render such an account, and so had on the day of writ purchased, to wit, 2 Feb., 3 Ed. II.; and of this he puts himself upon the country.

Issue is joined, the defendant finding six mainpernors.[49] Subsequently a jury at York finds that the defendant has, and on the day of writ purchased had, a messuage in the vill of Pontefract in the right of one Alice his wife, which is worth six shillings a year; and that he has not, so far as the jurors know, any other tenement in the said county or elsewhere. . . .

Afterwards, the defendant confesses that in the time aforesaid he received seventy-seven pounds of the plaintiff's money, and is ready to account. Three auditors are assigned, and he is committed to the Fleet. Afterwards, the account having been heard, the auditors record before the Justices here in the presence of the parties that the defendant is in arrear in thirty-three pounds, eighteen shillings and tenpence halfpenny. So he is re-committed to the Fleet until, etc.

Report from the Year-Book[50]

John Box brought the *Monstravit de Compoto* against Palmer.

Scrope: The defendant has lands whereby he may be justiced. We ask judgment of this writ, which is given by Statute[51] against those who have no lands or tenements by which they can be justiced. . . .

. . . *Herle*: He has only two-thirds of a house and four shillings worth of rent which he took in marriage with his wife.

STANTON, J.: He will have to say whether he has land or tenement in sufficiency.

Scrope: The statute is in our favour, and says nothing of sufficiency. We demand judgment.

BEREFORD, C.J.: We ought to maintain ancient writs wherever they can be maintained rather than the new ones. Since he has offered to aver that he has land and tenement whereby he can be justiced, it therefore behoves you to answer.

Malberthorpe: That would be a great hardship. For my bailiff might owe me two hundred pounds in arrears, and buy just two acres of land and two pennyworth of rent, and then I could never bring him to render account.

Scrope: It will be to the King's prejudice to maintain this writ of account, for as long as he has lands and tenements the Sheriff shall answer for the issues, and that is to the King's advantage.

Herle: We are ready to aver that he has no land or tenements whereby he can be distrained to render account.

Scrope: We are ready to aver that he has land and tenements whereby he can be distrained to render account.

The averment was received; it was said that he had no land.

---

[48] *Supra*, p. 268.
[49] See P. & M. II, 584-590.
[50] I venture to transcribe the translation given by Plucknett, *Statutes and their Interpretation in the Fourteenth Century*, pp. 182-3, in preference to that given by Maitland, *S.S. Vol.* 20, pp. 91-2.
[51] Statute of Marlborough, c. 23. *Supra*, p. 277.

PIRTON v. TUMBY
Y.B. 8 ED. II. (S.S. VOL. 41, p. 59)
A.D. 1315

Adam of Boston[52] brought a writ of account against William Tumby, and says that he wrongfully does not render him an account of the time when he was his bailiff in C.; and he says that William was his bailiff of a messuage in M. from a certain time to another certain time for linens and cloths; and he has frequently applied to him to render him an account thereof, but he wrongfully refuses to render one, to his, Adam's, damage of forty pounds.

Toudeby: We ask judgment, seeing that Adam supposes by his writ and his count that William was his bailiff and he seeks to charge him with the rendering of an account in respect of linens and cloths, and this is merely a matter of money, which cannot be recovered by this writ; for it speaks *de tempore quo ballivus suus*, etc., when it should have run *de tempore quo fuit receptor denariorum*. Judgment whether you can get from us an account of the sale of linens and cloths by this writ.

BEREFORD, C.J. *ad idem*: A writ running *de tempore quo fuit ballivus noster* infers that he is called on to render an account of such things as were capable of increase, as, for instance, your cows, sheep and fowls or the corn in your granary and the like. But in respect of linens and cloths the account can be of money only; or you might have said *de tempore quo fuit ballivus noster* of the messuage and *receptor noster* of the cloth.

Russell: I cannot sue him as the receiver of moneys, for then the averment would always be open to him that he was not the receiver of my moneys, for it might be that he had sold nothing.

Toudeby: You might then have brought your writ of Detinue of chattels against him. And so we say that he was never your bailiff of a messuage; ready, etc.

And the plaintiff joined issue. And this averment was put on the roll by BEREFORD, C.J. without any reference to linens or cloths. William Tumby found mainpernors.

Note from the Record

William Tumby of Boston . . . was summoned to answer Walter Pirton of Boston of a plea that he render him his reasonable account of the time when he was his bailiff in the vill of Boston (*ad respondendum . . . de placito quod reddat ei racionabilem compotum suum de tempore quo fuit ballivus suus in villa de sancto Botulpho*). And as to this the same Walter, by William Tinton his attorney, complains that, whereas the aforesaid William acted as his, Walter's, bailiff in the aforesaid vill of Boston from St. Barnaby the Apostle's Day in the thirty-third year of the reign of the lord King Edward, father of the lord King that now is, to Martinmas Day then next following, and throughout the said time had the care and administration of a messuage that was the same Walter's in the same vill and the duty of rendering to the same Walter his account of the profits accruing therefrom, the same Walter often requested the aforesaid William to render him his account thereof, yet the aforesaid William has hitherto refused and still does refuse to render him his account thereof, whereby he says that he has suffered loss and has damage to the amount of forty pounds. And thereof he produces suit, etc.

[52] The plaintiff's real name was Walter Pirton: see the Record, *infra*.

And William comes and denies force and injury, when, etc.; and he wholly denies that he was ever the bailiff of the aforesaid Walter in the aforesaid vill of Boston as the aforesaid Walter says. And of this he puts himself upon the country. And Walter does the like. . . .

BABBE v. INGE

Y.B. 8 Ed. II. (S.S. Vol. 41, p. 66)

A.D. 1315

One Stephen brought a writ of account against a certain Henry, and the writ claimed an account from him *de tempore quo fuit receptor denariorum ipsius Stephani, etc. ad communem utilitatem ipsius Stephani et Henrici.* And the writ was challenged by *Miggeley* because it said 'receiver of the moneys of the said Stephen, etc.' and afterwards said 'for the common profit, etc.,' whereas it ought to have said 'receiver of the moneys of the said Stephen and Henry'; and he asked judgment of the writ.

Stonor: Your deed is so couched, and the writ is in accordance with the deed; wherefore, etc.

BEREFORD, C.J.: It may be that Henry received Stephen's moneys for a moiety of the accruing profit, and of that you ought to give an account.— And he ruled that the writ was good.

And then *Miggeley* proffered on behalf of Henry an acquittance, which was denied; and thereupon an inquest was awarded.

Note from the Record

Henry Inge, merchant, in mercy for several defaults.

The same Henry was summoned to answer Stephen Babbe, merchant, of a plea that he render him his reasonable account of the time during which he, Henry, was the receiver of the moneys of the same Stephen accruing by any cause or from any contract whatsoever to the common profit of the same Henry and Stephen (*quod reddat ei racionabilem compotum suum de tempore quo fuit receptor denariorum ipsius Stephani ex quacunque causa et contractu ad communem utilitatem eorundem Henrici et Stephani preveniencium*). And as to this the same Stephen says by Hugh Bushey his attorney that, whereas the aforesaid Henry was the receiver of the moneys of him, Stephen, from the Tuesday next before the Feast of St. Mary Magdalene in the thirty-third year of the reign of the lord King Edward, father of the lord King that now is, until the Feast of St. Peter in Chains in the thirty-fourth year of the same King, father etc., and during that same time received at Dunstable of the moneys of the same Stephen thirty-one pounds, thirteen shillings and fourpence from the sale of the wool of the same Stephen by the aforesaid Henry to the common profit of both of them, to be accounted for to the same Stephen; yet, though the same Stephen often called upon the aforesaid Henry to render him his reasonable account thereof, the aforesaid Henry has hitherto refused to render him his account thereof, and still refuses; whereby he says that he has suffered loss and has damage to the amount of a hundred pounds. And thereof he produces suit, etc.

And Henry comes and denies force and injury, etc. And he fully admits that he was the receiver of the moneys of the aforesaid Stephen as the aforesaid Stephen says, but he says that the same Stephen cannot exact any account thereof from him. For he says that he, the same Henry, did at other time come to a settlement thereof with the aforesaid Stephen at Leighton Buzzard, to wit, on the Tuesday next before the Feast of the Translation of St. Thomas the Martyr in the fifth year of the reign of the King that now is, and the same Stephen did then in that same place by his writing acknowledge to him, Henry, that neither he, the same Stephen, nor his heirs or executors were entitled to make any further claim upon him, Henry, or to challenge the account. And he proffers that writing under the name of the same Stephen, which testifies this; and thereof he asks judgment, etc.

And Stephen says that he ought not on the pretext of the aforesaid writing to be barred from his action in this matter, for he says that that writing is not his deed. And he is ready to aver this by the country and by the witnesses named in the said writing.

So the Sheriff is commanded to cause to come here (*venire faciat*) on the quindene of the Holy Trinity Adam Coleman, one of the witnesses named, etc., and besides him twelve, etc. . . . to make recognition. . . . And it is to be known that the aforesaid impugned writing remains in the custody of Adam of Herwynton, the King's clerk.

REPPS v. REPPS
Y.B. 9 ED. II. (S.S. VOL. 45, p. 71)
A.D. 1315

Maude, the daughter of Edmund Repps, brought a writ of account against Lawrence Repps, and counted that he wrongfully, etc. during the time when he was her receiver of her moneys. And she said that Lawrence received them at Norwich on a certain day, etc., to wit, by the hand of Edmund her father twenty-five marks; and in the same place he received forty marks for cows and other chattels sold by her, whereof he ought to render an account.

BEREFORD, C.J.: You say that he had moneys from the cows, etc., which is a matter in issue. Your writ, therefore, should be of the time when he was your bailiff, and not your receiver.

Malberthorpe: We do not say that *he* sold our cows, etc., but that *we* sold them and that *he* received the moneys.

Upon this the bailiff of the franchise of Norwich came, and demanded the franchise.

Bacon: You ought not to have the franchise, for you should have demanded it before this, and no claim has been put forward hitherto.

Stonor: The writ says *receptor denariorum*, and makes no mention of any certain place where he was receiver. Therefore the bailiff has no need to make a claim, until the plaintiff counts [in his declaration]. Therefore he is within time.

And this was granted by the Court.

Bacon: He has nothing in the franchise by which he can be justiced. Therefore you ought not to have the franchise.

Stonor: Even though he had nothing in the franchise, you cannot on that account refuse the franchise; for, if a default is found in the franchise, then the cause will be re-summoned.

And, notwithstanding these objections, the franchise was allowed.[53]

---

[53] For another case of a successful claim by the city of Norwich, see *Scottow* v. *Birkeleghe* (1312) Y.B. 5 Ed. II (S.S. Vol. 33, p. 205).

Note from the Record

Lawrence Repps . . . was summoned to answer Maude the daughter of Edmund Repps of a plea that he render to her his reasonable account for the time when he was receiver of the moneys of the said Maude (*de placito quod reddat ei racionabilem compotum suum de tempore quo fuit receptor denariorum ipsius Matillidis*). And as to this the same Maude by William Tebaud her attorney says that, whereas the said Lawrence on the Monday next after the Feast of St. Gregory the Pope in the twenty-second year of the reign of King Edward, the father of the King who now is, received at Norwich of the moneys of her the said Maude twenty-five marks by the hands of the aforesaid Edmund, the father of her the said Maude, and also sixty pounds for the said Maude's oxen, cows, steers, wheat and barley sold there by the same Maude for the profit of her the said Maude and for him to render his account thereof when he should be so requested, yet the aforesaid Lawrence has hitherto refused to render to her his account and still refuses; whence she says that she has suffered loss and has damage to the value of one hundred pounds. And thereof she produces suit, etc.

And Lawrence comes. And thereupon the bailiffs of the liberty of the town of Norwich come and crave the court of their aforesaid liberty. And they are told to show to the court why such a liberty should be allowed to them. And thereupon the said bailiffs say that this liberty has been many times allowed to them in the time of the lord King who now is. And because it is found on an inspection of the rolls of the pleas here of Easter term in the third year of the lord King who now is that this liberty was allowed by a writ of the lord King who now is, by an order between one John of Bruges, plaintiff, and John Lay of St. Ives on a plea of account, as appears in the 83rd roll of the same term, therefore let them have their liberty in this plea.

And the bailiffs fixed a day for the parties at Norwich, Monday next after the Feast of St. Thomas the apostle. And they are told to show speedy justice to the parties, or the cause is to return.

THE BISHOP OF CHICHESTER'S CASE

Y.B. 11 & 12 Ed. III. (R.S.) p. 489

A.D. 1338

The Bishop of Chichester brought a writ of Account against R. de S. for the time that he was his bailiff of the manor of L., and also as receiver of his moneys; and he assigned the receipt by divers hands.

Trewith: Whereas you have supposed that he was your bailiff of the manor of L., there was a foreman in the same manor who had the care and administration of all the goods and chattels within the same manor and who was charged to render an account, and R. was sent there by the Bishop to be serjeant and overseer; without this, that he was his bailiff to render an account as he supposes by his writ. Ready, etc. And as to the charge of a receipt by divers hands, as to the whole charge, with one exception, he received the moneys by command of the Bishop and as messenger to pay several sums to divers persons, to whom he has paid them according to the command; without this, that he was his receiver of his moneys to account as he has supposed by his writ. Ready, etc. And as to the exception, he received this by the gift of the Bishop and not to account for it as he has supposed. Ready, etc.

Stouford: As to your statement that you were overseer and not bailiff, we will aver that you were our bailiff as we suppose by our writ and count. And as to all the rest, his plea amounts to no more than that he was not receiver as we suppose; and we will aver our writ.

SHARSHULLE, J.: As to the point that you wish to charge him as bailiff, he has admitted that he was your bailiff in one manner, but not in such manner as to create a duty to account; wherefore you must deny his statement as to the manner of acting as bailiff just as you must in your count against him as receiver. For he has admitted a receipt, and so you must either deny the manner of the receipt as alleged by him, or confess it and demur; for there is no doubt that for such a receipt as he has admitted there is a duty to account, since no other manner of action is available. And as to his statement that he will aver the payment, that may be put by way of answer to the auditors, when he shall come to account; for we are not auditors. Wherefore plead your plea on which you will demur.

Stouford: As to his being our bailiff, we will aver our writ.

And the averment stood.

Stouford: As to the receipt, you see clearly that he has admitted such a receipt as by law he must account for; and the payment to others which he has alleged will go by way of answer before the auditors. Wherefore we pray judgment of his admission and that he may go to account.

Trewith: And we demand judgment, since he has counted that we were his receiver to make a profit and to trade, and now he has admitted the contrary of this. And, moreover, he has asked for the account upon the whole of [the sums involved in] our pleading; whereas for one parcel thereof his count is bad, and so therefore is his [whole] action. Wherefore we pray judgment.

SHARSHULLE, J.: As to your point that he has acknowledged a receipt which was not for the purpose of making a profit or trading, you cannot turn this to your advantage; for it is a profit to him if you obey his order, even though it be not by way of trade. Since, therefore, he has acknowledged the receipt, he can have no other action save by Account, and the law will adjudge you to account. As to your other point—that, inasmuch as he has asked for the account as widely as you have admitted the receipt, including your statement that you received part as a gift, and inasmuch as he therefore admits a demand that you account for something for which no duty to account exists, his count and his writ should abate— his prayer is only that you do account, and not for any certain sum; for by a writ of account the action is only to obtain an account. But when he shall come before the auditors, then he will charge you with what you must answer for, and before them you will be saved from answering if there is anything for which you need not make account. Although, therefore, you say that as to one parcel you were not his receiver, no issue upon this may now be taken before us; but, since you have admitted that for the rest you ought to account, we can give no judgment save that you shall account. . . .

BASSET, J.: When a person offers a plea to a writ of account, such as a denial of parcel of the receipt or of the time during which he was bailiff, the plaintiff must aver his writ at to that parcel; and the inquest shall pass upon this before auditors are appointed. For the auditors cannot take an issue on a point which goes to traverse the writ. (To this most of the

Justices assented.) And when one brings a writ of Account, it is only to obtain an account, and the defendant will only be adjudged to account, so that the Court shall know from the plaintiff's count the certain sum beyond which he cannot charge him.

And then SHARSHULLE, J. said, after consulting with his colleagues, As to all the rest except one parcel, we award an account; and as to what he says the plaintiff gave him, this issue requires an inquest and we discharge you now until the inquest has passed upon it.

ANON
Y.B. PASCH. 41 ED. III. f. 10 pl. 5
A.D. 1368

In a writ of Account the defendant traversed the receipt; and it was found that the plaintiff bailed to the defendant £10 on condition that, if the defendant made him an assurance of certain land, the defendant should keep the £10, but that, if he did not make the assurance by a certain day, he should bail them back to the plaintiff. And the plaintiff said that he had not made the assurance by the day, etc.

Belknap: It is found that he was our receiver; wherefore we pray the account.

Cavendish: It is found that he was not your receiver to render account, but that you bailed to him certain moneys to bail back to you on a certain condition, for which you may have a writ of Debt, and not a writ of Account. Judgment of the writ.

Belknap: We cannot have a writ of Debt, for there is no contract on which we can count. . . .

Cavendish: If I bail certain moneys to you to bail to one John, he will have a writ of Account, because the property is in him as soon as you receive them from my hands, and he cannot have an action by a writ of Debt. But here at the time of the bailment the property was in him by whom the bailment was made, so that he shall have a writ of Debt and not a writ of Account.

WICHINGHAM, J.: When a thing is given on a condition, a man cannot know whose the property is until the condition is either performed or broken; but once the condition is broken, the property is deemed to have been all the time in the donor.

Cavendish: Surely not; for at the time of the bailment the property was in him who received the moneys, but on the breach of the condition an action accrues to the bailor to demand them by a writ of Debt.

THORPE, C.J.: Inasmuch as he may have an action of Debt or an action of Account, he may choose which of them to bring. Wherefore, albeit he may have a writ of Debt, this will not oust him from the action of Account.

And so he was adjudged to account.

CORE'S CASE
(1537) DYER, 20a

In the King's Bench in error the case was thus: That one John Core, grocer of London, brought an action of Debt against the administrators of one George Woddye, and counts upon this bill—

'Be it known to all men by these presents that I, George Woddye of London, have received of John Core the sum of twenty pounds sterling; of which twenty pounds sterling I, the forenamed George, to bear the adventure of the exchange to Roan and there to bestow the said twenty pounds in French prunes, for the behoof and use of the said John, and to see them safely shipped as I do my own wares; this done, the forenamed John to bear all manner of adventure and charge from the quay of Roan in France to his own house in the city of London; in witness whereof, etc.,' with a seal.

And averred in the court that Woddye had not bestowed the money in prunes; and upon this the defendants plead *plene administraverunt*,[54] and found against them; and this matter alleged in arrest of judgment; and yet judgment given.

And now there was error in this: That when the aforesaid Core, before the Justices of our Lord the King of the Bench, by his writ of Debt required against the aforesaid defendants twenty pounds and, in maintenance of his writ, declared on a bill made by the testator in his life-time and in the aforesaid declaration shewn, by this bill it appeared evident that by the law of the land a writ of Account might have been brought and maintained against the aforesaid testator in his life-time, and not a writ of Debt; nor can any writ of Debt by the law of the land be maintained against the administrator; wherefore they pray judgment and that the aforesaid judgment be revoked and annulled, etc.

Baker, Attorney-General, thought that the judgment should be reversed, for no action of debt lies for this against the testator; for the bailment was to the intent to have an increase and profit of the money, and not the money back, for which money no action of debt lies, but an action of account; for the money was delivered to the intent of being employed and bestowed in prunes, and not to be preserved entire for the use of the bailor. For the law is taken in our books to be that, if a man bail money to be bailed over, if it be not bailed according to the condition no action of debt lies, but account, for he shall not receive the money to retain it; but now since he did not make the delivery over, he was accountable to the bailor. . . . And although this receipt was testified by bill, yet it seems that it shall not alter the nature of the account; for it is only evidence and should not estop the testator from waging his law.'. . . And although the testator cannot wage his law, yet it is not good ground to say that the administrator or executors shall be charged.[55] As if a man before auditors is found in arrears and dies, the executor is not chargeable; yet the testator could not wage his law. . . . Wherefore the administrator shall not be charged, for that the thing remained always in the nature of an account, of which no action lies against administrators.

Montague, to the contrary: For I have learnt it to be law, that if a man deliver money to be bailed over, if the bailee do not perform the condition, he is a debtor for the money or accountable at the pleasure of the bailor. . . . For when a man hath received money and hath not employed

---

[54] See H.E.L. III, 586-7.
[55] This is a third argument. *Baker* argues (1) that account lies, and not debt: (2) that the deed in the present case was merely evidence of the obligation and not the obligation itself and would not have estopped the deceased from waging his law: (3) that, even if the deceased could not have waged his law, yet executors and administrators are never liable in account and should not, therefore, be made liable by wrongly changing the nature of the claim from account to debt.

and bestowed it according to the trust and condition, he is a guardian of the same money to my use, as my debtor if I will. For it is the more prejudice to me if I make my election for my action of debt, inasmuch as I shall only recover the naked sum which was bailed; but if I bring account, I shall recover the increase and profits of the same sum besides the sum. And when a man hath two actions given by the law, he may elect which he will. . . . As to that which is said, that this bill does not make the intestate a debtor, because there are wanting words obligatory, he clearly thought that the words ' I have received twenty pounds ' or ' I owe ' or ' I am bound to,' or if a man recite that ' Whereas he had one hundred pounds of money of I. S. he hath paid him forty pounds, and so there remains sixty pounds,' this is a good obligation and shall bind the executor; for every word which proves a man to be a debtor, or to have the money of any stranger in his custody, clearly, if it be by bill, shall make his executors debtors also. As if a bill be made that ' witnesseth that I have twenty pounds of I. S.' without other words, I shall be charged and shall be ousted of my law; for in our books . . . it is adjudged, That a man shall be ousted of his law, and the executor shall be bound. . . .

> [The majority of the Court, FITZJAMES, C.J., SPILMAN and PORTMAN, J.J., upheld the writ of Debt and affirmed the judgment; LUKE, J. dissenting.]

. . . SPILMAN, PORTMAN and FITZJAMES, Chief Justice, [considered] that the first judgment should be affirmed.

In the first place, admit that he had no bill evidencing the receipt, yet in the common opinion of the books it is in the election of the bailor to have an action of debt or account in such case. As in 41 and 42 Ed. 3,[56] it is ruled that if a man bail money to one upon a condition, that if the bailee make him assurance of certain land before such a day he shall retain the money for ever, but if not, to re-deliver it to the bailor; if the bailee do not perform this trust and condition, he is accountable for the sum or debtor to the bailor at his pleasure. The same is the law if money be delivered to traffic with or to be bailed over, if the bailee break his trust, the one action or the other lies for the bailor. So it is if I bail ten pounds to you to give away in alms for me, now you are accountable to me; for the property always rests in me until the alms be performed, and I may countermand the doing of that, and if you retain the ten pounds in your hands afterwards, I shall have a good action of debt against you for it.

And FITZJAMES thought in the case here that the property of the twenty pounds was in the bailee, because he had liberty by the bailment to make an exchange of the twenty pounds; yet he had it not so far but that the property vests back in the bailor if the trust be not observed, as is acknowledged by the defendant by the trial and also by the demurrer in law. And besides, if I bail twenty pounds to one to keep for my use, if the twenty pounds were not contained in a bag, coffer or box, an action of detinue doth not lie, because the twenty pounds could not be discovered or known to be mine, but debt and account lie at my pleasure there. So if I bail to one certain plate to keep for me, if he change the plate, I shall have an action upon the case or detinue at my election; in the time of Ed. 4.[57] So, by FITZJAMES, in the time of Hen. 7,[58] Frowicke being Chief Justice, this

---

[56] *Supra*, p. 285.
[57] 18 Ed. 4, f. 23, pl. 5. *Supra*, p. 113.
[58] 20 Hen. 7, f. 8, pl. 18. *Infra*, p. 351.

case was argued and ruled: A man bought twenty quarters of barley to be delivered at a certain place on a certain day; the vendor did not perform his contract, by which the vendee was driven to buy barley for his business, being a brewer, at a much greater price, etc.; the vendee upon this matter was permitted to bring an action upon the case, and adjudged maintainable; and so he might well have had an action of debt for the barley, but not detinue, for the property of the barley could not be known, for one quarter cannot be known from another quarter.

Then, it is to be considered to what effect this bill is, whether it be a sufficient obligation to charge executors. And it seemed to them all that it shall be. For if a man make such a bill, viz., ' This bill witnesseth that I, A. B., have borrowed ten pounds of C. D.,' without more, this shall charge the executors as well as a bond, and the testator should never wage his law against this bill. The law is the same, ' Memorandum, that such a one owes to B. ten pounds,' without more; if this bill be sealed and delivered as a deed, it is a bond good enough. . . . And although the executors are not expressed in an obligation, yet the law shall charge them, because they represent the estate of the testator. The law is the same of administrators; but the heir shall never be charged without express mention of heir. Therefore, inasmuch as this bill is evidence of the receipt of the twenty pounds by Woddye to the behoof and use of Core, and he hath not employed them accordingly, it is as strong as if he had been bound by words obligatory. Also it is a common maxim that against a specialty no man shall wage his law. . . . And besides, it is common doctrine that no action lies against executors where the testator could have his law; but here he could not. So if a man be retained in service for twenty shillings *per annum*; if the salary be in arrear and the master die, his executor shall be charged. So is the law with regard to the executor of one who has been boarded at the table of another, because the testator, by FITZJAMES in these cases, could not wage his law: so is the law for arrearages of an account. And so it shall be reasonable that the action lies, or otherwise the plaintiff will be without remedy and the defendant might retain the twenty pounds in his hands, which would be unreasonable. For it is clear law that no action of account lies against an executor or administrator, for the law does not intend them to have been privy to the account.

Wherefore it seemed that the judgment was good and affirmable, and so it was adjudged. *Quod nota.*

ℭ 13 ℰ

DEVELOPMENTS
OUTSIDE THE COMMON LAW
BEFORE THE SIXTEENTH CENTURY

JUSTICE in mediæval England was administered locally in a variety of tribunals—County, Borough and Manor courts, courts of the Fairs and courts of the Staple. Historians have condescended to their activities with an air of deprecation. Of the Borough courts, Sir William Holdsworth, after offering specimens of ' many kinds of contracts . . . actionable in local courts which would probably not have been actionable in the royal courts,' added that ' Borough justice was incapable of improvement sufficiently continuous to maintain an effective competition with royal justice.'[1] The impression left upon his mind by the published records of the Fair courts was ' that they were courts which dealt for the most part with petty transactions. . . . The forms of action, the procedure and the rules of law possess the same primitive characteristics as marked the business in other local courts.'[2] This attitude must be related to the complementary picture of mediæval England as an adolescent agricultural community, isolated from the main stream of European trade. ' All through the Middle Ages, England was economically in a backward state of development.'[3] Economic conditions must determine law and jurisdiction: contract is ever the handmaid of trade. But it is impossible to read such monographs as Dr. Power's *The Wool Trade in English Mediæval History* and the essays edited by Dr. Power and Professor Postan under the title of *English Trade in the Fifteenth Century* without a challenge to Holdsworth's view.[4] ' All through the Middle Ages,' to borrow his compendious phrase, England was an important commercial country.

The basis of its prosperity was wool, exported as raw material in the thirteenth and fourteenth centuries and in the fifteenth partly as

---

[1] *H.E.L.* II. 389. He cited as evidence the somewhat belated testimony of the Municipal Corporations Report of 1835.

[2] *H.E.L.* V. 113-4. See also P. & M. I. 643: ' From Henry II's day onwards civic has been falling behind royal justice, has been becoming antiquated and selfish '; and Pollock, *The Expansion of the Common Law*, p. 54, ' It may be taken as a safe rule throughout the formative period of the Common Law, that what the superior courts are doing to-day will be done by the inferior courts on some morrow not far off.'

[3] *H.E.L.* V. 113.

[4] Power, *The Wool Trade in English Mediæval History*, Ford Lectures (1941): Power and Postan, *Studies in English Trade in the Fifteenth Century* (1933).

raw material and partly as cloth.[5] But, though the chief, it was not the only article of commerce. England exported tin and pewter goods, coal and cheese, and imported linen and canvas from Flanders and Cologne, iron and fish from Scandinavia, timber, tar and pitch from the Baltic, furs, hemp and wax from Poland and Russia, beer from Bremen and Hamburg.[6] No class enjoyed a monopoly of trade. Sheep farming was shared between the demesne lands of manorial lords and peasant holdings: the thirteenth century was the ' heyday of demesne farming,' and the fifteenth century ' the day of the small man, when Hodge ruled the field.'[7] Nor were the merchants to be found only among the middle class. At the end of the fourteenth century the Earl of Kent owned a wine ship trading to Gascony and the Earl of Huntingdon a ' pilgrim ship ' to exploit the tourist traffic, while in 1464 the Earl of Warwick had eight ships under licence for the carriage of Bordeaux wine.[8] The monarch himself did not disdain the hazards or at least the profits of commerce. Edward IV owned and chartered ships for import and export, both on his own account and to meet his debts by lending his name to creditors who might thus avoid the customs duties and the regulations of the Staple. In June, 1464, five of his galleys cleared from Southampton with over £6,500 worth of undyed cloth; in June, 1470, a vessel unloaded for him at Sandwich 1,013 bales of woad, 27 butts of sweet wine, 32 barrels of alum, 7 bales of wax and 23 bales of ' paper scribable '; and in February, 1470, twenty-five ships entered or left the Port of London with miscellaneous cargoes owned by him or in his name— figs, raisins, oil, sugar, oranges, alum, rice, copper, lead, salt fish, wainscots, hats, cards, baskets, wire, pins, packthread, fans, soap, brushes and spectacles.[9] Well might an Italian visitor write in 1496 that ' the riches of England are greater than those of any other country in Europe, as I have been told by the oldest and most experienced merchants and also as myself can vouch from what I have seen. This is owing, in the first place, to the great fertility of the soil. . . . Next, the sale of their valuable tin . . .; but still more do they derive from their extraordinary abundance of wool, which bears such a high price and reputation throughout Europe.'[10]

[5] ' It was not for nothing that the Lord Chancellor of England was seated on a woolsack,' Power, *English Trade in the Fifteenth Century*, 39.
[6] Such were the imports and exports passing through the hands of the Hanseatic merchants: *English Trade in the Fifteenth Century*, 139-141. Other goods passed to and from the Mediterranean lands.
[7] Power, *The Wool Trade in English Mediæval History*, Lecture II, esp. at pp. 34 and 40.
[8] Kingsford, *The Beginnings of English Maritime Enterprise, History*, Vol. XIII, at p. 201.
[9] Scofield, *Life and Reign of Edward IV*, II. 404-428. Cf. Power, *English Trade in the Fifteenth Century*, 47-8.
[10] ' *A Relation of the Island of England*,' by the Secretary to the Venetian Ambassador (Camden Society, 1847), cited by Chrimes, *Sir John Fortescue*, at p. 186. See also the eulogy on London as the ' flower of cities all ' by the Scots poet, William Dunbar (A.D. 1460-1520).

The wool trade, as befitted so reputable an enterprise, was elaborately organised, and its details may be read in such contemporary documents as the Cely Papers, the letters and business memoranda of a family of London merchants, which survive for the years 1475-1488.[11] The Italian merchants bought either from middlemen or directly from the great religious houses or other large producers.[12] English merchants dealt almost invariably with middlemen. The Celys had travellers who rode out each Spring and Autumn and made their contracts with the Cotswold ' woolmen,' such as Thomas Midwinter of Northleach, from whom they bought wool to the value of £558 in 1482 and £753 in 1487. The raw material thus passed from producer to woolman, from woolman to London merchant, from London merchant to the firm's representative at Calais, and thence to the foreign buyer.[13] Each stage had its own established practice. The sale was by sample, and the price was payable as to one third in cash and as to two thirds on credit.[14] The wool was to be packed by ' an indifferent person of the fellowship of wool-packers ' in canvas ' sarplers,' loaded on pack-horses and delivered to the London merchant at the port of shipment. There it was taken over by the merchant, who had it weighed for custom dues, warehoused it at the quay until the fleet was ready to sail and engaged stevedores to load it on board.[15] Once at Calais, the representative of the London firm supervised its disembarkation, tested its quality and ultimately sold it to Dutch or Flemish buyers, again on the basis of one-third cash and two-thirds credit. The sales might be substantial: two Bruges partners in 1484 bought wool valued at £25,000 sterling. The sums outstanding on credit were covered by bills of exchange, to be accepted at the seasonal fairs held in Antwerp, Bruges and Bergen op Zoom. The Calais representative, if and when he was paid on the bills, must get his money to London. To ship the cash was clumsy and dangerous, and he therefore himself drew bills upon the English ' mercers,' who bought heavily at the Flemish fairs. ' The Staplers had Flemish money in

[11] The following account is derived from Power, *English Trade in the Fifteenth Century*, pp. 39-90. See also *Dunstable* v. *le Bal, infra*, p. 317.
[12] See *Pylate* v. *Cause, infra*, p. 319, and *Cotenni* v. *Prioress of Arden* (1303), S.S. Vol. 46, p. 69.
[13] By the Statute of Staples in 1353, to facilitate, *inter alia*, the regulation of a trade so vital as a source of royal revenue, all wool (with minor exceptions) had to be exported through London or Newcastle and sold at Calais. On the Staple system, see Power, *The Wool Trade in English Mediæval History*, Lecture V.
[14] The foreign merchants demanded longer credit than the English. Complaints were made in 1436 and 1437 of Lombards who bought on long credit in the Cotswolds, sold the wool for cash and lent the cash at heavy interest to English merchants—
      ' And thus they wolde, if ye will so beleve,
      Wypen our noses with our owne sleeve.'
Power, *English Trade in the Fifteenth Century*, p. 47, quoting the *Libelle of Englyshe Polycye*, a ' poem on the use of sea-power,' A.D. 1436.
[15] Dr. Power set out, at p. 59 of *English Trade in the Fifteenth Century*, the detailed accounts of George Cely for a single transaction. The cost of weighing was 1d. per sack, of porterage at the quay 3d. per sack, of chalking the address on the sarplers, ¼d. per sarpler, of freight to Calais, 3s. 4d. per sarpler.

Calais, where they sold, and in the marts, where they collected their debts; they wanted English money in the Cotswolds and London, where they bought. The mercers had English money in London, where they sold, and needed Flemish money at the marts, where they bought. So the Stapler on the continent delivered his money to a mercer and received a bill of exchange payable at a future date in London in English money."[16]

This series of transactions offered so many opportunities to ' contentious persons ' and the sums at stake were so considerable as to require adequate means of litigation. That the common law was not ignorant of commercial practice is shown by the frequent actions upon Statutes Merchant and Scripta Obligatoria, by the scope of Account and by the acceptance of Sale, in effect though not in principle, as a consensual contract in the second half of the fifteenth century.[17] But, while it recognized, it can scarcely be said to have satisfied the needs of commerce. With the important if belated exception of Sale, it offered no remedy for parol executory contracts; nor were Debt and Detinue, overcast by the shadow of compurgation, enticing actions for seller or buyer. The business man made his perennial complaint of the law's delays,[18] and the international character of trade presented its peculiar problems. One or other of the parties might be an alien. If he were the plaintiff, he could not sue at the common law; if he were the defendant, the chances of enforcing judgment against him were slight.[19] The contract, moreover, might have been made abroad or, though made in England, might require performance abroad. The difficulty here felt was one of ' venue.' Every action had to be assigned to a particular county in order to ensure the presence of jurors with local knowledge, and to ' lay the venue ' of a foreign contract might well seem impossible.[20] In 1375, however, a plaintiff, who wished to sue on a deed made at Harfleur in Normandy, was bold enough to describe the *locus in quo* as ' Harfleur in the county of Kent.'[21] The fiction appears to have been exploited by litigants even in domestic issues, when one county rather than another served their particular interests, and in 1382 Parliament intervened to check the abuse.

> ' To the intent that writs of Debt and Account and all other such
> actions be from henceforth taken in their counties and directed to the
> sheriffs of the counties where the contracts of the same actions did
> arise; it is ordained and accorded that, if from henceforth in pleas

[16] *English Trade in the Fifteenth Century*, p. 68.
[17] *Supra*, pp. 220-2, 228-9 and 270-1.
[18] Barbour, *Oxford Studies in Social and Legal History*, Vol. IV, p. 75, and S.S. Vol. 10, p. 10.
[19] Barbour, p. 76, and S.S. Vol. 10, Introduction, xlii, and cases there cited.
[20] *Venue = Visne = Vicinetum* (neighbourhood). Bracton, f. 309b, gives a specimen of a writ of *Venire facias*, whereby the sheriff is directed ' quod venire facias coram te . . . duodecim tam liberos quam legales homines de visneto tali per quos rei veritas melius sciri poterit.'
[21] *Pole's Case*. Y.B. 48 Ed. III. Hil. f. 2, pl. 6.

upon the same writs it shall be declared that the contract thereof was made in another county than is contained in the original writ, that then incontinently the same writ shall be utterly abated.' [22]

Despite the injunction, commercial pressure was strong enough to persuade pleaders, at intervals through the fifteenth century, to transpose continental towns to English counties. But the success of the device remained long in doubt, and contemporary petitions showed that plaintiffs found it expedient to seek the assistance of the Chancellor. [23]

LOCAL COURTS

The defects and uncertainties of the common law make it necessary to ask if the requirements of business could be met elsewhere. Were the local tribunals so unprogressive and so petty as Holdsworth suggested? Inquiry may be directed in turn upon the courts of the Boroughs, of the Fairs and of the Staple.

The sources cited by Miss Bateson in her two volumes on Borough Customs include one hundred and twenty-four charters, from Aberystwyth to Bury St. Edmunds and from Canterbury to Carrick-mac-Griffin in Ireland, and the 'Books' or 'Custumals' of various towns—the 'White Books' of London and Lincoln, the 'Red Books' of Bristol and Colchester, the 'Black Book' of Exeter, the 'Oak Book' of Southampton, the 'Chain Book' of Dublin. [24] The evidence, though necessarily scattered and desultory, throws light upon the activities of the Borough courts in matters both of substance and of procedure. That special rules should exist for the sale of goods is not surprising. In some towns a hand-clasp and in others the giving of earnest sufficed to bind the bargain. [25] But in truth their whole law of contract was more flexible than that of the common law, and Borough courts were enforcing informal covenants [25a] when the King's courts insisted upon seal. In the middle of the fourteenth century actions were brought at Nottingham for the breach of parol agreements to repair church ornaments, to employ the plaintiff as a wool-packer and to enter into partnership. [26] Counsel stated in a case of 1413 that ' there are divers actions which a man can have within the City of London which he

[22] 6 Rich. II. c. 2.
[23] See Holdsworth, *H.E.L.* V. 117-9: S.S. Vol. 10, Cases 3, 9, 18, 42, 55, 103, 125 and 129: Barbour, pp. 76-7. Barbour thus cites a petition, where the suppliants say '. . . a cause que les ditz obligacions furent fait a Caleys et non pas en Engletere, ils ne sachent en quel Countee d'engletere ils purront prendre leur accion pur trier la dite some.'
[24] Bateson, S.S. Vol. 18 and Vol. 21: for the sources, see Vol. 18, Intro. xviii-lvi. There was, not unnaturally, borrowing by one borough from another, and the customs of London, York and Winchester were particularly influential: see *History*, Vol. XXIII, p. 149.
[25] S.S. Vol. 18, p. 217, and S.S. Vol. 21, pp. lxxix-lxxxii.
[25a] For the methods of enforcement, and on process and execution generally in the Borough Courts, see S.S. Vol. 21, pp. xx-lxvii.
[26] See the cases cited by Maitland and Baildon, S.S. Vol. 4, p. 118.

cannot have at the common law, such as an action of covenant without specialty.'[27]   The Bailiffs of Scarborough testified in 1435 that

> 'afore the tyme of mynde it hath been used in the same town bi
> the custome then used and approved that plaints of covenant be
> maintainable within the said town as well upon covenants made by
> worde only as by writing at the commune lawe betwix any personnes
> sealed under their seals.'[28]

In 1480 the Abbot of St. Augustines brought an action of covenant against Richard Bayle in the Bristol Tolzey Court for the breach of a parol agreement to cure a certain William Hunt of his infirmity.[29]

Several boroughs catered expressly for merchants.   The custom of Ipswich provided that

> 'the pleas between foreigners (gents estraunges) which are called
> piepowder shall be pleaded from day to day if the plaintiff or the
> defendant asks for such adjournment.   Pleas in fair-time between
> foreigners passing through shall be pleaded from hour to hour, after
> dinner as well as before: that is to say, pleas attached during the
> fair-time.   And pleas attached by law marine, that is by foreign
> mariners and for those who only await their tide, shall be pleaded
> from tide to tide.'[30]

The White Book of London favoured 'foreign merchants,' not only by special rules of evidence where essential documents were outside the jurisdiction, but also by empanelling a jury 'half of denizens and half of foreigners dwelling in the town' to decide cases of 'contract, debt or trespass.'[31]   It even allowed actions to be brought within the City if the cause of action arose, not indeed outside England, but in any other part of the kingdom.

> ' In plaints of debt and account and other personal contracts made
> between merchant and merchant, if the plaintiff counts that the
> defendant at any merchant town or in a merchantable place within
> the kingdom bargained or bought from the said plaintiff any mer-
> chandise, or received his monies to pay or deliver to him or to render
> account in any place within the City of London; in such case the
> defendant by usage will be put to answer, notwithstanding that the
> contract is outside the city.'[32]

Commercial litigation was thus a feature of the Borough courts. In the courts of the Fairs it was predominant.   The right to hold a fair

[27] *Anon*, Y.B. 14 Hen. 4. f. 26, pl. 33.
[28] Cited by Vinogradoff, *Collected Papers*, II. p. 204, n. 4.
[29] Veale, *The Bristol Tolzey Court*, p. 9.   Similar cases may be noted in local courts other than those of Boroughs.   See cases heard in the reign of Edward II in the Bishop of Ely's court, S.S. Vol. 4, pp. 113-7; and, for instances in the Hundred Courts, Cam, *The Hundred and the Hundred Rolls*, pp. 182-3.
[30] Cited by Miss Bateson, S.S. Vol. 21 at p. 184; and see the custom of Waterford on the same page.   The 'foreigners' were non-burgesses rather than aliens.
[31] See *Whittington* v. *Turnebonis* (1421), *infra*, p. 314.
[32] See *Liber Albus* (R.S.) I. 212, 213, 215, 216, 292; and see Holdsworth, *H.E.L.* V, p. 104.   An interesting account of the working of the Law Merchant in the City of London is given by Dr. A. H. Thomas in his Introduction to the *Calendar of Select Pleas and Memoranda of the City of London*, A.D. 1381-1412 (1932).

or market, derived from the Crown, was usually accompanied by a grant of jurisdiction, and by the fifteenth century a court was assumed to be the normal incident of a fair.[33] It was known as a Court of Piepowder, apparently to commemorate the pedlars who trailed their dusty feet from market to market,[34] and, while open to local residents, was of peculiar interest to 'stranger merchants,' whether English or foreign. Its jurisdiction was wide in scope and without monetary limit. The president was the steward of the manor or the mayor of the borough to which the fair pertained, but, in the years of its greatness, the law was declared by the merchants themselves. In the reign of Edward IV, however, the common law courts identified the president with the judge and took the opportunity to assert their appellate rights.[35] The distinctive quality of the procedure was speed. Dr. Gross recounted the progress of a case heard at Colchester in 1458.

> 'The plaintiff sued for the recovery of a debt at 8 a.m., and the defendant was summoned to appear at 9 o'clock. He did not come at that hour, and the sergeant was ordered to distrain him to come at 10 o'clock, at which hour he made default. Similar defaults were recorded against him at 11 and 12 o'clock. At the latter session judgment was given in favour of the plaintiff, and appraisers were ordered to value the defendant's goods which had been attached. They made their report at 4 o'clock, and the goods were delivered to the plaintiff.'[36]

The importance of the courts declined in the second half of the fifteenth century, when they were not only controlled more strictly by the common law, but were confined by Statute to contracts made or business done during the actual days of the fair.[37] Their decay was accelerated in the sixteenth century by the new course of international trade and by the centralising tendencies of the age, and, though they lingered on into the nineteenth century, it was as the pale shadow of their early selves. The last ghost walked the unlikely streets of Hemel Hempstead in 1897.[38]

The fullest records extant are those of the Fair Court of St. Ives in Huntingdon from 1270 to 1324.[39] The right to hold a fair was

---

[33] e.g. Y.B. 12 Ed. IV. f. 9, pl. 24, and Stat. 17 Ed. IV. c. 2. For the fullest and most learned account of the Fair Courts, see Gross, Introduction to *Select Cases on the Law Merchant*, A.D. 1270-1638 (S.S. Vol. 23).

[34] An early use of the word is in Bracton, f. 334: 'propter personas qui celerem habere debent justitiam sicut sunt mercatores quibus exhibetur justitia pepoudrous.'

[35] Y.B. 6 Ed. IV. f. 3, pl. 9; and *Knyvet* v. *Stallon* (1472), S.S. Vol. 23, p. 126, a case removed by *certiorari* from the Piepowder Court of the Prior of Norwich.

[36] S.S. Vol. 23, Introduction, p. xxvi, and *Smythe* v. *Van Bondelin*, p. 122.

[37] Stat. 17 Ed. IV. c. 2, A.D. 1477.

[38] See Gross, Introduction, xix-xx. The decay of these, and other local courts, coincided with the rise of Assumpsit, which, in the early years of the sixteenth century, furnished the common law with a general contractual remedy: *infra*, Chap. 14. But in this context it is not easy to determine cause and effect.

[39] Cases from the years 1270-1324 were transcribed by Gross in S.S. Vol. 23, pp. 1-107, with the exception of the year 1275, previously excerpted by Maitland in S.S. Vol. 2, p. 130 *et seq.* Dr. Gross included in his volume a few cases from the

granted by Henry I. in 1110 to the Abbot of Ramsey. In the reign of Henry III the fair began on the Monday after Easter and lasted for four weeks, and under Edward II it lasted for six weeks. In the thirteenth and early fourteenth centuries it was an important centre for the traffic in wool, cloth and hides, and its cosmopolitan character is illustrated by a case of 1312. Complaint was made ' in a plea of trespass ' of nine defendants, including a chaplain, that they ' came and sang (carolaverunt) to the terror of the fair and to the great damage of the plaintiffs,' and the complainants included merchants of Louvain, Diest, St. Trond, Bruges, Ypres, Ghent, St. Omer, Caen, Dinant, the Bardi of Florence and ' all the merchants of England.'[40]

The cases of contract heard in the court were numerous and varied. The sale of goods raised issues familiar to modern lawyers. In *Long's Case* the defendant, sued for non-delivery, denied the existence of an agreement: there had been an offer, but no acceptance. In *Barton* v. *Bishop* a buyer admitted the contract but pleaded the breach of an express condition of quality. In *Dyer* v. *Grantham* the sale was by sample and the question was whether the bulk was equal to the sample.[41] The Letter or Writing Obligatory was an accepted instrument of payment and provoked as much litigation in the Fair as in the King's courts. in 1287 Henry Curteis of Leicester sued three merchants of Rouen for £8 sterling, the price of wool bought from him and his partner in the previous year at the Fair of Boston, which they had undertaken to pay to the plaintiff or to his attorney ' bearing the letter of obligation '; and in 1293 Sir William Hereford, citizen of London, similarly sued Ralph of Lyons for £42 3s. sterling on a *scriptum obligatorium.*[42] In these instances foreign debtors were involved: in *Hoppman* v. *Welborne,* where the terms of the instrument were set out at large, both parties were Englishmen.[43] The court entertained actions upon covenants without formality and apparently without distinguishing misfeasance and nonfeasance; and the cases ranged from simple contracts of service to elaborate partnerships, from undertak-

---

Fair courts of Carnarvon (A.D. 1325-6), of Wye in Kent (A.D. 1332), of West Malling in Kent (A.D. 1364), of Northwich (A.D. 1414), of Colchester (A.D. 1458), of Norwich (A.D. 1472), of Grantham (A.D. 1493-4), of Leicester (A.D. 1557-85), and of Halton (A.D. 1638).

[40] *Mill* v. *Pickard,* S.S. Vol. 23, p. 91. There is doubtful authority in the fifteenth century to suggest that a common law assault might be committed by words. In Y.B. Lib. Ass. 27 Ed. III, f. 134, pl. 11, a royal rent collector was received by the inhabitants of a town with ' mauvais paroles,' wherefore he dared not remain in the town, and this was held to constitute an assault and battery. But the reporter added, ' *Quare,* if the King had not been a party.' Contrast the remarks of Court and Counsel in *Browne* v. *Hawkins* (1478), *supra,* p. 139. In 1823 Holroyd, J. directed the jury in *R.* v. *Meade,* Lewin, 184, that ' no words or singing are equivalent to an assault ': see *The Circuiteers,* an Eclogue, given by Holdsworth, H.E.L. Vol. IX, Appendix:

' For Meade's case proves, or my Report's in fault,
That singing can't be reckoned an assault.'

[41] See the cases set out *infra,* at pp. 309-14.
[42] See S.S. Vol. 23, pp. 26 and 62.
[43] *Infra,* p. 312.

ings to carry goods, shoe horses or cure bald heads to agreements to pay brokerage and build houses to an exact specification.[44]

The Statute of Staples in 1353 necessarily provided for the legal incidents of the system which it established.[45]   On the one hand, a creditor was authorised to bring his debtor before the Mayor of a Staple town, there to acknowledge his debt, and the Mayor was empowered, in case of default, to levy summary execution upon the person or property of the debtor.[46]   On the other hand, a unique procedure was prescribed for the settlement of disputes in which merchants might be involved. ' All merchants coming to the Staple ' were to be ruled in ' all things touching the Staple,' and especially in actions of Debt, Covenant and Trespass, not by the common law nor by Borough custom, but by the Law Merchant; and, in any contract to which a merchant were a party even if it did not ' touch the Staple,' the plaintiff was, at his election, to sue either at common law or in the court of the Staple. The judges were to be the Mayor, ' having knowledge of the Law Merchant,' and two ' conveniable Constables,' and, where an alien merchant was affected, they were to be associated with two ' merchant strangers ' elected by the mercantile community. If the subject-matter of the dispute were the quality of the wool sold or the method of its packing, the award of commercial assessors was to be conclusive.[47]   Of the records of the staple courts few have been preserved and fewer published; but Dr. Gross offered two examples. The first case was heard in 1401 before the Mayor and Constables of the Staple of Westminster. The plaintiff, a grocer and a merchant of the Staple, claimed £28 as the balance of an account for the sale of spice. The subject-matter would seem to lie outside the category of ' things touching the Staple ' and to fall within the optional jurisdiction envisaged in chapter 8 of the Statute. The second case was heard in 1428 before the Mayor and Constables of the Staple of Exeter and arose out of a contract for the sale of woollen cloth. The plaintiff was a merchant of the Staple and he sued a merchant of Kingswear on the latter's undertaking to guarantee the payment of the price by ' stranger merchants ' of Normandy, Chester and Hull.[48]

Enough has been said to suggest that the commercial interests of mediæval England were more imposing and the instruments available for their sanction more adequate than has sometimes been allowed.

[44] See *Ribaud* v. *Russell, infra,* p. 308; *Waite* v. *Hamon, infra,* p. 308; *Colne* v. *Marshall, infra,* p. 309; *Eltisley* v. *Barber, infra,* p. 309; *Humfrey* v. *Flitt, infra,* p. 310; *Spicer* v. *Chapman, infra,* p. 311; *Moulton* v. *Byham, infra,* p. 313.
[45] *Supra,* p. 291, and *infra,* p. 315.
[46] *Statute of Staples,* cap. 9, *infra,* p. 315.   For a case involving protracted litigation upon an acknowledgment under the Statute, see *Duplage* v. *Debenham* (1484), S.S. Vol. 64, p. 75.   The process was in substance an application of the Statutes Merchant already created by legislation of Edward I: *supra,* pp. 239-41.   See Bailey, *Assignments of Debts in England,* 48 L.Q.R., pp. 268-271.
[47] Statute of Staples, cap. 8, 20, 21, 24; *infra,* p. 315.
[48] Gross, S.S. Vol. 23, Introduction, p. xxvii, and *Eliot* v. *Dyne,* p. 113, and *Pope* v. *Davy,* pp. 116-121.

Difficulties nevertheless arose which neither the common law nor Borough custom nor yet the Law Merchant, as administered in Fair or Staple courts, was competent to solve. Litigants who were outside the scope of Borough or mercantile custom might well find the common law restricted in substance or embarrassing in procedure. The operations of alien merchants, tenderly accommodated as they were, might react upon state policy and invoke the services of diplomacy. Recourse was therefore had, through one channel or another, to the Prerogative of the Crown.

THE COUNCIL AND THE CHANCELLOR

The King at first sought to avoid or to alleviate international acerbities either by intervening in the ordinary administration of justice or by encouraging the settlement of disputes before the Barons of his Exchequer. A group of cases in the reigns of Edward I and Edward II reveal his methods. In 1267 James le Roy of Dixmude began a protracted course of litigation by suing his partner for £500 alleged to be due to him on a balance of accounts.[49] By the partnership deed the plaintiff was to import cloth and spice into England and the defendant was to export wool to Flanders, and the loss or gain was to be shared in specified proportions. The defendant pleaded a deed, releasing him from all claims, which, he said, bore the seals of the plaintiff and his nephew, and the plaintiff replied by denying that either deed or seal was his. The case was remitted to a body of special commissioners appointed for Anglo-Flemish debts, who ordered the seals on the deed of release to be ' collated ' with those on the original deed of partnership.[50] The seals were found to ' agree in all respects,' and judgment was entered for the defendant. In 1278 the plaintiff complained to the King that the judgment had been induced by the defendant's deceit, and the King, ' pitying the poverty of the same merchant,' ordered the case to be re-opened by one of his justices, William of Norbury, who was to seek the assistance of a special jury and ' do justice to the parties according to the law merchant.' The jurors deposed that the collation of seals, though a normal common law process, was contrary to the law merchant, ' since in divers ways it was possible to contrive to obtain another person's seal, namely, either by loss of the seal or by means of forcible abstraction or by stealthy access in the night.' The defendant was re-examined, found guilty and ordered to discharge the debt by instalments, the last of which was paid into court in November, 1283.

In 1278 two citizens of Winchester were in dispute upon the sale of wool. The plaintiff complained to the King that he had bought

[49] *Le Roy* v. *Redmere*, S.S. Vol. 46, pp. 18-27; and see *Introduction*, pp. xxxii-iii.
[50] ' Collation of seals ' was a recognized method of deciding similar disputes at the common law, despite the obvious opportunities of fraud. See Glanvill, x. 12, and P. & M. II. 224.

from the defendant a large quantity of ' good merchantable wool,' warranted equal to sample, to be carried to St. Omer; but that, when the bulk was there examined, it was by no means equal to sample and was so ' vile and useless ' that the plaintiff ' stood in peril of death ' at the hands of the infuriated foreign buyers.   The King, anxious for the goodwill of the national trade, ordered the case to be specially heard before two Justices at the Assizes for Southampton, with the assistance of a jury of local merchants.[51]

These two cases, heard upon special instructions at the Assizes, may be balanced by three pleas before the Barons of the Exchequer. In 1299 and again in 1303 disputes arose on the forward sales over a number of years of the total wool crop of two religious houses.   The foreign buyers complained of non-delivery, and a number of interesting points were raised, including the effect of frustration caused by war.[52] In 1309 the agents of the Society of the Frescobaldi of Florence sued a merchant of Chipping Norton for a debt of £55, acknowledged by him under seal.   The defendant confessed the deed but pleaded that it had been made under duress.   Twelve merchants, half English and half Lombard, were impanelled to determine the issue of fact.[53]

In the fourteenth and fifteenth centuries foreign merchants addressed many petitions to the King's Council for extraordinary redress.[54]   Two instances, though their contractual significance is only incidental, illustrate the nervous reaction to diplomatic pressure.   The first was a chapter in the long history of litigation in which the Hanseatic merchants, as pioneers of the herring industry, were involved in the middle of the fourteenth century.   There was a double conflict of interests.   On the one hand, the English fishmongers, anxious to keep the foreigner out of their markets, indulged a familiar variety of complaints.   The Hansards in their own towns treated English merchants badly, they took currency out of the country, they would not patronise English inns but huddled jealously in their own communities.   For their part, the Hansards complained that their goods were seized on the high seas, that they were subject to exorbitant customs duties, and that they were not allowed to marry English women.   On the other hand, the English consumers alleged that their own fishmongers, by excluding the Hansards from the retail trade, ensured an artificial price for a basic article of diet.   In 1389 three Hansard merchants sought redress from the Council through the Chancellor, William of Wykeham, on the ground that the local courts, dominated by the fishmongers, denied them justice.   Their ship, laden with herring, had been seized by two Plymouth merchants, brought

[51] *Dunstable* v. *le Bal*, S.S. Vol. 46, p. 28, *infra*, p. 317.
[52] *Pylate* v. *Cause*, S.S. Vol. 46, p. 63, *infra*, p. 319, and *Cotenni* v. *Prioress of Arden*, S.S. Vol. 46, p. 69.
[53] *Le Feytur's Case*, S.S. Vol. 46, p. 79, *infra*, p. 320.
[54] See the cases collected by Leadam and Baldwin, S.S. Vol. 35.

into Weymouth and the cargo there sold at a loss. The Council ordered the proceeds of the sale to be delivered to them. The money was paid by the English merchants into the Chancery, but apparently went no further; and a second petition asked for it to be paid out to the Hansards.[55]

In the well-known *Carrier's Case* of 1473[56] the interplay of law and policy was conspicuous. An alien merchant had contracted with the defendant for the carriage of bales to Southampton. The defendant took the bales elsewhere, broke them open and converted the contents to his own use. As the common law did not recognize larceny by a bailee, the carrier could not normally have been prosecuted; but the foreign interests involved were formidable enough to ensure a debate ' in the Star Chamber before the King's Council.' The Chancellor, Bishop Stillington, in his dual capacity of politician and Churchman, sought to concentrate attention upon the question of *mens rea*: if the defendant had a guilty intent, technicalities should not impede justice. Chief Justice Brian opposed to this suspicious doctrine the classical position of the common law. As a bailee, the defendant might be liable in detinue, but not for trespass or felony.

> ' Where the party had possession by bailment and lawful delivery, there cannot afterwards be said to be felony or trespass touching this; for there can be no felony except with violence and *vi et armis,* and such thing as he himself holds he cannot take *vi et armis* nor against the peace.'

The Chancellor then sought to lift the debate to a higher plane.

> ' This suit is brought by a foreign merchant, who is come here with a safe conduct. He is not bound to sue according to the law of the land and abide a trial by twelve men and the other solemnities of the law of the land; but he ought to sue here. And in the Chancery it shall be determined in accordance with the law of nature, and for the speeding of merchants there should be suing there from hour to hour and from day to day.' [57]

The case was ultimately sent for argument before all the judges in the Exchequer Chamber. Chief Justice Brian was unrepentant; but his colleagues, not unmindful of the royal will, devised an ingenious compromise. They would not stomach the vague promptings of Natural

---

[55] S.S. Vol. 35, pp. xcviii and 76. So far as these incidents occurred on the high seas, the establishment of the Court of Admiralty soon after 1350 provided some redress. The Court, primarily concerned with such wrongs as piracy, also had a certain jurisdiction in contract, e.g. over charter-parties. See Marsden, *Select Pleas in the Court of Admiralty,* S.S. Vol. 6, especially at pp. xlvi and li. The records of the Court, however, begin only in 1524, and the earlier evidence is therefore fragmentary: see Plucknett, *Concise History,* 4th ed. pp. 623-4.

[56] S.S. Vol 64, p. 30.

[57] The Chancellor, in a later passage, identified the Law of Nature with the Law Merchant, ' which is law universal throughout the world.' He might have referred to Cap. 20 of the Statute of Staples, wherein the King undertook to do speedy justice to merchant strangers according to the Law Merchant ' without sparing any man or to drive them to sue at the Common Law '; *infra,* p. 317.

Law nor would they abandon the fundamental principles of trespass and larceny. It was possible, however, to distinguish the bale and its contents. Of the bale itself no larceny could be committed; but if the carrier ' broke bulk ' and abstracted the contents, the possession automatically revested in the bailor and the bailee became a trespasser. They thus reconciled expediency with the appearance of honour and were able to ' report to the Chancellor in the Council that, in the opinion of most of them, it was felony.'

The English litigant, when he felt the inadequacy of the common law, had not the political weapons of the more fortunate foreigner. But he could, and he did, state his grievance and seek his redress by petition to the Chancellor, at first as the Secretary of the Council and, at a later date, as himself the instrument of grace. In the early years of the fourteenth century the Chancellor did little more than summon the Council, but by the death of Edward III he had become its main-spring. The petition of the Hansards in 1389 was addressed to him, though the decree was pronounced by the Council as a whole. His status was emphasised and enhanced by the dignity or indolence which confined the sessions of the Council to term time. A Statute of 1412 entrusted the punishment of riot to the Council or the King's Bench, and ' to the Chancery in vacation.'[58] In the second half of the fifteenth century the Council was supplanted, even as an administrative body, by the more intimate departments of the Household,[59] and it is not surprising that the Chancery should be recognized as a separate court. The Chancellor made decrees in his own name and described himself as a ' Judge of Conscience.'[60]

The Chancellor was armed to dispense remedial justice, not only with the vague but none the less awful powers of the Prerogative, but with the more immediate weapon of Subpœna—the ' writ upon a certain pain '—whereby he could probe the conscience of the parties in a manner forbidden at the Common Law. That the Judges should at times be uneasy at the encroachment, real or fancied, upon their jurisdiction was not surprising;[61] but it must not be supposed that they indulged in a vendetta with the Chancellor. The relations between them, if competitive, were not unfriendly. They met in conference to exchange views or to find a joint solution of a delicate problem. In 1459 a litigant was advised by the Judges to seek the aid of the Chancellor, and Choke, in argument, described his Court as ' a court of

---

[58] Stat. 13 Hen. IV, c. 7.
[59] ' The Proceedings of the King's Council . . . end abruptly in 1461, and when a fresh series starts in 1540 they are the records of a radically different organization, the interval coinciding with the emergence of the King's Secretaries ': Galbraith, The Public Records, p. 55.
[60] Anon (1468), Y.B. Trin. 8 Ed. IV. f. 5, pl. 1. On the whole question of the relations between the Chancellor and the Council, see Leadam and Baldwin, Introduction to S.S. Vol. 35.
[61] See the cases cited infra, at p. 337.

record and as high a court as any the King has.'[62] The Chancellor
in turn might ask the advice of the Judges upon the propriety of a
Subpœna and defer to it against his own inclination.[63] Even where, as
in the *Carrier's Case*, public policy required exceptional provision for
the needs of a foreign merchant, he was prepared to accept a compromise which seemed at least to save the face of the law.

The formidable task awaiting the historian of Equity is indicated
by the mere presence in the Public Record Office of some 300,000
petitions, tied in bundles without index or classification.[64] Into this
appalling treasure-heap the American scholar W. T. Barbour, whose
brilliant career was cut short by untimely death, had the courage, in
Vinogradoff's words, 'to plunge boldly and to collect a sufficient
number of instances to frame conclusions as to the average methods
of Chancery in trying contract cases'; and it is upon his specimens
and observations that the student has as yet chiefly to depend.[65] Petitioners invoked the aid of the Chancellor both to fill the gaps of
the common law and to soften its asperities. Of the former process
three types of case are conspicuous. No surety was bound at the
common law save upon a deed. Conrad Goldsmyth of Tewkesbury
therefore complained that he had sold goods to Laurence Walker on
the understanding that Simkin Baker would accept liability for the
price, but that, after payment of part only, Walker had 'withdrawn
to strange places unknown' and that he had no remedy against Baker
'by the course of the common law.'[66] Nor did the mediæval common
law recognize a *quantum meruit* count: debt would lie only for a
pre-determined sum. Petitions were thus filed by a seller who alleged
that the buyer had agreed to pay 'selonque le prys que greynes furent
comunement venduz,' and by a complainant who had been asked to
do work for the defendant in Spain and had been promised a 'reasonable reward for his labour.'[67] Above all, the field of executory parol
agreements was open for the Chancellor's cultivation. John Whitehead alleged that he had recovered damages against Robert Orchard
for burning his mill and that Orchard was in prison for failure to
satisfy the judgment. The defendant, John Spring of Southampton,
had then promised Whitehead that, if the latter would discharge
Orchard, he would himself re-build the mill. Orchard was duly discharged but Spring failed to re-build, and Whitehead now asked that
he be 'rewled and juged as good cōnciens requyreth.'[68] A further

---

[62] *Anon*, Y.B. Hil. 37 Hen. VI, f. 13, pl. 3.
[63] *Anon* (1482), Y.B. Pasch. 22 Ed. IV, f. 6, pl. 18, *infra*, p. 325. See also Hemmant,
Introduction to S.S. Vol. 64, xiii-xiv.
[64] Introduction to S.S. Vol. 35, pp. xiii and xix.
[65] Barbour, *History of Contract in Early English Equity* (Oxford Studies in Social
and Legal History, Vol. IV); and Introduction, by Vinogradoff, at p. iv.
[66] *Goldsmyth's Case*, Barbour, p. 188, *infra*, p. 322. Cf. *Buckland* v. *Leukenore*
(S.S. Vol. 27, p. 9), *supra*, p. 266.
[67] See cases cited by Barbour, pp. 105-6.
[68] *Whitehead's Case*, Barbour, p. 225, *infra*, p. 323.

case of nonfeasance was disclosed by the homely facts of *Ellesmere v. Serle.*[69] The parties were in treaty for the sale of land, and, after an animated discussion conducted *coram publico,* terms were agreed, and all went together ' to the Swan beside Seynt Antonyes and there they dronke togederes upon the saide bargayn atte the coste of the saide Robert Ellesmere.' An appropriate deed was to be subsequently drafted; but at the appointed day, when the buyer tendered the price, the seller refused to execute the deed and the buyer ' lost his bargain.'

Petitioners were equally urgent where their complaints were accepted in principle by the common law, but its remedy was defective. They sought to avoid the technical rules which, in an action on a *debt sur contract,* enabled the debtor to wage his law and exonerated his personal representatives from liability. In one case Ralph Bellers asked the Chancellor to help him because he knew that his debtors ' would make their law against faith and good conscience ';[70] and in another the petitioner alleged that John Fairman, ' pur certeinz infir-mitez quy il avait ' had retained him at a fee of five marks, ' pur estre son fisision et luy faire d'estre seyn de son maladie.' He had, ' par son diligent labour ' cured his patient, but the latter had died before he was sufficiently convalescent to pay the fee. His executrix had refused to do so and the ' fisision ' now asked for a writ of Subpœna.[71] A purchaser of land might ask for Specific Performance because damages afforded no real satisfaction, or a debtor struggle out of the net into which he had been cast by the *stricti juris* nature of a deed.[72] The Chancellor's response to all these appeals, evidenced only too abundantly in such petitions, is corroborated by an occasional report in the Year Books. In 1468 a Subpœna was sued in the Chancery for the breach of a parol promise. The defendant argued that the plaintiff's only remedy lay in the Church courts. The Chancellor was short with him.

> '.You say that for breach of faith he must sue by the Canon Law; but in this case, because he is damaged by the non-performance of the promise, he shall have a remedy here.'

The defendant persisted that, had the plaintiff taken the trouble to obtain the defendant's promise under seal, he could have sued in Covenant, and that it was ' his folly not to have had a deed.' But the Chancellor dismissed the suggestion with the beneficent if uncomplimentary maxim, *Deus est procurator fatuorum.*[73]

[69] Cited by Barbour, pp. 117-8.
[70] *Bellers' Case,* Barbour, p. 182, *infra,* p. 321.
[71] *Fairman's Case,* cited by Barbour, p. 103.
[72] See *The Case of the University of Cambridge,* Barbour, p. 221, *infra,* p. 321; and *Godemond's Case,* Barbour, p. 231, *infra,* p. 324.
[73] *Anon* (1468), Y.B. Pasch. 8 Ed. IV, f. 4, pl. 11. Contrast *Anon* (1482). Y.B. Pasch, 22 Ed. IV, f. 6, pl. 18, *infra,* p. 325.

Such maxims indicate the broad foundations of the Chancellor's jurisdiction. He would do what ought to be done unfettered by form or technicality, and he did not shrink from the boldest expression of his thoughts. The law of man must accord with the law of God, and, as in some sense the vice-gerent of God, he could interpret its clauses and anticipate, by swifter if more transient measures, the ultimate sanction of eternal damnation.[74] The essence of contract, thus distilled, was no more than the obligation to keep a promise deliberately given for a legitimate purpose. In his own words, because a man was ' damaged by the non-performance of the promise, he shall have a remedy.'[75] The adoption of a principle so simple and yet so conclusive raises inevitably a question as to the relation between the Chancellor's activities in fifteenth-century England and the doctrines of the Canon Law.

The question has been much debated. Ames depreciated the reaction of ecclesiastical law upon English Equity, and Pollock and Maitland were aware of ' no English canonist who achieved anything for the law of contract.'[76] Vinogradoff, for his part, inclined to stress the influence of the Church, and Barbour felt himself ' driven to seek the source of the Chancellor's doctrines in the Canon Law.'[77] The problem may be approached from two angles. Attention may be focussed, on the one hand, upon the activities of the Church courts in England. That their jurisdiction in certain matters of contract was recognized appears from the law of usury. A Statute of 1341, re-stating a position previously acknowledged both by Glanvill and by Bracton, declared

> ' that the King and his heirs have cognisance of usurers dead, and that the Ordinaries of Holy Church have cognisance of usurers alive, as pertaineth to them, to compel them, by the censures of Holy Church upon their sin, to make restitution for usuries taken against the laws of Holy Church.'[78]

The Church courts used this power as late as the seventeenth century. In the reign of Elizabeth, a certain Thomas Wilcox was delated .by his neighbours as ' a horrible usurer, taking 1d. and sometimes 2d. for a shilling by the week. He has been cursed by his own father and

---

[74] See *Anon* (1489), Y.B. Hil. 4 Hen. VII, f. 4, pl. 8, *infra*, p. 326.

[75] *Anon* (1468), Y.B. Pasch. 8 Ed. IV, f. 4, pl. 11.

[76] Ames, *Lectures on Legal History*, pp. 124-7; and P. & M. II. 202. Cf. Pollock, in the Pollock-Holmes Letters, I. 145: ' Ames's evident desire to squeeze the ecclesiastical courts and the canonists out of the story is incompatible with the manifest pressure of their competition in matters of *fidei læsio.*'

[77] Vinogradoff, *Reason and Conscience in Sixteenth-Century Jurisprudence, Coll. Papers*, II. 190; and Barbour, *History of Contract in Early English Equity*, p. 167.

[78] 15 Ed. III, Stat. I, cap. 5. ' Cognisance of usurers dead '=the King's claim to the goods of the deceased. See also Glanvill, Book 7, c. 16, and Bracton, ff. 116b and 117. The practice of Holy Church was not always consistent with its doctrine. Thus Benvenuto da Imola, in his fourteenth century commentary on Dante, declared: ' He who practiseth usury goeth to hell, and he who practiseth it not tendeth to destitution.'

mother. For the space of two years he hath not received the Holy Communion, but every Sunday, when the priest is ready to go to the Communion, then he departeth the church for the receiving of his weekly usury, and doth not tarry the end of divine service thrice in the year."[79] More general questions of contract provoked persistent controversy. Already in the twelfth century Churchmen had accepted the principle of *læsio fidei*, whereby a Christian could pledge his hope of salvation to secure the payment of a debt or the fulfilment of a promise, and sought to control its consequences. The King was equally alive to the potentialities of a claim in which was implicit the whole law of agreement, and by the Constitutions of Clarendon in 1164 the power of the Church was confined to spiritual censure.[80] But for over three hundred years the relations between Church and State remained uneasy. In the thirteenth century craftsmen used the conception of *læsio fidei* to enforce trade union regulations.

> ' The smiths made a " confederacy," supported by an oath, with the object, as they declared, of putting down night-work, but, as was alleged in court, of preventing any but members of their organization from working at the trade, and summoned blacklegs before the ecclesiastical courts. The spurriers forbade anyone to work between sunset and sunrise, and haled an offending journeyman before the archdeacon, with the result that " the said Richard, after being warned three times by the Official, had been expelled from the Church and excommunicated, until he would swear to keep the ordinance." ' [81]

The Common lawyers retaliated in each generation with writs of Prohibition. In 1303 Chief Justice Bereford forbade the ecclesiastical judges to meddle with pleas of debt,[82] and a century and a half later the Exchequer Chamber had to repeat the admonition.

> ' If a man binds himself to pay another £40 on a certain day and he does not pay, and if the party sues him in a Court Christian *pro læsione fidei*, he shall have Prohibition.' [83]

The Chancellor was necessarily familiar both with the pretensions of the Church courts and with the doubtful efficacy of their sanctions, and he may well have determined to support with his own more drastic weapons a principle which he approved.[84]

[79] Cited by Tawney, *Religion and the Rise of Capitalism*, 162.
[80] Glanvill, x. 12, *supra*, p. 234. See Plucknett, *Concise History*, 4th ed., pp. 594-5, and P. & M. II, 193-202. The practical importance of the Church Courts in the England of the twelfth and thirteenth centuries is shown by the manual of procedure prepared under the title of *Summa Aurea* by William of Drogheda, who was murdered in a house in High Street, Oxford—still called Drawda Hall—in 1245. See Maitland, *Canon Law in the Church of England*, 107-116.
[81] Tawney, *Religion and the Rise of Capitalism*, 52.
[82] *Anon*, Y.B. 30 & 31 Ed. I. (R.S.) 492.
[83] *Anon*, Y.B. Pasch, 38 Hen. 6, f. 29, pl. 11.
[84] See the case of 1468, cited *supra*, at p. 304.

The alternative and wider approach demands an appreciation of the Canon Law as an international instrument.[85]   The Canonists started with the assumption that a simple promise was binding by its own intrinsic weight upon the conscience, and that failure or refusal to keep it was a breach of man's duty towards God. The translation of an ethical concept into law might seem to affront the maxim, ostensibly drawn from Roman jurisprudence and still held, with whatever practical mitigations, by the mediæval Civilians, *ex nudo pacto non oritur actio.*[86]   The Canonists sought a reconciliation by developing a doctrine of *Causa* which might serve, even if no more opaque than the Emperor's robes in the fable, to clothe the naked pact. They therefore declared that a pact was valid if it were adorned by an adequate *causa.* The definition of *causa* was a more embarrassing task and encouraged ingenious speculation, but, by the general consensus of opinion, the doctrine required the plaintiff to prove only that the promise had been made with a serious purpose. Unless his design was manifestly unreasonable or improper, the promisor was bound. Nor need his aim be commercial: benevolence, piety or the discharge of a moral obligation sufficed. The position was thus stated in the fifteenth century.[87]

> ' The question is whether a man is bound by a naked pact or simple promise. The answer is that he is so bound by canon law and in conscience, under pain of mortal sin, provided that a cause is expressed, as if I promise you ten pounds because you have sold me such a thing or have lent me the money, and so forth. But if it be so naked that no cause is added, he is not bound even in conscience; and the reason is that he is taken to have made the promise in error. . . . But notice that, if a man say, I promise to give you a hundred pounds, then the liberality of the promise is presumed to be the cause of the gift, and so it is not without cause. So, too, if anything is promised to a pious foundation, because he is taken to have bound himself for motives of piety. . . . No one is bound from whatever cause unless he has intended to bind himself. He is not required, under pain of mortal sin, to keep a naked pact, unless there exist a cause which requires him to be so bound by moral precept, as if I have promised my robe to my father, who is perishing with cold; for in such a case as this a man is bound, even if he never intended to be bound.'

That this doctrine was familiar to contemporary Englishmen appears from the comparison of Canon and Common Law written by Christopher St. Germain in the early sixteenth century and published under the title of *Two Dialogues between a Doctor of Divinity and a Student*

---

[85] See Vinogradoff, *Reason and Conscience in Sixteenth-Century Jurisprudence,* Coll. Papers, II. 190: Le Bras, in *Legacy of the Middle Ages* (Oxford, 1926), p. 321: Hazeltine, *Roman and Canon Law in the Middle Ages,* in 5 *Cam. Med. Hist.* 697: Plucknett, *Concise History,* 4th ed., pp. 285-9.
[86] Cf. Bracton, f. 99, *supra,* p. 236.
[87] In the *Summa* of Angelus Carletus, cited by Vinogradoff, *Coll. Papers,* II. at p. 201.

of the Common Law.[88] The Doctor explains the meaning of *Causa* after the style and almost in the words of the *Summa Angelica*. There is the same reference to what a later generation of English lawyers would call ' past consideration,' the same insistence on benevolence and piety as foundations of liability, the same reliance upon the Fifth Commandment as an exception to the normal requirement of intention. The Student unashamedly admits the refusal of the common law to countenance such latitude and approves its insular emphasis upon material interests. He retaliates by stressing the elusive properties of intention and slyly suggests that, if a gratuitous promise to Holy Church be binding, no argument can invalidate a similar promise to an individual Christian. The Dialogues were not published until 1523 and 1530 respectively, but St. Germain had lived half his life in the fifteenth century, and he may be said rather to have disseminated the thoughts imbibed in his youth than anticipated the new ideas by which his old age was beset.

It was in such an atmosphere and against such a background that the Chancellors made their contribution to the development of English contract. That upon occasion and within limits Canon Law and Equity might form a single front against the Common Law is shown by a passage in the first of the two Dialogues.[89] The Doctor refers to the common law rule that if a man, bound by deed to pay money, pays and fails to take a release by deed, or, having taken, loses it, he must pay again. On what ground of ' reason and conscience,' he asks, may this be justified? The Student confesses that the rule may hardly be supported in ethics, and falls back upon the argument that ' an obligation should not be lightly avoided by word of mouth ' and that individual hardship may not overset general convenience. Particular cases may, without injury to the policy of the law, be redressed in equity. ' If such default happen in any person, whereby he is without remedy at the common law, yet he may be holpen by a *subpœna*; and so he may in many other cases where conscience serveth for him.'[90] The Chancellor did not avow, even if he admitted to himself, the source of his inspiration, nor is there any evidence that he approved, and certainly none that he applied, the wilder extravagances of the Canon Law. But it is at least clear that he was adopting its central principle —the inherent validity of a promise—while the Common Law denied it.

[88] St. Germain was (probably) a member of Exeter College, Oxford, and (certainly) a member of the Inner Temple, born c. 1460 and died c. 1540. His First Dialogue was apparently published in Latin in 1523, though the first extant edition is of 1528. The Second Dialogue was published in English in 1530. See Winfield, *Chief Sources of English Legal History*, pp. 321-4. See the passages cited *infra*, p. 326, from Dialogue II, Ch. 24.

[89] Dialogue I, Chap. 12.

[90] The ' other cases ' are developed in Chaps. 17-20. Cf. the views of the judges in *Anon*, Y.B. Pasch, 22 Ed. 4, f. 6, pl. 18, *infra*, p. 325.

SOURCES

FAIR COURT OF ST. IVES
S.S. VOL. 23, ED. GROSS

A. RIBAUD v. RUSSELL
S.S. VOL. 23, p. 15

A.D. 1287

Gilbert Ribaud complains of William Russell and Walter Clerk of Haddenham. Pledge to prosecute, his faith[91]; pledge of the defendants, feathers.[92]

And Gilbert appears and complains of the said William and Walter, for that they unjustly detain from him and do not pay him 9s. 6d.; and unjustly because, whereas it was covenanted between him, Gilbert, and the said William and Walter, in the town of Bury St. Edmunds in the house of Alice Coterun, on the Monday before the feast of St. Nicholas last past, a year ago, that the said Gilbert should sell eleven sacks of feathers and that he should receive as his stipend 12d. for each sack, the said Gilbert as broker of the said William and Walter sold these sacks to a certain John Waterbailie of Provins. And after the said sale had been made, the said Gilbert firmly believed that his stipend, 9s. 6d., would be paid to him according to the covenant (*secundum convencionem*); but the said William and Walter have detained the said money from him and still detain it, to his damage a half-mark. And he produces suit.

The said Walter and William are present and deny all which should be denied word for word, and they are at their law. And because they cannot find pledges to make their law, the said Gilbert craves judgment against them, as against those who are convicted, both for the damages and for the principal.

Wherefore it is awarded that the said William and Walter make satisfaction to the said Gilbert and be in mercy for the unjust detention. They are poor: pledge, their bodies. And afterwards they were liberated, each on his own pledge of faith.

B. WAITE v. HAMON
S.S. VOL. 23, p. 13

A.D. 1287

John Waite complains of Hamon, the servant of Edmund Fytyl, for that the said Hamon unjustly detains from him 2s. of silver; and unjustly because, whereas the said John and Hamon covenanted at the last fair of St. Ives that the said Hamon should serve the said John for 3s. of silver from the Wednesday before the feast of St. Mark the Evangelist in that year during the fairs of St. Ives and Boston, the said Hamon broke the covenant at the fair of St. Ives and eloigned himself, so that the said John had no service from him. Wherefore the said John caused the said Hamon to be attached in the court of Sir John de Vaux,[93] and by the judgment of that court he recovered against the said Hamon the said 2s. and his damages to the amount of 20s. And from these damages he wholly released the said Hamon

---

[91] i.e., on his own recognizances.
[92] i.e., a pledge of those goods in which the defendants traded, as appears from the case itself.
[93] The holder of a court in his manor near Boston, during Boston fair.

on condition that the said 2s. should be paid to him; but as yet the said Hamon has paid him nothing of the said 2s. nor cared to pay. Moreover, he defamed him, John, before certain merchants, by which defamation the said John lost 12d. in carrying on his trade, to his damage and dishonour a half-mark. And he produces suit.

The said Hamon is present and denies all word for word, and wages his law; pledges of his law, Edmund Fytyl and John Sleaford.

C. COLNE v. MARSHALL
S.S. Vol. 23, p. 22
A.D. 1287

John, son of Alan of Colne, complains of Robert Marshall and his son Adam, and says that, whereas on Wednesday last he brought a certain horse of his to the workshop of the said Robert and Adam to have three of the said horse's feet shod with new shoes and to have a fourth shoe removed for 2d., the said Robert and Adam removed the shoe from one foot of the said horse and put a new shoe on another foot, but they broke their covenant as to the other two feet; wherefore the said John by the delay of the said Robert and Adam lost the sale of his horse on that day from the third to the ninth hour, to his damage a half-mark.

The said Robert and Adam are present and crave leave to make concord with John, and they make concord. And Robert and Adam put themselves in mercy, 6d. Pledges, Martin Jamot and Robert Baldwin.

D. ELTISLEY v. BARBER
S.S. Vol. 23, p. 36
A.D. 1288

John, son of John of Eltisley, complains of Roger Barber, for that he has unjustly broken a covenant with him; and unjustly because, whereas the said John was in the vill of Ramsey on the Monday after Epiphany last past, a year ago, in the house of Thomas Buck, the said Roger came there and undertook (*manucepit*) to cure his, John's, head of baldness for 9d., which the said John paid in advance. The next day, Tuesday, the said Roger put him in plaster and did likewise on Wednesday, and afterwards withdrew from the vill, so that, from that day to this, he would in no way interpose, to his, John's, damage a half-mark. And he produces suit.

The said Roger was present and denied tort and force, etc., and put himself on his law; and in finding pledges of his law withdrew from the bar without leave. Therefore the said John craved judgment against him as against one who is convicted.

Wherefore it is awarded that the said Roger make satisfaction to the said John for 9d., the sum claimed, and for his damages, which are remitted, and that he be in mercy 6d. for the trespass.

E. LONG'S CASE
S.S. Vol. 23, p. 39
A.D. 1291

Peter Long of London complains of Geoffrey of Cam[94] and says that he unjustly detains from him 600 ells of canvas, which he, Peter, through his

[94] Or possibly Caen.

broker, Hamon of Bury St. Edmunds, bespoke and bought from him in his booth in the vill of St. Ives, on the Friday after the feast of St. John before the Latin Gate, for 29s. the hundred and a farthing as a God's penny, to his damage 40s. And he produces suit.

The said Geoffrey is present and denies tort and force, etc., and says that he never sold the said canvas to the said Peter or to any broker of his; but he says that the said Hamon came to his booth and offered him 27s. for each hundred ells of the canvas and thereupon threw down a farthing as a God's penny,[95] against the will and without the assent of Geoffrey. And that this is true he craves may be inquired, and the adverse party does likewise; and a day is given them on Monday.

On that day the inquest comes and says that the said Geoffrey of Cam never granted the said canvas to the said Peter at the price alleged by the said Hamon, his broker. Therefore it is awarded that the said Peter be in mercy for his false claim. He is pardoned by Brother John of Eton (Warden of the Fair).

F. HUMFREY v. FLITT
S.S. VOL. 23, p. 43
A.D. 1291

Thomas Humfrey of Paris complains of John of Flitt for that he, John, has unjustly broken a covenant made with him, because, whereas he, John, was in the horse-market of the vill of St. Ives on Wednesday last, the said Thomas came there and covenanted with the said John that he, John, should carry for him to London for 12d. a certain bundle which was to be sold to a certain citizen of London, with the understanding that he should be in London at vespers on the following Thursday, and thereon he, John, received a farthing as a God's penny; but the said John tarried in St. Ives during the whole of the said Wednesday to his, Thomas's, damage 10s. And thereof he produces suit.

The said John is present and denies the words of court and the receipt of a God's penny and the whole contract, and he wages his law; pledges of his law, Gervase Godres and William Bellamy.

Afterwards he made his law sufficiently, and the said Thomas is in mercy 6d., which he has paid.

G. BARTON v. BISHOP
S.S. VOL. 23, p. 50
A.D. 1291

Hamon of Barton complains of William Bishop for that he unjustly detains and does not pay him 6s. for two barrels of salt haddock, which he, Hamon, sold to him on the bridge of St. Ives on the Thursday after the feast of the Apostles Philip and James in the nineteenth year of the reign of King Edward, which money he, William, was to pay on the following Saturday, and to bind this purchase the said William gave him a God's penny; and he has paid him nothing of the residue nor cared to pay, but has always hitherto detained it and still detains it, to his damage 20s.

---

[95] i.e., earnest. ' All over western Europe the earnest becomes known as the God's penny or Holy Ghost's penny (*denarius Dei*): P. & M. II. 208-9.

The said William is present and denies the words of court,[96] and fully acknowledges the contract and the delivery of a God's penny to the said Hamon, but says that the contract was made on condition that if the said fish should be suitable, as the said Hamon assured him that it was, and not corrupt, the contract and covenant between them should stand; but, because the said William found the said fish corrupt and fetid, he refused to accept it and wholly rejected it and remitted it into the hands of the said Hamon, who did therewith as he pleased. And that this is so he craves may be inquired; and the adverse party does likewise.

Afterwards they make concord, and William puts himself in mercy, 12d.; pledge, his body. He has paid [the fine].

H. SPICER v. CHAPMAN
S.S. Vol. 23, p. 77
A.D. 1300

John Spicer of Godmanchester appears against Peter Chapman of St. Ives and complains that the said Peter has unjustly broken a covenant with him; and unjustly because, whereas they, John and Peter, were together in the town of Huntingdon on the Saturday before Candlemas in the twenty-fourth year of the reign of King Edward, it was covenanted there between them that they should be partners to win or to lose in doing business in various parts of Scotland, and that the said John should make a journey to that country with horses laden with porret seed,[97] which he should sell and traffic there for the profit of both parties, as should seem to him expedient, and that a third of both gain and loss should be assigned to the said Peter. And the said Peter accepted this covenant as binding, and in confirmation thereof each gave the other a penny as a God's penny. And the said Peter gave to the said John 60s. for this business, and with the money thus received from Peter together with other money of his own he, John, bought porret seed and conveyed it to Scotland; and after he had transacted the said business there, he returned to Huntingdon on the Saturday after Mid-Lent in the same year, where he met the said Peter and delivered to him a horse worth 30s. as his share of the clear profit for the time being. And after the said Peter had received his share of the profit, he then offered to deliver to the said John a larger sum of money to continue their business, and the said John answered that he did not care to receive it until he should return from Scotland again. But, having returned from Scotland a second time on the Monday after the quindene of Easter in the said year, he met the said Peter in the town of Huntingdon and gave him at that time a horse with a good merchant's saddle worth 25s. as his share of the clear profit. And on the third journey of the said John to Scotland, which he undertook by the counsel and consent of the said Peter on the Monday after Septuagesima Sunday in the twenty-fifth year of the reign of King Edward, with three horses laden with porret seed with which and also with other merchandise he thought to do business there for his own profit and that of his said partner, he lost 33 marks. And on his return on the morrow of Easter Day in the said year he demanded that the said Peter

---

[96] i.e., traverses the formal allegations in the plaintiff's declaration. See Maitland, S.S. Vol. 2, p. 186, who suggests that the phrase is a corruption of ' words of course ' —*verba de cursu,* like *brevia de cursu.*

[97] Porret=onion or leek.

should make satisfaction to him for a third part of this loss according to the covenant made between them. Yet the said Peter in no way cared to do this, but forthwith demanded payment of the 60s. which he had delivered to the said John at the beginning of their partnership. Wherefore the said John, by reason of the injuries and grievances inflicted upon him by the said Peter, sold to the said Peter a messuage of his in Godmanchèster for 50s., and paid him 10s. in money; and moreover he delivered to the said Peter 10½d., which remained in the hands of the said John as clear profit from the two preceding journeys, to his great damage 100s., etc.

The said Peter is present and denies tort and force and all which should be denied, and he says expressly that he never made such a covenant with the said John; and that this is true he craves may be verified by a good inquest; and the adverse party does likewise. Therefore order is given to summon an inquest.

The inquest comes and says that the said Peter was never a partner of the said John as regards the transaction of the said business nor did he deliver to him any money save only 60s. by way of loan, in return for which the said John conveyed to him in perpetuity a certain messuage at Godmanchester for 40s. and two horses worth 20s. Therefore it is awarded that the said John recover nothing against the said Peter, but be in mercy for his false plaint.

I. HOPPMAN v. WELBORNE
S.S. Vol. 23, p. 86
A.D. 1302

Richard Hoppman of Lynn appears against Richard Welborne, citizen and draper of Norwich, who has been distrained by twenty pieces of cloth to come. And he complains of the said Richard Welborne, for that he unjustly detains from him and does not pay him £20 sterling; and unjustly because, whereas in the thirtieth year of the reign of King Edward the said Richard Hoppman had his cloth to sell in the fair of Stamford, the said Richard Welborne came there on the sixteenth day of April in the said year and received from him cloth from parts beyond the sea to the value of £33, whereof he was to have paid him, or his certain attorney bearing a writing obligatory made between them, £20 on Ascension Day in the said year at the fair of St. Ives and all the residue on the following feast of Holy Trinity in the town of Lynn. And of this £20 he has paid him nothing nor cared to pay, but has always hitherto detained the money to his great damage £10; and in proof thereof he makes profert of the said Richard Welborne's writing obligatory.

The said Richard Welborne is present and denies the words of court which should be denied, and craves that the said Richard Hoppman show in court if he has anything on his behalf whereby he can exact the said £20. And the said Richard Hoppman says that he has enough on his behalf, to wit, the writing obligatory of the said Richard Welborne, whereby he ought to recover his debt according to the law merchant.

And the said Richard Welborne craves and obtains a view of the said writing obligatory of which this is the tenor: —

> To all who shall see or hear this present writing Richard Welborne, citizen and draper of Norwich, greeting in the Lord. Know that I am indebted to Richard Hoppman, merchant of Lynn,

for £33 sterling for cloth bought and received at the time of the making of this present writing. Wherefore I am well content to pay the said Richard Hoppman, or his attorney bearing the present writing, fully and promptly at the times and places named below, to wit, £20 sterling at the fair of St. Ives on Ascension Day in the thirtieth year of the reign of King Edward and £13 sterling in the town of Lynn on the following feast of Holy Trinity. And I bind myself and my heirs and executors to make faithful payment thereof; and all my goods, wherever they may be found, may be distrained and detained by any sheriffs or bailiffs in whose jurisdiction they may be found for full payment of the said money and for complete restitution of all damages and expenses which the said Richard Hoppman or his attorney shall have sustained or incurred for default in the payment of the said money in the said way. In witness whereof I have put my seal to the present writing. Given at the fair of Stamford on the sixteenth day of April in the aforesaid year.

The said writing having been carefully examined, the said Richard Welborne afterwards comes and denies absolutely that this writing was ever his deed; and as to this he puts himself on an inquest of the merchants and others. And the said Richard Hoppman says that the said Richard Welborne unjustly denies that the said writing obligatory is his deed; and this he is ready to verify by a good inquest of the merchants who were at the fair of Stamford and others.

And because the merchants by whom the inquest should be made have left the fair, so that the said inquest cannot be made owing both to the small attendance at the court and to the claim of each party, a day is given to the said parties on the morrow of the coming feast of the Apostles Philip and James; and let the said twenty pieces of cloth be safely and honestly kept in the custody of Simon Wallis.

J. MOULTON v. BYHAM
S.S. VOL. 23, p. 103
A.D. 1317

John Byham and Simon Bateman were attached to answer Roger Moulton of a plea of covenant (*ad respondendum de placito convencionis*). And as to this, he complains that, whereas it was covenanted between them on the Sunday after the feast of Holy Trinity in the ninth year of the reign of the present King that the said John and Simon should build the said Roger a house in the vill of St. Ives, with the understanding that nothing of the old timber belonging to the said Roger should be put in the said house and that they should supply all that was needed from their own timber and that this should be of oak, and whereas the said Roger according to the agreement gave them for so building the said house a certain sum of money; the said John and Simon afterwards put alderwood and willow in the said house, contrary to the said covenant, to the damage of the said Roger, etc. And thereof he produces suit.

And the said John and Simon say that they put no timber of their own except oak in the said house, nor did they break any covenant as he alleges against them. And they crave that this be inquired; and the said Roger does likewise. Therefore order is given to cause a good inquest to come, etc.

The inquest comes and says that the said John and Simon broke their covenant with him, to his damage 2s. Therefore it is awarded that the said Roger recover, etc., and that the said John and Simon be in mercy 6d. Pledge of the said John, Nicholas Legge; pledge of the said Simon, William Gerold.

K. DYER v. GRANTHAM
S.S. VOL. 23, p. 105
A.D. 1317

John of Grantham, apothecary, and Bartholomew, his servant, were attached to answer Lawrence Dyer of a plea of covenant. And as to this he complains that, whereas on Friday the morrow of Ascension Day last past he, Lawrence, bought from the said John and Bartholomew in the vill of St. Ives in the booth of the said John a bale of plume alum containing 216 pounds for 26s. 9d. and a God's penny, which he paid on the pledge that the bale throughout was uniform with the sample thereof which had been shown to him; yet, when the said bale was emptied at Huntingdon on the following Tuesday, clay and earth mixed with the alum were found in the said bale contrary to the form of the said covenant (*contra formam convencionis predictæ*), and thus the alum was not uniform, to the damage of the said Lawrence, etc. And thereof he produces suit.

And the said John and Bartholomew come and deny tort and force, etc., and they fully acknowledge the said sale and pledge, as the said Lawrence alleges in his count; but they say that at the time when the said bale was delivered to the said Lawrence the said alum was uniform with the said sample in so far as such mineral alum could be or ought to be uniform. And they crave that this be inquired; and the said Lawrence does likewise. Therefore order is given to cause a good inquest to come, etc.

The inquest comes and says that the said alum is sufficiently uniform with the said sample. Therefore it is awarded that the said Lawrence take nothing by his plaint, but he in mercy 12d. for his false claim; pledge, a bale of alum.

PLEA ROLLS OF THE CITY OF LONDON [98]
WHITTINGTON v. TURNEBONIS
A.D. 1421

Richard Whittington, mercer, brought an action for debt against Stephen Turnebonis, merchant, for £296. In his bill he alleged that he had bought and had in his custody a certain Hugh Coniers, a prisoner of war taken in the battle of Agincourt and put to ransom at 1600 crowns, each crown being valued at 42d. in English money, and 16 marks of silver troy weight, each mark being valued at 20s., the whole amounting to £296; and that on 10 July 1420 in the parish of St. Michael de la Ryole the defendant agreed to pay that sum for the prisoner as soon as the plaintiff released to the prisoner all his right and claim in him for the ransom and should be prepared to hand him over to the defendant and obtain for the latter authentic letters under his seal witnessing the release; and that thereupon the plaintiff released his right to the prisoner and was ready to hand him over and obtain the

---

[98] *Calendar of Plea and Memoranda Rolls,* A.D. 1413-1437, ed. A. H. Thomas, LL.D. (1943), pp. 91-3.

aforesaid letters, but the defendant had not paid the money, though often requested to do so; to the plaintiff's damage £40.

The defendant . . . appeared on 27 February and said in protestation that the plaintiff had not released all right and claim to the prisoner and was not prepared to obtain the aforesaid letters; and for his plea he pleaded that the plaintiff was not ready to hand over the prisoner, and therefore no debt was owed.

The plaintiff prayed that the matter be inquired of by the country. The defendant, on the ground that he was an alien, prayed that one half of the jurors should be aliens, according to the form of the statute, which was granted.

On 5 March the serjeant returned the names of the jurors of the venue of the parish, viz., William Reynold, John Bacon, John Clerc, Thomas Walsyngham, John Brikles, John Synpston, John Tetford, Thomas Sutton and Edmund Salle, denizens; and Gerard Danidze, Francis Balby, Bartholomew Valerys, Paul Miliany, John Markannovo, John Abati, Nicholas Orlandini, Philip Saty and David Galganeti, aliens. . . .

Gerard Danidze and David Galganeti were challenged by the defendant, and Francis Balby, Bartholomew Valeris and John Markannovo by the plaintiff, as not having lands or rents to the annual value of 40s. according to the form of the statute,[99] and were removed from the jury. . . .

The serjeant was ordered to summon the jurors for 4 April with eight others, of whom half should be aliens. . . . [Six of the new jury were successfully challenged under the statute]. The plaintiff then prayed that ten other jurors be summoned, of whom half should be aliens. . . . [The next day the serjeant returned the names of four more English jurors], but declared that he could not find any aliens having the requisite annual value. The jury, thus being chosen, tried and sworn, . . . said on oath that the defendant owed the plaintiff £296 and assessed the damages at £10. On 10 April judgment was given that the plaintiff recover his debt and damages.

THE STATUTE OF STAPLES

27 ED. III. STAT. 2

A.D 1353

Cap. 8

We have ordained and established, That the Mayors and Constables of the Staple shall have jurisdiction and cognisance within the Towns where the Staples shall be,[1] and that all merchants coming to the Staple, their servants and household in the Staple, shall be ruled by the Law Merchant of all things touching the Staple, and not by the Common Law of the land nor

[99] 2 Hen. V, Stat. 2, c. 3 . . . 'No person shall be admitted to pass . . . on any inquest betwixt party and party in plea real or plea personal whereof the debt or the damages declared amount to 40 marks, if the same persons have not lands or tenements of the yearly value of 40 shillings.' As the above case shows, the effect of this statute was to limit the supply of qualified alien jurors with some severity.

[1] 'The Staple of wools, leather, wool-fells and lead, growing or coming forth within our said realm and lands, shall be perpetually holden at the places underwritten; that is to say, for England at Newcastle upon Tyne, York, Lincoln, Norwich, Westminster, Canterbury, Chichester, Winchester, Exeter and Bristol; for Wales at Caermarthen; and for Ireland at Dublin, Waterford, Cork and Drogheda; and not elsewhere '—Cap. I.

by the usage of cities, boroughs or other towns; and that they shall not implead nor be impleaded before the Justices of the said places in pleas of Debt, Covenant and Trespass touching the Staple, but shall implead all persons of whom they will complain as well such as be not of the Staple as those that be of the Staple which shall be there found, and in the same manner they shall be impleaded, only before the Mayor and Justices of the Staple, which shall be thereto deputed, of all manner of pleas and of actions whereof the cognizance pertaineth to the Ministers of the Staple: so always that of all manner of contracts and covenants made betwixt merchant and merchant, or whereof the one party is a merchant or Minister of the Staple, whether the contract or covenant be made within the Staple or without, and also of trespasses done within the Staple to merchants or to Ministers of the Staple by others, or by any of them to others, the party plaintiff shall choose whether he will sue his action or complaint (*sa accion ou sa querele*) before the Justices of the Staple by the law of the Staple or in other place by the Common Law. . . .

Cap. 9

To the intent that the contracts made within the same Staple shall be the better holden and the payments readily made, We have ordained and established, That every Mayor of the said Staples shall have power to take Recognizances of Debts, which a man will make before him in the presence of the Constables of the Staple or one of them; and that in every of the said Staples be a seal ordained, remaining in the custody of the Mayor of the Staple, under the seals of the Constables, and that all obligations which shall be made upon such Recognizances be sealed with the said seal . . .; and that the Mayor of the Staple, by virtue of the same letters so sealed, may take and hold in prison the bodies of the debtors after the term incurred, if they be found within the Staple, till they have made satisfaction to the creditor for the debt and damages; and may also arrest the goods of the said debtors found within the said Staple and may deliver the said goods to the said creditor by true estimation or may sell them at the best that a man may and deliver the money to the creditor up to the sum due. And in case that the debtors be not found within the Staple nor their goods to the value of the debt, the same shall be certified in the Chancery under the said seal, by which certification a writ shall be sent to take the bodies of the said debtors without letting them to mainprise, and to seize their lands and tenements, goods and chattels; and the writ shall be returned into the Chancery with the certificate of the value of the said lands and tenements, goods and chattels; and thereupon due execution shall be made from day to day in manner as it is contained in the Statute Merchant.[2] . . .

Cap. 20

Because we have taken all the merchant strangers coming into our said realm and lands into our special protection and moreover granted to do them speedy remedy of their grievances, if any be to them done; We have ordained and established, That if any outrage or grievance be done to them in the country out of the Staple, the Justices of the place where such outrages shall be done shall do speedy justice to them according to the Law Merchant

[2] *Supra*, p. 239.

from day to day and from hour to hour, without sparing any man or to drive them to sue at the Common Law. . . .

Cap. 21

. . . We have ordained and established, That in every town where the Staple is ordained a Mayor, good, lawful and sufficient, shall be made and established, having knowledge of the Law Merchant, to govern the Staple and to do right to every man after the laws aforesaid. . . . And in every place where the Staple is shall be two conveniable Constables . . . to do that which pertaineth to their office. . . .

Cap. 24

We will and ordain, That the merchant strangers shall choose two merchant strangers, whereof the one towards the South and the other towards the North shall be assigned to sit with the Mayor and Constables of the Staples . . . to hear the plaints touching merchant aliens that shall be moved before the said Mayor and Constables . . . to see that plain right be done to the said merchant aliens . . . ; and in case that debate rise betwixt them upon the discussing of any plea or complaint, the tenour of the same plea or complaint shall be sent before the Chancellor and other of our Council, to be determined there without delay. And also six persons shall be chosen, that is to say, four aliens, whereof two shall be of Almain and two of Lombardy, and two of England . . . ; that, when any question or debate shall arise or come amongst merchants of any unreasonable wool or improper packing according to the covenants made betwixt the sellers and the buyers, the said persons or four of them may before the Mayor of the Staple and the Officers by their oath say and amend as reason will, and thereupon credence shall be given to them without any contradiction.

SELECT CASES ON THE LAW MERCHANT
VOL. II
S.S. VOL. 46, ed. HALL

A. DUNSTABLE v. LE BAL
(at the Assises held in the County of Southampton)
S.S. VOL. 46, p. 28
A.D. 1278

The lord King commanded his beloved and trusty Salomon of Rochester and Master Thomas de Sutherington[3] that, whereas from the grave complaint of William of Dunstable, his citizen of Winchester, he had understood that, whereas the same William had bought from Robert le Bal' of Winchester 103 sacks of good merchantable wool sewn up in 86 sarplers,[4] namely, every sack out of 53 sacks for 8 marks and every sack out of the remaining 50 sacks for 6 marks, of which sarplers the same Robert in the presence of the aforesaid William caused 8 sarplers to be opened, namely 4 of the greater and 4 of the lesser price, whereof the same William had been content, and faithfully promised that the remaining wool sewn up in the sarplers was like

---

[3] Justices itinerant, holding the Assises in the County of Southampton.
[4] Sarpler = a large canvas sack for packing wool: used also as a measure of wool.

the wool opened; and whereas the said William, attaching faith to the statements of the said Robert herein, carried the whole of the wool aforesaid, save two sacks and a half which were stolen in the custody of the said Robert, to St. Omer: yet, when the same William caused it to be opened and exposed for sale at St. Omer, he found the wool sewn up in 68 sarplers, of which he had not made inspection, vile and useless and altogether differing from his agreement; whereby the same William, through the default of the aforesaid Robert herein, incurred a loss in his goods and merchandises of a hundred pounds.

And because the lord King is unwilling to leave such great malice unpunished, if it should have been perpetrated, he has appointed the aforesaid Salomon and Thomas to inquire in the presence of lawful and discreet merchants and citizens of Winchester by the oath of good and lawful men of the same city through whom the truth of the matter can best be known in the premises, and for swift and competent amends thereof to be made according to the law merchant.   Wherefore the aforesaid Salomon and Master Thomas commanded the Sheriff of Southampton that he should cause to come before them at Winchester in the Feast of St. Vincent in the sixth year so many and such good and lawful men of the city aforesaid as through them the truth of the matter might best and most fully be known and inquired.

At which day the aforesaid Salomon and Thomas came there. William and Robert came before them.   And William complains of the aforesaid Robert and says that, whereas he should have bought from the aforesaid Robert 103 sacks of good merchantable wool sewn up in 86 sacks, namely every sack out of 53 sacks for 8 marks and every sack out of the remaining 50 sacks for 6 marks, of which sarplers the same Robert in the presence of William himself caused 8 sarplers to be opened, namely 4 of the greater and 4 of the lesser price, of which he himself had been content, and faithfully promised that the remaining wool sewn up in the sarplers was like the wool opened; and whereas the same William, attaching faith to the statements of the said Robert, carried the whole wool aforesaid, save two sacks and a half which were stolen in the custody of the said Robert, to St. Omer; yet, when he had caused it to be opened there and exposed for sale, he found the wool sewn up in 68 sarplers, of which he had not made inspection, vile and useless and wholly differing from his agreement; whereby the same William and his men stood in peril of death in the foreign parts aforesaid.   And moreover he complains that, whereas he had bought the aforesaid 103 sacks of wool from the aforesaid Robert and had in good faith and according to the custom of the country handed them to him to be kept until he had sent for them, two sacks and a half, of the price of 20 marks, were abstracted thence by the aforesaid Robert and his household.   Whereby he says that he is damaged and has loss to the value of a hundred pounds.   And thereof he brings suit. . . .

[Robert le Bal' refuses to answer, but ' departs in contempt of the court.' The jurors find for William of Dunstable.]

. . . Wherefore it is awarded that the aforesaid William do recover the aforesaid price against the aforesaid Robert, and likewise his losses, which are taxed by good and lawful citizens and merchants at 20 marks.   And let the aforesaid Robert be taken, etc.

B. PYLATE v. CAUSE

(Before the Barons of the Exchequer)

S.S. VOL. 46, p. 63

A.D. 1299

William Cause of Lincoln was attached to answer James Pylate, yeoman of Walter, Bishop of Coventry and Lichfield, Treasurer of the lord King,[5] of a plea that he do render to him (James) 20 marks which he (William) owes to him; and whereof he proffered a certain writing in which is contained that in the year of Grace 1287, namely in the 15th year of the reign of the now King Edward, on the day of the Assumption of the Blessed Mary the Virgin, in the fair of St. Botolph, a covenant was made between William Cause, citizen of Lincoln, of the one part, and Everard of St. Venant and James Pylate, merchants of Douai, . . . of the other part, namely that the aforesaid William granted and sold to the aforesaid Everard and James all the wool of the house of Welbeck of the Premonstratensian Order, as well for the year of Our Lord 1290, namely for the 18th year of the now King Edward, as for the six years next and continuously following, namely every sack of good wool for 15 marks sterling and every sack of middling wool for 10 marks sterling and every sack of selected locks[6] for 8 marks sterling; whereupon [the agents of Everard and James] . . . have paid to the aforesaid William 20 marks sterling as earnest money (*in arris*) at the time of the making of the aforesaid writing, to be allowed to the same merchants in payment for the said wools in the last year of this covenant. And he (James) says that he did not receive the aforesaid wools except for the first three years, wherefore he asks for the said 20 marks to be restored to him according to the form of the said covenant.

And the aforesaid William Cause comes by his attorney and says that he is not bound to answer for the aforesaid 20 marks, because he says that [the plaintiff's agents] had the aforesaid wools from him for four years, and as to the residue of the time he was prepared every year at the Feast of St. James at Lincoln, according to the said covenant made between them, to have made delivery to [the plaintiff's agents] or to their attorneys, if they had come. And as neither the said merchants nor anyone in their name came after the aforesaid fourth year to seek the aforesaid wools, and also as in every year for a long time after the term appointed between them he retained and kept his said wools in expectation of the coming of the said merchants or of their attorneys, until the said wools or a large part of the same through this detention were deteriorated and the price of the same cheapened, on account of which he incurred very great loss, and no default remained in him but that the aforesaid merchants or their attorneys might have had and received the aforesaid wools, he craves judgment whether he is bound to answer for the aforesaid 20 marks.

And the aforesaid James says that he did not have the aforesaid wools save for the first three years, because he says that in the fourth year he himself was out of the Kingdom because of the war, and that the sea was then closed so that none was able to enter that Kingdom nor to transport anything therefrom. And this clearly appears by the date of the covenant aforesaid.

---

[5] Pylate, a merchant of Douai, is described as the Treasurer's yeoman in order to give the Barons of the Exchequer power to hear the case.
[6] 'Locks' were inferior or short wools.

And upon this they have a day, on the morrow of St. Michael. . . . On which day the aforesaid parties came; and they have a day, from day to day, etc.

C. LE FEYTUR'S CASE
(*Before the Barons of the Exchequer*)
S.S. VOL. 46, p. 79
A.D. 1309

Richard le Feytur of Chipping Norton was attached in London to answer Erneric de Friscobaldis and his fellows, merchants of the Society of Friscobaldi of Florence,[7] of a plea that he do render to him £55 which he owes to them. And as to this the same merchants proffer a certain writing which-they say is the deed of the said Richard; wherein is contained that the aforesaid Richard acknowledges himself bound to Betinus de Friscobaldis and Coppus Cottene and their fellows of the Society of Friscobaldi in £55 for 22 cloths of ray of Ghent bought from them in the Fair of St. Botulph, to be paid to the same Betinus or to his fellows or to anyone bearing this letter at London on the Eve of Christmas in the year of Grace 1304. And for this he binds himself and all his goods, etc. Dated in the Fair of St. Botulph, Thursday next after the Feast of the Assumption of the Blessed Mary the Virgin in the year aforesaid. And they say that the aforesaid Richard has unjustly detained from them the aforesaid £55 to this day and still detains them; to the loss of the said merchants £40. And thereof they produce suit.

And the aforesaid Richard in his proper person comes and defends all injury, etc. And he craves a view of the aforesaid writing. And, when he has had this, he well acknowledges that it is his deed, but he says that in no respect ought this to harm him; for he says that on the day of the execution of that writing the same Richard was imprisoned at Boston in the King's prison at the prosecution of the said merchants; and while he was thus in prison he made the aforesaid writing and signed and sealed it, through the distraint of prison; wherefore he is not bound to answer for this debt. And he craves that this be inquired of.

And the aforesaid merchants say that the aforesaid Richard made the said writing and sealed and signed it of his free will and out of prison; and this they likewise crave that it be inquired of.

Therefore a day is given further, in 15 days of the day of St. Michael. And the Sheriff of Lincolnshire is commanded that he cause to come here at that day, unless before that day (*nisi prius*) John de Sandale and Thomas de Cambridge[8] come to Boston, etc., twelve as well Lombard merchants as men of the parts of Boston to certify, etc. . . .

Afterwards, on Friday next before the Feast of St. Laurence in the third year of the reign of the now King Edward, the aforesaid merchants'[9] came before the aforesaid Thomas of Cambridge at Boston, and the aforesaid Richard came not. . . . Therefore, on his default, the taking of the inquisition is proceeded with. And the inquest comes, as well by Lombards as by men

---

[7] For this Society, see Renouard, *Les Relations des Papes d'Avignon et des Compagnies Commerciales et Bancaires de* 1316 *à* 1378 (1941), pp. 81, 570-2. The Society went bankrupt in 1312.
[8] Barons of the Exchequer.
[9] i.e., the plaintiffs.

of this Kingdom, according to a charter of King Edward, father of the King that now is, which the said merchants proffered and wherein it is willed that in every inquisition to be taken between Lombards and other men, whosoever they might be, the one half of that inquest is to consist of Lombards and the other half of men of England.

The jurors say by their oath that the aforesaid Richard made and executed the aforesaid writing by his good and free will and out of prison, and that the aforesaid merchants by reason of the unjust detention of the aforesaid debt had loss to the value of £20. Wherefore a day is given to the aforesaid merchants, at the aforesaid Quindene of St. Michael, at the Exchequer, to hear their judgment.

Afterwards, at that day, the aforesaid merchants ask leave to withdraw from their writ, and they have leave. And the said writing is delivered to them again.

PETITIONS IN CHANCERY

BARBOUR, *The History of Contract in Early English Equity*
(*Oxford Studies in Social and Legal History, Vol. IV*)

A. BELLERS' CASE
AFTER A.D. 1432 (BARBOUR, p. 182)
To hise fulgracius Lord the Chaunceller of England

Right mekely besechith Rauf Bellers that, for as moche as William Harper of Mancestre and Richard Barbour weren endetted to the seyde Rauf in certain sumes of mone withoute specialte to be payed unto the seyde Rauf or to hise certain attorne at certain dayes past, at the wheche dayes and longe aftir the seyde William and Richard weren required by the seyde Rauf to make hym payment of the seyde sumes, the wheche request the seyde William and Richard wolde not obeye in any wyse, soo that the seyde Rauf, consideryng that the seyde William and Richard wolde make hor lawe in that partie agens faithe and good conscience, sued to the Archebisshop of Yorke, at that tyme chaunceller of England, for remedie in that caas; apon the wheche suggestion the seyde chaunceller graunted under certain payne writtes severally direct unto the seyde William and Richard to apere afore hym in the chauncery, there to be examyned apon the seyde matere; by force of that oon of the seyde writtes the seyd Richard apered in the seyde chauncerie and there agreed with the seyd suppliant, and the seyde William myght nat be founde, soo that the writ direct unto hym stode in none effect: wherefore liketh to youre gracious lordeship to graunte a writ under a certain payn direct to the seyd William to aper afore yowe in the chauncerie, there to be examyned upon the matere afore-seyd for goddis luf and in werk of charite.

B. THE CASE OF THE UNIVERSITY OF CAMBRIDGE
AFTER A.D. 1433 (BARBOUR, p. 221)
To the full reverent Fader in god the Bisshop of Bathe, Chaunceller of England

Besecheth lowely your pore oratour John Langton, Chaunceller of the universite of Cantebrigge, that, where the seyd Chaunceller and universite by the assent and graunte of our soverain lord the Kyng have late ordeyned to founde and stablisse a college in the same toun, it to be called the universite college, and to endowe it with diverse possessions in relevyng of the sayd universitie and encresing of clergie thereof, And how late acorde took bytwix oon Sir William Bingham that the seyd Chaunceller and scolers shuld have a place of the seyd Sir William adjoyning on every side to the ground of the seyd Chaunceller and universite that they have ordeyned to bild her seyd college upon for the augmencacion and enlargeyng of her seyd college and to edifie upon certain scoles of Civill and other faculteez, and for to gif the seyd Sir William a noder place therfor, lyeng in the sayd toun betwix the Whit Freres and seint Johns Chirch, and do it to be amorteysed suerly after the intent of the seyd Sir William at the cost of the seyd Chaunceller and universite, as the ful reverent fader in god, the bisshop of Lincoln, in whose presence this covenaunt and acorde was made, wole recorde: And it is so, reverent lord, that the seyd Chaunceller and universite according to this covenaunt have ordeyned the seyd Sir William a sufficeant place lyeing in the seyd toun of Canterbrigge bytwix the said Whit Freres and seint Johns Chirch and extendyng doun to the Ryver of the same toun wyth a garden therto, which place is of better value then this other place is, and profred to amorteyse it at her own cost acordyng to the covenaunt forseyd, and therupon diverse costes and grete labores have made and doon late therfor: And also required diverses tymes the seyd Sir William to kepe and performe on his parte these seyd covenauntz, the seid Sir William now of self wille and wythoute any cause refusith it and will not doo it in noo wise:

Plese it to your gracious lordship to consider thes premisses and therupon to graunt to your seyd besechers a writ sub pena direct to the seyd Sir William to appere afore yow in the Chauncery of our lord kyng at a certain day upon a certain peyne by yow to be limited, to be examened of these materes forseid and therupon to ordeyne by your gracious lordship that the said Sir William may be compelled to do what trowth, good faith and consciens requiren in this caas, considering that, in alsomich as there is no writing betwix your seyd besechers and the seyd Sir William, thei may have noon accion at the comyn lawe, and that for god and in wey of charite.

C. GOLDSMYTH'S CASE
A.D. 1443-1450. (BARBOUR, p. 188)

To the most reverent Fader in God John Erchbysshop of Caunterbury Chauncellere of England

Besechuth humbully youre pore and contynuell oratoure, Conrade Goldsmyth, that, where oon Laurence Walkere the Saturday next before the Fest of the Purification of oure lady, the yere of the regne of the Kyng oure sovereyne lord, that is to say Kyng Harry the Sixte, att Teukesbury bought of youre seide besechere ii clothes and half of blankett for vii l. to be payode to the same besechere in the Fest of the Anunciacon of oure lady thenne next sewyng, for which payement as well and trewely to be made oon Symkyn Bakere of Teukesbury undertoke and bykame borowe for the seide Laurence, in as muche as the seide supliant wolde nothur have solde nor delyverode the seide clothe unto the seide Laurence butt only uppon trust of the seide Symkyn and that he wolde undertake for payement of the seide sume, which he feythfully promyttode unto the seide supliant that he schulde be satisfiode and payode therof atte his day, of which sume remayneth yett iii l. unpayode which nothur the seide Laurence nor the seide Symkyn yett hath satisfiode nor payode unto youre seide besecher; and the seide Laurence is wythdrawen to strange places unknowen, so that youre seide besecher may noo remedye have agenst hym, thaughe he sewe hym by wrytte, nor agenst the seide Symkyn by the cours of the comyn lawe:

Pleasith youre gracious Lordship to consyder these premissez and ther uppon to do the seide Conrade to have dewe remedye agenest the seide Symkyn, for the love of God and in Wey of Charyte.

Plegii de prosequendo: Ricardus Bury de Solbe in Com' Glouc.' Henricus Wakfeld de Camden in eadem Com'.

D. WHITEHEAD'S CASE

AFTER A.D. 1475. (BARBOUR, p. 225)

To the right reverent Fader in god the Bisshop of Lincoln Chaunceller of England

Mekely besecheth youre good and gracious lordship John Whithed, Esquier, that, wheras oon Robert Orchard late in an accion of waste suyd by the seid John Whitehed ageyn the seid Robert before the kinges Justices of his comone benche for brenning[10] of a water Mill, whiche the seid John Whithed had before leten to ferme to the seid Robert for terme of certeyn yeres, was condempnyd to the seid John Whithed in xxx l., and the seid Robert Orchard also at the suyte of the seid John Whithed, by processe thereuppon had, was for the same xxx l. in prison and execucon unto the tyme that John Spryng of Suthampton, Peautrer, grauntyd and feithefully promysed to the seid John Whithed that, if he wold relesse and discharge the seid Robert Orchard of his seid imprisonment and execucon and suffere hym to go at his liberte, that then the seid John Spryng at his owne propre cost and charge wold sufficiently and substancially edifie and bilde the seid mill ageyne bothe in tymber werk and stonys to the same expedient by a certeyn day nowe long tyme past: Wheruppon the seid John Whitched, trystyng the promysse of the seid John Spryng, at his desire immediatly relessyd and discharged the seid Robert Orchard of his seid execucon and lete hym go at large at his liberte, and howe be hit that the seid John Spryng before the seid day reedified not the seid Mill in fourme aforseid nor no part thereof, and that the seid John Whithed often tymes sythe the seid day hathe requyred the seid John Spryng to reedifie and bilde the seid Mill as ys aforeseid acordyng to his seid promyse, that to do at all tymes as yet he hath refusyd, contrairie to his seyd promysse, good feithe and conciens, of whiche youre seid besecher hathe no remedie by the comone law of this land:

Wherefor pleaseth hit youre good and gracious lordship, the premissis tenderly considered, to graunt a writ Suppena to be directed to the seid John Spryng, comandyng hym by the same to appere before the kyng in his Chauncery at a certayne day and undur a certeyne payne by your lordship to be lymitted, and ther to be rewled and Juged as good conciens requyreth, for the love of god and in wey of cheryte.

Plegii de prosequendo: Johannes Purvyer de London, Iremonger. Thomas Clyfton de eadem, Draper.

[10] i.e., burning.

E. GODEMOND'S CASE

A.D. 1480-1 (BARBOUR, p. 231)

*To the right reverend Fader in god and my gode lorde the Bisshope
of Lyncoln Chauncellar of Englonde*

Mekely besecheth your gode and gracious lordshipp youre Poure Oratour
Roger Godemond, that, where he afore this tyme uppon a X yere past
and more was bounde to one Alice Reme, Wedowe, by his syngle Obligacion
in X marke sterlyng paiable at a certeyn day in the said Obligacion specified,
and afterward the same Alice made her executours John Hale and one
Thomas Plane and died, after whos dethe youre seid Oratour truely paied
and full contented the seid executours of the dewete of the seid Obligacion,
trustyng by that payment to be discharged of the seid Obligacion, and lefte
the same Obligacion in the handys of the seid executours, trustyng that the
seid executours wolde have delyvered the seid Obligacion to your seid
besecher at all tymes when they hadde ben therto requyred; And afterward
the seid John Hale died, after whos dethe the seid Thomas Plane as executour of the seid Alice, not withstandyng the seid payment hadde and
contentacion of the Obligacion made, suethe an accion of dette nowe late
afore the kyngis Justice of the Comen Place upon the seid Obligacion agenst
your seid besecher, not dredyng god ne th'offens of his owne consciens,
intendyng bi the same accion shortly to condempne your seid besecher in the
seid X marke, because the seid payment can make no barr at the comen
lawe, and so to be twys satisfied upon the same Obligacion for one dewte,
contrary to all reason and gode conscience, whereof your seid besecher is
withoute remedy be the Comen lawe without your gode and gracious lordship to him be shewed in this behalf:

Please it therfor your gode and gracious lordship the premysses tenderly
to consyder and to graunte a writte Suppena to be directe to the seid Thomas
Plane, comaundyng hym bi the same to appere afore the kyng in his Court
of Chauncerie at a certeyn day and upon a certeyn peyn by your lordshipp
to be lemette, there to answer to the premysses and to bryng afore your seid
lordshipp the seid Obligacion to be cancelled, and ferthermore that he
may have ynyongcion[11] no further to procede in the seid accion at Comen
lawe till your seid lordshipp have examyned the premysses and sett such
rewle and direction in the same as shall accorde with reason and gode
consciens, and this for the love of god and in the Wey of Charite.

Plegii de prosequendo: Ricardus Somer de London, Gentilman.
Thomas Mey de London, Gent'.

Answer to the Petition.

*This is the answere of Thomas Plane oon of the executours of Alice Reme,
Wedowe, to the bill of complaynt of Roger Godmond.*

The seid Thomas Plane by protestacon sayeth that the mater conteigned in
the bill of compleynt of the seid Roger is not sufficient in lawe to put hym to
answere to the same; for plee, he sayeth that the seid Roger paid not the
seid X marcs nor non parcell thereof to the seid Thomas Plane ne to John
Hale his coexecutour in maner and forme as the seid Roger bi his seid
bille of complaynt hath surmyttyd; all whiche maters the seid Thomas Plane
is redy to averre as this court will award, and askith juggement and prayeth

---

[11] i.e., injunction.

to be dysmyssed out of this court wyth his resonable costys and expenses for his wrongfull hurte and vexacon in that behalf don, had or susteyned.

Endorsement on Petition.

Memorandum quod termino Sancti Michaelis, videlicet sexto die Novembris Anno, etc. XIX°, iniunctum fuit Thome Sharp, attorn' infranominati Thome Plane, quod ipse sub pena Centum marcarum minime prosequatur versus infranominatum Rogerum Godemond in quodam placito debiti super demandum decem marcarum coram Justiciis Regis de Banco suo, quousque materia infraspecificata plene determinata fuerit et discussa.

ANON
Y.B. PASCH. 22 ED. 4, f. 6, pl. 18
A.D. 1482

In the Exchequer Chamber before all the Justices of the one Bench and the other and in the presence of several Serjeants and Apprentices, the Archbishop of York, then Chancellor of England,[12] sought the advice of the Justices upon the grant of a Subpœna.

And he said that a complaint had been made to him that one was under obligation by Statute Merchant to another and had paid the money but had taken no release; and, notwithstanding this payment, the creditor sued out execution. And he said that the creditor, if he were examined, could not deny the payment. How then, Sirs, should I grant a Subpœna or not?

FAIRFAX, J.: It seems to me against all reason to grant a Subpœna, and by the evidence of two witnesses to subvert matter of record. For, where one is bound in this manner, he need not pay without acquittance or release. So, where a man is obliged on an obligation, he need not discharge his duty unless the obligee will make him an acquittance; and so it seems to me that this is his folly.

THE CHANCELLOR said that it was the common course in the Chancery to grant relief against an obligation; just as in the case of a feoffment upon trust, where the heir of the feoffee is in by descent or otherwise. For we find record of such cases in the Chancery.

HUSSEY, the Chief Justice of the King's Bench: When I first came into Court, which is not yet thirty years ago, it was agreed in a case by all the Court that, if a man had enfeoffed another on trust and if he died seised, so that the heir was in by descent, then the Subpœna would not lie; and there is good reason for this. For, just as, by a Subpœna, one descent might be disproved in the Chancery by two witnesses, so by the same reasoning twenty descents might be disproved; which is against reason and conscience. And so it seems to me that it is less harmful to make him who suffers his feoffee to die seised of his land to lose his land than to work a disinheritance by evidence in Chancery. And so, in the case of the Statute Merchant and also in that of the obligation, it is less harmful to make him pay again through his negligence than by two witnesses in the Chancery to disprove a matter of record or a matter in specialty. For it is all due to his negligence, since he need not have paid on the obligation before taking an acquittance or release from the plaintiff. Such is the law.

---

[12] Thomas Rotherham, Chancellor 1474-1483.

Whereupon the Chancellor said that it would seem great folly to enfeoff others of one's land.

And then the Chancellor agreed to the Statute Merchant, because it was matter of record.

ANON

Y.B. HIL. 4 HEN. 7, f. 4, pl. 8

A.D. 1489

A *Subpœna* was sued in the Chancery on this, that there were two executors and one, without the assent of his companion, released a man who was indebted to their testator. And it was argued that his intent should not in these circumstances be fulfilled, and a *Subpœna* was sued against the executor who released and against the debtor who was thus released.

Fineux said that no remedy lay here; for each executor has full and complete power and one may do everything that his companion might do, and so the release made by him was good.

THE CHANCELLOR[13]: *Nullus recedat a Curia Cancellariæ sine remedio;* and it is against reason that one executor shall have all the goods and shall make a release by himself.

Fineux: *Si nullus recedat sine remedio, ergo nullus indiget esse confessus.* But, Sir, the Law of the Land covers many things, and many things are sued here which are without remedy at the Common Law, and so these latter lie in conscience between a man and his confessor; and this is such a case.

THE CHANCELLOR: Sir, I know well that each Law is, or ought to be, in accord with the Law of God; and the Law of God is that an executor, who is of evil disposition, must not waste all the goods, etc. And I know well that if he does so waste and makes no amends or satisfaction, so far as he is able, or will not make restitution, so far as he is able, he shall be damned in Hell. And to make remedy for such an act as this, as I think, is well done according to conscience. And the will says, *constituo tales esse executores meos, ut ipsi disponant,* etc.; and so their powers are joint and not several, and, if one acts without his companion, he does so without authority. . . . .

DOCTOR AND STUDENT

Christopher St. Germain

DIALOGUE II—CHAP. XXIV[14]

What is a nude contract or naked promise after the laws of England, and whether any action may lie thereon.

Student: . . . . A nude contract is, when a man maketh a bargain or a sale of his goods or lands without any recompence appointed for it: as if I say to another, I sell thee all my land, or else my goods, and nothing is assigned that the other shall give or pay for it; this is a nude contract, and, as I take it, it is void in the law and conscience. And a nude or naked promise is, where a man promiseth another to give him certain money such a day or to build an house or to do him such certain service, and nothing is

---

[13] John Morton, Archbishop of Canterbury.
[14] The Second Dialogue of the Doctor and Student was first published, in English, in 1530. The edition cited above is that of William Muchall (1787).

assigned for the money, for the building, nor for the service; these be called naked promises, because there is nothing assigned why they should be made; and I think no action lieth in those cases, though they be not performed. Also if I promise to another to keep him such certain goods safely to such a time, and after I refuse to take them, there lieth no action against me for it. But if I take them, and after they be lost or impaired through my negligent keeping, there an action lieth.

Doctor: But what opinion hold they that be learned in the law of England in such promises that be called naked or nude promises? Whether do they hold that they that make the promise be bounden in conscience to perform their promise, though they cannot be compelled thereto by the law, or not?

Student: The books of the law of England entreat little thereof, for it is left to the determination of doctors; and therefore I pray thee shew me somewhat now of thy mind therein, and then I shall shew thee somewhat therein of the minds of divers that be learned in the law of the realm.

Doctor: To declare the matter plainly after the saying of doctors, it would ask a long time, and therefore I will touch it briefly, to give thee occasion to desire to hear more therein hereafter. First, thou shall understand that there is a promise that is called an *Advow*, and that is a promise made to God; and he that doth make such a vow upon a deliberate mind, intending to perform it, is bound in conscience to do it, though it be only made in the heart, without pronouncing of words. And of other promises made to a man upon a certain consideration, if the promise be not against the law, as if A. promise to give B. £20 because he hath made him such an house or hath lent him such a thing or other such like, I think him bound to keep his promise. But if his promise be so naked that there is no manner of consideration why it should be made, then I think him not bound to perform it: for it is to suppose that there were some error in the making of the promise. But if such a promise be made to an university, to a city, to the church, to the clergy, or to poor men of such a place and to the honour of God or such other cause like, as for maintenance of learning, of the commonwealth, of the service of God or in relief of poverty, or such other; then I think that he is bounden in conscience to perform it, though there be no consideration of worldly profit that the grantor hath had or intended to have for it. And in all such promises it must be understood that he that made the promise intended to be bound by his promise; for else commonly, after all doctors, he is not bound unless he were bound to it before his promise: as if a man promise to give his father a gown that hath need of it to keep him from cold, and yet thinketh not to give it him, nevertheless he is bound to give it, for he was bound thereto before. And, after some doctors, a man may be excused of such a promise in conscience by casualty that cometh after the promise, if it be so that if he had known of the casualty at the making of the promise he would not have made it. And also such promises, if they shall bind, they must be honest, lawful and possible, and else they are not to be holden in conscience, though there be a cause, etc. And if the promise be good and with a cause, though no worldly profit shall grow thereby to him that maketh the profit, but only a spiritual profit, as in the case before rehearsed of a promise made to an university, to a city, to the church or such other, and with a cause as to the honour of God, there it is most commonly holden that an action upon those promises lieth in the law canon.

Student: Whether dost thou mean, in such promises made to an university, to a city or to such other as thou hast rehearsed before, and with a cause as to the honour of God or such other, that the party should be bound by his promise, if he intended not to be bound thereby, yea or nay?

Doctor: I think nay, no more than upon promises made unto common persons.

Student: And then methinketh clearly that no action can lie against him upon such promises, for it is a secret in his own conscience whether he intended for it to be bound or nay. And of the intent inward in the heart man's law cannot judge, and that is one of the causes why the law of God is necessary, that is to say, to judge inward things; and if an action should lie in that case in the law canon, then should the law canon judge upon the inward intent of the heart, which cannot be, as me seemeth. And therefore, after divers that be learned in the laws of the realm, all promises shall be taken in this manner: that is to say, if he to whom the promise is made have a charge by reason of the promise, which he hath also performed, then in that case he shall have an action for that thing that was promised, though he that made the promise have no worldly profit by it. And if a man say to another, heal such a poor man of his disease or make an highway, and I will give thee thus much, and if he do it, I think an action lieth at the Common Law; and, moreover, though the thing that he should do be all spiritual, yet, if he perform it, I think an action lieth at the Common Law. As if a man say to another, fast for me all the next Lent and I will give thee twenty pounds, and he performeth it; I think an action lieth at the Common Law. And likewise if a man say to another, marry my daughter and I will give thee twenty pounds; upon this promise an action lieth, if he marry his daughter.[15] And in this case he cannot discharge the promise though he thought not to be bound thereby; for it is a good contract, and he may have *quid pro quo,* that is to say, the preferment of his daughter for his money. But in those promises made to an university or such other as thou hast remembered before, with such causes as thou hast shewed, that is to say, to the honour of God or to the increase of learning or such other like, where the party to whom the promise was made is bound to no new charge by reason of the promise made to him, but as he was bound to before; there they think that no action lieth against him though he perform not his promise, for it is no contract, and so his own conscience must be his judge whether he intended to be bound by his promise or not. And if he intended it not, then he offended for his dissimulation only; but if he intended to be bound, then if he perform it not, untruth is in him and he proveth himself to be a liar, which is prohibited as well by the law of God as by the law of reason. And furthermore, many that be learned in the law of England hold that a man is as much bounden in conscience by a promise made to a common person, if he intended to be bound by his promise, as he is in the other cases that thou hast remembered of a promise made to the church or the clergy or such other; for they say as much untruth is in the breaking of the one as of the other, and they say that the untruth is more to be pondered than the person to whom the promises are made.

Doctor: But what hold they if a promise be made for a thing past, as I promise thee forty pounds for that thou hast builded me such a house; lieth an action there?

---

[15] See *Anon,* Y.B. 37 Hen. 6, f. 8, pl. 18, *supra,* p. 249.

Student: They suppose nay; but he shall be bound in conscience to perform it after his intent, as is before said.

Doctor: And if a man promise to give another forty pounds in recompence for such a trespass that he hath done him, lieth an action there?

Student: I suppose nay; and the cause is for that such promises be no perfect contracts. For a contract is properly where a man for his money shall have by assent of the other party certain goods or some other profit at the time of the contract or after; but if the thing be promised for a cause that is past by way of recompense, then it is rather an accord than a contract; but then the law is that upon such accord the thing that is promised in recompense must be paid, or delivered in hand, for upon an accord there lieth no action. . . .

∽ *14* ∾

THE EVOLUTION OF ASSUMPSIT

THE mediæval common law was familiar both with the facts and with the idea of contract. But its favourite instruments of Covenant and Debt, though intrinsically capable of rich development, had been stunted by technical rules, the former by the insistence upon Seal, the latter by the doctrine of Quid pro Quo. Even when constrained to meet the needs of the parties to a sale of goods, it reacted, not by a change of heart, but by an artificial, if salutary, refinement upon existing principle. It could not bring itself to admit, at least within the scope of the older writs, the validity of mutual promises, through which alone a comprehensive law of contract could emerge and which was tacitly assumed in the local courts and boldly avowed by the Chancellor. If it wished to compete with its rivals, it must seek new remedies. The search was protracted.

A passing reference must be made to a case of 1348, not for its inherent importance, but because of the weight thrust upon it by modern and unfortunate reconstruction. A petitioner complained to the King's Bench, sitting at York, of the loss of his mare through the over-loading of a ferry.

> J. de B. complained by bill that G. de F. on a certain day and year at B. on the Humber had undertaken (*emprist*) to carry his mare in his boat across the river Humber safe and sound, but that the said G. so overloaded his boat with other beasts that by such overloading the mare perished, *a tort et damage,* etc.
>
> *Richmond*: Judgment of the bill, which supposes no tort in us, but rather proves that he should have an action by writ by way of Covenant or by way of Trespass.
>
> BANKWELL, J.: It seems that you did him a trespass when you overloaded the boat, whereby his mare perished. So answer over.[1]

The defendant's counsel then pleaded *not guilty,* and judgment was ultimately recorded against him. The case has sometimes been described as a landmark in the history of contract. Ames cited it as one of the ' earliest cases in which an *assumpsit* was laid in the declaration.'[2] Holdsworth used it to illustrate that ' special variety of trespass or deceit on the case which came to be known as the action of assumpsit.'[3] Professor Plucknett has exposed the inaccuracy of these statements. While the word ' emprist ' appears in the report,

---

[1] Lib. Ass. 22 Ed. 3, pl. 41. See the case set out and discussed by Professor Plucknett in his *Concise History,* 4th ed., pp. 441-2.
[2] *Lectures on Legal History,* p. 130.
[3] Holdsworth, *H.E.L.* III, p. 430.

the declaration, preserved in the record, made no mention of an *assumpsit*, but alleged the defendant to have ' received the mare to carry safely in his ship.' The action was not in case, which had yet to be born, but in trespass. The proceedings were initiated, not by writ, but by the less formal bill or *querela* which still lingered in the provinces and which explains the anomaly of trespass successfully applied without any direct and unauthorised act of interference. The case, in short, was not a precedent but a freak.

The action on the case, once admitted, offered a more fruitful soil for experiment. In *Waldon* v. *Marshall* in 1370 the plaintiff alleged that the defendant had undertaken (*manucepit*) to cure his horse, but had done his work so carelessly (*ita negligenter*) that the beast died. Counsel for the defendant urged that the action rested upon the fact of a promise and that the appropriate remedy, had there been a deed, was Covenant; but the writ was upheld because the defendant, by his negligent conduct, had caused the plaintiff damage.[4] In a similar case in 1375 the writ was quashed because, while the proof of an undertaking was vital to the plaintiff's success, he had omitted to lay a *venue,* so that the jury could not be summoned. Had this detail been in order, Chief Justice Cavendish would have supported it. ' For every little thing a man cannot always have a clerk to make a specialty for him.'[5] Already the essential difficulty had emerged. On the one hand, Bench and Bar alike saw the contractual implications and deplored the formality of Covenant. On the other hand, the new remedy at their disposal had its roots not in contract but in tort, and, cut after the pattern of trespass, demanded, in modern jargon, ' some positive act of negligent misfeasance.' What was to happen if the plaintiff proved no more than the failure to implement an undertaking? Could he sustain an action of Trespass on the Case where the defendant had done nothing at all?

The point was taken in the first decade of the fifteenth century. In 1400 and again in 1409 the plaintiff complained that the defendant had undertaken (*assumpsisset*) to build him a house and had not done so, and in each case he failed on the precise issue of misfeasance or nonfeasance.[6] If he relied upon a nonfeasance, he must produce a deed and sue in Covenant. The conclusion, if not irresistible, was to be expected. But, like other inferences drawn from technical premises, it must have seemed pedantic to a litigant whose damage was as serious in the one instance as in the other, and in *Watkins' Case* in 1425 the judges showed some inclination to retreat from the consequences of their logic.[7] The plaintiff, in an action of *Trespass sur ce cas,* alleged

---

[4] Y.B. Mich. 43 Ed. 3, f. 33, pl. 38, *supra,* p. 81.
[5] *The Surgeon's Case,* Y.B. Hil. 48 Ed. 3, f. 6, pl. 11, *supra,* p. 82.
[6] *Watton* v. *Brinth,* Y.B. Mich. 2 Hen. 4, f. 3, pl. 9, *infra,* p. 340; and *Anon,* Y.B. Mich. 11 Hen. 4, f. 33, pl. 60, *infra.* p. 340.
[7] Y.B. Hil. 3 Hen. 6, f. 36, pl. 33, *infra.* p. 341.

that the defendant had taken upon himself to build a mill by Christmas and had broken his promise. The defendant, though he ultimately traversed the facts and denied the breach, raised two interesting questions. He at first argued that the plaintiff should have stated in his declaration the price agreed upon for the work. If no price had been fixed, the builder, even when he had built the mill, could not have recovered any remuneration, since Debt admitted no *quantum meruit* count, and, in the absence of reciprocity, no action would lie against him. The argument was dismissed with the summary and somewhat specious comment that, as no business man would engage upon such a task for nothing, a fixed price must be assumed to exist. Counsel for the defendant then insisted on the distinction between nonfeasance and misfeasance. Martin, J. re-stated the orthodox position. If the plaintiff could prove only the breach of a promise, there was no liability: *aut conventio aut nihil*. If there was active misconduct, ' the covenant is thereby changed and made into a tort.' The other judges were prepared, had the course of the trial demanded such a sacrifice, to ignore the distinction and to allow Case on the simple ground of the damage suffered by the plaintiff.

These arguments were indecisive, and, while they revealed the sympathy of the judges, displayed also the embarrassing legacy of Trespass. Might its implications be avoided by using another formula? Between 1428 and 1433 three actions on the case were reported, based on the analogy not of Trespass but of Deceit.[8] In the first of these actions,[9]

> ' a man brought a writ *sur son cas* in the nature of a writ of Deceit. And he declared that a bargain had been made between the plaintiff and the defendant that the plaintiff should marry the daughter of the defendant and that the defendant should enfeoff the plaintiff and his daughter in such and such lands and tenements; and that he would not do this, but had married her to another. And the writ was that the plaintiff and the defendant *bargainassent*.'

Paston, J. quashed the writ because the facts disclosed no bargain in the eyes of the law. The contemplated marriage was not a sufficient Quid pro Quo for the conveyance of land, and the defendant's undertaking was therefore but a *nudum pactum*. ' As if I give or promise you my horse, this cannot be called a bargain.' The judgment, while it reflected the influence of Debt,[10] did not exclude the propriety of a similar writ upon more favourable facts; and a second attempt was made in 1430. A writ of *Deceit sur le Cas* was brought by the buyer

---

[8] *Anon* (1428) Y.B. Mich. 7 Hen. 6, f. 1, pl. 3: *Anon* (1430) Y.B. Mich. 9 Hen. 6, f. 53, pl. 37: *Somerton's Case* (1433), *infra*, p. 343. The experiment seems to have been foreshadowed by Babington, C.J. in *Watkins' Case, infra*, p. 341.
[9] *Anon* (1428) Y.B. Mich. 7 Hen. 6, f. 1, pl. 3.
[10] Compare the later discussion upon matrimony as a Quid pro Quo in Debt: *Anon* (1458) Y.B. 37 Hen. 6, f. 8, pl. 18, *supra*, pp. 226 and 249.

of a butt of wine for the breach of a warranty of quality.[11] Rolfe, for the defendant, excelled himself in the number and ingenuity of his pleas. He first took issue upon the Latin of the writ. The plaintiff had alleged the wine to have been warranted ' habilem et non corruptam,' whereas the word was ' abilem ' without the ' h.' The Court, however, was not interested in the niceties of classical scholarship. ' Some of the Chancery clerks say that it should be written with an "h" and some the contrary; wherefore, let it be.' Rolfe then submitted in turn that no warranty had been given, that, if it had, this had been done by a servant without authority, that the wine was in any event good and that, if it was not, the plaintiff, himself a vintner, could not fairly say that he had been deceived. Driven at length to a jury, he made his retreat not without dignity. ' It will be a great shame,' he said, ' to put this matter in the mouth of the *lais gens,* when it is a matter of law.'

The arguments indicate, at least, the atmosphere of contract in which the scope of the writ was discussed. There has been a tendency, however, to emphasise the claims of Deceit, as against Trespass, on the Case to be the ancestor of Assumpsit.[12] It is true that the meaning and effect of warranties on the sale of goods were most frequently canvassed through this medium.[13] To an age which did not seek to discriminate too nicely between one class of representation and another it came naturally to describe a breach of such a warranty as a fraud upon the buyer. But the wider suggestion that the problem of nonfeasance was to be solved more easily upon the analogy of Deceit than upon that of Trespass is scarcely sustained by the authorities. The third of the experiments in Deceit may be compared with a contemporary action of Trespass on the Case. In *Somerton's Case* in 1433[14] the plaintiff, in a writ fully flavoured with allegations of fraud, alleged that the defendant had undertaken (*assumpsit*) to procure for him the conveyance of a leasehold estate, but that he had betrayed his instructions to a stranger and had obtained the estate for him instead. The Court, while sympathetic to the plaintiff, unanimously repudiated nonfeasance as a sufficient ground of action and contrived to extract from the facts a ' constructive ' misfeasance. Three years later, in *Trespass sur son cas,*[15] the plaintiff complained that the defendant had

---

[11] *Anon,* Y.B. Mich. 9 Hen. 6, f. 53, pl. 37.

[12] e.g. Ames, *Lectures on Legal History,* p. 139.

[13] See, e.g. *Anon* (1472) Y.B. Trin. 11 Ed. 4, f. 6, pl. 10, *infra,* pp. 336 and 349; Fitzherbert, *Natura Brevium,* 98K; Blackstone, *Comm.* III. 164-5. Deceit on the case, however, had no monopoly of such actions. See *Anon* (1436) Y.B. 14 Hen. 6, f. 22, pl. 66, where the failure of the bulk to correspond with the sample was discussed on a writ of *Trespass* on the Case.

[14] *Infra,* p. 343.

[15] *Anon* (1436) Y.B. 14 Hen. 6, f. 18, pl. 58, *infra,* p. 344. See also *Tailbois* v. *Sherman* (1443) Y.B. 21 Hen. 6, f. 55, pl. 12, where the plaintiff sued in *Trespass sur son cas* for the non-delivery of two pipes of wine bargained and sold to him. The judges favoured the plaintiff, but, says the disconsolate reporter, ' the parties then made accord and nothing more was done in the matter.'

undertaken to obtain from a third party the release of certain interests in land, but had wholly failed to implement his undertaking. Newton, for the plaintiff, after offering examples of misfeasance, urged the extension of the principle to nonfeasance where, as in the case at bar, the plaintiff had suffered damage; and the two judges, whose views are recorded in the report, accepted the invitation without demur. Their too ready assent may well have been in advance of professional opinion, but, at least in this instance, the argument, rejected in Deceit, had prevailed in Trespass on the Case.

It would thus seem that, while the examples of Trespass and of Deceit each contributed to the gradual evolution of a contractual remedy, no essential distinction between the formulæ was taken by the mediæval lawyers. Through the one channel as through the other reasonable progress had been made during the first half of the fifteenth century. On the one hand, the judges had come to recognize the presence of an *assumpsit* as the core of the plaintiff's case. In *Marshal's Case* in 1441[16] a writ of *Trespass sur le cas* was brought against a veterinary surgeon, because he had assumed in London to cure a horse which afterwards died through his negligent misconduct. The arguments revolved around the familiar problem of *Venue*. It appeared that, while the horse died in London, the undertaking had been given at Oxford, and it was contended that the plaintiff had indicated the wrong neighbourhood for the selection of the jury. The decision turned upon the choice either of the undertaking or of the misconduct as the crux of the action. The judges, on the ground that without it no responsibility would have been incurred, chose the *assumpsit* and upheld the defendant. On the other hand, they inclined, though with more hesitation, to allow a writ for nonfeasance as well as for misfeasance. In *Doige's Case* in 1442[17] the plaintiff sued for the breach of an undertaking to make a feoffment of land by a certain day. John Doige had enfeoffed a stranger 'and so deceived him.' The defendant demurred on the ground that the only remedy was by writ of Covenant. The case was felt to be of major importance and was argued before all the judges in the Exchequer Chamber, where, after a diversity of opinion, it was adjourned, like too many of its fellows, without a conclusion. Two of the judges resolutely maintained the necessity of a misfeasance; but the majority favoured the plaintiff either by admitting the adequacy of a nonfeasance or by construing the facts with the same benevolence that had turned the scale in *Somerton's Case*. Chief Justice Newton, now free to substantiate the views which he had aired at the Bar, for his part felt no doubt. The deficiencies of Covenant, the demands of mutuality and the ties of conscience, all required the plaintiff's success.

[16] Y.B. Hil. 19 Hen. 6, f. 49, pl. 5, *infra*, p. 345.
[17] Y.B. Trin. 20 Hen. 6, f. 34, pl. 4, *infra*, p. 347.

The encouraging prospect thus opened was not destined to be realised in the second half of the fifteenth century. The task of the historian in this period is complicated—or perhaps only too drastically simplified—by recurrent gaps in the published evidence.[18]   From 1443 to 1471 there is no case of assumpsit in the printed reports and but one instance in 1472. From 1473 to 1486 the fog of law once more descends; and, after three cases in the latter year, there is again silence, save for a single note,[19] until 1503. These *lacunæ* are the more tantalising in that the Plea Rolls show a number of tempting actions to have been entered upon the lists of the courts. Thus, in the Common Bench for the Easter term, 1470,

> ' there are fifteen examples of assumpsit noted on the roll, and a number of other cases that seem to differ but little in nature from assumpsit. The actions of assumpsit include those brought for an incompetent operation of phlebotomy on a horse; for negligence in the care of a diseased horse by one who had agreed to have it in custody; for the bad shoeing of a horse so that the animal died; for the failure of the defendant to carry out the livery of seisin when he had promised it; for failure to build a suitable dovecote, fences or hedges, houses, or walls to keep out water; for failure to cure hides suitably and to make proper tiles.
>
> Actions of analogous nature are those in which the words *barganizasset* or *conduxisset* are substituted for *assumpsisset*. The failure to deliver seisin as bargained for occurs in this group just as in the assumpsit group. A more common action is that brought against a man who has bargained with another for the sale of a horse and has warranted the same horse to be well and able to work, whereas it proves to be diseased, ' collapsed with many infirmities ' and unable to labour. The words ' falso et fraudulenter ' sometimes appear in these cases. Again, impotent horses have been hired to do carting service from London to Boston, and short measures of grain or wine have been sold ' against the form of the bargain.' Thus action is brought against Robert Worth, warden of the Fleet, because he ' bargained ' to buy barrels of *threhalpeny ale*, but has not yet paid for them.' [20]

By such references the appetite is whetted but not satisfied. While the pressure of contractual problems would seem to have been felt almost as urgently at the common law as in chancery, it is idle to speculate on the judicial reaction to the obvious issues of trespass

---

[18] ie. published either in the Blackletter edition of the Year Books, or in the modern Rolls, Selden and Ames Foundation series. Further evidence very possibly *discurrit et latitat* in manuscripts awaiting transcription by competent hands. The phenomenon is not confined to legal literature. See Galbraith, *The Public Records*, p. 56: ' The reigns of Edward IV and Henry VII are perhaps the worst documented periods since the beginning of the Chancery enrolments in 1199.'

[19] Y.B. 5 Hen. 7, f. 41, pl. 7 (A.D. 1490). ' *Nota*, that it is said by several, that if one sells a thing and afterwards at another place he warrants it, this warranty is void, because it is not made on the bargain, and he will not have an action of Deceit on this.'

[20] Neilson, Introduction to S.S. Vol. 47, at pp. xxii-iii. The formidable nature of the researcher's task is indicated by the fact that on the rolls of this one court for this single term approximately 3,800 cases are entered: p. xix.

and deceit, of misfeasance and nonfeasance. All that may be done is to draw cautious inferences from the few published reports.

In an isolated action of 1472 the plaintiff sued in Deceit on the Case for the breach of a warranty given by a servant on the sale of his master's goods.[21] The judges first considered the question of vicarious liability, and distinguished the warranty of a servant from that of a third party. If given by the latter, it was but the gratuitous intervention of a stranger and, unless made by deed, had no effect. If given by the former, it must be received as the act of the master, whose sale it was and who alone could be sued. They then took a comprehensive survey of the doctrine of warranty. The buyer might obtain redress for its breach provided that he had relied upon the seller's skill or knowledge, that the defect was not patent, that the warranty was express and that it related to the existing state of the goods and was not a promise as to the future.[22]

In the three cases of 1486 the judges were unanimous in demanding proof of a misfeasance, even if, as in the previous generation, they were prepared, where necessary, to put a favourable construction upon the facts. In the *Shepherd's Case*,[23] Townshend, J. declared that, ' if a covenant is made with me to keep my horse or to carry my goods and nothing more done, then the action of Covenant lies and no other action; for in these cases he only fails to execute his promise.' In one of the other two cases, the plaintiff alleged that the defendant, after undertaking to obtain for him the lease of a manor, had procured it for a third party.

> *Vavasour*: This action will not lie unless he has done some act, and not for a mere nonfeasance; and here he has done nothing.
>
> BRIAN, C.J.: If it be agreed between you and me that you shall convey to me an estate in certain land, and if you then enfeoff another, shall I not have an *action sur mon cas*? Why, yes, of course I shall.
>
> And the Court was with him, because, when he took upon himself to make the feoffment, the conveyance to another was a great misfeasance.
>
> On this *Vavasour*, seeing the opinion of the Court, traversed the assumption.[24]

Judicial opinion was proclaimed unchanged as late as 1503. In a note ascribed to that year it was declared that,

[21] *Anon*, Y.B. Trin. 11 Ed. 4, f. 6, pl. 10, *infra*, p. 349.
[22] A pendant to the case is to be found in a note by Frowicke, C.J. in 1507, reported in Keilway, p. 91. ' If a man sells cloth to me or other things, and the cloth is to his knowledge bad, now I am deceived to his knowledge, and in this case, because he knows and yet sells, albeit he sells without warranty, yet he will be punished by writ on my case. But if he does not know, he will not be punished by writ on my case without warranty.'
[23] Y.B. 2 Hen. 7, f. 11, pl. 9, *supra*, p. 86.
[24] *Anon*, Y.B. Mich. 3 Hen. 7, f. 14, pl. 20. The third case is similar: *Anon*, Y.B. Hil. 2 Hen. 7, f. 12, pl. 15.

'where a carpenter makes a bargain to make me a house and does nothing, no action on the case lies, for it sounds in covenant. But if he makes the house improperly, the action on the case well lies.' [25]

To modern observers the judges may seem in these cases to have been throwing away the opportunity of expansion which their predecessors had been about to grasp. For this hardening of the legal arteries it is difficult to find a satisfactory explanation. Perhaps it is to be sought, not so much upon technical considerations, as through that elusive quality, the 'spirit of the times.' All ages are ages of transition, but some are more 'transitional' than others. Socially and politically, the fifteenth century 'was a time of striking contradictions, alike of progress and retrogression.'[26] Obsessed by the ever present fear of dynastic change and intimately acquainted with the weakness of the central government, the judges may well have shrunk, even within their own peculiar province, from any final and decisive step. While they looked forward to a single doctrine of Assumpsit, they looked back to the delictual origins of Case. Perhaps, on the other hand, no explanation is possible because none is required. In their impatience for a conclusion which seems, in retrospect, to have been inevitable, historians are apt to forget that, while still *in futuro,* it was but one of several possibilities. A painful and hesitant approach to a problem is no monopoly of the past. If in a hundred years of litigation the modern law of torts has still not wholly freed itself from the dogma of contractual privacy, it is the less surprising that the principle of contract took as long to emerge from the mediæval preoccupation with tort. A sense of proportion might rather demand applause for the feat of the judges in reaching an ultimate solution which utterly escaped the perspicacity of the Roman lawyers than deprecation at the time taken to produce it.

Whether a particular explanation be required or not, and whatever it may be, the note recorded in 1503 was the last unashamed pronouncement of the old order. With the turn of the century the judges no longer feared for the very foundations of the state. The local courts, which had served so long the needs of commerce, were in decay. The competition of the Chancellor, at first accepted if not with enthusiasm at least without resentment, had for some time grown irksome.[27] Case, moreover, had now become a generic form of action and the basic analogy of trespass had lost its power of attraction. In 1505 the liability for nonfeasance was admitted, almost

---

[25] Keilway, 50.

[26] Jacob, *Essays in the Conciliar Epoch,* pp. 173-4. Cf. the very title of Kingsford's book, *Prejudice and Promise in Fifteenth-Century England.*

[27] See the language of Fineux, C.J. in Y.B. Mich. 21 Hen. 7, f. 41, pl. 66, *infra,* p. 353; and cf., in another context, *Anon* (1482) Y.B. 21 Ed. 4, f. 23, pl. 6, where Fairfax, J. advised counsel to use 'actions sur les cases' more freely, so as to render *Subpœna* less attractive.

without argument.[28]   The buyer of twenty quarters of barley sued
for non-delivery.   He declared that the seller had taken upon himself
(*assumpsit super se*) to keep the barley safely until a certain day, and
then to make delivery, but that he had ' converted it to his own use
tortiously and to the damage of the plaintiff.'   The seller did not
deny that his conduct was as much a misfeasance as the feoffment
to third parties in the earlier cases, but insisted that the plaintiff had
chosen the wrong form of action: Debt lay,[29] but Case did not.   The
majority of the court accepted the contention.   Chief Justice Frowicke,
on the other hand, thought the plaintiff should have his election between
the one writ and the other, and, to avoid the monopoly of Debt,
stressed the tortious element in the action on the Case.   The
plaintiff might obtain compensation in Debt, but justice required the
defendant to be ' punished ' for the deceit which he had practised.
All the judges, however, agreed, and indeed assumed, that Case would
lie, in appropriate circumstances, for a nonfeasance.   Such an assertion, in the context, was an *obiter dictum*.   But in the following year
it was repeated by Chief Justice Fineux without qualification and
without demur.[30]

By thus enlarging the scope of Assumpsit the judges had cleared
the way for a general contractual remedy.   Nor need it be supposed
that this was a mere accident ' arising out of and in the course of their
employment,' a by-product of their energies as surprising as it was
salutary.   They had long perceived the implications of their arguments, set though they were in a delictual framework.   The reminis-
cences of tort remained, not only in the pleadings, with their language
of conversion and of deceit, but, for some years at least, in the
requirement that the plaintiff should prove his damage.   But the
principle of contract had at last been avowed, and the consequences
were at once apparent.   It was open to the common lawyers to
re-examine the relations between Debt and Case and to test the virtues
of the new action in supplying the defects of the old.   Debt, for
instance, would not lie against executors, who could not be heard to
wage their testator's law.   In 1521, therefore, a plaintiff tried the
experiment of suing in Case.[31]   He alleged that he had supplied goods
to X., whose credit was doubtful, on the verbal guarantee of Y., that
he had been paid by neither and that Y. had since died.   The Court
unanimously gave judgment against Y.'s executors on the ground that
the plaintiff had suffered by reliance upon the guarantee.   That this

---

[28] *Anon* (1505), *infra*, p. 351.

[29] Debt, and not Detinue, because the sale was of unascertained chattels, where no
property had passed.

[30] *Nota* (1506), *infra*, p. 353.   Fineux, C.J., K.B., had disapproved of the view of
Frowicke, C.J. C.P., in the case of 1505, that Action on the Case was there alternative to Debt: see *infra*, p. 353.

[31] *Anon*, Y.B. Pasch. 12 Hen. 8, f. 11, pl. 3.

result did not satisfy the profession appears from its review in 1536.[32] Fitzherbert, J., though he had been counsel for the plaintiff in the earlier case, had always disapproved of the decision, which rested upon no authority. ' Put the case out of your books,' he said, ' for it is without doubt not law.' But this rebuff did not impugn the character of Assumpsit. The refusal to countenance its use against executors was justified not in despite but because of the contractual principle, which was invoked to buttress the traditional arguments of compurgation. In the words of Fitzherbert, J., ' You shall not have *accion sur le cas* nor any other remedy; for, when the testator dies, this debt, due on a simple contract, dies also.'[33] When death did not intervene to break the chain of liability, Case might perhaps be substituted for Debt. In *Jordan's Case* in 1528,[34] the plaintiff had levied personal execution upon X., who lay in a debtor's prison. The defendant undertook, if the plaintiff would discharge him, to guarantee payment of the judgment debt. The plaintiff accordingly discharged X., but was not paid. To an action on the *assumpsit* defendant's counsel raised the objection, which had prevailed in 1505, that Debt was the only possible remedy, but was overruled. The judges were divided upon the question whether a benefit conferred upon a third party at the defendant's instance was a sufficient Quid pro Quo to sustain Debt; but they had no doubt that the action on the case was available.[35]

By the middle of the sixteenth century the modern conception of contract had in essence been formulated. The action of Assumpsit, through which it was expressed, was recognized as a distinct species of Case, resting upon the idea of ' promise,' just as the word ' contract ' was associated with the writ of Debt. Thus Rastell, in his Collection of Entries, has a sub-heading of *Accion sur le case sur Assumption,* with a cross-reference to *Accion sur le case sur le Promise.*[36] The case of *Andrew* v. *Boughey* in 1552 reflected the new attitude alike in thought and in language.[37] The plaintiff sued for the breach of a warranty of quality on the sale of goods. The defendant confessed and avoided by pleading accord and satisfaction. Judgment was given for the defendant on three grounds. First, on the hypothesis that a valid warranty had been given and broken, the breach had been purged by the subsequent accord and satisfaction, into the adequacy of which the court would not inquire. Secondly, the warranty appeared in fact to have been given after the conclusion of the original bargain,

---

[32] *Anon,* Y.B. Trin. 27 Hen. 8, f. 23, pl. 21.
[33] See also Brooke, New Cases, pl. 304 (A.D. 1546): ' It was agreed that action sur le cas does not lie against executors *sur l'assumption del testator,* although they have assets.'
[34] Y.B. Mich. 19 Hen. 8, f. 24, pl. 3, *infra,* p. 353.
[35] Cf. the earlier doubts upon the question of Quid pro Quo, *supra,* p. 226.
[36] *Supra,* pp. 90 and 92.
[37] 1 Dyer, 75a, *infra,* p. 355. The case was reported by Dyer under the general heading of ' Assumpsit.'

so that the defendant could not in law be bound by it.[38]   Thirdly, the plaintiff had not declared the price to be payable at a future date, and it must be assumed against him that it was payable at once.   Payment was therefore a condition precedent to the obligation of the seller to deliver the goods and no evidence had been offered to show that it had been satisfied.   In the words of the Sale of Goods Act, three and a half centuries later, ' unless otherwise agreed, delivery of the goods and payment of the price are concurrent conditions.'[39]

SOURCES

WATTON v. BRINTH
Y.B. MICH. 2 HEN. 4, f. 3, pl. 9
A.D. 1400

One Laurence Watton brought a writ *forme sur son especial matter* against Thomas Brinth, and the writ was thus:—*Quare cum idem Thomas ad quosdam domos ipsius Laurentii bene et fideliter infra certum tempus de novo construendo apud Grimesby assumpsisset, prædictus tamen Thomas domos ipsius Laurentii infra tempus prædictum, etc. construere non curavit ad dampnum ipsius Laurentii decem librarum, etc.;* and he counted accordingly.

Tirwhit: Sir, you see well how he has counted of a covenant and of this shows nothing: judgment, etc.

Gascoigne: Since you make no answer, we demand judgment and pray our damages.

Tirwhit: This is merely a covenant.

Bryn: So it is; and peradventure if he had counted, or in the writ mention had been made, that the thing had been commenced and then by negligence not done, it would have been otherwise.

HANKFORD, J.: He could have a writ on the Statute of Labourers,[40] and this carpenter is an artificer, whereby you might have a good action against him on the Statute; but you know well that a man cannot have an action of covenant against his servant if he does anything against his covenant, if there is no deed about it.

RICKHILL, J.: Because you have counted on a covenant and shown nothing for it, you shall take nothing by your writ, but be in mercy.

ANON
Y.B. MICH. 11 HEN. 4, f. 33, pl. 60
A.D. 1409

A writ was brought against a carpenter *sur tiel mattere*, that, whereas he had undertaken to make the plaintiff a new house within a certain time, he had not made the house, *a tort,* etc.

---

[38] Cf. *supra*, p. 335, n. 19, and *Roscorla* v. *Thomas* (1842) 3 Q.B. 234.
[39] Sale of Goods Act, 1893, s. 28.   The third point taken by the Court rested on the failure by the plaintiff to frame his declaration with sufficient clarity.   Had he alleged and proved an agreement for credit, the delivery would have been due before payment.   But the declaration was at the best ambiguous, and the ambiguity must be construed against him.
[40] See Holdsworth, H.E.L. II. 460-4.

Tildesley: Sir, you see well how this matter sounds in a manner of covenant, of which covenant he shows nothing. Now therefore we ask judgment if he shall have an action without a specialty.

Norton: And we ask judgment, sir; for if he should have made my house badly and should have destroyed my timber, I should have had an action sure enough on my case without a deed.

THIRNING, C.J.: I grant well in your case, because he shall answer for the tort he has done, *quia negligenter fecit*. But if a man makes a covenant and shows nothing done beyond the covenant, how shall you have your action against him without specialty?

HILL, J.: He could have had an action on the Statute of Labourers in this case, supposing him to have been retained in his service to make a house, but this action is too feeble. Because, therefore, it seems to the court that this action, which is taken at common law, is founded on a thing which is a covenant in itself, of which nothing is shown, the court awards that you take nothing by your writ, but be in mercy.

WATKINS' CASE
Y.B. HIL. 3 HEN. 6, f. 36, pl. 33
A.D. 1425

A writ of Trespass was brought by one W. B. against Watkins of London, mill-maker. And he counted by *Strangeways sur ce cas*, that is to say, that on such a day and year in London in such a ward he took upon himself (*emprist sur luy*) to make a mill for the said plaintiff; and he showed that the mill was to be all ready and built by the following Christmas, but that by this time the mill was not built, *a tort* and to the damage of the plaintiff ten marks.

Rolfe: Judgment of the writ: for by the writ it is supposed that the defendant should make a mill, and he has not declared for certain how much he should have for the making.

Strangeways: Since you have said nothing, we ask judgment and pray our damages.

BABINGTON, C.J.: If I bring a writ of Deceit against one, for that the defendant was my attorney and that by his negligence I have lost my land, etc., in this case I must declare how he was retained by me, or else the writ shall be abated. So here.

MARTIN, J.: I do not know that I have seen in the Law that a writ *sur tiel mattere* lies, where no tort is alleged in the writ, but only that the defendant has promised to do something and he has not done it; for in such case a good writ of Covenant lies, supposing that he has a specialty. But if he had made a mill which was not good but altogether badly made, then a good writ of Trespass would lie. Suppose we put the case that a farrier makes a covenant with me to shoe my horse, and by his negligence he lames my horse, on this matter shewn a good writ of Trespass lies, for, notwithstanding that in the rehearsal of the matter a covenant is supposed, I say that, inasmuch as he has done badly what he had covenanted to do, the covenant is thereby changed and made into a tort, for which a good writ of Trespass lies. But in the case at bar there is no such thing; for no tort is alleged in the writ by any feasance, but only a nonfeasance, which sounds only in covenant.

BABINGTON, C.J.: I think the contrary. Put the case that one makes a covenant with me to roof my hall or a certain house by a certain time, and within this time he does not roof it, so that by default of the roofing the furniture of the house is all damaged by the rain; in this case I say that I shall have a good writ of Trespass *sur le mattere monstre* against him who made the covenant with me. So too I shall recover damages because I have suffered loss by the not making the mill.

COKAYNE, J.: To the same intent. As to the first argument, that he should have declared that he made the covenant with him for a sum certain, it seems to me, Sir, that he has thus declared in effect. For it is not to be supposed that he should make the mill for nothing, and so it is all one as if he had expressly said so in his pleading, and on the matter shown the writ is well enough. And put the case that one makes a covenant to repair certain ditches on my land, and he does not do so, so that by his default the water which should run into the ditches floods my land and destroys my corn; I say that I shall have a good writ of Trespass for this nonfeasance. So here.

Rolfe: On the first point, it seems to me that he should have made express mention in the writ what he is to have; and I say that there is a great difference where one agrees to do a thing and where one is a common labourer. For one who is a labourer is put in certainty by the Statute,[41] whereby, notwithstanding that nothing is said in the covenant as to what he shall have, the servant shall have a good action of Debt against me for his salary according to the Statute. But if I make a covenant with one to go with me or to do a certain thing, and I do not say for certain what he is to have for his feasance, in this case I say that the covenant is void for both parties; for if he does not perform the covenant I will never have action against him, and no more shall he, if he performs the act, demand anything for his work, unless it is expressed for certain what he shall have. So it seems to me that, if this action *sur cest mattere* is to be maintained, the principal thing which is the cause of the action should be expressly declared in the writ, and that is the covenant, which is not good unless it be stated for certain what he is to have.

Strangeways: I think the contrary. And as to what Master Martin has argued, that, because no tort is supposed by the writ, the writ should not lie, Sir, it seems to me that it will lie. For suppose one makes a covenant with me to be my servant, and then I order him to go out with my cart and he refuses, I say that I shall have a writ of Trespass against him for this refusal; and this is a mere nonfeasance. So here.

MARTIN, J.: That I grant well; for the refusal is a departure from your service, for which a good action lies. But truly, as it seems to me, if this action be maintainable *sur cette mattere,* for every broken covenant in the world a man shall have an action of Trespass.

BABINGTON, C.J.: All our talk is vain; for as yet they have not demurred in law.

Wherefore he said to *Strangeways* and *Rolfe,* Plead and say what you will, or demur; and then there can be debate and dispute enough.[42]

Wherefore *Rolfe* pleaded over, and said that, long after the time when it was supposed that he made the covenant, that is to say, on such a day, etc., the defendant came to the plaintiff in such a ward and said to him that the mill was quite ready and built, and asked him when he would have

[41] i.e., Statutes of Labourers.
[42] i.e. You must either demur in law and thus fight on the law, or plead and fight on the facts: decide first which you will do.

the mill, and discharged himself completely of the mill. And so we demand judgment if the action lies.[43]

Strangeways: He did not discharge himself.

Issue joined.

Quare de l'opinion de MARTIN.[44]

SOMERTON'S CASE

Y.B. 11 HEN. 6, HIL. f. 18, pl. 10: PASCH. pl. 1: TRIN. pl. 26 [45]

A.D. 1433

Writ[46]

The King to the sheriff, greeting, etc. Distrain John Colles of Northaston . . . to show why, whereas the said William Somerton retained at Northaston the aforesaid John Colles to be of his counsel for the purchase of the manor of Northaston from John Boteler to the aforesaid William and his heirs, or at least to procure a term of years therein, for a certain sum paid to the said John Colles by the aforesaid William as agreed between them under a certain form of agreement, and whereas the aforesaid John Colles agreed and undertook (*assumpsit*), for the said certain sum as promised between them, to obtain the aforesaid manor to the said William and his heirs, or at least a term of years to be held from the aforesaid John Boteler, yet the aforesaid John Colles, by collusion between himself and John Blunt at Northaston, contriving basely to defraud the said William in this behalf, maliciously revealed all the counsel of the said William in this behalf to the aforesaid John Blunt, and there and then falsely and fraudulently became of the counsel of the same John Blunt and, contrary to his aforesaid promise and assumption, procured the said manor to the said John Blunt for a term of years to be held of the aforesaid John Boteler, to the damage of the said William, etc.

Argument.

. . . COTTESMORE, J.: The matter of the writ is single enough.[47] For if I retain you to serve me, and you undertake to serve me, that is no double matter; since he does not undertake to do anything more than he is retained to do, and so it is all one thing. So, if I retain you to make me a house, and you grant that you will make the house, this is but one thing, and you will be in default if you misframe the timber and ruin the house. And in the same way, if I retain a Surgeon to aid me, and he undertakes to aid me, and he gives me contrary medicines, whereby I am harmed, here is a good action on the case. So here. . . .

[43] The ' prefabrication ' suggested by this plea was a common mediæval practice. See John Harvey, *Gothic England* (1947) at p. 38: ' In most parts of the country the ordinary small house or cottage was built of timber framing, the panels filled with hurdles or wattling and daubed over with clay or a composition of clay, lime and chopped straw. . . . Quite frequently houses were framed by the carpenter at his yard, often placed beside a river, then transported in parts by barge or wagon to the site, and there erected in order. Every timber had to be marked at the joints with corresponding numerals to permit of correct assembly. These marks may often be seen quite clearly from the street, as on the Grammar School, Stratford-on-Avon, built by master carpenter John Hasill in 1427.'

[44] Note by the reporter.

[45] The case was argued and reported in three different terms. See Plucknett, *Concise History*, 4th ed., p. 605, n. 3.

[46] Y.B. 11 Hen. 6 Pasch., f. 25.

[47] He is repelling the defendant's argument that the writ improperly contained a double allegation: (1) that the defendant was *retained*, (2) that he *undertook* to act as the plaintiff's counsel.

MARTIN, J.: . . . To allege that one retains another to do a certain thing, and that he undertakes to do it, this is not double; as if I sell to you a tun of wine and I warrant the wine to be sound and not corrupt. Likewise you shall have an action supposing that one sells you a horse and warrants the horse to be sound in its limbs and he knows the horse to have a certain malady. So here; for the cause of the action is neither the retainer nor the warranty, but the cause is that the other has discovered his counsel and has become of counsel with another.

BABINGTON, C.J.: To the same intent. For if I retain one to purchase a manor for me, and he does not do so, I shall not have any action against him without a deed; but, if there had been a deed, I could have had an action of Covenant because he had not done what he was retained to do. But if he becomes of counsel with another in this matter, then, because I have been deceived, I shall have *accion sur mon cas,* for he is bound to keep my counsel when he is retained by me. But if a man shows his title-deeds to a man of Law, who afterwards becomes of counsel with another and then discloses the said title-deeds to him, he shall not have an action against him on this matter, because he did not previously retain him. As for the suggestion that he warranted to him to purchase the manor, for this matter he will have no action other than an action of Covenant; and for this he must have a deed to the effect that he was retained to buy the manor, etc., and that he warranted to him to do this. But this is only a covenant, and, if he has no deed, he cannot have an *accion of Trespass sur son cas;* for there is no more than a covenant broken. But if he betrays his counsel and becomes of counsel for another to purchase this manor for him, now here is a deceit for which I shall have *accion sur mon cas.* . . .

COTTESMORE, J.: To the same intent. And I say that matter which lies wholly in covenant can by malfeasance *ex post facto* be converted into deceit. For if I warrant to purchase for you a manor, notwithstanding that I fail to do this for you, no action will lie for these bare words without a deed to this effect. And in the same manner, if I warrant to pay you £20 without deed, you shall not have an action, since the warranty sounds in covenant. So here, the retainer of the one part and the warranty of the other sound wholly in covenant; yet, when he has become counsel for another, that is a deceit and changes all that came before, which was but covenant between the parties, and for this deceit he shall have *Accion sur son cas.* . . .

ANON

Y.B. 14 HEN. 6, f. 18, pl. 58

A.D. 1436

Trespass was brought by one R. *sur son cas.* And he counted that the plaintiff had bargained for certain land for a certain sum from the defendant, and he showed everything in detail, and that the covenant of the defendant was that he should cause third parties to make release to him within a certain time and that they had not so released; and so the action accrued to him.

Ellerkar: This action sounds in the nature of a covenant, wherefore he should have had a writ of Covenant, and not this writ.

Newton: In as much as you acknowledge the trespass and show no other matter, we demand judgment.

Ellerkar: I think your writ should abate, for several similar cases have been adjudged in the law before now. Thus, in the case that I make a covenant with a carpenter to make me a house within a certain time and he does not do so, I shall have no action save by a writ of Covenant. And the law is the same if one takes upon himself to shoe my horse and he does not do so, no other action shall I have save a writ of Covenant; and so, if he does not do it and there is no specialty, the action fails. So here, he has taken upon himself to make a stranger release, which is a covenant, and he shows that he has not released, which is nothing but a covenant broken; wherefore I think the writ should abate.

Newton: I think the contrary, and that the writ is good. In the case of the carpenter which *Ellerkar* has put, I agree well that it is law that, if a carpenter makes a covenant with me to make a house good and strong and of a certain form and he makes me a house which is weak and bad and of another form, I shall have an action of *Trespass sur mon cas*. So, too, if a farrier makes a covenant with me to shoe my horse well and properly and he shoes and lames him, I shall have a good action. So, too, if a leech takes upon himself to cure me of my maladies and he gives me medicines but does not cure me, I shall have *Action sur mon cas*. Again, if a man makes a covenant with me to plough my land in good season and he does so in unseasonable time, I shall have *Action sur mon cas*. And the cause in all these cases is that there is an undertaking and a matter in fact beyond that which sounds in covenant. So, in the case at bar, he has taken upon himself that a stranger shall release to the plaintiff, which is an undertaking, and, inasmuch as this has not been done, the plaintiff has *tort*, as in the cases before rehearsed.

PASTON, J.: I think the same. As to what has been said, that, if the carpenter takes upon himself to make me a house and does not make it, I shall not have *Accion sur mon cas*, I say, Sir, that I shall. And, Sir, if a farrier makes a covenant with me to shoe my horse and he does not do it, and I go on my way and my horse has no shoes and is ruined for lack of shoes, I shall have *Accion sur mon cas*. And if you, who are Serjeant at Law, take upon yourself to plead my cause and do not do it, or do it in some other manner than I wish, whereby I suffer loss, I shall have *Accion sur.mon cas*. So it seems to me that in the case at bar the writ is good.

JUYN, J.: I agree. And, as PASTON has said, if the farrier does not shoe my horse, I shall have an action against him as much as if he had shod him and lamed him. For all this is dependent upon the covenant and accessory to it, and, as I have an action for the accessory, so I shall have an action for the principal.

PASTON, J.: That is very well said.

MARSHAL'S CASE
Y.B. HIL. 19 HEN. 6, f. 49, pl. 5
A.D. 1441

Writ of *Trespass sur le cas* against one R. Marshal, for that the defendant assumed upon himself in London to cure the plaintiff's horse of a certain malady, and that he *adeo negligenter et improvide imposuit medicinas, etc., quod equum, etc.*

Portington: To this we say that at Oxford in the county of Oxford we assumed to cure the horse of some such infirmity as you speak of, which we have sufficiently done; without this (*sans ceo que*),[48] that we assumed to cure your horse in London. Ready, etc.

Markham: That is no plea. For I suppose by my writ that by his negligence he has killed my horse, and this is the essence of my complaint and of my action, which he must therefore traverse, and not the *assumpsit*. Thus, in the case of a carpenter who assumes upon himself to make me a house good and sufficient and does not do it, I shall not have an action against him; which proves that it is the misfeasance which is the cause of the action and which, therefore, must be traversed.

NEWTON, C.J.: I think the plea is good. For suppose that he assumed to cure your horse at Oxford, as is alleged, and that he did so, and that then in London your horse had the infirmity again and that then gratuitously (*de son bon gre*) he applied his medicines and your horse died; now for this that he did gratuitously you shall have no action. Or suppose that my horse is sick and I come to a surgeon to have his advice and he says that one of his own horses had a similar sickness and that he applied a certain medicine to him and so he will do now to my horse; and this he does and my horse dies; shall the plaintiff have an action? Why, no. Nor shall he in our case, unless he assumed upon himself, etc.; and it is this assumption which the defendant must traverse, as he has done.

PASTON, J., to *Markham*: You have not shown that he is a common surgeon to cure such a horse; wherefore, even if he has killed your horse by his medicines, yet you shall not have an action against him without an assumption; which proves well that the *sans ceo* should be taken on the assumption.

Fortescue: As to *Markham's* argument that, if a carpenter assumes upon himself to make me a house and does not, I shall not have an action, and that this proves that the assumption is not the cause of the action and so the traverse is not to be taken upon it; I say that, in any case where one assumes to do a thing and does not do it, I shall have a good action for the nonfeasance, and the traverse should come on the assumption. Wherefore the assumption is the cause of the action, and so it follows that the *sans ceo* should be taken on the assumption. For suppose I have a ruinous house and a carpenter assumes upon himself to repair it well and truly by a certain day and he does not, whereby my house is completely destroyed, now I shall have an action against him, and the traverse can well be taken on the *assumpsit*. So here, while it is by his negligence that the horse died, yet it is because he assumed upon himself to cure the horse and has not done so that he shall have an action; as in the case where the house was lost by his negligence. So I think the plea to be good enough.

AYSCOUGH, J.: I think that it is the *assumpsit* which gives the action, just as much as if he had warranted. Suppose I sell you a hundred sarplers of linen with a warranty that they are good and merchantable and then you find the sarplers full of moths; now this warranty is as much the cause of your action as the corruption of the linen, and on this warranty the *sans ceo* can well be taken. So here in this case the assumption is the cause of the action, because the issue can well be taken on that; just as in an action on the Statute of Labourers the retainer can be traversed as well as the departure from service.

Markham: The writ is, that he *negligenter et improvide medicinas apposuit;* and so it seems that by these contrary medicines he killed him,

---

[48] *absque hoc: supra*, p. 143, n. 66.

and thus the cause of his action is the killing of the horse, which I think he must traverse.

NEWTON, C.J.: *Negligenter apposuit* is not to the point. If I have a malady in my hand and he applies a medicine to my heel, by which negligence my hand is maimed, yet I shall have no action unless he had assumed upon himself to cure me.

Markham: Then by your leave we will imparl.

DOIGE'S CASE

Y.B. TRIN. 20 HEN. 6, f. 34, pl. 4[49]

A.D. 1442

A bill of Deceit was brought against John Doige in the King's Bench. And the plaintiff counted that he bargained with the said John on such a day and year to buy from the said John so much land for £100 to him paid, of which land he was to enfeoff the said plaintiff within fourteen days, and that the said John enfeoffed one A. of the same land and so deceived him. And the defendant demurred on this bill, for that, on the matter thus shown, the plaintiff should have a writ of Covenant and not this action. And now in the Exchequer Chamber,

AYSCOUGH, J.: If a carpenter takes upon himself to make me a house and does not do so, I shall not have a writ of Trespass, but only an action of Covenant, provided that I have a specialty; but if he makes the house badly, I shall have an action of *Trespass sur mon cas;* for this misfeasance is the cause of my action. So in our case, if the defendant had kept the land in his hands without making feoffment, then the plaintiff would only have a writ of Covenant; and I think the case is all one when the defendant makes feoffment to a stranger and when he keeps the land in his hands. Wherefore the action does not lie. . . .

Wangford: The defendant has done some wrong, on which the action of Deceit is founded; for by the act of enfeoffing a stranger he has disabled himself from making feoffment to the plaintiff unless he buys back the land afterwards and enfeoffs him. . . . So, if I retain a man to buy for me a manor for a certain sum and then he buys it for himself, on this I shall have an action of Deceit. And so in our case.

Stokes, to the same intent: Suppose I retain one who is skilled in the law to be of counsel with me in the Guildhall at London on a certain day and he does not come on that day, whereby my cause is lost, now he is liable to me in an action of Deceit; and yet he has done nothing. But because he has not done what he undertook to do and I am thereby damaged, he is liable in Deceit.

PASTON, J.: Suppose a man bargains to enfeoff me, as in our case here, and he afterwards enfeoffs another, and then he re-enters and enfeoffs me and the other ousts me. Now here the action of Covenant may not be brought, because he has at last enfeoffed me according to his covenant; and yet the deceit remains upon which an action may be based. Wherefore it does not always follow that where there is a covenant the action of Deceit will not lie.

Babthorpe: Suppose the defendant had enfeoffed a stranger, reserving to himself an estate tail, and had then enfeoffed the plaintiff, is not this a great deceit? Of course it is; and yet it sounds in covenant. Wherefore, etc.

[49] See another transcription by Dr. Hemmant, SS. Vol. 51, p. 97.

AYSCOUGH, J.: If the feoffment has been made wrongly by such a fraud, it is a wrong in the nature of a misfeasance. But in our case no feoffment is made to the plaintiff, properly or improperly, and so there is nothing done save the breach of covenant.

NEWTON, C.J.: The defendant has disabled himself from keeping his covenant with the plaintiff because he has enfeoffed another and, moreover, the day has passed by which the feoffment should have been made. To what effect, then, is the plaintiff to have a writ of Covenant, when the defendant cannot be held to any covenant with him, unless he has a specialty? To no effect; and so, since the plaintiff has made a firm bargain with the defendant, the defendant can demand the purchase price by a writ of Debt, and in conscience and in right the plaintiff ought to have the land, even though the property cannot pass to him in law without livery of seisin. For it would be strange law (*merveillous Ley*) that a bargain should be made whereby the one party will be bound by an action of Debt and yet be without remedy against the other. Wherefore the action of Deceit well lies.

FORTESCUE, C.J.[50]: If by a deed of indenture I lease land to a man for a term of years and then I oust him within the term, and peradventure twenty years after the end of the term he brings an action of Covenant against me, the action lies well; and yet he cannot recover the term itself, but damages only. So in this case. And as to the argument that, because he has disabled himself from executing the covenant, the action of Deceit lies, I will put you a case where the party has disabled himself and yet no action lies save Covenant. For suppose I make a lease for a term of years to *Paston,* and then I lease the same land to *Godrede,* who goes into occupation: now I have disabled myself from giving *Paston* his lease, and yet he shall have only a writ of Covenant against me. Wherefore, etc.

PASTON, J.: Because a man can have a writ of Covenant, it does not follow that he shall not have a writ of Deceit; for perchance all the covenants are kept and yet he is deceived. For suppose a carpenter takes upon himself to make me a house of a certain length and width and height, which he does, but makes default in the joinery or some such thing, which is outside the covenant; now the action of Covenant will be of no use to me because he has kept all the covenants, and yet I shall have an action of *Trespass sur mon cas* for his misfeasance. So here, though I can have a writ of Covenant, yet, since he has disabled himself as aforesaid, I shall have Deceit. Wherefore, etc.

NEWTON, C.J.: If I bail a certain sum of money to *Paston* to bail over to *Fortescue,* now, if *Paston* does not do this, he will be liable to me in an action of Account and also in an action of Debt, and it is at my pleasure which I shall bring[51]; but when I have brought the one, the other is extinguished. So in this case here there are two actions, Covenant and Deceit, and so the party may bring Deceit if he wishes. Wherefore, etc.

FRAY, C.B.: If the defendant in our case had ousted his feoffee and had then enfeoffed the plaintiff, now all the covenants would be fulfilled; and suppose that later the feoffee were to oust the plaintiff, is the plaintiff to have no action now because he could not have an action of Covenant? Surely, he shall.

---

[50] He became Chief Justice of the King's Bench on Jan. 25, 1442. Newton was Chief Justice of the Common Pleas.
[51] See *supra,* p. 272.

PASTON, J.: It is not true that in every bargain there must be a covenant. For if I buy from you a horse without your warranting him to be sound, here there is no covenant, and yet there is a bargain; and if he is unsound I shall have a writ of *Trespass sur mon cas* against you and shall allege that you sold him to me, knowing him to be unsound. A case came before the Common Bench, where the plaintiff bargained to have 14 bales of grain from the defendant and the defendant sold them to him, knowing the said grain to be diseased, and the action was upheld. [But look at the record of this case: for there it was warranted that the said grain was merchantable].[52] Wherefore it is right that the plaintiff should have an action of Deceit on such a bargain even if, had he a specialty, he could also have a writ of Covenant.

WESTBURY, J.: If a man, after such a bargain as in our case and before the feoffment, made a Statute Merchant[53] and then made the feoffment, the party should have a writ of Deceit. So here.

FORTESCUE, C.J.: If this case be law that *Newton* has put, then indeed there would be no question of the law in our case; for if each party is bound by action on a bargain, then it will be proper to maintain this action of Deceit.

PASTON, J.: Come then to this case.

FORTESCUE, C.J.: Willingly. I would agree that, if I buy a horse from you, now the property in the horse is in me, and for this you shall have a writ of Debt for the money and I shall have Detinue for the horse on this bargain. But that is not so in our case. For, though the plaintiff has a right to have this land in conscience, yet the land does not pass without livery. Wherefore, etc.

PASTON, J.: In our case the contract is good without specialty, and a good contract will bind both parties. What reason is there, then, that the one shall have an action of Debt and the other shall have no action? There is no reason, since in right (*en droit*) he should have the land.

Et adjornatur.

ANON

Y.B. TRIN. 11 ED. IV, f. 6, pl. 10

A.D. 1472

Action of Deceit was brought by one against another for that, whereas the plaintiff bought in London from the defendant certain cloths, the defendant warranted each cloth to be of a certain length, whereas they were not of such length. The defendant said that one B., long before the said sale, was possessed of the said cloths as of his own proper goods, etc., and, being so possessed, the said defendant, as servant to the said B. in his house, sold them, etc., *ut supra;* without this (*sans ceo*), that he sold them in the manner alleged, etc. And the Court said that he should have pleaded that the said B., by the defendant his servant, sold, etc.

Pigot: It is all one; for it is the same to say that I, by my master's command, paid so much money, and to say that my master paid through me.

Fairfax: I think the plea is not good. For though the property was in B., yet this does not matter, for he shows that the sale was in *market overt* and then in such a case the property is not material; for even if it were in

---

[52] These words would seem to have been inserted by the reporter.
[53] *Supra*, p. 222.

a stranger, yet by this sale he will be excluded; and now, though he shows that the defendant sold these things, yet he does not deny that he warranted them, *ut supra*. Wherefore the action is rightly maintained against him.

Pigot: In such an action of Deceit as this upon a sale and bargain with warranty, if he traverses the bargain, that goes to all. Then here we have shown that we ourselves did not sell, but that it is B.'s sale and that the defendant was only his instrument and minister. For the master shall have an action of Debt for the money for which they were sold, but on the warranty made by the servant to the man on the master's sale he shall not have an action of Deceit.

CHOKE, J.: If a man sells to me, and a stranger warrants that it is good and sufficient, on this warranty made by parol I shall not have an action of Deceit, but, if it were by deed, I may have an action of Covenant. So it is necessary that the bargain was part of the contract, or otherwise I shall not have an action of Deceit against the warrantor. Now here the sale is the sale of the master and the warranty is the act of the servant, and therefore on this warranty I shall not have an action against the servant. If a man undertakes to cure me of a certain malady and he gives me such medicines as to make me worse, I shall have *action sur mon cas* against him; but if he undertakes as above and then commands his servant to give me medicines or to plaster me, whereby I am made worse, I shall not have an action against the servant but against the master. So, too, if one undertakes to shoe my horse and orders his servant, who lames him, the action lies against the master.

LITTLETON, J.: Although this sale is the sale of the master, yet it is made by the servant, and perchance if he had not warranted the thing the plaintiff would not have bought it; and so, as he warranted it and the sale was made through him, it is reasonable that, if he be deceived, he should have an action of Deceit. And, Sir, if my servant sells a horse to you on the terms that you shall give the master twenty pounds for the horse and to the servant twenty shillings, in this case the servant shall have an action of Debt for the twenty shillings.

BRIAN, C.J.: These twenty shillings may be for his labour. But, Sir, it seems here that the action of Deceit will not lie in this case, for it is the sale of the master and not of the servant. And, as has been said, in one case the warranty is traversable and in another it is not. For if I sell to a man twenty sheep for killing and they are corrupt, yet, even if I have warranted them, he shall not have an action of Deceit on the warranty and so the warranty need not be traversed; for, until they are dead, I cannot know whether they are corrupt or not. But if you put trust and confidence in me, then, if I deceive you, you shall have an action of Deceit. So if I sell mutton to be eaten and it is corrupt, you shall have an action of Deceit, even if I have not warranted it.

NEALE, J.: In your case the cause is that it is forbidden by law to sell bad food.

BRIAN, C.J.: If a man sells to me seed and warrants that it is good, and it is bad, or that it is seed of such a country, and it is not, I shall have an action of Deceit, for I cannot know this, but the seller can know it well. But if he warrants that the seed will grow, such a warranty is void, for it is not for him to warrant this, but God. And, if a man sells me a horse and warrants that it has two eyes, and it has not, I shall not have an action of Deceit, for I can know this for myself from the beginning.

LITTLETON, J.: Because you have good view of him at the time of the bargain, the bargain is good, even if the horse be blind, etc. But if a man sells cloth which perchance is beyond the sea and warrants it to be of a certain length, and it is not, I shall have an action of Deceit, for it may be that this warranty is the cause of the bargain.

CHOKE, J.: If I sell a horse and warrant that he will go thirty leagues in a day, now, if he will not, there shall be no action of Deceit. For a man should warrant only such things as exist at the time of the warranty and he cannot warrant any future act.

Fairfax: If I buy goods from a man with a warranty and the warranty is of some thing of which I could have notice by my five senses at the outset, then, if they are not as warranted, I shall not have an action; as if he sells me red cloth and warrants it to be blue, for I can know this by my eyes at the time of the sale.

BRIAN, C.J.: If the buyer in your case were blind, he should have an action of Deceit.

Fairfax: If a man sells me certain cloths and warrants them to be of such a length, and they are not, I shall have an action of Deceit, for I cannot by merely looking at them know their length, but only by a collateral proof, that is, by measurement; and so, since I have given credence to you as to their length and you have deceived me, it is right that I should have an action of Deceit.

ANON
Y.B. MICH. 20 HEN. VII, f. 8, pl. 18[54]
A.D. 1505

A man brought an *Action sur son cas* for that, whereas he had bought from the defendant 20 quarters of barley to be delivered to the plaintiff at a certain day and place, the defendant converted the said quarters to his own use; whereby the action accrued to him.[55]

KINGSMILL, J.: This action does not lie, but it is proper for him to have action of Debt; for the property is not changed by the bargain, since the thing is unascertained and he must have what the defendant delivers and it is at the defendant's pleasure what grain he will deliver. For if he buys 20 quarters from another, he can satisfy the plaintiff with these; wherefore the property is not in the plaintiff, any more than the money which the plaintiff is to pay to the defendant. . . .

FISHER and VAVASOUR, J.J. were of the same opinion.

FROWICKE, C.J. thought the contrary: As to what is said, that the plaintiff cannot take the 20 quarters nor has the property in them by the bargain, this is not to the point. For the defendant has done an act against my bargain and to my deceit, whereby I am put to loss, and so it is right that he should be punished for this misdemeanour by the *action sur le cas* which has been brought. If I sell ten acres of land, parcel of my manor, and covenant further to make title by such a day, and before the day I sell all the manor to another, in this case *action sur le cas* lies against me; and so

[54] Also reported Keilway, p. 69 and p. 77, as in Mich. and Hil. 21 Hen VII.
[55] In Keilway, p. 77: 'in an action of *Trespass sur le Case* the plaintiff counted that he had bought from the defendant 20 quarters of malt for a certain sum of silver paid beforehand, which he left with the defendant for safe keeping until a certain day was past, and that the defendant *super se assumpsit* to do this and to keep good custody until the day, but that the defendant had converted the said malt to his own use tortiously and to the damage of the plaintiff, etc.'

if I sell ten acres of my woods and then sell all the woods to another; or if I covenant, for money, to make a house by such a day, and I do not do it, *action sur le cas* lies for the nonfeasance. So here he has sold 20 quarters of barley to the plaintiff to be delivered by a certain day, and he has not done so but has converted them to his own use; wherefore he should be punished by *accion sur le cas*. And although he can have Debt, it does not follow that he cannot have this action. For if I bail money to one to bail over and he converts it to his own use, I can have action of Account, Debt or *Action sur le cas*. So, too, where a thing is bailed to one to keep, and he converts it to his own use, Detinue lies and also *Action sur le cas*, as was shewn here before in the case of *Cheeseman*. But in this case here it is good to examine and consider of the matter.

And on this the case was adjourned.

And on another day,

KINGSMILL, J.: This action does not lie, but he will be put to his action of Debt. For the bargain must be taken equally between the parties, not more for the one than for the other, unlike the case of a gift; and so, no more than the seller can take the money for the thing bought, can the buyer take the thing which is unascertained, as here. And by the very terms of this bargain he cannot take the corn, for it must first be measured out. And suppose that he had no corn at the time of the bargain, but that he bought it afterwards, or that he has since sold the corn which he had at the time of the bargain and then buys other corn, he can deliver it on the proper day and it will be well; which shows that he [the buyer] had no interest in the grain at the time of the bargain, and he must therefore sue in Debt. But if I sell the grain that is in my barn or my house, I cannot deliver other grain, for perchance there is no grain so good in the whole country; for which Detinue lies. And where a general action lies, a special *Accion sur le cas* will not lie; as where Assise of Nuisance lies, *Accion sur le cas* lies not; and so here. But for a nonfeasance, *Accion sur le cas* lies; as if an attorney does not execute his office or a labourer does not do his service in tending my land; for by this I am damaged, and no general action lies.

FISHER and VAVASOUR, J.J. to the same intent: For there is a diversity where the thing bought is certain and where it is uncertain. Where it is uncertain, the buyer cannot take without the delivery of the other; but where it is certain, he can. Wherefore in this case, since it is not certain what grain the buyer shall have (for, as has been said, he can buy other grain and deliver it to the plaintiff at the day, and this will discharge him), the plaintiff has no interest in the grain, and so he must sue in Debt.

FROWICKE, C.J. to the contrary: Each man must be punished according to his default. While, then, Debt lies for the grain, yet, because he has deceived him, this is a greater tort than the detention of the grain or than the non-payment, and for this he cannot be punished in the other action as he can be in this action. For if I deliver money to one to deliver over to my attorney for my costs in some suit, and he delivers it to my adversary, in this case the delivery is a greater damage to me than the non-delivery; and yet Debt lies against the bailee. But, though Debt lies, yet *Action sur le cas* also lies for the misdemeanour; and so these actions are founded on different grounds. And where I am bound in an obligation on condition of paying a less sum, and I deliver the less sum to my servant to pay over, and he does not pay, in this case Debt lies or Account for the non-payment; but, because by the non-payment I have forfeited my obligation, I have suffered a great tort for which I shall have *Action sur le cas*. And so in this case, because by the conversion to his own use of the grain the plaintiff is deceived, so he has greater damage than by the non-delivery of it, and so, as I think, the action here lies. As to KINGSMILL'S remark, that where Nuisance lies the *Action sur le cas* lies not, I agree well, for the one is real and the other merely personal, and such actions cannot be brought together; but it is otherwise here. Suppose I covenant to enfeoff a man of one acre, parcel of my manor, and I sell all the manor to another, here *action sur le cas* lies for this deceit; and so in the case at bar, because he sells to the plaintiff 20 quarters of barley and then converts them to his own use. This is a deceit and a misdemeanour, for which the action lies.[56]

[57]And, coming from Westminster, I heard Master FINEUX say that, to his mind, the action of Debt lies, in which he shall recover damages for all this misdemeanour, and not this action.

NOTA
Y.B. MICH. 21 HEN. VII, f. 41, pl. 66
A.D. 1506

Note, that if one makes a covenant to build me a house by a certain day, and he does nothing about it, I shall have *Action sur mon cas* on this nonfeasance as much as if he had been guilty of a misfeasance; for I am damaged by this: *per* FINEUX, C.J. And he said that it has thus been adjudged, and he held it to be law. And so it is, if one makes a bargain with me that I shall have his land to me and my heirs for £20 and that he will convey the estate to me if I pay him the £20, that, if he will not convey the estate to me according to the covenant, I shall have an *accion sur mon cas*, and I will not need to sue out a *Subpœna*.

JORDAN'S CASE
Y.B. MICH. 19 HEN. VIII, f. 24, pl. 3[58]
A.D. 1528

In the King's Bench one *Jordan* brought a writ *sur son cas*. And he recited in the writ that, whereas the plaintiff had one *Tatam* in execution in the

---

[56] Keilway, at p. 78, adds, in his report of the judgment of FROWICKE, C.J.: 'If I bail my goods to a man for safe keeping and he takes the custody upon himself (*emprist le custodie sur luy*), and my goods are lost for default of good custody, I shall have action of Detinue or action on my case at my pleasure, and shall charge him by these words—*super se assumpsit*. And if I sue my action of Detinue and he wages his law, I shall be barred in my action on my case because I had my choice and chose Detinue, and this was at my peril, and I have lost the advantage of the action on my case. . . . And if I covenant with a carpenter to make me a house and pay him £20 to make it by a certain day, and he does not make it by the day, now I have a good action on my case because of the payment of my money, and yet it sounds only in covenant; and without payment of money in this case, no remedy. Yet, if he makes the house and does it badly, an action on my case lies. So also for the nonfeasance, if the money is paid, action on the case lies. And so it seems to me in the case at bar that the payment of the money is the cause of the action on the case, without any alteration of property.'

[57] Note by the reporter. Fineux, C.J. was Chief Justice of the King's Bench, as Frowicke, C.J. was Chief Justice of the Common Pleas.

[58] There has been much confusion in the dating of this case. Brooke's Abridgment, *Accion sur le Case*, pl. 5, gives 27 Hen. VIII.: the Black-letter page heading to the term is 26 Hen. VIII, and to the case itself 19 Hen. VIII. As Brooke, J., who appears in the case, died in May, 1529, the last date must be preferred.

Counter[59] for a certain debt recovered against him, the defendant *assumpsit super se* to the plaintiff that, if the said plaintiff would discharge the said *Tatam* from execution, he would pay the debt to the plaintiff by such a day if the said *Tatam* had not paid him before; and he showed that he discharged the said *Tatam* from execution and that the said *Tatam* had not paid before the day. Wherefore, etc. The defendant traversed the assumption, and on this they were at issue.

And at *Nisi Prius* in London the plaintiff gave in evidence that the defendant came to the plaintiff's wife, the plaintiff being absent, and *assumpsit super se* to the wife that, if the plaintiff, her husband, would discharge the said *Tatam* from the execution, he would pay the debt to the husband on such a day if *Tatam* had not paid it before; and then the said plaintiff came to his house and his wife told him, and he agreed to the assumption and on this discharged the said *Tatam* from the execution. The defendant said that this evidence was not good because the wife could be no party to such an assumption without the command of her husband or without agreement made before, and so the assumption was void and the subsequent agreement of the husband could not make it good.

And it seemed to the Justices at *Nisi Prius* that the exception was not good. Wherefore the defendant made a bill of exceptions and one of the Judges sealed it; and then the verdict was given for the plaintiff. And now, at a day in Banc, the defendant put the aforesaid matter in arrest of judgment.

Knightly: You shall not have judgment. For this assumption of the plaintiff's wife in her husband's absence was not good; for the wife cannot do any act which will prejudice her husband. . . . [The Court drove him to another argument]. . . . Yet again it seems that this action will not lie, for he could have had an action of Debt in this matter and then he should not have a writ *sur son cas,* for this he shall have only if there is no other remedy.

TOTA CURIA: That is not so. For in many cases one may have an *action sur son cas* where he could have some other remedy; and so, for this matter, it is good enough.

BROOKE, J.: It seems to me that the assumption made to the plaintiff's wife in his absence is good unless the husband disagrees. . . . And as to the point that the plaintiff should have had a writ of Debt and not this action, I think the contrary. For I understand that one shall have Debt only where there is a contract; and the defendant has not *quid pro quo,* but the action is founded only on the assumption, which sounds merely in covenant; and if it was by specialty the plaintiff would have an action of Covenant. But, since he has no specialty, to my mind he has no remedy if he has not *action sur son cas.* And a case was adjudged since I have been Judge here,[60] that a stranger came with a man to a Baker of London and said to the Baker, Give this man as much bread as he wants and if he does not pay you I will; and the Baker delivered certain bread to the man, who did not pay him, and the Baker brought his *action sur son cas* on the special matter against the stranger, and the stranger demurred in law; and it was adjudged clearly that the action lay, and the Baker recovered. So in this case.

SPELMAN, J., to the same intent: First, because this matter comes before us on a bill of exceptions, I will speak to that. And I think the defendant

[59] A debtors' prison in the City of London.
[60] Brooke became a Judge in 1520 and died in May, 1529.

should not have the advantage of this bill to arrest judgment. . . . [He put a technical objection and then dealt with the relations of husband and wife, *ut supra*]. . . . Then, admitting the assumption to be good, what action shall the plaintiff have? I think it is at the election of the plaintiff to bring a writ of Debt or another action; for in several cases the Law gives two ways for a man to come to his remedy. As if I bail goods to you and you burn my goods or suffer them to be consumed by moths; now it is in my election to bring the one action or the other, that is, writ of Detinue or *Accion sur mon cas* at my pleasure, provided that, when I have had the one, I shall not have the other. And if I am disseised, I can elect to bring a writ of *Entry sur Disseisin* or a Writ of Right. So I think that the plaintiff should recover.

PORT, J., to the same intent. . . .

FITZ JAMES, C.J. to the same intent: [After dealing with the other points, *ut supra*]. . . . Then, shall he have an action of Debt or this action? It seems to me that he shall not have an action of Debt. For here there is no contract and the defendant has not had *quid pro quo;* wherefore he has no remedy if he has not *accion sur son cas*. So, if a stranger in London buys a piece of cloth, and I say to the merchant, If he does not pay you by such a day, I will; here there is no contract between the merchant and me, and he will not have an action of Debt against me. So, too, if one is arrested for debt and I say to the creditor, Be you content to let him go free and if he does not pay you I will; now, if the debtor does not pay the debt, the creditor can have *accion sur son cas* against me, but not action of Debt. So, too, in the case of delivery of bread that has been put, the plaintiff could not have a writ of Debt. Wherefore, in the case here, because there is no contract between the plaintiff and the defendant, the plaintiff cannot have an action of Debt, but only this action.

And then the plaintiff had judgment.

Quod Nota.

ANDREW v. BOUGHEY

1 DYER, 75a

A.D. 1552[61]

The declaration was, That the defendant ' on such a day, year and at such a place, undertook for twenty marks (the moiety of which was in hand, paid, and the residue agreed between them to be paid within a certain time) that he would deliver at such a place, within four days after such a Feast, four hundred pounds weight of good and merchantable wax; but the defendant, not regarding his promise and undertaking, and intending to defraud the plaintiff of all the profit that he should have by the said bargain and to draw him into disgrace and infamy, afterwards, *sc.* on such a day which was before the Feast, did deliver to the plaintiff at the said place three hundred and seventy-three pounds weight of wax, falsely and deceitfully mixed with resin and turpentine, etc., as parcel of the said four hundred pounds, asserting and warranting the said three hundred and seventy-three pounds to have been good, proper and merchantable, when it was not so;

---

[61] The action was brought in the King's Bench, of which the judges were Cholmley, C.J., and Mervin, Bromley and Portman, J.J.

and that the said plaintiff, confiding in the assertion and promise of the said defendant in this behalf and believing the said wax to have been good, etc., afterwards sold it to one B. for twelve pounds, and afterwards the wax became forfeited to the mayor and sheriffs of London, according to a custom; whereby the plaintiff was not only compelled to pay back the twelve pounds to B., but by occasion of the aforesaid false mixing of the said wax was much hurt and brought into great infamy on that account, etc.'

To this the defendant, '*protestando*[62] that the said three hundred and seventy-three pounds which were delivered to the plaintiff were of good and merchantable wax, etc., for plea says, That before the said Feast at such a place the plaintiff and defendant did agree that, if the defendant would deliver immediately to the plaintiff one cake of wax weighing twenty pounds, the plaintiff would accept that in recompense as well for the aforesaid three hundred and seventy-three pounds as for the residue which was to be delivered,' and pleaded this execution in certain, with the acceptance by the plaintiff accordingly, etc.

Whereupon the plaintiff demurred in law, because the deceit, which is the effect and substance of the matter (*ut dicitur*), is not answered.

And the bar seemed good enough. For the effect and substance of this action is that the defendant hath not performed his bargain, *sc.* with good and merchantable wax, but that it was corrupted and mixed, as above, and deceitful, for which the plaintiff has received satisfaction and recompence by the cake and his own acceptance, and, although it were not of one hundredth part of the value of his loss, yet by his own accord and agreement this injury is dispensed with. And in all actions in which nothing but amends is to be recovered in damages, there a concord carried into execution is a good plea. . . .

And it seems here also that the deceit is not material. For the plaintiff in his declaration hath alleged that, after the undertaking and the contract made and before the Feast at which the wax should be delivered, *sc.* on the third of September, etc., the defendant made the affirmation and warranted that the wax was good, etc., to which the plaintiff gave faith and credit, which is the cause of his deceit; for without a precedent trust a man cannot be deceived. And here the warranty and promise of the goodness of the wax was void and of no force in law, because it was not made immediately upon the contract but a month after; and that is not good according to 5 H. 7. 41. b.[63] And then from first to last, if the promise and warranty that the defendant made on the said third day of September be void, then is the confidence and faith given to it by the plaintiff in vain and of no force; and then it follows of course that the plaintiff was not nor could be deceived by the intendment of the law. The deceit therefore is immaterial and needs not to be answered.

And it seems for another cause that, although the plea were not good, still the plaintiff shall not recover. For if it appear to the Court that the plaintiff in any action have not good cause to have his action, the Court will never give judgment for him. Here it appears in the beginning of the count that ' for ' twenty marks, the moiety of which was in hand paid and

[62] On *protestation* as a pleader's device, see Stephen on Pleading, 2nd ed. (1827) pp. 256-9.
[63] Y.B. Trin. 5 Hen. VII. f. 41, pl. 7: ' *Nota,* that it is said by several that, if one sells a thing and afterwards at another place the seller warrants it, this warranty is void, because it was not made *sur le bargain;* and the buyer shall not have an action of Deceit.'

the other moiety was to be paid 'at a certain time agreed on between them,' etc. *Non constat* whether that time was past or to come, at the time of this action brought; and if it was past, as it shall be intended most strongly against the plaintiff, and the money not paid or legally tendered, then the contract and undertaking is void. For this word—'for'—makes the contract conditional; as, '*for* a marriage to be had I covenant to make an estate, etc.,' if the marriage do not take effect, I shall be discharged from the covenant. The law is the same of an annuity granted *pro consilio impendendo;* cease to give counsel, and the annuity ceases. . . . Also, if a man grant to one a way over his land and he for having this way grant him a rent charge; if the one be stopped, the other is stopped. So it is in contracts; as if, ' for an hawk to be delivered to me on such a day, you shall have my horse at Christmas,' if the hawk be not delivered at the day you shall not have the action for the horse, etc. Here then the strength of the matter (which may be variously taken and expounded) shall be construed against the party who shews or pleads it, *sc.* that the time of the payment was prior to the time of the deliverance or at the very time of the deliverance or, at most, within one year afterwards; and here were almost two years between the Feast when it was to have been delivered and the time of the action brought; and then the declaration should have been, ' At a certain time yet to come agreed on between the parties, etc.' . . .

∽ 15 ∾

THE SUBSEQUENT DEVELOPMENT
OF ASSUMPSIT

A.

INDEBITATUS ASSUMPSIT

THE attempt had been made in *Jordan's Case* in 1528 to establish Assumpsit as a substitute for Debt, and two of the four judges had approved.[1] Such a course was clearly favourable to a plaintiff. He would be able not only to avoid the inveterate wager of law, but also, perhaps, to reach the representatives of a deceased debtor who, unless he could produce a deed, would remain immune. The attack upon the representatives, indeed, had already been launched, and, after an initial victory, had been repulsed.[2] But so practical a problem was bound to be forced repeatedly upon the attention of the courts, and in *Norwood* v. *Read* in 1558 the attack was renewed.[3] A buyer brought an action on the case against the executors of a deceased seller for the non-delivery of goods. Counsel for the defendants, while they pressed the stale argument of wager of law, sought to freshen it by rationalisation. The archaic form, it was suggested, concealed a live issue. On the existing law of evidence executors could be assured of their testator's liability only if this appeared under seal: in the absence of a deed it must be doubtful whether the liability had in truth been incurred, or, if originally incurred, whether it had not subsequently been discharged. Moreover, to allow the action in one instance against representatives was to allow it in all. Assumpsit had become a general contractual remedy. 'Every contract executory is an *assumpsit* in itself.' Despite this reasoning, the Court of Queen's Bench delivered judgment for the plaintiff. Plowden, however, after reporting the decision, noted the doubts entertained of its propriety by ' many wise and learned men in our law.' The profession had not been convinced, and the campaign was not yet over.

Apart from this particular problem, the advantages of Assumpsit were so patent that it was bound to be popular with litigants. The first edition of Rastell's Entries, published in 1566, offered three precedents of ' actions sur le case in lieu de action de Dett.'[4] But an obstacle

---

[1] *Supra*, pp. 339 and 353.
[2] *Supra*, p. 339.
[3] *Norwood* v. *Read*, 1 Plowden, 180.
[4] *Supra*, p. 93.

had yet to be surmounted which, if technical, was none the less formidable. Lawyers, nursed upon the forms of action, were initially prejudiced against a development which confused their categories, and to allow upon the same set of facts two writs so eminently diverse as Case and Debt was patently irregular. An objection, which, in happier circumstances, might have been confined to the scholar in his study, was reinforced by the instinct of cupidity. The Court of Common Pleas, which enjoyed a monopoly of Debt, was moved to defend, as the Queen's Bench for the same reason to attack, a vested interest. For thirty years an unsavoury internecine war was waged. A plaintiff in either court, who sued in Case, must declare not only that the defendant had incurred a debt, but also that he had undertaken to discharge it. But was the ' undertaking ' a fact which he must prove in evidence or a fiction introduced merely to give colour to the suggestion of *assumpsit* and no more traversable than the allegations of ' loss ' and ' finding ' in the writ of Trover? The Common Pleas insisted on the fact, the Queen's Bench on the fiction. As late as 1600 the Exchequer Chamber, packed with the judges of the Common Pleas and of the Exchequer, upset, on this issue, the judgment of the Queen's Bench.[5]

So open a conflict became a scandal, and in *Slade's Case* in 1602 it was at last terminated.[6] John Slade brought an action upon the case in the Queen's Bench against Humfrey Morley. He declared that he had bargained and sold standing crops to Morley, that Morley had ' assumed and promised ' to pay a fixed price for them and that he had failed to do so. The jury in a special verdict found that the crops had been sold but that there had never been any express assumpsit to pay the price. The judges felt that they must make up their minds once and for all whether an implied assumpsit would suffice, and the case was twice argued before the members of all three courts in a special session of the Exchequer Chamber.[7] The view, so long and so obstinately held by the Queen's Bench, was vindicated. Case was accepted as a general alternative to Debt (save where the plaintiff had to rely upon a deed), and, when so used, the ' assumpsit ' might be a pure fiction.

The common law was now committed to two species of Assumpsit: *Special Assumpsit,* where the undertaking was express, and *Indebitatus Assumpsit,* where it might be implied from the mere existence of a previous debt.[8] The creation of the latter species enabled the doubtful

---

[5] See *Edwards* v. *Burre* (1573) Dalison, 104, and *Maylard* v. *Kester* (1600) Moore, 711.
[6] 4 Co. Rep. 91a, 92b, *infra,* p. 371.
[7] The second argument, sustained by Coke for the plaintiff and Bacon for the defendant, must have been an outstanding forensic exhibition.
[8] Cf. Stephen on *Pleading,* so late as 1827: ' *Indebitatus assumpsit* is that species of the action of assumpsit in which the plaintiff first alleges a debt and then a promise in consideration of the debt. The promise so laid is, generally, an *implied* one only.' (2nd ed. p. 350, note 5.)

liability of the personal representatives to be finally settled. An attempt was made in *Pinchon's Case* in 1612 to re-open the decision in *Norwood* v. *Read*.[9] Counsel for the defendants took two points. On the one hand, they tried once more to make wager of law palatable in a new environment by stressing its place in the contemporary rules of evidence. On the other hand, they advanced the argument or murmured the incantation, *Actio personalis moritur cum persona*. Assumpsit, though lately adapted to contract, was in essence tortious and as such within the ban of the alleged maxim. Neither argument prevailed. The judges were not prepared to rationalise what they wished to avoid. Wager of law was no more than an incident of Debt and inappropriate to Assumpsit. Nor were they impressed by a doubtful Latin text. Whatever its origin, Assumpsit was no longer delictual; and, even if it were, the ban extended only to such torts as caused personal injury, such as Assault and Battery.[10] The decision, on a long view, made for justice, but its immediate consequences were not altogether happy. So long as the law of evidence forbade the examination of the litigants and therefore, in an oral contract, of the only persons likely to know the facts, the way was open, if not to perjury, at least to a process of conjecture which might or might not be intelligent. One of the by-products of the decision was the Statute of Frauds, of which it may justly be said that the cure was worse than the disease.[11]

B.

QUANTUM MERUIT

Before the seventeenth century the common law afforded no remedy where services were rendered or goods delivered by one person to another in circumstances which raised a presumption that they were to be paid for, but where no precise sum had been fixed by the parties. Debt would not lie in the absence of a previously ascertained price.[12] Assumpsit would not lie without an express promise.[13] Account would not lie since the facts did not fall within the range of relationships exclusively countenanced by the law.[14] But during the first quarter of the seventeenth century Assumpsit was extended to

---

[9] *Pinchon's Case*, 9 Co. Rep. 86b, *infra*, p. 374. For *Norwood* v. *Read*, see *supra*, p. 358.

[10] Cf. *Anon* (1521) Y.B. 12 Hen. 8, f. 11, pl. 3, where Fineux, C.J. said of *Actio moritur cum persona*, that it applied only 'where the hurt or damage is corporal, as if one beats me and dies, there my action is gone.' For the history of the alleged maxim, see Winfield, 29 Col. L.R., 244-9.

[11] See Plucknett, *Concise History*, 4th ed. pp. 610-1, and *Rabel*, 63 L.Q.R., 174.

[12] *Young* v. *Ashburnham* (1587) 3 Leonard, 161. The strange decision in *Waring* v. *Perkins* (1621) Croke Jac. 626, that Debt would lie on a *quantum meruit* for work and materials, must be regarded as a belated aberration.

[13] The suggestion to the contrary to be found in the discussion in *Watkins' Case* (1425) *supra*, pp. 332 and 342, stands alone and precedes by three-quarters of a century the emergence of Assumpsit as a contractual remedy.

[14] *Supra*, p. 273.

meet the situation through an implied undertaking to pay a reasonable sum. The inference was easily drawn in the case of the ' common callings.' As the law imposed on the one party a certain standard of conduct, so it might require from the other the discharge of all proper expenses. It was accordingly said in 1609 that

> ' it is an implied promise of every part, that is, of the part of the innkeeper that he will preserve the goods of his guest, and of the part of the guest that he will pay all duties and charges which he caused in the house.' [15]

The principle was applied in the following year to the case of the common carrier. The plaintiff in *Rogers* v. *Head*[16] declared that,

> ' whereas the defendant is a common carrier from London to Leatherhead . . . *et retrorsum,* and he delivered to him £3 to be delivered at the Black Boy in Southwark; the defendant, in consideration of the premises and for that the plaintiff did undertake *rationabiliter* to content him for the carriage, promised safely to carry it thither and to deliver it at the said sign to the plaintiff. . . .'

The Court sustained the declaration,

> ' because a carrier may demand as much as is reasonable and the other is bound to pay it; and it is the usual course to appoint a tailor to make a garment or a smith to shoe his horse and that he will content him; and such a contract is good enough.'

It is to be observed that the claim was already regarded as normal even outside the common callings; and within the next twenty years successful actions were brought to recover *tantum quantum meruit* by professional men and tradesmen and even by plaintiffs who, though not carrying on any business, had undertaken a particular service for the defendant.[17]

The action upon a Quantum Meruit,[18] thus established, raised a question of classification. Was it to be regarded as but a particular application of the general Indebitatus Assumpsit authorised by the judgment in *Slade's Case,* or was it a distinct species of Assumpsit? The former view was not without its attraction. Whether a price had been fixed beforehand or was left to be determined subsequently by the verdict of a jury, the obligation derived from the receipt of

---

[15] *Warbrook* v. *Griffin* (1609) 2 Brownlow, 254.

[16] (1610) Croke Jac. 262. So, in the *Six Carpenters Case* (1610) 8 Coke Rep. 146a, the Court said *obiter* that an action would lie against a tailor for clothes made, though no price were agreed upon; for ' the putting of his cloth to the tailor to be made into a gown is sufficient to prove the special contract, for the law implies it.'

[17] See *Hall* v. *Hemming* (1616) 3 Bulstrode, 85; *Hall* v. *Walland* (1621) Croke Jac. 618, *infra,* p. 377; *Rolt* v. *Sharp* (1627) Croke Car. 77, *infra,* p. 378.

[18] In the latter half of the seventeenth century a refinement was admitted, whereby *Quantum Meruit* was confined to the case of work done, and a count of *Quantum Valebant* was used for the price of goods supplied: *Boult* v. *Harris* (1676) 3 Keble, 469; *Webb* v. *Moore* (1691) 2 Ventris, 279; Blackstone, *Comm.* III. Chap. 9, *infra,* p. 392. But in the above pages *Quantum Meruit* will be used as a general appellation for both classes of cases, unless otherwise specified.

goods or services and the promise to pay might be said, in English if not in law, to rest upon the fact of a precedent debt. On the other hand, the adoption of this view was obstructed by a technical difficulty. It was held by one school of lawyers that the range of Indebitatus Assumpsit was limited to the class of cases formerly covered by the writ of Debt; and, if their contention were sound, it followed *ex hypothesi* that Quantum Meruit must lie outside this range.[19] Whatever the academic merits of the respective arguments, the predominant opinion of the seventeenth and eighteenth centuries seems to have segregated Quantum Meruit as an individual type of Assumpsit. In none of the cases in the first half of the seventeenth century was a precedent debt alleged by the plaintiff in his Declaration.[20] It is true that in the reign of Charles II practice became unsettled, and actions essentially based upon a Quantum Meruit were pleaded in the language of Indebitatus Assumpsit.[21] But even at this time there were clear indications of the contrary opinion. In *Jermy* v. *Jenny*,[22] the plaintiff declared

> ' that, whereas the defendant on the 8th of June, 1655, at Layston, in consideration that the plaintiff at the special instance and request of the defendant would thenceforth admit, entertain and board the defendant and his retinue in the house and family of the plaintiff and would find, provide and allow to and for the defendant and his retinue meat, drink and lodging and horse-meat for his horses whensoever and so often as it should please the defendant to repair and come to the dwelling-house of the plaintiff, the defendant did assume and promise to pay to the plaintiff so much money for the same as he should reasonably deserve, upon request.'

Towards the close of the seventeenth and during the first half of the eighteenth century professional opinion hardened in favour of the earlier precedents. It became usual for a plaintiff to declare alternatively upon an Indebitatus Assumpsit, where he claimed a fixed sum of money, and upon a Quantum Meruit, where he claimed a reasonable sum.[23] Nor was the distinction between the counts a mere point of pleading. In *Smith* v. *Johnson* in 1698,[24] in answer to a Declaration thus framed in the alternative, the defendant asked leave to pay money

---

[19] On this school of thought, see *infra*, p. 365. The difficulty of the classification is illustrated by two passages in Jackson, *History of Quasi-Contract*. On p. 42, the learned author says, ' During the seventeenth century it became settled law that indebitatus assumpsit would lie to charge a defendant on an implied promise to pay what is reasonable '; and on p. 105, ' [in quantum meruit claims] the facts are analogous to those which would create a debt, but there is no debt created, so that a quantum meruit and ordinary [*sic*] indebitatus assumpsit must be distinguished.' Compare Ames, *Lectures on Legal History*, pp. 89-90.

[20] See cases cited *supra*, p. 361, n. 17.

[21] e.g. *King* v. *Locke* (1663) 1 Keble, 422, and *Tate* v. *Lewen* (1672) 2 Wms. Saunders, 371.

[22] (1661) Sir T. Raymond, 8.

[23] See the precedent cited in Lilly's Entries, *infra*, p. 378; and *Wood* v. *Newton* (1746) 1 Wilson, 141.

[24] 12 Mod. 187.

into court as a complete discharge of any obligation he might have incurred. The Court, while it was ready to allow the motion as an answer to the Indebitatus Assumpsit, refused it as to the Quantum Meruit. ' For who can tell what a man deserves until it be tried? ' The distinction was emphasised by Wood in his Institutes.[25]

> ' Where an Indebitatus Assumpsit is brought for goods sold and delivered, there you must prove a price agreed on; otherwise the action will not lie. . . . Where a Quantum Meruit is laid, you need not prove any price agreed on, but only that the work was done and what you deserve for the same. So that in an action for work done, it is the best way to lay a Quantum Meruit with an Indebitatus Assumpsit. For if you fail in the proof of an express price agreed, you will recover the value. So an action on the case will lie on an implied Assumpsit for a Quantum Valebant,[26] where an innkeeper, etc., furnishes another with meat, drink, etc., or where a tradesman delivers goods at no certain price; and, in an action for goods sold, it is the best way to lay a Quantum Valebant with an Indebitatus Assumpsit, for the reason above.'

C.

QUASI-CONTRACT

The older writs availed in a number of cases which were independent of agreement. Debt lay to enforce penalties imposed by statutes and bye-laws and to collect customary dues and judgment debts; and it had also been used to recover money paid for some specific purpose which the payee had wholly failed to implement.[27] The essence of Account was a duty, not voluntarily assumed, but derived from a relationship thrust by the law upon the parties. Such was the explanation of the ' constructive ' bailiffs and receivers and of the liability to return money paid by mistake.[28] Assumpsit, on the other hand, once severed from its tortious stock, was associated with the consensual conception which was wanting in the older writs. But any possibility of confining its scope to the realisation of this idea was frustrated by the success of Indebitatus Assumpsit. If it was to be used as a general alternative to Debt, it must, of necessity, accept the legacy of claims outside the limits of agreement. Already by 1677 the now familiar, if unfortunate, title of Quasi-Contract had been introduced to designate such claims;[29] and the various specimens may, for convenient analysis, be arranged in two main groups.

The first group comprised the duties to pay fixed sums of money imposed by statute, bye-law or custom. The use of Indebitatus

---

[25] See the 9th edition (1763), Book IV, Chap. IV, at pp. 555-6.
[26] For *quantum valebant*, see *supra*, p. 361, n. 18.
[27] *Supra*, pp. 222-3.
[28] *Supra*, pp. 272-3.
[29] *City of London* v. *Goree*, 3 Keble, 677: *infra*, p. 382, n. 83.

Assumpsit to enforce these duties had been foreshadowed by the practice of the Queen's Bench in the later years of Elizabeth,[30] but its general adoption was reserved for the reign of Charles II. Between 1660 and 1685 actions were persistently and successfully brought. Perhaps the most striking case is that of the *City of London* v. *Goree*.[31] The plaintiffs claimed in Assumpsit the amount of dues customarily levied upon foreign goods exposed for sale within their boundaries. The jury, in a special verdict reminiscent of the proceedings in *Slade's Case*, found the custom to exist, but that the defendant had made no express promise to discharge it. Upon this verdict the Court unanimously gave judgment for the plaintiffs. They allowed that, as the defendant had not agreed to pay, his liability could not be based upon contract; but as it was equally clear that no tort had been committed, it could only be described as arising *quasi ex contractu*.[32] Whatever the difficulties of nomenclature, they were prepared to subscribe unequivocally to the doctrine that, where Debt would lie, there also lay Indebitatus Assumpsit. This view, convenient and popular as it was, could not be indulged without offence to more precise minds. Sir John Holt, in particular, with that curious combination of common sense and pedantry which distinguished him, sturdily resisted the application of a form of action, now generally identified with contract, to facts manifestly not contractual. In *Shuttleworth* v. *Garnett*,[33] where the plaintiff brought Indebitatus Assumpsit for a fine due to him, as lord of the manor, on the admission of a copyhold tenant, counsel for the defendant stressed the impropriety of a contractual action to enforce a duty derived from the tenure of land. Holt, as Chief Justice, seized the opportunity to obscure the issue among the mysteries of real property and the problems involved in the administration of assets; but he could not persuade his colleagues to disregard the precedents of the last twenty-five years, and he found himself in a minority of one. Twelve years later he fought a last delaying action to postpone, if he could not avert, the perpetuation in the law of what, with too nice a discrimination, he regarded as a solecism. The City of York claimed, in Indebitatus Assumpsit, the amount of a fine due under their bye-laws upon the refusal of the defendant to fill the office of sheriff.[34] Sir Bartholomew Shower, for the defendant, giving a new twist to an old word, put a simple but incisive question. 'How can there be any privity or assent implied, when a fine is imposed on a man against his will? ' Chief Justice Holt wanted no further invitation

---

[30] See the cases cited by Jackson, *History of Quasi-Contract*, pp. 40-1, especially *Lord North's Case* (1588) 2 Leonard, 179.
[31] (1677) 2 Levinz, 174: 3 Keble, 677: 1 Ventris, 298. See also *Mayor of London* v. *Gould* (1667) 2 Keble, 295, *Barber Surgeons of London* v. *Pelson* (1679) 2 Levinz, 252, and *Mayor of London* v. *Hunt* (1682) 3 Levinz, 37.
[32] Cf. Justinian, *Institutes*, Book III, Title XXVII, pr.
[33] (1688) 3 Mod. 240: Carthew, 90; *infra*, p. 381.
[34] *City of York* v. *Toun* (1700) 5 Mod. 444: 1 Ld. Raymond, 502,

to intervene. ' We will consider very well of this matter; it is time to have these actions redressed.' But, although he accepted with relish a motion to adjourn the case—' till Doomsday '—he dared not pronounce judgment against the plaintiff. Authority was too strong, and the view of the majority in *Shuttleworth* v. *Garnet* prevailed.

The second group offered a luxuriant crop of cases identified by the requirement that the defendant should account to the plaintiff for his ill-gotten or gratuitous gains. As early as 1628 the King's Bench allowed a plaintiff to recover in Case money which she had paid under a mistake induced by the defendant's fraud.[35] But in this, as in the first group of quasi-contracts, it was not until after the Restoration that Indebitatus Assumpsit was adopted as the regular and appropriate form of action. The development of a remedy which general considerations of justice might seem to demand was temporarily threatened by the view, sustained in some quarters, that its range was not merely indicated by the scope of Debt but restricted to it. ' Indebitatus Assumpsit,' it was said in 1697, ' will lie in no case but where Debt lies.'[36] Such a statement, however, could never have been literally accepted without impugning the contemporary admission that ' Indebitatus will lie wherever the plaintiff may have an account ';[37] and it was fortunately realised that the machinery of the past was not an adequate indication of the needs of the present.

The cases were brought within a common formula whereby the plaintiff claimed a sum of money as ' had and received by the defendant to his use.'[38] They may be discussed under four heads. The plaintiff might sue for money which the defendant had obtained by misconduct. In the earlier precedents an account was sought of profits made in the exercise of an office wrongfully usurped—as clerk of a court, steward of an honour or controller of customs.[39] In these cases, though the language of delict was freely indulged, no actual tort might have been committed. But the principle was soon applied so as to allow Indebitatus Assumpsit as an alternative to such a tort as trover. The advantages of the new remedy were considerable: the pleadings were simpler, the action was not extinguished by death, and the plaintiff need not, as in trover, declare and prove the precise value of the goods which the defendant had converted to his use.[40] The plaintiff might

---

[35] *Lady Cavendish* v. *Middleton* (1628) Croke, Car. 141. The form of action was not Indebitatus Assumpsit, but rather an ' innominate' action on the case: see Jackson, *History of Quasi-Contract*, p. 9, n. 2.

[36] *Hard's Case*, 1 Salkeld, 23; and see *Bovey* v. *Castlemain* (1696) 1 Ld. Raym., 69.

[37] *Aris* v. *Stukeley* (1678) 2 Mod. 260, *infra*, p. 381, n. 79. See also *Asher* v. *Wallis* (1708) 11 Mod. 146, and *Moses* v. *Macferlan, infra*, p. 387.

[38] See the pleadings in *Chandler* v. *Vilett* (1671) 2 Wms. Saunders, 117, *infra*, p. 379. The phraseology reflects the formalistic influence of Account.

[39] *Woodward* v. *Aston* (1676) 2 Mod. 95: *Aris* v. *Stukeley* (1678) 2 Mod. 260, *infra*, p. 381, n. 79: *Howard* v. *Wood* (1680) *infra*, p. 380.

[40] *Hussey* v. *Fiddall* (1698) 12 Mod. 324; and *Lamine* v. *Dorrell* (1705) 2 Ld. Raymond, 1216, *infra*, p. 384. For the advantages of *Indebitatus Assumpsit* see Winfield, *Province of the Law of Tort*, pp. 141-6, and Lord Mansfield in *Moses* v. *Macferlan, infra*, p. 388.

seek, in the second place, to recover money paid by mistake; as where an underwriter had paid on a policy of marine insurance under the erroneous assumption that the ship had been lost. By the beginning of the eighteenth century the courts were not only familiar with such questions, but had grappled with the complications introduced where the transaction was tainted with illegality, and were exploring the implications of the maxim, *In pari delicto potior est condicio defendentis*.[41] The plaintiff, thirdly, might have been forced to pay money by the exercise of some improper authority or influence. It was irrelevant whether the constraint were public or private. In *Newdigate* v. *Davy*[42] the victims of the illegal Court of High Commission set up by James II took advantage of the Revolution to secure the return of the penalties imposed upon them; and in *Astley* v. *Reynolds*[43] the Court condemned the extortion of money by duress not only of the plaintiff's person but also of his goods. Finally, the action was available when money had been paid on a consideration which had wholly failed. Thus in *Martin* v. *Sitwell*[44] the plaintiff was allowed to recover the amount of a premium which he had paid on a policy of insurance, where it later appeared that there was no insurable interest.

The single strand running through all these decisions was the unfair advantage secured by the defendant at the plaintiff's expense. While it would be scarcely flattering to the discernment of the judges to suppose them unconscious of its existence, it is equally true that it was not avowed as an *a priori* concept of English jurisprudence. But the precedents were so numerous and the current of opinion so steady that it wanted but the advent of a dominant personality to proclaim the principle of unjust enrichment as a single and all-sufficient *ratio decidendi*. To the generous mind of Lord Mansfield the invitation was irresistible, and in *Moses* v. *Macferlan* he expressed what had for so long been implicit.

> ' In one word, the gist of this kind of action is that the defendant, upon the circumstances of the case, is obliged by the ties of natural justice and equity to refund the money.'[45]

If a person had obtained money which honesty forbade him to keep, the law would supplement the pressure of conscience. If, on the other hand, it had been paid to him, without legal sanction indeed, but in discharge of an honourable obligation, the court would not require its restoration. The principle had the defects of its qualities. The elasticity which enabled justice to be done between party and party encouraged speculative litigation and the occasional embarrassment of

[41] See *Tomkins* v. *Barnet* (1693) Skinner, 411, *infra*, p. 384; *Lamine* v. *Dorrell*, *infra* p. 384; and *Astley* v. *Reynolds* (1731) 2 Strange, 915, *infra*, p. 386.
[42] (1694) 1 Ld. Raymond, 742.
[43] *Infra*, p. 386.
[44] (1690) 1 Shower, 156, *infra*, p. 383; and see *Helmes* v. *Hall* (1705) 6 Mod. 161.
[45] (1760) 2 Burrow, 1005, *infra*, p. 389.

judicial idiosyncrasy. But it remained for a hundred and fifty years
the mainspring of Quasi-Contract, and not until the twentieth century
was it seriously challenged.[46]

The triumphant progress of Assumpsit in all its branches was
attested by Blackstone in his Commentaries.[47]   He divided contracts
into the two classes of *express* and *implied*. *Express* contracts were
sub-divided into the three species of ' debts,' ' covenants ' and ' promises.'   A debt was a fixed sum of money ' due by certain and express
agreement '; but the Writ of Debt, formerly ubiquitous, was now confined in practice to the recovery of sums granted by deed.   In ' simple
contracts ' it had been replaced by Indebitatus Assumpsit, whereby the
plaintiff could not only avoid wager of law, but would escape the
necessity of proving, at his peril, the precise amount claimed in his
writ.   This advantage had been noticed by Chief Justice Parker in
1714.

> ' If you bring Indebitatus Assumpsit for £10 for a horse sold,
> and if it was sold for more or less, yet the plaintiff shall recover
> what it was sold for. But if Debt be brought on that contract, if it
> come out to be more or less, the plaintiff cannot recover, for it is a
> *præcipe quod reddat* so much money in particular.' [48]

The Writ of Covenant, on the other hand, was still in common use
where the defendant had broken an undertaking under seal to do a
particular act and where no precise sum had been agreed as the price
of the breach. A ' promise ' was described by Blackstone, in a lingering
if unconscious echo of mediæval controversies, as ' in the nature of a
verbal covenant,' lacking only ' the solemnity of writing and sealing to
make it absolutely the same.' The remedy here was universally by
Assumpsit.

The review of *implied* contract was vitiated by the ambiguity of the
epithet. Blackstone, like others before and since, applied it indiscriminately to liabilities based upon a genuine, if tacit, agreement and
to liabilities imposed by the law independently of agreement. The
word was used in the first sense to indicate the scope of *quantum meruit*
and *quantum valebant,* and in the second sense to explain the action
for money had and received. He was even tempted, without apparent
appreciation of the elision, to slip from the language of jurisprudence
into that of political science and to justify the recovery of a judgment
debt or a statutory penalty as grounded upon the Social Contract.
It is, in truth, apparent that these heterogeneous causes of action were
connected only by the historical accident of their vindication by the
common remedy of Assumpsit.

[46] See Fifoot, *Lord Mansfield,* pp. 141-157 and 245-9.
[47] Book III, Ch. 9: *infra,* p. 389.   Blackstone's Commentaries, unlike the original
Lectures on which they were based, reflected the influence of Lord Mansfield's
early judgments.
[48] *Vaux* v. *Mainwaring,* Fortescue, 197   See *supra,* p. 230.

D.

THE COMMON COUNTS

The procedural advantages which suggested the action for money had and received as a substitute for trover were not exhausted by this single development.[49] They served rather as a general recommendation of Indebitatus Assumpsit. As early as 1586 prudent lawyers had observed that, by using the new form of action, they could economise the truth which, if they were to declare in Debt, they must publish *in extenso*. ' In an action upon the Case . . . the plaintiff needs not to show any certainty of the contract or other circumstances how or in what manner the debt did accrue or begin.'[50] In 1680 it was preferred, as an ' expeditious remedy,' to Special Assumpsit;[51] and its superiority was emphasised by Lord Mansfield in *Moses* v. *Macferlan*.

> ' One great benefit, which arises to suitors from the nature of this action, is that the plaintiff need not state the special circumstances from which he concludes that *ex æquo et bono* the money received by the defendant ought to be deemed as belonging to him. He may declare generally " that the money was received to his use," and make out his case at the trial.'[52]

Litigants might thus hope to avoid the more egregious errors to which they were exposed by an extended form of pleading, and, by minimising the preliminary statement of their case, commit its merits to the mercies of judge and jury.[53]

By the close of the seventeenth century the practice was approved of confining the declaration to a general indication of the cause of action without condescending to particular facts. In 1694 it had been challenged and vindicated.[54] The plaintiff had declared that ' the defendant was indebted to him in so much money for work and labour done and performed at the instance and request of the said defendant,' and it was objected that the circumstances should have been set out in detail. The Court approved the declaration.

> ' The only reason why the plaintiff is bound to shew wherein the defendant is indebted is that it may appear that 'tis not a debt on record or specialty, but only upon simple contract; and any general words by which that may be made to appear are sufficient.'

In the early years of the eighteenth century such a pleading had become ' every day's experience.'[55] Thus encouraged, practitioners set themselves to evolve, within the framework of Indebitatus Assumpsit, a series of stylised and yet simple forms of declaration which should

---

[49] *Supra,* p. 365.
[50] *Manwood* v. *Burston* (1586) 2 Leonard, 203.
[51] *Howard* v. *Wood,* Sir T. Jones, 126, *infra,* p. 380.
[52] *Infra,* p. 388.
[53] The perils of pleading extended even to the abuse of Latin. For an amusing, if scandalous, example, see *Gardner* v. *Fulford* (1668) 1 Levinz, 204.
[54] *Hibbert* v. *Courthope,* Carthew, 276.
[55] *Per* Strange, *arguendo,* in *Hayes* v. *Warren* (1731) 2 Strange, 933.

mitigate the dangers of prolixity and at the same time satisfy as many exigencies as possible. These 'Common' or 'Indebitatus' Counts, as they were called, were the favourite devices of the eighteenth century and survived as the daily instruments of litigation until 1852. Stephen, in his classic treatise on Pleading, gave six varieties: for goods sold and delivered, for work done, for money lent, for money paid by the plaintiff to the use of the defendant, for money had and received and for money due on an account stated.[56] Bullen and Leake, in a valedictory review, added two others—for goods bargained and sold and for money due as interest; and explained, in a sentence, the design of the whole series.

> 'Simple contracts, express or implied, resulting in mere debts, are of so frequent occurrence as causes of action that certain concise forms of count have been devised for suing upon them, in which it is sufficient to state the cause of action by a general description, reserving the particular circumstances of the debt to be given in evidence.'[57]

The convenience of the common counts was evident; but they were not without blemish. The lack of candour, vital to their success, sometimes did no more than postpone the difficulties until the parties had come into court. As the issues had not been clarified by the pleading, the defendant might be unaware of the precise complaint made against him and unprepared with the evidence required to meet it. Their range, moreover, though wide, was not unlimited. They could not be used to obtain unliquidated damages nor, unless such failure was due to the defendant's fault, by a plaintiff who had not himself discharged his obligations. Ample scope was thus left for controversy upon the comparative propriety of Indebitatus and of Special Assumpsit. In *Power* v. *Wells* the plaintiff had given his mare and twenty guineas to the defendant in return for the defendant's horse, warranted to be sound. The plaintiff alleged that the horse was in fact unsound and sought to recover the twenty guineas as money had and received to his own use. The form of action would seem at first sight well conceived, but the plaintiff was ultimately non-suited. The essence of his case was the condition of the horse, and a breach of warranty could be pursued only on a special Assumpsit.[58] Even when the facts fell undoubtedly within the ambit of the Common Counts, it was not always easy to select the significant variety. There was, for example, a dark borderland between the respective spheres of *goods sold and delivered* and of *work and materials*. Pleaders sought to avoid the

---

[56] *Infra*, p. 393.
[57] Bullen and Leake, *Precedents of Pleading*, 3rd ed. (1868) p. 35. The count *for goods bargained and sold* lay where, although the property had passed, the goods had not been delivered.
[58] *Power* v. *Wells* (1778) 2 Cowper, 818. See also *Weston* v. *Downes* (1778) 1 Douglas, 23, and *Payne* v. *Whale* (1806) 7 East, 274.

necessity of selection by telling the same tale in as many different ways as there were types of count; and Campbell, reporting an action by a farrier for work and materials, deplored the extravagant results of timidity.

> ' In cases of this sort it is not unusual to find at least ten counts in the declaration—two for work and labour as a farrier, etc.—two for work and labour generally—two for goods sold and delivered —and the four money counts, not omitting money lent, which can never be of any use except where there is the specific contract of the lending and borrowing of money.' [59]

It was not surprising that when, in 1834, the judges, urged reluctantly upon the tide of reform, sought to re-cast their procedure, they should have attacked the indiscriminate use of these counts. They might thus diminish the protracted confusion of a trial and, even more happily, foster that system of Special Pleading which Stephen had so lately and so unexpectedly erected into a science. The New Rules of that year, of which Baron Parke was, if not the only, at least the prime begetter, while they preserved the Common Counts, confined the plaintiff to the choice of a single specimen. Upon this initial selection he was to stake his whole fortune and to the elucidation of this one issue all the evidence was to be marshalled. The purpose was beneficent; the result disastrous. Never were the reports so encumbered with technicality. Plaintiffs were constantly non-suited, after the most gratifying display of erudition, on the threshold of success. Baron Parke was driven to confess himself at a loss to interpret the language of his own rules.[60] The ultimate solution was necessarily more drastic. The Common Law Procedure Act of 1852 destroyed alike the sacred mysteries of Special Pleading and the ruder machinery of the common counts, and, perhaps with too ingenuous an optimism, required from each litigant little more than a naked statement of his case. The new procedure was thus welcomed by Smith in his *Action at Law*.

> ' Every declaration and subsequent pleading, which clearly and distinctly states all such facts as are necessary to sustain the action, defence or reply, as the case may be, will be sufficient, and it is not necessary to state these facts in any technical or formal language or manner, and judgment will be given according to the very right of the cause and the matter of law appearing in the pleadings. In accordance with this principle all statements which need not be proved, such as . . . the statement of losing and finding and bailment in actions for goods or their value; the statement of acts of trespass having been committed with force and arms and against the peace of

---

[59] *Clark* v. *Mumford* (1811) 3 Campbell, 37.   See also Stephen on *Pleading*, pp. 316-8.
[60] The rules, published in Hilary Term, 1834, are set out in the notes to the Appendix to 5 Barnewall and Adolphus.   For an account of their effect and of Baron Parke's own difficulties, see Fifoot, *Lord Mansfield*, pp. 232-241.   See also Bullen and Leake, 3rd ed. pp. 35-6.

our lady the Queen; the statement of promises which need not be proved, as promises in indebitatus counts and mutual promises to perform agreements, and all statements of a like kind, which formerly encumbered pleadings, are now to be omitted.' [61]

In contract as in tort the judges were left, unprotected by the forms of action, to meditate upon principle.

S O U R C E S

SLADE'S CASE
4 Coke Rep. 91a, 92b
A.D. 1602
Record

Devon, ss.[62] *Memorandum*: At another time, that is to say, the term of St. Michael last past, before the lady the Queen at Westminster came *John Slade,* by *Nicholas Weare,* his attorney, and brought here into the Court of the said lady the Queen, then there, a certain Bill against *Humphrey Morley,* in the custody of the Marshal, etc., of a plea of Trespass upon the Case; and there are pledges of suit, to wit, *John Doe* and *Richard Roe,* which Bill followeth in these words:

ss. Devon, ss.

John Slade complaineth of *Humphrey Morley,* in the custody of the Marshal of the Marshalsea of the lady the Queen, before the Queen herself,[63] for this,

That, whereas the said *John,* the 10th day of November in the 36th year of the reign of the said lady Elizabeth, now Queen of England, etc., was possessed for the term of divers years then and yet to come of and in one close of land with the appurtenances in Halberton in the county aforesaid called *Rack Park,* containing by estimation eight acres, and, so thereof being possessed, the said *John* afterwards, that is to say, the said 10th day of November in the 36th year aforesaid, had sowed the said close with wheat and rye, which wheat and rye in the close aforesaid . . . afterwards, that is to say, the 8th day of May in the 37th year of the reign of the said lady the now Queen, were grown into ears;   ,

The said *Humphrey,* the aforesaid 8th day of May in the said 37th year aforesaid . . ., in consideration that the said *John* then and there, at the special instance and request of the said *Humphrey,* had bargained and sold unto the said *Humphrey* all the ears of wheat and corn which did then grow upon the said close . . ., did assume, and then and there faithfully promised, that he the said *Humphrey* £16 of lawful money of England to the aforesaid *John* in the Feast of St. John the Baptist then next following would well and truly content and pay;

---

[61] Smith, *Action at Law,* 10th ed. (1868) pp. 76-7. For a general review of the nineteenth-century reforms in procedure, see Hepburn, *Historical Development of Code Pleading in America and England,* in *Essays in Anglo-American Legal History,* II. 643.

[62] see *supra,* p. 64, n. 63.

[63] i.e., in the Queen's Bench.

Yet the said *Humphrey*, his assumption and promise aforesaid little regarding, but endeavouring and intending the said *John* of the aforesaid £16 in that part subtilly and craftily to deceive and defraud, the said £16 to the said *John* according to his assuming and promise hath not yet paid nor any way for the same contented him, although the said *Humphrey* thereunto afterwards, that is to say, the last day of September in the 37th year of the reign of the said lady the now Queen aforesaid at Halberton aforesaid by the said *John* was oftentimes thereunto required, but the same to pay him or any way to content him hath altogether refused and doth yet refuse; whereupon the said *John* saith he is the worse and hath damage to the value of £40, and thereof he bringeth Suit, etc. . . . .

Report

John Slade brought an Action on the Case in the King's Bench[64] against Humfrey Morley . . . and declared that . . . the defendant, in consideration that the plaintiff, at the special instance and request of the said Humfrey, had bargained and sold to him the said blades of wheat and rye growing upon the said close . . ., assumed and promised the plaintiff to pay him £16 at the Feast of St. John the Baptist then to come; and for non-payment thereof . . . the plaintiff brought the said action. The defendant pleaded *Non assumpsit modo et forma;* and on the trial of this issue the Jurors gave a special verdict, *sc.* : —

> That the defendant bought of the plaintiff the wheat and rye in blades growing upon the said close as is aforesaid, *prout* in the said Declaration is alleged, and further found that between the plaintiff and the defendant there was no other promise or assumption, but only the said bargain.

And against the maintenance of this action divers objections were made by *John Doddridge*, of Counsel with the defendant. 1. That the plaintiff upon this bargain might have ordinary remedy by action of Debt, which is an action formed in the Register, and therefore he should not have an Action on the Case, which is an extraordinary action and not limited within any certain form in the Register. . . . The second objection was, That the maintenance of this action takes away the defendant's benefit of Wager of Law and so bereaves him of the benefit which the Law gives him, which is his birthright. For peradventure the defendant has paid or satisfied the plaintiff in private betwixt them, of which payment or satisfaction he has no witness, and therefore it would be mischievous if he should not wage his Law in such case. . . . The defendant shall not be charged in an action in which he shall be ousted of his Law, when he may charge him in an action in which he may have the benefit of it.

And as to these objections the Courts of King's Bench and Common Pleas were divided; for the Justices of the King's Bench held that the action (notwithstanding such objections) was maintainable, and the Court of Common Pleas held the contrary. And for the honour of the Law and for the quiet of the subject in the appeasing of such diversity of opinions (*quia nil in lege intolerabilius est eandem rem diverso jure censeri*), the case was openly argued before all the Justices of England and Barons of the Exchequer, *sc.*, Sir John POPHAM, Kt. C.J. of England, Sir Edm. ANDERSON, Kt. C.J. of the Common Pleas, Sir W. PERIAM, Chief Baron of the Exchequer,

[64]*Sic.*

CLARK, GAWDY, WALMESLEY, FENNER, KINGSMILL, SAVIL, WARBURTON and YELVERTON, in the Exchequer Chamber, by the Queen's Attorney-General[65] for the Plaintiff and by *John Dodderidge* for the Defendant; and at another time the case was argued at Serjeant's Inn by the Attorney-General for the Plaintiff and by *Francis Bacon* for the Defendant. And after many conferences between the Justices and Barons it was resolved that the action was maintainable and that the plaintiff should have Judgment.

And in this case these points were resolved.

1. That altho' an action of Debt lies upon the contract, yet the bargainor may have an Action on the Case or an action of Debt at his election; and that . . . in respect of infinite precedents (which *George Kemp,* Esq., Secondary of the Prothonotaries of the King's Bench shew'd me) as well in the Court of Common Pleas as in the Court of King's Bench . . ., to which precedents and judgments, being of so great number in so many successions of ages and in the several times of so many reverend Judges, the Justices in this case gave great regard. . . .[66] So that in the case at Bar it was resolved that the multitude of the said judicial precedents in so many successions of ages well prove that in the case at Bar the action was maintainable.

2. The second cause of their Resolution was divers judgments and cases resolved in our books where such Action on the Case on *Assumpsit* has been maintainable, when the party might have had an action of Debt. . . .

3. It was resolved, That every contract executory imports in itself an *Assumpsit,* for when one agrees to pay money or to deliver any thing, thereby he assumes or promises to pay or deliver it; and therefore, when one sells any goods to another and agrees to deliver them at a day to come, and the other in consideration thereof agrees to pay so much money at such a day, in that case both parties may have an action of Debt or an Action on the Case on Assumpsit, for the mutual executory agreement of both parties imports in itself reciprocal Actions on the Case as well as Actions of Debt; and therewith agrees the judgment in *Read* and *Norwood's* Case.[67]

4. It was resolved, That the plaintiff in this Action on the Case in *Assumpsit* should not recover only damages for the special loss (if any be) which he had, but also for the whole debt, so that a recovery or bar in this action would be a good bar in an action of Debt brought upon the same contract. So, *vice versa,* a recovery or bar in an action of Debt is a good bar in an Action on the Case on *Assumpsit.* . . .

5. In some cases it would be mischievous if an action of Debt should be only brought, and not an Action on the Case; as in the case *inter Redman* and *Peck,*[68] [where] they bargained together that for a certain consideration *Redman* should deliver to *Peck* 20 quarters of barley yearly during his life, and for non-delivery in one year it was adjudged that an action well lies, for otherwise it would be mischievous to *Peck*; for, if he should be driven to his action of Debt, then he himself could never have it, but his executors and administrators; for Debt does not lie in such case 'till all the days are incurred, and that would be contrary to the bargain and intent of the

---

[65] Coke.
[66] Here follows a discussion of the place of Precedent in the contemporary law which, while of some general interest, is not germane to the particular purpose of this book.
[67] *Norwood* v. *Read* (1558) 1 Plowden, 180, *supra,* p. 358.
[68] *Peck* v. *Redman* (1552) Dyer, 113a.

parties. . . . Also it is good in these days in as many cases as may be done by the Law to oust the defendant of his Law and to try it by the Country, for otherwise it would be occasion of much perjury.

6. It was said, That an Action on the Case on *Assumpsit* is as well a formed action, and contained in the Register, as an action of Debt, for there is its Form. Also it appears in divers other cases in the Register that an Action on the Case will lie, altho' the plaintiff may have another formed action in the Register. . . . And therefore it was concluded that in all cases when the Register has two writs for one and the same case it is in the party's election to take either. But the Register has two several actions, *sc.* Action upon the Case upon *Assumpsit* and also an Action of Debt, and therefore the party may elect either.

And as to the objection which has been made, that it would be mischievous to the defendant that he should not wage his Law, forasmuch as he might pay it in secret: to that it was answered that it should be accounted his folly that he did not take sufficient witnesses with him to prove the payment he made. But the mischief would be rather on the other party; for now experience proves that men's consciences grow so large that the respect of their private advantage rather induces men (and chiefly those who have declining estates) to Perjury . . . ; and therefore in Debt, or other action where Wager of Law is admitted by the Law, the Judges without good admonition and due examination of the party do not admit him to it. . . . And I am surpriz'd that in these days so little consideration is made of an oath, as I daily observe. . . .

PINCHON'S CASE

A.D. 1612

From the Record

COKE'S ENTRIES—ACTION SUR LE CASE, 1

Edward Pinchon, knight, and *Richard Weston,* knight, executors of the last will and testament of *Jeremy Weston,* late of Roxwell in the county of Essex, knight, the deceased executor of the last will and testament of *Rose Pinchon,* late of Whittle in the county of Essex, widow, deceased, complain of *Thomas Legate,* esquire, executor of the last will and testament of *John Legate,* late of Bonchurch in the county of Essex, esquire, deceased, in the custody of the Marshal of the Marshalsea of our lord the King, in the presence of the King that now is, for that, to wit,

Whereas the aforesaid *Rose* in her lifetime, to wit, on the 7th day of February in the year of Our Lord 1595 at Whittle in the county of Essex, gave by way of loan to the aforesaid *John Legate* in his lifetime 200 pounds of lawful money of England, the said *John,* in consideration thereof, then and there undertook (*super se assumpsit*) and faithfully promised the aforesaid *Rose* in her lifetime, that he, the said *John Legate,* would well and faithfully pay to and content the said *Rose,* her executors and administrators, 200 pounds of lawful money of England when thereto requested;

Yet the aforesaid *John Legate* in his lifetime and the aforesaid *Thomas* after the death of the said *John,* not regarding the promise and assumption of the aforesaid *John Legate* made in his lifetime, but the aforesaid *John* in his lifetime, contriving and fraudulently intending craftily and subtilly to deceive and defraud the aforesaid *Rose* in her lifetime and the aforesaid *Jeremy* after the death of the said *Rose* of the aforesaid 200 pounds, and the aforesaid *Thomas* after the death of the said *John,* likewise contriving and fraudulently intending craftily and subtilly to deceive and defraud the aforesaid *Edward* and *Richard* after the death of the said *Rose* and *Jeremy* of the aforesaid 200 pounds, although the aforesaid *John* in his lifetime by the said *Rose* in her lifetime and by the aforesaid *Jeremy* after the death of the said *Rose* was often required, and although the aforesaid *Thomas* after the death of the said *John* by the aforesaid *Edward* and *Richard* . . . was likewise required, and although goods and chattels of the aforesaid *John Legate,* belonging to him at the time of his death, came after the death of the said *John* to the hands of the aforesaid *Thomas* and still remain in the hands of the said *Thomas* sufficient both to pay and discharge all debts and funeral expenses of the same *John* and to satisfy the aforesaid *Edward* and *Richard* of the aforesaid 200 pounds, have not paid nor has either of them paid the aforesaid 200 pounds;

Whereby the said *Edward* and *Richard* have totally lost diverse profits which they could have had and enjoyed with the aforesaid 200 pounds by buying, selling and bargaining, to the damage of the said *Edward* and *Richard* of 240 pounds. . . .

From the Report
9 Coke Rep. 86*b.*

. . . The defendant pleaded *Non assumpsit,* etc., and it was found for the plaintiffs; and upon the verdict judgment given for the plaintiffs, upon which judgment a Writ of Error was brought. And in this case the principal Error which was assigned was, That no *Action upon the Case upon Assumpsit* for payment of the said debt lies against executors.

And it was argued for the plaintiff in the Writ of Error[69] that the action did not lie. For it is a maxim in Law that executors shall not be charged with a simple contract, and that for two reasons: one, because by the presumption of Law they can't have knowledge either of the beginning of the debt, being made by word without writing, or of the continuance of it, because the testator might pay it privately betwixt themselves; and therefore it is adjudged in 15 *Ed.* 4, 16*a* that an action of Debt lies not against executors for the testator's diet, altho' it be of necessity; and if an action *on the Case* should lie against executors, it would impugn the said maxim of the Common Law; for every contract executory implies an *assumpsit* in law, and by consequence the executors should be charged with every contract executory, which would be directly against the said maxim. Another reason was added: that this action on the case on Assumpsit is *actio personalis quæ moritur cum persona,* for the Entry in this case is *in placito transgressionis super casum* and therefore lies not against executors; no more than, if a gaoler suffers one who is in execution to escape, the plaintiff might have an *action on the Case* at the Common Law against the gaoler, but after the death of the gaoler no action lies against his executors, for that was grounded upon a wrong, which *moritur cum persona.* . . .

And this case depended on consideration divers terms; and after many arguments on both sides and conferences had amongst the Judges, viz., Coke, Chief Justice of the Common Pleas, Tanfield, Chief Baron, Warburton, J., Baron Snigge, Baron Altham, Foster, J. and Baron

---

[69] i.e., the original defendant.

BROMLEY, it was resolved by them all *una voce, nullo contradicente,* that
the Action on the Case in the case at bar did well lie against the executors,
and that, not only without impugning any rule or reason of Law or any
book resolved in the point, but also well warranted and confirmed by divers
authorities in Law, Judgments and Resolutions late and antient.

And as to the objections which have been made (for the confuting of
them is a confirmation that the action doth well lie), to the first it was
answered, That the said book in 15 *Ed.* 4, 16*a.* is that Debt lies not against
executors upon a contract for the testator's diet.   But the reason thereof
is not (as hath been urged) because the executor can't have knowledge of the
contract nor of the continuance thereof, because the testator might have
privately paid it, but the reason of the law which is given in the Book in
the same case is because the testator might have waged his Law. . . . And
the like judgment is in the same year, *fol. 25. a,* that an action of *Debt* lieth
not against the executors (and the reason of the judgment is . . . that a
man shall never have an action against executors where the testator in
his life-time might have waged his Law), and the reason thereof is because
the executors shall be deprived of the benefit of waging Law, if an action
will lie against them; which reason strongly proveth that in the case at Bar
the action will lie against the executors, because the testator in an *Action on
the Case* on this *Assumpsit* could not wage his Law, and therefore his
executors shall not be deprived of it. . . .

[The Judges then examined several cases in the Year-Books and declared
that the resolution in *Slade's Case*[70] had altered the former law].

. . . [Wherefore] if an *Action on the Case on Assumpsit* lies upon every
contract executory, it follows that, forasmuch as the testator could not wage
his Law, the action shall lie against his executors.   And therefore also it is
true that an action *on the Assumpsit* made by the testator will lie against
executors, because in such action the testator could not wage his Law; as
in the same case an action of Debt lies not against executors because in such
action the testator might have waged his Law.   So no birth-right or privilege
of the subject is taken away by this Resolution, but thereby justice and right
is advanced, for as much as the creditor shall be paid his just and true debt.
And the executors, who in truth have the goods in another right, *sc.* to pay
the debts, etc. of the testator, shall not convert them to their private use
without paying the just and true debts of the testator; for that would be
against justice and right and against the office of executors, who are but
ministers and dispensers of the goods of the dead; and, notwithstanding the
testator's death, yet the debt remains, for death is no discharge of the debt,
and it would be a great defect in the law that no remedy should be given
for it. . . .

As to the other objection, that this personal action of Trespass on the
Case *moritur cum persona;* although it is termed *Trespass* in respect that
the breach of promise is alleged to be mixed with fraud and deceit to the
special prejudice of the plaintiff and for that reason is called *Trespass* on
the Case, yet that doth not make the action so annexed to the persons of
the parties that it shall die with the persons; for then, if he to whom the
promise is made dies, his executors should not have any action; which no
man will affirm.   And an action *sur Assumpsit* upon good consideration,
without specialty, to do a thing, is no more personal, i.e. annexed to the
person, than a covenant by specialty to do the same thing. . . .

[70] *Supra,* p. 371.

HALL v. WALLAND

CROKE, JAC. 618

A.D. 1621

Error of a Judgment in the Common Bench in an Assumpsit, where the Plaintiff declared that, whereas William Mabbs was possessed of such land in Melton Mowbray *pro termino diversorum annorum* of the demise of John Woodward, Esq., and whereas there was communication betwixt the said William Mabbs and the Defendant for his estate and interest, the Defendant, 27 April, 18 Jac. at Melton Mowbray aforesaid, in consideration the Plaintiff would procure the said John Woodward to license the said William Mabbs to assign his Lease and interest to the said John Walland, promised he would pay all his charges and as much as he deserved for obtaining thereof, not exceeding 44s.; and alleges *in facto* that he *postea, viz.* 27 *Junii apud Melton Mowbray prædictum,* procured the said John Woodward to grant this licence, and that he paid unto him therefor 20s., and the ingrossing thereof cost 40s., and he deserved for his pains 10s.; and that the Defendant, *licet requisitus,* had not paid, etc. The Defendant hereupon demurred, and adjudged for the Plaintiff, and Error brought.

The first Error assigned was because it is not shewn in what county Melton Mowbray was; so it doth not appear where the land lies nor where the promise was made. *Sed non allocatur.* . . .

[Two other technical objections taken and disallowed]. . . . Fourthly, That he alleges the promise to be, to pay *tantum quantum meruerit,* and avers that he deserved 20s.,[71] which is an uncertain and void promise, for it cannot appear what he deserved; and then, entire damages being given, it is ill for this cause, and the judgment erroneous for all.

Sed non allocatur. For such promise to pay *tantum quantum meruerit* is certain enough, and he shall make the demand what he deserves; and if he demand too much, the Jury shall abridge it according to their discretion. And in proof thereof two precedents were shewn, the one in *Hilary* 17 *Jac.,* betwixt *Ive* and *Chester,* where a tailor brought such an action and alledged a promise to pay *tantum quantum meruerit* for the making of such garments, and recovered[72]; the other in *Hilary* 11 *Jac.* betwixt *Shepherd* and *Edwards,* where a physician brought such an action upon a promise to pay *tantum quantum meruerit* for such a cure, and avers that he cured him and deserved £100.[73] And of that opinion was all the Court here. Wherefore the Judgment was affirmed.

---

[71] *Sic.*

[72] *Ive* v. *Chester* (1619) Cro. Jac. 560. The plaintiff as executrix of a deceased tailor declared that 'the defendant, in consideration the testator would buy and pay, for the defendant, these wares, *viz.,* 24 yards of lace, 11 yards of velvet, 3 yards of broadcloth, and would make for him a cloak, promised not only to pay unto him such sums as he should expend for the said wares, but would pay unto him as much as he deserved for making the said cloak.' The defendant successfully pleaded infancy and that the goods were not necessaries.

[73] *Shepherd* v. *Edwards* (1616) Cro. Jac. 370. The plaintiff, a physician, declared that 'in consideration that at the defendant's request he would with his best skill apply wholesome medicines for the curing the defendant of his disease . . ., the defendant assumed and promised to pay unto him upon request such a sum of money as the plaintiff for his labour and counsel *in et circa curationem morbi prædicti mereret.*' The plaintiff further declared that he had cured the defendant and 'that he well deserved an hundred pounds for his labour and counsel bestowed about the curing of the said disease.' After a verdict for the plaintiff, 'the plaintiff had judgment, although it was objected *quantum mereret* was insufficient and uncertain.'

ROLT v. SHARP
CROKE CAR. 77

A.D. 1627

Error in the Exchequer Chamber of a Judgment given in an Assumpsit in the King's Bench; where the Plaintiff declared, That he at the request of A. S. made a gown and petticoat for the said A. S., which lay by him because they were not paid for; that the Defendant, in consideration the plaintiff would deliver to the said A. S. the said gown and petticoat, assumed and promised to the Plaintiff that he would pay as much as the gown and petticoat were reasonably worth; alleging *in facto* that he upon that promise delivered the said gown and petticoat to the said A. S., and that then it was reasonably worth fifteen pounds, and that he had requested the Defendant to pay it, and he had not paid it. The Defendant pleads *non assumpsit*, and found against him, and Judgment for the Plaintiff.

And now Error assigned, That the declaration is insufficient, because it is alledged he promised to pay and he doth not shew to whom he should pay it, so it is uncertain unto whom the payment should be made. Secondly, there is not any consideration for the Defendant to be charged, for he hath not any benefit by the delivery to A. S. Thirdly, he doth not alledge that he delivered them to A. S. to her own proper use, and then the delivery to her is not material. Fourthly, the promise to pay for them *tantum quantum*, etc., is insufficient.

But all the Justices held that the declaration is good. For as to the first, That he promised to the Plaintiff to pay, although he doth not say to whom he should pay, it is good enough; for it shall be intended to the Plaintiff and to pay to another is idle. For the Plaintiff made the cloaths and the promise was to him to pay; therefore it shall be intended to be paid unto him. . . . To the second, that the consideration is good; for the delivery of those garments out of his hands at the Defendant's request is a good and valuable consideration. To the third, that the delivery to A. S. at his request is a very good consideration. To the fourth, it is the usual way to lay down uncertainly, *viz.*, that he should pay for it *tantum quantum meruit*, etc., and then to aver what it is reasonably worth; which being the common course and always allowed, Judgment was therefore affirmed.

TOMKINS v. ROBERTS
[74] JOHN LILLY : A COLLECTION OF MODERN ENTRIES

A.D. 1701

Action on the Case

Middlesex

Martin Tomkins complains of *Thomas Roberts* in the custody of the marshal, etc., for that, to wit,[75] whereas the said *Thomas*, the 30th day of September in the 12th year of the reign of the Lord William the third now King of England, etc. at Westminster in the county aforesaid, was indebted to the said *Martin* in 50 pounds of the lawful money of England for wines by him the said *Martin* to the same *Thomas*, and at his special instance and request, before sold and delivered; and the said *Thomas* so therein being

[74] See *supra*, p. 64
[75] Here follows a count in *indebitatus assumpsit* for wines sold and delivered.

indebted, he the same *Thomas* in consideration thereof afterwards, to wit, the day, year and place aforesaid, assumed upon himself and to the same *Martin* then and there faithfully promised that he the same *Thomas* the said 50 pounds with interest to the same *Martin*, when thereunto afterwards he should be requested, would well and faithfully pay and content: Nevertheless, the said *Thomas*, his promise and assumption in form aforesaid made not regarding, but contriving and fraudulently intending him the said *Martin* of the said fifty pounds with the interest thereof in this behalf craftily and subtilly to deceive and defraud, the said fifty pounds with the interest thereof to the same *Martin* hath not yet paid nor him for the same hitherto in any wise contented, altho' the same *Thomas* afterwards, to wit, the 1st day of May in the 13th year of the reign of the said now Lord the King, and often after at Westminster aforesaid in the county aforesaid, by the same *Martin* to do it was requested, but the same to him hitherto to pay, or otherwise in any wise to content, hath altogether refused and yet doth refuse.

[76]And whereas also that the said *Martin* afterwards, to wit, the 1st day of October in the 12th year abovesaid at Westminster aforesaid in the county aforesaid, at the special instance and request of him the said *Thomas*, had sold and delivered to him the said *Thomas* other wines, the said *Thomas* in consideration thereof afterwards, to wit, the same day, year and place last mentioned, assumed upon himself and to the said *Martin* then and there faithfully promised that he the said *Thomas* so much money as he the said *Martin* for the wine last mentioned should reasonably deserve to have to the same *Martin*, when thereto afterwards he should be requested, would well and faithfully pay and content: And in fact the same *Martin* says that he for the wine last mentioned reasonably deserved to have of the said *Thomas* sixty pounds of like lawful money of England, and thereof the said *Martin* afterwards, to wit, the same day, year and place abovesaid, to the same *Thomas* gave notice: Nevertheless the said *Thomas*, his promise and assumption aforesaid last mentioned not regarding, but fraudulently intending the same *Martin* of the said sixty pounds in this behalf craftily and subtilly to deceive and defraud, the said sixty pounds or any penny thereof to the said *Martin* hath not yet paid, altho' often requested, etc., but the said *Thomas* the same to him hitherto to pay or for the same in any wise to content hath altogether refused and yet doth refuse, to the damage of the said *Martin* sixty pounds. And therefore he produces the suit, etc.

CHANDLER v. VILETT

2 WMS. SAUNDERS, 117

A.D. 1671

From the Record[77]

WILTSHIRE, to wit: Be it remembered that heretofore, to wit, in the term of St. Michael last past, before our lord the king at Westminster came *Thomas Chandler*, who is within the age of twenty-one years, by *John Ridley* his guardian specially admitted by the court here, and brought into the

---

[76] Here follows a count on a *quantum meruit*.

[77] This case is cited here for the form of pleading. It was subsequently argued, not on the form of the action, but on the question whether the Statute of Limitations could be pleaded against an infant: 2 Wms. Saunders, 120.

court of our said lord the king then there his certain bill against *Richard Vilett*, gent., in the custody of the marshal, etc., of a plea of trespass upon the case, which said bill follows in these words, to wit:

WILTSHIRE, to wit: *Thomas Chandler*, who is within the age of twenty-one years, by *John Ridley*, his guardian specially admitted by the court here, complains of *Richard Vilett*, gent., being in the custody of the marshal of the marshalsea of our lord the king before the king himself, for that whereas the said *Richard*, on the 1st day of May in the 17th year of the reign of our lord Charles the second now king of England, etc. at Highworth in the said county, was indebted to the said *Thomas* in £50 of good and lawful money of England for money by the said *Richard* before that time had and received to the use of the said *Thomas*, and, being so indebted, he the said *Richard* in consideration thereof undertook and then and there faithfully promised the said *Thomas* that he the said *Richard* would well and faithfully pay and satisfy the said £50 to the said Thomas;

And whereas also the said *Richard* afterwards, to wit, on the said 1st day of May in the 17th year aforesaid at Highworth aforesaid in the county aforesaid, was indebted to the said *Thomas* in £12 of like lawful money for other money by the said *Richard* before that time likewise had and received to the use of the said *Thomas*, and, being so indebted, he the said *Richard* in consideration thereof undertook and then and there faithfully promised the said *Thomas* that he the said *Richard* would well and faithfully pay and satisfy the said £12 to the said *Thomas;*

Yet the said *Richard*, not regarding his said several promises and undertakings, but contriving and fraudulently intending craftily and subtilly to deceive and defraud the said *Thomas* in this behalf, has not paid the several sums, amounting in the whole to £62, to the said *Thomas*, nor has he in any wise satisfied him for the same (although to do this he the said *Richard* afterwards, to wit, on the 1st day of August in the 21st year of the reign of our said lord the now king at *Highworth* aforesaid in the county aforesaid, was requested by the said *Thomas*), but to pay him the same has hitherto altogether refused and still refuses, to the damage of the said Thomas of £80; and therefore he brings suit, etc.

HOWARD v. WOOD

A.D. 1680

Report in 2 Levinz, 245

Assumpsit for money received for his use. And upon *non assumpsit*, and special verdict, the case was: —

The Queen having granted to the plaintiff Sir Robert Howard the Stewardship of the Honour of Pomfret for years, to be held from the end of a former term, in which Stewardship were comprised several Courts Leet as well as Courts Baron, the first term being ended, the defendant, by a grant subsequent to that grant made to the plaintiff, held the court and received the money; for which the plaintiff brought his action for the fees. . . .

Report in Sir T. Jones, 126

. . . . It was objected that this action does not lie, but a special action according to his case. . . . This action is not only improper, but also contrary to the truth of his case. For the plaintiff declared in *assumpsit* for monies received by the defendant to the use of the plaintiff, and the Jury found the defendant received the monies to his own use, claiming the office of Steward in his own right and the monies as fees incident to the office, which he had exercised against the plaintiff's will, and no otherwise due than for the exercise of the office. This money was incident to the tort done by the defendant in the exercise of the office; and where a receipt depends merely on a tort, there can be no contract or privity and without them no debt, and by consequence *indebitatus assumpsit* does not lie. . . .

But it was resolved by the whole Court[78] that the action lay. For it is an expeditious remedy and facilitates the recovery of just rights; and this manner of action hath now prevailed for a long time and the point hath been ruled often by the Judges in their circuits and actions frequently brought in this manner. And already on solemn argument in the Court of Exchequer in the case of Dr. Aris,[79] who brought such action for the profits of the office of Comptroller in the port of Exeter, it was resolved by the Lord Chief Baron and all the Court that the action lay. And it was said by the Court here that, if the case had now first come in judgment, the Court would not allow the action. But for the frequent practice of allowing it, and in respect to the said judgment already given in the Exchequer, and for maintaining a conformity in judgment with the other Courts, the whole Court agreed that the action lay. And Judgment was given for the plaintiff.

SHUTTLEWORTH v. GARNETT

A.D. 1688

Report in 3 Mod. 240

[The plaintiff declared] that the defendant was tenant of customary lands held of the manor of A., of which manor B. was lord; that a fine was due to him for an admission; that upon the death of the said lord the manor descended to W., as his son and heir, who died; and the plaintiff, as executor to the heir, brought an *indebitatus assumpsit* for this fine. He declared also that the defendant was indebted to him in twenty-five pounds for a reasonable fine, etc. The plaintiff had a verdict and entire damages.

It was now moved in arrest of judgment that an *indebitatus* will not lie for a customary fine, because it does not arise upon any contract of the parties, but upon the tenure of the land, for upon the death of the lord there is a relief paid. For there must be some personal contract to maintain an action of *debt* or an *indebitatus assumpsit*. . . . Secondly; where the

---

[78] King's Bench: Scroggs, C.J., Pemberton, Dolben and Jones, J.J.

[79] *Aris* v. *Stukely* (1678) 2 Mod. 260. *Pollexfen*, for the defendant, argued, *inter alia*, that 'a general *indebitatus assumpsit* will not lie here for want of a privity and because there is no contract. It is only a tort, a disseisin, and the plaintiff might have brought an assise for this office . . . or an action on the case for disturbing of him in his office; and that had been good, because it had been grounded on the wrong.' Counsel for the plaintiff argued, *e contra*, 'that an *indebitatus assumpsit* would lie here; for where one receives my rent I may charge him as bailiff or receiver; or if any one receive my money without my order, though it is a tort, yet an *indebitatus* will lie, because by reason of the money the law creates a promise, and the action is not grounded on the tort but on the receipt of the profits in this case.' 'THE COURT: An *indebitatus assumpsit* will lie for rent received by one who pretends a title; for in such case an account will lie. Wherever the plaintiff may have an account, an *indebitatus* will lie.'

cause of an action is not grounded upon a contract, but upon some special matter, there an *indebitatus assumpsit* will not lie; and therefore it will not lie upon a bill of exchange or upon an award or for rent, though there is a privity both of contract and estate, without a *special assumpsit*.

E contra, it was argued that the action lies; for, though a fine savours of the realty, yet it is a certain duty. In all cases where *debt* will lie upon a simple contract, there an *assumpsit* will lie likewise. It is true this does concern the inheritance, but yet it is a contract that the tenant shall be admitted paying the fine. It has been also maintained for money had and received out of the office of register for the plaintiff's use,[80] and for scavage money due to the mayor and commonalty of London,[81] which is also an inheritance. It is a contract implied by law, and therefore the action is well brought.

Dolben, Eyre and Gregory, Justices, in Michaelmas 1 Will. & Mary were of that opinion; and judgment was given for the plaintiff.

But the Chief Justice [Holt] was of another opinion. For he held that, if the defendant had died indebted to another by bond and had not assets besides what would satisfy this fine, if the executor had paid it to the plaintiff, it would have been a *devastavit* in him.[82] Suppose the defendant promises, in consideration that the plaintiff would demise to him certain lands, that then he would pay the rent; if the defendant plead *non assumpsit,* the plaintiff must prove an express promise or be non-suited. Also here is no tenure or custom set out.

Yet, by the opinion of the other three Justices, the plaintiff had his judgment.

Report in Carthew, 90

. . . Holt, *Chief Justice,* was of opinion that the administratrix might bring an action of *Debt,* and that it was her proper remedy. But an *Assumpsit* is an action of an inferior nature, and if it will lie for this duty, then the duty itself is in its nature inferior to a debt on a bond, which debt must therefore be paid by an executor before this duty; but this would be very strange, because the fine issues out of the lands and is meerly in the realty. . . .

Nota. It was admitted by all that *Debt* would lie for a Fine upon an admittance to a copyhold.

And, in arguing this case, that of the *Lord Mayor of London and Goree*[83] was cited, which was lately adjudged *in Banco Regis,* which was an *assumpsit* for a sum certain due for *Scavage* (which is a certain and customary duty for all goods and merchandizes imported in London); and there it was adjudged that the action would lie notwithstanding the duty was the inheritance of the Lord Mayor.

To which Holt, Chief Justice, replied that the cases were not parallel,

---

[80] *Woodward* v. *Aston* (1676) 2 Mod. 95.

[81] *City of London* v. *Goree* (1677) 2 Levinz, 174: 3 Keble, 677: 1 Ventris, 298.

[82] 'A *Devastavit* is a mismanagement of the estate and effects of the deceased, in squandering and misapplying the assets contrary to the trust and confidence reposed in them, and for which executors and administrators shall answer out of their own pockets as far as they had, or might have had, assets of the deceased.' Bacon, Abridgment, *Executors and Administrators,* (L) 1.

[83] *City of London* v. *Goree* (1677), 2 Levinz, 174: 1 Ventris, 298: 3 Keble, 677. In 3 Keble, 677, it is said: 'this is a duty that ariseth *ex quasi contractu* and not *ex delicto,* though it was originally but a charge upon the subject, for, it being agreed that Debt lieth, *a fortiori* an *indebitatus.*'

for the duty of *scavage* doth arise out of things in the personalty; but the duty in the principal case issued out of the realty.

But Judgment was given for the plaintiff by three Judges against the opinion of the Chief Justice.[84]

MARTIN v. SITWELL

1 SHOWER, 156

A.D. 1690

Indebitatus Assumpsit for £5 received by the defendant to the plaintiff's use. *Non assumpsit* pleaded.

Upon evidence it appeared that one Barkdale had made a Policy of Assurance upon account for £5 premium in the plaintiff's name and that he had paid the said premium to the defendant, and that Barkdale had no goods then on board, and so the policy was void and the money to be returned by the custom of merchants.

At the trial I urged these two points.[85] 1st, That the action ought to have been brought in Barkdale's name, for the money was his, we received it from him, and if the policy had been good 'twould have been to his advantage; and upon no account could it be said to be received to Martin's use, it never being his money. Besides, here may be a great fraud upon all insurers in this, that an insurance may be in another man's name, and, if a loss happen, then the insurer shall pay, for that some *cestui que trust* had goods on board; if the ship arrives, then the nominal trustee shall bring a general *indebitatus* for the premium, as having no goods on board.

To all which the Lord Chief Justice HOLT answered, That, the policy being in Martin's name, the premium was paid in his name and as his money, and he must bring the action upon a loss; and so, upon avoidance of the policy, for to recover back the premium. And as to the inconveniences, it would be the same whoever was to bring the action, and therefore the insurers ought with caution to look to that before-hand.

Then, 2ndly, I urged that it ought to have been a Special Action on the Case upon the custom of merchants. For this money was once well paid, and then by the custom it is to be returned upon matter happening *ex post facto*. I argued, if the first payment were made void, then the Law will construe it to be to the plaintiff's use, and so an *indebitatus assumpsit* will lie. But when a special custom appoints a return of the premium, an *indebitatus* lies not, as for money received to the plaintiff's use, but a Special Action on the Case upon that particular custom.

---

[84] Holt, C.J. nurtured his resentment at the decision: see *Hussey* v. *Fiddall* (1698) 12 Mod. 324, where he says, '[*Indebitatus Assumpsit*] has been held to lie for a fine by custom; but surely that was hard, for it was to leave matter of law to a jury'; and *Smith* v. *Airey* (1705) 6 Mod. 128, where he says, 'An *indebitatus* has been brought for a tenant-fine, which I never could digest.'

[85] Of Sir Bartholomew Shower, Wallace says: 'In 1687 the author was made Recorder of London, but . . . in 1688 was obliged to resign his place in favour of Sir George Treby. He belonged to the Tory party, and of course is pretty well abused by Macaulay, Lord Campbell and other English historians, in whose veins Whiggery flows instead of blood. He probably did not give the "Whig dogs," as Johnson called them, any special privileges when they deserved to be hanged, and on this account was called by them the "Man-hunter." He died in 1701, and, as he had attained to but the 43rd year of his age, it is evident that he must have been an able and laborious lawyer.' Wallace on the *Reporters*, p. 394.

To which Chief Justice HOLT answered me with the case adjudged by WADHAM WYNDHAM,[86] of money deposited upon a wager concerning a race, that the party winning the race might bring an *indebitatus* for money received to his use, for now by this subsequent matter it is become as such. And as to our case, the money is not only to be returned by the custom, but the policy is made originally void, the party for whose use it was made having no goods on board; so that by this discovery the money was received without any reason, occasion or consideration, and consequently it was originally received to the plaintiff's use.

And so Judgment was for the plaintiff against my client.

TOMKYNS v. BARNET
SKINNER, 411
A.D. 1693

Upon a trial at Guildhall in an *Indebitatus Assumpsit* for money received to the use of the plaintiff, the case was that the plaintiff was co-obligor with J. S. to the defendant, and between J. S. and the defendant there was an usurious contract. The plaintiff paid part of the money to the obligee and, after, pleaded the Statute of Usury upon this bond, and this was adjudged an usurious bond; upon which he brought this action for the money paid before the bond was proved usurious; and the question was if the action lay.

And HOLT, Chief Justice,[87] seemed to incline strongly that it did not lie. For here there was a payment actually made by the plaintiff to the defendant in satisfaction of this usurious contract; and if they will make such contracts, they ought to be punished; and he was not for encouraging such kinds of *Indebitatus Assumpsit*. And though the case was objected, that if a man pay money upon a Policy of Assurance, supposing a loss where there was not any loss, that in such case this shall be money received to the use of the payer, he admitted it, because here the money was paid upon a mistake; the same law if it was upon a fraud in the receiver. But in the principal case he was of opinion *ut supra,* and said that he would not encourage these actions; but that it is like the case of bribes—he who receives it ought to be punished, and he who gives them ought not to be encouraged by any way to recover his money again.

LAMINE v. DORRELL
2 LD. RAYMOND, 1216
A.D. 1705

In an *indebitatus assumpsit* for money received by the defendant to the use of the plaintiff as administrator of J. S., on *non assumpsit* pleaded, upon

---

[86] Judge of the King's Bench, 1660-1668. The case referred to is not reported.
[87] In the report of the case given in 1 Salkeld, 22, the presiding judge is said to be TREBY, C.J. But there are other details in Salkeld's report which not unfairly provoked Lord Mansfield in *Smith* v. *Bromley,* Douglas, 670, at p. 672, to denounce it as 'stuffed with such strange arguments that it is difficult to make anything of it.' There is much to justify the observation wrung from HOLT, C.J. in *Slater* v. *May,* 2 Ld. Raym. 1071, at p. 1072, referring specifically to 4 Mod. Rep., but more generally applicable to contemporary standards of reporting, that 'the inconveniences of these scambling reports will make us appear to posterity for a parcel of blockheads.'

evidence the case appeared to be that J. S. died intestate possessed of certain Irish debentures; and the defendant, pretending a right to be administrator, got administration granted to him, and by that means got these debentures into his hands and disposed of them. Then the defendant's administration was repealed and administration granted to the plaintiff, and he brought this action against the defendant for the money he sold the debentures for. And it being objected upon the evidence that this action would not lie, because the defendant sold the debentures as one that claimed a title and interest in them and therefore could not be said to receive the money for the use of the plaintiff which indeed he received to his own use, but the plaintiff ought to have brought *trover* or *detinue* for the debentures, the point was saved to the defendant; and now the Court was moved and the same objection made.

POWELL, J.: It is clear the plaintiff might have maintained *detinue* or *trover* for the debentures; and when the act that is done is in its nature tortious, it is hard to turn that into a contract, and against the reason of *assumpsit*. But the plaintiff may dispense with the wrong and suppose the sale made by his consent, and bring an action for the money they were sold for as money received to his use. It has been carried thus far already. *Howard* and *Wood's* case is as far[88]; there the title of the office was tried in an action for the profits.

HOLT, C.J.: These actions have crept in by degrees. I remember, in the case of Mr. *Aston*,[89] in a dispute about the title to the office of clerk of the papers in this court, there were great counsel consulted with; and Sir William Jones and Mr. Saunders were of opinion an *indebitatus assumpsit* would not lie, upon meeting and conferring together and great consideration. If two men reckon together and one overpays the other, the proper remedy in that case is a special action for the money overpaid or an account; and yet in that case you constantly bring an *indebitatus assumpsit* for money had and received to the plaintiff's use. Suppose a person pretends to be guardian in socage and enters into the land of the infant and takes the profits, though he is not rightful guardian, yet an action of account will lie against him. So the defendant in this case pretending to receive the money the debentures were sold for in the right of the intestate, why should he not be answerable for it to the intestate's administrator? If an action of *trover* should be brought by the plaintiff for these debentures after judgment in this *indebitatus assumpsit,* he may plead this recovery in bar of the action of *trover,* in the same manner as it would have been a good plea in bar for the defendant to have pleaded to the action of *trover* that he sold the debentures and paid to the plaintiff in satisfaction. But it may be a doubt if this recovery can be pleaded before execution. This recovery may be given in evidence upon not guilty in the action of *trover,* because by this action the plaintiff makes and affirms the act of the defendant in the sale of the debentures to be lawful, and consequently the sale of them is no conversion.

Afterwards, the last day of the term, upon motion to the Court they gave judgment for the plaintiff. And HOLT said that he could not see how it differed from an *indebitatus assumpsit* for the profits of an office by a rightful officer against a wrongful, as money had and received by the wrongful officer to the use of the rightful.

[88] *Howard* v. *Wood, supra,* p. 380.
[89] *Woodward* v. *Aston,* (1676) 2 Mod. 95.

ASTLEY v. REYNOLDS

2 STRANGE, 915

A.D. 1731

In an action for money had and received to the plaintiff's use, the case reserved for the consideration of the court was that above three years ago the plaintiff pawned plate to the defendant for £20, and at the three years' end came to redeem it; and the defendant insisted to have £10 for the interest of it, and the plaintiff tendered him £4, knowing £4 to be more than legal interest. The defendant refusing to take it, they parted; and at some months' distance the plaintiff came and made a second tender of the £4, but, the defendant still insisting upon £10, the plaintiff paid it and had his goods; and now brings this action for the surplus beyond legal interest.

For the plaintiff it was insisted by *Reeve, Filmer* and *Draper* that the action lay; the plaintiff not being *particeps criminis* and having paid the money, not upon the foot of an usurious contract, but by compulsion. They agreed the case in *Salkeld,* 22,[90] that if he had been party to the fraud he could not maintain the action. But here, they said, the money was extorted; and extortion and usury differ in this, that one is given freely and the other involuntarily, and a man shall avoid a deed by duress of his goods as well as of his person. And it is observable that all the laws against usury are for the punishment of the lender and not of the borrower, and that it is not pretended that there was any agreement about the interest at the time of the loan. And a case was cited of *Wilkinson* v. *Kitchin,*[91] where money was given to a Newgate solicitor to lay out in bribes, and it was held by HOLT, C.J., that it might be recovered back from him in an *indebitatus assumpsit,* though it appeared he had disposed of it according to his directions.

E contra, it was argued by *Marsh* and *Fazackerly* that there was no colour to say the plaintiff paid it either by mistake or force, it being stated that he knew the £4 he tendered was beyond the legal interest; and he did it with his eyes open, having another remedy for his goods by trover after tender of the legal interest; and it falls within the rule *volenti non fit injuria.*

Et per curiam.[92] The cases of payments by mistake or deceit are not to be disputed; but this case is neither, for the plaintiff knew what he did, and in that lies the strength of the objection. But we do not think the tender of the £4 will hurt him, for a man may tender too much, though a tender of too little is bad; and where a man does not know exactly what is due, he must at his peril take care to tender enough. We think also that this is a payment by compulsion. The plaintiff might have such an immediate want of his goods that an action of trover would not do his business. Where the rule *volenti non fit injuria* is applied, it must be where the party had his freedom of exercising his will, which this man had not. We must take it he paid the money, relying on his legal remedy to get it back again.

The plaintiff had judgment.

---

[90] *Tomkyns* v. *Barnet*: see *supra,* p. 384.
[91] (1696) 1 Ld. Raymond, 89. But cf. *Anon* (1695) Holt, 35.
[92] Lord Raymond, C.J.K.B., and Page, Probyn and Lee, J.J.

MOSES v. MACFERLAN
2 BURROW, 1005
A.D. 1760

[Moses had procured from Jacob four promissory notes for 30s. each, value received. These he indorsed to Macferlan under a written agreement that the indorsement should not involve him in liability. When the notes were not met, Macferlan sued Moses in a Court of Conscience,[93] and in that court the Commissioners refused to recognize the written agreement and held Moses liable on his indorsement. Moses paid the £6 involved, and now sought to recover it from Macferlan in the King's Bench by an action for money had and received to his use.]

. . . All this matter appearing upon evidence before Lord Mansfield at *nisi prius* at Guildhall, there was no doubt but that, upon the merits, the plaintiff was intitled to the money; and accordingly a verdict was there found for Moses . . . for £6 (the whole sum paid into the Court of Conscience); but subject to the opinion of the Court upon this question, ' whether the money could be recovered in the present form of action or whether it must be recovered by an action brought upon the special agreement only.' . . . The Court, having heard the counsel on both sides, took time to advise.

LORD MANSFIELD now delivered their unanimous opinion in favour of the present action.

. . . Many other objections, besides that which arose at the trial, have since been made to the propriety of this action in the present case.

The 1st objection is, ' that an action of *debt* would not lie here, and no *assumpsit* will lie where an action of *debt* may not be brought.' Some sayings at *nisi prius,* reported by note takers who did not understand the force of what was said, are quoted in support of that proposition. But there is no foundation for it. It is much more plausible to say that where *debt* lies, an action *upon the case* ought not to be brought. And that was the point relied upon in *Slade's Case*[94]; but the rule then settled and followed ever since is that an action of *assumpsit* will lie in many cases where *debt* lies and in many cases where it does not lie. A main inducement, originally, for encouraging actions of *assumpsit* was to take away the wager of law; and that might give rise to loose expressions, as if the action was confined to cases only where that reason held.

2nd objection: ' That no *assumpsit* lies except upon an express or implied contract; but here it is impossible to presume any contract to refund money which the defendant recovered by an adverse suit.'

Answer: If the defendant be under an obligation, from the ties of natural justice, to refund, the law implies a debt and gives this action, founded in the equity of the plaintiff's case, as it were upon a contract (*quasi ex contractu,* as the Roman law expresses it). This species of *assumpsit* (for money had and received to the plaintiff's use) lies in numberless instances for money the defendant has received from a third person, which he claims title to in opposition to the plaintiff's right and which he had, by law, authority to receive from such third person.

3rd objection: ' Where money has been recovered by the judgment of a Court having competent jurisdiction, the matter can never be brought over again by a new action.'

---

[93] Courts of Conscience were courts for the speedy recovery of small debts, set up by statute in London and elsewhere. See Blackstone, Comm. III. 81.
[94] 4 Co. Rep. 92b. *Supra,* p. 371.

Answer: It is most clear that the merits of a judgment can never be over-haled by an original suit[95] either at law or in equity. Till the judgment is set aside or reversed, it is conclusive as to the subject-matter of it to all intents and purposes.

But the ground of this action is consistent with the judgment of the Court of Conscience: it admits the Commissioners did right. They decreed upon the indorsement of the notes by the plaintiff, which indorsement is not now disputed. The ground upon which this action proceeds was no defence against that sentence. It is enough for us that the commissioners adjudged 'they had no cognizance of such collateral matter.' We cannot correct an error in their proceedings, and ought to suppose what is done by a final jurisdiction to be right. . . . The ground of this action is not that the judgment was wrong; but that (for a reason which the now plaintiff could not avail himself of against that judgment) the defendant ought not in justice to keep the money. . . . Money may be recovered by a right and legal judgment; and yet the iniquity of keeping that money may be manifest upon grounds which could not be used by way of defence against the judgment. Suppose an indorsee of a promissory note, having received payment from the drawer or maker of it, sues and recovers the same money from the indorser, who knew nothing of such payment. Suppose a man recovers upon a policy for a ship presumed to be lost, which afterwards comes home; or upon the life of a man presumed to be dead, who afterwards appears; or upon a representation of a risque deemed to be fair, which comes out afterwards to be grossly fraudulent. . . .[96]

This brings the whole to the question saved at *nisi prius, viz.,* 'whether the plaintiff may elect to sue by this form of action for the money only, or must be turned round to bring an action upon the agreement.'

One great benefit, which arises to suitors from the nature of this action, is that the plaintiff need not state the special circumstances from which he concludes that *ex æquo et bono* the money received by the defendant ought to be deemed as belonging to him. He may declare generally 'that the money was received to his use,' and make out his case at the trial.

This is equally beneficial to the defendant. It is the most favourable way in which he can be sued. He can be liable no further than the money which he has received, and, against that, may go into every equitable defence, upon the general issue. He may claim every equitable allowance; he may prove a release without pleading it; in short, he may defend himself by everything which shews that the plaintiff *ex æquo et bono* is not intitled to the whole of his demand or to any part of it.

If the plaintiff elects to proceed in this favourable way, it is a bar to his bringing another action upon the agreement; though he might recover more upon the agreement than he can by this form of action. And therefore, if the question was open to be argued upon principles at large, there seems to be no reason or utility in confining the plaintiff to an action upon the special agreement only. But the point has been long settled, and there have

[95] i.e. as opposed to proceedings by way of appeal.

[96] Lord Mansfield clearly felt some embarrassment in dealing with this third objection, that the King's Bench could not, at least otherwise than by way of appeal, reverse the decision of a competent court; and his contention that he was not in fact reversing it, but supplementing it by considering facts which it could not entertain, is perhaps more specious than convincing. Lord Kenyon in *Marriot* v. *Hampton* (1797) 7 T.R. 269, decisively repudiated the inference that a decision, lawfully reached, could thus be set aside as it were by a side-wind. But this latter judgment did not impair the general principle for which Lord Mansfield was contending.

been many precedents. I will mention to you one only, which was very solemnly considered. It was the case of *Dutch* v. *Warren*,[97] an action upon the case for money had and received to the plaintiff's use. . . .

This kind of equitable action, to recover back money which ought not in justice to be kept, is very beneficial, and therefore much encouraged. It lies only for money which *ex æquo et bono* the defendant ought to refund. It does not lie for money paid by the plaintiff, which is claimed of him as payable in point of honour and honesty, although it could not have been recovered from him by any course of law: as in payment of a debt barred by the Statute of Limitations, or contracted during his infancy, or to the extent of principal and legal interest upon an usurious contract, or for money fairly lost at play; because in all these cases the defendant may retain it with a safe conscience, though by positive law he was barred from recovering. But it lies for money paid by mistake; or upon a consideration which happens to fail; or for money got through imposition (express or implied); or extortion; or oppression; or an undue advantage taken of the plaintiff's situation, contrary to laws made for the protection of persons under those circumstances. In one word, the gist of this kind of action is that the defendant, upon the circumstances of the case, is obliged by the ties of natural justice and equity to refund the money.

Therefore we are all of us of opinion that the plaintiff might elect to waive any demand, upon the foot of the indemnity,[98] for the costs he had been put to; and bring this action to recover the £6, which the defendant got and kept from him iniquitously.

BLACKSTONE : COMMENTARIES
Book III : Ch. 9
Of Injuries to Personal Property

. . . Hitherto of injuries affecting the right of things personal in *possession.* We are next to consider those which regard things in *action* only; or such rights as are founded on and arise from *contracts.* . . . The violation or non-performance of these contracts might be extended into as great a variety of wrongs as the rights which we then considered[99]; but I shall now endeavour to reduce them into a narrow compass by here making only a twofold division of contracts, *viz.,* contracts *express* and contracts *implied,* and considering the injuries that arise from the violation of each and their respective remedies.

Express contracts include three distinct species, debts, covenants and promises.

1. The legal acceptation of DEBT is a sum of money due by certain and express agreement. As by a bond for a determinate sum; a bill or note; a special bargain; or a rent reserved on a lease; where the quantity is fixed and unalterable and does not depend upon any after-calculations to settle it. The non-payment of these is an injury for which the proper remedy is by action of *debt,* to compel the performance of the contract and recover the specifical sum due. This is the shortest and surest remedy; particularly where the debt arises upon a specialty, that is, upon a deed or instrument under seal. So also, if I verbally agree to pay a man a certain price for a certain parcel

[97] (1722) 1 Strange, 406.
[98] i.e., the special agreement between the parties.
[99] Blackstone refers back to his Commentaries, Book II, Ch. 30.

of goods, and fail in the performance, an action of debt lies against me, for this is also a *determinate* contract: but if I agree for no settled price, I am not liable to an action of debt, but a special action on the case according to the nature of my contract. And indeed actions of debt are now seldom brought but upon special contracts under seal, wherein the sum due is clearly and precisely expressed; for in case of such an action upon a simple contract, the plaintiff labours under two difficulties. First, the defendant has here the same advantage as in an action of *detinue,* that of waging his law or purging himself of the debt by oath, if he thinks proper. Secondly, in an action of debt the plaintiff must recover the whole debt he claims or nothing at all. For the debt is one single cause of action, fixed and determined, and which, therefore, if the proof varies from the claim, cannot be looked upon as the same contract whereof the performance is sued for. If therefore I bring an action of debt for £30, I am not at liberty to prove a debt of £20 and recover a verdict thereon; any more than, if I bring an action of *detinue* for a horse, I can thereby recover an ox. For I fail in the proof of that contract which my action or complaint has alleged to be specific, express and determinate. But in an action on the case on what is called an *indebitatus assumpsit,* which is not brought to compel a specific performance of the contract but to recover damages for its non-performance, the implied *assumpsit,* and consequently the damages for the breach of it, are in their nature indeterminate; and will therefore adapt and proportion themselves to the truth of the case which shall be proved, without being confined to the precise demand stated in the declaration. For if *any* debt be proved, however less than the sum demanded, the law will raise a promise *pro tanto,* and the damages will of course be proportioned to the actual debt. So that I may declare that the defendant, *being indebted* to me in £30, *undertook* or promised to pay it, but failed; and lay my damages arising from such failure at what sum I please: and the jury will, according to the nature of my proof, allow me either the whole in damages or any inferior sum. . . .

2. A COVENANT also, contained in a deed, to do a direct act or to omit one, is another species of express contracts, the violation or breach of which is a civil injury. As if a man covenants to be at York by such a day or not to exercise a trade in a particular place, and is not at York at the time appointed or carries on his trade in the place forbidden, these are direct breaches of his covenant; and may be perhaps greatly to the disadvantage and loss of the covenantee. The remedy for this is by a writ of *covenant;* which directs the sheriff to command the defendant generally to keep his covenant with the plaintiff (without specifying the nature of the covenant) or shew good cause to the contrary; and if he continues refractory, or the covenant is already so broken that it cannot now be specifically performed, then the subsequent proceedings set forth with precision the covenant, the breach and the loss which has happened thereby; whereupon the jury will give damages in proportion to the injury sustained by the plaintiff and occasioned by such breach of the defendant's contract. . . .

3. A PROMISE is in the nature of a verbal covenant and wants nothing but the solemnity of writing and sealing to make it absolutely the same. If therefore it be to do any explicit act, it is an express contract, as much as any covenant; and the breach of it is an equal injury. The remedy indeed is not exactly the same: since, instead of an action of covenant, there only lies an action upon the case for what is called the *assumpsit* or undertaking

of the defendant; the failure of performing which is the wrong or injury done to the plaintiff, the damages whereof a jury are to estimate and settle. As if a builder promises, undertakes or assumes to Caius that he will build and cover his house within a time limited, and fails to do it; Caius has an action on the case against the builder for this breach of his express promise, undertaking or *assumpsit,* and shall recover a pecuniary satisfaction for the injury sustained by such delay. So also in the case before-mentioned, of a debt by simple contract, if the debtor promises to pay it and does not, this breach of promise entitles the creditor to his action on the case, instead of being driven to an action of debt. Thus likewise a promissory note, or note of hand not under seal, to pay money at a day certain, is an express *assumpsit;* and the payee at common law, or by custom and act of parliament the indorsee,[1] may recover the value of the note in damages, if it remains unpaid. . . .

From these *express* contracts the transition is easy to those that are only IMPLIED by law. Which are such as reason and justice dictate, and which therefore the law presumes that every man has contracted to perform; and, upon this presumption, makes him answerable to such persons as suffer by his non-performance.

Of this nature are, FIRST, such as are necessarily implied by fundamental constitution of government, to which every man is a contracting party. And thus it is that every person is bound and hath virtually agreed to pay such particular sums of money as are charged on him by the sentence, or assessed by the interpretation, of the law. For it is part of the original contract, entered into by all mankind who partake the benefits of society, to submit in all points to the municipal constitutions and local ordinances of that state of which each individual is a member. Whatever therefore the laws order any one to pay, that instantly becomes a debt, which he hath beforehand contracted to discharge. . . . On the same principle it is (of an implied original contract to submit to the rules of the community whereof we are members) that a forfeiture imposed by the by-laws and private ordinances of a corporation upon any that belong to the body . . . immediately creates a debt in the eye of the law . . .; for which the remedy is by action of debt. The same reason may with equal justice be applied to all penal statutes, that is, such acts of parliament whereby a forfeiture is inflicted for transgressing the provisions therein enacted. The party offending is here bound by the fundamental contract of society to obey the directions of the legislature and pay the forfeiture incurred to such persons as the law requires. . . .

A SECOND class of implied contracts are such as do not arise from the express determination of any court or the positive direction of any statute; but from natural reason and the just construction of law. Which class extends to all presumptive undertakings or *assumpsits;* which, though never perhaps actually made, yet constantly arise from this general implication and intendment of the courts of judicature, that every man hath engaged to perform what his duty or justice requires. Thus,

1. If I employ a person to transact any business for me or perform any work, the law implies that I undertook or assumed to pay him so much as his labour deserved. And if I neglect to make him amends, he has a remedy for this injury by bringing his action on the case upon this implied *assumpsit;* wherein he is at liberty to suggest that I promised to pay him

---

[1] 3 and 4 Anne, c. 9.

so much as he reasonably deserved, and then to aver that his trouble was really worth such a particular sum, which the defendant has omitted to pay. But this valuation of his trouble is submitted to the determination of a jury, who will assess such a sum in damages as they think he really merited. This is called an *assumpsit* on a *quantum meruit.*

2. There is also an implied *assumpsit* on a *quantum valebant,* which is very similar to the former; being only where one takes up goods or wares of a tradesman, without expressly agreeing for the price. There the law concludes that both parties did intentionally agree that the real value of the goods should be paid; and an action on the case may be brought accordingly, if the vendee refuses to pay that value.

3. A third species of implied *assumpsit* is when one has had and received money of another's without any valuable consideration given on the receiver's part: for the law construes this to be money had and received for the use of the owner only, and implies that the person so receiving promised and undertook to account for it to the true proprietor. And if he unjustly detains it, an action on the case lies against him for the breach of such implied promise and undertaking; and he will be made to repair the owner in damages, equivalent to what he has detained in such violation of his promise. This is a very extensive and beneficial remedy, applicable to almost every case where the defendant has received money which *ex æquo et bono* he ought to refund. It lies for money paid by mistake, or on a consideration which happens to fail, or through imposition, extortion or oppression, or where undue advantage is taken of the plaintiff's situation.[2]

4. Where a person has laid out and expended his own money for the use of another at his request, the law implies a promise of repayment, and an action will lie on this *assumpsit.*

5. Likewise, fifthly, upon a stated account between two merchants or other persons, the law implies that he against whom the balance appears has engaged to pay it to the other, though there be not any actual promise. And from this implication it is frequent for actions on the case to be brought, declaring that the plaintiff and defendant had settled their accounts together, *insimul computassent* (which gives name to this species of *assumpsit*) and that the defendant engaged to pay the plaintiff the balance, but has since neglected to do it. But if no account has been made up, then the legal remedy is by bringing a writ of *account, de compoto,* commanding the defendant to render a just account to the plaintiff or shew the court good cause to the contrary. In this action, if the plaintiff succeeds, there are two judgments: the first is, that the defendant do account (*quod computet*) before auditors appointed by the court; and, when such account is finished, then the second judgment is, that he do pay the plaintiff so much as he is found in arrear. This action, by the old common law, lay only against the parties themselves, and not their executors, because matters of account rested solely in their own knowledge. But this defect, after many fruitless attempts in parliament, was at last remedied by Statute 4 Anne, c. 16, which gives an action of account against the executors and administrators. But, however, it is found by experience that the most ready and effectual way to settle these matters of account is by bill in a court of equity, where a discovery may be had on the defendant's oath, without relying merely on

---

[2] Blackstone here cites Lord Mansfield's judgment in *Moses* v. *Macferlan* (1760) 2 Burrow, 1005, at p. 1012, which he incorporates in his text. *Supra,* p. 389.

the evidence which the plaintiff may be able to produce. Wherefore actions of account, to compel a man to bring in and settle his accounts, are now very seldom used; though, when an account is once stated, nothing is more common than an action upon the implied *assumpsit* to pay the balance.

STEPHEN ON PLEADING
DECLARATION IN ASSUMPSIT [3]

In the King's Bench

—— Term, in the —— year of the reign of King George the Fourth.

Wiltshire, to wit: C. D. was attached to answer A. B. of a plea of trespass on the case. And thereupon, the said A. B., by —— his attorney, complains: —

For that, *whereas*[4] the said C. D. heretofore, to wit, on the —— day of —— in the year of our Lord ——, at —— in the county of ——, was indebted to the said A. B. in the sum of —— pounds of lawful money of Great Britain for divers goods, wares and merchandizes by the said A. B. before that time sold and delivered to the said C. D. at his special instance and request; and being so indebted, he, the said C. D., in consideration thereof afterwards, to wit, on the day and year aforesaid at —— aforesaid in the county aforesaid, undertook and faithfully promised the said A. B. to pay him the said sum of money when he, the said C. D., should be thereto afterwards requested:

And whereas also[5] the said C. D. afterwards, to wit, on the day and year aforesaid at —— aforesaid in the county aforesaid, was indebted to the said A. B. in the further sum of —— pounds of like lawful money for work and labour, care and diligence, by the said A. B. before that time done, performed and bestowed in and about the business of the said C. D. and for the said C. D., at his like instance and request; and being so indebted, he, the said C. D., in consideration thereof afterwards, to wit, on the day and year aforesaid at —— aforesaid in the county aforesaid, undertook and faithfully promised the said A. B. to pay him the said last-mentioned sum of money when he, the said C. D., should be thereto afterwards requested:

And whereas also[6] the said C. D. afterwards, to wit, on the day and year aforesaid at —— aforesaid in the county aforesaid, was indebted to the said A. B. in the further sum of —— pounds of like lawful money for so much money by the said A. B. before that time lent and advanced to the said C. D. at his like instance and request; and being so indebted, he, the said C. D., in consideration thereof afterwards, to wit, on the day and year aforesaid at —— aforesaid in the county aforesaid, undertook and faithfully promised the said A. B. to pay him the said last-mentioned sum of money when he, the said C. D., should be thereto afterwards requested:

And whereas also[7] the said C. D. afterwards, to wit, on the day and year aforesaid at —— aforesaid in the county aforesaid, was indebted to the said A. B. in the further sum of —— pounds of like lawful money for so

---

[3] The ensuing precedent is taken from the second edition of Stephen on *Pleading* (1827) at p. 312. The learned author has explained that, subject to certain rules and conditions, the plaintiff may join several counts in the same declaration, and the above is an example of the process.
[4] Here follows a count for goods sold and delivered.
[5] Here follows a count for work done.
[6] Here follows a count for money lent.
[7] Here follows a count for money paid.

much money by the said A. B. before that time paid, laid out and expended to and for the use of the said C. D. at his like instance and request; and being so indebted, he, the said C. D., in consideration thereof afterwards, to wit, on the day and year aforesaid at —— aforesaid in the county aforesaid, undertook and faithfully promised the said A. B. to pay him the said last-mentioned sum of money when he, the said C. D., should be thereto afterwards requested:

And whereas also[8] the said C. D. afterwards, to wit, on the day and year aforesaid at —— aforesaid in the county aforesaid, was indebted to the said A. B. in the further sum of —— pounds of like lawful money for so much money by the said C. D. before that time had and received to and for the use of the said A. B.; and being so indebted, he, the said C. D., in consideration thereof afterwards, to wit, on the day and year aforesaid at —— aforesaid in the county aforesaid, undertook and faithfully promised the said A. B. to pay him the said last-mentioned sum of money when he, the said C. D., should be thereto afterwards requested:

And whereas also[9] the said C. D. afterwards, to wit, on the day and year aforesaid at —— aforesaid in the county aforesaid, accounted with the said A. B. of and concerning divers other sums of money from the said C. D. to the said A. B. before that time due and owing and then in arrear and unpaid, and, upon that account, the said C. D. was then and there found to be in arrear and indebted to the said A. B. in the further sum of —— pounds of like lawful money; and being so found in arrear and indebted, he, the said C. D., in consideration thereof afterwards, to wit, on the day and year aforesaid at —— aforesaid in the county aforesaid, undertook and faithfully promised the said A. B. to pay him the said last-mentioned sum of money when he, the said C. D., should be thereto afterwards requested:

Yet he, the said C. D., not regarding his said several promises and undertakings, but contriving and fraudulently intending craftily and subtilly to deceive and defraud the said A. B. in this behalf, hath not yet paid the said several sums of money or any part thereof to the said A. B. (although oftentimes afterwards requested). But the said C. D. to pay the same or any part thereof hath hitherto wholly refused and still refuses, to the damage of the said A. B. of —— pounds; and therefore he brings his suit, etc.

---

[8] Here follows a count for money had and received.
[9] Here follows a count for money due on an account stated.

‿ *16* ‿

CONSIDERATION

[With a Note on ACCORD and SATISFACTION]

A

THE ORIGIN OF THE DOCTRINE

THE revival of historical interest among Anglo-American jurists in the later years of the nineteenth century naturally directed attention upon the central feature of their law of contract. In the dearth of direct evidence as to the origin of the doctrine of consideration, it was perhaps equally natural that they should have indulged in intelligent reconstruction. Holmes found himself able to trace the doctrine back to the technicalities of Debt.[1] Assuming, as he did, that consideration was to be defined in the alternative—as a benefit conferred on the promisor or as a detriment incurred by the promisee—it was comparatively easy to identify 'benefit' with the idea of Quid pro Quo. To associate the phrase with 'detriment' was a more formidable task; and he was driven to admit not only that the latter element entered the law through Assumpsit, but also that the result was the co-existence of 'two inconsistent theories,' the one prevalent in the old action and the other in the new. But, though his theory might thus be embarrassed, he was not prepared to abandon it, and he felt able to explain the doctrine, in its final form, as a modification of the original requirement of Debt.

It is true that the idea of Bargain, so significant in the later law, was the basis of Debt sur Contract. It is true that, so late as 1600, the Court in *Brett's Case* used Quid pro Quo as a synonym for consideration.[2] It is also true that, in the latter half of the fifteenth century, the severity of Quid pro Quo had been relaxed so far as to allow a seller of goods to sue in Debt before he had made delivery.[3] But such facts do not suffice to deflect the criticism to which Holmes' thesis has generally been subjected.[4] The language of *Brett's Case* was a lonely anachronism. The incidents of Sale were rationalised, if at all, on the basis not of promise but of property, and were not only an avowed exception to the general rule but such an exception as went far to prove the rule. The decisive objection to the thesis is that the most

---

[1] Holmes developed his thesis in *The Common Law*, Lecture VII.
[2] Croke, Eliz. 755; *infra*, p. 421.
[3] *Supra*, pp. 227-9.
[4] e.g., Ames, *Lectures on Legal History*, pp. 129-130; Barbour, *History of Contract in Early English Equity*, pp. 60-1.

prominent feature in the modern doctrine of consideration—the binding character of mutual promises—was foreign to the very nature of Debt.[5]   Debt was 'real,' Assumpsit 'consensual'; and the latter epithet represents, not a modification of the former, but its antithesis. The inconsistency which Holmes confessed and sought to avoid was in truth fatal to his views; and, once admitted, the rest of his reasoning was a non sequitur.

Ames avowed, and indeed insisted upon, the two strands woven into the history of the doctrine.

> 'It seems impossible to refer consideration to a single source.   At the present day it is doubtless just and expedient to resolve every consideration into a detriment to the promisee incurred at the request of the promisor.   But this definition of consideration would not have covered the cases of the sixteenth century.   There were then two distinct forms of consideration: (1) detriment; (2) a precedent debt.' [6]

Of these two forms the first was to be found at the beginning of the sixteenth century,[7] the second not until its middle years.   The first was the hall-mark of Special Assumpsit, the second, ultimately derived from Debt, was imbedded in Indebitatus Assumpsit.   But the judges, once they had evolved a comprehensive remedy for all parol contracts, looked about them for some single expression which might denote the grounds upon which it would lie.   'Consideration' had been used by lawyers for a hundred years, but in the merely general sense of reason or motive.[8]   This word they now appropriated to their current purpose and invested with particular significance.

Holdsworth followed Ames, but disturbed the balance of his argument by stressing one of its sides at the expense of the other.[9] 'Detriment' was not only anterior in time to 'benefit' but superior in importance.   The one was essential and inevitable, the other auxiliary and accidental.   By thus ante-dating the element of detriment both Ames and Holdsworth, it would seem, fell into error.   They identified a later contractual conception with the conditions necessary to success when, in the reign of Henry VII, the judges first allowed the action on the case upon a bare non-feasance.[10]   The emphasis upon detriment, said Holdsworth,

---

[5] See, e.g., the judgments in *Anon.* (1458), *supra*, p. 249, and in *Jordan's Case* (1528), *supra*, p. 353.
[6] *Lectures on Legal History*, p. 129; and see generally pp. 129-30, 143-48.
[7] For this assertion Ames relied on the case of 1505 and the note of 1506, set out *supra*, at pp. 351-3.
[8] See examples of its early use (a) in conveyancing, e.g. in a settlement executed by Sir John Fortescue in 1461, published by Miss Scofield in E.H.R. XXVII, 323: 'And the consideracion of the makyng of the forseyde estate was . . .'; and in Y.B. 20 Hen. 7, f. 11—a grant 'made on good consideration, for the elder brother is bound by the law of nature to aid and comfort his younger brother'; (b) in legal literature, e.g. *Doctor and Student, supra*, pp. 326-9; (c) in legislation, e.g. Stat. 32 Hen. 8, c. 42—'Wherefore, in consideration of the premises, be it enacted . . .'
[9] H.E.L. VIII, pp. 3-11.
[10] See the case of 1505 and the note of 1506, *supra*, pp. 351-3.

'is clearly the direct result of the fact that assumpsit was originally an action in tort; for it followed that the gist of the action was, not the benefit got by the defendant-promisor, but the detriment incurred by the plaintiff-promisee on the faith of the defendant's promise.'[11]

But between the tortious and the contractual aspects of assumpsit a gulf is fixed across which no logical bridge can be built. In the tort, as it presented itself to the lawyers of the early sixteenth century, the plaintiff must have suffered damage as a result of the defendant's breach of undertaking, and he thus incurred a 'detriment' in the primary meaning of the word. In the contract no damage need be proved, and 'detriment' was applied in a more artificial sense, to denote the promise or act tendered by the plaintiff to procure the defendant's undertaking. In the tort the judges concentrated upon the consequences of the defendant's default, in the contract upon the facts present at the time of his undertaking and in exchange for which it was given. The vital nature of the distinction may be re-stated in the language of proof. While assumpsit was still wholly tortious, the plaintiff had to prove an undertaking by the defendant, its breach and the resultant damage. When it became contractual, he had, as before, to prove the undertaking and the breach, but he had also to show that he himself had bought that undertaking by the simultaneous offer of a counter-promise or act; and in this last requirement lay the essence of consideration. The contrast, if obscured by the indiscriminate use of the word 'detriment,' is complete. It is no more possible to explain the metamorphosis of assumpsit in terms of evolution than to see in the developed doctrine of consideration the apotheosis of Debt.

Salmond detected the breach of continuity.[12] The history of Assumpsit was the perversion of a delictual into a contractual remedy, and a doctrine appropriate to the one was not likely to suit the other. It was therefore necessary, in his opinion, to seek the origin of consideration outside the common law altogether and to look for a principle, already fully constructed, which might be introduced into Assumpsit *ab extra*. Such a principle he discovered in the *causa* of the Canonists, as translated by the Chancellor into the language of fifteenth-century England. The theory was admittedly conjectural.

> 'It is difficult to say exactly when the equitable principle of consideration became established in Assumpsit. There is a singular dearth of evidence on the point, but the change must have taken place between the end of the reign of Henry VII, when assumpsit was extended to nonfeasance, and the beginning of the reign of Elizabeth, when the rule appears as perfectly familiar.'[13]

[11] H.E.L. VIII, p. 10.
[12] *Essays in Jurisprudence and Legal History*, pp. 187-224.
[13] *Ibid*, at p. 221.

But Barbour, fresh from his heroic incursions into the arcana of Equity, felt himself able to corroborate.[14] The very idea of promise as the essence of liability, while it was foreign to Debt and to delictual Assumpsit, was the mainspring of the Chancellor's intervention. What was more likely than that the Elizabethan lawyers should have borrowed without acknowledgment from the rivals whose competition they wished to overcome?

Despite the charm of the theory, Salmond and Barbour must be allowed to be the victims of their own enthusiasm. Among the diversity of uses to which the word ' consideration ' was put, it undoubtedly served to acclimatise the Canonist *causa* and to invoke the aid of the Chancellor. But while it is possible, though by no means necessary, to assume that the Common law took the name from Equity, it does not follow that it took the doctrine. The promise which the Chancellor enforced was, in content and in character, very different from that which became the burden of Assumpsit. Where the one was as wide as morality and as warm as conscience, the other was commercialised into the price of a bargain. The very purpose of consideration as a technical doctrine was to deny the precept that a single and simple promise was binding of its own inherent validity. Neither Salmond nor Barbour attempted to explain how a generous principle thus came to be at once attenuated and coarsened; and there is nothing in the published cases by which the transformation can be traced.

It is, however, always simpler and more gratifying to destroy than to construct. Any expectation that the doctrine may be approached through the medium of a preconceived, or even of a coherent, theory is doomed to disappointment. It is the congenital weakness of legal historians to pursue the mirage of continuity, and in the present context their perspective has too often been distorted by peering into the past through nineteenth-century spectacles. Consideration has come to be regarded, not only as technical in the sense of an individual element in the action of assumpsit, but also as inherently artificial and as inviting, therefore, the peculiar attention of professional inquirers. But neither in origin nor in nature is it occult. Contract in any legal system may be based upon the principle either of promise or of bargain, and the one has no innate superiority over the other. The Elizabethan judges, though the choice was not consciously present to their minds, were impelled by every tradition of the common law to prefer the principle of bargain. Gratuitous promises were associated with the writ of Covenant and were excluded from the province of Debt sur contract. During the early experiments with Assumpsit the idea of reciprocity was constantly asserted, and St. Germain made his Student reject, because of this idea, the suggestion that a past

[14] *History of Contract in Early English Equity,* pp. 59-65 and 166-8.

benefit might support an obligation.[15]   The large commercial interests
of the new age sought a general sanction not for charitable gifts but
for business enterprise.   In such an environment it is not surprising
that the judges should have required some material inducement to the
defendant's undertaking.   This requirement the plaintiff might meet
in one of two ways.   He might discharge the burden, to which the
proceedings in Debt had long accustomed litigants, of proving that
he had conferred a benefit upon the defendant; or he might show that
he had bought the defendant's promise by the tender of his own.   Act
or promise was the price to be paid for success in the new consensual
action of Assumpsit.   The doctrine is thus neither an exotic imported
from a more luxurious jurisprudence nor, though a domestic invention
of the common law, need its source be pursued with care and cunning
through the labyrinth of the past.   The ' mystery of consideration '
which the Victorian lawyers found so fascinating[16] becomes no more
than the practical answer to an urgent problem.

B.

THE ESTABLISHMENT OF THE DOCTRINE

The compulsive quality of mutual promises was established by the
judges in a number of cases between 1550 and 1560.   In *Pecke* v.
Redman in 1555[17] the parties had agreed that the defendant ' should
deliver or cause to be delivered to the plaintiff twenty quarters of barley
every year during their two lives, and that the plaintiff should pay
four shillings for each quarter.'   The plaintiff sued on the defendant's
default over a period of three years.   The argument went off upon the
question ' whether the plaintiff shall recover damages in recompense
of the whole bargain as well for the time to come as for the past ';
but the court had no doubts upon the substance of the plaintiff's case.
In *Joscelyn* v. *Shelton* in 1557[18] the plaintiff declared ' that the defendant, in consideration that the son of the plaintiff should marry the
daughter of the defendant, assumed and promised to him four hundred
marks in the seven years next ensuing.'   The plaintiff lost because
he had sued before the lapse of the full time allotted for payment; but
the propriety of the consideration, even if to modern eyes it would not
seem to have ' moved from the promisee,' was not questioned.[19]   By

---

[15] See, for reciprocity in Debt, *Anon* (1458) Y.B. 37 Hen. 6, pl. 18, *supra*, p. 249; in
Assumpsit, *Watkins Case* (1425) Y.B. 3 Hen. 6, pl. 33, *supra*, p. 341; *Anon* (1428)
Y.B. 7 Hen. 6, f. 1, pl. 3, and *Doige's Case* (1442) Y.B. 20 Hen. 6, pl. 4, *supra*,
p. 347.   For *Doctor and Student*, see *supra*, p. 326.
[16] See Ames, *Lectures on Legal History*, p. 129.
[17] 2 Dyer 113a.   See also *Andrew* v. *Boughey* (1552) 1 Dyer 75a, *supra*, p. 355.
[18] 3 Leonard, 4.
[19] The rule that consideration must move from the promisee was clearly laid down
in *Bourne* v. *Mason* (1670) 1 Ventris, 6, *infra*, p. 424.

the accession of Elizabeth the principle was established, and the note of a reporter in 1589, that ' a promise against a promise will maintain an action upon the case' was remarkable not as a novelty but as the belated recognition of a *fait accompli*.[20]

The adoption of this principle at once distinguished Special Assumpsit and Debt. The 'benefit' essential to the latter was irrelevant in the former. The court was to be concerned ' not so much with the profit which redounds to the defendant as with the labour of the plaintiff': a promise ' will support an action on the case, for although it is not beneficial to the defendant, it is chargeable to the plaintiff.'[21] It was a corollary of the distinction that the plaintiff, when he relied upon a promise, need not allege its fulfilment, but only his readiness to fulfil it. The doctrine of consideration involved the assumption that his own outstanding undertaking, not yet discharged by performance or by subsequent agreement, was itself actionable and therefore a ' charge' upon him. In the words of Chief Justice Popham in *Wichals* v. *Johns,* ' there is a mutual promise, the one to the other, so that, if the plaintiff doth not [discharge his promise], the defendant may have his action against him; and a promise against a promise is a good consideration.'[22]

The proof of a benefit, while not necessary to success in Special Assumpsit, was retained in the law through the contemporaneous development of Indebitatus Assumpsit. A form of action, contrived as a measure of convenience to supersede Debt, had to accept the legacy of Quid pro Quo. The situation was appreciated as early as 1558,[23] and thirty years later its implications were avowed. Coke, supporting a plea of infancy, argued that 'every consideration that doth charge the defendant in an *assumpsit* must be to the benefit of the defendant or charge of the plaintiff, and no case can be put out of this rule.' As the debt in the case at bar had been incurred during infancy, it was without legal sanction and a promise to satisfy it in return for a forbearance to sue could be described neither as a benefit to the one party nor as a charge upon the other.[24] In 1587 an attempt was made to analyse more precisely the ingredients of consideration. Chief Baron Manwood was himself the plaintiff in an action on the case.[25] He succeeded, not altogether unexpectedly, in the court of first instance and was then taken on a writ of error into the Exchequer Chamber, where the case was twice argued, chiefly upon niceties of pleading, and ultimately

---

[20] *Strangborough* v. *Warner,* 4 Leonard, 3.
[21] *Webb's Case* (1577) 4 Leonard, 110, *infra,* p. 415: *Baxter* v. *Read* (1585), 3 Dyer, 272b. See also *Foster* v. *Scarlett* (1587) Croke, Eliz. 70, and *Preston* v. *Tooley* (1587) Croke, Eliz. 74.
[22] (1599) Croke, Eliz. 703. See also *Gower* v. *Capper* (1596) Croke, Eliz. 543, *infra,* p. 420, and *Whitcalfe* v. *Jones* (1599) Moore, 574.
[23] *Norwood* v. *Read,* 1 Plowden, 180.
[24] *Stone* v. *Wythipol* (1588) Croke, Eliz. 126.
[25] *Manwood* v. *Burston* (1587) 2 Leonard, 203.

adjourned. But its interest lies in the definition of consideration offered by the Chief Baron as counsel in his own behalf.

> 'There are three manners of considerations upon which an Assumpsit may be grounded:
>
> 1. A debt precedent:
> 2. Where he to whom such a promise is made is damnified by doing anything or spends his labour at the instance of the promisor, although no benefit cometh to the promisor; as I agree with a surgeon to cure a poor man (who is a stranger unto me) of a sore, who doth it accordingly, he shall have an action:
> 3. Or there is a present consideration.' [26]

The first of these alternatives testified to the successful encroachment of Indebitatus Assumpsit upon Debt. The third accepted the validity of mutual promises as the basis of Special Assumpsit. Upon the meaning of the second opinions have differed. Holdsworth imagined it to recall the achievement of the judges in the early years of the sixteenth century in expanding the scope of Case so as to embrace the effects of nonfeasance. 'It is clear,' he said, 'that the second of these considerations originates in the extension of the action of assumpsit to cover certain kinds of nonfeasance in breach of an undertaking.'[27] Pollock, on the other hand, agreed with Vinogradoff that it related, not to Assumpsit, but to Debt.[28] The latter view seems preferable. The facts supposed are that B. requests A. to do work for C., and promises him in return a sum of money. A. does the work and sues for the reward. It is the very situation envisaged by the judges when in 1458 and again in 1528 they inquired whether a benefit conferred at the defendant's request upon a third party would be a sufficient Quid pro Quo to sustain Debt.[29] Both the language and the illustration of the Chief Baron had been anticipated in *Doctor and Student,* from which they may well have been borrowed. According to the Student,

> 'If he to whom the promise is made have a charge by reason of the promise, which he hath also performed, then in that case he shall have an action for that thing that was promised, though he that made the promise have no worldly profit by it. And if a man say to another, heal such a poor man of his disease or make an highway, and I will give thee thus much, and if he do it, I think an action lieth at the Common Law.' [30]

---

[26] *Manwood* v. *Burston,* 2 Leonard, 203, at p. 204.
[27] H.E.L. VIII, p. 7. Holdsworth's view may, perhaps, be identified with that of Ames. See the latter's remarks on the passage from *Doctor and Student,* cited below, in *Lectures on Legal History,* pp. 142-3. It is supported by Potter, *Historical Introduction to English Law,* 3rd ed., p. 465.
[28] Pollock, *Principles of Contract,* 12th ed., p. 132, n. 11; Vinogradoff, *Coll. Papers,* II. pp. 202-3.
[29] See *Anon* (1458) Y.B. 27 Hen. 6, pl. 18, *supra,* pp. 226 and 249; and *Jordan's Case* (1528), *supra,* pp. 339 and 353.
[30] *Supra,* p. 328. Similar language and illustrations were used by the Court in discussing the scope of Debt in *Anon* (1458), *supra,* p. 251. The use of the word 'charge' both by St. Germain and by the Judges in 1458, and the idea that the

The definition in *Manwood* v. *Burston,* while it reflected once more the duality of the doctrine, served also to emphasise the equal importance to the Elizabethan lawyers of each of its aspects. To resolve consideration, after the fashion of the late nineteenth century, into the single element of detriment is unhistorical. But it is undoubtedly upon the exchange of promises that retrospective interest is centred. At least as a general ground of liability such an exchange was a novelty, and its implications required and received the more detailed analysis. The principle was no sooner accepted than limits had to be set to its application. A plaintiff could not be allowed to ' buy ' the defendant's undertaking with a promise that was manifestly worthless or improper. The danger was apparent: to discover a touchstone of validity was not so easy. The judges decided from the outset that they would make no attempt to strike a financial balance between the two promises.[31] The bargain which they were to enforce was the work of the parties themselves and was not to be audited in the courts. Any service, however trifling, undertaken by the plaintiff at the defendant's request would sustain a counter-promise; the defendant was presumably the best arbiter of his own interests. So it was declared in 1587 and again in 1596 that ' when a thing is to be done by the plaintiff, be it never so small, this is a sufficient consideration to ground an action.'[32] The judges, indeed, were rather at pains to uphold a doubtful bargain than extreme to mark what was amiss. In *Grisley* v. *Lother*[33] the plaintiff declared

> ' that, where she had a daughter, which was heir apparent to her husband, the defendant's testator, in consideration that she, at his special instance and request, would give her consent that he should have that daughter to wife, did assume and promise that he would give her £100.'

The defendant argued that, as the mother was not the daughter's guardian, her consent to the marriage was superfluous. But the action was sustained.

> ' The mother hath by the law of nature and in the affection of the daughter and the confidence arising in her counsel and direction a special stroke to incline the daughter's mind either one way or other; and the desire of her consent and the working of it shews that

---

benefit conferred, at the defendant's request, on a third party may equally be regarded as a duty imposed on the plaintiff which has been thereby ' discharged,' may seem at first sight to anticipate the later use of ' detriment' in the context of Consideration. But. though the words are akin, the principles embodied are diverse. The ' charge,' which the plaintiff, suing in Debt, had performed, was a substantial loss to himself and a substantial gain to the third party; as, indeed, it must have been to be offered as the equivalent of Quid pro Quo. The so-called ' detriment' of modern Consideration need be no more than the giving of a promise. It is, in truth, the later use of the word ' detriment' which is misleading.

[31] See *Andrew* v. *Boughey* (1552) 1 Dyer, 75a, *supra*, p. 355.

[32] *Sturlyn* v. *Albany*, Croke, Eliz. 67, and *Knight* v. *Rushworth*, Croke, Eliz. 469, *infra*, p. 420. See also *Preston* v. *Tooley* (1587) Croke, Eliz. 74.

[33] (1614) Hobart, 10.

so the defendant conceived it; and therefore it shall be presumed of importance to have her consent, which, being granted at his suit and request, shall be accounted consideration sufficient.'

Consideration, therefore, did not need to be 'adequate'; but it had still to be 'sufficient.' So vague an epithet was to be amplified only at the cost of much litigation. Two lines of development may be followed. On the one hand, the judges had to decide if a plaintiff might purchase the defendant's promise by the abandonment of a pre-existing claim. By the death of Elizabeth they had resolved that such a forbearance was a sufficient consideration, provided that the facts, if assumed to be true, disclosed a good cause of action. To encourage the extortion of a promise under the pressure of an empty threat was *pessimi exempli*.[34] Throughout the seventeenth century this principle was elaborated, and nice points were raised upon the length of time for which the forbearance might be offered. Must the plaintiff forbear in perpetuity and, if not, must he engage for a fixed term of years or would a 'reasonable' time be accepted?[35] But, if on occasion obscured by detail, it remained unimpaired until the nineteenth century. The forbearance to pursue a doubtful claim was then upheld by the courts, even though, had the claim been tested, it would prove to have been unfounded. 'Otherwise,' said Lord Bowen, 'you would have to try the whole cause to know if the man had a right to compromise it.'[36] The ruling of the modern judges is convenient: the logic of their predecessors is impeccable.

What was the effect, on the other hand, of a promise by the plaintiff to do an act which he was already bound to do by virtue of some outstanding duty? Where the duty was imposed by the general law, there was no room for doubt. A man was not to be bribed to perform a public office. So it was held in 1603 that a promise to pay money to a sheriff to induce him to execute a writ was void.[37] Where the obligation derived from a private contract the position was less obvious. The contract might have been previously made between the same parties or it might have been made by the plaintiff with a third party. The first alternative came before the Court in *Greenleaf* v. *Barker*.[38] John Barker was bound on an obligation to pay £5 to Thomas Greenleaf on November 1st. He alleged an agreement whereby he was to pay this money to Greenleaf on the 3rd of November without further

---

[34] *Tooley* v. *Windham* (1591) Croke, Eliz. 206, *infra*, p. 419, and *Stone* v. *Wythipol* (1588) Croke, Eliz. 126. See also *Sturlyn* v. *Albany* (1587) Croke, Eliz. 67, *infra*, p. 420, and *Bane's Case* (1611) 9 Co. Rep. 91a.

[35] See *Baker* v. *Jacob* (1611) 1 Bulstrode, 41: *Brickendell's Case* (1611) 1 Bulstrode, 91: *Linger* v. *Broughton* (1617) 3 Bulstrode, 206: *Cooks* v. *Douze* (1632) Croke, Car. 241: *Tolson* v. *Clerk* (1636) Croke, Car. 438.

[36] *Miles* v. *New Zealand Alford Estate Co.* (1886) 32 Ch. D. 266, at p. 291. The older and more logical rule was first abandoned in *Longridge* v. *Dorville* (1821) 5 B. & Ald. 117.

[37] *Bridge* v. *Cage* (1603) Croke, Jac. 103.

[38] (1590) Croke, Eliz. 193, *infra*, p. 418.

pressure in return for Greenleaf's promise to deliver to him a third party's bond for twenty shillings. Upon this agreement he sued in assumpsit and won. A writ of error was brought into the Queen's Bench on the ground that there was no consideration for Greenleaf's promise, and, though no final conclusion was reached, the two judges present accepted this contention. Barker, when he undertook to pay 'without suit or trouble' two days after the date originally assigned for payment, did no more than promise to fulfil his existing duty. This opinion, while it did not stand alone,[39] was balanced by the realistic suggestion, made in other Elizabethan and Jacobean cases, that cash in hand was different alike in quality and in value from a mere chose in action, and that actual payment by a debtor might therefore be sufficient consideration for a new promise by the creditor.[40] The merits of these rival views were not finally assessed until the early years of the nineteenth century, when Lord Ellenborough in *Stilk* v. *Myrick*[41] settled the law in accordance with the opinion expressed in *Greenleaf* v. *Barker*.

The judges were invited to examine the second alternative in two cases in 1600 and in a third in 1616.[42] In *Sherwood* v. *Woodward* the plaintiff had sold cheese to the defendant's son and the defendant now promised to guarantee payment 'in consideration the plaintiff would deliver' it to his son. The defendant, sued upon this promise, pleaded that the plaintiff, in undertaking delivery, was doing 'no more than what the law appoints'; but the plaintiff won, apparently on the ground that the original contract required him, not to make delivery, but only to suffer the cheese to be removed. In *Brett's Case*, A. had boarded his son with the plaintiff for three years at £8 *per annum*. During the first year A. died without having paid any part of the fee, and A.'s widow now undertook to satisfy the plaintiff if the latter would fulfil his original engagement with her husband. The widow was held to her promise. In *Bagge* v. *Slade* A. and B. were sureties for C., and each was responsible for the full amount. A. promised B. that, if B. would pay the whole debt, he would repay him as to one half. B. paid the debt and sued A., who pleaded the absence of

---

[39] See *Richards* v. *Bartlet* (1584) 1 Leonard, 19, *infra*, p. 415, and *Dixon* v. *Adams*, (1597) Croke, Eliz. 538. The argument was complicated by the intrusion of the doctrine of Accord and Satisfaction: see NOTE, *infra*, p. 412.

[40] e.g. *Reynolds* v. *Pinhowe* (1595) Croke, Eliz. 429: 'Speedy payment excuses and prevents labour and expense of suit'; and *Hubbard* v. *Farrer* (1635) 1 Viner, Abr. 306, pl. 17: 'It is a good consideration for the obligee to have money in his purse, it being before only a chose in action.' See Ames, *Lectures on Legal History*, pp. 331-2.

[41] (1809) 2 Camp. 317.

[42] *Sherwood* v. *Woodward* (1600) Croke, Eliz. 700, *infra*, p. 421; *Brett's Case* (1600) Croke, Eliz. 755, *infra*, p. 421: *Bagge* v. *Slade* (1616) 3 Bulstrode, 162. On these cases and the whole problem, see Davis, *Promises to perform an existing duty*, 6 C.L.J. 202. The position is made even more obscure than its inherent complexity warrants by the difficulty, often present, of discovering whether the consideration relied on was an act or a promise. In *Sherwood* v. *Woodward* and in *Brett's Case*, it would seem to have been a promise; but *Bagge* v. *Slade* is more doubtful.

consideration. Judgment was once more given for the plaintiff. None of the cases is satisfactory. In the first the judges avoided the issue by discovering a fresh obligation, and in the others the difficulties were never discussed at all. But, so far as any general inference is justified, they would seem to support as sufficient consideration a promise to fulfil a contract previously made between the plaintiff and a third party.[43]

The problems arising upon the exchange of promises, if a first charge upon the energies of the judges, did not exhaust their responsibilities. An act was to be received, equally with a promise, as the price of the defendant's undertaking. Must the act be done simultaneously with that undertaking, or would a previous performance suffice? If the latter view prevailed, it was further necessary to distinguish a material inducement from the mere sentiment of gratitude for a past benefit. The dilemma was not unfamiliar to English lawyers: it was present in the earlier law of sale and it had been discussed by St. Germain in his Doctor and Student.[44] But it was now aggravated by the emergence of Indebitatus Assumpsit, where the plaintiff in terms referred to an already existing debt and based the defendant's promise upon it.

The point was taken as early as 1568 in the case of *Hunt* v. *Bate*.[45] A.'s servant had been arrested upon a charge of trespass. B. and C., ' two citizens of London, who were well acquainted with the master,' offered bail ' in consideration that the business of the master should not go undone.' Afterwards, A., ' upon the said friendly consideration,' undertook to indemnify the good citizens against any expense to which they might be put. B. had, in the sequel, to pay £31, and sued A. on this undertaking. It was held that his action must fail,

> ' because there is no consideration wherefore the defendant should be charged for the debt of his servant, unless the master had first promised to discharge the plaintiff before [bail had been given]; for the master did never make request to the plaintiff to do so much for his servant, but he did it of his own head.'

The case was cited and its reasoning approved in 1585 in *Sidenham* v. *Worlington,* and, with the famous judgment of the Common Pleas in *Lampleigh* v. *Brathwait,* the distinction between ' executed ' and ' past ' consideration may be said to have been drawn with tolerable lucidity.[46] A double test was to be applied. The act of the plaintiff

---

[43] A similar obscurity shrouds the interpretation of a further group of three cases in the mid-nineteenth century. See Davis, 6 C.L.J. 202.

[44] See Y.B. Trin. 5 Hen. VII, f. 41, pl. 7, cited in *Andrew* v. *Boughey, supra,* at p. 356; and *Doctor and Student, supra,* p. 328.

[45] 3 Dyer, 272a.

[46] *Sidenham* v. *Worlington* (1585) 2 Leonard 224, *infra,* p. 416, and *Lampleigh* v. *Brathwait* (1616) Hobart, 105, *infra,* p. 423. The solution here reached is substantially that of the modern law, though Bowen, L.J. in *Stewart* v. *Casey* [1892] 1 Ch. 104 detected some change of emphasis.

must have been requested by the defendant and it must have been done in the way of business and not as the office of friendship. The request, the act and the subsequent promise of remuneration might then be described, without too severe a strain, as the component elements of a single transaction.

The one exception to the proof of a material inducement which the judges were tempted to allow was a tribute to domestic life. A father might be liable upon a promise made out of affection for his child, though it was otherwise without consideration. The indulgence was narrowly restrained. A mother, whose feelings were at least as strong, had no corresponding duty to provide for her offspring, and her ' natural affection,' therefore, while potent to raise a use, would not support an assumpsit.[47]

By the first years of the seventeenth century the doctrine of consideration may thus be said to have been assimilated into the law. It was established as the criterion of success in an action for the breach of any contract not under seal. The meaning of ' sufficiency ' had been indicated if not defined, and the frontiers marked between ' executory,' ' executed ' and ' past ' consideration. But the antithesis of ' detriment and benefit,' which Victorian judges repeated as a confident formula, was as yet no more than a convenient phrase, and the principle which it reflected still lay open to the impression of new minds and new necessities.

C.

THE INFLUENCE OF LORD MANSFIELD
AND
NINETEENTH-CENTURY REACTION

Lord Mansfield, when in 1756 he became Chief Justice, set himself to prune the ' Gothick ' superfluities which marred the symmetry of the common law. He would liberalise the whole conception of contract and, in particular, would moderate the undue influence of consideration. The temper of the age, rational and cosmopolitan, was propitious.[48] Nor had the doctrine itself, though now two hundred years old, been defined so firmly as to preclude a fresh examination. Contemporary jurists had approached it with circumspection. To Bacon it was to be explained as ' a cause or occasion meritorious, that requires a mutual recompense in fact or in law ': Viner repeated the explanation, but added that ' loss was as good a consideration for a

---

[47] *Marsh* v. *Rainsford* (1588) 2 Leonard, 111, *infra,* p. 418; *Harford* v. *Gardiner* (1588) 2 Leonard, 30; *Brett's Case* (1600) Croke, Eliz. 755, *infra,* p. 421; *Bourne* v. *Mason* (1670) 1 Ventris, 6, *infra,* p. 424; *Dutton* v. *Poole* (1677), *infra,* p. 425.
[48] Cf. contemporary developments in France, as seen, e.g., in Pothier.

promise as benefit or profit': Blackstone was content to describe it as 'the recompense given by the party contracting to the other.'[49]

The judicial attitude of the last sixty years encouraged the belief that rationalisation was possible. The line of demarcation between 'executed' and 'past' consideration, long since drawn, was becoming faint with age, and there were a number of occasions on which, though still by way of exception, previous conduct might sustain a subsequent assumpsit. Where a promise would have been binding but for the intervention of some special rule of law, and this rule had either ceased to operate or was in the nature of a privilege which the defendant had foregone, the cause of action, if dormant, revived, and, if originally absent, was supplied. So it was held in 1699 that a promise to pay a debt barred by the Statute of Limitations enabled the creditor to sue, because the debtor 'had waived the benefit of the Statute.'[50] A second exception sprang from the new attitude of the courts to the problems of infancy. An agreement made by an infant had originally been deemed void so that a promise to discharge it given after coming of age was without consideration.[51] But by the end of the seventeenth century the judges had revised their opinion. In the words of Chief Justice Holt, 'when the defendant under age borrowed money of the plaintiff and afterwards at full age promised to pay it, this is a good consideration for the promise and the defendant shall be charged.'[52] The change of mind was supported by a more discriminating use of language: an infant's agreement was no longer void, but voidable. In *Loyd* v. *Lee*[53] his position was contrasted with that of the married woman. The defendant had given a promissory note during her husband's life, and, after his death, 'in consideration of forbearance' assumed to pay it. Pratt, C.J. refused to allow her to be sued. The note was 'absolutely void, and forbearance, where originally there is no cause of action, is no consideration to raise an assumpsit.' It might be otherwise, he added, 'where the contract was voidable.' The more generous interpretation of the doctrine, which these exceptions to the ban upon past consideration might be taken to invite, was reinforced from two opposing directions. On the one hand, the 'natural affection' of a father had availed to validate his promise because it was balanced by a 'natural duty' to support his children; and the Law of Nature, so dear to eighteenth-century philosophy, might be coaxed to yield moral injunctions of a more general efficacy. On the other hand,

---

[49] Bacon's Abridgment (1736), *Assumpsit* (c): Viner's Abridgment (1751) pp. 405-411: Blackstone's Lectures, first delivered in 1753 and still in manuscript. See the transcription, made by courtesy of All Souls College, Oxford, in Fifoot, *Lord Mansfield*, p. 127.
[50] *Hyling* v. *Hastings*, 1 Ld. Raym., 389, 421.
[51] *Stone* v. *Wythipol* (1588) Croke, Eliz. 126, *supra*, p. 400.
[52] *Ball* v. *Hesketh* (1697) Comberbatch, 381, followed in *Southerton* v. *Whitlock* (1726) 1 Strange, 690.
[53] (1719) 1 Strange, 94.

the pressure of commercial interest had secured a peculiar dispensation for the negotiable instrument. Consideration was to be presumed from its very existence and would, in any event, be satisfied by proof of an antecedent debt.[54]

In this favourable environment Lord Mansfield led two assaults upon the doctrine. In his first and bolder attempt he sought to destroy the status of consideration as an essential and independent element in the action of Assumpsit and to reduce it to the level of evidence. If the intention of the parties to bind themselves could be discovered by other means, such as the presence of writing, it was superfluous. He seized his opportunity in 1765 in the case of *Pillans* v. *Van Mierop*.[55] An Irish merchant named White had drawn a bill of exchange upon the plaintiffs, merchants at Rotterdam. The plaintiffs promised to accept it if White would name a responsible firm in London who would reimburse them. White named the defendants, and the plaintiffs honoured the bill. Up to this moment there had been no direct contact between the plaintiffs and the defendants; but at a later date the defendants, at the plaintiffs' request, promised in writing to accept their bill for the same amount. Before it was presented White became a bankrupt, and the defendants refused to implement their promise. In the Court of King's Bench the defendants argued that the only consideration which could be proved was past and that this would not support an assumpsit. The argument was rejected. The judgments display an embarrassing variety of *rationes decidendi*. Lord Mansfield took two points. In the first place, this was a commercial case and by the custom of merchants, which was an integral part of English law, no consideration was required. In the second place, the function of the doctrine, even where no business interest was involved, was merely evidentiary, and its absence could be compensated by the presence of writing. The separate, but equally dubious, analogies of the Deed and of the Statute of Frauds were invoked to support this new and startling proposition. Mr. Justice Wilmot, while he was able to detect in the facts a tincture of consideration, accepted both Lord Mansfield's points, but preferred the second. The distinction between written and oral contracts was fundamental; and, while the older cases were ' strange and absurd,' the doctrine had been ' melting down into common sense of late.' Mr. Justice Yates and Mr. Justice Aston emphasised the commercial aspect of the case.

The broad influence of *Pillans* v. *Van Mierop* was reflected ten years later in *Williamson* v. *Losh*.[56] The defendant, as executor of John Losh, was sued in assumpsit upon the following ' promissory note.'

---

[54] *Meredith* v. *Chute* (1702) 2 Ld. Raym., 760.
[55] 3 Burrow, 1663, *infra*, p. 427.
[56] (1775), cited by Langdell in his *Cases on Contract* (1871) p. 180.

> ' I, John Losh, for the love and affection that I have for Jane Tiffin, my wife's sister's daughter, do promise that my executors, administrators or assigns, shall pay to her the sum of £100 of money one year after my decease, and a caldron and a clock, a wainscot chest and a bed and bed-clothes and seven pudden-dishes. As witness my hand this 16th day of February, 1763.'

Jane Tiffin subsequently married the plaintiff. The defendant admitted that he had proved the will and that he had sufficient assets to satisfy the demand made upon him, but pleaded the absence of consideration. The judgment of the King's Bench survives in a single sentence.

> ' The court held that, the instrument being in writing and attested by witnesses, the objection of *nudum pactum* did not lie.'

The *ratio decidendi,* if it may be conjectured from such scant material, would appear to be the distinction between written and oral agreements, but a commercial flavour is still perceptible. The somewhat peculiar document upon which the plaintiff sued was apparently invested with the insignia of a negotiable instrument.

The challenge to orthodoxy was too audacious, and in 1778 it was decisively repelled. In *Rann* v. *Hughes* Lord Mansfield had held an administratrix liable upon a written promise, made in her personal capacity, to pay a debt due by the deceased to the plaintiff.[57] The judgment was reversed in the Exchequer Chamber and the reversal sustained in the House of Lords. Buller, for the plaintiff, urged uncompromisingly the intrinsic validity of a written agreement. He dared to impugn the sanctity of the Deed. To affix a seal was notoriously a farce, and, if so trivial an act dispensed with consideration, why should it be required where the parties, by embodying their terms in a document, even if unsealed, had attested their serious purpose? But two centuries of precedents were not to be ' melted down into common sense.' The general opinion of the judges, accepted by the Lord Chancellor, declared the antithesis of written and oral agreements to be heretical; and consideration remained a vital element in all contracts not under seal.

In his second line of attack Lord Mansfield was less ambitious. Assuming the necessity of consideration, he took advantage of the reluctance of his predecessors to explain its meaning in authoritative language and offered a new and revised version. The pressure of moral sentiment, already faintly felt, and the avowed, if exceptional, instances of past consideration seemed to invite the construction of a broad and accommodating principle. In *Trueman* v. *Fenton*[58] the defendant in December, 1774, bought linen from the plaintiff and gave

---

[57] 4 Brown, P.C. 27, and 7 T.R. 350, n: *infra,* p. 430. The presence of writing, though it did not appear on the Declaration, was presumed, even in the House of Lords, to exist.

[58] (1777) 2 Cowper, 544. See also *Atkins* v. *Hill* (1775) 1 Cowper, 284.

him in payment two promissory notes. The notes were not met, and in January, 1775, the defendant became a bankrupt. In February the defendant asked the plaintiff to cancel both notes and offered him a new note for a smaller sum in full satisfaction. The plaintiff accepted the offer and agreed not to claim in the bankruptcy proceedings. In April the defendant obtained his discharge and was sued upon the latest note. He argued that the original debt was merged in the bankruptcy and that the plaintiff must fail for lack of consideration. 'As to that,' said Lord Mansfield, ' all the debts of a bankrupt are due in conscience, notwithstanding he has obtained his certificate; and there is no honest man who does not discharge them, if he afterwards has it in his power to do so.' The court would, therefore, imply a ' fair consideration for the note.' This decision, while it must be set against, could still be reconciled with, the judgment in *Rann* v. *Hughes* delivered in the following year. The rebuff which Lord Mansfield there received enhanced rather than diminished the charm of his alternative approach to the problem. The debtor who acknowledged a statute-barred debt, the adult who recognised a youthful liability, the discharged bankrupt who found himself in unexpected if precarious affluence—all these were bound in honour, and the law should add its more prosaic sanction. The House of Lords had not defined the doctrine upon the pre-eminence of which they insisted, and, by supplying the omission on his own terms, Lord Mansfield would kiss the rod and yet avoid humiliation. In *Hawkes* v. *Saunders* in 1782[59] the plaintiff sued once more on an undertaking by an executrix to pay a legacy. The assets of the estate were admitted to be more than adequate to meet the liabilities, and this happy circumstance not only explained the defendant's promise[60] but enabled *Rann* v. *Hughes* to be distinguished on the facts. Consideration was not to be interpreted so narrowly as to require proof of an ' immediate benefit ' to the promisor or an ' immediate loss ' to the promisee. Whenever a defendant was under a moral duty to pay money and subsequently promised to pay, the pre-existing duty sufficed to support the promise.

The principle of moral obligation was accepted by Lord Mansfield's successors. It was avowed and applied in 1803 in *Cooper* v. *Martin*.[61] The plaintiff had married a widow with four children and had maintained them during infancy. The eldest son, when he came of age, undertook to pay the cost of his maintenance, and the plaintiff sued on this promise. There was no previous request by the defendant to which it could be related and the facts could not be brought within

---

[59] 1 Cowper, 289, *infra,* p. 433.
[60] Until 1830 (when the law was altered by 11 Geo. IV and 1 Will. IV, c. 40), if a testator named no residuary legatee, the executor, after carrying out the provisions of the will and satisfying the debts, could keep the balance of the estate for himself; and there was thus an inducement to promise payment to the creditors out of his own pocket.
[61] 4 East, 76.

the traditional limits of executed consideration. But Lord Ellen-borough had no difficulty in supporting the action. 'Having done an act beneficial for the defendant in his infancy, it is a good considera-tion for the defendant's promise after he came of age. In such a case the law will imply a request.' Professional opinion, it is true, was not uniform. The reporters, Bosanquet and Puller, entered a *caveat* in their note to the case of *Wennall* v. *Adney*.[62] The scattered instances upon which Lord Mansfield had relied all assumed the presence of an antecedent legal duty, fortuitously barred by a temporary obstacle, and his broad generalisation was without precedent. But such criticism was not echoed from the Bench for another generation. In *Lee* v. *Muggeridge* in 1813[63] Lord Mansfield's doctrine was regarded as so firmly rooted as to be impervious to argument. A married woman had asked the plaintiff to lend money to her son-in-law, and the loan was duly made. After her husband's death she promised the plaintiff in writing that her executors should re-pay him. In an action against the executors, the plaintiff admitted that the woman, while a *feme covert,* could not bind herself, but contended that the promise which she had given as a widow converted a moral into a legal obligation. After hearing the authorities cited by the defendant, Sir James Mans-field told counsel for the plaintiff that they need not trouble themselves to reply. It was impossible to conceive 'a stronger moral obligation than is stated upon this record.' Mr. Justice Gibbs was still more emphatic. The plaintiff's contention was indisputable, and 'counsel for the defendant did not dare to grapple with the position.'

Judicial scepticism was first evident in 1831, when Lord Ten-terden felt bound to observe 'that the doctrine that a moral obliga-tion is a sufficient consideration for a subsequent promise is one which should be received with some limitation.'[64] But it was not decisively repudiated until 1840. Lord Denman, in his judgment in *Eastwood* v. *Kenyon*,[65] adopted the critical note of Bosanquet and Puller, 'which has been very generally thought to contain a correct statement of the law.' The principle of moral obligation was dis-covered by Lord Mansfield on one of his not infrequent excursions from the narrow path of orthodoxy, and it was not warranted by the occasional eccentricities which his predecessors had tolerated. In repelling the heresy, Lord Denman conceived himself to be 'justified by the old common law of England.' His appeal to history must be allowed. Whatever its value in the modern law, the doctrine of con-sideration still rests upon the foundations laid by the Elizabethan lawyers.

[62] 3 B. & P. 247, at pp. 249-253, *infra,* p. 435. The case was decided in 1802, but the report was not published until 1804.
[63] 5 Taunton, 36, *infra,* p. 437.
[64] *Littlefield* v. *Shee* (1831) 2 B. & Ad. 811.
[65] (1840) 11 Ad. & El. 438, *infra,* p. 440.

NOTE

ON

ACCORD AND SATISFACTION

The current definition of Accord and Satisfaction is that of Lord Justice Scrutton.[66]

> 'Accord and satisfaction is the purchase of a release from an obligation, whether arising under contract or tort, by means of any valuable consideration, not being the actual performance of the obligation itself. The accord is the agreement by which the obligation is discharged. The satisfaction is the consideration which makes the agreement operative.'

The underlying problem may be simply stated. X. owes Y. £100. X. either (a) pays or promises to pay Y. £50 or (b) performs or promises to perform some other act on the understanding that Y. will forgo his original claim. Is the claim thereby discharged? The doctrine has had a long and chequered history and still admits of controversy. Two particular questions emerge. On the one hand, if such an accord is made between the parties, must it be executed before it may operate as a discharge or will an executory agreement suffice? What, on the other hand, is the relation of the doctrine to that of consideration? An intimate connection has long been assumed[67], but the assumption has been attacked as unhistorical.

> 'The rule is commonly thought to be a corollary of the doctrine of consideration. But this is a total misconception. The rule is older than the doctrine of consideration and is simply the survival of a bit of formal logic of the mediæval lawyers.' [68]

It is certainly true that the genesis of the doctrine is to be found in the fifteenth century within the ambit of Debt. It was discussed by the judges in 1455.[69] Danvers, J. expressed the opinion that, 'if a man be indebted to me in £20, and I take from him 12d. in satisfaction of these £20, in this case I will be barred from the remainder.' Moyle, J. preferred the illustration of a substituted performance. 'Suppose I am obliged to you on condition of giving you a horse, and afterwards I give you a hanaper or other thing and you accept and receive it, you will be barred from demanding any horse afterwards by your own acceptance.' Forty years later the problem was still seen from these distinctive points of view. Whereas Fineux, J. held the original claim to be discharged no less by part payment than by the

---

[66] *British Russian Gazette, Ltd.* v. *Associated Newspapers, Ltd.* [1933] 2 K.B. 616, at pp. 643-4. The definition was adopted from Salmond and Winfield, *Law of Contracts.*

[67] See *Foakes* v. *Beer* [1884] 9 A.C. 605, and Law Revision Committee, *Sixth Interim Report.*

[68] Ames, *Lectures on Legal History,* p. 329. See also Holdsworth, H.E.L. VIII, pp. 20-3, 80-5.

[69] *Anon,* Y.B. 33 Hen. 6, Mich. f. 48, pl. 32.

receipt of a novelty, Chief Justice Brian stated the rule almost in modern terms.

> ' The action is brought for £20, and the concord is that he shall pay only £10, which appears to be no satisfaction for the £20; for payment of £10 cannot be payment of £20. But if it was of a horse which was to be paid according to the concord, this would be good satisfaction, for it does not appear that the horse be worth more or less than the sum in demand.' [70]

This latter view was accepted by the full Court of Common Pleas in 1563, where a note by the reporter emphasised the resolution of a doubt;[71] and the celebrated dictum in *Pinnel's Case*[72] assumed it to be established law. The plaintiff in this case sued in Debt on a bond for £8. 10s., due on November 11, 1600. The defendant pleaded that, at the plaintiff's request, he had paid him £5. 2s. 2d. on October 1st. The Court, while they gave judgment for the plaintiff on a point of pleading, intimated that, but for the technical flaw, they would have found for the defendant. Merely to pay part of the original claim could never be a discharge; but it was otherwise where the debtor went outside his obligations either by doing some fresh act or, as in the case at bar, by meeting the creditor's request for payment at an earlier date.

Ames' description of the rule as a relic of mediæval scholasticism is thus an unnecessary condescension. Debt rested on the idea not of promise but of duty, and it is not surprising that the judges should ultimately have refused to recognize a part performance as a discharge of that duty. The wonder is rather that they should have allowed it to be discharged by a substituted act. It was at least inevitable that they should have disdained a merely executory accord. The ' real ' nature of Debt, as illustrated in its requirement of Quid pro Quo, demanded the actual receipt of a benefit, and, in this context, the word ' satisfaction ' was invested with no artificial or attenuated significance. ' It is agreed,' said Brian, C.J., ' that the concord alone is not to the purpose, but the concord with satisfaction; and so the performance of the concord is the whole substance of the plea.'[73]

So long as the rule was confined to Debt, it was to be accepted as inherent in the nature of the writ. The development of Assumpsit might seem to involve its re-examination. As early as 1552 a plea of Accord and Satisfaction was received by the King's Bench to a declaration in the new form of action,[74] and in *Richards* v. *Bartlet* in 1584 it

---

[70] *Anon* (1495) Y.B. 10 Hen. 7, Mich. f. 4, pl. 4.
[71] Dalison, p. 49, pl. 13.
[72] (1602) 5 Coke Rep. 117a, *infra*, p. 422.
[73] *Anon*, Y.B. 10 Hen. 7, Mich. f. 4, pl. 4. See also Danvers, J. in *Anon*, Y.B. 33 Hen. 6, Mich. f. 48, pl. 32: ' Where a man has *quid pro quo*, in this case it will be deemed a satisfaction '; and cf. *Doctor and Student, supra*, p. 329.
[74] *Andrew* v. *Boughey*, 1 Dyer, 75a, *supra*, p. 355. The defendant here had done an act which he was not originally bound to do.

was related to the doctrine of consideration.[75]   A buyer, sued for the price of goods, pleaded an agreement by the seller to accept 3s. 4d. in the £, and ' that he hath been always ready to pay the said sum newly agreed.'   The plea was held bad, first, because a promise to pay part of the price was not sufficient consideration to forgo the balance, and secondly, because, even assuming it to be sufficient, the promise had not been performed.   The transference of the rule from Debt to Assumpsit and its assessment in terms of consideration have been severely criticised.[76]   A plaintiff suing in Assumpsit must prove consideration for the defendant's undertaking, but no similar burden should be laid upon a party who seeks to use a promise as a weapon, not of offence, but of defence.   An element essential to the formation is irrelevant to the discharge of a contract.   The new orientation of the rule, however, while unnecessary in its inception and unfortunate in its sequel, was not unintelligible.   Assumpsit was not based, like Debt, upon the idea of duty, and Accord and Satisfaction had to be re-stated in more appropriate language.   It was not unnatural that the judges should treat the plaintiff's promise to forbear as binding only on the same conditions as any other undertaking within the scope of Assumpsit and should demand the presence of consideration.[77]

As in Debt, therefore, so in Assumpsit, though for other reasons, the defendant, to escape liability upon the original claim, must prove some new element either in party, time or act.   But the judges did not admit at once the full consequence of their argument.   Since the essence of consideration lay in the validity of mutual promises, they should logically have received the promise of a novelty, no less than its performance, as a sufficient satisfaction.   The second resolution in *Richards* v. *Bartlet*[78] shows that they hesitated to take this step; and, indeed, it was not taken until 1682.[79]   Even now opinion was divided. While Comyns in his *Digest* declared that ' an accord with mutual promises to perform is good, though the thing be not performed at the time of the action,' Chief Justice Eyre in 1794 insisted on performance.[80]

---

[75] 1 Leonard, 19, *infra*, p. 415.   See also *Greenleaf* v. *Barker* (1590) Croke, Eliz. 193, *infra*, p. 418; *Dixon* v. *Adams* (1597) Croke, Eliz. 538, and *Goring* v. *Goring* (1602) Yelverton, 10.

[76] See Pollock, *Principles of Contract*, 12th ed., p. 147, and Ames, *Lectures on Legal History*, pp. 329-336.

[77] Ames (*Lectures on Legal History*, pp. 331-3) was of opinion that Accord and Satisfaction was not based on the doctrine of consideration until Lord Ellenborough's judgment in *Fitch* v. *Sutton* (1804) 5 East, 230, and cited a number of seventeenth-century cases to support his contention, especially *Bagge* v. *Slade* (1616) 3 Bulst. 162, and *Rawlins* v. *Lockey* (1639) 1 Vin. Abr. 308, pl. 24.   But these were cases, not of Accord and Satisfaction, but of promises by the defendant to perform part of his existing contractual duty in return for the plaintiff's promise to do some new act; and, as such, their evidence may scarcely outweigh the testimony of *Richards* v. *Bartlet* and of the other cases cited *supra*, n. 75.

[78] *Infra*, p. 416.

[79] *Case* v. *Barber*, Sir T. Raymond, 450, *infra*, p. 426.   Cf. *Goring* v. *Goring* (1602) Yelverton, 10, and *Peytoe's Case* (1611) 9 Coke Rep. 77b, at p. 80b.

[80] *Lynn* v. *Bruce*, 2 H.Bl. 317, citing *Allen* v. *Harris* (1696) 1 Ld. Raym. 122.   Comyns' *Digest* was first published 1762-7.

' Satisfaction ' stuck in the judges' throats. ' Accord executed is satisfaction—accord executory is only substituting one cause of action in the room of another, which might go on to any extent.'[81]   Only in 1831 was Comyns' view finally upheld and logic vindicated.[82]   In the result the word had to be stripped of its primary meaning and interpreted as a synonym for consideration.

In its original setting of Debt the doctrine of Accord and Satisfaction was not misplaced.   Its translation into the terms of Assumpsit and into the language of consideration may be a matter of regret but scarcely of reproach.   If in the modern law it is an anomaly, the abolition of the forms of action offered the opportunity for its revision, and the failure of the House of Lords in 1884 to grasp that opportunity reflects rather upon their timidity than upon the intelligence of their predecessors.[83]   It has now to be removed by Statute or avoided by judicial virtuosity.[84]

SOURCES

WEBB'S CASE

4 LEONARD, 110

A.D. 1577

In an action upon the case the plaintiff declared that, whereas Cobham was indebted to J. S. and J. S. to the defendant, the said defendant, in consideration that the plaintiff would procure the said J. S. to make a letter of attorney to sue the said Cobham, promised to pay and give to the plaintiff £10.

It was objected that here was not any consideration for to induce the *assumpsit;* for the defendant by this letter of attorney gets nothing but his labour and travel.   But the exception was not allowed of.   For in this case, not so much the profit which redounds to the defendant as the labour of the plaintiff in procuring of the letter of attorney is to be respected.

RICHARDS v. BARTLET

1 LEONARD, 19

A.D. 1584

Dorothy Richards, executrix of A., her former husband, brought an action upon the case upon a promise against Humfrey Bartlet, and declared that, in consideration of two weighs[85] of corn delivered by the testator to the defendant, he did promise to pay to the plaintiff ten pounds.   To which the defendant said that, after the *assumpsit,* the plaintiff, in consideration that

[81] Per Eyre, C.J. in *Lynn* v. *Bruce,* 2 H.Bl. 317.
[82] Per Parke, J. in *Good* v. *Cheesman* (1831) 2 B. & Ad. 328.
[83] *Foakes* v. *Beer,* 9 A.C. 605.
[84] e.g. *Central London Property Trust, Ltd.* v. *High Trees House, Ltd.* [1947] 1 K.B. 130, *per* Denning, J.
[85] A ' weigh ' or ' wey ': ' a standard of dry-goods weight, varying greatly with different commodities.'   O.E.D.

the said two weighs were drowned by tempest and in consideration that the defendant would pay to the plaintiff for every twenty shillings of the said ten pounds three shillings and four pence, *sc., in toto* thirty-three shillings and four pence, did discharge the said defendant of the said promise; and averred further that he hath been always ready to pay the said sum newly agreed; upon which there was a demurrer.

And the opinion of the whole Court[86] was clearly with the plaintiff. First, because that here is not any consideration set forth in the bar by reason whereof the plaintiff should discharge the defendant of this matter; for no profit but damage comes to the plaintiff by this new agreement, and the defendant is not put to any labour or charge by it; therefore here is not any agreement to bind the plaintiff. . . . See *Onlies' Case,* 19 Eliz., Dyer.[87] Then, admitting that the agreement had been sufficient, yet, because it is not executed, it is not any bar. And afterwards judgment was given for the plaintiff.

SIDENHAM v. WORLINGTON

2 LEONARD, 224

A.D. 1585

In an action upon the case upon a promise the plaintiff declared that he at the request of the defendant was surety and bail for J. S., who was arrested into the King's Bench upon an action of £30, and that afterwards for the default of J. S. he was constrained to pay the £30; after which the defendant, meeting with the plaintiff, promised him for the same consideration that he would repay that £30, which he did not pay; upon which the plaintiff brought the action. The defendant pleaded *non assumpsit,* upon which issue was joined, which was found for the plaintiff.

Walmsley, Serjeant, for the defendant, moved the Court that this consideration will not maintain the action, because the consideration and promise did not concur and go together; for the consideration was long before executed, so as now it cannot be intended that the promise was for the same consideration. As if one giveth me a horse and a month after I promise him £10 for the said horse, he shall never have Debt for the £10 nor Assumpsit upon the promise; for there it is neither contract nor consideration, because the same is executed.

ANDERSON, C.J.: This action will not lie; for it is but a bare agreement and *nudum pactum,* because the contract was determined and not *in esse* at the time of the promise. But, he said, it is otherwise upon a consideration of marriage of one of his cousins, for marriage is always a present consideration.[88]

[86] Queen's Bench: Wray, C.J.: Ayloffe, Gawdy and Clench, J.J.

[87] *Onely* v. *Earl of Kent* (1577) 3 Dyer, 355b. An action on the case was brought against husband and wife, ' that, in consideration the plaintiff had used great pains and expended great sums about the affairs, suits and quarrels of the wife during her widowhood [by a previous marriage], she undertook and promised' to repay him and pay a further £200. She pleaded that two leases were held by the plaintiff to her use and that she had agreed that he should retain them for himself in satisfaction of all claims. It was held that here was no good accord: (1) because the leases were already in law the plaintiff's and the wife enjoyed only a ' naked promise and confidence to have them, for which is no remedy in law, but a *subpœna* lies '; (2) because, as the uses were not to take effect at once but only *in futuro,* they were executory only and not executed, and so no good satisfaction.

[88] This is a reference to an anonymous case cited in the report of *Hunt* v. *Bate,* 3 Dyer, 272a, where the marriage was at the request of the defendant.

WINDHAM, J. agreed with ANDERSON, C.J.: And he put the case in 3 *Hen.* 7[89]: if one selleth a horse unto another, and at another day he will warrant him to be sound of limb and member, it is a void warranty, for that such warranty ought to have been made or given at such time as the horse was sold.

PERYAM, J. conceived that the action did well lie: And he said that this case is not like unto the cases which have been put on the other side. For there is a great difference between contracts and this case; for in contracts upon sale the consideration and the promise and the sale ought to meet together, for a contract is derived from *con* and *trahere*, which is a drawing together, so as in contracts everything which is requisite ought to concur and meet together, *viz.* the consideration of the one side and the sale or the promise on the other side. But to maintain an action upon an *Assumpsit* the same is not requisite; for it is sufficient if there be a moving cause or consideration precedent, for which cause or consideration the promise was made. And such is the common practice at this day. For in an action upon the case upon a promise, the declaration is laid that the defendant, for and in consideration of £20 to him paid, *postea*, that is to say, at a day after, *super se assumpsit*; and that is good; and yet there the consideration is laid to be executed. And he said that the case in *Dyer*, 10 *Eliz.* 272[90] would prove the case. For there the case was that the apprentice of one Hunt was arrested when his master Hunt was in the country, and one Baker, one of the neighbours of Hunt, to keep the said apprentice out of prison, became his bail and paid the debt. Afterwards Hunt, the master, returning out of the country, thanked Baker for his neighbourly kindness to his apprentice and promised him that he would repay him the sum which he had paid for his servant and apprentice. And afterwards upon that promise Baker brought an action upon the case against Hunt, and it was adjudged in that case that the action would not lie, because the consideration was precedent to the promise and was executed and determined long before. But in that case it was holden by all the Justices that, if Hunt had requested Baker to have been surety or bail and afterwards Hunt had made the promise for the same consideration, the same had been good, for that the consideration did precede and was at the instance and request of the defendant.

RHODES, Justice, agreed with PERYAM: And he said that if one serve me for a year and hath nothing for his service, and afterwards at the end of the year I promise him £20 for his good and faithfull service ended, he may have and maintain an action upon the case upon the same promise, for it is made upon a good consideration. But if a servant have wages given him, and his master *ex abundanti* doth promise him £10 more after his service ended, he shall not maintain an action for that £10 upon the said promise; for there is not any new cause or consideration preceding the promise.

Which difference was agreed by all the Justices. And afterwards, upon long and good advice and consideration had of the principal case, Judgment was given for the plaintiff. And they much relied upon the case of *Hunt* and *Baker*, 10 Eliz. Dyer, 272. See the case there.

[89] The reference should be to Y.B. 5 Hen. 7, f. 41, pl. 7; *supra*, p. 356, n. 63.
[90] *Hunt* v. *Bate* (1568) 3 Dyer, 272a. The defendant's name, in the account of the case given above in *Sidenham* v. *Worlington*, is wrongly stated as *Baker*.

MARSH v. RAINSFORD

2 Leonard, 111

A.D. 1588

In an Action upon the Case the case was, that a communication was had between the parties that the plaintiff should marry the daughter of the defendant, in consideration of which the defendant promised the plaintiff to give him £200; but they could not agree upon the days of payment of it. After which they stole away the defendant's daughter and secretly married her without the defendant's knowledge. Yet afterwards the defendant gave his consent to it and allowed of the said marriage, and, in consideration of the said marriage, promised to pay the plaintiff £100.

Egerton, Solicitor-General, for the defendant: That the action upon this matter will not lie. For here the consideration is precedent to the promise, whereas the consideration in such cases ought to be future and subsequent. And, as the case is here, the plaintiff is out of the course of consideration of marriage; for he hath stolen away and married his wife without the knowledge or consent of her father. See such case, 10 Eliz. Dyer, 272.[91] The servant of one A. is arrested in London, and two friends of his master bail him; and afterwards A. promiseth to them for their friendship to save them harmless from damages and costs, etc. It was holden that the action doth not lie, for here is not any consideration, for the bailment was of their own heads, and it is executed before the promise. But if the master, before the enlargement of his servant, had requested the plaintiff for to bail his servant and he had so done, the action would have lien.

Wray, C.J.[92]: Although the consideration be precedent, yet, if it were made at the instance of the other party, the action would have lain. But here the natural affection of the father to his daughter is sufficient matter of consideration. If one cometh to a Serjeant at Law to have his counsel and the Serjeant doth advise him, and afterwards the client in consideration of such counsel promiseth to pay him £20, an action lieth for it.

And so, *Popham*[93] said, it had been adjudged in the Exchequer. And it is a common action in this Court, in consideration *quod querens deliberasset* to the defendant, etc., he promiseth to pay so much. And it was late adjudged betwixt *Style* and *Smith,* if a physician, who is my friend, hearing that my son is sick, goeth to him in my absence and helps and recovers him, and I, being informed thereof, promise him in consideration etc., *ut supra,* to give to him £20, an action will lie for the money.

And afterwards in the principal case Judgment was given for the plaintiff.

GREENLEAF v. BARKER

Croke, Elizabeth, 193

A.D. 1590

Error of a judgment given in an Assumpsit at Canterbury.

The said J. B. brought an Assumpsit and declared that, whereas the said J. B. was indebted to the said T. G. by obligation in five pound, to be paid upon the first of November following, in consideration that he,

---

[91] *Hunt* v. *Bate* (1568) 3 Dyer, 272a.
[92] Chief Justice of the Queen's Bench. The puisne judges were Shute, Gawdy and Clench, J.J.
[93] At this time Attorney-General; he succeeded Wray as Chief Justice in 1592.

the third of November, at the instance and request of the plaintiff[94] would pay him the said five pound without suit or trouble, he assumed to deliver him a Bond in which J. S. was indebted to him in twenty shillings with a letter of attorney to sue for the debt; and upon this Declaration after verdict Judgment was given for the plaintiff; and upon this judgment Error was brought.

1. *Error.* That the consideration was not good, for he did no more than the law did compel him to do, viz. to pay the money that was due before. And so was the opinion of GAWDY and FENNER[95]; for he payeth no more than was due. But if it had been paid before the day, it is otherwise; for every consideration must be for the benefit of the defendant or some other at his request, or a thing done by the plaintiff for which he laboureth or hath prejudice. . . . [They cited, *inter alia, Sidenham* v. *Worlington, supra*, p. 416]. . . .

2. *Error.* The assumpsit is void. For it appeareth not that the plaintiff could have any benefit of it; for it is not to sue and recover the twenty shillings to his own use and so is rather a charge. And of that opinion was GAWDY : FENNER, *contra.* . . .

But both conceiving that there was no consideration and so a plain error, WRAY being absent, they were both of opinion to reverse the Judgment. . . .

[The case was ultimately adjourned].

T O O L E Y v. W I N D H A M
CROKE, ELIZ. 206
A.D. 1591

Assumpsit. For that there were controversies between him [the plaintiff] and the defendant for the profits of certain lands, which the father of the defendant had taken in his lifetime, and that he had purchased a Writ out of Chancery against the defendant to the intent to exhibit a Bill against him; upon the return of the Writ for the said profits, the defendant, in consideration he should surcease his suit, promised to him that, if he could prove that his father had taken the profits or had the possession of the said land under the title of the father of the plaintiff, he would pay him for the profits of the said land; and said *in facto* that he had proved that the father of the defendant had taken the profits under the title of the father of the plaintiff. And, upon *non assumpsit,* it was found for the plaintiff.

Coke: This is no consideration; for the suit in Chancery was unjust, and then the staying of it is no good consideration. . . .

CURIA: It is no consideration. For if the father of the defendant did take the profits, it is not reason his son should answer for them; and so the suit in Chancery is unjust, and the staying of it no good consideration. But if the suit had been for evidences or otherwise, the staying of it had been a good consideration. But here it is for a personal tort, for which neither the executor or heir are to answer.

And *Trin. 33 Eliz.,* it being moved again, all the Court held it no good consideration. For he did not alledge that he was heir or executor, and so had no colour to charge him; and, if it had been so alledged, yet no cause to charge him for a personal tort. And it was adjudged for the defendant.

[94] i.e., the plaintiff in error, the defendant to the assumpsit.
[95] Justices of the Queen's Bench. The other judges were Wray, C.J. and Clench, J.

KNIGHT v. RUSHWORTH

CROKE, ELIZ. 469

A.D. 1596

Assumpsit. The case was that one Mary Rushworth had entered into a Bond of Two Hundred Pound to the plaintiff; and Mary Rushworth gave all her goods to the defendant to pay her debts. The defendant, pretending that this Bond was read to the said Mary Rushworth as an obligation of One Hundred Pound only and so void, assumed to the plaintiff that, if he and two witnesses would depose before the Mayor of Lincoln that the obligation was read to Mary Rushworth as an obligation of Two Hundred Pound, he would pay it. Whereupon the plaintiff with two others came before the Mayor of Lincoln, and there deposed upon a Book accordingly; and hereupon brought this action; whereto it was demurred.

Yelverton, for the defendant, moved that this action lies not; for there is not any consideration besides this oath, which is unlawful, and therefore void.

Hearn: It is not material whether the consideration be for the plaintiff's benefit; for if it be any charge or trouble to the defendant it sufficeth, as in *Albany's* Case[96]; and he conceived the oath to be lawful enough, he being before the Mayor. . . .

ANDERSON, C.J. C.P.: The travail of coming before the Mayor is a very good consideration. And truly the oath is not illegal, being taken before him. And the smallness of a consideration is not material, if there be any. . . .

WALMSLEY, J. agreed.

BEAUMONT and OWEN, J.J. doubted herein at first; but afterwards they agreed with their Companions that the consideration was sufficient and lawful.

Wherefore it was adjudged for the plaintiff.

GOWER v. CAPPER

CROKE, ELIZ. 543

A.D. 1596

Assumpsit: and [the plaintiff] declares, Whereas the defendant was indebted unto him by Bill in £20, the defendant, in consideration the plaintiff assumed unto him to deliver him the said Bill, assumed to procure two sufficient sureties to be bound to the plaintiff for the payment of the said £20. And

---

[96] *Sturlyn* v. *Albany* (1587) Cro. Eliz. 67. 'The case was, The plaintiff had made a lease to J.S. of land for life, rendering rent; J.S. grants all his estate to the defendant; the rent was behind for divers years; the plaintiff demands the rent of the defendant, who assumed that, if the plaintiff could shew to him a Deed that the rent was due, he would pay to him the rent and the arrearages. The plaintiff alledgeth that upon such a day, etc., at Warwick, he shewed unto him the Indenture of Lease by which the rent was due, and notwithstanding he had not paid him the rent and the arrearages due for four years. Upon *non assumpsit* pleaded, it was found for the plaintiff. . . . And it was moved in arrest of judgment that there was no consideration to ground an action, for it is but the shewing of the Deed, which is no consideration. . . . But it was adjudged for the plaintiff; for, when a thing is to be done by the plaintiff, be it never so small, this is a sufficient consideration to ground an action. And here the shewing of the Deed is a cause to avoid suit. . . .' *Semble,* in *Hearn's* argument in *Knight* v. *Rushworth*, the words 'plaintiff' and 'defendant' have been transposed by the reporter.

[he] alledgeth *in facto* that he delivered the said Bill to the defendant and that he, intending to deceive the plaintiff, produced two sureties to be bound, that were of no value. The defendant pleads that the plaintiff had not delivered unto him the said Bill.

And it was thereupon demurred; and, without argument, adjudged for the plaintiff. For the alledging that he had delivered the Bill was but surplusage; for the consideration was the promise to deliver it, and therefore he needed not have alledged that he delivered it. But a promise against a promise is a sufficient ground for an action. And although it be alledged that he found sureties, yet, when it is alledged that they are insufficient (which is allowed by the defendant's plea and demurrer), it is all one as if he never had found sureties.

Wherefore it was adjudged for the plaintiff.

SHERWOOD v. WOODWARD
CROKE, ELIZ. 700
A.D. 1600

Assumpsit. Whereas [the plaintiff] sold to the defendant's son certain weights of cheese, the defendant, in consideration the plaintiff would deliver the said cheese to his said son, assumed that, if the son did not pay for them, then he would. And for non-payment the action was brought.

Upon *non assumpsit* pleaded, and found for the plaintiff, it was moved by *Godfrey* in arrest of judgment that this was not any consideration; for it is no more than what the Law appoints, to deliver that which he sold, the property whereof is in the son by the sale.

But GAWDY and FENNER, J.J. held it to be a good consideration; for it is an ease to the bargainee to have them without suit, which, peradventure, otherwise he could not have had. And although the bargainee may take them in this case, the bargainor is not bound to deliver them; and there is a new act done by him upon this agreement, and it is an ease to the vendee. And 12 Hen. 7[97] is that, to deliver the goods of the party himself at another place, is a good accord.

Wherefore, *ceteris Justiciariis absentibus*,[98] they adjudged it for the plaintiff.

BRETT'S CASE
CROKE, ELIZ. 755
A.D. 1600

Assumpsit. The case was: That William Dracot, first husband to the *feme*,[99] sent his son to table with the plaintiff for three years and agreed to give unto him for every year £8, and died within the year. The *feme* during her widow-hood, in consideration of her natural affection to the son and in consideration that the son should continue during the residue of the time with the plaintiff, promised to the plaintiff to pay unto him

---

[97] *Semble*, the reference should be Y.B. 10 Hen. 7, Mich, f. 4, pl. 4.
[98] The other Judges of the Queen's Bench were Popham, C.J. and Clench, J.
[99] The defendants were 'J.S. and his wife': the 'feme' was the wife of J.S. and the widow of William Dracot.

£6 13s. 4d. for the tabling of the son for the time past and £8 for every year after that he should continue there with the plaintiff. Afterwards she married the defendant, and the plaintiff brought his action as well for the £6 13s. 4d. as for the tabling for the two years following.

And *Warburton* moved that this action lay not. First, because it was an entire contract by her first husband for the entire year, which cannot be apportioned. Secondly, because natural affection is not sufficient to ground an *assumpsit* without *Quid pro Quo*. Thirdly, that this is a contract, for which action of Debt lies, and not this action.

But all the Court[1] held that the action well lay. For as to the first, it is well apportionable, because, it being for Tabling which he had taken, there ought to be recompense, although he departed within the year or that the contractor died within the year. To the second, they agreed that natural affection of itself is not a sufficient consideration to ground an *Assumpsit*, for, although it be sufficient to raise an use, yet it is not sufficient to ground an action without an express *Quid pro Quo*. But it is here good because it is not only in consideration of affection, but that her son should afterward continue at his table, which is good as well for the money due before as for what should afterwards become due. And as to the third, true it is that, if the contract had been only for the Tabling afterwards, then Debt would have lain, and not this action. But in regard it is conjoyned with another thing for which he could not have an action of Debt (as it is here for this £6 13s. 4d.), an action upon the Case lies for all; as debt with other things may be put into an arbjtrament.[2]

Wherefore it was adjudged for the plaintiff.

PINNEL'S CASE

5 COKE REP. 117a

A.D. 1602

Pinnel brought an action of Debt on a Bond against Cole of £16 for payment of £8 10s. the 11th day of November, 1600. The defendant pleaded that he at the instance of the plaintiff before the said day, *scil.* 1st October ..., paid to the plaintiff £5 2s. 2d., which said £5 2s. 2d. the plaintiff accepted in full satisfaction of the £8 10s.

And it was resolved by the whole Court[3] that payment of a lesser sum on the day in satisfaction of a greater cannot be any satisfaction for the whole, because it appears to the Judges that by no possibility a lesser sum can be a satisfaction to the plaintiff for a greater sum; but the gift of a horse, hawk or robe, etc. in satisfaction is good. For it shall be intended that a horse, hawk or robe, etc. might be more beneficial to the plaintiff than the money in respect of some circumstance, or otherwise the plaintiff would not have accepted of it in satisfaction. But when the whole sum is due, by no intendment the acceptance of parcel can be a satisfaction to the plaintiff.

But in the case at Bar it was resolved that the payment and acceptance

[1] The Court of Common Pleas: Anderson, C.J., Glanvill, Walmsley and Kingsmill, J.J.
[2] At the date of this case (1600), the Common Pleas had not yet accepted the view of the Queen's Bench as to *indebitatus assumpsit. Supra,* p. 359.
[3] Court of Common Pleas: Anderson, C.J., Walmsley, Kingsmill and Warburton, J.J.

of parcel before the day in satisfaction of the whole would be a good satisfaction in regard of circumstance of time; for peradventure parcel of it before the day would be more beneficial to him than the whole at the day, and the value of the satisfaction is not material. So, if I am bound in £20 to pay you £10 at Westminster and you request me to pay you £5 at the day at York and you will accept it in full satisfaction of the whole £10, it is a good satisfaction for the whole; for the expences to pay it at York is sufficient satisfaction.

But in this case the plaintiff had Judgment for the insufficient pleading. For he did not plead that he had paid the £5 2s. 2d. in full satisfaction (as by the Law he ought), but pleaded the payment of part generally, and that the plaintiff accepted it in full satisfaction. And always the manner of the tender and of the payment shall be directed by him who made the tender or payment, and not by him who accepts it. And for this cause Judgment was given for the plaintiff. . . .

LAMPLEIGH v. BRATHWAIT

Hobart, 105

A.D. 1616

Anthony Lampleigh brought an Assumpsit against Thomas Brathwait, and declared that, whereas the defendant had feloniously slain one Patrick Mahume, the defendant, after the said felony done, instantly required the plaintiff to labour and do his endeavour to obtain his pardon from the King; whereupon the plaintiff upon the same request did, by all the means he could and many days' labour, do his endeavour to obtain the King's pardon for the said felony, *viz.* in riding and journeying at his own charges from London to Roiston, when the King was there, and to London back, and so to and from Newmarket, to obtain pardon for the defendant for the said felony; afterwards, in consideration of the premises, the said defendant did promise the said plaintiff to give him one hundred pound; and that he had not, etc., to his damage one hundred and twenty pound.

To this the defendant pleaded *Non Assumpsit,* and found for the plaintiff, damage one hundred pound. It was said in arrest of judgment that the consideration was passed. But the chief objection was, that it doth not appear that he did anything towards the obtaining of the pardon but riding up and down, and nothing done when he came there. And of this opinion was my brother WARBURTON; but myself and the other two Judges were of opinion for the plaintiff, and so he had judgment.[4]

First, it was agreed that a mere voluntary courtesy will not have a consideration to uphold an Assumpsit. But if that courtesy were moved by a suit or request of the party that gives the Assumpsit, it will bind; for the promise, though it follows, yet it is not naked, but couples itself with the suit before and the merits of the party procured by that suit, which is the difference. Pasch. 10 Eliz., Dyer, 272, *Hunt* v. *Bate*[5]; see *Oneley's Case,* 19 Eliz., Dyer, 355.[6]

Then, to the main point, it is first clear that in this case, upon the issue *Non Assumpsit,* all these points were to be proved by the plaintiff:

[4] The Court was the Common Pleas, and the Judges were Hobart, C.J., and Warburton, Foster and Winch, J.J.
[5] *Supra,* p. 417.
[6] *Supra,* p. 416, n. 87.

1. That the defendant had committed the felony, *prout*, etc.
2. Then that he requested the plaintiff's endeavour, *prout*, etc.
3. That thereupon the plaintiff made his proof, *prout*, etc.
4. That thereupon the defendant made his promise, *prout*, etc.

For wheresoever I build my promise upon a thing done at my request, the execution of the act must pursue the request, for it is like a case of commission for this purpose.

So then the issue found *ut supra* is a proof that he did his endeavour according to the request, for else the issue could not have been found; for that is the difference between a promise upon a consideration executed and executory, that in the executed you cannot traverse the consideration by itself, because it is passed and incorporated and coupled with the promise. And if it were not indeed then acted, it is *nudum pactum*. But if it be executory, as, in consideration that you shall serve me a year, I will give you ten pound, here you cannot bring your action till the service performed. But if it were a promise on either side executory, it needs not to aver performance, for it is the counter-promise, and not the performance, that makes the consideration. . . .

BOURNE v. MASON

1 Ventris, 6

A.D. 1670

In an Assumpsit the plaintiff declares that, whereas one Parry was indebted to the plaintiff and defendants in two several sums of money and that a stranger was indebted in another sum to Parry, there being a communication between them, the defendants, in consideration that Parry would permit them to sue in his name the stranger for the sum due to him, promised that they would pay the sum which Parry owed to the plaintiff; and he alledged that Parry permitted them to sue and that they recovered.

After *Non Assumpsit* pleaded and a verdict for the plaintiff, it was moved in arrest of judgment that the plaintiff could not bring his action, for he was a stranger to the consideration.

But in maintenance thereof a judgment was cited in 1658 between *Sprat* and *Agar* in the King's Bench, where one promised to the father, in consideration that he would give his daughter in marriage with his son, he would settle so much land. After the marriage the son brought the action, and it was adjudged maintainable. And another case was cited of a promise to a physician that, if he did such a cure, he would give such a sum of money to himself and another to his daughter, and it was resolved that the daughter might bring an Assumpsit.

Which cases the Court[7] agreed. For in the one case the parties that brought the Assumpsit did the meritorious act, tho' the promise was made to another; and in the other case the nearness of the relation gives the daughter the benefit of the consideration performed by her father. But here the plaintiff did nothing of trouble to himself or benefit to the defendant, but is a mere stranger to the consideration. Wherefore it was adjudged *quod nil capiat per billam*.

---

[7] King's Bench: Kelyng, C.J., Morton, Twisden and Rainsford, J.J.

DUTTON v. POOLE

SIR T. RAYMOND, 302 : 2 LEVINZ, 210

A.D. 1677

[8] In Trespass upon the Case, the plaintiffs declare that, whereas Sir Edward Poole, Knight, father of the said Grizil,[9] was possessed and lawfully interested of and in certain timber trees growing in a certain park called Oaksey Park in Wiltshire, and 1 *May 26 Car.* 2 intended to cut down and sell the same to raise portions for his children, of which said intention the defendant having notice, he the said defendant, then at Sherborn in the County of Gloucester, in consideration that the said Sir Edward at the defendant's special instance and request would forbear cutting the said trees, did promise the said Sir Edward that he the said defendant would well and faithfully pay to the said Grizil £1,000. And the plaintiffs in fact say that the said Sir Edward after the making the said promise did not cut any of the said trees, and yet the defendant did not pay the said Grizil whilst she was sole, nor the said Sir Ralph and Grizil or either of them after their marriage, the said £1,000, though thereunto requested, *ad damnum* £1,000. . . .

. . . [10]After verdict for the plaintiff upon *Non Assumpsit*, it was moved in arrest of Judgment that the action ought not to be brought by the daughter, but by the father, or, if the father be dead, by his executors; for the promise was made to the father, and the daughter is neither privy nor interested in the consideration. . . . And divers cases were cited for the defendant . . . and [especially] a case lately resolved *in Com. Banc. inter Norris* and *Pine, intrat. Hil.* 22 & 23 *Car.* 2, where the case was—' If you will marry me, I will pay your children so much ' ; and, the action being brought by the children, adjudged it lay not.

On the other side it was said, If a man deliver goods or money to H. to deliver or pay to B., B. may have an action, because he is to have the benefit of the bailment. So here the daughter is to have the benefit of the promise. So if a man should say, Give me a horse and I will give your son £10, the son may bring the action, because the gift was upon consideration of a promise to the son. And the father is obliged by natural affection to provide for his children, for which cause affection to children is sufficient to raise a use to them out of the father's estate; and therefore the daughter had an interest in the consideration and in the promise. . . .

Upon the first argument WYLDE and JONES, *Justices,* seemed to think that the action ought to be brought by the father or his executors, tho' for the benefit of the daughter, and not by the daughter, being not privy to the promise nor to the consideration. TWYSDEN and RAINSFORD seemed *contra.* And afterwards, two new Judges being made, *scil.* SCROGGS, Chief Justice in lieu of RAINSFORD,[11] and DOLBEN in lieu of TWYSDEN, the case was argued again upon the reasons aforesaid.

And now SCROGGS, C.J. said: That there was such apparent consideration of affection from the father to his children, for whom nature obliges him to provide, that the consideration and promise to the father may well extend to the children. And he and JONES remembered the case of *Norris v. Pine,* and that it was adjudged as aforesaid. But SCROGGS said,

[8] From the report in Sir T. Raymond, 302.
[9] Daughter to Sir Edward Poole and afterwards wife to and co-plaintiff with Sir Ralph Dutton.
[10] From the report in 2 Levinz, 210.
[11] Sir William Scroggs displaced Sir Richard Rainsford as Chief Justice of the King's Bench on May 31, 1678, and was himself dismissed three years later.

He was then and still is of opinion contrary to that judgment. DOLBEN, J. concurred with him that the daughter might bring the action; JONES and WYLDE *hæsitabant*. But next day they also agreed to the opinion of the *Chief Justice* and DOLBEN. And so Judgment was given for the plaintiffs, for the son[12] hath the benefit by having of the wood and the daughter hath lost her portion by this means.

And, *nota*, upon this Judgment error was immediately brought; and *Trin.* 31 *Car.* 2 it was affirmed in the Exchequer Chamber.

CASE v. BARBER
SIR T. RAYMOND, 450
A.D. 1682

The plaintiff declares in an *Indebitatus Assumpsit* for £20 for meat, drink, washing and lodging for the defendant's wife, provided for her at the request of the defendant. . . . The defendant pleads that, after the making the said promise, etc. and before the exhibiting the said Bill, *viz.* such a day, it was agreed between the plaintiff and the defendant and one Jacob Barber, his son, that the plaintiff should deliver to the defendant divers clothes of the defendant's wife, then in her custody, and that the plaintiff should accept the said Jacob, the son, for her debtor for £9, to be paid as soon as the said Jacob should receive his pay due from His Majesty as Lieutenant of the ship called the *Happy Return,* in full satisfaction and discharge of the premises in the Declaration mentioned; and avers that the plaintiff the same time did deliver to the defendant the said clothes and that she accepted the said Jacob the son as her debtor for the said £9, and that the said son agreed to pay the same to the plaintiff accordingly; and that the said Jacob afterwards, and as soon as he received his pay as aforesaid, *viz.* 27 April, 32 Car. 2, was ready and offered to pay the said £9, and the plaintiff refused to receive it; and that the said Jacob hath always since been and still is ready to pay the same, if the plaintiff will receive it. . . . The plaintiff demurs.

And it was alledged by the defendant's counsel that the plea is good. For although in *Peytoe's Case*[13] and formerly it hath been held that an accord cannot be pleaded unless it appears to be executed, yet of late it hath been held that upon mutual promises an action lies, and consequently, there being equal remedy on both sides, an accord may be pleaded without execution as well as an arbitrament and by the same reason that an arbitrament is a good plea without performance. To which the Court[14] agreed. For the reason of the law being changed, the law is thereby changed; and anciently remedy was not given for mutual promises, which now is given. . . .

But in this case at Bar judgment was given for the plaintiff for two reasons.

1. Because it doth not appear that there is any consideration that the son should pay the £9, but only an agreement without consideration.

2. Admit the agreement would bind, yet now by the Statute of Frauds and Perjuries, 29 Car. 2, this agreement ought to be in writing, or else the

[12] i.e. the defendant, son and heir to Sir Edward Poole.
[13] (1611) 9 Co. Rep. 77b. See at p. 80b: '*Nota* Reader, the best and most secure form of pleading of an Accord is to plead it by way of Satisfaction and not by way of Accord; for if he pleads it by way of Accord, he ought to plead the precise execution thereof in the whole, and if he fails of any part thereof, his plea is insufficient.'
[14] Court of King's Bench: Pemberton, C.J.; Raymond, Dolben and Jones, J.J.

plaintiff could have no remedy thereon. And though upon such an agreement the plaintiff need not set forth the agreement to be in writing, yet when the defendant pleads such an agreement in Bar, he must plead it so as it may appear to the Court that an action will lie upon it, for he shall not take away the plaintiff's present action and not give him another upon the agreement pleaded.

PILLANS v. VAN MIEROP

3 BURROW, 1663

A.D. 1765

On Friday 25th of January last Mr. Attorney-General *Norton* on behalf of the plaintiffs moved for a new trial. He moved it as upon a verdict against evidence; the substance of which evidence was as follows.

One White, a merchant in Ireland, desired to draw upon the plaintiffs, who were merchants at Rotterdam in Holland, for £800, payable to one Clifford, and proposed to give them credit upon a good house in London for their reimbursement, or any other method of reimbursement.

The plaintiffs, in answer, desired a confirmed credit upon a house of rank in London as the condition of their accepting the bill. White names the house of the defendants as this house of rank, and offers credit upon them. Whereupon the plaintiffs honoured the draught and paid the money, and then wrote to the defendants, Van Miérop and Hopkins, merchants in London (to whom White also wrote about the same time), desiring to know whether they would accept such bills as they, the plaintiffs, should in about a month's time draw upon the said Van Miérop's and Hopkins' house here in London for £800 upon the credit of White. And they, having received their assent, accordingly drew upon the defendants. In the interim White failed, before their draught came to hand or was even drawn; and the defendants gave notice of it to the plaintiffs and forbad their drawing upon them. Which they nevertheless did; and therefore the defendants refused to pay their bills.

On the trial a verdict was found for the defendants.[15] . . . [On a motion for a new trial the case was twice argued; and on the second argument],

Serjt. Davy (for the defendants): . . . A promise to pay a past debt of another person is void at Common Law for want of consideration, unless there be at least an implied promise from the debtee to forbear suing the original debtor. But here was a debt clearly contracted by White with the plaintiffs on the credit of White, and there is no promise from the plaintiffs to forbear suing White. A naked promise is a void promise: the consideration must be executory, not past or executed.

LORD MANSFIELD asked if any case could be found where the undertaking holden to be a *nudum pactum* was in writing.

Serjeant Davy—It was antiently doubted whether a written acceptance of a Bill of Exchange was binding for want of a consideration. It is so said somewhere in *Lutwyche*.

LORD MANSFIELD: This is a matter of great consequence to trade and commerce in every light.

[15] Mainly on the suggestion of fraud on the part of the plaintiffs; a suggestion considered by Lord Mansfield to be against the weight of the evidence.

If there was any kind of fraud in this transaction, the collusion and *mala fides* would have vacated the contract. But . . . it seems to me clear that there was none. . . .

If there be no fraud, it is a mere question of law. The Law of Merchants and the Law of the Land is the same. A witness cannot be admitted to prove the Law of Merchants: we must consider it as a point of law. A *nudum pactum* does not exist in the usage and law of merchants.

I take it that the ancient notion about the want of consideration was for the sake of evidence only; for when it is reduced into writing, as in covenants, specialties, bonds, etc., there was no objection to the want of consideration. And the Statute of Frauds proceeded upon the same principle.

In commercial cases among merchants the want of consideration is not an objection.

This is just the same thing as if White had drawn on Van Miérop and Hopkins, payable to the plaintiffs. It had been nothing to the plaintiffs whether Van Miérop and Co. had effects of White's in their hands or not, if they had accepted his bill. And this amounts to the same thing: ' I will give the bill due honour ' is, in effect, accepting it. . . . This is an engagement to accept the bill, if there was a necessity to accept it, and to pay it when due; and they could not afterwards retract. It would be very destructive to trade and to trust in commercial dealing, if they could. There was nothing of *nudum pactum* mentioned to the Jury; nor was it, I dare say, at all in their idea or contemplation.

I think the point of law is with the plaintiffs.

Mr. Justice WILMOT: The question is whether this action can be supported upon the breach of this agreement.

I can find none of those cases, that go upon its being *nudum pactum*, that are in writing: they are all upon parol.

I have traced this matter of the *nudum pactum*, and it is very curious. . . . [It is] echoed from the Civil Law—*ex nudo pacto non oritur actio*. Vinnius gives the reason in *Lib. 3. Tit. De Obligationibus, 4to Edition*, 596.[16] If by stipulation (and *a fortiori* if by writing) it was good without consideration. There was no radical defect in the contract for want of consideration. But it was made requisite in order to put people upon attention and reflection and to prevent obscurity and uncertainty; and, in that view, either writing or certain formalities were required. *Idem*, on *Justinian, 4to Edition*, 614. Therefore it was intended as a guard against rash inconsiderate declarations. But if an undertaking was entered into upon deliberation and reflection it had activity, and such promises were binding. Both Grotius and Puffendorff hold them obligatory by the Law of Nations. *Grot. Lib. 2. c.* 11 : *De Promissis. Puffend. Lib. 3. c. 5.* They are morally good and only require ascertainment. Therefore there is no reason to extend the principle or carry it further.

There would have been no doubt upon the present case according to the Roman Law, because here is both stipulation (in the express Roman form) and writing.

Bracton (who wrote *temp. Hen.* 3) is the first of our lawyers who mentions this. His writings interweave a great many things out of the Roman Law. In his third Book, *Cap.* 1. *De Actionibus,* he distinguishes between

---

[16] Vinnius (Arnold Vinnen), Dutch jurist, A.D. 1588-1657. He was responsible for a famous edition of the Institutes of Justinian.

naked and clothed contracts. He says that *Obligatio est mater actionis,* and that it may arise *ex contractu multis modis, sicut ex conventione, etc., sicut sunt pacta conventa quæ nuda sunt aliquando, aliquando vestita, etc.*[17]

Our own lawyers have adopted exactly the same idea as the Roman Law. *Plowden,* 308*b.* in the case of *Sheryngton* v. *Strotton*[18] mentions it; and no one contradicted it. He lays down the distinction between contracts or agreements in words (which are more base) and contracts or agreements in writing (which are more high); and puts the distinction upon the want of deliberation in the former case and the full exercise of it in the latter. His words are the marrow of what the Roman lawyers had said. ' Words pass from men lightly ': but where the agreement is made by Deed, there is more stay. . . . ' The delivery of the Deed is a ceremony in law, signifying fully his good will that the thing in the Deed should pass from him who made the Deed to the other. And therefore a Deed, which must necessarily be made upon great thought and deliberation, shall bind, without regard to the consideration.'

The voidness of the consideration is the same in reality in both cases, and the reason of adopting the rule was the same in both cases; though there is a difference in the ceremonies required by each law. But no inefficacy arises merely from the naked promise. Therefore, if it stood only upon the naked promise, its being in this case reduced into writing is a sufficient guard against surprise; and therefore the rule of *nudum pactum* does not apply in the present case. I cannot find that a *nudum pactum* evidenced by writing has been ever holden bad, and I should think it good; though where it is merely verbal it is bad. Yet I give no opinion upon its being good *always,* when in writing.

Many of the old cases are strange and absurd. So also are some of the modern ones, particularly that of *Hayes* v. *Warren.*[19] It is now settled that, where the act is done at the request of the person promising, it will be a sufficient foundation to graft the promise upon. In another instance the strictness has been relaxed; as, for instance, burying a son,[20] or curing a son[21]; the considerations were both past, and yet holden good. It has been melting down into common sense of late times.

However, I do here see a consideration. If it be a departure from any right, it will be sufficient to graft a verbal promise upon. Now here White, living in Ireland, writes to the plaintiffs ' to honour his draught for £800, payable ten weeks after.' The plaintiffs agree to it on condition that they be made safe at all events. White offers good credit on a House in London, and draws; and the plaintiffs accept his draught. Then White writes to them ' to draw on Van Miérop and Hopkins '; to whom the plaintiffs write to inquire if they will honour their draught. They engage that they will.

---

[17] *Supra,* p. 236.

[18] *Sharington* v. *Stratton* (1566) 1 Plowden, 298, at p. 308. Plowden, as is clear from the passage cited, identifies ' writings ' and ' Deeds.'

[19] (1732) 2 Strange, 933. Counsel, in this case, sought to meet the objection of past consideration by asking, ' Why should not gratitude be a good consideration? ' But the Court declined the invitation. ' It does not appear that this work was for the benefit of the defendant, and we must take it to be a past consideration.' The Court, it is true, rested their decision to some extent upon the form of pleading and thus offered bolder spirits a way of escape.

[20] See *Church* v. *Church* (1656) referred to in Sir T. Raymond, at p. 260: ' In assumpsit the plaintiff declared that, whereas the plaintiff had at his own charges buried the defendant's child, the defendant promised to pay him his charges; and, though there was no request laid, yet judgment was given for the plaintiff.'

[21] *Style* v. *Smith,* referred to in *Marsh* v. *Rainsford,* 2 Leonard, 111, *supra,* p. 418.

This transaction has prevented, stopped and disabled the plaintiffs from calling upon White for the performance of his engagement . . . ' to give them credit on a good House in London for reimbursement.' So that here is a good consideration. The Law does not weigh the *quantum* of the consideration. The suspension of the plaintiffs' right to call upon White for a compliance with his engagement is sufficient to support an action, even if it be a suspension of the right for a day only or for ever so little a time.

But to consider this as a commercial case. All nations ought to have their laws conformable to each other in such cases. *Fides servanda est*: *simplicitas Juris Gentium prævaleat. Hodierni mores* are such that the old notion about the *nudum pactum* is not strictly observed as a rule. On a question of this nature—whether by the Law of Nations such an engagement as this shall bind—the Law is to judge. . . .

[YATES, J. and ASTON, J. concurred].

RANN v. HUGHES

4 BROWN, P.C. 27: 7 T.R. 350, n.[22]

A.D. 1778

[The plaintiffs, as executors of Mary Hughes, declared that ' divers disputes ' had arisen between Mary Hughes and one John Hughes, which had been referred to arbitration; that the arbitrator had awarded that John Hughes should pay to Mary Hughes £983 0s. 2½d.; that John Hughes died intestate, possessed of effects sufficient to discharge the award; that the defendant, Isabella Hughes, was the administratrix; that the defendant, ' as administratrix aforesaid, became liable ' to pay the said sum to the plaintiffs, as executors of Mary Hughes; ' and being so liable, the said Isabella, in consideration thereof, afterwards, to wit, on the same day and year last aforesaid at Westminster aforesaid undertook and to the said Joseph and Arthur then and there faithfully promised to pay them the said sum of money in the said award mentioned.']

. . . The cause was tried before LORD MANSFIELD at the sittings in Westminster Hall after Trinity Term, 1774, when the jury found a verdict for the plaintiffs on the first count of the declaration, that the defendant did make the promise therein alledged, and gave the plaintiffs £483 damages and 40s. costs. The jury also found that the defendant Isabella had fully administered the effects of John Hughes.

In Michaelmas Term, 1774, a motion was made by the defendant in the Court of King's Bench to set aside the verdict and for a new trial. But the Court were unanimously of opinion that the verdict was well founded, both on the facts and the law of the case; whereupon in Easter Term, 1775, judgment was entered up against the defendant generally for £547 damages and costs.

Soon afterwards the defendant brought a writ of error in the Exchequer Chamber, where the case was twice argued; and in Michaelmas Term. 1776, the judgment of the Court of King's Bench was reversed.

But to reverse this judgment of reversal, the plaintiffs brought a writ of error in Parliament.

---

[22] The pleadings and arguments are to be found in 4 Brown, P.C. 27; and the judgment of Skynner, L.C.B. in 7 T.R. 350, n.

[*Buller* and *Dunning*, for the plaintiffs in error, set themselves, *inter alia*, to meet the objection that, ' supposing this to be a promise to pay the debt out of the effects of the administratrix, yet that promise was void in law '].

. . . ' The second objection, that the promise was void, was supported on two grounds; 1st, that it did not appear by the declaration that the promise was in writing; 2dly, that there was no consideration for the promise. As to the first ground, it is an adjudged point that the Statute of Frauds, which requires such promise to be in writing, makes no alteration in the mode of pleading, and, therefore, though the promise be not expressly alledged in the declaration to have been made in writing, yet it must necessarily be presumed to have been so; for, if it had not been so proved at the trial, which in fact it was, the plaintiffs could not have obtained a verdict, and, after a verdict, everything is presumed which was necessary to be proved on the trial.

And as to the second ground, it was submitted that, in the case of a promise in writing, which this must be taken to be, it is not necessary to alledge any consideration in the declaration; but, if it were necessary, there was a sufficient consideration for the promise appearing upon this declaration. In reason, there is little or no difference between a contract which is deliberately reduced into writing and signed by the parties without seal, and a contract under the same circumstances, to which a party at the time of signing it puts a seal or his finger on cold wax. In the case of a deed, i.e. an instrument under seal, it must be admitted that no consideration is necessary; and in the year 1765 it was solemnly adjudged in the Court of King's Bench that no consideration was necessary when the promise was reduced into writing.[23] That opinion has since been recognized in the same Court and several judgments founded upon it[24]; all which judgments must be subverted and what was there conceived to be settled law totally overturned, if the plaintiffs in this cause were not entitled to recover. But, further, if a consideration were necessary, a sufficient one for the promise appeared upon the declaration in this case. The defendant was the administratrix of John Hughes, she had effects of his in her hands, she was liable to be called upon by the plaintiffs in an action to shew to what amount she had assets and how she had applied them; and under these circumstances she promised to pay the demand which the plaintiffs had against her. . . .

[25]After argument the following question was proposed to the Judges by the Lord Chancellor[26]: ' Whether sufficient matter appeared upon the declaration to warrant after verdict the judgment against the defendant in error in her personal capacity ' ; upon which the Lord Chief Baron SKYNNER delivered the opinion of the Judges to this effect.—

It is undoubtedly true that every man is by the law of nature bound to fulfil his engagements. It is equally true that the law of this country supplies no means nor affords any remedy to compel the performance of an agreement made without sufficient consideration. Such agreement is *nudum pactum ex quo non oritur actio;* and whatsoever may be the sense of this maxim in the civil law, it is in the last-mentioned sense only that it is to be understood in our law. The declaration states that the defendant, being indebted as administratrix, promised to pay when requested, and the judgment

---

[23] *Pillans* v. *Van Miérop,* 3 Burrow, 1663, *supra,* p. 427.
[24] None seems to have survived save *Williamson* v. *Losh* (1775), cited by Langdell in his *Cases on Contract* (1871) p. 180; *supra,* p. 408.
[25] Henceforth the citation is taken from the report in 7 T.R. 350, n.
[26] Earl Bathurst.

is against the defendant generally. The being indebted is of itself a sufficient consideration to ground a promise, but the promise must be co-extensive with the consideration unless some particular consideration of fact can be found here to warrant the extension of it against the defendant in her own capacity. If a person, indebted in one right, in consideration of forbearance for a particular time promise to pay in another right, this convenience will be a sufficient consideration to warrant an action against him or her in the latter right. But here no sufficient consideration occurs to support this demand against her in her personal capacity; for she derives no advantage or convenience from the promise here made. For if I promise generally to pay upon request what I was liable to pay upon request in another right, I derive no advantage or convenience from this promise, and therefore there is not sufficient consideration for it.

But it is said that, if this promise is in writing, that takes away the necessity of a consideration and obviates the objection of *nudum pactum,* for that cannot be where the promise is put into writing, and that, if it were necessary to support the promise that it should be in writing, it will after verdict be presumed that it was in writing; and this last is certainly true. But, that there cannot be *nudum pactum* in writing, whatever may be the rule of the civil law, there is certainly none such in the law of England. His Lordship[27] observed upon the doctrine of *nudum pactum* delivered by Mr. Justice WILMOT in the case of *Pillans* v. *Van Miérop,*[28] that he contradicted himself and was also contradicted by Vinnius in his Comment on Justinian.

All contracts are by the laws of England distinguished into agreements by specialty and agreements by parol; nor is there any such third class as some of the counsel have endeavoured to maintain as contracts in writing. If they be merely written and not specialties they are parol, and a consideration must be proved. But it is said that the Statute of Frauds has taken away the necessity of any consideration in this case. The Statute of Frauds was made for the relief of personal representatives and others, and did not intend to charge them further than by common law they were chargeable. His Lordship here read those sections of that Statute which relate to the present subject. He observed that the words were merely negative and that executors and administrators should not be liable out of their own estates, unless the agreement upon which the action was brought or some memorandum thereof was in writing and signed by the party. But this does not prove that the agreement was still not liable to be tried and judged of as all other agreements merely in writing are by the common law, and does not prove the converse of the proposition, that when in writing the party must be at all events liable.

He here observed upon the case of *Pillans* v. *Van Miérop* and the case of *Losh* v. *Williamson,* Mich. 16 Geo. 3 in *B.R.*[29]; and, so far as these cases went on the doctrine of *nudum pactum,* he seemed to intimate that they were erroneous. He said that all his brothers concurred with him that in this case there was not a sufficient consideration to support this demand as a personal demand against the defendant, and that its being now supposed to have been in writing makes no difference. The consequence of which is that the question put to us must be answered in the negative.

And the judgment in the Exchequer Chamber was affirmed.

[27] The report here slides into *oratio obliqua,* which impairs its elegance, if it does not deflect the argument.
[28] *Supra,* p. 427.
[29] *Supra,* p. 408.

HAWKES v. SAUNDERS

1 Cowper, 289

A.D. 1782

This action was brought against the defendant in her own right; and the declaration stated that George Saunders by his will bequeathed a legacy of £50 to the plaintiff; that he appointed the defendant his executrix; that she proved the will; that goods and chattels came to her hands more than sufficient to pay all the testator's debts and legacies; by reason whereof she became liable to pay the legacy, and, being so liable, in consideration thereof she promised to pay it.

Lord Mansfield: . . . It is admitted at the bar that, after verdict, it must be taken to have been a promise in writing and that there were assets. If so, the whole case is reduced to this single point: whether the circumstance of the defendant having assets sufficient to pay all the debts and legacies is, or is not, a sufficient consideration for her to make a promise to pay the legacy in question? As to that point, the rule laid down at the bar as to what is or is not a good consideration in law goes upon a very narrow ground indeed; namely, that, to make a consideration to support an *assumpsit*, there must be either an immediate benefit to the party promising or a loss to the person to whom the promise was made. I cannot agree to that being the only ground of consideration sufficient to raise an *assumpsit*.

Where a man is under a legal or equitable obligation to pay, the law implies a promise, though none was ever actually made. *A fortiori,* a legal or equitable duty is a sufficient consideration for an actual promise. Where a man is under a moral obligation, which no court of law or equity can enforce, and promises, the honesty and rectitude of the thing is a consideration. As if a man promise to pay a just debt, the recovery of which is barred by the Statute of Limitations; or if a man, after he comes of age, promises to pay a meritorious debt contracted during his minority, but not for necessaries; or if a bankrupt, in affluent circumstances after his certificate, promises to pay the whole of his debts; or if a man promise to perform a secret trust or a trust void for want of writing by the Statute of Frauds.

In such and many other instances, though the promise gives a compulsory remedy where there was none before either in law or equity, yet, as the promise is only to do what an honest man ought to do, the ties of conscience upon an upright mind are a sufficient consideration. But an executor who has received assets is under every kind of obligation to pay a legacy. He receives the money by virtue of an office which he swears to execute duly. He receives the money as a trust or deposit to the use of the legatee. He ought to assent if he has assets. He has no discretion or election. He retains what belongs to the legatee and therefore owes him the amount. . . . The legacy in such a case is a demand clearly due from the executor upon various grounds of natural and civil justice, and may be recovered from him by process of law. In such a case a promise to pay stands upon the strongest consideration.

Let us see then what the facts are in the present case. The executrix knows the state of her testator's affairs and of his property. It might consist of chattels which she might not choose to dispose of. It might consist of leases which she had no mind to sell; and, having a full fund to pay the demand, which the plaintiff had a right to recover if he pleased, she, in consideration of that fund, promises to pay. I cannot think this is not a sufficient consideration. I am of opinion it is amply sufficient. It is not like the case of *Rann* v. *Hughes*[30]; for there, there were no assets nor any averment of assets stated in the declaration. But in this case there was a full fund; and therefore she was bound in law, justice and conscience to pay the plaintiff his legacy.

Mr. Justice WILLES and Mr. Justice ASHHURST were of the same opinion.

BULLER, J.: I am entirely of the same opinion. . . . I shall give my opinion singly on this point: whether an obligation in justice, equity and conscience, to pay a sum of money be, or be not, a sufficient consideration in point of law to support a promise to pay that sum?

If such a question were stripped of all authorities, it would be resolved by enquiring whether law were a rule of justice or whether it were something that acts in direct contradiction to justice, conscience and equity. But the matter has been repeatedly decided. In *Stone* v. *Withypol*[31] the Court say ' It is an usual allegation for a rule that everything which is a ground for equity is a sufficient consideration.' So in *Wells* v. *Wells*,[32] the Court presumed an equitable right in the plaintiff which did not appear on the declaration, and held that to debar herself of that was a good consideration. These authorities alone are sufficient to shew that the ground taken in the argument at the bar is not large enough.

But to come closer to the consideration now in question, in *Camden* v. *Turner, C.B.* sittings after *Trin. 5 Geo. I*,[33] KING, C.J. held that an action for money had and received lay against an executor for a legacy, which he had owned lay ready for the plaintiff, whenever he would call for it. . . . Lord KING held that his owning the money lay ready was an assent and admission of assets and a sufficient consideration. In *Reech* v. *Kennegal*,[34] Lord HARDWICKE expressly holds that assets coming to an executor's hands is a sufficient consideration to support a promise, and he puts that case upon the same footing as a promise in consideration of forbearance. His Lordship says, ' At law, if an executor promises to pay a debt of his testator's, a consideration must be alledged; as of assets come to his hands, or of forbearance, or if admission of assets is implied by the promise. Otherwise it will be but *nudum pactum* and not personally binding on the executor.' In *Trewinian* v. *Howell*[35] it was adjudged that ' having assets ' is a good consideration for a promise, and the judgment . . . was affirmed; and two other cases are there cited where the same point had been so determined. Lastly, the case of *Atkins* v. *Hill*[36] is in point. The declaration was the same and the objection the same as in the present case, and the Court unanimously held that the promise was good and that the action well lay.

I agree with my lord, that the rule laid down at the bar as to what is or is not a good consideration is much too narrow. The true rule is that, wherever a defendant is under a moral obligation or is liable in conscience and equity to pay, that is a sufficient consideration. Some of the cases which I have mentioned go fully to that extent. But even if the narrow rule which has been mentioned were adopted as the true rule, yet in this case I think the consideration is sufficient; for here is both a loss to the plaintiff

---

[30] *Supra*, p. 430.
[31] Buller, J. here cites from the report of *Stone* v. *Withypol* (1588), Latch, 21. Compare the fuller report of the case in Croke, Eliz. 126.
[32] (1670) 1 Ventris, 40.
[33] Unreported.
[34] (1748) 1 Ves. Sen. 123.
[35] (1588) Croke, Eliz. 91.
[36] (1775) 1 Cowper, 284.

and a benefit to the defendant, arising from that which is the consideration of the promise. The loss to the plaintiff is that the effects which are liable to the payment of the legacy have not been so applied; but the defendant has detained them in her own hands for other purposes. The benefit to the defendant is that she has received those effects and has them still. The defendant is bound in conscience to apply the effects towards the discharge of the debts and legacies; she is a trustee for that purpose and is guilty of a breach of trust in not so doing; and it is admitted that a breach of trust is a good ground for action.

Therefore I agree in opinion with the rest of the Court that this rule in arrest of judgment ought to be discharged.

NOTE TO

WENNALL v. ADNEY

by the reporters, J. B. Bosanquet and C. Puller, in
3 B. *and* P. 249[37]

An idea has prevailed of late years that an express promise, founded simply on an antecedent moral obligation, is sufficient to support an assumpsit. It may be worth consideration, however, whether this proposition be not rather inaccurate and whether that inaccuracy has not in a great measure arisen from some expressions of Lord Mansfield and Mr. Justice Buller, which, if construed with the qualifications fairly belonging to them, do not warrant the conclusion which appears to have been rather hastily drawn from thence. . . .

[The learned reporters then referred to and cited from *Atkins* v. *Hill*, 1 Cowp. 284, *Hawkes* v. *Saunders*, 1 Cowp. 289, and *Trueman* v. *Fenton*, 1 Cowp. 544[38]; and continued]

Of the two former cases it may be observed that the particular point decided in them has been over-ruled by the subsequent case of *Deeks* v. *Strutt*, 5 T.R. 690.[39] And it may further be observed that, however general the expressions used by Lord Mansfield may at first sight appear, yet the instances adduced by him as illustrative of the rule of law do not carry that rule beyond what the older authorities seem to recognize as its proper limits; for in each instance the party bound by the promise had received a benefit previous to the promise. Indeed it seems that in such instances alone as those selected by Lord Mansfield will an *express* promise have any operation, and there it only becomes necessary because, though the consideration was originally beneficial to the party promising, yet, inasmuch as he was not of a capacity to bind himself when he received the benefit or is protected from liability by some statute provision or some stubborn rule of law, the law will not, as in ordinary cases, *imply* an assumpsit against him. The same observation is applicable to *Trueman* v. *Fenton*, that being an action against a bankrupt on a promise made by him subsequent to his certificate respecting a debt due before the certificate.

There is, however, rather a loose note of a case of *Scott* v. *Nelson* (Westminster Sittings 4 Geo. 3, *coram* Lord Mansfield—see Espinasse,

---

[37] The date of the case is Nov. 26, 1802; but the report was published in 1804.
[38] *Supra*, pp. 409-10 and 433.
[39] The 'particular point,' on which in *Deeks* v. *Strutt* Lord Kenyon joined issue with Lord Mansfield, was the competence of a common law court to hear a suit for a legacy. Lord Kenyon did not dispute Lord Mansfield's view of consideration.

N.P. 945), in which his Lordship is said to have held a father bound by his promise to pay for the previous maintenance of a bastard child. And there is also an anonymous case, 2 Shower, 184, where Ld. Ch. J. Pemberton ruled that 'for meat and drink for a bastard child an indebitatus assumpsit will lie.' Although the latter case does not expressly say that there was a previous request by the defendant, yet that seems to have been the fact, for Lord Hale's opinion is cited to shew 'that where there is common charity and a charge,' the action will lie; which seems to imply that, if a charge be imposed upon one person by the charitable conduct of another, the latter shall pay; and though he adds 'and undoubtedly a special promise would reach it,' that expression does not necessarily import a promise subsequent to the charge being sustained, but may be supposed to mean that where a party is induced to undertake a charge by the engagement of another to pay, the latter will certainly be liable even though he should not be so where the charge was only induced by his conduct without such engagement. The case of *Watson* v. *Turner* (Bull. N.P. 147) has sometimes been cited in support of what has been supposed to be the general principle laid down by Lord Mansfield, because in that case overseers were held bound by a mere subsequent promise to pay an apothecary's bill for care taken of a pauper; but it may be observed that 'this was adjudged not to be *nudum pactum,* for the overseers are bound to provide for the poor'; which obligation, being a legal obligation, distinguishes the case. Indeed, in a late case of *Atkins* v. *Banwell* (2 East, 505) that distinction does not seem to have been sufficiently adverted to, for *Watson* v. *Turner* was cited to shew that a mere moral obligation is sufficient to raise an *implied* assumpsit, and, though the Court denied that proposition, yet Lord Ellenborough observed that the promise given in the case of *Watson* v. *Turner* made all the difference between the two cases, without alluding to another difference which might have been taken, viz., that, though the parish officers were bound by law in *Watson* v. *Turner,* the defendants in the principal case were not so bound, because the pauper had been relieved by the plaintiffs as overseers of another parish, though belonging to the parish of which the defendants were overseers.

In the older cases no mention is made of moral obligation; but it seems to have been much doubted whether mere natural affection was a sufficient consideration to support an assumpsit, though coupled with a subsequent express promise. Indeed Lord Mansfield appears to have used the term *moral obligation,* not as expressive of any vague and undefined claim arising from nearness of relationship, but of those imperative duties which would be enforceable by law were it not for some positive rule, which, with a view to general benefit, exempts the party in that particular instance from legal liability. On such duties, so exempted, an express promise operates to revive the liability and take away the exemption, because if it were not for the exemption they would be enforced at law through the medium of an implied promise. In several of the cases it is laid down that, to support an assumpsit, the party promising must derive a benefit or the party performing sustain an inconvenience occasioned by the plaintiff. . . .

[The learned reporters then cited and discussed a number of seventeenth-century cases, e.g. *Brett's Case* (Croke, Eliz. 755) and *Lampleigh* v. *Brathwaite* (Hobart, 105),[40] and concluded]

[40] *Supra,* pp. 421 and 423.

An express promise, therefore, as it should seem, can only revive a precedent good consideration which might have been enforced at law through the medium of an implied promise had it not been suspended by some positive rule of law, but can give no original right of action if the obligation on which it is founded never could have been enforced at law, though not barred by any legal maxim or statute provision.

LEE v. MUGGERIDGE
5 TAUNTON, 36
A.D. 1813

This was an action of *assumpsit,* brought in consequence of GRANT, M.R. having dismissed a bill filed by the same plaintiff against the same defendants to obtain payment of the bond hereinafter mentioned, but with liberty for the plaintiff to bring forth such action at law as he might be advised.[41]

[Mary Muggeridge, then wife to John Muggeridge, requested the plaintiff to lend to her son-in-law, Joseph Hiller, £1,999 19s. The plaintiff agreed to do so if Mary Muggeridge would execute a bond, binding her separate property to cover the amount of the loan with interest. Mary Muggeridge executed the bond and the plaintiff lent the money to Joseph Hiller. John Muggeridge later died, and, as Joseph Hiller had not repaid the loan, Mary, now a widow, wrote to the plaintiff ' that it was not in her power to pay the bond off, that her time here was but short, and that it would be settled by her executors.' On November 1st, 1811, Mary died, and the defendants were her executors. The plaintiff sued the defendants in assumpsit, declaring that they had been ' requested by the plaintiff to settle the bond, that is to say, to pay the principal money and interest so omitted to be paid by J. Hiller, according to the form and effect of such promise and undertaking of Mary in her lifetime so by her made; but that they, not regarding such promise and undertaking of Mary, did not nor would, when so requested or at any time since, settle such bond or pay the principal and interest, and the same remained wholly unpaid.' The Jury found a verdict for the plaintiff, and it was now moved in arrest of judgment that no sufficient consideration was shown for the promise of the deceased.]

. . . *Lens* and *Best,* Serjts. [for the plaintiff] . . . admitted that when the deceased gave the bond, being covert, she had no power thereby to bind herself, but contended that, notwithstanding that, the promise, which after she was liberated from all restriction she gave in confirmation of the bond, was obligatory on her. The same payment which was recited to be the consideration of the bond is a sufficient consideration for the subsequent promise. This differs nothing from the case of infancy and the many other cases which subsist in the English Law, where, though a party is not compellable to make a promise, yet, if he does make it, the promise shall be compulsory on him. In certain cases where the law destroys the remedy, as in the case of the Statute of Limitations, a subsequent promise, operating by the old consideration, will revive the remedy. . . . Lord Mansfield thought the rule of *nudum pactum* was too strict and that it was competent for parties to make their own agreements on deliberation, and, if they did so think fit to make them, that they must be subject to them. It is now fully recognized in the law that, if there be, even in the strictest morality, the foundation

[41] 1 Vesey & Beames, 118. Grant, M.R. here held that ' where a married woman reserves no power of disposition over her property during coverture, there are no means by which she can dispose of it while she remains covert.'

for a promise and the promise be accordingly made, it is binding. It is a new *ligamen,* though not a new consideration; for if there were a new consideration, it would be clearly good. In *Goodright d. Carter* v. *Straphan*[42] Lord Mansfield held that an account stated by a widow, allowing interest on a mortgage executed by her during coverture, a direction given by her in writing to her tenant to attorn to the mortgagees and a paper whereby she purported to surrender the possession, amounted to a delivery by her in her widowhood of the mortgage deed, holding her previous delivery during coverture to be absolutely void.

MANSFIELD, C.J.[43]: That was certainly a very strong case, and I very well remember the surprise I felt at the time when it was decided, because it was making those acts of the widow equivalent to a formal re-delivery of the deed; and others were much surprised at it. But it strongly recognizes the principle that a moral obligation is a good consideration. . . .

Lens and *Best,* Serjts.: The doubt on that case has always been on the form in which Lord Mansfield applied the principle, not on the principle itself. There cannot, however, be a stronger case of moral obligation than the present, for the giving this bond of the deceased was the inducement to the plaintiff to lend the money. In *Trueman* v. *Fenton*[44] Lord Mansfield and the rest of the Court fully recognize the principle and found on it their decision that a bankrupt, promising after he has obtained his certificate to pay a debt thereby barred, is bound by his promise. In *Barnes* v. *Hedley*[45] a promise to pay the principal money lent on an usurious security, with legal interest, was held valid; and many cases to the like effect are there cited. Although no reasons are assigned for the judgment, it must necessarily have proceeded on the ground that a moral obligation will support a promise to pay.

Shepherd and *Vaughan,* Serjts., *contra*: . . . The feme covert never had the money; neither can a feme covert by any means create a debt from herself, so that on the declaration the case stands thus, that she, not being indebted, was not liable, and, in consideration of her not being liable, she undertook to pay. If this money had been advanced, not on her bond but on her mere promise, a subsequent promise to pay, made when she first became discovert, would be merely void. A bygone debt from a third person would be no consideration for a promise to pay. There must be an agreement not to sue, or some new consideration moving to the promisor or from the lender. . . . There is no mutuality or connection between this consideration and this promise, for the whole transaction had an end before the deceased was discovert. The law does not recognize the principle to the extent stated, that every moral obligation of any sort or kind whatever would be a good consideration for a promise. There must be a mutuality. This cannot be a stronger case than if the money had been advanced to the feme covert herself; yet in *Loyd* v. *Lee*[46] it was held by Pratt, C.J., where a married woman gave a note as a feme sole, and, after her husband's decease, in consideration of forbearance to sue promised payment, that

---

[42] (1774) 1 Cowper, 201.
[43] Chief Justice of the Common Pleas, 1804-14. He was no relation to Lord Mansfield, and his name had originally been *Manfield.* Foss, *The Judges of England,* VIII, p. 335, says of him: ' he was an amiable man, but had not got rid of the habit of swearing, which was too prevalent in his earlier years. So great was the annoyance that he resigned his post in Hilary vacation, 1814.'
[44] (1777) 1 Cowper, 544.
[45] (1809) 2 Taunton, 184.
[46] (1719) 1 Strange, 94.

the note was not barely voidable but absolutely void, and that forbearance, where originally there was no cause of action, is no consideration to raise an assumpsit. In *Barber* v. *Fox*[47] an assumpsit by the heir to pay the bond of his ancestor, in consideration of forbearance to sue, was held void. . . .

MANSFIELD, C.J.: The counsel for the plaintiff need not trouble themselves to reply to these cases. It has been long established that, where a person is bound morally and conscientiously to pay a debt though not legally bound, a subsequent promise to pay will give a right of action. The only question therefore is whether upon this declaration there appears a good moral obligation. Now I cannot conceive that there can be a stronger moral obligation than is stated upon this record. Here is this debt of £2,000 created at the desire of the testatrix, lent in fact to her, though paid to Hiller. After her husband's death she, knowing that this bond had been given, that her son-in-law had received the money and had not repaid it; knowing all this, she promises that her executors shall pay. If then it has been repeatedly decided that a moral consideration is a good consideration for a promise to pay, this declaration is clearly good. This case is not distinguishable in principle from *Barnes* v. *Hedley*.[48] There not only the securities were void, but the contract was void; but the money had been lent, and therefore, when the parties had stripped the transaction of its usury and reduced the debt to mere principal and interest, the promise made to pay that debt was binding. Lord MANSFIELD's judgment in the case of *Doe d. Carter* v. *Straphan*[49] is extremely applicable. Here in like manner the wife would have been grossly dishonest, if she had scrupled to give a security for the money advanced at her request. As to the cases cited of *Loyd* v. *Lee*[50] and *Barber* v. *Fox*,[51] there was no forbearance, and those cases proceeded on the ground that no good cause of action was shewn on the pleadings.

[HEATH and CHAMBRE, J.J. concurred].

GIBBS, J.: I agree in this case that the plaintiff is entitled to recover. It cannot, I think, be disputed now that, wherever there is a moral obligation to pay a debt or perform a duty, a promise to perform that duty or pay that debt will be supported by the previous moral obligation. There cannot be a stronger case than this of moral obligation. The counsel for the defendant did not dare to grapple with this position, but endeavoured to shew that there was no case in which a subsequent promise had been supported, where there had not been an antecedent legal obligation at some time or other; from whence he wished it to be inferred that, unless there had been the antecedent legal obligation, the mere moral obligation would not be a sufficient consideration to support the promise. But in *Barnes* v *Hedley* certainly *Hedley* never was for a moment legally bound to pay a farthing of that money for which he was sued; for it appears to have been advanced upon a previously existing usurious contract, and whatever was advanced upon such a contract certainly could not be recovered at any one moment. The borrower, availing himself of the law so far as he honestly might and no further, reducing it to mere principal and interest, does that which every honest man ought to do in like circumstances, promises to pay it; and that promise was held binding. . . . It is therefore clear that

---

[47] (1671) 2 Saunders, 134.
[48] (1809) 2 Taunton, 184.
[49] (1774) 1 Cowper, 201.
[50] (1719) 1 Strange, 94.
[51] (1671) 2 Saunders, 134.

this rule[52] must be discharged upon the ground that, wherever there is an antecedent moral obligation and a subsequent promise given to perform it, it is of sufficient validity for the plaintiff to be able to enforce it.

EASTWOOD v. KENYON
11 AD. & EL. 438
A.D. 1840

[On the death of John Sutcliffe, his infant daughter Sarah was left as his sole heiress. The plaintiff, acting as her guardian, spent money on her education and for the benefit of her estate, and for this purpose borrowed money from one Blackburn, to whom in return he gave a promissory note. Sarah, when she came of age, promised the plaintiff to pay the amount of this note. She later married the defendant, who also promised to pay the amount of the note. The plaintiff sued the defendant on this promise.

At the trial the plaintiff had a verdict. The defendant moved to arrest judgment on two grounds: (1) that the agreement was caught by the Statute of Frauds, (2) that the declaration showed no consideration for the promise. The Court held that the agreement was not within the Statute of Frauds, and then proceeded to consider the second point].

LORD DENMAN, C.J.: . . . The second point arose in arrest of judgment, namely, whether the declaration showed a sufficient consideration for the promise. It stated, in effect, that the plaintiff was executor under the will of the father of the defendant's wife, who had died intestate as to his real estate, leaving the defendant's wife, an infant, his only child; that the plaintiff had voluntarily expended his money for the improvement of the real estate whilst the defendant's wife was sole and a minor; and that, to reimburse himself, he borrowed money of Blackburn to whom he had given his promissory note; that the defendant's wife, while sole, had received the benefit, and, after she came of age, assented and promised to pay the note, and did pay a year's interest; that after the marriage the plaintiff's accounts were shewn to the defendant, who assented to them, and it appeared that there was due to the plaintiff a sum equal to the amount of the note to Blackburn; that the defendant in right of his wife had received all the benefit, and, in consideration of the premises, promised to pay and discharge the amount of the note to Blackburn.

Upon motion in arrest of judgment this promise must be taken to have been proved and to have been an express promise, as indeed it must of necessity have been, for no such implied promise in law was ever heard of. It was then argued for the plaintiff that the declaration disclosed a sufficient moral consideration to support the promise.

Most of the older cases on this subject are collected in a learned note to the case of *Wennall* v. *Adney*,[53] and the conclusion there arrived at seems to be correct in general, ' that an express promise can only revive a precedent good consideration which might have been enforced at law through the medium of an implied promise, had it not been suspended by some positive rule of law; but can give no original cause of action, if the obligation on which it is founded never could have been enforced at law, though not barred by any legal maxim or statute provision.' Instances are given of

---

[52] i.e. the rule *nisi* to arrest judgment.
[53] (1802) 3 B. & P. 249, *supra*, p. 435.

voidable contracts, as those of infants ratified by an express promise after age, and distinguished from void contracts, as of married women, not capable of ratification by them when widows—*Loyd* v. *Lee*[54]; debts of bankrupts revived by subsequent promise after certificate; and similar cases.

Since that time, some cases have occurred upon this subject, which require to be more particularly examined. *Barnes* v. *Hedley*[55] decided that a promise to repay a sum of money with legal interest, which sum had originally been lent on usurious terms but, in taking the account of which, all usurious items had been by agreement struck out, was binding. *Lee* v. *Muggeridge*[56] upheld an *assumpsit* by a widow that her executors should pay a bond given by her while a feme covert to secure money then advanced to a third person at her request. On the latter occasion the language of MANSFIELD, C.J. and of the whole Court of Common Pleas is very large and hardly susceptible of any limitation. It is conformable to the expressions used by the Judges of this Court in *Cooper* v. *Martin*,[57] where a stepfather was permitted to recover from the son of his wife, after he had attained his full age, upon a declaration for necessaries furnished to him while an infant, for which, after his full age, he promised to pay. It is remarkable that in none of these was there any allusion made to the learned note in 3 *Bosanquet and Puller* above referred to, and which has been very generally thought to contain a correct statement of the law. The case of *Barnes* v. *Hedley* is fully consistent with the doctrine in that note laid down. *Cooper* v. *Martin,* also, when fully examined, will be found not to be inconsistent with it. This last case appears to have occupied the attention of the Court much more in respect of the supposed statutable liability of a stepfather, which was denied by the Court, and in respect of what a Court of Equity would hold as to a stepfather's liability, and rather to have assumed the point before us. It should, however, be observed that LORD ELLENBOROUGH, in giving his judgment, says, ' the plaintiff having done an act beneficial for the defendant in his infancy, it is a good consideration for the defendant's promise after he came of age. In such a case the law will imply a request, and the fact of the promise has been found by the jury'; and undoubtedly the action would have lain against the defendant whilst an infant, inasmuch as it was for necessaries furnished at his request in regard to which the law raises an implied promise.

The case of *Lee* v. *Muggeridge*[58] must, however, be allowed to be decidedly at variance with the doctrine in the note alluded to, and is a decision of great authority. It should, however, be observed that in that case there was an actual request of the defendant during coverture, though not one binding in law; but the ground of decision there taken was also equally applicable to *Littlefield* v. *Shee*,[59] tried by GASELEE, J. at Nisi Prius, when that learned judge held, notwithstanding, that, ' the defendant having been a married woman when the goods were supplied, her husband was originally liable, and there was no consideration for the promises declared upon.' After time taken for deliberation, this Court refused even a rule to shew cause why the nonsuit should not be set aside. *Lee* v. *Muggeridge* was cited on the motion and was sought to be distinguished

[54] (1719) 1 Strange, 94.
[55] (1809) 2 Taunton, 184.
[56] (1813) 5 Taunton, 36, *supra,* p. 437.
[57] (1803) 4 East, 76.
[59] (1831) 2 B. & Ad. 811.
[58] (1813) 5 Taunton, 36, *supra,* p. 437.

by LORD TENTERDEN, because there the circumstances raising the consideration were set out truly upon the record, but in *Littlefield* v. *Shee* the declaration stated the consideration to be that the plaintiff had supplied the defendant with goods at her request, which the plaintiff failed in proving, inasmuch as it appeared that the goods were in point of law supplied to the defendant's husband and not to her. But LORD TENTERDEN added that the doctrine that a moral obligation is a sufficient consideration for a subsequent promise is one which should be received with some limitation. This sentence, in truth, amounts to a dissent from the authority of *Lee* v. *Muggeridge,* where the doctrine is wholly unqualified.

The eminent counsel who argued for the plaintiff in *Lee* v. *Muggeridge* spoke of Lord Mansfield as having considered the rule of *nudum pactum* as too narrow, and maintained that all promises deliberately made ought to be held binding. I do not find this language ascribed to him by any reporter and do not know whether we are to receive it as a traditional report or as a deduction from what he does appear to have laid down. If the latter, the note to *Wennall* v. *Adney*[60] shews the deduction to be erroneous. If the former, LORD TENTERDEN and this Court declared that they could not adopt it in *Littlefield* v. *Shee*. Indeed, the doctrine would annihilate the necessity for any consideration at all, inasmuch as the mere fact of giving a promise creates a moral obligation to perform it.

The enforcement of such promises by law, however plausibly reconciled by the desire to effect all conscientious engagements, might be attended with mischievous consequences to society; one of which would be the frequent preference of voluntary undertakings to just debts. Suits would thereby be multiplied, and voluntary undertakings would also be multiplied, to the prejudice of real creditors. The temptations of executors would be much increased by the prevalence of such a doctrine, and the faithful discharge of their duty be rendered more difficult.

Taking then the promise of the defendant, as stated on this record, to have been an express promise, we find that the consideration for it was past and executed long before, and yet it is not laid to have been at the request of the defendant . . . ; and the declaration really discloses nothing but a benefit voluntarily conferred by the plaintiff and received by the defendant, with an express promise by the defendant to pay money. . . .

In holding this declaration to be bad because it states no consideration but a past benefit not conferred at the request of the defendant, we conceive that we are justified by the old common law of England.

Lampleigh v. *Brathwait*[61] is selected by Mr. Smith[62] as the leading case on this subject, which was there fully discussed, though not necessary to the decision. HOBART, C.J. lays it down that 'a mere voluntary courtesy will not have a consideration to uphold an *assumpsit*. But if that courtesy were moved by a suit or request of the party that gives the *assumpsit,* it will bind; for the promise, though it follows, yet it is not naked, but couples itself with the suit before and the merits of the party procured by that suit, which is the difference': a difference brought fully out by *Hunt* v. *Bate*,[63] there cited from *Dyer,* where a promise to indemnify the plaintiff against the consequences of having bailed the defendant's servant, which the plaintiff had done without request of the defendant, was held to be made

[60] 3 B. & P. 249, *supra,* p. 435.
[61] (1615) Hobart, 105, *supra,* p. 423.
[62] In the first volume of his Leading Cases (1st ed. in 1837).
[63] (1568) 3 Dyer, 272a, *supra,* p. 405.

without consideration; but a promise to pay £20 to plaintiff, who had married defendant's cousin at defendant's special instance, was held binding.

The distinction is noted, and was acted upon, in *Townsend* v. *Hunt*,[64] and indeed in numerous old books; while the principle of moral obligation does not make its appearance till the days of Lord MANSFIELD, and then under circumstances not inconsistent with this ancient doctrine when properly explained.

Upon the whole we are of opinion that the rule must be made absolute to arrest the judgment.

[64] (1635) Croke Car. 408.

INDEX